Ъ

Ing. Rudolf Pecinovský, CSc. is a graduate of *Faculty of Nuclear Science and Physical Engeneering at Czech Technical University in Prague*. He obtained his Ph.D. (CSc.) degree at *Institute of Information Theory and Automation, Czechoslovak Academy of Sciences*. He is a lector at *Faculty of Informatics and Statistics, University of Economic, Prague, Faculty of Information Technology, Czech Technical University in Prague* and at *College of information Management, Business Administration and Law*. He published more than 40 textbooks.

OOP – Learn Object Oriented Thinking and Programming

by Rudolf Pecinovský, CSc.

ʙ

2013

This book is published both in printed as well as PDF form. You can find the detailed information about it at http://pub.bruckner.cz/titles/oop, where you can also download the PDF version.

OOP – Learn Object Oriented Thinking and Programming

Copyright © Rudolf Pecinovský, 2013

Translation Irena Mihovičová

Published in the Czech Republic by Tomáš Bruckner, Řepín – Živonín, 2013
Academic Series

This book was reviewed by
    Doc. MUDr. Jiří Kofránek, CSc., Charles University in Prague,
    Doc. Ing. Vojtěch Merunka, Czech University of Life Sciences Prague,
    Doc. Ing. Miroslav Virius, CSc., Czech Technical University in Prague

Trademark Notice: Product or corporate names may be trademarks or registered trademarks, and are used only for identification and explanation without intent to infringe.

Paperback printed on demand and worldwide distributed by Lightning Source UK Ltd. Pitfield UK and Lightning Source Inc. La Vergne TN US. New prints are available for ordering in every bookstore.

Visit us at http://pub.bruckner.cz

ISBN 978-80-904661-8-0 (paperback)
ISBN 978-80-904661-9-7 (PDF)

Reaction of Readers

I consider this book to be unique, above all due to the fact that the author has realized the importance of knowing the object programming than throwing out hundreds of statements and functions. The book is written in an autobiographical way which I noticed first time in textbooks and especially in programming textbooks. Thanks to it I had really good feeling from reading the book. Another aspect that I appreciated is a lot of available animations. Due to them I always knew what and where I should do. The book thus becomes pleasantly simplified, which has a great affect for beginning young programmers as for example me. I have no reservations to this book and I can only warmly recommend it to all who are powerlessly swamped in the object oriented programming world.

Ladislav Janeček
a beginning programmer

What I appreciated in the book, it was among other things the fact, that the author explained the terms in an interesting style and that, at the very beginning; he explained items which are usually explained in more advanced courses, but which have important consequences. I always appreciate progressive explaining, so that you cannot meet a situation when you are reading a code and you do not understand it because you are missing certain advanced knowledge. When reading the book, the author does not press on the reader to quickly write the code and so the reader starts to write down the source code after learning the OOP basics. I would recommend this book to anybody who wants to learn OOP. Anyway, I felt sorry for one thing, and it is that I did not know the book when I started to learn the OOP.

Martin Škurla
a programmer

Programming is my hobby. I recommend the books of Rudolf Pecinovský to all who really want to get into the secret of OOP and do not want to finish at programs of "Hello World" type. The book is really suitable even for real beginners, especially for the so called "perpetual" beginners, who would like to learn programming, but the topic seems to them too complicated and discouraging. Majority of current books can teach you to develop simple programs from the beginning, but they mention OOP only marginally, as if it would be something extra. Terms like design patterns are unknown for them. Luckily the exceptions do exist. This is one of them. If not Mr. Pecinovský, I could be a perpetual beginner, maybe only pseudo OOP programmer.

Martin Staněk
an intermediate advanced student

All the literature which I have read until now on OOP was only a dry theory that I was not able to apply in practice. I am glad that I discovered this book. It helped me to transfer the theory to practice. With impatience I am expecting another volume of the book, with which I can get to the core of the OOP.

Stanislav Hruška
a self-learner programmer

You cannot find a lot of Czech textbooks of programming, where you "yourself" could make a program for car races at the end of the book. And what is the dream of each young beginning programmer? To program a game and show it off to friends. In case you are really interested in programming, this book can really help you in your long way. Programming is not a matter of several weeks or months, but you can become a good programmer within several years.

Sophisticated examples and accompanying animations are an important part of the technical text. Examples and animations are made out in a top professional quality and are added to each chapter of the book. Examples, animations, development environment *BlueJ* as well as Java, this is all FREE, without any charges! All is functioning in Windows as well an in Linux.

The book is written according to the methodology *Design Pattern First*; the object oriented programming (OOP) and draft patterns are contemporary phenomenon. The presentation is ambitious, but can be mastered. I would recommend this book to all who really have a serious interest in OOP.

This book is according to my opinion very suitable as a textbook of programming for high schools as well as for universities for branches aimed to information technologies.

Jiří Kubala,
an IT teacher, High School of Informatics, Ostrava-Poruba

This book presents the OOP in a little bit different way compared to other textbooks. Not only because it is written as a dialogue of an "I-Know-Nothing" and "A Wise-Old-Man", but the way how it presents the Object Programming differs from current programming textbooks.

It's difficult to say whether it's a better way, but it's fully suitable for me and I think it may be fully suitable also for those readers who started programming hundred times and hundred times they failed. I can describe it as if you would unsuccessfully cut a piece of wood, and suddenly, when you put your saw to the other hand, you could cut it somewhat more easily. And that's the case of this book.

Despite I already knew many paragraphs from other books, this one enabled me to see certain matters from a different view. I appreciate a lot that the book shows an already developed program, i.e. not only independent examples, but you can see relations among separate parts of the program.

I also welcome the possibility to see the videos/animations at the author's websites which are of great help in case the text is not fully understandable or the description by words would be too long.

I am looking forward for the second volume of this book.

Tibor Bako
an OOP beginner

This is an ideal book for beginners as well as for experienced programmers. It is written in a style which is attractive and keeps attentiveness for the firstly named. The needed knowledge and skills are gradually presented in a pleasant, gentle and natural style and immediately demonstrated and reinforced by examples and exercises. To more experienced programmers it provides a different view (and according to me the proper one) on object oriented programming.

Vít Grafnetter
a programmer

Contrary to a number of other programming textbooks which I have read, this one does not overload the reader with only a lot of new statements, but teaches him real programming. And it makes it in a very original and comprehensible form. Despite the fact it is determined to younger beginning readers, it was a great contribution for me.

Michal Palas
a high school student

Dedicated to my wife Jaruška
and to my children Stephanie, Pavlínka, Ivanka and Michal

Brief Content

Acknowledgement xx

Preface xxi

Author's Foreword xxiii

Part 1: Interactive Mode 1

1 The Prologue... 2

2 The OOP – Get Acquainted 10

3 We Are Sending First Messages... 18

4 The Test Class 25

5 The Messages Requiring a Value... 33

6 The Messages Requiring an Object.. 43

7 The Messages with Parameters.. 50

8 The Object Type Parameters... 59

9 The Expedition into the Interior of Instances... 68

10 The Interface 77

11 The Interface Continued 89

12 The Introduction into Design Patterns 100

13 The Inheritance of Interface Types 108

14 Mediator and Listener 121

Part 2: Basics of Creating OO Programs 133

15 The First Code.. 134

16 The First Constructor... 144

17 Parameters 150

18 The Fields and the Methods.. 157

19 Implementation of an interface 169

20 Comments... 181

21 Using of this... 194

22 Overloading.. 202

23 The Local Variables... 212

24 Methods Returning a Value 221

25 The Crate 231

26 Strings and How to Work with Them 240

27 A Bit of Logic 251

28 Class Methods and Fields 263

29 Refactoring of the Code 276

30 Static Constructor – Class Constructor 289

31 Debugger 308

32 Creating of an Standalone Application 319

Part 3: Advanced Creating of OO Programs 329

33 Packages 330

34 Linking of Instances 346

35 Decorator 366

36 Teaching Cars to Turn 380

37 Controlling from Keyboard 390

38 Containers and Maps 407

39 Further Programming Constructions 420

40 The Factory Method Second Time 434

41 The Loops 444

42 Lists and Their Ordering 469

43 The Array 483

44 The Finale 494

Index 495

Detailed Content

Acknowledgement...xx

Preface...xxi

Author's Foreword..xxiii

Part 1: Interactive Mode 1

1 The Prologue 2
    Methodology Used 3
    The Presentation Concept 3
    The Accompanying Animations 4
    What You Will Need 5
        File Manager...5
        JDK and JRE..6
        BlueJ Environment..6
        Professional IDE..7
    Working with BlueJ 8
    Review 8

2 The OOP – Get Acquainted 10
    The Object Oriented World 10
        The Objects..10
        The Classes 11
        The Messages...12
        The Structured vs. Object Oriented Program 13
    The First Project 13
        The Graphic Language UML 14
        Classes in the Project...15
    The Compilation 16
    Review 17

3 We Are Sending First Messages 18
    The Instances and References to Them 19
    Creating a New Instance 20
        The Object Bench..22
        The Messages Sent to Instances 22
    The Virtual Machine 23
    Review 23

4 The Test Class...25
    The Test Fixture 25
    Creating the New Class...26
    Creating the Test Fixture...27
    Creating the Test..28

Methods and Constructors 30
Review 31

5   The Messages Requiring a Value 33

Return Type 34
Obtaining the Return Value 35
Primitive and Object Types 35
References to Objects 38
Record of Method Calling 39
The getXxx and setXxx Messages/Methods 40
Review 41

6   The Messages Requiring an Object 43

The Rules for Creating the Identifiers 43
Getting the Reference to the Returned Object 45
The Instance of String Type 46
How to Write the Strings 46
Memory Management – Garbage Collector 47
Using Methods Returning the Value in Tests 47
Review 48

7   The Messages with Parameters 50

The Meaning of Parameters 50
The Object Construction Using Parameters 50
The Dialog Structure for Sending Messages with Parameters 51
The Example Continued 53
Once More the Object vs. the Reference 53
The Parameters of String Type 54
The Animation 56
Exercise 56
Review 58

8   The Object Type Parameters 59

The Significance of Quotation Marks when Entering the Strings 59
The Class Object 60
The Object Type Parameters 62
Direct Passing of the Message Return Value 63
Briefer Record of Messages 65
Exercise 65
Review 66

9   The Expedition into the Interior of Instances 68

Fields of Instances and of Classes 68
Working with the Fields 69
The Messages Requesting a Field Value 70
Field Accessibility 71
Test Fixture Extending 72
Monitoring of Field Values 72
Static Fields – Class Fields 73
Exercise 74
Review 75

10 The Interface 77

Motivation 77
Interface vs. Implementation 78
Interface as a Data Type..80
    Interface versus `interface` 80
Practical Usage 81
    Preparation of a New Project..81
    Importing the Class from Another Project...................................84
Implementation of an `interface` by the Class 85
Exercise...86
Review 87

11 The Interface Continued 89

Readiness for the Future Extension 89
    The Example: Multishape 89
Test Class of the Class..91
Variable Number of Parameters..93
The Design Pattern *Prototype* 96
Verifying of the Multishape Functioning...97
Exercise...98
Review 98

12 The Introduction into Design Patterns 100

Design Patterns...100
Examples of Design Patterns...101
    Library/Utility Class 101
    Simple (Static) Factory Method 101
    Singleton...101
    Enumeration Type – Multiton 102
    Servant 102
The Implementation of More Interface Types..103
Exercise..106
Review 107

13 The Inheritance of Interface Types 108

Hierarchy of the Types 108
Three Types of Inheriting...110
One `interface` Missing 111
Signature versus Contract..112
Definition of a New Interface Type 113
New Hierarchy of the Interface Types 113
Inheriting of the Interface Types..115
Documentation of the Project 116
Exercise..118
Review 118

14 Mediator and Listener...121

    Observer – Listener – Subscriber 121
    The Mediator...122
Dependency Injection 124
How to Prevent Mutual Cancelling of Shapes.......................................124
The Canvas Manager and Its Project..125

    Recursion 130
  Other New Features 130
  Exercise 131
  Review 131

Part 2: Basics of Creating OO Programs 133

15 The First Code 134
  The New Empty Class 134
  Files in *BlueJ* Projects 134
  The Source Code of the Empty Class 137
  Constructor 140
  Adjustment of Presets 141
  Exercise 142
  Review 142

16 The First Constructor 144
  Definition of the Constructor 144
  Name of the Constructor 145
  The Working Constructor 146
  Source Code Formatting 147
  More Complex Example 148
  Exercise 149
  Review 149

17 Parameters 150
  Parameters and Arguments 150
  Renaming the Class 152
  The Test Class of the Light Class 154
  Exercise 154
  Review 155

18 The Fields and the Methods 157
  The Light Has to Learn 157
  Introducing Fields 158
  Encapsulation and Implementation Hiding 158
  The Assignment of the Value to the Field 160
  Method Definitions 161
  The Qualification 161
  The Conflict of Names of a Field and of a Parameter 162
  Exercise 164
  Review 167

19 Implementation of an interface 169
  Interconnecting the Source Code with the Class Diagram 169
  The Abstract Methods and Classes 170
  Implementation of a Method Declared by an Implemented Interface 171
    The @Override Annotation 173
  The Interface and the Class File 174
  Test Class 174

Exercise...177
Review 179

20 Comments 181

Commenting Parts of a Code 181
Comments in Java..182
Documentation Comments...183
Documentation of the Classes and the Whole Project.........................184
The Standard Class Template 184
Formatting of the Documentation Comments...186
    Javadoc Tags..187
    Comments Marking Sections of the Source Code...........................188
Empty Method's Pattern 191
Exercise...192
Review 192

21 Using of this 194

The Hidden Parameter this..194
Unsuitable Copying of the Code 196
The Details of the Constructor's Work 197
Adjustment of the Constructors Using this 199
Exercise...200
Review 200

22 Overloading 202

Further Constructors 202
Overloading of the Methods 205
The Identifiers of Parameters 206
The Identification of the Called Method 207
The Basic Arithmetic Operators 207
Exercise...209
Review 210

23 The Local Variables 212

The Auxiliary Methods 212
The Local Variables 213
Fields × Parameters × Local Variables 214
    The Applicability (The Range of Validity)..214
    The Initialization (Assigning the Initial Value) 215
    The Lifetime 216
Position and Module Setting...216
The Constants and the Magic Values 218
Exercise...219
Review 220

24 Methods Returning a Value...221

Fields versus Properties..221
The Accessory methods...222
The Properties Saved in the Fields..222
Returning of the Values Obtained by Calculation 224
Object Equality Testing...224
Test of Returning the Proper Value 225

Exercise..228
Review 229

25 The Crate 231
The Fields Representing a Set of Values 231
Passing Parameters by Value and by Reference 231
Crate / Transport Object 233
The Constants 234
Methods Working with the Crate 235
Exercise..237
    1. Put the project 125b_Crate_Start into operation...237
    2. Import the classes Light, Arrow, TrafficLight and Car and put them into operation 238
    3. Supplement and Test these Classes 238
Review 239

26 Strings and How to Work with Them...240
Problems with Comparing the Objects...240
Concatenation of the Text Strings..241
Text Representation (Text Signature) 241
Line Ending 243
The Escape Sequence...244
The Standard Output 246
    Terminal Window 247
The Standard Error Output 248
Exercise..249
Review 249

27 A Bit of Logic 251
Problems with Objects Comparing...251
The Cast Operator (Type) 252
Numerical Comparison Operators < <= == >= > != 253
Operators and their Arity 253
Comparison of Objects..254
Logical Complement Operator ! 254
Conjunction (Conditional-And) Operators && and & 255
Disjunction (Conditional-Or) Operators || and | 256
Type Comparison Operator instanceof 256
Contract of the equals(Object) Method 258
Value Types and Reference Types 259
    Reference Types 259
    Value Types...259
Exercise..260
Review 260

28 Class Methods and Fields 263
Counted Objects 263
Static Fields..263
Order of Modifiers...264
Program Modifications...264
Innovation of the toString() Method 266
Town...266
    Entering 267

An Analysis 268
   Exercise 273
   Review 274

29 Refactoring of the Code 276
   What is Refactoring 276
   How to Solve Our Problem 277
   The IModular Interface 277
   A Servant Class 279
   The Method auxSwapPositionsWithCheck 279
      Generalization of a Method 281
      Adjustment for Arrows 281
      Adaptation of Test Classes 283
   The testPositionSize Test Method 283
      Generalization of a Copied Method 284
      Adapting the Method to Different Requirements 284
   Exercise 287
   Review 288

30 Static Constructor – Class Constructor 289
   Class Constructor – Static Constructor 289
   The Call class 297
   Loading and Initializing of a Class 299
      Details of Class Initializing 300
   What Should Be Remembered 302
   Procedure of Instance Creating 303
      Details on Constructing an Object Once Again 303
   Instance Instruction 305
   Exercise 305
   Review 305

31 Debugger 308
   The Importance of Debugger 308
   Activating of the Debugger 308
   Debugger's Window 310
   Stepping through / Tracing the Program 311
   The Call Sequence Panel 313
   Return Stack 314
   Local Variables 316
   Stepping through Test Methods 316
   Exercise 317
   Review 317

32 Creating of an Standalone Application 319
   Assignment 320
   The Dispatcher Class 321
   The IUFOFactory Interface 321
   Design Pattern Factory Method 322
   The IUFO Interface 322
      The move(int) Method 323
      A Constructor 324
      Controlling by Direct Message Sending 325

Controlling from a Keyboard...325
Creating a Standalone Application 326
The Main Class of an Application..326
Creating Executable Archives...327
Exercise...328
Review 328

Part 3: Advanced Creating of OO Programs 329

33 Packages 330
Packages and Folders...330
Big Programs and Their Problems 331
Conventions for Project Names...331
Creating Packages in *BlueJ*...332
The package statement..335
Tree of Packages 335
Simple and Full Names 336
Package java.lang...337
The import Statement..337
Package Name Convention 339
Change in Package Dividing...340
Why the Star Notation is Unsuitable 343
Exercise...343
Review 344

34 Linking of Instances..346
Conditions, the Future Objects Have to Meet..346
The RoadField Class...347
The Ring Class 352
The Design Pattern *Builder*..352
The RingBuilder Class 352
Creating of Rings...357
Static Import..360
The RingTest Class 361
Exercise...361
Review 364

35 Decorator 366
Recursion..366
Analysis of Error Message 367
Multimover Class and IMultimovable Interface..370
Ambitions of Objects..371
Design Pattern *Decorator* 372
The Circular Class 373
Test Completing..377
Exercise...379
Review 379

36 Teaching Cars to Turn..380
Reference Area and Relative Coordinates 380

Creating of Objects Turned to Entered Direction 382
Effective Re-drawing of Modified Objects 384
Block 385
The IDirectable Interface... 386
Decorator DirectableCircular 387
Exercise.. 389
Review 389

37 Controlling from Keyboard 390

The Controller 390
Preparation of the Race 394
Conditional Statement – the if Statement 395
Using a Block 396
The IRacer Interface 396
Premature return 398
Embedded Conditional Statement 399
Time Measurement 400
Automatic and Explicit Casting 401
Finishing the Race Class 402
Exercise.. 405
Review 406

38 Containers and Maps 407

Containers and a Library of Collections 407
Dictionaries and Maps... 408
Member Classes 409
The Map<K,V> Interface and the HashMap<K,V> Class 412
      Generic Types and Type Parameters... 412
      Interface vs. Implementation 413
      Initialization 413
The Registration.. 414
The Check of Transits.. 416
The End of the Race 417
The IRace Interface 417
Exercise.. 418
Review 418

39 Further Programming Constructions 420

Collections that Can Be Received from a Map 420
Collection Library 421
The for(:) Loop 423
Race for Several Rings 424
Increment and Decrement Operators... 425
Exceptions and Their Throwing 428
Further Corrections in Older Classes 430
Exercise.. 431
Review 431

40 The Factory Method Second Time................................434

Problems with Variant Rings... 434
The IRingFactory Interface 435
More Complex Factory 436

Complete Conditional Statement 437

Methods with a Variable Number of Parameters 438

The Classic for Loop 439

Exercise 442

Review 442

41 The Loops 444

Size of a Road-field 444

The Lazy Initialization 445

Determining of Lower and Upper Limits 447

Leaving the Loop from Inside of Its Body 448

The Sequence of if … else if 449

Side Effects of Methods 451

Loops Taxonomy 452

The while Loop – the Loop with a Condition at the Beginning 453

The do … while Loop – the Loop with a Condition at the End 454

The switch Statement 456

Change of the Module for Ring 457

The ParallelRace Class 461

Exercise 468

Review 468

42 Lists and Their Ordering 469

Enum Types 469

Enum Type Using 470

The State Diagram 470

The Lists 472

Modifications of the ParallelRace Class 473

Sorting the List Content 476

Native (Natural) Sorting 476

Alternative Sorting and the Design Pattern Command 478

Exercise 480

Review 481

43 The Array 483

Declaration of an Array Variable 483

Creating and Initializing an Array 484

Methods with a Variable Number of Parameters 485

How to Use the Array 486

Sorting of the Array Content 488

How to Express Numbers with Words 488

Exercise 492

Review 492

44 The Finale 494

Index 495

Acknowledgement

I would like to express my thanks to all who helped me in my way to successful completing of this book, both by direct contributing to its content and form, as well as by providing space and means for its creation.

Above all I would like to thank to my wife Jaruška who was my greatest support and whose endless patience and accommodativeness above all in the final hectic period of completing the handwriting enabled me to finish the book in a reasonable date. Great thanks belong also to my children who helped me in finding mistakes in the text as well as in accompanying programs and took over also some of my other duties.

My great thanks go also to a group of volunteers who at electronic conferences accepted my challenge for reading the created manuscript, drawing my attention to possible discrepancies or badly understandable parts of the lecture. The final form of the text arose thanks to particularly Tibor Bako, Vít Grafnetter, Stanislav Hruška, Ladislav Janeček, Jiří Kubala, Michal Palas, Pavel Říha, Martin Staněk, Josef Svoboda and Martin Škurla. Their comments helped remarkably to improve the text quality and remove certain discrepancies.

Also Jarmila Pavlíčková and Luboš Pavlíček who are my colleagues in teaching programming at the University of Economics contributed to the resultant shape of the text. The book reflects many of the results from our (sometimes quite excited) debates on modern programming principles and on ways, how to present these principles to our students.

I would like to say thanks also to the associated professor Mr. Vojtěch Merunka with whom I discussed some principles included into the general conception of the book. His requirement to include into the book several of my ideas for users, who do not intend to create new programs, inspired me to comprise the explanation on an interface into the interactive part. He also supported me in my intention not to include an explanation concerning the inheritance of implementation into the first volume.

I have to express my great thanks also to all colleagues in ICZ Company whose knowledge and rich practical experience enabled me to watch the real needs of practice and accommodate my choice of explained topics as well as the way of lecturing from far near distance. Moreover, they drew my attention to interesting papers and reported on attended conferences dealing with topics of the modern programming itself.

My thanks belong also to authors of *BlueJ* program, due to which the explanation can be organized in such a way so that the students become acquainted with all important principles without being diverted by writing programs. This means they can start programming in the moment these key principles have already "got under their skin".

Preface

This book is a textbook of programming in Java language for beginners. The Java programming language is nowadays the most spread programming language. Programming textbooks for beginners are known and used already a half of century.

That's why you could consider it useless to make out another textbook on programming and above all in the most usual Java. The author (Rudolf Pecinovský) was surrounded by a wide competition. Despite it he succeeded to write a book, which is significantly better and completely different than others. Everybody can recognize it already at the beginning, namely due to three reasons.

Firstly, this textbook did not emerge accidentally. Such a book cannot be written without a long-term professional experience. Writing the text has been preceded by years of preparation, practical programming and teaching experience as well as years of active presentations at professional conferences, in scientific magazines etc. People of my generation used to meet a number of programming languages and styles during their professional life. I myself remember hot debates between adherents of a "common" and structured programming. Then we experienced a period of fighting between adherents of C language and of Pascal language, which resulted in more generalized controversy between the defenders of using the industrial programming language for teaching and supporters of the language less used in industry, yet allegedly more suitable for teaching. The pioneer period of object programming run within such a debate. The professional community in the Czech Republic and in Slovakia remembers well that in all those phases Rudolf Pecinovský did participate and his views and ideas, coming from any period, did not lose its validity and correctness. We can find them in this book. Rudolf Pecinovský does not pretend that he understands everything, he is not afraid to present a speculation or a question. It is the proof of the highest professionalism and familiarity with object programming.

Secondly, this book is written in an unusual form of a dialogue between two persons: the author of the book and his friend, who represents the reader. Author's friend puts questions and the author answers. A number of topics refer one to the other; new questions result from the previous answers. After several minutes of reading you get a feeling, as if you would lay the questions yourself. The author succeeded to evoke a feeling of identification of the reader with the book protagonist. The same form of a dialogue we can find in works of Sokrates, Plato, Cicero, St. Augustin, Komensky, Galileo and others. According to classical authors the dialogue is one of the pillars of the European thinking. His pragmatic contribution comes from the understanding and perception that a man can make a mistake or maintains a position of single-track viewpoint and that he can help to meet someone else's view. Meeting and clashing of opinions leads to a better view of participants, they had before the meeting. This can be documented also by a translation of the Greek expression "dia-logos" that can be expressed as "through the word" or more freely "through the language". This book has features of such a dialogue: The author is able to clearly and understandably explain his opinion. He listens to the views and arguments of others, understands them, thinks about them and reacts to them.

Thirdly, the professional publications in our country are written usually in a different way. They use a sterile passive voice and third person of singular (e.g. "it is done", "it means that") or first person of plural (e.g. "we have", "we propose"). Using of "me" and "you" is not considered as suitable for professional literature in the Czech Republic. Rudolf Pecinovský showed that it is possible; however, you should know how to do it. And he rounds off his effort with an accurate Czech language and brilliant Czech terminology without using anglicisms.

This book should be read by not only beginners in Java – to whom the book is primarily determined – but also by all those, who would like to learn programming or teach programming in any modern object programming language. The book content, quality of processed examples, theories, dialogues and gradation of the explanation give more than sufficient proof that Rudolf Pecinovský knows what he speaks about. This book is a pride of an original Czech professional literature. Regardless the fact that you already know Java or you are practically using it, you should read this book, use it as your handbook, and study it very carefully.

Doc. Ing. Vojtěch Merunka, Ph.D.
Faculty of Economics and Management,
Czech University of Life Science, Prague;
Faculty of Nuclear Sciences and Physical Engineering
Czech Technical University in Prague

Author's Foreword

This book is a result of a long-period experimenting with the way how to teach contemporary programming. I tried to teach programming maybe in all types of schools. I gave lessons at basic schools, secondary schools, for groups of people interested in programming. At present I teach programming at the Faculty of Informatics and Statistics of the University of Economics and at the same time I give courses for professional programmers in ICZ Company. I recognize in my courses, that the secondary and university type schools produce a number of programmers who are programming in certain "modern" language, but in fact they do not know the programming in a modern way. Their schools thought them programming in the same way as I learned more than 30 years ago. Programming has changed significantly since that time; however, these changes did not penetrate into lessons at a number of schools.

The book you hold in your hands significantly differs from a majority of programming textbooks that you can meet at present. It does not try to teach you any language, but it strives to teach you thinking in such a way so that you would be able to use all advantages of modern programming. At the same time it tries to show you that the modern object oriented programming is far close to current man's way of thinking than you could notice at the first sight (and then majority of textbook is willing to admit).

I aimed to write this book in such a way so that a clever secondary school student could use it. It is outlined as a conversation between me and my good friend – let's say my child. I verified in several previous textbooks, that the form of a dialogue brings a number of advantages:

☞ You can follow the explanation thread much easily.

☞ On places where the students are discomfited or are not clear you can insert an additional question which may digress from the main topic for a while, but which contributes to better understanding of current explanation and possible connections of the reader and that's why he understands the subsequent explanation better.

☞ Lessons can be served in small portions which – as certain reviewer said "you succeed to read during pissing pause in a rattlesnake area".

The book is divided into three parts.

☞ In the first one you work with the developing tool in an interactive mode, when the user appears to be one of the program's objects and sends messages to other objects. This means he is in the center of all events and communicates with surrounding program parts without knowing programming. In this part I will explain all basic principles of object oriented programs which we shall use in future parts.

☞ In the second part the explanation will be quicker. You will learn how to create simple programs in which you shall gradually apply all principles, you have learned in the first part. We shall also prepare basic stones for a program which we will build up in the next program part.

☞ In the third part the explanation will become again a bit quicker. I shall start explaining principles, that belong to basic principles of object oriented programming, but a lot of which are far behind the horizon of subject matter presented in current courses. Gradually we shall create a program for simple car races with several participants. You will use components of this program in the last lesson for demonstrating the simple program simulating the operation in a simplified city with streets and crosses controlled by traffic lights.

At the beginning I said that I do not intend to teach any language, but programming. However, if we would like to create the above mentioned programs, we need certain language. I have chosen Java, which has a lot of advantages:

☞ It is the most popular programming language for a lot of years, used by more than 6 million programmers. It's indicated that Java will keep its leading position even for future times.

☞ It is one of the simplest languages used in professional practice, which means it is easy to learn it. Anyway, it is easier, than learning other languages optimized for professional programmers who offer mass of various peculiarities that are never used by a significant part of programmers.

☞ All tools you need for the development of not only simple but also very extensive programs used in great companies or in the state administration you can get free of charge.

☞ Developing tools as well as created programs run in all current operational systems, which means, it is not important if you develop the program under *Windows*, *Linux* or *MacOS*. The developed program will be operating in any of them and you can transfer it from one PC to the other without any problem.

☞ It is the most frequent language in university courses of programming.

☞ For me it is also important due to the fact that there is no development tool determined especially for teaching in initial courses of programming. This tool offers a lot of important functions, which are not offered by any other tools, despite they are more elaborated.

However, the used language is not important because I don't want to teach you Java, but I want to teach you programming in a modern way, i.e. object oriented programming. That's why I shall present only Java's most essential items and we will concentrate above all on how you should think when developing the programs, to which items you should aim, what to suppress to backside and how to arrange it so that it would not come back as an unexpected boomerang. I would like to engage in more detailed and systematic explanation of all broached topics in the following volume.

I admit that this publication as a book for beginners is a bit thick. It's caused by the fact that everything is explained in details and at examples which we pass through step by step, and you can see which suitable solutions are proposed and why. The explanation is supplemented by a number of queries, by which my "partner" assures that she understood the explanation well, or on the contrary, she is asking questions concerning unclear items.

The book was arising two and half years. It began as a serial on the *Sun* company pages under the title *Object Oriented Thinking in Java*. When I came to an agreement with the ComputerPress publishing house on the Czech edition, I stopped working at this serial and devoted my time only to the book. Several volunteers who were willing to read the whole book text and pointed out the discovered mistakes and insufficiencies in explanation enrolled to me. They were beginning as well as advanced programmers, even teachers. Despite the endeavor of all these people there may be some mistakes or inaccuracies.

Part 1:

Interactive Mode

In this part you will hear the explanation what does it mean the object oriented programming, then we shall exploit the fact that the used development environment enables working in an interactive mode in which the user becomes one of the program objects and can communicate with other objects. In this mode I will show you the most important rules of cooperation with individual objects that create the program. Rules will be subsequently used for managing the development of programs in other parts of the book.

1 The Prologue

What you will learn in this lesson
In this opening lesson you will meet the style of explanation and the basic tools used during this
explanation.

Project:
In this lesson we start working with the 101a_Shapes project.

1.   I would like to learn programming. My friends told me that the best programming language for beginners is Java. That's why I'd like to ask you for your help.

I agree with your friends that Java is one of the best languages for entering into the world of programming. Moreover, according to a number of statistics it is the most widely used language. I will not enumerate all its advantages, but believe, that your friends advised you really well. With pleasure I will help you with your entering the programmer's universe.

2.   They also advised me not to pick up the textbook which is concentrated on the language rules and libraries overview, but supposes at the same time that I will learn programming by myself.

This is a frequent problem of a number of textbooks and courses. They focus on "here's what the language can do". In opposition, my courses (and thus also this book) focus on "here's how to use it well and stay out of troubles". Don't be afraid, we shall concentrate above all to programming, and I promise not to speak about language rules and libraries offer sooner than we will really need to know them.

However, I have to warn you in advance that I teach programming in a little bit different way than majority of textbooks. That is to say I teach it according to the methodology *Architecture First*, which is rather young (it occurred on 2004). Its advantage – compared to other methodologies – is that you will not find out in later courses of advanced programs that knowledge and skills gained at the beginning were not the best form of programming and that you should start programming in rather different way.

3.   Why it's presented in such a way when it's known that it's not quite well?

A lot of teachers assume that they cannot teach how to design an architecture of a program when the students don't know to write down a program, how to code it and test it. Therefore, the courses for beginners mostly concentrate on how to write down a simple program, whilst designing a program and its architecture is presented only in very advanced courses. Disadvantage of this approach is that introductory course students often learn bad habits and only hardly they get rid of them in advanced courses.

For a long time there was no methodology which would be able to change this unpleasant state. Fortunately, at the turn of the century new teaching tools appeared enabling a development of new methodologies which eliminate these problems. However, it is not the proper time for explaining all details just now. After we shall meet the passages that made troubles to beginners in current way of teaching, I will let you know.

Methodology Used

4.   It's not necessary to explain all details, but at least you could imply a bit how it differs from the previous ones.

The main difference between the *Architecture First* methodology and other methodologies is that it changes the order of explanation. The *Architecture First* methodology is based on two main principles:

☞   The tools facilitating the program development are more and more sophisticated. In many cases it is sufficient to suggest only, what should be programmed, and the tools send this requirement to the embedded code generator which creates the needed program. The last area, which yet resists to this automation for a long time, is the design of the program architecture, which means the arrangement of the main components and design of the rules for their cooperation."

☞   One of the important pedagogical patterns called *early bird pattern* says: *"Organize the course so that the most important topics are taught first. Teach the most important material, the "big ideas", first (and often). When this seems impossible, teach the most important material as early as possible."*

The above mentioned propositions imply that if we are confident that the last activity which will be soon left to programmers will be primarily (and almost entirely) the design of the program architecture , we should teach it from the very beginning or very soon despite some subjects, that were formerly explained at the beginning, would be postponed or left out. Therefore, the *Architecture First* methodology suggests teaching students firstly the basic architectonical principles to be able to design the program (teaching them how to think in the object oriented way).

A lot of courses start with explaining the basic principles, but they only explain them and don't incorporate them immediately in developing a program, because students still do not know, how to do it. *Architecture First* methodology lets the creation of the designed program to a code generator. Only when the students come beyond the code generator capabilities they start to learn how to code the constructions themselves.

The Presentation Concept

5.   It looks interesting. I hope you will not rush me to absorb these principles quickly. As you know I need to assimilate new knowledge. I don't want to compete in passing the course as quickly as possible. Some of my friends wanted to learn programming quickly and after that they were discovering for several months what their textbooks and courses skipped to be quicker. They have to learn all these things, but it took much more time to them.

Here you can apply the well-known saying *Haste makes waste*. We shall not hurry up and whenever anything will be unclear to you, please, do ask me. I will not try to teach you quickly, but I will try to teach you correctly.

As I have already told you, for some time you will not feel that you are learning programming. You will have a feeling that we are only playing with the computer. However, in this initial phase you have to learn a lot of terms, connections and regularities so that later on you could understand further topics much better and quicker. Nearly in each of my courses there are students who underestimate this initial phase and subsequently they reproach themselves for useless problems because they were not careful enough.

6.   On the other side I am afraid, that when we start going through all items carefully, we will pass through only few of them.

I agree with you. But it can be solved. Let's divide the whole course into several volumes. In this volume (i.e. in this book) we will make only some first excursion into the world of object oriented programming. An excursion where our goal will not be a presentation of topics to all details, but where I will rather try to give you a basic idea what the object oriented programming means and how to proceed in creating the object oriented programs. Simply you should receive a general overview of this area. At the same time you will learn a lot of skills that standard courses don't present not even in advanced courses of programming. (At this occasion I have to remember a reader who read another of my books and then he wrote me: "I thought I am not any programmer's rookie. But after I have read your textbook I opened up my eyes and mouth.")

In the next volume we will firstly go back to all what we skipped during this general overview and then we will start studying certain areas deeply. We will also mention other areas, which are not mentioned in current programming textbooks.

The Accompanying Animations

7.   It all looks attractive. Do you think you will be able to explain everything sufficiently illustratively to me? I mean I need firstly to try it several times, before I remember it.

I will do my best. Furthermore, in first lessons the text explanation will be accompanied by animated demonstrations in flash format at your disposal at the address

    http://edu.pecinovsky.cz/animations

In case your browser knows to open flash animations (nowadays practically all browsers know it), you can open them and practice everything what the animation shows at the screen.

First of all let me give you few advices how you can control them. All accompanying animations have two sets of controlling elements.

☞   Green buttons with arrows located in bottom corners of the animated picture.

☞   Silver control bar under the animated picture.

The animation stops after presenting an action so that you could see the result. Often a callout textbox appears (possibly with an arrow) bringing an information about the current animation or some other additional information.

The green button with an arrow to the right activates further animation running. You will use them in case you would like to continue. The green button with an arrow to the left returns the animation to previous stop and you will use them in case you would like to run the last sequence once more.

The silver control bar enables stopping the animation at any moment and repeated activating. For stopping and activating the animation you will find a button at its left edge. The control bar will also enable you to move immediately to any place of the animation. This you will achieve by clicking on the control bar on which the slider runs. The slider then moves to the place on which you clicked and sets the animation in a corresponding way. You will activate the animation by pressing the button on the left edge of this control bar.

> *Animation 1.1: Animation describing its own handling –* LOOTP_101a_Handling
> *So that you could test the described animation handling, I prepared for the beginning an animation with the well-known card game FreeCell.*

At the beginning analogous animations will be included in each lesson; some of them (e.g. the current one) will include more animations. They are mostly recorded in resolution 1000×600 pixels so that you could put the browser with activated animation aside the screen (or on a second screen) and you would have some place for experiments. When preparing these animations I supposed that you will open them and after each stop you will try repeating aside at the display what the animation has just shown you.

What You Will Need

8.   I am looking forward for presentation with animations. What I will need for it?

Besides taste for studying you will need the development tools, with which you will analyze the accompanying programs and create your own programs. Good news is that you can download all necessary tools from internet free of charge.

9.   You said "all necessary tools". Does it mean that we shall need more than one tool?

Good estimation. At the beginning we will need JDK and *BlueJ*. Further you can add more comfortable professional environment. I will give you a notice in a proper time and will let you decide yourself.

File Manager

10.   Don't throw unknown names on me and better explain what it means.

Don't be afraid, I will explain everything to you. Before I start to speak about tools, which are necessary for programming, I would like to mention an important tool that you will use in every work with your computer. It is a file manager.

I was thinking for a long time how to show you what happens on a disk during the work. I wanted to use a manager that is free of charge but I didn't want to use the file manager that is a part of an operational system because thus I would discriminate those who are working with different operating system.

At the end I discovered a file manager **muCommander.** It is free of charge and it is written in Java which means it will operate in all systems where JRE (see further) is installed. That's why I will use it in my excursions to a disk and for the research which files occur/don't occurs there.

You can find it at the address http://www.mucommander.com. I don't press on you to download it; you can use your favorite file manager. I only wanted to tell you which file manager I'm using for pictures and animations.

JDK and JRE

11.   Well, I notice. And now you could tell me something about the tools for which you started to use the strange abbreviations.

JDK (Java Development Kit) is a denomination for a package of programs containing all necessary elements for the development of programs in Java language. Its installation file has about 100 MB (I am speaking about version 7, later versions can be larger) and you can download it at the address http://java.sun.com/javase/downloads. You will find there offers for downloading JDK with various additions. Skip it over and download only JDK itself. We will not need any additions at this moment and before we shall need them, the new ones will occur.

When installing the JDK you will install in fact two environments: JDK itself, (we have already said that it is an environment with tools acting for development of your applications), and JRE (Java Runtime Environment), which is an environment that has to be installed at the computer, where we want to use these applications.

JRE is significantly simpler and is necessary for all those who want to activate programs in Java. However, at present it is usually installed at majority of computers. It is installed as a part of JDK so that you could not only develop the application, but also test it, how it will run at computers of your brilliant program users who may have installed only JRE at their computers.

You have to start with installing the JDK because the development environment that we will use requires JDK's previous installation.

12.   When JDK contains all we need why to download any other environments?

Due to the fact that handling the programs that are part of JDK are not known as being very user-friendly – majority of them can be controlled only from the command line. It's convenient to some programmers[1], but majority of them use certain development environment, which mediates the communication between the programmer and the relevant JDK programs, and is much user friendly. These environments mostly offer a whole set of tools that make the work easier.

Comfortable environments that offer a majority of tools needed for program developing are usually marked with an abbreviation IDE (Integrated Development Environment) which should evoke that these programs have integrated more functions in the only program.

BlueJ Environment

13.   Does it mean that we shall download also some IDE?

Yes, we will download the *BlueJ* environment, which is an integrated development environment that was designed especially for introductory courses and which we will use in first lessons of our course. You can download it at the address http://www.bluej.org.

---

[1]   Number of textbooks use working with a command line as the only possibility. Their authors claim that a student can best recognize basic principles of a platform. However, it seems to me that I could ask the bus driver to get from Paris to Rome by walking, because only thus he can understand how far apart both cities are.

Unfortunately, the default configuration which you will download does not use all possibilities offered by the *BlueJ* environment. Therefore I use a little bit different configuration in my courses. So I would advise you to have a look at my pages http://edu.pecinovsky.cz/bluej_config, where the preconfigured version is prepared for downloading. It has a configuration that we will use in our course. These pages are continuously updated and you can get there the last information on recommended versions and how to set its configuration to be convenient with materials of this course.

14.   You told me that there are further development environments. Why have you chosen just *BlueJ*?

The main advantage of this environment is that handling with it is so simple that you can learn it within few minutes. Contrary to it learning of some professional IDE takes so much time and effort as learning Java. And moreover, the *BlueJ* environment offers some special "teaching functions" which you surely will appreciate but which are not offered by professional development environments. This environment is also fully localized in many languages; it will be highly appreciated by those who are not so familiar with English language. (However, only versions for English, Czech and Slovak languages are offered at my pages.)

Professional IDE

15.   Well, so we have JDK and IDE. Why did you tell that at the last third I will be able to transfer to another environment?

Some programmers reproached me in internet discussions that I do not use professional environment. My answer is simple: any professional environment of Java does not offer such functions which I consider to be important for the initial lessons. And moreover, the *BlueJ* environment was designed in the way so that the beginner should not be amused by fighting with the environment and could concentrate on the lectured topics.

But simplicity of *BlueJ* environment is redeemed by the fact that it offers really only basic functions. Therefore, a lot of students give up their time and effort for learning at least basic functions of some professional development environment, because they know that their endeavor will return many times in future designing of programs.

In case you would like to sacrifice your comfort and learn handling with IDE, whose knowledge will save you a lot of time in developing more complex programs, I recommend the *NetBeans* environment which belongs to the best available development environments. You can theoretically use this environment since the moment when we will leave the interactive mode and will start to write the source code. Until the end of this course I will use *BlueJ*, but in case you would like to continue in the advanced course, *NetBeans* will be used there.

You can download the *NetBeans* environment at the address http://www.netbeans.org. However, at the same address from which you downloaded JDK you can download even the whole set JDK+*NetBeans*. I would recommend downloading and installing them separately, because then you will be able to update *NetBeans* and JDK independently.

The second, not less good choice is the *Eclipse* environment which you can download at the address http://www.eclipse.org/downloads. The third famous IDE is *IntelliJ IDEA*, which you can download at the address http://www.jetbrains.com/idea/download.In case you would meet programmers who work with this environment and they would be willing to advise you, you can follow them without any problems.

Working with *BlueJ*

16.   I have downloaded and installed JDK as well as *BlueJ*, so we can start.

Before we begin the programming itself let's have a look how to work with the *BlueJ* environment. Firstly, download the file with accompanied programs which you will find at the address `http://books.pecinovsky.cz/lootp`. It is a self-extracting file containing all projects which we will use during the course. Then activate the accompanying animation at `http://edu.pecinovsky.cz/animations/LOOTP_101b_IDE_BlueJ`, open the project `101a_Shapes` according to instructions and have a try so that you could be concentrated at the explanation itself and working with the environment would not amuse you.

> *Animation 1.2:* BlueJ *environment and how to work with it –* `LOOTP_101b_IDE_BlueJ`
> *Basics of the work with the environment should not be explained by words only; the best is to show it. All necessary explanation is therefore placed at this animation.* **Majority of presented topics in this animation is not discussed in the textbook; however, in further text I suppose you know it.**

Review

Let's review what you learned in this lesson (some of the following items are not in the text but in accompanying animations):

☞   This book is the first volume of a series. It should offer the basic overview of object oriented programs and their development.

☞   The explanation follows the *Architecture First* methodology that teaches first the key properties of programs together with some basic architectonic principles and only after it the coding rules.

☞   This textbook presents topics which are not presented in current programming courses, despite the fact they are generally considered as very important.

☞   This textbook will be followed by another volume that will return to areas which we could not explained now and will present further important topics neglected in current courses.

☞   The development environments serve for developing the programs. The basic development tool for developing programs in Java is JDK – Java Development Kit.

☞   The user, who wants only to run programs written in Java, will manage with the JRE (Java Runtime Environment).

☞   Tools from JDK package do not have too much comfortable development environment and therefore majority of programmers use an IDE – integrated development environment.

☞   At the course beginning we shall use IDE *BlueJ*, which is specially designed for introductory courses of programming. In the next volume we will transfer to professional IDE *NetBeans*.

☞   The *BlueJ* application window is divided into three panels: the button panel, the object bench and the class diagram.

☞   In IDE *BlueJ* we work with projects.

☞ A standard project has its own folder where all its files are placed. We recognize the folder with *BlueJ* project according to its icon in a dialog box for projects opening.

☞ *BlueJ* is able to open also projects placed in the JAR and ZIP archives. These projects can be opened as NON-BLUEJ projects. During opening them, *BlueJ* automatically creates a folder named according to the opened archives, unrolls the archives content into it and works further with it as with *BlueJ* project.

☞ You open the existing project by the command **File → Open**. *BlueJ* opens a dialog box, in which it shows only folders. The folders containing a *BlueJ* project are marked by a special icon.

☞ In case the opened project is among the twelve lastly opened projects we can open it quickly from the sub-offer evoked by a command **File → Reopen**.

☞ When opening the project, its name is written in the title bar of the application window. At the same time its class diagram is read and depicted.

☞ Rectangles in class diagram represent classes featuring in the project.

☞ The class rectangle can be caught by a mouse and drawn to another place.

☞ The size of the class rectangle can be changed by catching and drawing its right bottom corner.

☞ By clicking with the mouse in a free space followed by drawing you define a selected block. All classes in this block, as well as all classes that are somehow touched by this block, will be marked as selected.

☞ Selected class is marked by bolding its edge.

☞ Selected rectangles can be shifted at the same time or you can change their measure.

Project:
No significant changes were made in the 101a_Shapes project.

2 The OOP – Get Acquainted

What you will learn in this lesson
In this lesson you will become acquainted with objects and classes, you will learn what it means when objects mutually send messages. You will learn what the basic difference between the old structured program and the newer object oriented one is. At the conclusion you will make acquaintance with the graphic language UML and you will meet our first project drawn in this language.

Project:
In this lesson we continue in using the 101a_Shapes project.

The Object Oriented World

17.   **I have already learned opening and closing the project as well as manipulation with classes (better say with corresponding rectangles in class diagram) according to the animation, and you could start explaining what the classes are like.**

Let me start a bit broader. The Object Oriented Programming comes out of the understanding that each program is a simulation of a real or virtual world.

☞   The program for accounting administration simulates the acting of the company and their customers concerning the orders, supplies, invoices and payments. The simulation is synchronized with the real life by making a real invoice, registering real received payments etc.

☞   The program for playing chess simulates acting in certain virtual chess world, in which two armies attack one other, and one army is handled by the player and the second one by the computer.

☞   Drawing program simulates an action in a virtual world of geometric shapes which mutually react in multiple way (i.e. mutually communicate and impact one another).

And thus we could pass program by program.

   Note on terminology:
   An expression *Object Oriented Programming* is long, that's why we often use an abbreviation **OOP**. If we do not speak just about programming, we often use instead of the long *object oriented* only simple **OO** – e.g. OO analysis or OO program.

The Objects

The world is created by **objects**. Therefore, if the program should successfully simulate events in this world, it has to know how to work with objects.

We are willing to consider persons, animals and things as objects in current life. Object oriented programming generalizes such understanding of objects. In OO programs we take as objects also the characteristics (color, taste, smell …), events (connecting, interruption …), states (calmness, movement, anger …) and generally **everything, what we can call with a noun** including such abstract "objects" as beauty, welfare or life.

18.   How can be a beauty taken as an object?

By many ways. You can e.g. characterize the level of beauty of some object by a number from -5 to +5 and put this characteristic as object representing the given beauty.

The Classes

19.   It's a little bit strange, but it's understandable. Please, go on.

In bigger programs there are thousands and tens of thousands of objects. So that we could reasonably work with them, we need certain classification. When you will have all your papers on the table, you surely will not be able to work with them well and you will sort them into groups according their topics.
    Similar situation is with the objects. We can divide them into groups with very similar characteristics. These groups are named **classes**. Objects belonging to certain class are named as **instances of this class**. E.g. your as well as my computers are instances of a general class of personal computers.

20.   Then what's the difference between an object and an instance?

Strictly speaking minimal. They are both almost mutually substitutable synonyms. The expression *object* is preferred in situations when we speak about general objects, whilst the expression *instance* is preferred in situations when you want to stress that the given object belongs to some class (the object is an instance of XYZ class). They are not substitutable only in the very rare cases, when the object under discussion is not an instance of any class.

21.   You told me that all what we can name by a noun is an object. This means that also the class has to be an object.

You are true. A class is also an object. It is an object which keeps information characterizing its instances and as the only one it is able to create instances. But don't task your mind with it. After you will be a little bit more experienced, you will take it as quite usual. And when I return to your previous question, in some languages (e.g. in Java) the class is an object which is not an instance of any class.

22.   An object keeping the information on instances – that's too abstract for me and I don't want to wait for being more experienced. Could you explain it at some example just now?

I will try it. Imagine that you are one of the objects of a program simulating the world you are living in. A while ago I told you that both your and my computers are instances of a class of all computers. Similarly the table on which the computer is standing is an instance of a class of all tables, and a chair on which you are sitting is an instance of a class of all chairs.

The class knows how to create its instances – thus you could consider it as a factory for your instances. In case you will need a new computer, you will ask the computer class for a new instance and in case it will be possible, the class will create it. In case you will need a new car, you will ask the car class and it will create the required car for you.

The Messages

23.   It's a pity that the real word doesn't operate in such way. How the addressed class recognizes which kind of computer or car I want?

You are sending your requirement as a message. A detailed specification of your requirement could be a part of this message – we say that you are **sending a message with parameters**.

24.   Well, I asked the car class for a car and I obtained a car. But how I would arrive to my aim with this car in the program?

You are identically proceeding all the time: your object, i.e. the object representing you, will send a message to the object of car to reach the required place. Well, it would be suitable to get in before that. If I would use a hypothetical language in which I write firstly the addressed object and then the name of the message which I am sending, followed by possible parameters of this message, the resultant program might look out as follows:

```
a_car open

a_car get_in me
a_car close
a-car go_to destination
```

25.   As I see the car opens and closes itself. In case of a usual car, I should open and close it myself. But with getting in – I don't understand. Why I should say to the car that I am getting in?

The car does not close itself; it closes in reaction to your message. And in a real world you give over the message by taking the handle or pushing the door. In the virtual world of the computer program the message looks out a little bit different, but the result is the same: the door will open, respectively close.

26.   Well, maybe. And why I have to say to the car that I am getting in and I cannot get in without telling it to the car?

Because the omnipresent physics, which would tell it to the car instead of you, is missing in the program. When you get in the car in real life you place your xyz kilos (pounds) into it and your car immediately knows that you are in. In the computer program this physics has to be replaced by the programmer and it is he/she who has to give over the relevant information explicitly (= publicly).

27.   Does it mean that when I want for example to sit down at the chair I have to send a message as well?

Of course, in the real world I will sit down at a chair and, depending on my weight and the chair quality, the chair will bear me or not. At the same time, depending on the underlayment, the chair, I am going to sit on, can sink.

In an OO program the object getting to sit down (in this case the object representing me) sends a message how many kilos (pounds) is just going to sit down on the chair to the object representing the chair. The object of chair will evaluate if it will bear the object getting to sit down (me in this case) and if yes, it will send a message about the change of loading its feet to its underlayment. The underlayment answers, if the chair will sink and how much. The chair will evaluate the situation and will send info to the object getting to sit down concerning how the action turned out.

In case we would like to improve the program, when evaluating the reaction of an object getting to sit down, the object of chair could send a message to an object representing the surrounding air that it's creaking. It would send this message to all objects that can react to a sound – e.g. also to my ears (better said to an object representing my ears). And, my ears can evaluate this creaking (let's skip over my brains for simplifying the program) and recommend me not to tease the chair.

The Structured vs. Object Oriented Program

28.   It looks like the program is nothing else than permanent sending messages from one object to the other one.

That's exact. A current, structured program is usually defined as a sequence of statements which defines how the given problem should be solved. (Well, it is not accurate, but for a majority of structured programs this definition is suitable.) Opposite to it the object oriented program could be defined as **a set of objects and messages that are sent among these objects.**

Different characterization of both types of programs leads also to a different analysis of problems and subsequent solutions. I tell it so that you would not be surprised that some of your friends understand the programming in different ways. For a long time there was only structured programming and even now a number of contemporary textbooks do not teach different types of program proposals. They teach you programming in object oriented languages and use objects and classes in their programs, but they are not teaching you object thinking. But that's what I would like to teach you in my course.

The First Project

29.   What about to finish the theory and try a practical example.

I agree. Opposite to current usage we will not create any program like *Hello, World* – let's leave it for textbooks of syntax. We want to concentrate to program architecture and that's why we shall work with nontrivial (= not very simple) projects immediately at the beginning.

30.   Do you think that it is reasonable to start with – how you say – nontrivial projects, despite I don't know anything about programming?

Don't be afraid, their complexity will be sufficiently small so that you would be able to understand their architecture, but on the other hand, sufficiently big so that you could recognize as much as possible when studying the work with objects.

We shall start with a 101a_Shapes project in which you became acquainted with *BlueJ* environment in the accompanying animation and practice your manipulation with classes in class diagram. Please, open it so that we could speak firstly about further details concerning the class diagram.

The Graphic Language UML

31.   I've opened it. What will you tell me about it?

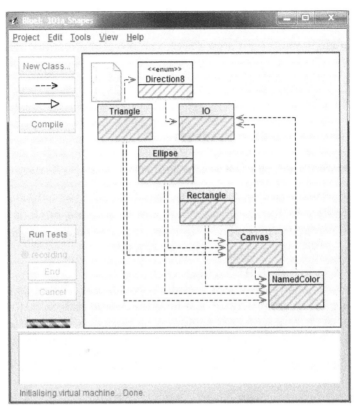

Figure 2.1
The BlueJ application window with an open 101a_Shapes project

In the accompanying animation at the end of the last lesson you learned that the biggest area of the application window of *BlueJ* environment is taken by the so called *class diagram*. The class diagram is one of the diagram set by which the proposals of object oriented programs are depicted in the graphic language UML (Unified Modeling Language).

The UML language is used by top programmers for program design even before they sit down to the text editor and start writing program in some programming language. The UML language makes the proposal of program architecture easier. The programmers clear up mutual relations of its particular future parts and the resultant program is proposed more quickly and reliably. Therefore I will try to teach you first object thinking on class diagrams and only after it we shall start to think over how to write down various functions in a code. Knowing the UML and the ability to speak in it belongs to the obligatory skills of a modern programmer.

32.   You told me that the class diagram is one of the UML diagrams. Could another one be better?

There are altogether 13 diagrams and each of them serves to a different purpose. The class diagram describes the general program architecture at the level of classes and for our purposes it is the most useful for the time being. After you will be more advanced and we shall solve some more complex tasks, I will show you further ones.

Classes in the Project

33.   We wanted to start working on a project and again we came to a theory.

Don't be afraid, we will already start working on our project. As I told you, each rectangle in the class diagram represents a class. There are seven classes defined in the current project:

☞   Instances of Ellipse, Rectangle and Triangle classes represent the corresponding geometrical figures. If during creating the instance there is yet no canvas (see further), the class will require creating it.

☞   The instance of the Canvas class represents a canvas on which the geometrical figures are drawn. This class ensures having only one instance so that all geometrical shapes would be drawn on the same canvas.

☞   Instances of the NamedColor class represent colors of the canvas and of painted shapes. The class in its birth defines several basic colors, but others can be created as well.

☞   Instances of the Direction8 class represent 8 cardinal and secondary points; those are directions to which the triangle can be turned.

☞   The IO class does not have any instance and even does not enable to create any. It does not need any instances – all messages are sent directly to the class which provides all arrangements. The IO class gained its name from the expression *Input/Output*. It covers the communication with the user in a project (i.e. input and output of information) through dialog boxes in which we can either provide or receive information. Besides that it can stop running the program for certain time, if necessary.

34.   Why the Direction8 class is colored in a different way than other classes?

I will start a little bit broadly. Some classes have special characteristics, to which we would like to draw your attention. UML enables to draw an attention to these specialties through the so called **stereotypes**, which means short, mostly one-word names of the given feature closed in «guillemets» («French quotation marks», «angle quotes») and in case of the class located above a class title. Moreover, *BlueJ* enables to color the classes marked by stereotypes with the color assigned to this stereotype in a configuration file.

The Direction8 class is defined as the so called **enum type** or **enumerated type**, which means that all its instances were defined beforehand and therefore no others can be created. These instances are created in advance and you can ask the class for them any time.

35.   Why there are arrows pulled among classes?

Arrows mark dependence among classes. E.g. the arrow going from Canvas class to Color class announces that the Canvas class is dependent on the Color class. You cannot create a canvas that would have no color.

Similarly all geometrical shapes are dependent on the Color class because they also need to have a color. Moreover, these shapes are dependent on Canvas class, because it is the only one place where they can be drawn and prove their existence.

36.   What does it mean the sheet of paper in the left upper corner?

It stands for the text file called README.TXT, which is usually a part of the project. Author of the project can write basic information for users into this file. By clicking at the icon you will open the file and you can write down your own notes.

37.   Well, everything is clear and we can start the programming.

For the time being we will not be programming. Don't mix programming and coding. First I have to remind, that we will not write a code at the beginning. As I've said earlier, we will start first with learning the architectural principles and we will delegate the code writing to a code generator. We will play with classes and instances for a while so that you would understand how the object oriented program is working. And only after that we shall start coding.

38.   I am not much excited of it. Why do you think playing with classes and objects could help me in my subsequent programming?

Programming is not only coding but also designing the architecture of the program. Many programmers, who start with learning how to code a program at first, have later problems with designing a good architecture. The inversed way, where we first learn architectural principles and only then the code writing, doesn't bring such problems. Don't worry; you will learn how to code the program in the next part.

We start working in the interactive mode. Let's try to play that we are part of the program – an object which is sending messages to other objects. At the same time I will explain you why other objects react to our messages in the way they react. I will show you how our messages have to look out so that we would evoke a required reaction of objects receiving our messages.

The Compilation

39.   Well, how should I send a message?

So that you could send messages to individual program parts, the program has to run. Firstly it needs to be compiled. When being compiled the program is converted from a form understandable for a man (we create it in such a form) into a form, which the computer is able to process much quicker. As soon as some class is compiled, *BlueJ* enables to communicate with it.

40.   How can I recognize if the class is compiled?

Simply. In *BlueJ* the classes which are not yet compiled have the lower part of its rectangle in class diagram hatched. After compilation the hatching disappears.

41. I suppose that the compilation starts with pressing the button Compile at the button panel.

Yes, it is one of the possibilities. The fact that a class compilation started is indicated by a change of its rectangle color. After the compilation the rectangle returns to its original color and at the same time the hatching disappears. And again you can see everything in the accompanying animation.

Animation 2.1: Compilation of classes in the BlueJ environment – L00TP_102a_Compilation
Animation shows the dependence of compilation succession on the mutual dependence of individual classes in a project.

Review

Let's review what you have learned in this lesson:

☞ The term *object oriented* can be sometimes replaced by an abbreviation OO.

☞ Object oriented programming is marked with an abbreviation OOP.

☞ OOP comes out of the knowledge that all programs are a simulation of the real or of the virtual world.

☞ The world is created by objects which reciprocally interact. Programming languages have to describe properly both objects as well as their interactions.

☞ Interactions of objects from the simulated world are described in the program as messages that objects send one to the other.

☞ A more detailed specification of our requirements is passed through the data called message parameters.

☞ The object oriented program is a description of a set of objects and their interactions written in some programming language.

☞ In OOP we include into objects everything what we can call with a noun.

☞ In modern programming the graphic language UML is used for program designing.

☞ UML defines 13 diagrams for different phases of the program development. For our purposes the most useful is the class diagram.

☞ Rectangles in class diagram represent classes performing in the project.

☞ Arrows between classes symbolize dependences. The class, from which the arrow leads, is dependent on the class, to which the arrow points.

☞ Some classes have special features on which an attention should be drawn. In UML we can do it through stereotypes, which mean short, mostly one-word names of the given feature closed in «Guillemets» («French quotation marks»).

☞ By hatching the lower rectangle's part *BlueJ* announces that the class is not yet compiled.

☞ We ask for compiling of all project classes by pressing the **Compile** button at the button panel.

Project:
No significant changes were made in the 101a_Shapes project.

3 We Are Sending First Messages

What you will learn in this lesson
In this lesson you will send your first message and will create the first instance. You will become acquainted with the object bench and meet the explanation what is the virtual machine and how it resets.

Project:
In this lesson we continue in using the 101a_Shapes project.

42.   The project is compiled. And I repeat my question: "How should I send a message?"

As I told you already last time, you can send a message only to the class that has been compiled. Immediately as the class is compiled you can start sending the messages. A list of all messages, to which the given object (in this case the class) understands and which therefore can be sent, is enumerated by *BlueJ* in the context menu of each object. (To be precise, it is a list of commands, and when they are entered, *BlueJ* sends the corresponding message to the object.) The only objects which we see for the time being are classes. Therefore we will send our messages to classes. Click with the right button on any class and look through its context menu. Figure 3.1 shows what you can see after opening the context menu of the Rectangle class.

Red commands in the lower part of the menu represent messages which can be sent to the development environment. However, for now we will not pay attention to them and we shall concentrate on black commands in the upper part of the menu which represent messages that can be sent to the class. By entering these commands you ask *BlueJ* to send the corresponding message to a given class and announce the result.

43.   Why the "black list" is divided into two parts?

The horizontal line separates commands (messages) requiring the class to create a new instance from commands for sending other messages. Notice that the commands requiring creation of a new instance are quoted as the first (they are considered as more important) and start with the word **new**.

44.   Why there are so many commands requiring a new instance?

Because in various situations you have various requirements for creating the instance. Let's have a look at the rectangle, the context menu of which is shown in figure 3.1; sometimes you can have precise requirements for where the rectangle should be created, how large it should be and what should be its color, the other time you will not care about it and you will be satisfied with a default setting.

Therefore the class is able to receive the message in which all adjustable characteristics of the created object are set. Besides that it also offers "zero variant" of the message in case you have no special requirements for the created object, respectively when you are satisfied with default setting.

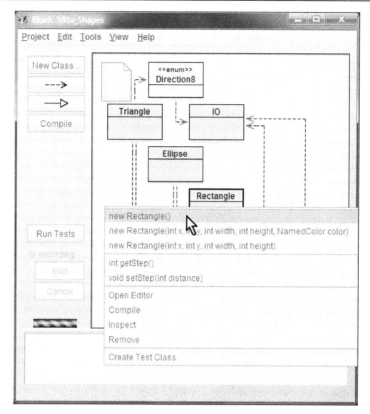

Figure 3.1
The context menu of the Rectangle *class*
(there may be a different order of commands it the context menu in your computer)

The Instances and References to Them

45. **By sending the** new Xxx **message I am asking for an instance. How the class will give me over the created instance?**

At this moment I would like to point out that in a majority of modern programming languages the object never receives the required instance, but only a **reference** to it. And we turn to instances by way of these references. We work with references similarly as e.g. with telephone numbers. In case we need to call somebody, we have to know firstly his telephone number. Usually we have numbers of people to whom we call under their names. If you want to call e.g. Fred, you find the record marked as Fred in your telephone list and the telephone dials the recorded number. (In contemporary telephones you do not know the number itself – you only find the name "Fred" and the telephone picks up the proper number itself.)

Similarly it is in programs. In case you want to send a message to an object (you want to "phone" it up) you have to know the reference to this object (to know its telephone number). Similarly as in the telephone, you save all references and other values of the program to memory places marked by names according to which you recognize what is saved there. You only must not forget to save the information which you intend to use later.

Entitled places in memory where various figures are saved (e.g. the above mentioned references) are called by the programmers as **variables**, because the program can change their content (e.g. the content of the variable of my account state will increase with each salary – at least I hope). Names of these variables and generally of all named entities in the program (classes, messages etc.) we call **identifiers** because they help us to identify individual entities (variables, classes, methods …).

Terminological   **Note:**

In case I will have a reference to an object saved in the xyz variable, I will speak about this reference briefly as about xyz reference or xyz object. It seems to me that thus the sentences can be formulated more clearly. In case I will be afraid of misunderstanding I will express precisely and speak about the xyz variable with a reference to an object, if need be, about the reference saved in xyz variable.

As I've said, the only objects to which we could turn until now were the classes. They are unambiguously identified by their names. But, in case we would like to save a reference to an object into a variable, we have to think out a name, according to which we recognize what is saved in it. Let's try it.

Creating a New Instance

46.   Let's do it! I will try to send the most simple, i.e. the "zero variant" of a message asking for creation a new rectangle – exactly according the figure 3.1.

This will be the best first step. We will ask to create a default version of a new instance of Rectangle class. *BlueJ* fortunately knows that in case you would like to work with the received reference sometimes in future, you have to name it. Therefore it will ask you to give a name (an identifier) to the created instance (to be precise the name of the variable into which the reference to the created instance will be saved) before it sends a message to the class. It will offer you a name derived from the name of the class the instance of which is being created. I recommend accepting the offered name now. Later we shall speak about the rules that have to be kept in case you would like to give your own names to instances.

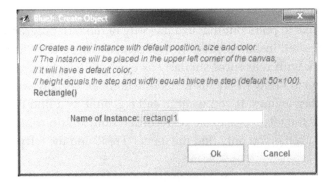

Figure 3.2: The dialog box for parameterless creation of an instance

47. I've confirmed the name, and two red rectangles appeared: one of them opened a new window to be visible, the second one, rounded and described, has appeared below under the class diagram.

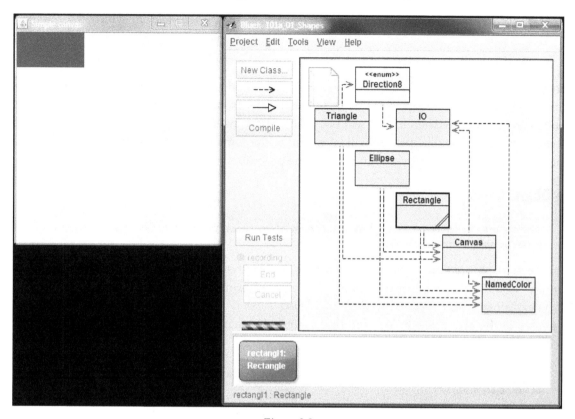

Figure 3.3
Creating of the first instance

Let's review what has happened:

1. The Rectangle class received your requirement for a new instance. It created the instance and wanted to draw it on a canvas. Therefore it asked the Canvas class for its instance.

2. The Canvas class realized that there is no such an instance existing and it created this instance. At this occasion it asked the operational system for a new application window, whose working area would represent this drawing canvas.

3. The Canvas class passes the reference of the freshly created canvas to the Rectangle class, and then the Rectangle class required painting of the freshly created rectangle.

4. The canvas instance paints the required rectangle and announced to Rectangle class completing its activities.

5. By this the Rectangle class declared the creation of a rectangle as completed and gave over the reference to it to the claimant, i.e. the *BlueJ* environment.

6. *BlueJ* has prepared a new variable, named in the way we have ordered, and put the received reference to the freshly created rectangle into it. Then, it placed the rounded rectangle, repre-

senting this variable (and so a reference to the created instance), under the class diagram into an area marked **object bench**. This rounded rectangle has always two-line description:

☞   The first line serves as the name (identifier) of the variable, in which the reference is placed.

☞   Under it there is the name of the class the instance of which is the referred object.

In the next requirement for creating a new graphic object (it does not have to be a rectangle) the above mentioned process will be repeated. The result will differ from the last one, because the Canvas class already has its instance. Therefore, it will not create a new instance, but it will only return a reference to the existing one. The new picture will be drawn to the same canvas as the previous one. Each next creation of graphic shape will undergo by the same procedure.

The Object Bench

48.   Why the area under the class diagram is called an *object bench*, when the variables are saved in it? Should it better be named *variables bench*?

After we start programming you will learn that besides the variables into which the references are saved, we also use the variables into which the values of primitive type are saved (what does it mean will be explained in the section *Primitive and Object Types* on page 35). However, these variables are not shown in the object bench. You can find there only variables where the references to objects are saved, and therefore it has the name object bench.

49.   A while ago you told me that the canvas instance is created. Why the variable with a reference to canvas is not in the object bench?

In the object bench only those references can be seen for which you explicitly ask. References to objects that are handed over among objects during processing the message cannot be seen. (It would not be wise, because there are thousands of those references.) But in case you would like to have the reference to canvas instance, you can require the Canvas class for it. For the time being we will not use it, so we will be glad if it would not hamper in the stack.

The Messages Sent to Instances

50.   Can I send messages also to objects to which the variables in the object bench refer?

Yes, of course. When you have at your disposal a reference to an object, you can send a message to it. The procedure is similar as for sending messages to any class in the class diagram – you will send the message (to be precise you ask *BlueJ* to send it) by entering the corresponding command from the context menu of the addressee class.

Try how it is possible to send messages to created objects and how the addressed objects will react on them. For the time being, limit yourself to parameterless messages starting with the word **void**. (I will explain its meaning in future, when we will speak about other types of messages.) You can see an illustration of such usage in the accompanying animation

Animation 3.1: Creating of new objects ad sending first messages – LOOTP_103a_First_messages
Animation will repeat what we have already told in the text, i.e. it will show creating new instances of
various classes and sending simple messages to these instances.

Notice one aspect during your experimentation: all instances of the same class define identical set of messages to which they understand. This set of messages is adjusted by the class during creating the given instance and it is adjusted in the same way for all its instances.

As you can see at instances of `Ellipse` and `Rectangle` classes, the instances of various classes can understand to the same set of messages. However, this is only a consequence of the fact that both classes create instances with nearly identical features, so that their classes have defined an identical set of messages for them to which they can understand.

The triangle characteristics are also almost identical. However, triangles compared to rectangles and ellipses have also a definition of the direction to which they are turned. The set of messages to which the triangles understand is therefore richer by messages working with the direction.

After we will work with instances of `Color` and `Direction8` classes, you will see that their set of messages to which they can react is quite different. However, always it will be valid that all instances of one class understand the common set of messages defined by their mother class.

The Virtual Machine

51.   At the end of the animation you were speaking about a resetting of a virtual machine. What does it mean and why we have to reset it?

Virtual machine is a name for a program which carries out your compiled program. By the fact that the program is not passed directly to the processor but it is submitted to the virtual machine, you reach the advantage that the use of your programs will not be restricted to only one specific processor and operating system, but you will be able to open your program anywhere where the relevant virtual machine operates. At present there is hardly any computer, which would not have the Java installation.

By resetting the virtual machine you arrange that the computer will forget everything what you have done until that time, and will start since the beginning. Thus you cannot be afraid that there will be some garbage left after you.

52.   And what about when I wouldn't want to forget?

Things that should not be forgotten will be saved into a file. And you can pick them up anytime during the next session. I will show it to you next time.

Review

Let's review what you have learned in this lesson:

☞   In the interactive mode you are sending the messages to object by entering the corresponding command in their context menu.

☞   Black items in the upper part of context menus represent messages to a given object; red items in the lower part represent messages that can be sent to the development environment.

☞ Messages sent to a class are also divided into two parts: in the upper part there are messages which require creating a new instance, the lower part contains remaining messages.

☞ The classes frequently offer whole groups of messages with same names. Particular messages within such a group differ by required parameters.

☞ The named places in the memory in which various values are located (e.g. the above mentioned references) are called *variables*.

☞ To have a good overview of separate entities of the program (classes, variables, messages …) and to be able to distinguish them, we assign names to them. Names of the variables, classes and other entities of the program are called *identifiers*.

☞ Modern programming languages mostly do not allow working directly with objects, but only with *references* to objects. Whenever we send a message to an object, we send it via a reference to this object.

☞ The variables containing references to objects for which we have asked in an interactive mode, are depicted by *BlueJ* in the *object bench* placed under the class diagram. They are represented by rounded rectangles with two-line description:

　　☞ the first line contains the name of a given variable,

　　☞ the second line contains the name of a class whose instance is the referred object.

☞ When we ask a class for a new instance, *BlueJ* firstly asks us which name (identifier) should be assigned to the variable into which the reference will be saved, and through which we shall send messages to the given instance.

☞ After creating the instance *BlueJ* creates a rounded rectangle representing the given object in the object bench, precisely the variable containing a reference to this object.

☞ In the object's context menu there is a list of commands corresponding to the messages that can be sent to the given object.

☞ All instances of the same class understand to a set of the same messages.

☞ The virtual machine is a program which carries out our programs.

☞ By resetting the virtual machine the information which is not saved becomes forgotten.

Project:
No significant changes were made in the 101a_Shapes project.

4 The Test Class

What you will learn in this lesson

In this lesson you will create your first class – the test class. You will see what it is the test fixture and how it is defined. After that you will define your first tests. At the conclusion you will become acquainted with what is the difference between the message and the method.

Project:

In this lesson we continue in using the 101a_Shapes project.

53.   Last time you told me that all what I would like to remember I can save into a file before the resetting of virtual machine. Can I save also my experiments?

Yes, you can – e.g. by defining a special class which you will teach to react to certain message by re-playing your actions. *BlueJ* knows to follow your operation and to create a program that can repeat it, if required. It works similarly as macro recorders in some programs.

54.   That's what I would like to try.

Why not? I would like to tell you only that this mechanism is provided by *BlueJ* only for test classes. You have to program other kinds of classes in a classic way, i.e. to write down their program as a properly formulated text. But before you start writing the programs yourself, let's use this *BlueJ* ability and let it write the programs instead of you.

55.   Why the test class has such an extraordinary position?

I think it is due to the fact that the concept of tests exploited in the *JUnit* library, which *BlueJ* uses, has several features that make programming of test preparation easy. Moreover, very often the tests consist from only simple sequence of messages sent after the test will run using the previously prepared data. Authors of *BlueJ* utilized these advantages, and students now can create simple programs even when they do not know programming at all.

The Test Fixture

56.   Well, so show me how I can create such a class.

First of all I have to tell you something about test classes generally, so that you would know why you should do certain things just in the way I will show you.

As you surely assessed from the chapter's title, test classes serve for testing of programs. But a single test is mostly not sufficient for testing some part of the program. However, it's often appropriate that the whole group of tests start at the same initial state. You can consider the test class as an object which is able to define a group of tests with a common initial state. The initial state, common for tests in the particular test class, is marked as the *test fixture*. In case we ask the test class to start any prepared test, it creates firstly a test fixture and subsequently verifies it.

Therefore, we have to show to the test class how it should prepare the test fixture and only then we can do various experiments with it, i.e. various tests.

Creating the New Class

57.   If I understand it properly, we will start with creating the test fixture.

Not so fully. Before starting to create a fixture, we have to create a test class. Let's start with creating this class.

58.   Don't take me at my word – it's clear. So show off!

You ask for creating a new class e.g. by pressing the button **New Class** on the button panel. *BlueJ* opens the dialog box, in which you have to enter the name of the new class and which class type *BlueJ* has to create.

Let me postpone for a while the explanation of the rules according to which the names are created and I will advise you simply to call the new class **Tests**. Adjust the **Class Type** switch to **Unit Test** because I told you a while ago that *BlueJ* is willing to program only the test class. Confirm your assignment. *BlueJ* creates a new class, gives the name Tests to it and places it in a free room of class diagram.

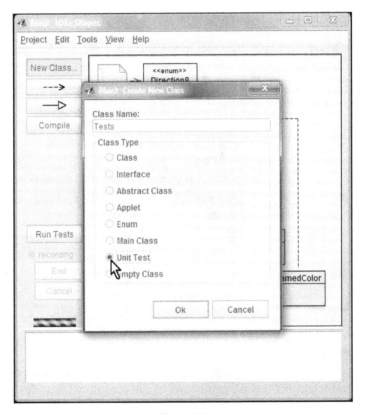

Figure 4.1
Creating a new test class named Tests

As we have already said the test class has a special position. *BlueJ* points it out by a stereotype «unit test» and it assigns a special color to it similarly as to other classes marked with a stereotype.

59.   By a stereotype? What does it mean?

Don't try to suggest that you are bigger forgetter than me. We were speaking about stereotypes in the section *Classes in the Project*, on page 15. Stereotype means a short text closed in «Guillemets» («French quotation» marks), which is written above the class title in the class diagram and indicates its rarity – e.g. that it is a test class.

60.   Why you name the class Tests, when all other class names are in singular?

Because the identifier Test is used by the *JUnit* library, which is responsible for managing our tests (you will meet this identifier in the section *Test Class* on page 174), therefore we have to think out a different name for this purpose.

Creating the Test Fixture

61.   Well, I have a class. So let's dive to the fixture! What should I do?

Anything new what you would not know. You will start with resetting the virtual machine and then you will send messages that will bring the system into a state in which the tests should start. *BlueJ* will watch your activities and on your request it will convert them into a program that creates a fixture and brings the program to the required state.

62.   Wait a minute! I have to say somehow that since now I start showing how to create the test fixture.

BlueJ remembers all actions since the last virtual machine reset. In case you will do something, what BlueJ would not remember, before showing the actions, which BlueJ has to remember, you have to re-set the virtual machine. However, the reset is also performed as a side effect of the compilation. Then, if you will show something immediately after compilation, you do not have to reset the virtual machine explicitly.

63.   Yes, I understand. But what should I say when I want to stop?

You will send a message **Executed Actions ▶ Test Fixture**, that can be found in the test class context menu (see figure 4.2). *BlueJ* then creates the corresponding program. You can try its functioning by sending a message **Test Fixture ▶ Object Bench**, after which *BlueJ* runs the created program and fulfill the object bench with the relevant references – the test fixture.

64.   I have created a rectangle, an ellipse and a triangle we played with last time. When I asked to create a tool, new arrows appeared in the class diagram.

That's good. *BlueJ* stretched the dependence arrows from the test class to classes of graphic shapes. Please, shift the test class a bit to the right and you will see that there are arrows from it going to Rectangle, Ellipse and Triangle classes (see figure 4.3). That happened because the test class became dependent on these classes. Each sending a message to some object creates a dependency of the sender on the addressee. That is because each change of the addressee's behavior causes a potential change in the behavior of the sender. The Tests class asks all shape classes for their instances and therefore it is dependent on them and *BlueJ* show these dependences in the class diagram.

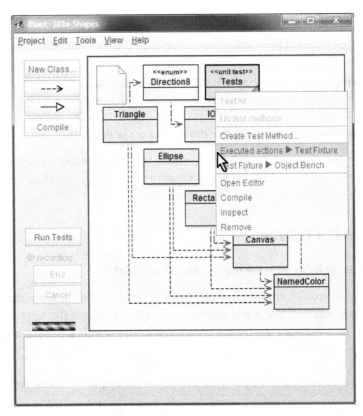

Figure 4.2
The request for converting the remembered executed actions to a program for creating a test fixture

Creating the Test

65.   You are true. Well, I have the fixture. How I should prepare a test now?

I recommend you to reset the virtual machine to agree with *BlueJ* on the initial state of the program before the test beginning. Then open again the context menu of the test class (see figure 4.2) and enter the command **Create Test Method**. By this you are sending a message to *BlueJ* that you would like to show a test of the fixture created by this class and let *BlueJ* to create it.

   BlueJ opens a dialog asking for the name of the created test (see figure 4.4). Let's say that you will call it testMovements as in the figure 4.4.After entering the name the test class creates a test fixture. At the same time *BlueJ* "lights up" the indicator **Recording** and "revives" the buttons **End** and **Cancel** for ending and canceling the performed test respectively.

   After entering the name the test class creates a test fixture and *BlueJ* starts recording what you are doing. At the same time it will switch on the **Recording** indicator which will draw an attention by a red "light" to recording the test commands, and "revive" the buttons **End** and **Cancel** for ending and canceling the performed test respectively.

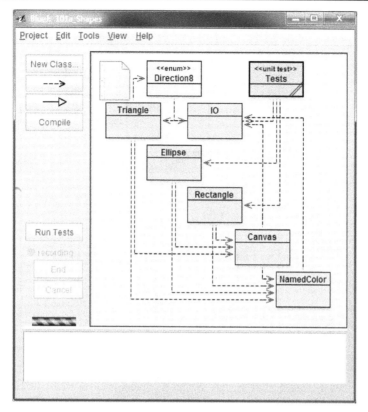

Figure 4.3
Dependences of the test class after the definition of the test fixture

If you would realize during the showing that you made a wrong step, you press the **Cancel** button and you can start once again.

In case everything goes properly, you press the button **End** after finishing the test. *BlueJ* then "switches off" the **Recording** red light, deactivates the buttons **End** and **Cancel**, converts the remembered actions to a program, and inserts this program to the source code of the test class. Then it includes a command to the test class context menu by which you can evoke this program.

I tried to demonstrate all what we were speaking about in an accompanying animation. Start it and try it once more.

> *Animation 4.1: Creating of test class and its fixture – LOOTP_104a_Tests_class*
> *The animation shows how the new test class is created, how creating of test fixture is interactively defined, and how it is possible to enter interactively the tests cooperating with this tool.*

66.   All was operating. I was only wander why there was a blank area left on the original position of the moved shape despite there was another object under it.

Objects are shifted identically as if drawn on a paper. Firstly they have to be rubbed out at the original position and then drawn again at a new position. However, because the objects do not know mutually about themselves, they cannot send a message to objects lying under them so that they should redraw. This is your turn; you have to ask the objects to redraw.

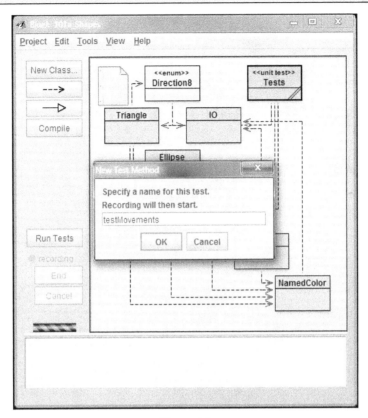

Figure 4.4
Question on the test name

I intentionally made it so simple and we could say also clumsily, so that you would have a motivation when you will work with more sophisticated canvas, because at first you will have to learn several other constructions and regularities for it.

67.   I know a number of simply managed programs that don't operate so silly and I don't need anything else for their controlling.

Of course, I could tailor the program so that it would not operate so foolishly. But our aim is not to shift the objects. You are learning programming. When I would arrange the program to operate smartly, I would have to hide certain constructions because you would not understand them yet. After you would meet them later on you would be surprised why you should use them if you did not need them before.

Please, be patient a while, we will soon come up to an explanation.

Methods and Constructors

68.   Well, I will try it. But I've one more question. You always say that I am sending messages to objects but in context menu there is mentioned that we are asking *BlueJ* to create a test method. What does it mean the method?

The method is a part of a program that takes care about an object's reaction to a given message. Each message that the object understands, has assigned to the corresponding method that will take care about the relevant reaction. Thus each message sending is converted to the corresponding method calling. Until an appropriate method for a certain object (a class, an instance) is defined, the object cannot receive corresponding messages.

When you will write programs you will define classes and their methods. Up until now *BlueJ* environment defined methods instead of us. We presented something to *BlueJ* and it defined a method which was able to repeat the presented action.

The programmers do not mostly speak about *sending messages*, but about *method callings*. Both expressions are synonyms, similarly as an *object* and an *instance*. When we are speaking at a more abstract level of problem description, we use rather *message sending*; when we are speaking about a code, we prefer an expression *method calling*.

Even the program that creates a test fixture is a method. When we are sending a message so that the class would start the test, *BlueJ* in cooperation with the test class provides to call firstly the method which creates the test fixture, and only after that the method which performs the test with the just created fixture.

When I mentioned methods I should tell you that methods that take care about constructing a new object are called **constructors**. Constructing an object is made in two phases:

1. First of all the virtual machine receives a message in the form new Xxx, where Xxx is a name of a class whose instance we want to create. The virtual machine designates a place in a memory and prepares some system components which are necessary for proper operating of each object.

2. Then the special method is called, that creates (constructs) an object of a given class in the allocated memory and returns a reference to the created object to the calling program. Because this method constructs the object, we call it a **constructor.**

69. **It's strange. I would say that the main merit in constructing the object belongs to the virtual machine, which finds out and prepares the memory, where the created object will dwell.**

Constructing an object can be mostly compared to producing a cup or a jar. A memory provided by a virtual machine is something like clay. Until we have no clay we cannot produce any cup. However, creating the cup is a care of a potter who creates it according to his ideas. The potter is represented by a constructor in the program. It accommodates the designated memory to such a form so that it could serve as a required object.

Review

Let's review what you have learned in this lesson:

☞ The *BlueJ* environment is able to follow our acting, to convert it to a program and save it in the test class.

☞ Because the test class has non-standard features from the *BlueJ* environment view (*BlueJ* is able to program it itself), its name is supplemented by a stereotype «unit test» in class diagram and its rectangle is colored by a different color than ordinary classes have.

☞ A stereotype is a short text closed in «Guillemets» («French quotation marks»), which is written in the class diagram above the class name and reminds its specialty – e.g. that it is a test class.

☞   Test classes mostly contain a set of several tests working with the same initial set of objects. This initial set of objects is named *test fixture*. Each test class has its own fixture.

☞   We can create a test fixture in such a way that after compilation of classes or resetting the virtual machine we show how it would be created. After a command **Executed Actions ▶ Test Fixture** in the context menu of the test class for whose tests we create this fixture, *BlueJ* defines a method based on presented activities and this method will be started up before each test of this class.

☞   We can start up a program creating the test fixture also independently by entering the command **Test Fixture ▶ Object Bench**. *BlueJ* then fulfills the object bench with references to objects from the fixture.

☞   We ask creating the test by the **Create Test Method** command in the context menu of the test class. First of all *BlueJ* asks for the name of the created test (method) and then revives buttons for ending and cancelling the test together with the record indicator of carried out actions at the button panel.

☞   Showing is completed by an **End** button at the button panel. *BlueJ* then defines a test method which is able to repeat the presented activities. Then it adds a command into the context menu of the relevant test class which evokes this test.

☞   The method is a part of a code defining a reaction of an object to a given message. Expressions *message sending* and *method calling* are mutually equivalent.

☞   Creating of an object is carried out in two phases:

   ☞   first of all the virtual machine allocates a needed place in a memory,

   ☞   then a required object is created at this place and a reference is sent to the claimant.

☞   A method which takes care about constructing an object in the allocated memory and giving over a reference to a constructed object is called a **constructor**.

Project:
The resulting project shape to which we proceeded at the end of the lesson is in the `104z_Tests` *class project.*

5 The Messages Requiring a Value

What you will learn in this lesson
In this lesson you will learn messages that return a value. You will read the explanation what does it mean data type, how primitive and object data types differ and you will become acquainted with all primitive types. You will learn working with references to objects, how sending messages can be recorded, respectively method calling, as well as why names of some messages/methods have a prefix get, respectively set.

Project:
In this lesson we continue in using the 104z_Tests class project.

70. **I've already enjoyed sending messages. Last time you promised to tell me something about messages that start neither with** new, **nor** void. **I would say that it's just the proper time.**

You are true, let's go on. Messages which we used to send to created instances until now required a certain (visible) action (e.g. shifting or redrawing) from instances. However, in programs we often don't need so that the instance would do something, but it should reveal something (mostly about itself). In other words, we want so that it gave us information.

To be able to work effectively with the received information we need to know what it is like. You are working quite differently with numbers, rectangles or with a text. Therefore, in instance and class context menus the commands – by entering of which we send messages – start with a name of data type which has the return value. The only one exception is commands requiring creation of an instance that have the new keyword in front of the name of the return value type.

71. **Which return value? We did not lend anything to an object; we only send a message to it.**

Take it as an expression used by the programmers. You send a message to an object and the object executes your command. When you ask it for an action, it only announces fulfilling the task. In case you ask it for information it provides you with this information (value) after finishing the action. Programmers say about this operation that the object *returns* the required value and the transmitted information itself is called the *return value*. Take it as you send a message and the required information is returned to you.

72. **Well, I'll cope somehow with it. Go on with the explanation.**

Until now we worked with two kinds of messages:

☞ Messages whose activation commands in the context menu started with the word new. These messages could be sent only to a class. The class reacting to this message creates a new instance and returns a reference to it. (As we have already said you never get an object but through a reference you can send messages to it.)

☞ Messages whose activation commands in the context menu started with a word *void*. After sending such messages the addressed object did what you have asked but did not return you anything.

Now we add a third type of messages, i.e. messages in which we ask a value. Commands leading to sending these messages begin in context menus by a name of return value type (return type).

Return Type

73.   Please show it to me at an example.

Well, the virtual machine is reset so we can start since the beginning. In case you will have a look into the context menu of the Triangle class (see figure 5.1), in the second part you will find the message as follows:

```
int getStep()
```

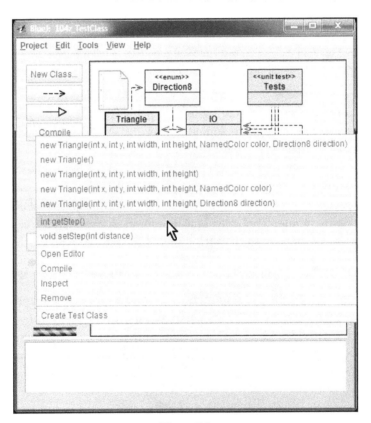

Figure 5.1
We are sending the getStep() message

The word int at the beginning of the command is an abbreviation of a word *integer* and says that the addressed object (in our case the Triangle class) returns an integer in reaction to this message. I can reveal you that it will be a number of picture elements (shortly *pixels*) by which the random instance of the Triangle class shifts when we send a message to this instance requiring to shift without mentioning how much it should shift. (Until now we did not send any shifting messages but soon we shall see that we can send also a message to an instance specifying how much it should shift.)

Obtaining the Return Value

74.   And how I will learn what the object answered to me?

When you will send such a message, *BlueJ* takes over the return value from an object, opens a dialog box and shows you what the addressed object answered to you (see figure 5.2).

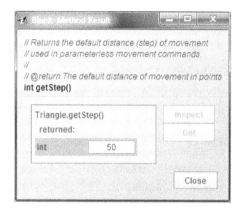

Figure 5.2
The dialog box with a return value message

75.   And now I should verify if it's not talking rubbish, I mean if it returned me the proper value.

I have prepared a little animation which shows you all. Firstly it asks the Rectangle class about the step's default size, then requires an instance; and then it asks the instance for its coordinate, requests it to shift, and again asks for its coordinate. Activate your animation and try to do all operations. Of course, you can try also other moves.

> *Animation 5.1: Sending messages requiring to return the value – LOOTP_105a_Return_primitive_value*
> *The animation will show how to send messages which require returning of some value from an addressed object.*

Primitive and Object Types

76.   This was really simple. But I noticed the NamedColor getColor() command in the context menu of the rectangle instance. I tried it but it did not return me any color – only an arrow appeared instead of a return value.

It's little bit more complicated with colors because colors (contrary to numbers) are instances of object data type NamedColor.

77.   How "contrary to numbers"? When you were explaining the OOP principles, you told that everything what can be named by a noun is an object in OOP. So why a number is not an object?

In pure OOP it is really as I told you. But the Java authors wanted so that the resulting program might work as quickly as possible even on the very slow processors and therefore they divided all data types into three groups:

☞   A degenerated type void represents a special one-element group; it serves only to programmer's proclamation that there is a method which does not return anything. It cannot be used in other cases and therefore you cannot define a variable of this type.

☞   Next eight data types that have a direct support in instruction sets of contemporary micropro-cessors were named *primitive data types*. (Values of these types will be sometimes labeled as *primitive values*.) The virtual machine converts work with them directly to relevant instructions of a given processor. Values of primitive types are often generally marked as *primitives*.

☞   All other data types (there is more than 20,000 types in a standard library) are included into *object data types*. Working with them is quite different.

78.   What does it mean a standard library?

A library means a set of classes which create certain complete set and which you can use in your pro-gram. A standard library is a part of Java installation. The others have to be gained and included into the program. But we will speak about it in details at the final part of the course.

79.   You always operate with some data types. What does it mean the data type?

Data type (shortly only a type) is a name for three features specifying properties of values, which we will name as data of a given type. The data type specifies:

☞   a set of permissible values,

☞   a way of saving these values in a memory (for now we will not be interested in it and processing of this information will be left to a virtual machine),

☞   operations which can be carried out with values of a given type (including the message specifi-cation that can be sent to a given object).

In other words: the data type tells you what you can expect from values of a given type and what you can do with them. Thus the program's working effectiveness increases and the number of faults which you can do during the program decreases. However, I will speak about it several times in future.

> **Note:**
> If you read the previous items, you would see immediately, that void is not a real data type, but only a marking which should be written down to a place where the identifier of a data type belongs.

80.   Which data types are primitive?

I would divide them into two groups. The following ones belong to those more used:
boolean   Logic values true (yes), and false (no).

char	*Characters.* Besides numbers and letters of all alphabets, including the Chinese, Japanese and Korean also other characters belong here, such as notes, cartographic characters etc.
int	Integers ranging approximately ± 2 billion (±2.10^9).
long	Long integers ranging approximately ±9.10^18.
double	Real numbers ranging approximately 10^±308 stored with the precision approximately 15 valid ciphers and used mostly in scientific technological calculations (they are not used in operations working with money due to rounding faults).

The remaining types are not used too often (we will not use them in our course at all) and are listed only to make the picture complete:

byte	Integers from -128 to 127.
short	Integers ranging approximately ±32 000.
float	Real numbers ranging approx. 10^±38 stored with precision approximately 6 valid figures.

Note:

The British mathematician George Boole (1779–1848) showed that we can work with logic values similarly as with the arithmetic ones and founded bases of a discipline called *Boolean algebra* or *Boolean logic*. In programming languages that introduce a type for logic values this type is often called at his honor boolean.

81.   Well, I have further questions, but maybe they will be answered when I will start working with primitive date types. Now I'd like to know how it is with those object types?

The type of object is defined by the class whose instance the object is. (You will learn further possibilities with time, but until now let's deal with a class only.) Therefore the type is marked by the name of a given class. Thus we can say that the instances of Rectangle class are objects of Rectangle type.

As I have already said, we work with objects in a different way than with values of primitive types. They all emerge in a designated area of memory called a *heap* and you can address them only through references to them. I mentioned references in the section *The Instances and References to Them* on page 19. Once more I remind that whenever you want something from the object, i.e. whenever you want to send a message to an object, you will send it through the object reference. On the contrary, whenever you require an object, you will receive only a reference to it instead of the object itself.

82.   You really told it. I only don't know why it's so complicated?

It may be strange to you but the main reason is the programmer's work productivity and robustness ("foolproofness") as well as reliability of resulting programs. When the program is running there are various objects appearing and disappearing and somebody has to allocate a memory to them and clean up the "deceased" objects. This activity is provided by a special part of a virtual machine marked as *memory manager* or (according to its main function) a *garbage collector*.

An experience proved that if the memory manager, whose functioning is of key significance, has to work reliably, we have to keep it without any intervention. Therefore the programmers can turn to objects only through a mediator which is its reference.

Before I started working in Java, I was programming more than 15 years in C++. First few weeks of programming in Java I permanently complained that this or that might be programmed better and more effectively in C++. However, after few weeks I discovered that despite the fact I am always complaining, I work twice quicker than when I would use C++. The main merit was due to the memory manager – it overtook activities in which the programmers currently make faults. Thus Java did not allow me to make a lot of mistakes which would be usual when working with C++ and which would hamper the whole development. Since that time Java is my favorite.

References to Objects

83.   I don't know how I can increase the productivity by making something complicated.

But in fact it's really not complicated. It is similar as with the television. Formerly you have to go to the TV and press or turn the relevant button. Now the TV producers complicated the situation by adding a remote control. But majority of people whom I know like this little complication and find it useful.

   Please, consider the reference to an object as the remote control of an object which is otherwise non-attainable. This idea is useful for explanation of further features of references.

   ☞   As soon as you lose or damage the remote control (= the reference), you lose simultaneously any possibility to affect further operation of managed object.

   ☞   You can manage one TV with several remote controls simultaneously. The TV will react independently to all commands sent from any remote control. Similarly it is with objects. You can have several references to one object and the object will react independently to any reference which handed over your message.

84.   Certain remote controllers can control several devices together. Can I send messages to several objects through one reference?

Yes and no. However, you don't have enough knowledge yet for fully understanding the answer. Ask this question later when we will go over the type casting.

85.   How I can lose or damage a reference?

You will lose it in case you ask for it and forget to save it. You destroy it in case you save something else to the variables where it is saved (it cannot be done in an interactive mode but when you start writing the code, you will do it many times). In both cases such abandoned object which is not used any more will become a catch of the garbage collector which will most probably definitely destroy it so that its place in memory could be allocated to a newly created object.

86.   Why only most probably? Does the garbage collector have to release the space?

When it decides that releasing of that memory is complicated and that the obtained result doesn't correspond to the needed effort, it may abandon this attempt. It leaves the memory blocked by the object despite nobody needs that object and it only fills its place.

87.   I would say that we were speaking a lot about it and that now you should show me how I can work with objects.

It is simple. Ask the Tests class for a test fixture and then ask some of the created objects for its color. *BlueJ* opens a dialog in which it announces that the addressed object returns a reference to the required object. The fact that the addressed object does not return you a value but only a reference is represented by an arrow at the text field position. *BlueJ* enables to add this reference to the object bench. Then you can work with it as with any other object, i.e. to send messages to it and thus impact its functioning or obtain information.

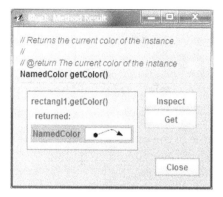

Figure 5.3
The dialog with the returned reference to an object

You can ask for including a reference into the object bench by pressing the button **Get**. *BlueJ* then asks you how the included reference should be named (precisely how the variable to which the reference is saved should be named) and puts it into the object bench. You can use this reference in the same way as reference received during creating new instances.

88.   Before I will name it, please, tell me what was the other button entitled Inspect for?

This you will use in case you would like to have a look into the object. But now I want to stay outside for a moment.

Record of Method Calling

89.   I'll try to stand it. I see that always I am asked to think out a name. Should you explain me already, how such name should be created?

Today I would not like to overload you with further information and that's why I will postpone explanation on rules for creating names (as I have already told you we call them *identifiers*) for next time.

Today I will tell you good-bye saying other items. Due to reasons which overlap the explanation framework, the object cannot distinguish messages that differ only by a type of return value. Therefore each object can offer the only one message with a given name and given set of parameters offering additional information.

When entering the command for sending a message (the relevant method calling) the information on expected type of return value is not mentioned – even without this info the message is unambiguously determined. (*BlueJ* writes the message type in the name of the context menu command only due to the fact that the beginners can easily orientate). Programmers are accustomed to it. Mostly they do not quote this type of return value in the text, when they mention which method they called (which message they sent) or which method is necessary to be called for.

Therefore, in the first example, the programmer would tell or write that he/she "called the getStep() method of the Triangle class", or he/she would connect both pieces of information (i.e. the addressed object and the method's name) and would tell that he called a method

```
Triangle.getStep()
```

In programs, the object's name to which we are sending a message (i.e. the name of the class or of the variable in which the reference to this object is located) is written in front of the identifier of the forwarded message and separated by a dot. As far as the second example is mentioned I would say: "I called the getColor() method of a rectangle1" or I would briefly put down:

```
rectangle1.getColor()
```

The empty brackets behind the name of the called method indicate that it is a method without parameters. If it would have any parameters, they would be quoted in these brackets. (We will speak about methods with parameters in some of future lessons.)

As you can see at figures 5.2 on page 35 and 5.3 on page 39, this kind of recording is used also in *BlueJ* in dialog boxes with return value. We will use it in further text as well.

The getXxx and setXxx **Messages/Methods**

90. **Why the messages are named so strangely:** getStep **and** getColor**?**

This is a general convention how to call messages that ask for values of some object properties. Names of these messages always start with the word get, followed (without any space) by the name of the detected property as in case of the message getColor(), about which we have spoken a while ago.

In case the detected value is of boolean type, the word get can be replaced (and mostly is replaced) by the word is. The isVisible() message is an example and you can send it to your canvas.

On the contrary, messages that adjust the values of object properties start with a word set. The message called setBackgroundColor which you can send to the canvas is an example.

The words get, set and is are used as prefixes independently which language you are using for naming the given properties.

91. **Such convention is strange. Could we use the native prefixes from our language instead of it?**

This is not a good idea. This convention is worldwide spread and used by a lot of various tools that offer a number of very useful functions. These tools rely just on the fact that the processed program keeps the above mentioned convention.

Further on, the programmers have got it under their skin so deeply that they do not think over it. They even use slang names *getters* and *setters* for methods defining answers to these messages. If you would name your messages/methods for detecting and adjusting the values of properties in a different way, you would catch them unawares (and most likely also make them angry).

92. **You told me that they have slang names. Do they have any "non-slang" names?**

Collectively they are named **accessory methods**, because you approach to the values of object properties with their help. The getXxx and isXxx methods are named **accessor methods** or **accessors** and the setXxx methods as **mutator methods** or **mutators**.

Review

Let's review what you have learned in this lesson:

☞ Three kinds of messages can be distinguished in context menus of objects (including classes):

☞ Commands starting with a keyword new are sending messages requiring creating a new instance. After processing such message the addressed class passes (*returns*) a reference of a created instance to the claimant. These commands are only in context menus of classes.

☞ Commands starting with a keyword void are sending messages requiring an action, and when this action is carried out the addressed object does not return anything.

☞ Other commands start with a name of the *return value* type, i.e. the value (value means also a reference to an object), due to which the message is sent (mostly) and which, after processing, the addressed object gives back to the claimant – professionally: which it returns.

☞ A library means a set of classes that create a compact set and that you can use in your program.

☞ The standard library is a part of Java installation.

☞ The term *data type* determines trio of features specified as follows:

☞ a set of permissible values,

☞ the way of saving these values in the memory,

☞ operations that can be carried out with values of this type.

☞ Java divides the types into three groups:

☞ Degenerated date type void.

☞ Eight basic date types that have a direct support in instruction set of majority of processors are indicated as *primitive date types* and operations with them are converted directly to instructions of the relevant microprocessor.

☞ The remaining date types are named *object types*. We communicate with their values, i.e. with separate objects only through references to them.

☞ Values of primitive types are often named by collective name primitives.

☞ Boolean, char, int, long, double and void belong among the frequently used primitive types.

☞ The object type is defined by a class whose object is an instance. The type is therefore named by a name of a given class.

☞ *BlueJ* writes the return values of primitive types directly in a dialog box after completing the required action.

☞ In case you send a message asking for an object, you always will receive only a reference to this object. *BlueJ* enables you to name it and save it in the object bench.

☞ The described way of working with objects does not allow making the most usual mistakes and contrary to older languages (e.g. C++) it increases the productivity of work roughly twice.

☞   We can compare the work with references of an object to managing the TV through the remote control.

☞   In case we lose a reference we lose any possibility to impact further operating of the referred object at the same time.

☞   When mentioning the message sending, respectively the method calling, we need not indicate the return value type. We quote the addressed object (the class name or the variable name with a reference to an instance), followed by a dot, name of the method and parentheses with potential parameters.

☞   For names of messages (and corresponding methods) by which we detect or adjust the values of objects properties Java has the following convention:

    ☞   Names of messages asking for the property value begin with a prefix get, followed by a name of a given property. In case the detected property is of boolean type, we may use a prefix is.

    ☞   Names of messages adjusting the property value start with a prefix set, followed again by the property name.

☞   These messages and methods for detecting or adjusting the values of object properties are called *accessors and mutators*.

☞   The accessor and mutator methods are called *getters* and *setters* in slang.

Project:
No significant changes were made in the 104z_Tests *class project.*

6 The Messages Requiring an Object

What you will learn in this lesson
In this lesson you the rules for creating the identifiers will be explained and you will learn working with messages returning value of object types. You will see how the values of String type are assigned and at the conclusion you will become acquainted with how the methods returning a value should be used in tests.

Project:
In this lesson we continue in using the project 104z_Tests class.

The Rules for Creating the Identifiers

93.   Last time you promised to tell me how the names are created.

You are true – and the promises should be fulfilled, shouldn't they? First of all I would like to remind that we use the term *identifiers* for names, because they identify particular entities in the program. Rules for creating the identifiers in Java language are only four. The identifiers have to suit the rules as follows:

☞   They may contain only letters (all letters including diacritical or Japanese marks), digits and $ (a dollar) and _ (an underlining) characters, however it is recommended not to use the $ character.

☞   They cannot start with a digit.

☞   They are case sensitive, the uppercase and lowercase letters are different – hello, Hello and HELLO are three different identifiers.

☞   They mustn't be any of the language keywords, i.e. any of the following 50 words:

abstract	continue	for	new	switch
assert	default	if	package	synchronized
boolean	do	goto	private	this
break	double	implements	protected	throw
byte	else	import	public	throws
case	enum	instanceof	return	transient
catch	extends	int	short	try
char	final	interface	static	void
class	finally	long	strictfp	volatile
const	float	native	super	while

94.   What does it mean the keywords?

The keywords are words, which have defined its meaning in the given programming language. We have already met some of them (keywords int, new, void …), and we will reveal the meaning of others step by step in further lessons.

95.   You told that identifiers may contain any letter. So can I have for example an identifier ☺?

Smilie is not a letter but a common symbol. You can use only the characters, which the Unicode character set classifies as a letter.

96.   Can I try drafting of identifiers?

Of course, create instances of particular classes and try to assign various identifiers to the created variables into which the references to these instances will be saved. When you would try to assign an identifier of already existing variable, *BlueJ* will warn you and will ask different assignment. However, you can examine that identifiers varying only by size of letters (capital vs. small) are considered as different ones.

The created variables can be immediately cancelled – it is sufficient to enter the command **Remove** in their context menu. Of course, you can immediately assign the identifier of the removed variable to the newly created one. After you finish playing with it, reset the virtual machine and let *BlueJ* create the test fixture once again.

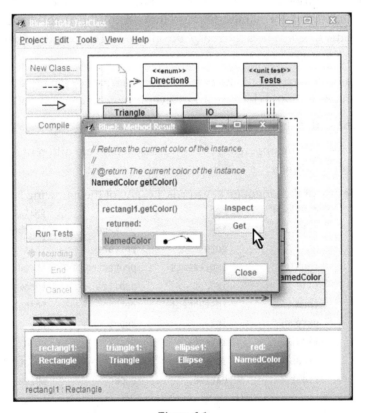

Figure 6.1
The object bench with an added reference of the rectangle color

Getting the Reference to the Returned Object

97.   Will I need my knowledge of creating the names or (when I would like to speak in a sophisticated way) identifiers also in another cases besides for creating new instances?

Of course, for example when you will call a method which returns a reference to an object, you would probably like to save this reference and you will have to think out an identifier of the variable into which you will save it. Ask e.g. for the rectangle color and press the button **Get** in the subsequently opened dialog. *BlueJ* will ask you for the name of the variable into which it should save the obtained reference. Because you know that its color is red, put it into the reference name, and i.e. enter the name red. *BlueJ* will create a variable with such name and will add it into the object bench (see figure 6.1).

98.   The dialog box did not close after adding the reference into the bench. Why?

BlueJ expects that you might want to use the second service of this window, which is the possibility to look into the given instance. But we will postpone it for later time. At present we could use the window for showing how to manage the object with the help of several references. Ask the window for the reference once more and name it e.g. RectColor to remember, whose color it is.

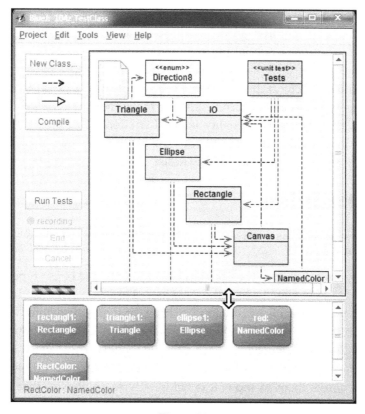

Figure 6.2
The enlarged object bench

99.   Nothing has happened.

Nothing? At the right edge of the object bench a scroll bar appeared announcing that the bench contains another line of references. Because we will not need to see the whole class diagram for a while, you can take the separating bar between the class diagram and the object bench and shift it up (see figure 6.2). Then you will see that *BlueJ* added another reference in the next line.

The Instance of String Type

100.   Yeah, it's there! What shall we do with it?

Maybe you can send the message

    String getName()

to the instance and ask for the name of its color. Now I only wanted you to realize that you can have several references which may refer to the same instance. In case you would decide to send a message to an instance, it doesn't matter which reference you will use for it. The result will be always the same.

101.   I asked the reference RectColor for the name of the referred color and *BlueJ* really opened a window in which I learned that the color is named "red". I was only wondering why there is a button Get in the window, when the window shows a value (see figure 6.3).

The message you have sent required an object of String type, which is an object type, but has a special position among object types. Its instances are text strings, i.e. sequence of characters, which we consider to be one object. Because we work with text strings very often, this type has certain privileges that make the programmer's work easy. Their exceptionality in *BlueJ* environment proves the fact that among other things you can see their value (i.e. the text they represent) in dialog **Method Result**.

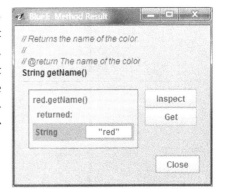

Figure 6.3
A dialog box with the name of the rectangle color

How to Write the Strings

102.   Why is the word red in quotation marks when all texts were without quotation marks until now?

This is connected to those privileges. The String type is the only one object type whose value (i.e. the relevant text) can be written directly into the program. Then you need to differ whether you are speaking about a text that is a value of certain text string, or when the entered text indicates the keyword or certain identifier in a program. Quotation marks serve to determining the texts which are values of String class. Therefore, whenever you will write the text string which is a value of the String class, you have to put it in quotation marks. However, when printing the strings, the quotation marks are not used. *BlueJ* requests them in input text fields only to emphasize that this is really the text string, and to remind you how the text strings are entered in a program.

103. Can you show me using of text strings at an example?

We will use the text strings after you will learn sending messages with parameters, it means in the next lesson. I will show it to you and you will try it.

Memory Management – Garbage Collector

104. I wanted to ask just one question. In the previous lesson you told me that in case I lose the reference, I cannot get it back.

Exactly, the only exception is that you would save the reference beforehand. In case there is no reference to the given object (neither yours nor of anybody else), you really cannot get it back.

105. But a while ago you showed me how I can get a reference to a given color. This should mean there is a way.

This is a different situation. In the presented example we used the fact that each instance of a rectangle (and of course of any other geometric shape) remembers its color. You can ask for it anytime and it will return you the remembered reference. But I was speaking about a situation when nothing is referred to a given object, all references are cancelled and there is no possibility to ask for.

As soon as nothing is referred to this object, you cannot get a reference to it, but it is more than likely that the object will be cancelled as well, i.e. removed from the memory.

You should know, that *garbage collector* is regularly looking through the heap, i.e. through the memory where the objects are saved, and in case it discovers an object with no reference, the garbage collector can cancel it and release the relevant memory for future usage.

106. You told me, that the garbage collector can remove it, but not that it will remove it.

I've answered the similar question in the previous lesson (question 86), but I can answer again in other words.

The garbage collector needs a part of the processor's capacity. Not to spend more processor's time than is necessary for the work, it doesn't devote too much time to cancelling these objects in case it would take more work than how much memory place would be obtained by removing them. In case the garbage collector will not consider removing of such useless object from a heap effective, it will leave it there.

However, if the garbage collector would remove such relict or not, has no impact on the fact that you have zero chance to get a reference to it.

Using Methods Returning the Value in Tests

107. I wanted to define the re-coloring of a rectangle as a test and *BlueJ* protested.

You are true. It is little bit more complicated in tests, because *BlueJ* does not know if you would like to verify that the called method returned the proper value. The window opened during defining the tests has therefore a checkbox **Assert that** (see the mouse cursor at figure 6.4) accompanied by other fields.

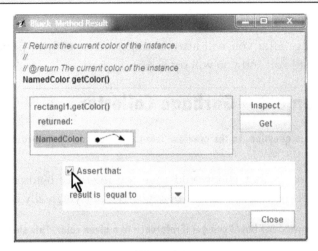

Figure 6.4
The window for sending a message with return value while creating the test

For the time being we will not use this possibility, and so please clear the checkbox. In case you would not cancel the check, *BlueJ* would warn you by a dialog box 6.5. Don't press the button **Continue** in any case, because you would agree with recording the fault and the program could not be compiled. Ask *BlueJ* to get back by pressing the button **Go back** and then clear the checkbox instead of entering the expected return value. Entering of return value tests will be discussed later on.

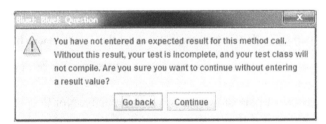

Figure 6.5
A verifying dialog, if we really want to create a program with a fault

Review

Now I would like to review what you have learned in this lesson. Start up the accompanying animation and then get through items of the following review.

> *Animation 6.1: Sending of messages requiring the return of a reference to an object –*
> `LOOTP_106a_Return_object`
> *The animation repeats what was explained during the lesson, i.e. it obtains a reference to an object in several ways and draws an attention to a special window form in test definition.*

Let's review what you have learned in this lesson:

☞   We use the term **identifiers** for the names of entities featuring in programs (classes, objects, messages ...).

☞ The identifiers have to fulfill three rules:

  ☞ They may contain only letters, digits and symbols $ and _.

  ☞ They cannot start with a digit.

  ☞ They cannot concur with any of keywords.

☞ Java identifiers are case sensitive, the uppercase and lowercase letters are interpreted as different.

☞ *BlueJ* enables to change the relative size of class diagram and of object bench by shifting the separating edge.

☞ The program has no chance to get back the reference to an object to which anything is referred.

☞ An object, to which nothing is referred, becomes a candidate for removing.

☞ A memory in which the objects live (a heap) is regularly controlled by the *garbage collector*. If it discovers an object to which nothing is referred, it can remove such object and release the memory for future usage.

☞ String type is an object type whose instances represent text strings and which has certain privileges among other object types.

☞ Texts that are values of String class instance should be entered in quotation marks.

☞ In dialogs with return values *BlueJ* does not depict only an arrow for text strings as for objects of other types, but writes there directly the relevant text string closed in quotation marks.

☞ In case you will send a message requiring a return value in the test definition, *BlueJ* opens a dialog box which enables to enter the return value test. Provisionally, please, clear the checkbox **Assert that**.

☞ In case you forget clearing the checkbox, *BlueJ* will verify in the following dialog if you really want to enter the program with an error. If not, you can return to a previous dialog box by pressing the button **Go back** and clear the checking.

Project:
No significant changes were made in the 104z_Tests class project.

7 The Messages with Parameters

What you will learn in this lesson
In this lesson firstly the meaning of parameters will be explained and you will learn how to construct objects applying the parameters. Once again using the reference will be presented and finally how to use the test classes for creating a picture and its animations.

Project:
In this lesson we continue in using the 104z_Test_class project.

The Meaning of Parameters

108. **You have spoken about parameters when we started sending messages which require creating an instance. What is so strange with them that you decided to devote the whole lesson to them?**

Only by establishing the parameters of sent messages the programming starts to be really interesting. Parameters enable to specify in details what you exactly expect from an object to which you are sending the given message. At non-parametric messages we often depended on default setting and, of course, they did not have to meet our requirements.

Working with parameters is not difficult. When sending messages requiring parameters, *BlueJ* opens a dialog box in which it prepares an input field labeled with its name and type for each parameter (very often you can estimate its purpose from its name).

Moreover, it copies the documentation comments into the dialog, which means that when the author of the given class is a decent programmer, you would have complete information at your disposal and you can assign the data properly.

The Object Construction Using Parameters

109. **I'd welcome an example which would clarify this item once again.**

Well, we will start again by resetting the virtual machine. Then we will try to create our "popular" triple-object composed of a rectangle, an ellipse and a triangle, but this time we will locate them to a different place and we will change their size. Let's start again with a rectangle – you should send the following message for creating a rectangle with an entered position:

```
new Rectangle(int x, int y, int width, int height)
```

As you see, the message has four parameters. Presentation of parameters in parentheses behind the message is called the *declaration*. In each declaration firstly the type of the declared parameter is written followed by a name of a given parameter. Individual declarations are separated by commas.

According to the declared type you can recognize which kind of data you should enter, and on the other hand, according to it the computer recognizes what can be expected from you and how to prepare for it. Thus, the effectiveness of the program is increased, but mainly, the number of faults, you can make when creating the program, is decreased. We will discuss this question several times in future.

110.   How should I enter the values of parameters?

I have already told you. After entering the command for sending the message with parameters *BlueJ* opens a dialog box in which it asks for parameter values. In addition when the message returns a reference to an object, it asks you also for the name of the variable into which the returned reference should be saved.

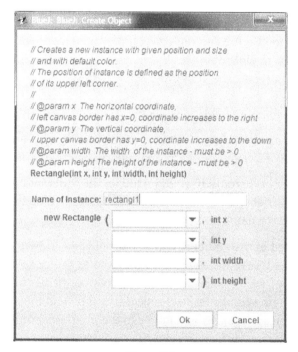

Figure 7.1
The dialog box for entering the parameter values

The Dialog Structure for Sending Messages with Parameters

111.   At the beginning you started enumerating of what I can find in the dialog box. Before going on, please, explain, what this window offers.

That's a good idea. Please notice at figure 7.1 that this window is divided by a horizontal line into two parts. The upper one contains a copied documentation of the called method. For the time being, please don't pay attention to neither slashes nor "@" characters prefixing the words *param*; when you will learn writing comments, I will explain you their meaning. For now, please remember that a good programmer puts the so called **documentation comment** before the method definition, in which he explains what the given method is doing, how it is used, what the meaning of particular parameters is and what it returns[2]. *BlueJ* copies this comment and locates it into the upper half of a dialog box which is opened when calling the method with parameters.

Under the comment you can find a **method header**, from which you can recognize its return type, its name (constructors have no name applicable in the source code, therefore the method is presented as nameless) and a list of its parameter declarations in parentheses; at each of them you can find its type followed by its name. Individual parameters are separated by commas.

The method header will be always presented, so that you can have at least basic information even when you will work with a program written by a dauber who thinks that writing comments is beneath his dignity – the intellectual surely handles even a chaos!

We will meet method headers elsewhere – *BlueJ* uses them in context menus as "names" of commands for sending a corresponding message. *BlueJ* adds a keyword new before the method header only at commands requiring the class for creating its instance.

Let's have a look below the dividing line.

In case it would be a method returning the object type value, there will be an input field under the separating line, in which *BlueJ* will offer you the name of a variable, into which the reference to a returned object is saved. You can accept it or enter your own. In case of a method that doesn't return anything, this field is missing.

Then there is a section containing fields representing the statement calling the method:

☞   If it is a requirement for creating an instance, as in our diagram, you can find the new keyword followed by the name of a class whose instance we are creating.

☞   If it is an ordinary method, you will find a name of an addressed class (see figure 7.3 on page 55) or the name of a variable with a reference to an addressed object (see figure 6.3 on page 46) followed by a dot and the name of the called method.

The method name is followed by parentheses with input fields for individual parameters, each field at separate line. To outline the transcript as close as possible to the code realizing the corresponding statement in a program, *BlueJ* writes commas behind individual fields (future parameters). However, contrary to the correct program statement, *BlueJ* repeats the type and the name of the given parameter behind each input field in the dialog. This will not be in the program, but it serves to better orientation in parameters and to knowing which field belongs to which parameter.

112.   **Oh, it was dozens of things! I'm afraid I will not remember it. Never mind, when I would like to brush it up, I will get back and read it once more. You told that the method header announces the return type and the method's name. Those are two things, but in the dialog box at figure 7.1 there is only** Rectangle. **So how is it?**

The dialog box at figure 7.1 is a reaction to the constructor calling (we were speaking about constructors in the section *Methods and Constructors* on page 30). The constructor can be considered as a nameless method, which means there is only a return value type in the header, i.e. the type of a created object.

---

[2]   I remind that the term a method means a code which defines how the object will react to the corresponding obtained message.

The Example Continued

113.   Well, I will presume that I already know the dialog and therefore I would switch on the example. So I require creating a rectangle – will it be a special one?

We will make twice bigger rectangle than the last one and a little bit shifted to the middle of the canvas. For now, we will keep the offered reference name and enter the coordinates [50; 50], the width being 200 and the height being 100.

114.   Good. I entered the values you have ordered and I added also two remaining objects (an ellipse and a triangle) for which I entered the same parameter values.

Well, you could make use of the fact that each input field has its scroll list with lastly entered values, but it doesn't matter, you can try it next time.

And now we will replace the original test fixture by the freshly created trio. Ask again the Tests class to create a test fixture; and after it will warn you that the tool has been already created and will ask you if it should be replaced (see figure 7.2), let it replace.

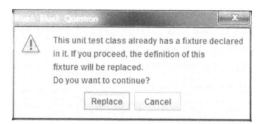

Figure 7.2
The dialog asking confirmation of requirement for replacing the fixture

And now try to start both prepared tests. In case you proceeded exactly as I told you, they both should operate.

Once More the Object vs. the Reference

115.   You are true, it really works! How it is possible that it operates despite we have quite different objects in the fixture?

As I have already told you, programs in Java do not work with objects but with references to objects. In case the variable with the reference will have the same name and will refer to an object of the same type (i.e. to an instance of the same class), the program will not notice any change and will turn to the reference regardless to which object it refers.

References now refer to new objects, but variable names are the same. Therefore the test methods have no chance to notice any change and they will work with new fixture without any opposing. Only we know that by way of the same variables they now turn to different objects, because their references refer to other objects.

I will try to outline it at an example from life. Imagine that you are a head of a department whose staff-members are working all over the world and you communicate with them only by e-mails. The staff-members are objects to which you are sending messages and their e-mail addresses are names of references by way of which you send them your messages.

When a staff-member asks his colleague to deputize for him for a certain time and the colleague starts to repeat instead of him, i.e. when your reference starts to refer to someone else, who will react to your messages instead of the original object, you cannot recognize it, until you will be told. The same situation is in the program.

The Parameters of String Type

116.   I see. When we came to these objects — you have said that we work with objects in a different way than with primitive type values. Is this valid also for parameters?

Of course, as we have already mentioned, you do not work with the objects themselves, but only with their references, by way of which you communicate with these objects. Everything is then a little bit more complicated. Therefore I would like to postpone the work with object parameters for the next lesson.

Now I would limit myself only to text strings, to be precise to instances of String class. As we said in the previous lesson, instances of the String class have certain privileges in Java, which enable to work with them in certain situations similarly as with primitive type values. We showed that *BlueJ* doesn't substitute their values by an arrow symbolizing the reference in dialog boxes, but similarly as at primitives it writes directly their value – the relevant text.

Speedily we remarked that the second privilege of String class instances is that you can assign the values of text strings directly – you can only put the assigned text into quotation marks. Strings are the only objects, for which Java defines the possibility of direct assigning. We can use it just now.

We are starting with improving our fixture. I don't like the way of testing when I see directly the results and I cannot compare them with the initial state. We will change it now and we will learn how to work with text strings.

We will use the IO class service (I remind that the IO name arose from an abbreviation of In-put/Output), which is able to open the dialog with a message for the user on request and to stop the program running until the user confirms reading the message.

Please, reset the virtual machine, request the Tests class for our favorite texture and then send the message

   void inform(Object text)

to the IO class. *BlueJ* opens the dialog with the request for an object (more precisely for a reference to an object), which is a parameter of this message (see figure 7.3). The parameter is the String class instance, which fortunately enables to assign values of its instances directly. However, as we said in the section *How to Write the Strings* on page 46, we write down the text representing the value of the String class instance in quotation marks. Enter e. g. the following text (don't forget the quotation marks):

   "Fixture prepared"

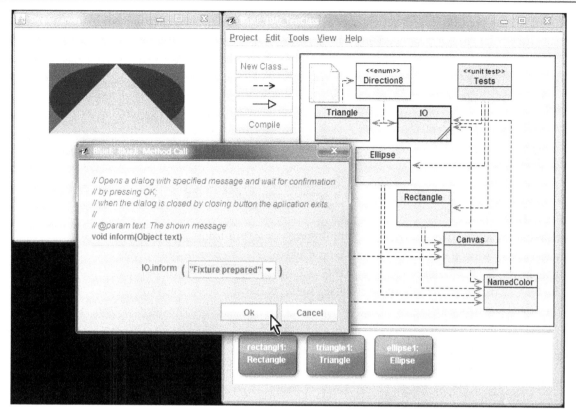

Figure 7.3
Sending the IO.inform("Fixture prepared") *message to the* IO *class*

The class reacts by opening the dialog at figure 7.4 in which the entered text is written down. Press the **OK** button and the demonstration how to create the test fixture is finished.

Figure 7.4
The announcement about creating the fixture

Now request *BlueJ* to convert the executed actions into method preparing the test fixture for the Tests class (the fixture itself did not change, we only replenish the accompanying action) and confirm that the original test fixture should be replaced (more precisely the program that creates the texture should be replaced).

Then try loading of the test fixture and verify that opening of the required dialog box as well as announcement on fixture readiness is really a part of it. Finally try some of our tests to see how opening of the dialog and connected state freezing makes the action, carried out with objects in the fixture, more visible.

To make the possible future repeating easy, I prepared another little accompanying animation that demonstrates the above described actions. In case of problems, please start it and do everything precisely according to the animation.

Animation 7.1: Sending messages with parameters – LOOTP_107a_Messages_with_parameters
Animation repeats what was explained during the lesson, i.e. it shows sending messages with parameters and the possibility of fixture modification.

The Animation

117. I would return to our test. When I tried it all three operations executed at once. Could it be arranged so that they appear gradually?

Of course, the actions were carried out step by step, only the computer is so quick that it seemed as if they would be done at once. In case you would like to see the course of the test, we should do it similarly as in projecting the movies: to stop the accomplishing for a while after each change. And it's no problem. You can send the following message to the IO class:

```
void pause(int milliseconds)
```

The class stops the program for the entered number of milliseconds. Define a new test, name it e.g. testAnimatedMovements and define it so that it would wait a quarter of a second (i.e. 250 milliseconds) after each shift.

Exercise

118. We are always doing exercise with your triplet. Couldn't we start drawing anything more interesting?

Until we did not finish sending messages with parameters, it was not possible. But now you know enough to create more interesting picture as a test fixture and examine all what we have explained until now.

I will offer you three themes for test class which you could create. You can see their realization at figure 7.5. Create the test fixture which will draw the initial picture (the upper one) and open the window with the message on readiness of the object. Then define the test which animates this picture in the way you can see at the lower figure. The precise assignments are as follows:

☞ Define the House test class. Its test fixture creates a little house with a chimney and opens a dialog with the House prepared message. Name the variables into which you will give individual parts of the little house as building, chimney and roof.

   Then define the test method testSmoke in this class which will supplement the smoke. Call the individual smoke objects (ellipses) as s1, s2 and s3.

☞ Define the Face class. Its test fixture draws a rectangle face and opens a dialog with the Face prepared message. Name the variables, into which you will put individual parts as head, leftEye, rightEye, nose and mouth.

   Define the testSmile test method in this class, which evokes a smile by enlarging the height of the mouth ellipse and covering its upper half by a rectangle. Name the variable into which you will give the reference covering the rectangle lip.

☞ Define the Robot test class. Its test fixture will draw a silhouette of a simple robot and will open a dialog with the Robot prepared message. Name the variables into which you will call its separate parts as head, body, legs, leftHand and rightHand.

Define the testSweep test method in this class which will sweep with the robot's hand. You will not need any other object for it.

I will not dictate you the size of separate objects. Try to deduce it from information that the canvas measures 300×300 pixels. In case you will not strike, nothing will happen.

Figure 7.5
The possible form of created objects

In case you would need a more expressive hint, you can have a look at the animated solutions. The sample solution can be found at the final project of this lesson. Try to propose your own pictures and their animations.

Animation 7.2: Exercise A Little House – LOOTP_107_e1_House
The animation presents creating the House class, a test fixture which draws a little house at the canvas and the testing method which paints smoke above the chimney.

Animation 7.3: Exercise A Face – LOOTP_107_e2_Face
The animation presents creating the Face class, a test fixture which draws a square shape face at the canvas and the testing method which depicts a smile.

Animation 7.4: Exercise A Robot – LOOTP_107_e3_Robot
The animation presents creating the Robot class, a test fixture which draws a robot at the canvas and the testing method which raises his right (from the observer's view) hand.

Review

Let's review what you have learned in this lesson:

☞   Parameters enable to specify more precisely what we request from the object by sending the relevant message – e.g. when creating pictures we can enter a required position as well as a size of the created object.

☞   In the interactive mode values of parameters are assigned in a dialog, which *BlueJ* opens after entering a command for sending a message with parameters.

☞   *BlueJ* divides the dialog for entering the parameters with a horizontal line into two parts:

   ☞   In the upper part there is the method's documentation comment copied together with its header.

   ☞   In the lower part there is the calling of the given method accompanied by repeated information on types and names of individual parameters.

☞   In the header there is the type of a return value, the method's name and in parentheses there is a list of parameters' declarations separated by commas, where each declaration contains the parameter's type and name.

☞   The constructor can be evaluated as a nameless method and therefore we can find only a type of a return value (a class, whose instance is being constructed) in its header and the name is missing.

☞   In case we request the test class to save another test fixture (this test class has already defined its test fixture), *BlueJ* will ask us if we really want to replace it, and in case of confirmation it replaces the original program by a new one.

☞   We reminded again that we never work directly with objects in Java, but always only with references to objects.

☞   If we change the reference contents, the programs working with these references will send their messages to the newly referred objects.

☞   Objects of String type present text strings. If we want to assign a value of a parameter which is a text string we assign the relevant text closed in quotation marks.

Project:
The resulting project form to which we came at the end of the lesson after making all exercises is in the
107z_Parameters project.

8 The Object Type Parameters

What you will learn in this lesson

In this lesson you should remind firstly the significance of quotation marks for assigning text strings, then you will become acquainted with an Object *class and you will see how it is possible to work with object type parameters. Further you will learn how you can pass the received return value of the sent message as a value of a newly sent message parameter.*

Project:

In this lesson we continue in using the 107z_Parameters *project.*

The Significance of Quotation Marks when Entering the Strings

119. **Last time we entered a text that should be written in a dialog box. What would happen if I would forget to enter the quotation marks?**

BlueJ would try to interpret the assigned text as a program. You can try it immediately. Ask again the IO class for opening an information box and enter the name of the variable with a reference to an ellipse, i.e. the name:

```
ellipse1
```

into the input field. Confirm your input and the IO class will open a dialog with a text characterizing the given ellipse, i.e. with the following text:

```
Ellipse_1[x=50, y=50, width=200, height=100, color=blue)
```

Now enter again the command for sending this message, but this time close the entered text on both ends with quotation marks. Then the entered text will be

```
"ellipse1"
```

As you surely will estimate, the subsequently opened window will show only the following text:

```
ellipse1
```

And now let's try a trick: enter gradually the names of the variable with an ellipse and a triangle separated by a space into the input field, i.e. write

```
ellipse1 triangle1
```

BlueJ will read the input and will try to interpret it. It will not succeed (the couple of identifiers written in the program as above mean nothing), and therefore it will announce an error – you will find the following record under the input field:

```
Error: ';' expected
```

Because the assignment is incorrect, *BlueJ* will not accept it, but will leave it in the input field for a revision. Please, put the whole text into quotation marks. After that the input field will be as follows:

```
"ellipse1 triangle1"
```

In case you will confirm this innovated assignment, the IO class will open the dialog box and will write down the expected text:

```
ellipse1 triangle1
```

And finally an advice: even the fields expecting the object type values do remember the last accepted inputs. If you would like to enter some of the latest values once more, you can find it in the list – see figure 8.1.

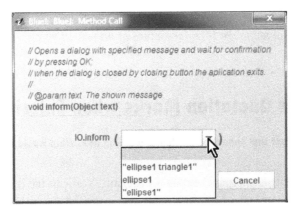

Figure 8.1
The list of lastly entered (correct) values

The Class Object

120.   All the time you are presenting, how various text strings are given over to the inform(Object) **method, but as the command shows in the context menu as well as the dialog box at figure 8.1, this method has a parameter of the** Object **type, not of the** String **type. However, you told me that in the parameter, there has to be the value of such type, which the given method takes into account, otherwise it cannot be processed. But in this case we transgressed against this principle and despite of it everything operated. Why?**

As I told you at the beginning, the OOP supposes that everything is an object. At the same time I told you that the objects with common features are put into classes. All objects have a common property that they are objects. So Java defines an Object class for them. All objects which you can meet in the program will be instances of the same Object class. Therefore, if the method declares that it expects an Object type parameter, it means that you can pass a reference to any object in this parameter.

So that the Object class would include really all objects, its definition has to be very general. Therefore special classes are defined for objects with special features – e.g. classes in our project. These specialized classes are marked as **child classes of the** Object **class** (you can meet also the terms subclasses or derived classes).

The fact that an object is an instance of some child class does not change the fact that it's at the same time an object. The child class only describes special features of its instances; features that a general object does not need – e.g. we can define their location or dimension. In case the parameter is of the Object type, you can pass any instance of object type as its parameter, even any value of a primitive type, because the compiler will wrap it into an object if need be.

The Object class defines nine methods and thus it arranges that all objects understand to corresponding nine messages. These methods can be used by instances of the child classes; we say that the child classes **inherit** them from the Object class. Therefore, besides methods defined by its mother class, each instance has also methods inherited from the Object class. *BlueJ* presents these methods in the submenu **Inherited from Object**. Majority of these methods are determined for advanced programming techniques. We shall use only two of them in this book: the toString() method and the equals(Object) method.

Inheriting of classes will be discussed in details in the next course (= in the following volume of this book). Now I can only tell you that in case the child class does not like an inherited definition of certain method, it can define its own one. We say that the newly defined method overrides the inherited one. *BlueJ* then indicates at commands corresponding to this "better defined" method **[overridden in Xxx]** in the menu of methods inherited from the Object class, where Xxx marks the name of a child class which defined its own version of a given method (see figure 8.2). As soon as some class overrides the parent (i.e. inherited) version of a method, its instances will use this "improved" method whenever, when a relevant message will be sent to them.

As I have already told you we will deal with class inheritance in the next volume. I am speaking about it just to explain you what *BlueJ* shows in its context menus.

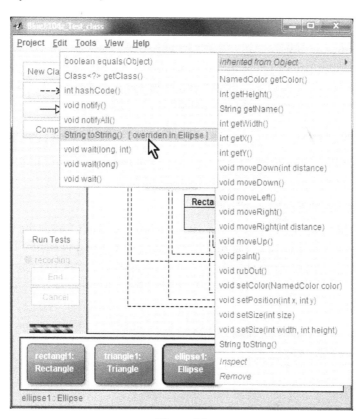

Figure 8.2
The list of inherited methods and their possible overrides

The Object Type Parameters

121.   We came from texts to general objects. Last time you told me that we will leave it for the next lesson. So what you can tell me about them?

In case you need to assign a value of primitive type to a message parameter, you simply take it and assign it. In case you use the interactive *BlueJ* mode, in which we are working, you simply write down the given value into the input text field. You can do it also with a text string – *BlueJ* itself will convert it to a relevant object and will pass the reference to this object in the message parameter.

It is more complicated with values of other object types. At first you have to gain the reference to be passed – mostly by sending a message to an object and the requested reference comes as a return value of this message. Let's have a look how to do it.

Reset the virtual machine and ask the Tests class for our favorite fixture. Then ask the rectangle for its color, save the received reference into an object bench in the variable RectColor. We have already done it, so you can go on easily.

Now, in the triangle1 context menu enter the command

```
void setColor(NamedColor color)
```

Then *BlueJ* opens a dialog of this message and asks you to enter a reference to a color that you want to pass to the triangle.

You can enter the reference in various ways. The most simple is to enter the name of the variable in which the reference is saved. If you have it in the object bench, you can only click on it and *BlueJ* will write down its name instead of you.

Try it. Activate the input field (click into it) and then click on the variable RectColor in the object bench. *BlueJ* will write its name into the input field. Now confirm the input and the triangle1 will gain the entered color, i.e. it obtains the rectangle's red color.

122.   It really changed its color! But what should I do when I would like to use a color that no created object has?

You can require it directly in the NamedColor class. Look at its context menu. In the message list that can be sent to the class you can find also the following message

```
NamedColor getNamedColor(String colorName)
```

You enter a name of the color you want to use (it's a string, so don't forget the quotation marks), and the class will return you a reference to the required color. Save it in a variable. Then send the message adjusting the new shape color to the shape, you want to recolor, enter the name of the just obtained variable into the input field (now it is a name, so without the quotation marks), and confirm the dialog and the shape will recolor.

123.   But how I recognize which colors the class knows?

You will ask – send the following message

```
void showDefinedNames()
```

to the class NamedColor. The class then opens a dialog where you can find names of the colors defined until now.

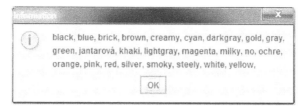

Figure 8.3
Known names of colors

Start up the accompanying animation and look at it step by step. Then try something similar.

Animation 8.1: Messages with object type parameters – LOOTP_108a_Object_parameters
This animation presents the operations demonstrated until now, i.e. it shows how to send messages with parameters of object types.

Direct Passing of the Message Return Value

124.   All's operating as you've described, but I've an impression that it's possible to do it more simply. Can I request the instance directly?

Yes, there is one possibility. Until now we proceeded in the way that firstly we sent a message to an object, the addressed object returned us a reference to a requested object which we saved into the variable in the object bench. Then we sent a message to which we passed the name of this variable in the parameter.

We can join these two steps into one. In case we know that the returned reference is needed only for passing it as a parameter and we will not need it any more, we can skip over saving it into the object bench. *BlueJ* enables to write down the calling of a relevant method (I remind: the method is a code defining the reaction to a message) directly to the text field. Then the returned reference is not saved and is passed as a parameter's value.

125.   I see! So in case I would like to set to our triangle the same color as of the lower rectangle...

Then you would enter sending the message setColor(NamedColor) in the local triangle offer and in the subsequently opened dialog you would enter the following text in the input field for the colors

    rectangl1.getColor ()

Then *BlueJ* sends a message getColor() to the object referred by the variable rectangl1 and passes over the received reference as a parameter of the setColor(NamedColor) message. Next it sends this message to the triangle. As you can see from figure 8.4, the result really corresponds with sending the message

    triangle1.setColor(rectangl1.getColor ())

However, you can ask for the color not only the created instances, but you can request directly the NamedColor class, which offers you several messages, called getNamedColor for this purpose.

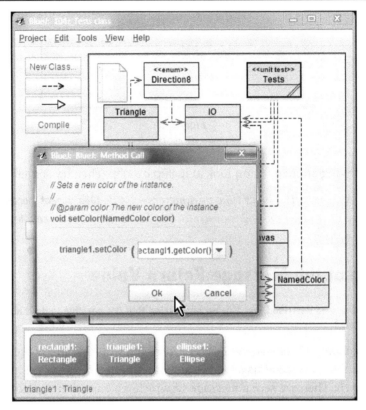

Figure 8.4
Entering of parameter's value as a return value of a called method

126. Well, if I would like to set e.g. yellow color, I should write into the input field NamedColor.getNamedColor
(NamedColor)**?**

In the section *How to Write the Strings* on page 46 you can find an explanation that it is necessary to differ when you are speaking about a text which is a value of some text string and when the entered text represents a keyword or an identifier of a program. Texts which are values of String class instances have to be closed between quotation marks. When you enter yellow without quotation marks, *BlueJ* starts to look for the variable called yellow. But you wanted to enter the name of a color directly, which means you have to enter into an input field the following text

    NamedColor.getNamedColor("yellow")

**127. When I can write message sending (or method invocation) into the input field, maybe I could enter anything
    what should be done firstly.**

You are true. You can enter an expression into the input field. The result of this expression is a value and its type corresponds to the relevant parameter's type. *BlueJ* evaluates the expression and in case it will correspond to the language rules, it will be executed and the result will be passed as a parameter's value.

Briefer Record of Messages

128. **Now I will digress a bit. You've told that for setting the color I should send a message** setColor(NamedColor) **to a triangle. This was a typo, wasn't it? In context menus this message is written as** void setColor(NamedColor color) **and you mentioned it few paragraphs ago.**

No, it was not a typo. Remind how I explained in section *Record of Method* Calling on page 39 that programmers do not quote the return value type in references on used methods. The same laziness causes that they do not quote names of parameters. The compiler recognizes which message do you send (and which method it should call) according to its name and number and types of passed parameters. Neither the parameter's names nor the method's return value play a role in it.

Therefore, the programmers in their references on methods quote only data important for the compiler, i.e. the method's name and its types of parameters. They skip both the return type as well as the names of particular parameters. As I have already told, *BlueJ* quotes this additional information so that the beginners, for whom it is determined, could easily orientate. And I mean, when *BlueJ* spoils you, I could start with briefer way of identifying the methods so that you would become familiar with them.

This "briefer" record may have two possible forms:

☞ If I would only refer to a message (method) without having on mind a real value of the passed parameter, I will quote only parameters' type at their places, e.g. setColor(NamedColor).

☞ If I would know parameters' values of a given message, I will write down the message in the same form as *BlueJ* writes in the dialog box (and how you will write in the program) – e.g. that you have to send a message setPosition(50,100) to the ellipse or directly that you should send the message ellipse1.setPosition(50,100).

Exercise

129. **Well, if you are so intensively thinking of my good, please, give me some examples where I could verify how I understand to all what we debated today.**

I would suggest improving the classes you created last time. Please, supplement the test classes from exercise in the previous lesson by tests which use parameters of object types.

☞ Fulfill the House class by the test testColor, which will color the roof to red and the building to ochre. You will get the necessary colors by sending the following message Yellow getNamedColor(String colorName).

☞ Fulfill the Face class by the test testBlink, which blinks with the left eye (from the user's view), i.e. firstly change the eye's color to the color of the face (the eye disappears) and then returns to the original color. You will receive the necessary colors by sending a message NamedColor getColor() to required objects, i.e. to the face and to the blinking eye.

☞ Fulfill the Robot class by the test testColor, which will color the robot's body to cyan and his hands to steely.

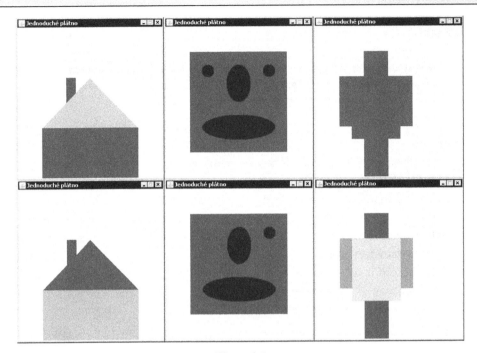

Figure 8.5
The possible result of added tests

In case you would need a more significant prompter, you can see the animated solutions. Sample solutions can be found again in the lesson's final project.

Animation 8.2: The exercise A House – LOOTP_108_e1_House
This animation will show you a modification of Home class from the previous exercise. It adds the testColor test which changes the roof to red and the little house to ochre.

Animation 8.3: The exercise A Face – LOOTP_108_e2_Face
This animation will show you a modification of Face class from the previous exercise. It supplements the testBlink test which blinks with the left eye (from the user's view), i.e. changes the eye's color firstly to the face color (the eye disappears) and then back to the original color.

Animation 8.4: The exercise A Robot – LOOTP_108_e3_Robot
This animation will show you a modification of Robot class from the previous exercise. It adds the testColor test which colors the robot's body to azure and his arms to steely.

Review

Let's review what you have learned in this lesson:

☞ When declaring the message we firstly write down the return value type followed by a message name. When sending the message we do not write the return value type, but again we have to put down to whom the message is sent.

☞ In message parameters declaration you should quote firstly the parameter's type, then its name. When sending the message you do not write the parameters types, but only their values.

☞ The values of object parameters can be entered by writing the variable with a reference to a relevant object into the input field.

☞ If we click on the reference in the object bench, *BlueJ* copies its name into the active text field.

☞ *BlueJ* remembers several previously entered values of a given type. Therefore if you want to use once again some of these values, you can open the associated list with the remembered values and select the value in the list.

☞ In *BlueJ* you can enter a method calling or generally any expression returning the needed value into the input field. *BlueJ* verifies it and in case of valid Java expression, it will be evaluated and the result will be passed as a value of the parameter in whose field the given expression is recorded.

☞ The compiler distinguishes forwarded messages (called methods) according to their names and number and type of their parameters. It ignores the return value types as well as name of parameters

☞ When mentioning methods, the programmers often mention only those characteristics of methods, which are controlled by a compiler. Therefore they do not mind neither the return value type of the given method, nor names of its parameters. *BlueJ* quotes them in context menus only for better orientation of beginners.

Project:
The final form of the project to which we came at the end of the lesson after completing all exercises is in a project 108z_Object_parameters.

9 The Expedition into the Interior of Instances

What you will learn in this lesson
In this lesson we will carry out an expedition into the interior of instances. You will learn what does it
mean fields and what is the difference between instance fields and class fields. You will see how to send
messages requiring a field value and how it is possible to extend the previously created test fixture.
Finally you will recognize how it is possible to monitor the field value during program's functioning.

Project:
In this lesson we continue in using the project 108z_Object_parameters.

Fields of Instances and of Classes

130.   How the instance recognizes where it should paint them, where it should shift or which color should have its shape?

So that the object could correctly react to our messages, it has to keep information describing the **state of an object**. The variables, where this information is saved, are called **fields.**

> **Note:**
> Some authors use the term *variable* instead of *field*. The classic OOP uses the term *attribute* for object data. Certain textbooks prefer it (me too), but I wanted to accommodate the Java habits and terminology of *Java Language Specification* and therefore I use the term *field*.

Each class defines which fields its instances will have (all instances of the same class have always the same set of fields) and which fields will belong to the class itself. Each instance has its own set of **instance fields** and controls it. Despite the fact that a set of instance fields is the same for all instances of the same class, values saved in these fields can differ in individual *instances, because state of these instances may differ.*

Opposite to it the **class fields** are common to a given class and to all their instances. In other words, all instances of a given class share fields of its class. As soon as any of them (class or any of its instances) will change the value in any class field, since this moment all instances will work with this new value.

You can imagine it as if all members of your family would share one bank account (class field), but each of them would have its own billfold (instance field) with current cash. As soon as someone changes the account state, it will touch immediately each of them. However, the state of their cash in a wallet is a private matter of each of them and its change will not influence directly wallets of other family members (unless the wallets would be refilled from the common account.

Terminological note:
Class fields are often called *static fields*. It is justified by language syntax and is a historical inheritance from the language C++. When we will come up to their declarations in a program, it will be more clear.

Working with the Fields

131.   Maybe I understand the notion of fields. But now, please, explain me what I can do with them.

BlueJ offers you a possibility to look into the interior of each object and to watch the values of its fields. Furthermore, you can also get a reference of the public fields of object type, which is saved in the object bench.

132.   But how then I recognize that the given field is a public one?

Don't be afraid, it will be written (together with its name and type) in a dialog which will open after your request for inspecting the instance interior.

133.   I see! It starts to be interesting. Please show me, how to do it.

It's simple. A while ago you wanted to get an instance of NamedColor class. So let's have a look what this class offers. Open its context menu and enter the command **Inspect**. *BlueJ* then opens an object inspector window which you can see at figure 9.1.

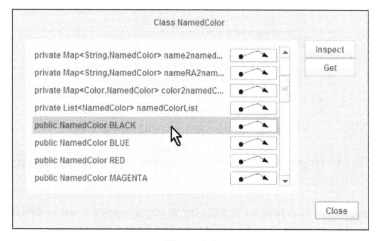

Figure 9.1
The outlook into the interior of NamedColor class

The window shows a list of fields; it's too many of them and you have to use scrollbar to see them all. The first fields are not interesting for us because they are **private**, but below them you can find a group of **public** fields representing separate colors.

When you click on some of them (let's take the field BLACK), buttons **Inspect** and **Get** will get "live". After pressing the button **Inspect** another object inspector dialog opens, which enables to investigate the interior of a selected instance. Delay it to a time when you will know more, and now press the button **Get**. Another window will open, in which *BlueJ* asks you for a name of a reference that *BlueJ* afterwards saves into the object bench.

The Messages Requesting a Field Value

134.   Last time you showed me how I can enter the method invocation into the input field which would return the required reference. Can I request for a reference to a field value?

You can send a message to an object in which you directly ask for value of its public field – in this case we would ask the NamedColor class for a reference to its color. If you will write down the code for sending this message into the input field for a given parameter, *BlueJ* sends the corresponding message to the addressed object and passes the received value as the value of the given parameter.

Such message is entered as the usual message: you address the object to which you are sending the message, and then you write a dot, followed by the message name, which is a field's name whose value you are requesting for. The only one difference is that you cannot add any parameters to the requirement for the field value, and thus there are no parentheses after the field's name. In case you will ask the NamedColor class for a value of a field BLACK, you will simply write the following (be careful in differing the small and capital letters):

        NamedColor.BLACK

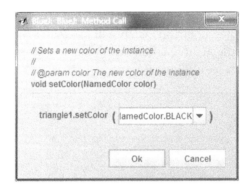

Figure 9.2
The message requiring for a reference to a black color

Once more I would like to emphasize that you can request only values of public fields. Others might be only inspected.

135.   I did not understand why I have to write NamedColor.BLACK**, if recently it was sufficient to write only** red **for a red color.**

Maybe you are touching the section *Getting the Reference to the Returned Object* on page 45. But at that place the red identifier was the name of the variable with a reference to an existing auxiliary object. But now you asked how it can be arranged so that you might not need any auxiliary object. That was why I showed you that you can ask the class for the requested object directly in the place where you pass the obtained reference as a parameter. In other words, this time we have no BLACK variable and that's why *BlueJ* does not accept this name. Firstly you have to send a message requesting the color. Therefore you have to enter both the addressee (NamedColor class), as well as the message name = the name of the requested field.

Field Accessibility

136. You said, that I can request only values of public **fields. I would like to know, what is the publicity of fields like?**

The modifier public does not deal with any publicity, but specifies only access rights to the given object, i.e. who may ask for a value of the given field and adjust it, if need be. That's why it is called an access modifier.

In the inspector window of the NamedColor class which you can see at figure 9.1, first few fields are marked by private access modifier and the following ones are marked as public. The fields with public modifier can be used by everybody, who can use the relevant object (in our case the NamedColor class). Opposite to it, the fields marked with private modifier serve only for the **internal needs** of the given class and its instances, and no one has an access to them.

137. Should I understand it that I can choose who will be allowed to work with particular field in the program?

It's a long story. For now I will only tell you that the ability to encapsulate the processed data together with operations which work with these data (i.e. to locate them in the same shell – an instance or a class) as well as to hide totally the implementation details (as programmed here), are considered as the most important features of object oriented programs. You can imagine that each object says:

Everybody may know, what I am able to do,
but nobody can snoop
how I am doing it and why I know what I know.

As I have said, the object keeps information in fields which enables to fulfill successfully its function. When proposing an object the programmer has to carefully think over which kind of information will be open to other objects and which will be only for a private need of the given object.

Prevailing majority of fields is usually marked as private. However, in some cases the programmer comes to a conclusion that it would be useful to open them also for other objects and then they are marked as public.

As I have already indicated, this topic is far more extensive and complicated which means we will come back to it many times in future.

138. Well, then I'll remember that I can freely work only with fields marked as public. But how it is possible that the values of other fields can be seen in the browser window, if you told me a while ago that they are private and thus secret for others?

Because you work in the development mode and the system is always willing to reveal items which nobody can discover in the standard mode.

The object inspector enables e.g. current monitoring of changes of field values (including the private ones) of an object. You can utilize it especially in a situation when the program starts to make suspicious things and you need to find out why.

Test Fixture Extending

139.　Aha, I see, this starts to be interesting. Give me an example.

Well, but our existing fixture is a little bit featureless for such tests because all its objects have the same position and size. To make it more varied, let's start with extending the test fixture by a set of objects created by sending parameterless messages.

140.　Would it be strange if the readiness of a fixture will be announced and after confirmation of a dialog box further objects will be added in it?

Don't be afraid, we will use the reverse procedure. Let's use the fact that *BlueJ* remembers all actions since the last reset of the virtual machine and we will prepare default versions of our favorite objects. Only after it we will ask for a fixture containing objects created with the assistance of parametric constructors whose installation is completed by opening of a dialog which announces the readiness of the fixture.

Not to confuse our program we have to call the newly added objects with names that differ from objects in the fixture. The names of references to objects in the fixture finish with the digit one. Because the new objects will arise by using parameterless messages, we will replace the offered one by zero at the end of their names.

As I have told you after creating a new triplet of objects we request reading up the fixture. Its objects are then added to those who already have been created and their successful completing will be announced by the final dialog. You confirm it and ask *BlueJ* for saving the new program version which creates the test fixture of the Tests class. Then you will continue working with this version of the fixture.

Animation 9.1: Completing the fixture by another set of shapes – OOPNZ_109_A1_DoplneniPripravku
The animation repeats the explained items. It shows how it is possible to adjust creating the fixture so that the fixture would include further objects.

Monitoring of Field Values

141.　I have a newly created test fixture and I can start working with it.

Let *BlueJ* save the fixture into the object bench, select the triangle1 object and enter the command **Inspect** in its context menu. *BlueJ* opens the inspection window (see figure 9.3).

And now try to change the position and/or the size of a given diagram and look at the dialog box, how the values of its fields are changing.

You can even have a look into several objects at the same time and observe that after each action the proper field of a proper object is changed.

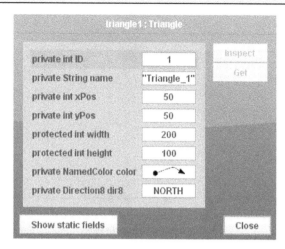

Figure 9.3
Fields of a triangle1 instance

Static Fields – Class Fields

142.   What is the button **Show static fields** for?

As I told you in the previous lesson, the class also has its fields, which are common to all its instances. By pressing this button you open an inspection window which shows fields of the given class..

In the previous lesson you opened this window by entering the command **Inspect** in the class context menu. The command **Show static fields** is only another way how to open this window and how to have a look at values of class fields.

143.   Why they are called static?

This is more due to historical reasons. You can explain it for example that these fields are all at the same place (therefore static), and all instances of the given class can see them if they need to learn their immediate value.

144.   Please, give me an example, in which I can see that all instances share the class field.

Why not? When we were playing with triangles we can continue playing with them. Ask for an inspection of fields of Triangle class. One of them is step. Its value determines how far the object will shift after sending a parameterless message for shifting.

As you can see at figure 9.4, the field is private, so that you can neither recognize its value nor adjust it directly. But you can adjust it by sending a public message

```
void setStep(int distance)
```

Set the value of this field e.g. to 25 and then send parameterless messages to both triangles requiring their shifting. The distance by which they will shift is equal to a new value of the field step.

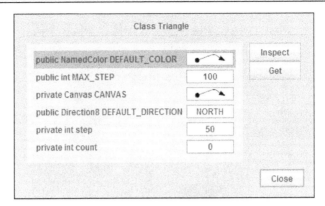

Figure 9.4
The fields of Triangle class

145. There is a zero in the last field named count **at the class inspector dialog at figure 9.4. However I have there number two. Why?**

In the field count the class counts how many instances it has created. The diagram shows zero, because I took the window after resetting the virtual machine when no instance have been yet created. You opened the window after creating the test fixture, when there were two triangles created. Try to make out another triangle and you will see how the field value will increase again.

So that you could repeat everything and examine it, I prepared again a little accompanying animation, which would show you all what was debated here. Start it up and try to repeat all. Then try yourself something similar.

> *Animation 9.2: Fields and how to work with them – OOPNZ_109_A2_UtrobyObjektu*
> *The animation shows how you can look into objects interior and recognize values of their fields.*

Exercise

146. Which exercise did you prepare for me today?

Supplement the creating of fixtures in test classes from exercises of the previous lesson.

☞ The test fixture of House class immediately draws properly colored little house which will have cyan window and brown door. Ask for the color by a requirement for a field value (e.g. NamedColor.AMBER) and pass the obtained object to the constructors directly. Don't forget that the identifiers of color fields contain only capital letters.

☞ The fixture of Face class adds a green elliptic body to the rectangle face, which will be seen only partly (the ellipse will reach out of the canvas edging below).

☞ The fixture of Robot class immediately draws properly colored robot and it also draws two black circles instead of feet.

If you would need a more significant clue, you can have a look at the animated solutions. Sample solutions can be found again in the final project of the lesson.

Figure 9.5
The possible shape of created objects

Animation 9.3: The exercise A Little House – LOOTP_109_e1_House
The animation will present a modification of House *class from the previous exercise according to an input of this lesson.*

Animation 9.4: The exercise A Face – LOOTP_109_e2_Face
The animation will present a modification of Face *class from the previous exercise according to an input of this lesson.*

Animation 9.5: The exercise A Face – LOOTP_107_e3_Robot
An animation will present a modification of Robot *class from the previous exercise according to an input of this lesson.*

Review

Let's repeat what you have learned in this lesson:

☞ The object keeps information concerning its state in fields.

☞ Certain authors use the term *variable* instead of *field*, certain others use the term *attribute*.

☞ All instances of a given class have the same set of fields.

☞ Both instances, as well as the class itself, may have their own fields.

☞ Fields of a class are common to both the class as well as to all its instances.

☞ *BlueJ* enables to examine fields of each object through the object browser which we call by a command **Inspect** from the object context menu.

☞ The window of object browser enables to gain the value (the reference to an object) of the public fields of object type.

☞ When sending the message with parameters you can write a code into the input field. This code sends a message and returns the value instead of a requested parameter value. The returned value will be then used as a value of a given parameter.

☞ Accessibility of field values for other objects can be specified through *access modifiers*. They are also shown in the browser window.

☞   Fields can be either public or private. The values of `public` fields are accessible for all objects for which the "owner" of these fields is available.

☞   `Private` fields serve only for an internal need of a given object and no one else has an access to them.

☞   The object inspector window updates the shown values of object's fields after processing each message.

Project:
The resulting shape of a project to which we came at the end of the lesson after passing through all exercises is in the `109Z_Inside_instances` project.

10 The Interface

What you will learn in this lesson
In this lesson you will learn what does it mean an interface and what is the difference between an interface and an implementation. You will become acquainted with a kind of data type called interface *and its advantages when it is appropriately used in a program. After that you will see how it is possible to import a class from another project and finally how to define that a class implements the given interface.*

Project:
In this lesson we are opening a new project entitled 110a_Interface_added.

Motivation

147.   It seems that you have told me everything about objects and that we could start programming.

I would like to present you one more construction. It often makes troubles to programmers. Therefore I want to introduce it as soon as possible. According to my experience, this construction is problematic mainly to programmers who are used to think in a way typical for structured programming, whilst it doesn't matter which programming language they are using. Quite often I meet this situation with students who passed through a course of object programming, but some key constructions were presented to them at the end of the course, so that they did not have enough of time to adopt and master them. To avoid such problems, I would like to present this construction even before your first attempt to create your own code. This important construction is the interface.

But firstly I will start with a little repeating. In the section *The Messages Sent to Instances* on page 22 I presented that all instances of the given class are equipped with the same set of methods and therefore they know how to react at the same set of messages. In the section *Briefer Record of Messages* on page 65 we mentioned that the message is unambiguously determined by its name, by the number of parameters and by the types of individual parameters. In other words: the message sender has to pass the value of a type declared in the message declaration in each parameter.

The message requirement for getting only the value of the declared type in the parameter is a little bit limiting, because we have to define a special method for each type, whose value we would like to use in the given parameter. However, if we would add a new class into our project, whose instances would work with our graphic objects, we would have to define a special method for each of our shapes.

148.   Could you explain it at an example?

I will try it. All three kinds of graphic objects in our project are able to shift to an entered position. But they shift in jumps. In case you install a class, whose instances will be able to shift the graphic objects smoothly (let's call it e.g. Mover), each type of shifted objects will need to have a definition of a separate method – one would have to know shifting the rectangles, another one ellipses and the third one triangles. In case you would add into your program another graphic shape, e.g. stars, you would have to define another method for them in Mover class. You surely feel yourself that all these methods will be very similar one to another and they will differ only by the type of parameter, in which they would receive the graphic object, which should be smoothly moved at a canvas.

But let's remind what we have said about data types. In the section *Primitive and Object Types* on page 35 I mentioned that the data type says which values the data of a given type can acquire and what you can do with them. It provides information to a program about what this object knows, which messages it can receive and what you can require in them. But all graphic objects know nearly the same: to inform about their position, size and color, to paint and rub out themselves, to shift, and to change their color and their size. (The triangle is also able to tell the direction to which its peak is turned and can adjust a new direction, but this little difference can be skipped over.) From a certain viewpoint we could consider individual types of graphic shapes as special cases of some more general type, whose objects are able to react to the above mentioned messages.

Interface vs. Implementation

149. **What you say is an interesting remind of what I should know, but I don't know where the novelty is that may cause me troubles.**

I am coming to it. When I happen to meet this topic during my lectures, I like to ask my students if they know who Janus was– the Roman Empire's god of entrances and exits, beginnings and endings (January is named after him). Janus had two faces: one was looking into the future, the other one into the past. Similarly it is with the program: its two faces are the interface and the implementation:

☞ **The interface** of a given entity (= of a program's part – a module, a class, a method…) specifies what the given entity knows and how to communicate with it. In case of an object it says which messages can be sent to it (to which messages the object understands) and how the object reacts to them. It is important to remember that an **interface doesn't solve anything, it only promises**, what the given entity can provide. We could say that the **interface summarizes what the surrounding program should know about the given entity**.

☞ Opposite to it, the **implementation** provides that the given entity would do exactly what its interface promises. Good programmers usually strive to make most difficult any attempts to reveal the implementation. The less the surrounding program knows about the implementation of a given entity, the easier is to change this implementation in future. As soon as any information escapes, it cannot be guaranteed that anybody will not use it. Then, when I would change any generally known feature, I would have discover all who use it (or who even might use it) and have a look how much I have to change also these parts of the program. And that would be a lot of work.

150. **But if I would be programming and I would add my own class to a project, then I would know how the other programs are composed, wouldn't I?**

This is just the joke: you will know it, but you will look like you don't know it. Moreover, the compiler will try to take care so that you would not utilize fully this knowledge.

151.   Are you playing with me? How the compiler can recognize if I utilize knowing how certain class is programmed?

After you will start programming I will show you how you can explain to the compiler, what you consider as implementation details which shouldn't be disclosed. The compiler then keeps an eye so that nobody would use these parts of a program.

To be more precise what I have on my mind: I will show you how you can present only a class interface, so that you would not be distracted by implementation details. Open the context menu of any class and enter a command **Open Editor**. *BlueJ* opens an editor window, similar to a window at figure 10.1. There is a part of Mover class documentation which we have already discussed and with which we will work. (I have chosen its documentation because it has only few constructors and methods, and after a slight shift I succeeded to put all into a screenshot.)

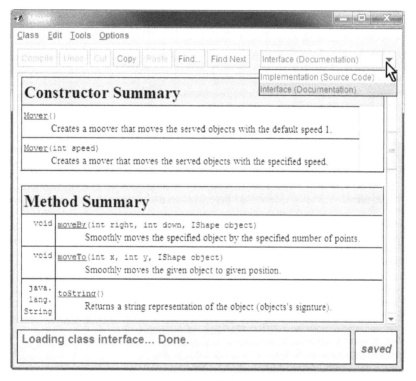

Figure 10.1
The class documentation

Please notice the pull down list at the right edge of editor's button panel. As the mouse pointer shows, you can choose in this list if the window will show an implementation, i.e. the source code, or a class interface derived from documentation comments (I mentioned this in the section *The Dialog Structure for Sending Messages with Parameters* on page 51).

The documentation, which is a description of the interface, is presented in Java as a web page. At the figure 10.1 I picked up a part of it with tables briefly characterizing both constructors and all three methods which this class offers. There is a characteristic of the whole class above them; below them you will find a detailed description of individual constructors and methods. In case you work with a class and its instances you should be satisfied with information you find in this window.

In case you switch to implementation in the pull down list, the source code of the given class will be shown in the window, i.e. the way how I have programmed it (a class implementation). You will work with the source code after you will learn the introductory presentation with OOP and start creating the code itself. So hold on a while, it will not last a long time.

Interface as a Data Type

152.   **I already know how I will learn which interface belongs to a certain class, i.e. which methods I can call (which messages I can send to it). But it seems to me that it is too little to an announced novelty.**

You are true. That's why I will return to theory for a while. As I like to say:

The only one constant of contemporary programming is the certainty
that the assignment will soon change.

Therefore the programmer has to prepare his programs in such way so that the possible changes could be included as easy as possible. After what was said a while ago, it is obvious that the programmers will adjust the program's implementation in the easiest way at such moment when they will be sure that any change will not influence any of the fellow workers of their program (any of the objects, their program depends on). Not to impact any colleagues by a change of implementation the programmers have to be sure that they are not dependent on it. This can be reached e.g. by the fact that the program will look like there is no implementation. I cannot be dependent on anything what does not exist.

153.   **Such a tale! If I understood properly, when the program has no implementation, it cannot do anything.**

I didn't tell it has no implementation. I told that it looks like not having any one. This is what also the Java authors realized and why they installed into their language a special kind of data type – an `interface`. The `interface` does not have (contrary to classes) any implementation[3]. Theoretically it also cannot have any instances, because it is necessary to do something for their creation, but the implementation responsible for every "work" is missing here.

This seemingly blind lane is solved by the fact that Java allows declaring implementation of certain `interface` by classes. But they have to guarantee that their instances would be able to properly react to all messages which the implemented `interface` declares. As a "reward" instances of these classes can pass off themselves as instances of the implemented `interface`.

Interface versus `interface`

154.   **You are confusing me a bit. How should I understand this title?**

The term *interface* is used in two meanings:

---

[3]   In Java 8 an interface can suggest a default implementation, but we will discuss this possibility only in the second volume.

☞ Firstly, it is a sum of generally known characteristics of any program's entity, about which we were speaking at the beginning. Each class, each method, each field and the whole program have its interface. It is what others know about the given entity.

☞ Secondly, this term is used for the program's construction, which we might consider as syntax representation of interface and which behaves as a class without any implementation.

Mostly you recognize from the context which from these two meanings the speaker has on his mind. In the following text when I will want to emphasize that I speak about the program's construction I will write it with the monospaced font used for programs – interface – or use the term *interface type*. In case I will speak about a general interface of the given entity, I will write it with *italic – interface*. If you would not be sure, which meaning I have on my mind, don't hesitate to ask me.

155. You told that interface can define the data type. Then, such methods could exist which would have parameters of this type. If I understood properly I can pass any of instances which pose as instances of the given interface in these parameters.

Exactly, and that is the greatest advantage of this construction. You can define a method that expects a parameter of a given interface type and when calling the method you can pass an instance of any class, which implements this interface, as this parameter. Opposite to methods with which we were working until now, and in parameters of which you can pass an instance of the only one type (if not considering an Object type), this method can work with more general parameters and their mother class can be any class implementing the declared interface.

Practical Usage

156. Let's return to the main presentation. You explain everything too generally. Please get off your abstract exegesis and try to show me what you strived to explain the whole time at a practical example.

Well, I will try to show it step by step at an example. In the part on motivation I was speaking about the Mover class, which should know to shift fluently your graphic shapes. If you would define this class without using an interface, you would have to define a separate method for each kind of graphic objects – one for triangles, another one for rectangles and the third one for ellipses. And now, please, imagine that you would like to define one method for shifting to an entered position and the second method for shifting by an entered distance. Each of these methods should be defined three times, so altogether we would have six methods. With each additional function you should have to add another three methods.

Preparation of a New Project

157. I understood until now. But I don't have any shifting class, nor any interface, so for now I have nothing to solve.

Well, let's right the wrongs. Leave your current project and open the project 110a_Interface_added, where a Mover class is added (I showed you its documentation a while ago) and IShape interface – see diagram 10.2.

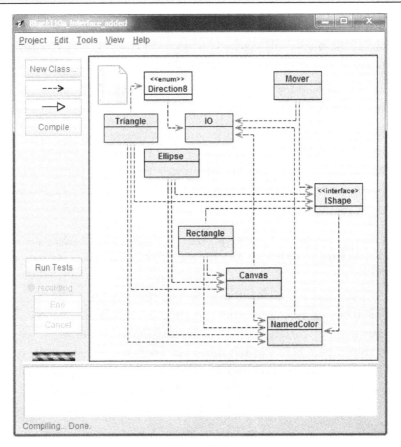

Figure 10.2
The initial look of a project 110a_Interface_added

As you see, not only a class and an interface were added in the project, but also lines telling who is dependent on whom. We would like to add further lines that would show which class implements the IShape interface. Then the class diagram would be so overloaded, that you couldn't orientate in it. Therefore we would ask *BlueJ* to stop drawing the dependency lines and then we will reorganize the whole class diagram so that we could work better with it.

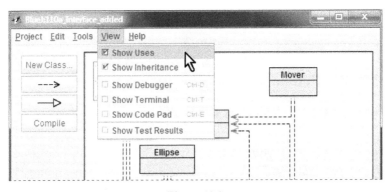

Figure 10.3
Cancelling the dependency lines

158. How should I ask *BlueJ* not to draw the dependency lines?

It is simple. You open a **View** menu and clear the option **Show Uses** – see figure 10.3. *BlueJ* then stops to show dependencies.

As I have already told you we will not stop at this point. We will make all classes in the diagram smaller and reorganize them according to figure 10.4. (If you forgot how to do it, open the animation LOOTP_101b_IDE_BlueJ – *BlueJ environment and how to work with it* once more, and go through it.

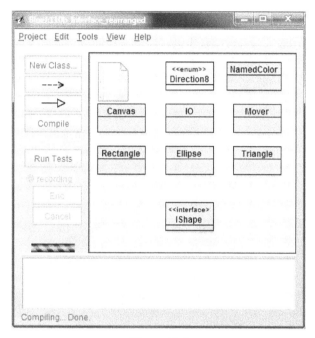

Figure 10.4
The project's look after diminishing and reorganizing of classes – project 110b_Interface_rearranged

159. Why should I make the classes smaller?

Because immediately we will import our test class from the previous project. Occasionally *BlueJ* inserts the rectangle at a place where already a rectangle of another class is placed and moreover, *BlueJ* puts it to the bottom. In case we want to find it, we have to move a bit with each of rectangles to discover the relevant one. The same can happen when you insert a new class into a project. When you diminish all class rectangles a little bit, the new or imported classes will be always sticked out so that you can take them and shift them into a position which would suit to you.

160. This is a good idea. I see that IShape **has its stereotype as well as a different color.**

Surely, we depict an interface in a class diagram similarly as an ordinary class, and yet it is not an ordinary class, we point out its exceptionality by a stereotype <<interface>> and we stress it also by a different color.

Moreover, I adopted a convention that is used by a number of programmers, although it is not quite current in Java: I put a letter I in front of names of all interface types (therefore the interface does not have the name Shape, but IShape). Majority of all my students say that it helps them to be well oriented in the program.

Importing the Class from Another Project

161.   And now let me know, what it means importing.

From time to time it happens that you deposited a class which you could use in another of your projects. Importing a class is a smart possibility how to include this class into your project. We will use it in our course several times.

A while ago I told you e.g. that we will import a test class from the previous project, i.e. from project 109z_Inside_instances. Not to speculate over how much you diverged from a sample solution, which I will ponder in further explanation, I prepared a subfolder Extension_10 in the project folder. This subfolder is not a project because it does not contain any package.bluej file, but you can find a source code of all classes in it that we will gradually import.

I will prepare also other imported files for you in this way. In the project folder you sometimes will find a subfolder Extension_xx, where xx will be a number of the lesson in which we will import the given files. There will be e.g. source codes which would be uncompilable with the initial version of the project, and which might be imported only after we will adjust the project a bit. I think it's useless to explain it more, you will see it.

162.   How a class from somewhere else can be imported into a project?

Look into a menu **Edit** for the command **Add Class from File.** *BlueJ* then opens a standard open dialog. Find a folder in it with the file you want to add. It is meaningful to add only source files, i.e. files with the extension java. Look in the folder of this project and find a subfolder Extension_10. Pick up the file Tests.java, confirm your input and *BlueJ* adds a rectangle of Tests class into the class diagram. Diminish it to a size of other rectangles, put it to a place convenient for you, compile it and try if all tests in the new project are running.

163.   If I understood it properly, I could import the class from anywhere, not only from this project or another one.

You are true. You can import a class from any place from which your file manager is able to read – even from a flash memory, if need be, to which a file was saved by any of your friends. But as I have already told you, you can import only source files with the extension java. In case of importing anything else *BlueJ* would revolt.

164.   Well, the class is imported and compiled. What should I do further?

Now we start experimenting with interface. Reset the virtual machine and request the test class for a fixture. Then ask the Mover class for a new instance. As the context menu (or the figure 10.1 on page 79) will show you, the Mover class offers two constructors, i.e. two possible messages requiring an instance. The one-parametric constructor requires the speed by which the created mover should shift the committed objects; by sending the parameterless message you require creating a mover with the speed 1.

Implementation of an `interface` by the Class

165.   I've created a mover and I added it to the object bench. What else?

If you open a context menu of the created mover (or if you would have a look into its documentation on page 10.1), you see that you can send two messages to it requiring a fluent shift of an object. After sending the message

    moveTo(int, int, IShape)

the mover takes the object passed in the third parameter and shifts it fluently to the position, the coordinates of which are defined in the first and the second parameter. The message

    moveBy(int, int, IShape)

will request to shift the object passed in the third parameter by a distance entered in the first and the second parameter.

Both messages require the third parameter of IShape type. Open now the IShape interface in the editor, and some of the graphic shape classes in another window besides it. Put both windows alongside and compare the method tables in their documentations. You will see that our class implements all messages required by this `interface` and so nothing should prevent the class to pass off its instances as instances of the given `interface`.

166.   You are true, it's all there. So I can start fluent shifting.

Sorry, this is what you cannot do. In case you will try to pass a reference to an instance of this class to some of the above mentioned Mover's methods as a reference to an object, which should be shifted, *BlueJ* would oppose and it will show you an error message

    Error: incompatible types - found Ellipse but expected IShape

in the dialog under the input fields. This means that an instance of IShape type was expected at a given place, but instead of it an instance of Ellipse type was found. The problem is that an ellipse theoretically could be considered as an instance of IShape type, because it implements all the declared methods, but the Ellipse class did not announce that it would apply for this possibility. Only instances of those classes that explicitly declare implementation of the given `interface` may pose as instances of certain `interface`.

167.   My goodness, why it needs enrollment? Why it's not sufficient that the instance knows everything what is needed?

In some languages it is sufficient, in some of them not. Java belongs to those more rigorous. The fact that a class will explicitly declare the implementation of an `interface` is a promise and the compiler can check if the class really fulfilled its promises and that all its instances may be used in situations in which the program requires instances of that `interface`.

168.   You told me that only some languages are so strict. What's the problem when in other languages the programs also operate?

Always you can choose only one possibility. The more tolerant languages check the object's ability to receive a message only at a moment when the message is being sent. But this is time consuming. The more rigorous languages can move this control to a compiling phase and thus they significantly strengthen the program's efficiency.

169.   Well, then how the class should enroll to the `interface` **implementation?**

You will enroll it. Generally, there are two ways: either you would adjust the source code (I will explain it in some of the future lessons), or you will show your intention and *BlueJ* will do it. Then you ask only for compilation and you make the verification if the compiler has no objections. The procedure is simple as follows:

1. Press the button on the left side with the triangle head arrow (in further text it is called an **implementation arrow**).
2. Move the mouse pointer to a class which will implement the `interface`.
3. Press the mouse button – thus you will anchor the arrow's root, and then draw the arrow's head to the `interface` which the given class wants to implement.
4. Release the mouse button. *BlueJ* then draws a dashed triangle head arrow to the implemented `interface`. At the same time it adjusts the source code in such way so that it would announce to the compiler that the class decided to implement the relevant `interface`. Because the source code of implemented class will change, *BlueJ* announces that this class was not compiled. At the same time even the `Tests` class will become not compiled, due to (as you surely remember from previous lessons) it is dependent on these classes.

Please, draw now stepwise the implementation arrows from all graphic shape classes to the `IShape` interface and let the whole project being compiled (as we know, the virtual machine resets at the same time). Then create the mover instance again and try to shift certain object by this mover.

170.   Oh, it operates!

And now try creating the test method which would shift the zero set objects similarly as the `Movements` test shifts objects of the first set, but this time use the mover. To examine both mover methods we will shift the triangle by 50 points down and then we shift the ellipse to the position [100, 0].

Again I have prepared a little additional animation so that you may repeat and examine everything. It will present you all what we have debated. Start it and try to repeat all. Then try something similar.

> *Animation 10.1: The interface and its usage – OOPNZ_110_A1_Interface*
> *The animation will show you a class import into a project and subsequently the defending of* `interface` *implementation by a class. It will show you how it is possible to use* `Mover` *class for realizing the fluent shifting.*

Exercise

171.   I've repeated all with the assistance of the animation and now I expect input in which I can exercise that I perceived the topic properly.

A big portion of today's information was theoretical and I don't have any bigger practical applications on my mind. Please, try the following simple tasks:

☞ In the subfolder `Extension_10` you will find the source codes of sample solutions for classes `House`, `Face`, and `Robot` from the previous lesson. Please, import them.

☞ Define the test `testSmoothSweep` at the picture with a robot, in which one arm fluently raises upwards and subsequently lowers down.

☞ Define the test `testSun` at the picture with a little house, in which a yellow sun slowly goes above the little house. In case you want the sun would properly appear from behind the left window side (the sun is always going from left to the right at our hemisphere) you have to create first a sun with the horizontal coordinate higher than 0 and immediately slide it behind the left edge, and subsequently the mover gets it out from this place.

☞ Define the test `testCap` at the picture with an angular face, to which a triangle cap goes from above to the face. You will have to solve a similar problem as in the previous case with the sun.

Review

Let's review what you have learned in this lesson:

☞ Review from the previous lessons:
  ☞ All instances of the given class are equipped with the same set of methods.
  ☞ The message is unambiguously determined by its name and types of individual parameters.
  ☞ Only an instance of a given type can be passed over in the parameter.

☞ The entity *interface* specifies what the given entity knows and how to communicate with it.

☞ The *interface* does not solve anything, only promises what the given entity can provide.

☞ The *interface* resumes what the program should know about the given entity.

☞ An implementation provides so that the given entity would do exactly what its *interface* promises.

☞ The only one constant of contemporary programming is the certainty that the assignment will soon change.

☞ In case you will open a class in an editor, you can choose if you would like to see an *interface* (documentation) or a source code (implementation).

☞ To be easily changed, it is profitable if the surrounding program does not know anything about the entity implementation details, because it should not be dependent at it.

☞ The `interface` construction installs the data type that has only an *interface* and no implementation.

☞ Interface types are marked with a stereotype «`interface`» in the class diagram. *BlueJ* color them green in our configuration.

☞ For better orientation in a program we will put a letter I at the beginning of interface names.

☞ Java enables to implement an `interface` to classes.

☞ The class implementing certain interface can pose its instances as instances of an implemented interface.

☞ For implementing the interface it is not sufficient so that the class would implement all its declared methods; the class has to enroll explicitly to this implementation.

☞ In *BlueJ* a class can enroll to an interface implementation by drawing the implementation arrow (a triangle head arrow) from the implementing class to the implemented interface.

☞ The term interface is used in two meanings:

  ☞ The summary of characteristics of the given entity visible to the surrounding program. If I want to emphasize this meaning, I write the term in *italics – interface*.

  ☞ The program construction defining the data type without implementation. In case it will be needed to stress this meaning in a text, I will type it in the monospaced font – interface.

☞ In case an interface is declared as a type of message parameter, then an instance of any class which implements this interface can be passed as this parameter.

☞ You can import to your project any class from another project by the command **Edit → Add Class from File**.

Project:
The resulting form of a project to which we came at the end of the lesson after completing all exercises is in the 110z_Interface project.

11 The Interface Continued

What you will learn in this lesson
In this lesson you will import the Multishape *class and you will see how it becomes a worthy part of our project thanks to the* interface *implementation. You will learn how it is possible to define the test class of a particular class and what some of its characteristics are. Further you will come to know that a method can have a beforehand unknown number of parameters. A design pattern* Prototype *will be shown to you and you will read what are the advantages of using the factory method that produces copies contrary to using a constructor.*

Project:
In this lesson we continue in using the 110z_Interface *project.*

Readiness for the Future Extension

172.   I realized in the last lesson that interface **serves to defining the data type for a parameter in which we want to pass the values of different types. Then I can pass an instance of any class implementing this** interface. **Did I understand it properly?**

It is one of many possible usage of this construction. Gradually I will show and explain you plentiful further possibilities. Now, I would like to show you one profitable feature of our existing solution: in case we would add a quite new class into the project and it would implement the IShape interface, we will be able to use also the mover for it and fluently move its instances.

What is the conclusion of it? In case the interface is the parameter's type, I can pass as a parameter not only instances of contemporary classes, which implement this interface, but I gain a method which is prepared for instances of all such classes declared in future. So I am prepared for easy implementation of a number of improvements that may lead to a definition of such classes.

The Example: Multishape

173.   You are true. Thus I can save a lot of programming in future. Show me please an interesting example in which I can see that it was worthy to do it.

I have one interesting example. If you look into the project folder you will find there a subfolder Extension_11. There is a source code of Multishape class in it. Please, import it into our project. After a possible adjustment its class diagram should look out as at the figure 11.1.

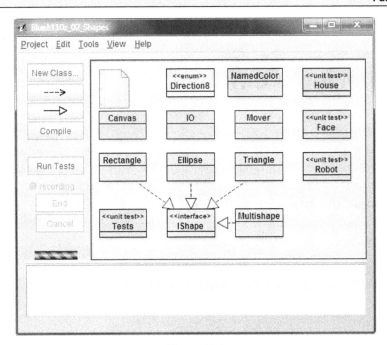

Figure 11.1
The project with Multishape class

174.   What is the Multishape class like? How its instances do look out?

The instances of this class are shapes acquired by completing several simpler shapes. Whole this composition behaves as one shape with which you can work similarly as with the original simpler shapes: you can shift it, change its size or ask for its properties.

175.   Do you mean by completing several simpler shapes that you take several shapes, you put them into a picture and then you announce: "This is a new multishape"?

Maybe it sounds strange to you, but you are nearly true. You really can assemble a more complex shape from simple shapes and then you ask the Multishape class to create a new shape which is a copy of your original complex. This shape will become a simple shape that can be included into assembling even more complicated shapes.

176.   Well, I like it. So what we will put together?

I would not think out too much complicated things, what about to take our basic triple-shape which we have in two issues in our test fixture. Then we could create another one in which this newly created multishape could participate.

Test Class of the Class

177.   I agree, tell me, what I should do.

Today's project will be a bit more extensive and that's why we will do it in several phases. I will try to tell and teach you something new in each of them. Let's start with information that for each class *BlueJ* enables to create a test class of its own.

178.   The test class belonging to each class? How do you mean it?

For each class *BlueJ* can define a test class which will be associated with it. If you want to use this possibility, the support for testing should be activated. *BlueJ* with our configuration has this support set. When you use a configuration without it, enter the command **Tools → Preferences**, open the **Miscellaneous** card in the opened dialog and set the option **Show unit testing tools** (see figure 11.2).

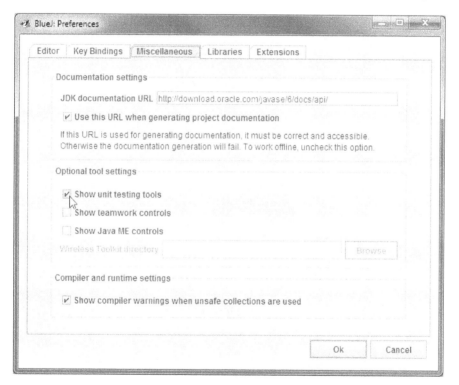

Figure 11.2
Activation of depicting the tools for testing

Setting this option evokes emerging of the button **Run Tests** together with the indicator **Recording** and buttons **End** and **Cancel** at the button panel. Since this time these control elements will be a permanent part of the panel.

At the same time the new command **Create Test Class is added** at the end of the context menu of all classes (see figure 11.3). By entering this command you ask *BlueJ* to create a test class associated with the given class. *BlueJ* then creates a new test class named **XxxTest**, where **Xxx** represents the class name for which you are creating the given test class, and which will be associated with the created test class.

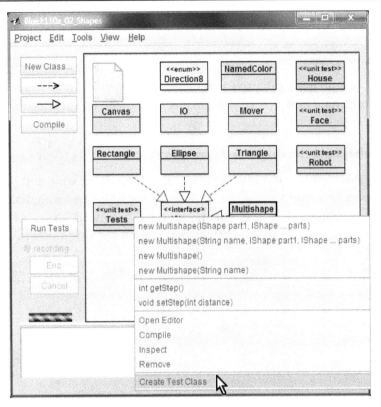

Figure 11.3
Asking for the test class associated with the given class

179.   You always speak about associating. What is so special on it?

The associated test class is inserted behind its tested class in the class diagram and shifted northeast-ern (i.e. to the right top) so that its name could be read. You cannot move with the associated test class. Its position is unambiguously determined by a position of the relevant tested class. Check that after each shifting of tested class its associated test class immediately leaps to its constant relative position, whilst the test class itself cannot be shifted at all. However the size of the test class can be changed.

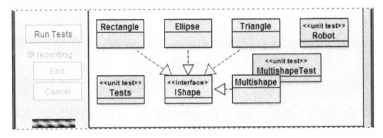

Figure 11.4
The test class associated with the given class

Variable Number of Parameters

180.   Well, I've created the test class MultishapeTest. **What now?**

Prepare the test fixture for the created test class.

1.   Reset the virtual machine.

2.   Send a requirement for creating a new instance to Multishape class, precisely a message

new Multishape(String name, IShape part1, IShape... parts)

The *BlueJ* opens the dialog in the figure 11.5.

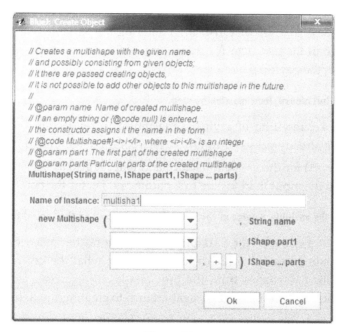

Figure 11.5
Entering the variable number of parameters

181.   What strange buttons are on the right next to the third input field?

To explain them I return back to figure 11.3. Please, notice that the command for sending the message and requiring creating a new instance has three dots between the type and the name of the second parameter. (Of course, you can find them also in the method header in the upper part of a dialog and once more as a determination of a type at entered parameters.) They symbolize the fact that the number of parameters of the given type at this place is not known in advance and can differ between individual sending the given message. The language definition also does not exclude the possibility to quote no parameter at this place. Then, it is impossible to determine the number of needed input fields in the dialog box for parameters in advance. This problem is solved in *BlueJ* by buttons marked with [+] and [–]:

☞   Pressing the button [+] adds a new empty field behind the given input field,

☞   on the contrary, pressing the button [–] removes the input field on the left side of the button (as I have said already, all fields of the second parameter can be removed).

Thus, you can prepare as many input fields as many parameters you need to pass. All prepared input fields have to be fulfilled. In case any field is left empty, *BlueJ* writes an error message at the bottom margin of a dialog box and refuses the take over the parameters.

Moreover, the order of entered parameters is very important. Shapes entered sooner are placed below the shapes entered later. In case you would like to create your testing composition, you have to enter firstly a rectangle, then an ellipse and finally a triangle to the last parameter.

182. It means me to make out a zero rectangle, an ellipse and a triangle?

Theoretically it would be possible. We could even ask the Tests class for creating the test fixture and use its instances. But it has a disadvantage: these instances would hamper in the instance stack even in time when you would not need them. Let's use the fact that in the section *Direct Passing of the Message Return* Value on page 63 we learned that instead of entering the variable with a reference to an object you can send a message in the text field for parameter which returns this value. The returned value can be used as a value of the passed parameter.

183. Don't take it amiss, but please, lead me step by step.

Surely, first two steps, i.e. resetting of a virtual machine and requesting for a new instance of the Multishape class, we have already passed through, so let's continue with the third step:

3. Enter a name (e.g. m1) for the created instance and enter it also as a string (don't forget the quotation marks) into the input field for the first parameter, i.e. for the name of the created instance

184. Why I have to enter the variable's name of the multishape twice and on the second time in quotation marks?

The entered string is not a name of the variable, but a name of the instance itself. Each instance of Multishape class has its name through which you can indicate what the given multishape represents. (In case we would define e.g. shapes from the previous lesson exercises as multishapes, we could name them e.g. house, face and robot). But let's again return to creating the fixture.

4. Enter the command (or better said statement) for the first parameter – in our case the statement: new Rectangle().

185. Why there are no buttons "+" and "−" at this field?

I again return to the figure 11.3. You can see there are four messages for creating a new multishape there. When you send a message without any shape parameter, the class Mutlishape works in a little different mode – I'll show it soon. The parameter part1 forces that you have to enter at least one shape in this mode. But I would like to continue in creating the fixture.

5. Increase the number of parameters for entered parts to two by pressing the button "+".

6. Enter: new Ellipse() into the input field of the first of them.

7. Enter: new Triangle() into the input field of the second of them.

8. Confirm your inputs by pressing **OK** and the variable m1 will appear in the object bench with a reference to the created multishape.

186. **Until now it goes according to our expectations. Now, will we create a test fixture based on existing activities or will we create another multishape?**

I would create another multishape. And I would show you another way of creating these shapes, when the new multishape will not be created in one step, but it will be gradually completed from individual parts. At the same time I would like to show you that another multishape can be a part of such shape because each multishape is an instance of IShape interface.

 This procedure has a disadvantage: the created multishape cannot be seen and you have to surmise its current state or draw it at a paper.

187. **Well, I'd rather see it all, but I hope it will be sufficiently simple so that I'll be able to observe it. Please, go on and I'll stop you in case of necessity.**

9. Ask once again to create a new multishape, but this time by sending a message new Multishape(String). This message does not ask creating a complete new multishape, but only starts its creating. The Multishape class only prepares an empty instance, into which you will add shapes, from which the multishape will be composed.

10. In case you want to have the same fixture as I have, enter an instance also for the variable to which the reference of a created instance will be saved, the name m2 (don't forget to close the parameter into quotation marks) and confirm your input.

 The variable m2 appears in the object bench referring to the just created instance. But as I said a while ago, the instance is not yet finished. It's only an intermediate product that does not contain any parts.

11. Send a message addShapes(IShape...) to m2 instance, and pass a reference to m1 instance as a parameter to this message, i.e. send the message m2.addShapes(m1). Thus you will enter the whole multishape m1 (more precisely a copy of its current form) as the first part of the created instance m2. However, you cannot see anything at the canvas – you have only to believe it.

12. Decrease the width of the multishape m1 to one third and its height to one half by sending the message m1.setSize(33,25).

13. By sending the message m1.setPosition(33,25) shift your multishape m1 to a position which is inside the triangle in the newly created multishape m2. Again it is not seen but you can verify it in a while.

14. Send the message m2.addShapes(m1) to the newly created instance m2. By this you add a copy of the new form of the multishape m1 as its further part.

15. Send the message m2.creationDone() to m2 instance by which you finish its completing; since this time it is fully usable.

16. Send the message m1.setPosition(150,0) to m1 instance, by which you shift it so that it might be seen after drawing m2 instance.

17. Send the message m2.paint() by which you depict the newly created instance. Now you can verify if the multishape m2 is really composed of a copy of the initial form of m1 multishape and an added copy of diminished and shifted m1 – the objects should be arranged as on figure 11.6.

18. Send the message IO.inform("Multishapes prepared") to the IO class and subsequently confirm the opened dialog.

19. Ask the MultishapeTest class to save the previous activity as an activity creating the test fixture.

20. Try the created definition of a new fixture. Reset the virtual machine and request the MultishapeTest class to create the fixture and save the variables with its objects into the object bench.

Figure 11.6
The test fixture with two multishapes

The Design Pattern *Prototype*

188.   All passed but I have to admit that I feel confused a bit. How it is possible to insert the m1 multishape into the created m2 multishape twice?

The point is that the Multishape class never uses an object passed in a parameter for constructing an instance. Instead of it, the class requests this object for its copy. Then when you change the object, its copy does not change and the multishape keeps its form.

189.   The class requests this object for its copy? Is it possible?

When you look into the documentation of IShape interface, you will find also a method copy() among declared methods, which returns an instance of IShape type. The contract of this method says that by its calling you receive an object's copy, whose method you called. Thus the constructor of Multishape class can simply let its arguments make their copies.

Using this method is particularly advantageous in a situation when the original (i.e. copied) object is rather complex or when you cannot discover all parameters required by the constructor. And this is our case. The constructor of Multishape class receives an object in a parameter about which it is known only that it is an instance of IShape interface. Even its class is unknown and so its new instance, which would be a copy of this object, could not be requested.

The design pattern *Prototype* which recommends teaching the objects to make out their own copies (i.e. to equip them with a method capable to do it) solves similar situations. Then it is a matter of the given object if it uses a constructor or another mechanism for making a copy. The addressed object knows which class is its parent class and which constructor should be called. It knows all its visible as well as hidden properties and thus it can make out its really perfect copy. This could be hardly done in case the information would be taken only from the object's (general!) *interface*.

190.   Then the copying method can serve as a substitute constructor.

Yes, to some extent. You cannot create any instance of a given class with its help, but if you are satisfied with a copy of an existing instance for the given purpose, it is often significantly simpler (sometimes even the only possible) way to create the required instance.

191.   If I remember it well, you told me sometimes at the beginning that the only possibility how to create a new instance is to use `new` with constructor's calling.

This holds true in case when you need to create quite a new object. But when you need to create only a copy of a previously created object, there are substituting means existing. Messages requiring a copy of an addressee are one of them. Now, I would not like to dwell on it and let's return to an explanation how to define a method realizing an answer to this message.

Verifying of the Multishape Functioning

192.   You are true. Let's return to our multishapes. I would like to try if they really would behave as the other shapes do including fluent shifting and changes of their size.

It's a good idea. Let's define a test method which would verify all these assumptions. We have already verified the leap shifting as well as size changes during the fixture's definition, so now we can examine the smooth ones. To be sure I will lead you again step by step, despite I think you would be able to do it alone. And of course, you can try it on projects of closing exercises once again.

1.   Reset the virtual machine.

2.   Tell the MultishapeTest class that you want to create a new test method. To continue in being traditional, call it testSmoothResizing.

3.   Create a mover's instance. Not to be detained by smooth shifting, set a bigger speed – e.g. 10.

4.   Ask the mover to shift the m1 object by 100 points to the right. You will see how fluently it will move the object without influencing its copies in m2 multishape.

5.   Ask the mover to shift m2 object to a position [100, 100]. Again you can see that the picture is moving as a whole and that m1 object does not influence shifting of its copies.

6.   Close the test record.

Now, when everything is remembered and saved, ask the MultishapeTest class to run the whole test once again so that you could enjoy it.

193.   The test we prepared in this lesson shifted only with the whole shape. However, the method in Tests class, named by the same name, shifted only with parts of the whole shape. How can I arrange so that e.g. only triangle would move in our triple shape?

This couldn't be done. A multishape always poses as a whole. In case you would like to move only with its one part, it would be similar if you would like to move with only one peak of the triangle.

This property of the multishape is a consequence of the fact that it is composed from copies of its parameters. Thus, it becomes independent on whether somebody enlarges or shifts any part of the completed multishape. Only a pattern, according to which the given part of the multishape was created, can be enlarged or shifted. But the general behavior or appearance of the multishape cannot be influenced.

Exercise

194.   Well, but in exercises at the end of the previous lessons you wanted me to prepare some simple animations. I thought I could create all my pictures with the assistance of a multishape. But how I should animate a picture, when the multishape cannot be changed?

The only one thing I can advise you is not to include those parts into the multishape which you would like to discolor or move. Try to supplement pictures with the aid of a multishape without animations, and instead of animating you can shift the pictures or change their size and produce their copies. Creating composed shapes whose individual parts can be influenced independently towards the whole – this will be a topic of our future lessons after we will start writing the code. Don't be afraid, we are close to it.

Review

I tried to show all what we debated once again in the accompanying animation. Turn it on and try everything in it once more.

Animation 11.1: The multishape and the test class of the class – OOPNZ_111_A1_Multishape
The animation will show the import of `Multishape` class creating its test class, definition of its fixture and creating a test.

Let's review what you learned in this lesson:

☞   One of the possible usages of the `interface` construction is the parameter's definition in which you can pass instances of all classes that implement the given `interface`.

☞   Such solution has an advantage that you can use it without any adjustments also in case you add quite a new class into the project. It is sufficient if this class will implement the relevant `interface`.

☞   The `Multishape` class enables to compile several simpler shapes into a bigger whole which then poses as a new shape.

☞   Multishapes can be also composed of previously created multishapes.

☞   An *associated test class* can be created to each class of the project in *BlueJ*.

☞   You can ask creating a test class in the class context menu. However, the command for creating the test class will appear only after switching on the test support.

☞   In case you want to have a possibility to create associated test classes you need to check the option **Show unit testing tools** in **Preferences** window in the **Miscellaneous** card.

☞ For creating the associated test class you can ask by assigning a command **Create Test Class** in the class context menu.

☞ This test class will be inserted in class diagram under its test class and shifted right up, so that it would be possible to read its name.

☞ It is not possible to move independently with the associated test class in the class diagram. This class automatically keeps its relative position towards its associated tested class.

☞ Another consequence of association is an automatic running of a compilation of the test class after the compilation of the tested class. Therefore it is not needed to ask for it solo.

☞ If triple dots appear in the head between the type and the parameter's name, it means that you can enter any number of parameters at this place, including zero (i.e. no) parameters.

☞ *BlueJ* solves the variable number of parameters by adding the buttons [+] and [−], with the aid of which you can adjust the needed number of input fields.

☞ Keep the order of entered parameters.

☞ In case the created object should not be dependent on changes of objects that the constructor receives as parameters and which should become parts of the created object, it is suitable to use copies instead of these objects.

☞ The design pattern *Prototype* recommends teaching objects how to create their own copies. They can often solve situations when it is necessary to create objects without having information for their direct creating.

Project:
The resulting project form to which we came at the end of the lesson after passing all exercises is in the 111z_Multishape *project.*

12 The Introduction into Design Patterns

What you will learn in this lesson

In this lesson you will see the design patterns as well as patterns used in our project in details. After that you will learn how the class can concurrently implement several interface types and what are the advantages for the programmer emerging from it.

Project:

In this lesson we continue in using the 111z_Multishape project.

195.   You told me in the previous lesson that before transition to a new project I have to learn something. What is it?

I wanted to present you the design patterns and to show you how it is possible to improve our example with the mover.

Design Patterns

196.   Design patterns? What is it?

The design patterns are programming analogy of mathematical formulas. They advise you how to solve certain type of tasks. They do not say that the designed solution is the only one possible, but everybody knows, that it is adequately universal and, above all, verified in time.

   Look for example at the well-known formula for solving the quadratic equation. You have learnt in the school that the solution of the equation

$$ax^2 + bx + c = 0$$

you can receive by substituting the appropriate values in the following formula

$$x = \frac{-b \pm \sqrt{b^2 - 4ac}}{2a}$$

Nobody forces you to use this formula (except being examined in the school). There is a number of quadratic equations that can be solved quicker without the formula. Nevertheless, in majority of cases using the above formula is the best and most suitable way of solution.

   If you learn to use this formula you gain several advantages:

☞   You get the solution quicker because you will not be pressed to think how to solve the task.

☞   You significantly decrease the probability of a fault you could do if you would only invent the solution.

☞   By using the formula you receive also a related terminology, which makes the communication easier. When you say to your colleague that the discriminant is negative, he immediately knows, what does it mean for solving the problem and you do not need to explain extensively how it is with the ability to solve the quadratic equation.

By using the design patterns you gain the same advantages.

197. I know the advantages of mathematical formulas, but despite it I don't understand how the programmer's analogy could look out.

The mathematical formulas are directives to which you install numbers. The design patterns are directives, to which classes and objects are installed.

Examples of Design Patterns

198. Well, I start to feel what they are about. Could you give me an example?

Yes, of course. There are several of them in the project which we used until now. We used another of them in the last two lessons and further they will be used in the project with which we are starting to work since this lesson.

Library/Utility Class

The simplest design pattern used in our project is the *Library Class* for which also the name *Utility Class* is used. It is a class which serves as a box for statistical methods and fields (in our project there is a class IO serving like that). It does not need to create any instances. And when it does not need them, it is suitable to exclude creating them. This can be reached by closing its constructor to surrounding objects. Without available constructor nobody can create any new object.

Simple (Static) Factory Method

The *Simple Factory Method* for which also the name *Static Factory Method* is used is a statistical method which returns a reference to an instance of its class. Thus it can be used similarly as an operator new with a contractor. Contrary to the operator new it can decide itself, if it calls new and allows to create a new instance or if it returns a reference of an existing instance to the applicant. Its further advantageous properties will be discussed later.

A simple factory method in our project is e.g. the method getCanvas(), by which we request the class Canvas for its instance, or the set of methods getNamedColor(???), by which we ask the class NamedColor for its instance.

Singleton

Sometimes we need a class which has only one instance. This problem is solved by the design pattern *Singleton*. It recommends:

☞ to exclude the constructor (otherwise as much instances can be made out as you would like),

☞ to offer a simple factory method for getting a reference of an instance which returns the reference to the same instance – the singleton.

According to this pattern there is a class Canvas defined in our project which guarantees that several not-communicating canvases will not be wandering through our display and that all pictures we would draw will be drawn at the same canvas.

Enumeration Type – Multiton

We could consider the class which defines the enum type as a generalization of a singleton. The singleton has an only one instance; the *enumeration type* called also shortly *enum type* (*Multiton* is also used) has more instances. These instances are named beforehand, so that they are known and we cannot add any other during the program's running. The enum type has got its name according to listing of its instances – we call it enum because its instances are defined by an enumeration.

The enum type (similarly as the singleton) has an inaccessible constructor, so that it would be not possible to create further instances. Contrary to the singleton, all its instances are defined as its public fields. That's why you do not receive references to them exclusively by a factory method, but in most cases you request directly for a given field.

The only one enum type in our project is the type Direction8.

Servant

The design pattern *Servant* solves the problem how to add a supplementary functionality to a group of classes without inserting nearly the same method into each of them and violating by this the principle not to repeat the same or the very similar code. It recommends to define (or gain by another way) a new class whose instances would be able to mediate the realization of supplementary functioning.

We can assume that the instances of this new class act as servants of the operating instance which we can equip with the supplementary functioning. So that the servant could properly serve, it must be in accord with the served object. Therefore, the servant class comes in pair with the interface which declares what the served objects have to know so that the servants could assist them. The servant methods mediating this supplementary functionality have an instance of this interface in the range of their parameters. The required supplementary functionality can be obtained by sending a relevant message with the served object passed as a parameter.

We have already met the design pattern *Servant* when we solved the problem of smooth shifting of our objects in previous parts. Instances of Mover class operated as servants, our graphic objects were the served objects and the IShape interface was a required interface that had to be implemented by all served objects.

199. According to your explanation it seems to be simple, so why they are so brilliant?

Majority of design patterns is really simple and comprehensible. It is rather a matter of realizing how the given problem can be solved. Many of those patterns belong to the group of: "It's so simple – why I didn't have such an idea myself?" However, their detailed explanation is a bit more extensive, compared to the brief view I have provided to you just now.

The biggest contribution of design patterns is the idea of a set of formulas for programming similarly as for the mathematics and physics. But I have to admit that the programmers were not the first who came with such idea. They were inspired by an architect Christopher Alexander, who came with a thought to apply basic design patterns in architecture in the 70ties of the last century. His views were interesting for several programming gurus who started to apply them in programming at the end of the 80ties. And when in 1995 the famous book *Design Patterns* was published, the idea of design patterns started to spread with a snow-ball effect in the programming world. At present, the programmers who do not know any design patterns are not considered as worthy by big software companies.

This is also one of the reasons why I tried to present you the design patterns since the beginning of the course. Now we have learnt basic characteristics of the first few of them and I will present several others to you in course of the following lessons.

The Implementation of More Interface Types

200. You told me at the lesson's beginning that you want to show me how it is possible to improve our example with the mover.

That's right. I have said that we used the design pattern *Servant* to learn our shapes moving fluently. I have also said that the servant class occurs in pair with the IShape interface which declares what the assisted objects have to know, so that they may be assisted in all respects. However, our IShape interface declared also a number of methods that were not needed by movers for their work. To give you an example it concerns to methods getWidth() and copy().

201. You are true. And which methods would then be sufficient to the movers?

The movers would be satisfied if the assisted objects would be able to say their current position and adjust the new one.

202. I think that they didn't have to be able to say their current position because (as you told) the whole shifting is only repeated adjusting of new, a little bit shifted positions.

You are true, but to calculate to which positions the mover shall gradually locate the object, it has to know the object's current as well as the target position. The target position can be recognized in parameters, the information on current position can be obtained from the shifted object.

To sum up: the mover would be satisfied with objects which are able only to say and adjust their position, but, because its methods require a parameter of IShape type, the fluently shifted objects have to know (unnecessarily) a number of other skills.

203. I see, it didn't cross my mind. Does it mean that we should define the IShape interface more modest?

Neither this would be good. The IShape interface shows what our shapes know to do and in case we would "restrain" them we could meet a task in near future which would require so that the objects would understand to a message and would know how to react, but which is not mentioned by the interface.

204. Which for example?

For example, when we would like to teach the objects to change fluently not only their position but also their size. The servants that would provide such functioning would be satisfied with objects that are able to say their current size and adjust the new one.

205.   You are true. So what's your advice?

We will proceed in two phases. In the first phase, please remove the current class Mover (by entering the command **Remove** in its context menu). In the second phase find a subfolder Extension_12 in the project folder and import a modified version of the Mover class from it. It differs from the original one only by the fact that its methods shift objects of IMovable type, which is an interface which, of course, you have to import together with the Mover class.

> **Note**:
>
> When you will import this class as well as the interface, don't forget that *BlueJ* supports the simultaneous import of multiple source files. It is sufficient to add further files into the selection range in the dialog for entering the imported files while pressing the button CTRL. I remind this convention just to be sure, because you certainly know it from *Windows*.

206.   The newly added class and interface types are marked as not compiled. Should I compile them?

If you will be more attentive, you will see that the classes Tests and MultishapeTest are marked as not compiled because both of them cooperated with the Mover class which we have removed. We replaced it by the new class, but we cannot deceive *BlueJ* – it will not believe until it compiles the classes. And it is good because in the new adjustment these classes cannot be compiled. As we have said the new mover does not use parameters of IShape type, but uses the parameters of IMovable type.

If you open the documentation of an IMovable interface, you will discover that its declared methods are only a sub-set of methods declared by IShape interface. As I have already shown in the section *Implementation of an interface by the Class* on page 85, it is not sufficient to define all required methods to pass the class instance off as an instance of certain interface. You have to explicitly inscribe to its implementation. And you did not do it yet.

So draw the implementation arrows from all four graphic classes also to an IMovable interface (see figure 12.1). Then the compiler will be satisfied and everything will be O.K.

207.   Does it matter when the class implements several interface types?

No, it doesn't matter. By implementing the interface the class only pledges that its instances will implement all methods that are declared by the given interface. When the class decides to implement several interface types it has only to provide implementing of all methods declared by all implemented interface types.

I like to compare it with a common life. The objects also alternate their *interfaces* in it. Imagine that you are in a restaurant and you are served by a man who "implements" an *interface* the *waiter*. In this moment you do not bother if he knows e.g. to drive a car, you need so that he would be able to serve you. When he finishes his working hours, he sits e.g. in a car and goes to see his friends. During his way he implements an *interface* the *driver* and in case a policeman would stop him, he should be checked only if he implemented properly this interface. When he arrives to his friends, they can play e.g. football. In this moment he starts implementing an *interface* the *football player* and again, it is not relevant what else he knows.

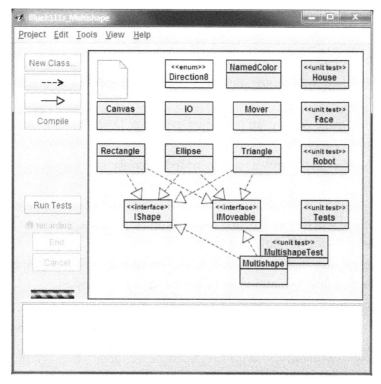

Figure 12.1

The class diagram after importing Mover and IMovable types and supplementing of new implementations

Similarly it is in the program. In the given moment the object acts as an instance of some interface and other objects that communicate with this object can send only such messages to it, which are permissible for the instance of the given interface. After some time the object can act as an instance of a different interface and thus it again limits the set of acceptable messages. And due to the fact that the compiler knows what the object acts as in the particular moment, the compiler can check if the object does not receive anything else than what instances of the given interface can know. Thus, in the compile-time it can catch a lot of errors which would otherwise appear in the runtime and might have very unpleasant consequences.

208. And what about when two interface types declare the same method? How can be determined, which one should be called?

If two different interface types declare a method with the same head, we have to take into account that both declarations will be implemented by one method. In other words: the implementing class will assume that there are two declarations of the same method. (You will meet such example in the next lesson.)

In case each method should do something different, you would have to solve this possible clash and one of those methods should be renamed or you would have to find another solution. (Don't ask me which one; I will explain it after it will be needed.)

Exercise

209. So what will I train today?

Last time you trained fluent shifting, so today try a smooth enlargement and reduction. Proceed as follows:

1. Import another three types from the folder Extension_12: the Resizer class and interface types IResizable and IChangeable.

2. Draw the implementation arrows to both added interface types from all classes implementing the IShape interface. It means four arrows will go to each interface.

3. The class diagram will become chaotic, so you have to reorganize it – e.g. according to figure 12.2. But still there will be more arrows than would be pleasant, next time I will show you how to get rid some of them without losing the functionality.

4. Look on which services the instances of Resizer class offer to you and define the test methods by which you examine fluent enlarging and decreasing of your shapes.

This time I will not tell you how precisely you have to examine the smooth change of size. Involve your own fantasy. In case you would need an inspiration, you can have a look at the test testSmoothResizing in the class MultishapeTest in the final version of today's project.

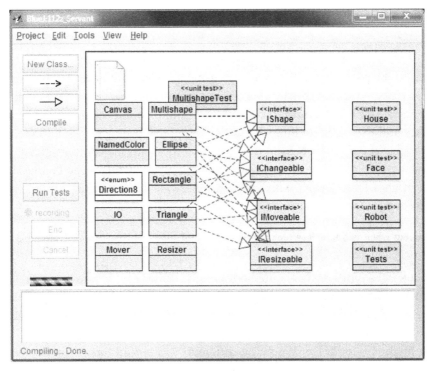

Figure 12.2
The class diagram before test for smooth size change

Review

I tried to show all what we debated until now in the additional animation. Turn it on and try everything once more in it.

Animation 12.1: More interface types – OOPNZ_112_A1_MoreInterfaceTypes
The animation will show the explained items, i.e. importing of further interface types and the definition of implementing several interface types by one class.

Let's repeat what you have learned in this lesson:

☞ The design patterns are programming parallels to mathematical formulas to which, instead of numbers, the classes and objects and sometimes also methods are installed.

☞ Knowing the design patterns helps to create a quick, effective and easy adjustable program.

☞ The design pattern *Utility Class* called also *Library Class* serves only as a box for static methods. It does not need any instances and therefore it should have inaccessible constructor.

☞ The design pattern *Simple Factory Method* (called also *Static Factory Method*) is a static method which is defined by classes instead of the inaccessible constructor.

☞ The design pattern *Singleton* pattern proposes how to define a class which will have only one instance.

☞ The design pattern *Enumeration Type* called also shortly *Enum type* or *Multiton* defines a fixed set of instances known in advance and does not allow to create further instances.

☞ The design pattern *Servant* shows how to add functionality to a group of classes without adding nearly the same method to each of them.

☞ The class, whose instances act as servants, has an associated `interface` which specifies what the instance that should be served by the servant, has to know.

☞ The class can implement several interface types simultaneously.

☞ Objects of the program are similar to objects in real life – they also act in various situations similarly as instances of various interface types.

☞ Identical declarations of a method in various interface types are considered as declarations of the same method. In case the class implements several interface types and several of them declare the same method, all these methods are implemented at the same time by only one method.

Project:
The resulting form of the project which we reached at the end of the lesson after passing through all exercises is in the 112z_Servant project.

13 The Inheritance of Interface Types

What you will learn in this lesson
In this lesson you will continue in working with interface types. You will learn how the data types create inheritance hierarchies and you will see three types of inheritance. Then I will explain what the difference between a signature and a contract is and you will meet the first definition of an interface. Then we shall adjust the hierarchy of interface inheritance in this project and finally how it is possible to create project documentation.

Project:
In this lesson you continue in using the 112z_Servant project.

210. Recently I've got rid of some arrows but my class diagram was again full of them at the last lesson's end. Shall I switch off showing of arrows again?

No, the implementation arrows are immensely important for understanding the project architecture. But today I will show you only how the number of arrows can be decreased without losing any interesting information.

Hierarchy of the Types

211. I am eager – go on and explain!

The idea is simple and uses a mechanism which is called inheritance. Principally, you can often find a group of instances with common special properties among instances of certain type. They can be defined as a **subtype**, which characterizes this specialized group of objects. This subtype is often called a **child** of an original type. Logically the original type is called a **parent type** of given subtypes. And when I speak about the terminology, I would like to mention that the parent is sometimes called a **basic type** and the descendant are called **derived types**. The following table shows all terms in use:

Parent type	–	Child type
Ancestor	–	Descendant
Basic type	–	Derived type
Supertype	–	Subtype

A basic feature of inheritance is that the instance of the child type inherits all properties and abilities of its parent. Due to the fact that we know a bit more about the child type (we know its specialization), we can equip its instances by other properties and abilities which ensue from its specialization.

212. Well, you shoot the terminology as from a machine gun, but I didn't hear any example.

The inheritance of types is usually illustrated at an example of animal as well as vegetable species. Completing of such example is your turn but when we are sitting at the PC, we can try one example of this kind. In case we have an object of PC type, we know that it is suitable for a number of various tasks but we cannot say more about its possible usage.

To estimate better what you can require from the given computer, you should define the subtypes of the general PC – let's say hall computers (supercomputers, mainframes, minicomputers), desktop computers, portable computers (notebooks, tablets, smartphones) and embedded computers (e.g. in a car, microwaves etc.). Besides it, there is surely a number of computers that cannot be included in any of the above mentioned kinds.

As mentioned in parentheses, each type has its subtypes. If we have a look at the other side of the inheritance tree, we could say, that computers are a special kind of electronic devices, the electronic devices are a special kind of general devices and so we could continue in generalizing so long so that we would get to some fully general object.

213.   Well, I understand what it means to include objects into certain hierarchy and surely I could give you an example just from the animal world which you have avoided – e.g. that dogs are a special type of mammals and mammals are a special kind of animals. But be so kind and let me know, why such classifying?

You ask properly. It is important to know **what the object is**, but let's admit that in programming we are more interested in **what the object knows** or what I can require from it. When we return to computers it's useful to know that the given PC is a notebook because you can derive a lot of its properties, but no less important is knowing under which operating system it works and which programs are installed in it etc.

In case I speak about animals, it's useful to know if the given animal is a dog, a gnat, an elephant or a guinea pig. But in case you already know that the given animal is a dog, a lot of people are not interested in its variety but more to which commands the animal understands, how often it is necessary to walk out with it etc. However, this is a different category of properties. To give you an example from life: besides a dog we used to have a tom cat and it learned to obey the dog's orders better than a lot of dogs we used to meet. In many ways we could treat it as a dog. So it is similar in programming, i.e. that you can treat an object of a certain type as if it would be something else.

The fact that the given animal is e.g. a dog does not necessarily mean that it knows how to retrieve. On the other hand you can define a type CanRetrieve, into which you will include all objects properly reacting to the relevant message. On one side, instances of this type might be dogs, but on the other hand, we could include maybe falcons and other domesticated bird raptors, dolphins or trained robots.

214.   Examples you mentioned were surely interesting but I'd like to ask you to put an example that is a bit closer to programming. The example which would give me an idea what it would mean for me in programming.

I am going to do it. From my previous longer outlining you should come up to a conclusion that the most important thing in programming is not the class of a given object, but its *interface* (I don't have on my mind an interface construction, but really a general *interface*), i.e. what you can require from the object and what the object can offer you.

Let's take our project. There are classes of graphic shapes (Ellipse, Rectangle, Triangle, Multishape) and besides them also the classes which could be marked as auxiliary ones. We could monitor e.g. the focuses and half-axis of an ellipse, what is the length of separate triangle sides and a lot of further information which we have learned in mathematics and which characterize a particular graphic shape. For our purposes is, however, more useful when we know that it is able to draw the given shape, when we know to adjust its position and size as well as some other properties.

When we look to our servant classes, their requirements are even more modest. The mover is satisfied when the served object is movable (i.e. it knows to tell and adjust its position), the resizer is satisfied if the object is resizable (i.e. the object knows to tell and adjust its size) and one of its demanding methods insists on the fact that the served object has to be changeable (we could say it is movable and resizable at the same time).

As I have shown you last time, requirements for what the object should know can be declared through the interface construction. When we would like to deal with inheritance, it would be more advantageous to deal with above all the inheritance of interface. The interface does not divide the objects according to what they are, but according to what they are able to do. Thus the hierarchy of interface specifies the inheritance based on the abilities of objects.

Three Types of Inheriting

215. Should I understand it that besides the interface inheritance (i.e. inheritance of interface types) there is also something like class inheritance?

Yes, it is. And when the inheritance is explained in current programming courses, usually the class inheritance is explained as the first one. Students are explained how it is recorded in a program and what it can be used for. Unfortunately, they only rarely learn all its snags and dangers and there are really a lot of them. Due to it their programs are not overflowing with stability.

If I want to be precise, the OOP distinguishes even three types of inheriting:

☞ **Inheriting of type** corresponds with *interface* inheriting in programs. This inheritance is a key one in programming. If I would inherit the *interface* of my parent, I will offer the same as my parent (and maybe even something more, but let's disregard it now), and therefore I will be able **to impersonate as a parent instance**. This inheritance applies not only in inheriting of *interfaces* (a general object property), which we shall debate in this lesson, but also in implementing the interface (a special kind of data type) by the class (another kind of data type). From the view point of types inheriting it is possible to consider the implemented interface as one of the parents of classes which implement them.

☞ **Inheriting of implementation** which asserts itself in inheriting of classes. During it I take over not only its *interface* but also all its implementation. Therefore, I don't have to define my own method, but I can use the parent one. But just in implementation inheritance there is a lot of treacherousness about which I have spoken and therefore we will avoid it in the first part of our course.

☞ **Natural inheriting** speaks about how you perceive the specialization of objects regardless how we program it. We have been explained in the school that e.g. the square is a special kind of rectangle which has all its sides of the same length. The square thus can be theoretically defined in the program as a descendent of a rectangle. But this would be valid only until the time when our application would require so that the rectangles would be able to change their sizes independently. The square is not able to do it, because it has to have all its sides of the same length.

A properly proposed program has all these three aspects of inheritance in accord. However, it is not simple to reach it and in a number of programs the individual aspects are mutually in contradiction. This is also one of the reasons why the textbooks' authors often avoid explaining these problems.

Consequences of such missing explanations are a false usage of inheritance which we often meet in programs.

As you might understand, it is really not simple to explain the inheritance well, and it is very desirable so that the students should already have certain knowledge and skills and would be able to put things into coherence. To avoid it I will ignore the fact that there are three types of inheritance and when I will speak about inheritance I will concentrate only to the type inheritance, to be precise to the interface types inheritance. The remaining aspects of inheritance, together with an explanation how to harmonize them, will be debated in the next course (= in the next part of the book).

As far as the class inheritance is mentioned, we will limit roughly on what we have already debated in the section *The Class Object* on page 60. To be sure I repeat once more:

☞ All classes are descendants of the Object class. Thus they inherit its whole *interface* as well as its implementation.

☞ If the inherited implementation of some method does not suit to certain class, it can define its own implementation. Then, the implementation defined in their mother class will be used for instances of a given class regardless to which instance they pose as.

One interface Missing

216. I reconcile with the fact that for now I will not receive any information about implementation inheritance. What will you tell me about the *interface* inheritance or (more generally said) type inheritance?

Don't be afraid, it will not be so extensive. I told you that instances of child type are in fact instances of parent type which have some special properties. Knowing of these special properties is for me, a programmer, additional information which enables me to define further methods for these instances (i.e. to teach them understanding to further messages), methods for the realization of which the special properties of this subtype are necessary.

Let's have a look at our project. If I will have objects, which will know only what the IMovable interface requires from them, I can only locate them to various positions and possibly move them smoothly with the mover. To profit from it, they should be painted at the canvas. We neglected this until now because we didn't meet any object which would be movable and wouldn't be able to paint themself at the canvas. But it means that all movable objects should know how to be painted at the canvas.

We can look at it on the other way around. The movable objects are interesting for us only in case they can be painted. We could say that the movable objects are a special subset of all objects that can be painted. Their specialty lies in the fact that besides they can be painted, they also can tell and adjust their position at the canvas.

A while ago we stated that if we have a set of objects with special properties it is suitable to define a special type for them which is a descendant of their original type. However, now we are at a reverse position. We have a descendant but we do not have parents. We need a parent which would characterize all objects that know how to be painted at the canvas.

What such an object should know? To be precise, to which messages it should understand? What do you think?

217. It's simple – it should be able to be painted. It should understand the paint() **message – it's understandable for all our graphic objects.**

I knew you would fall into the trap. We send the paint() message to an object in case when someone erased a bit of it and we want to paint it as a whole again. But when you send a message to move to a position, at which it is just now, i.e. a message

```
object.setPosition(object.getX(),object.getY())
```

it will probably repaint. After all, it will paint itself after each position adjustment as well as after each adjustment of the size or of a color.

218. Well, you have caught me now. To which messages it should understand?

Attention, a surprise: to no one. We don't have to require so that it would understand to any messages, i.e. so that its class would not define any methods, but we are satisfied with a promise to know to be depicted at the canvas.

219. Probably you are true, but how it can promise it?

A trick: we will leave him to implement an interface (let's call it IPaintable), which will not require implementing of any method, but it will only request to promise that it will know something.

Signature versus Contract

220. Something is wrong here. In the section *Implementation of an interface by the Class* **on page 85 you told that the class has to enroll to** interface **implementation so that the compiler could check if it fulfills what it promised. But how can be anything checked if the class doesn't have to implement any method?**

In chapter *The Interface* on page 77 I told you that each program's entity has two faces: an *interface* and an implementation. Now I add another piece of information: the *interface* has also two faces: a signature and a contract.

A signature (sometimes you can meet the term *a header*) comprehends everything what the compiler can check (everything, what we find in the declaration). The data type declares its name in and a set of declared fields and methods (messages), the methods declare their name in, type of return value and types of separate parameters. (To be precise this is in Java and similar languages. Some languages are more modest in this respect.) We could say that the signature specifies how the given entity should look out in the program.

The **contract** specifies what the given entity should know and for what it can serve. This cannot be verified by the compiler (possibly sometimes in the future), this has to be checked by the programmer himself (or he can find a tester for it).

Because I know how you are keen into examples, I will try to repeat it at an example of a method setPosition(int,int).

☞ Signature of this method comprises that it is public, it does not return anything (it has declared the void return type), its name is setPosition and it has two parameters, both of them are of int type.

When quoting the signature also the declared names of parameters are sometimes stated. But it is only for the better orientation of the reader in the meaning of individual parameters. If I would state the full signature of the quoted method, I would probably copy its heading and wrote as follows (the same is quoted for the class documentation):

```
public void setPosition(int x, int y)
```

☞   We would include into the contract that after calling this method the object really will move to a position with the given horizontal and vertical coordinates, so that when we would ask for its position it should quote just the coordinates we have adjusted. Thus the contract of the method setPosition(int,int) is connected with methods of position getting at the same time.

If I would get back to our IPaintable interface, its signature would limit only to its name and all its meaning for the rest of the program would lie in its contract, i.e. in the fact that class instances, which implement them, can be painted at the canvas.

221.   You have just thought out this interface without methods or it is currently used?

The interface types without methods are not so extraordinary and they have their own name – they are called **tag interfaces** (i.e. interface types) or **marker interfaces**.

Definition of a New Interface Type

222.   Will we import this interface from somewhere?

Yes, you can do it, I have prepared it but due to the fact that it does not declare any methods, you can define it yourself.

223.   So shall we start writing a code?

Not immediately, but in this case it is sufficient to add a new interface into the class diagram. Try it. Press the button **New Class** in the left panel. The dialog box **Create New Class** in which the *BlueJ* asks you for the name of the created class and its type. Assign the name IPaintable and set the switch **Class Type** to the state **Interface** (see picture 13.1).

New Hierarchy of the Interface Types

224.   The interface was created. If I understood it properly, I should put on implementation arrows to it from all graphic classes. But the number of arrows will again increase and you've said we shall decrease it.

You are right; we will decrease it, so don't draw anything. On the contrary, you will start with cancelling the majority of existing arrows. Click gradually on each arrow that does not lead to an IShape interface (these are the only ones to be kept), and thus you will pick it out. (In case you would have troubles to hit the arrow, click on its head – it is bigger).

You can recognize that you succeeded to select the arrow according to the fact that *BlueJ* will draw it bold. Click on the

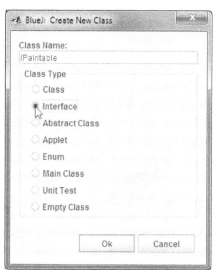

Figure 13.1
Creating a new interface

selected arrow once more, this time with the right button. Thus you will open its context menu with the only command **Remove**. Enter this command and the arrow disappears.

225.   I have cancelled all shapeless arrows. And what now?

Rearrange the interface types and stretch the arrows among them according to the figure 13.2.

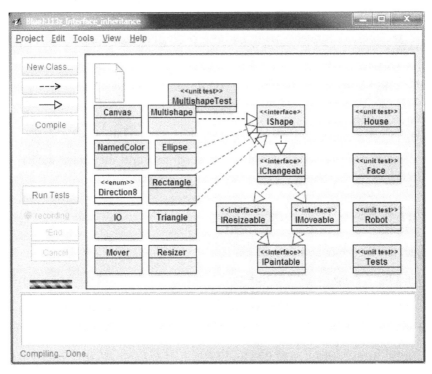

Figure 13.2
The new hierarchy of interface types

226.   There are implementation arrows among interface types at the figure. But the `interface`, **cannot implement anything.**

This time those are not implementation arrows but arrows of inheritance which are always oriented from the descendant to its parents. According the UML rules, the inheritance arrows should not be dashed, but *BlueJ* paints all arrows pointing to interface types as dashed. You can recognize the difference according to the arrow's root: if it is an `interface`, it is inheritance, if it is a class, it is an implementation.

After you will stretch all arrows, start the tests to examine that you did not influence the functionality by changing the architecture.

227.   You are true; it operated even in the new arrangement. But you should explain where you pushed me.

Let's start with the `IPaintable` interface. I said that all objects which you want to move and inflate, should know how to be drawn, and that the movable and inflatable objects are only a special case of more general drawable objects. Therefore you stretched the inheritance arrows from both of them to the IPaintable interface, so that you would indicate that the interface types IMovable and IResizable are its descendants.

Similarly it is in the next layer. When you will have a look to the documentation of the IChangeable interface, you will see that it declares all methods of IMovable and IResizable interface types. We could say that the changeable object is a special kind of movable object, which can change also its size, respectively a special kind of a resizable object that can change also its location. Thus the interface fulfilled the condition for becoming the descendant of both mentioned interface types. By stretching the inheritance arrows we have created an interface with two parents. (Contrary to people, the interface types can have any number of parents.)

Similarly it is with the IShape interface. The objects posing as instances of this interface are special cases of changeable objects which can react to a group of commands requiring creating of their copy, painting them on the canvas and rubbing them out from the canvas.

Inheriting of the Interface Types

228. Well, you've explained me why I should put up the arrows in the way I did. But I cannot understand what its advantage in the program is.

You have already seen the first advantage – the program is more transparent and its architecture, i.e. the way of arranging separate data types and their mutual links, is more comprehensible. As I have already told, all inheritance definitions come out of the fact that the descendant characterizes a certain subset of ancestor's instances. The following basic rule of the OOP ensues from it: **the descendant's instance can pose as a parent's instance at any time**.

When you know, that e.g. an Ellipse implements the IShape interface, then you know at the same moment that it implements all parent interface types and can pose as an instance of any of them. The mover requires the parameter of IMovable type. When you know that ellipses can pose as an instance of the IShape interface it is logic that they can pose also as an instance of IMovable interface and be assisted by movers. That's why all our tests were operating.

229. You told that the descendant's instance can pose as an ancestor's instance at any time. The ellipse (and generally any of our shapes) can pose as an instance of IShape interface. May I consider them as descendants of this interface?

Of course, you should take it as that all arrows with triangle head indicate the inheritance. Our classes of graphic shapes are descendants of interface types implemented by them according to the class diagram and all descendant's rights and duties pass to them.

230. Descendant's rights and duties? What is it?

Everything ensues from the basic rule which was postulated by Barbara Liskov in 1988 (sometimes it is marked with an abbreviation LSP – Liskov Substitution Principle) which I emphasized with a bold a while ago. This principle is in reality even more rigorous:

> **The instance of subtype has to be able**
> **to pose as a fully-fledged ancestor's instance at any time[4].**

It is its duty and its right ensues from it: when it is able to pose as a fully-fledged ancestor's instance, nothing can hamper it posing as such instance. After you will know the OOP a little bit more, you will recognize that a significant part of inheritance characteristics are connected with this rule.

231.   You outlined that there are further advantages.

Another advantage is appreciated particularly by programmers because they don't have to copy the repeated declarations. At the beginning I told you that the descendant's instance would inherit all properties and abilities of the ancestor. It inherits its properties by inheriting all its methods – in case of an interface it inherits all ancestors' declarations of methods and so they do not have to be quoted once more.

However, one consequence ensues from this: if the class decides to implement certain interface, it has to implement not only all its methods, but also all methods declared by any of its possible ancestors independently to the fact if they are or are not stated in the definition of the implemented interface.

Documentation of the Project

232.   I suppose that if I'd like to program such class, I'd have a look into the documentation of an implemented interface and I'll find there all methods which I should define.

Yes and no. You will find only those methods in the interface documentation, which the given interface declares. In case it does not declare certain methods, but only inherits them, you can find only their list in the documentation, and the detailed description of the contract can be found in parent's documentation.

However, for now I showed you only the documentation which the *BlueJ* depicts in editor's window. But it is not completed because it doesn't contain hypertext references among individual project's classes (e.g. you cannot directly move from the descendant's documentation to ancestor's documentation). First of all you have to create the complete project documentation.

233.   Slip it here. How can I do it?

So that I could explain it clearly, I have to modify our project a bit. For now all interface types declare both the inherited as well as the added methods, and that's why I cannot show you how to proceed when you need to learn something about a method that is inherited but the interface does not declare it itself.

---

[4]   Exactly: If S is a subtype of T, then objects of type T may be replaced with objects of type S (i.e., objects of type S may be substituted for objects of type T) without altering any of the desirable properties of that program (correctness, task performed, etc.).

   More formally: Let $q(x)$ be a property provable about objects x of type T. Then $q(y)$ should be provable for objects y of type S where S is subtype of T.

Remove the interface types IShape, IChangeable and IPaintable from the project and import their source codes instead of them from the subfolder Extension_13 of the folder of this project. If certain arrow will not depict after the import, stretch it once more.

234.   I am ready. What now?

Open the menu **Tools** and enter a command **Project Documentation**. *BlueJ* will ask the javadoc program which is a part of JDK to generate a complete documentation and will open it in your preferred browser.

Figure 13.3
The documentation of projects and its cross references among separate types

The browser will open the created documentation in a window with two panels: all types (i.e. classes and interface types) are motioned in the left one, and in the right one, there will be the documentation of the type you click on in the left panel. At the beginning there will be a documentation of Canvas class, because it is the first in the alphabet, and the left list starts with it.

235.   For now it all corresponds. What shall I do with the documentation?

Click on the left on the IChangeable interface, and the page (see figure 13.3) will occur on the right. It will offer you a number of useful hypertext references compared with the editor's page:

☞   The initial name of the interface is followed by a list of hypertext references to all ancestors under the title **All Superinterfaces**. If you click on any of them, you will get to its documentation.

☞   Further you will find a list of hypertext references to all found descendants under it, entitled **All Known Subinterfaces**.

☞   It is followed by a list of hypertext references to all found classes that implement the given interface under the title **All Known Implementing Classes**.

The table entitled **Method Summary** which has to comprehend a list of all declared methods is empty in case of IChangeable interface, because it does not declare any methods, but only inherits them. (If it would decide to declare the inherited method, it would be present for the case that precising the contract would be a part of this declaration.)

The table with an overview of declared methods is followed by a sequence of tables; each of them is devoted to one ancestor and contains hypertext references to all methods inherited from this ancestor. So, if you need to learn anything about each of these methods, you only click on it and you will get the required information.

236.   I am interested in how the documentation generator recognized that "the instance of IChangeable interface represents geometric shapes..." as well as further affirmations described in the documentation.

The so called **documentation comments** are an integral part of the code to which the decent programmers write information for those who would like to use the code sometimes in future. These comments contain the proper description of the contract about which we have spoken a while ago. After we will write the code I will ask you to include them into your programs automatically.

Exercise

237.   Phew, I'd say that there were too many new things in this lesson. Have you prepared an exercise for me?

Not today, because this lesson was rather informative. Maybe it would be better if you could go through the whole project's documentation within the exercise framework and have a look which new pieces of information it provided to you. Later on, when you will be searching something particular, you may use it.

Review

I tried to show all what we were discussing here in the accompanying animation. Turn it on once more and have a try.

Let's repeat what you have learned in this lesson:

☞ The architecture of the program – this is a way of arranging the individual types and their mutual relations.

☞ In case you find a set of instances with common special properties among instances of certain type, it is useful to define a special subtype for them.

☞ The couple (supertype → subtype) is also called (basic type → derived type), respectively (parent type → child type), respectively (ancestor → descendant).

☞ The relation between the supertype and subtype is called inheritance.

☞ In programming we are usually more interested not in "what the object is", but "what the object knows", i.e. what we can require from it.

☞ Requirements for object's abilities are usually declared through a construction of an interface.

☞ The interface inheritance concerns of objects' abilities, i.e. the instances of child interface have to know all what the instances of parent interface know, i.e. they have to understand to messages that are declared in the parent interface.

☞ All graphic objects in our project are special cases of objects which know to draw themselves. We can specify that they are instances of the IPaintable interface, which requires this ability.

☞ The interface types of each entity have two components:

   ☞ The signature which represents the part of the interface that can be checked by a compiler. It specifies how the given entity should look out in the program.

   ☞ The contract which comprehends properties that cannot be checked by the compiler. It specifies what the given entity should know and which it can serve for.

☞ The interface, which does not declare any methods and specifies only a contract, is called *tag interface* (also called a *marker interface*).

☞ The new interface is defined by pressing the button **New Class** at the left panel. Subsequently its name should be entered in the opened dialog box and we set the state **Interface** in the switch **Class Type**.

☞ The child interface inherits all methods of its parent. Therefore, the class that implements certain interface has to implement also all methods declared by its possible ancestors.

☞ The child interface may declare – but does not need to declare – once more the inherited methods.

☞ The program's architecture can be more transparent by suitable definition of the inheritance.

☞ The class implementing certain interface can be considered as subtype of this interface and the implemented interface as the supertype of the given class.

☞ Besides the `interface` inheritance also the implementation inheritance is used. However, this brings a lot of trickiness and therefore I will not explain it in this introductory course.

☞ When installing the `interface` we always have to respect the *Liskov substitution principle* (LSP) which says that instance of a subtype has to be able to fully-fledged pose as an instance of its supertype any time.

☞ The documentation depicted in the editor's window is not completed because the hyper-text references aimed to another classes do not occur in it.

☞ You ask creating a full documentation of the whole project by entering the command **Tools → Project Documentation**.

☞ The full project's documentation can be opened in a default browser in the window with two panels:

    ☞ The left panel contains a list of all classes of the project.

    ☞ The right panel contains the documentation of the class or `interface` selected in the left panel.

☞ Only methods which the given `interface` declares are quoted in the `interface` documentation in the table of methods.

☞ Methods that are only inherited are quoted in special tables devoted to all individual parent types.

Project:
The resulting form of the project to which we came at the end of the lesson after passing all exercises is in the 113z_Interface_inheritance project.

14 Mediator and Listener

What you will learn in this lesson
In this lesson I will present you the design patterns Observer and Mediator and we will speak about the principle of the dependency injection. Then you will become acquainted with a new project's concept which – thanks to using the described patterns and principles – will provide that the shapes will not mutually rub out one another.

Project:
In this lesson we open the new project entitled 114a_CanvasManagerStart.

238.   Rubbing out of shapes in their original position before changing their position or size looks quite silly. Could you do something with it?

You cannot do much against mutual rubbing out of shapes in the current project. The problem is that shapes painted in canvas do not know one about the other and so they cannot ask the shape whose part was rubbed out to redraw itself as was done at the beginning with the partly rubbed out rectangle. If you would like to prevent the mutual rubbing out, each shape should have to know about all other shapes so that it could point them out that they should repaint themselves. Can you imagine how complicated it would be?

Therefore we exchange the project once again for such project that would enable us to solve these problems. But before that, I will present you two design patterns used in this project.

Observer – Listener – Subscriber

239.   Well, go on.

One of the typical tasks that the programmer has to solve is when the object waits that certain event occurs (e.g. pressing a button). You can program the waiting so that the given object (the observer) will permanently monitor the object of its interest (maybe the keyboard) and check if the expected event has arisen. But it will spend a part of the processor's time for it, whilst the processor could do more useful things (if you have seen the second Shrek movie, you surely remember the Donkey who was asking the whole way: "Are we there yet?").

The design pattern *Observer* recommends to choose quite different strategy – that is used in car radio receivers when the CD listening is interrupted at a moment of broadcasting the traffic news. The observer (the driver) is registered at the monitored object (he tunes in to the relevant station in our case) and then he stops to follow it and pursues his work (he drives the car and listens the CD). When the observed object meets the expected event, it gives an announcement to all registered observers who can subsequently react to this event.

Note:

This strategy is often called **The Hollywood Principle** and is characterized by a slogan: "Don't call us, we shall call you". This sentence is often used e.g. when you are interested in being engaged in movie's crew as extras and characterizes the principle of this design pattern.

If the monitored object has to inform all observers on the emerged event, it has to know how to say it. It defines an `interface` for this purpose, which has to be implemented by all registered observers, i.e. by all objects that want to be informed about changes of the observed object. This `interface` declares which message the monitored object should send to all registered if the expected situation would come.

240.   Why the pattern is called the observer? When I observe something then I see that the given event came and no one has to announce it to me.

The term *Observer* is a semi-official name of the given pattern. However, I admit that I don't like it as well because if you observe something you cannot do too many other things (e.g. you hardly can drive and watch the screen if there are any important news). Therefore some authors (including me) prefer pair of terms *broadcaster –listener* instead of *observed – observer*, because if you only listen you can do a number of other things. However, probably the most fitting name pair is *publisher –subscriber*, because the subscriber has to be really registered even in our world.

Fortunately, it is not so much important which term we will use. It is important to understand the principle of pattern's functioning and how to use it. Let's revise:

☞   The observed object (broadcaster, publisher) is associated with an `interface` that defines the message sent by the observed object (broadcaster, publisher) to the observers (listeners, subscribers). This interface must be implemented by all observers (listeners, subscribers), because only the instance of this interface can be registered.

☞   Each observer (listener, subscriber) has to be registered at the observed object (broadcaster, publisher) firstly.

☞   When the awaited event arises, the observed object (broadcaster, publisher) sends the message declared in the associated interface to all registered objects. Reactions of the notified objects are individual (they know, why they are waiting for the announced event).

The Mediator

241.   This was the first pattern; and the second one?

Similarly as in our project with the canvas, also in other programs there are often situations when a number of objects need to mutually communicate. But it is not suitable so that every instance could directly communicate with each other instance because, thus a number of mutual relations might arise as a potential source of mistakes and they could make troubles to subsequent program adjustments. Therefore the design pattern *Mediator* suggests creating one object which will be a mediator in all mutual communications – such a telephone exchange. A number of mutual relations will cease because all objects will turn to only the mediator, who will send a message to the required addressee if need be (see figure 14.1).

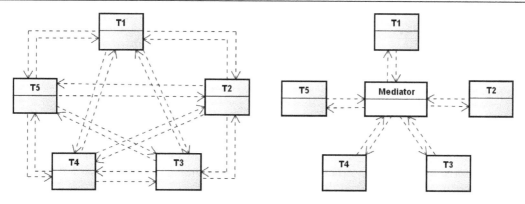

Figure 14.1
Mutual dependencies before and after introducing the Mediator

If an object would want to draw the others' attention to some event, it informs the mediator and the mediator passes the needed information to other engaged addressees. It's the same as with the telephone exchange. By dialing a number you announce to the telephone exchange with whom you want to speak and the exchange provides to inform the addressee.

The mediator has to define certain mechanism which enables to pass over the forwarded message to addressees as effectively as possible. Usually the design pattern *Observer* is used for it. All objects that want to communicate register at the mediator-transmitter as its listeners. The object that wants to tell anything to others, passes the message to a mediator and tells if the message should be passed to certain particular object (a set of objects) or to all. The mediator then contacts all addressees and sends them the message.

242. You said that by communicating of each with everybody a number of dependencies arise. Why the communicating objects should be dependent one on another? If I only tell something to an object I am not dependent on it.

Oh, no, even if you simply tell something to certain person (i.e. you send a message), you care about him so that he would understand your message. (In case you don't care about him, you do not have to bother with saying it.) Therefore you need so that he would understand the language of the given message. Thus you are dependent on a language to which the message receiver understands. When the message receiver gets e.g. deaf, you have to change fundamentally the message language. In other words, the message sender is always dependent on the receiver. As soon as the receiver's abilities change, you have to check if you have to adjust also the sender, so that he would send the message in such form in which the receiver is able to process it.

Theoretically the receiver is not dependent on the sender. We could say that he doesn't take care about from whom he received the message. He has received a message so he reacts to it. If two objects mutually communicate, they are simultaneously senders as well as receivers and thus they are dependent one on another.

Dependency Injection

243.   But it will not be much easier. When certain receiver would change, then I should check the mediator. When I will have to modify it, I will have to touch all receivers, because each of them is a sender at the same time, and so round and around.

Oh no, as I have mentioned, the mediator uses mostly the design pattern *Observer* (see the figure 14.2). It is therefore associated with an `interface` that defines the format of messages which the mediator sends to the registered objects. Thus every object, which would like to receive messages from its colleagues through the mediator, should be registered at the mediator. And as we said, it has to be registered as an instance of the associated `interface`. Thus the mediator communicates only with instances of the associated `interface` and it is dependent only on this `interface`, which is usually defined to suit to the mediator. This means the instances communicating with the mediator have to accommodate. Until you change the mediator's definition or its `interface` (this may sometimes occur), no requirements on changes for the communicating instances will come from this side.

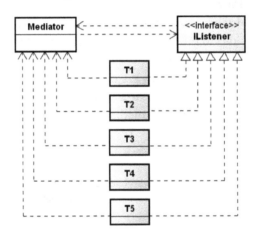

Figure 14.2
Mediator using the Observer (Listener, Publisher) design pattern

This technique is one of the *Dependency Injection* techniques – instead of being dependent on others, I will arrange so that they would be dependent on me. This realizes the more general *Dependency Inversion Principle (DIP)* which says that we should do the programming in such way so that the higher level objects would not be dependent on lower level objects – e.g. so that the managing objects would not be dependent on administered objects. (In our case the mediator poses as a managing object because it coordinates the communication of communicating objects.)

How to Prevent Mutual Cancelling of Shapes

244.   Well, do you think I have sufficient skills so that you could present me the new project?

I would say that you as well as the time are matured. As I have already told at the beginning of this lesson, the basic problem of the current solution is that the changed object does not know the others and therefore it cannot advise them that they should repaint themselves, because they may have a part rubbed out. If we would like to set it right, the newly painted object should register at all objects painted until now, so that they could inform about their changes. But this would lead to vast inform-ing each object about the others and to sending messages to all, which would considerably complicate the whole project.

As I have already told, the design pattern *Mediator* advises to create a new object in such case, a mediator which would mediate all communication among objects. The new graphic shape would not be necessarily registered at all others, but it would be sufficient to register at the mediator. Similarly it would be sufficient to inform the mediator that certain object changes its position or shape and the mediator would send a message to all other shapes to redraw.

This mediator could operate as a manager of the canvas which supervises if all other objects are re-drawn in proper time. The object that would like to be depicted at the canvas has to be registered at its manager. It has to announce any change of its outlook so that the manager could start redrawing. The manager gradually informs all registered objects from below up and asks them to redraw themselves. Thus it is provided that all objects will be properly depicted, even in case that the changing object is between two others, as meat in a hamburger.

So that this concept would really operate, it is necessary to provide that the canvas would be inac-cessible for all who might do mischief. In other words, the possibility to draw at the canvas should be open only for those who would register at the canvas manager. This can be achieved by such ar-rangement that e.g. to draw at the canvas would be possible for the only one object – a painter. It will be the only one that would be able to draw the required picture. All which would like to be portrayed would have to draw through this painter. The canvas manager will pass this painter at a moment when it asks the objects to redraw.

The Canvas Manager and Its Project

245.   You are always speaking about how the project should look like. What about to show the project?

You are true. As it is stated at the lesson's beginning, the new project can be found in the folder 114a_CanvasManagerStart. You can see its class diagram at figure 14.3.

Before we start to analyze is, please, compile it and then import the classes Tests and MultishapeTest from the previous project which you have created in preceding lessons, or from the subfolder Extension_14 of this project folder.

246.   They are imported. But the class MultishapeTest did not associate with the class Multishape and remained up quite alone.

The test classes do not associate with their tested "companions" during importing, even when they are imported together in the source project. But *BlueJ* enables another trick. Enter a command for creating a test class in the context menu of Multishape class. *BlueJ* starts to execute it and discovers that in the project there is already a class with the name planned for the test class. So it does not strive to think out a different name but announces this fact to you in a dialog and will not create any class. However, the side effect of this experiment is an association of the existing test class with its tested class.

But if you don't want to associate them, you don't have to do it. Simply put them into the class di-agram as it suits you. The only one what you will lose, is the automatic attempt for compilation of the associated (i.e. test) class after the compilation of the class to which it is associated.

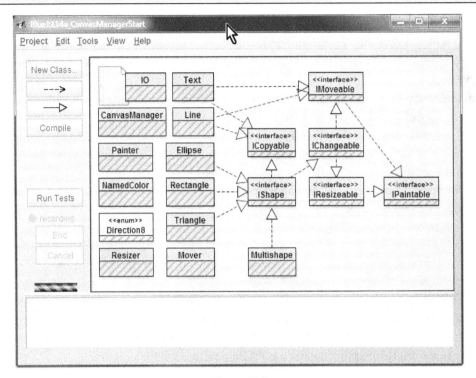

Figure 14.3
The project 114a_CanvasManagerStart

247. When you say it so generally, it looks like I can associate whatever with anything.

Yes, you can, you need only to add an appropriate line into the file package.bluej, in which you announce which class is associated to your class. Similarly, when the association of the class with its test class hampers to you, it is sufficient to take away the relevant line from the package.bluej file and the association will be cancelled. If you are interested in it, you surely will derive the necessary operations from the package.bluej file yourself. However, I wouldn't like to discuss it as this is a specialty connected with *BlueJ*.

248. Well, but now I have another problem: I tried the tests and they behave strangely.

That is the consequence of the fact that the depicting of shapes is done a little bit different in this project, and therefore we will have to adjust the test fixtures. Then everything will operate as it should do. (So I asked you firstly to compile the project and only then to import the two test files.)

As I've told the object that wants to be depicted at the canvas should have been firstly registered at the canvas manager, i.e. at the instance of CanvasManager class by sending a message add(IPaintable) and by passing itself in its parameter. However, our objects don't do it, which means they will be depicted at the canvas only when the method, creating a fixture, or the test method will send them the paint() message. Its contract in this project says that it registers its object at the canvas administrator.

As you surely remember, previously we called this method only in case we wanted so that the damaged object would be repainted. In other words, in the current project the shape will appear at the moment when we have asked it in the last project to redraw itself.

249. Well, so what should I do?

Reset the virtual machine and start to create a test fixture of some of the tested classes. Don't forget to register the created objects before you close creating the fixture at the `CanvasManager`. You have two possibilities: either you will send a message `paint()` to an instance and the instance will register itself at the canvas manager, or you ask the `CanvasManager` class for a reference to its instance by sending a message `CanvasManager.getInstance()` and you save this reference into the variable for which I use a mnemonic name `CM` (of course, you can call it by a different name). After it you will register each created object at the manager by sending a message `add(IPaintable)`. The registered object immediately appears at the canvas.

250. Due to the fact that the `CanvasManager` class does not offer any possibility to send a message starting with `new`, I estimate that the canvas manager will be a singleton, similarly as the `Canvas` was.

You are true. The canvas manager is a singleton and the canvas, on which the objects are depicted, is its private property, and you can get close to it only when you are allowed. To be more precise, when the manager gives you the painter which – when required – outlines the relevant object.

251. And how can I get the painter?

I will start with a detour. The `IPaintable` interface is not a tag interface in this project, but it requires an implementation of the method `paint(Painter)`. The canvas manager will call this method at the moment when it will ask the given object to repaint. At this occasion it passes also the needed painter in its parameter.

252. But when once the object gains the painter, it can leave it and continue painting whenever it wants.

Yes and no. This mechanism has to prevent the objects to cancel and redraw themselves without any control, i.e. so that the programmers would not have to think out how to paint the object properly at the proper time and not to confuse it by mistake. This mechanism practically eliminates any mistakes. Especially when you take into account that it is useless to hold the painter, because it may not operate in a while, as something may change and you will need a different painter for a new canvas.

253. Why a new canvas?

Because the picture should be repainted many times per second and each repaint is prepared at a new canvas whilst the old one is shown to the user. By this way the shown picture doesn't blink due the permanent repainting.

254. Well, to sum up: all classes are adjusted in the new project so that they would cooperate with the canvas manager, and when I adjust the fixture, the tests will run.

Exactly, to be sure I will repeat how you should create the fixtures, because you will create them once again. (I recommend you to reset the virtual machine before each creating.):

☞ The class `Tests`

1. The objects `rectangle0`, `ellipse0` and `triangle0` (*BlueJ*) are created through parameterless constructors, i.e. on coordinates [0, 0] with the size [100, 50].

2. The objects rectangl1, ellipse1 and triangle1 are all created on coordinates [50, 50] and have the size [200, 100].

3. Gradually enroll all created objects at the canvas manager – e.g. by sending a message paint() to each of them. They will appear gradually after you will send this message. Therefore I recommend sending the message to objects in the order in which you have created them.

255.   **Stop! You told me that the objects have to be firstly enrolled and only after it they will be able to depict themselves. But now you say that they will be enrolled when being depicted.**

Watch out! This is a different message. The canvas manager asks the enrolled objects to be able to react to message paint(Painter). But this is a message paint(), and after its receiving the object enrolls itself at the canvas manager. As you can see, the message has a bad name. Two messages with the same name, each of them doing something different, should not occur in projects. I have prepared this as a trap for students to show them which problems such inappropriate name can cause.

256.   **Well, I swallowed the ball. Go on.**

4. Despite you requested instances to register themselves at the canvas manager, I would add a field with the reference to the manager's instance into the fixture because it may suit in future. Name the field CM.

5. At the conclusion send a message inform(Object), to which you pass the text "Fixture prepared", to the IO class, i.e. send the message IO.inform("Fixture prepared").

6. Ask the Tests class to save the hitherto activity as a test fixture.

7. Run the testSmoothMovements() method to ensure that the new project works as expected.

☞   The class MultishapeTest

8. Reset the Virtual machine.

9. Send a message getInstance() to CanvasManager class. Request for a reference in the subsequently opened dialog and save it into the variable CM. You established the variable CM with a reference to the canvas manager last time, but you didn't use it and enrolled the instances by sending a message paint(). Now we will start using the manager for real.

10. Create a multishape m1 by calling its constructor with a variable number of parameters, enter the name "m1" and gradually enter the calling of parameterless constructors of classes Rectangle, Ellipse and Triangle to input fields for separate shapes (see figure 14.4).

11. Send a message add(m1) to the canvas manager. Thus you will depict a multishape m1. Don't pay any attention to a dialog showing that only one shape was added and close it.

12. Create a multishape m2 called "m2" with the aid of the constructor Multishape(String).

13. Send a message add(m2) to the canvas manager. Nothing will be seen at the canvas because the multishape does not yet contain anything.

14. Send a message addShapes(m1) to multishape m2. Be careful to send the message really to the multishape and not to the canvas manager.

Don't be afraid that the canvas will not visually change, because there will be now two same multishapes: once m1 and once its copy which became a part of m2.

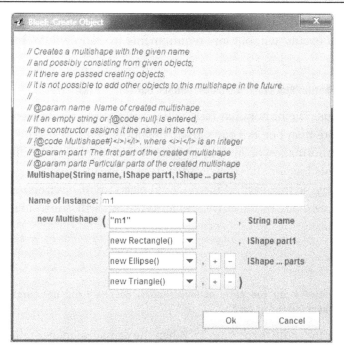

Figure 14.4
Calling of constructor with variable number of parameters

15. Move the multishape m1 by sending the message
    m1.setPosition(33, 25)

    Then the multishape m1 peeps out behind the multishape m2.

16. Diminish the multishape m2 by sending the message:
    m1.setSize(33, 25)

    The multishape m1 again hides behind the multishape m2.

17. Send the message m2.add(m1) to the multishape m2. After sending it you will see a copy of a current form of a multishape m1 in the depicted multishape m2.

18. To enjoy the new properties of the current project let's change a little bit the original conception of the test fixture. Ask the Mover class for creating a mover with a speed 5. Save the received reference into the variable mover.

19. Ask the mover to shift the multishape m1 to a position [150; 0]. You will see how the multishape will appear from under its bigger sibling and moves to the entered position.

20. Announce the multishape m2 that its composing is finished, i.e. send a message m2.creationDone().

21. Send a message
    IO.inform("Multishapes prepared")

    to IO class.

22. Ask the class MultishapeTest to save the hitherto activity as a test fixture and confirm, that the previous fixture will be replaced.

And now try to run the tests. You will see that the shapes which were covered during various changes will appear in their full beauty without any requirements for redrawing. This was already provided by the canvas manager.

257.   When I pressed the button Run Tests, a window jumped out entitled Tests results.

Sorry, I was not precious. The button **Run Tests** will gradually run all defined tests. The window **Run Tests** appears when more than one test runs. In this window you can see the results of particular test together with detailed information about failed tests. We will return to this subject later.

Running multiple tests together has one disadvantage in the interactive mode: if more tests run one after another, it is suitable so that each of them would clean up its environment. However, this is not possible in the interactive mode in the current *BlueJ* version. I will return to it, when we will discuss the interior of the test class.

Recursion

258.   How it is possible, that I can see parts of multishapes, despite I did not enroll them at the canvas? The multishape enrolls them instead of me?

No, it is sufficient when the multishape enrolls. When the canvas manager will ask to redraw itself, i.e. when the canvas sends the message paint(Painter), the multishape will ask gradually each of its parts to redraw by the painter, i.e. the multishape send the message paint(Painter) and pass the painter in a parameter, and thus the operation recursively repeats.

259.   What does it mean that the operation recursively repeats?

We speak about recursive calling when certain method calls itself directly or indirectly. The multishape should redraw in our example, i.e. the canvas manager called its paint(Painter) method. A part of the multishape is another multishape. Therefore the "parent" multishape asks for redrawing, i.e. it calls its paint(Painter) method. This means that the multishape method was called from the same multishape method. And this is a recursive calling.

There are thick books about recursive calling and its possibilities. We will speak about it when we will discuss some more demanding expressions of object oriented programming in this course.

Other New Features

260.   How the square grid arose? I didn't paint any.

This project brings two new classes: the Text class, the instances of which represent text strings paintable on the canvas, and the Line class, the instances of which represent lines with specified end points and color. The canvas manager uses the lines for painting a grid that should help you to estimate the coordinates of the analyzed object. You can learn the size of the grid square by calling the getStep() method and set it by the setStep(int) method.

In addition the canvas manager offers the setStepSize(int,int,int) method that (beside the step specified in the first argument) allows also setting the number of grid rows and columns.

Exercise

261.   What you will recommend me for training today?

We left your animated pictures for few lessons. Please, brush them up and let them run in a new project. You have to up-date not only creating of test fixtures, which you will supplement by enrolling of individual shapes to the canvas manager, but also of certain tests – above all those, where new objects arise. They also have to enroll at the canvas manager, so that they could be seen.

However, numerous tests may stay without any change. The robot will properly wave and the figure will wink with eyes even without any modifying. A pleasant surprise can be expected at the little house and its testChangeColor test, even after you will adjust it. The original version repainted the building and in the latest fixture its color did not change, only the window and the door disappeared. And now the building will only change its color without any side effects. To see it, you have to enter the test once more and change the building's color – e.g. to the yellow one.

Review

I tried to present all what we have debated now in the accompanied animation. Run it and try everything once more.

Animation 14.1: The interface inheritance – OOPNZ_114_A1_SpravcePlatna
The animation will repeat what was explained in course of this lesson, i.e. importing the classes into a new project and running the tests.

Let's review what you have learnt in this lesson:

☞   The design pattern *Observer* solves the problem when one object or more objects expect revealing certain event of the observed object. The pattern recommends the following procedure:

   ☞   Define the interface in which we declare the message that the observed object intends to send to all enrolled observers after the event begins. – In our case it is the IPaintable interface with the paint(Painter) method.

   ☞   Implement this interface by all observers. – In our case by all classes of graphic objects which we would like to depict at the canvas.

   ☞   Define a method of the observed object through which the objects can register. The parameter of this method will be the interface instance implemented by the observers. – In our case it was a method add(IPaintable).

   ☞   Enroll (register) all observers at the observed object. – In our case register all graphic objects which we want to depict (they are observers) at the canvas manager (it poses as an observed object).

   ☞   Whenever an expected event occurs, the observed object "rings round" all registered observers, i.e. calls their method declared in an interface which all observers have to implement. – In our case whenever the canvas should be redrawn, the canvas manager asks the depicted object one after another to depict by a delivered drawer.

☞ We often use pairs of terms *Broadcaster – Listener* or *Publisher – Subscriber* instead of *Observer – Observed*.

☞ The design pattern *Observer* realizes the so called *Hollywood Principle*, characterized by a slogan: "Do not call us, we will call you."

☞ The design pattern *Mediator* solves a situation when a number of objects need mutual communication. During direct communication a number of mutual dependencies significantly growths. Therefore the pattern recommends creating a mediator, which mediates the separate objects communication. The communicating objects are then dependent only on the mediator.

☞ Passing the messages by the mediator is usually realized by implementing the design pattern *Observer*.

☞ Implementing the pattern *Observer* is one of the techniques of *dependency injection*. Thus the object provides not to be dependent on any object with which it communicates, but on the opposite so that these objects would be dependent on it.

☞ The dependency injection implements the *Principle of Dependency Inversion*, which requires so that the managing object would not be dependent on the managed objects.

☞ The managing object as well as the mediator is represented in our project by the instance of CanvasManager class.

☞ All objects that want to be depicted at the canvas have to implement the IPaintable interface and as instances of this interface they have to be registered at the canvas manager.

☞ Each time, when the outlined object changes its look, it has to ask the canvas manager for redrawing the canvas.

☞ When redrawing the canvas, the manager calls gradually the method paint(Painter) for all registered objects, and passes the drawer in its parameter, which is the only one object, that can draw at the canvas.

☞ When converting the test classes from the old project with a canvas to the new one with a canvas manager it is sufficient to adjust the fixture definition.

Project:
The resulting form of a project to which we came at the end of the lesson and after completing all exercises is in the 114z_CanvasManager project.

Part 2:

Basics of Creating
OO Programs

In this part you will learn to write simple programs and apply the rules you have met during the work in an interactive mode. You will start with the simplest programs which will be gradually made perfect in each lesson.

15 The First Code

What you will learn in this lesson
In this lesson the interactive mode will be abandoned. Firstly the concept of files from which the BlueJ project consists will be presented to you together with the significance and meaning of separate groups of files. Then you will create an empty class and you will hear its definition.

Project:
In this lesson you return back to the project 113z_Interface_inheritance.

262.   I'd say it's enough of playing with objects and we should start programming something real.

I would like to explain you few basic phrases, but I understand your impatience, so I will postpone the explanation for a while. We have discussed the key principles and we can go on coding, i.e. to the definition of our programs in the text form. That's why we will try a real definition of a new class today.

263.   Hurray! I have been already afraid I will not live to see it.

Don't be sarcastic and close the opened project. For a while we will go back to the original project with an ordinary canvas. I will return to the new project after you will learn defining methods with parameters. Don't be afraid, it will be quick.

The New Empty Class

264.   Don't tense me up. What should I start with?

Let's start the same way as with creating the test class, i.e. pressing the button **New Class**. But in subsequently opened window we adjust the switch **Class Type** to the state **Empty Class**. To be stylish we will call this class **Empty** (see figure 15.1).

   BlueJ creates a new class and depicts it in the class diagram (I recommend to relocate it into a free space and decrease it to a size corresponding with the size of its neighbors). In case you will have a look at the disc folder where the project is saved, you will see a new file Empty.java, in which the source code of the created class is located.

Files in *BlueJ* Projects

265.   I have found the file Empty.java, but there was a mass of other files. Could you briefly explain me, what are these files like?

I agree with you that it's the highest time to explain which files you can find in the project folder. There are the following types of files:

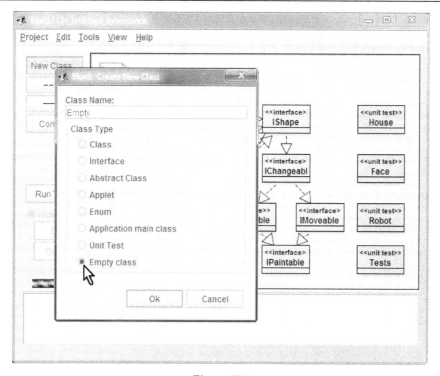

Figure 15.1
Creating the empty class

☞ ***.java** – files with the extension java are source files of programs which are created by a programmer. Those are the text files containing the source code or programs. We will create these files during the whole course.

☞ ***.class** – files with the extension class are created by a compiler. They are the compiled versions of source files of the same name which are often marked as **class files**.

☞ ***.ctxt** – files with the extension ctxt are auxiliary files created by *BlueJ* program. *BlueJ* saves certain information in them discovered during the source code analysis. This information helps to increase the comfort of the user's interface.

☞ **package.bluej** – a file created by *BlueJ* where the complete information on an application window is saved, as well as the class diagram and editing windows of particular classes. The position and the size of the application window is adjusted here as well as of particular classes together with their mutual dependencies depicted by arrows, the position and size of editing windows of separate classes, the mode in which the windows open (documentation × implementation), associating of test classes with their tested classes and some other items.

266. There are more files with class **extension than with extensions** java **or** ctxt.

It can easily happen. You can find internal classes which are defined inside certain classes as well as an interface determined for their internal need. Each class and each interface (also those, which are defined inside other classes or interface types) has its class file. Therefore, when compiling certain source files, more files with the class extension are arising (more class files).

267.   If I understood it well, during transferring the project to another PC I don't have to transfer all files.

Files with extensions class and ctxt are created in each compilation. During transferring the project to another PC it is sufficient to transfer only the source files (i.e. files with the extension java) and if you want to keep information saved in the file package.bluej, then including this file.

268.   Nothing will happen when I cancel them?

Come to see it. Close the project (you do not have to close the whole application, it's sufficient to close only the project), delete all files with extensions class and ctxt, and open the project again. The project will look out the same, only hatching will appear symbolizing that the classes are not compiled, i.e. that the class files which were younger than the corresponding java files do not exist.

269.   Can the files be deleted without closing the project?

Some of them yes, some of them no. Anyway, the externally executed changes in the file of open project (i.e. when you jump aside from *BlueJ* with an open project to some file manager and you start rummaging in the project folder), may lead *BlueJ* to incorrect state because there is something different at the disc than the application supposes. Therefore it is better to close the project before any external operation with files in the project folder, then to carry out the given operation and open the project again.

As I have already told you, it is not necessary to close the whole application. It is sufficient to close the project and after amendments you can open it again. Opening the project is far quicker than opening the whole application.

270.   So the only one really dangerous action is deleting the source code?

I would precise: *unwanted* deleting of the source code. You often create a file only for tests and you want to delete it at the end of your experimenting. You do not have to close the project and start up the file manager. In case you need to remove certain class, you can adjust the command **Remove** in its local offer. *BlueJ* then deletes the class from the diagram and at the same time it deletes also all corresponding files from the disc. (You can try it – delete the classes HouseFace and Robot, we will not use them anymore.)

However, besides source files I recommend not to delete files **package.bluej**.

271.   What would happen so horrible? You told that *BlueJ* remembers only auxiliary information and it can be found any time once again, can't be?

Again I can tell you, try it. Close again the project and re-name the files **package.bluej** (you can delete them, but renaming is sufficient). In case you try to open now the project again, *BlueJ* will oppose. According to the presence of **package.bluej** *BlueJ* recognizes that it deals with its project.

However, when you delete this file by mistake, you can outwit *BlueJ* simply by creating an empty file **package.bluej** in the project folder. *BlueJ* opens the folder as its project, but because it will not find any information in the file package.bluej on classes whose source files it discovered in this folder, *BlueJ* puts them at any place in the class diagram. But when you close the project and change the file package.bluej for the original one, you again receive your well-known project after opening.

Another possibility how to open the project, in which the file package.bluej is not present, is to use a command **Open Non BlueJ** in the menu **Project**. But when processing this command *BlueJ* strives to include into the project also the subfolders which, sometimes, is reverse of what you really want. Luckily, *BlueJ* warns you in any sign of danger and you can withdraw your command. (You can test it with projects in which the folders with class source codes are located, which we have imported during the lessons – e.g. project 110 – 112).

I will not ruminate on this topic further. I tried to show you everything in the accompanying animation. You can find there also the explanation and demonstration of certain operations and properties of *BlueJ* environment about which we were not speaking here, but whose knowledge I consider useful for further work.

> *Animation 15.1: Files in* **BlueJ** *projects – OOPNZ_115_A1_SouboryVProjektechBlueJ*
> *The animation will show the explained parts concerning the project files, both the source files as well as files created during compilation. Moreover, it shows also some other properties which were not explained but which we will use later on.*

The Source Code of the Empty Class

272.   Speaking about files in *BlueJ* project was interesting, but a little bit off the point. I would like to discover already how the source code looks like and how I should program the class itself.

We do go on it. Open the class Empty in an editor. You can open the editor with the class source code by several ways. You can double-click on the given class in the class diagram or you can open its context menu and enter the command **Open Editor** (see figure 15.2). In case the editor depicts the class

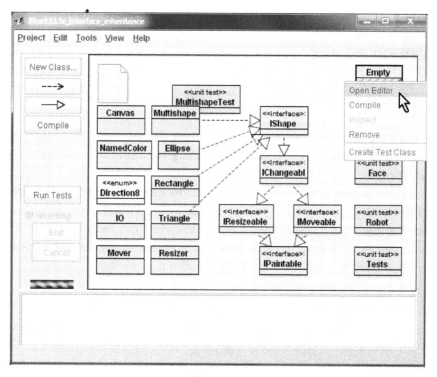

Figure 15.2
The command for opening the editor with source code

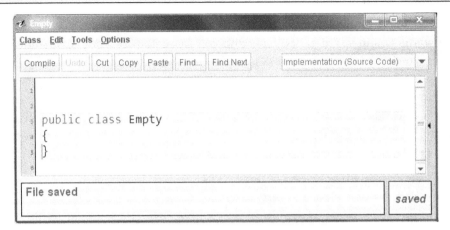

Figure 15.3
The editor with the source code of the class Empty

documentation instead of the source code, it is sufficient to enter that you want to depict the source code in the unrolled list at the tool panel as is showed in figure 10.1 in the section *Interface vs. Implementation* on page 78.

Then *BlueJ* opens the editor with the source code of the given class (see figure 15.3).

As you see the source code is very simple. The significance of separate part is as follows:

☞ public

The keyword announcing that the class is public and therefore anybody can send messages to it. It is possible to define the class without using the keyword public, but such class has certain limitation. Therefore we will not use this possibility and situations when it might be suitable will be presented after some time.

☞ class

The keyword class announces that we intend to define a class.

☞ Empty

After the keyword class the **name** or the **class identifier** follows, which has to fulfill the rules I have explained in the section *The Rules for Creating the Identifiers* on page 43. The convention requires starting the class name with a capital letter.

Besides that **the name of the public class has to be identical with the name of the file in which its source code is saved including the size of individual characters**. (Logically it results in the fact that the source code of only one public class can be in one file.) The file with the source code has to have the extension java. But you don't have to take care about it because *BlueJ* immediately creates the relevant file and names it correctly.

☞ {}

All up-to-now explained parts create the **class header**, according to which the compiler recognizes its basic characteristics. The **class body** closed in braces follows after the head. Due to the fact that our definition is still empty, also the braces are empty. With the exception of two precisely specified statements (we shall speak about them later) everything has to be defined within the class body in Java language.

273. Why the beginning of the definition is in red and the rest in black?

This is a **syntax highlighting**, which started to be used in the middle of the 80ies of the last century and which is practically a compulsory function of all programming editors today. According to it, various formats are used for various parts of the program. *BlueJ* is quite modest in this respect and uses only a color for highlighting (it does not use the bold, underlined or italic fonts). It stresses only keywords, comments and text strings (both will be explained to you further).

274. And what does it mean the syntax?

The syntax is a set of rules describing how we can write the program. And those are just the rules which I described a while ago, i.e. that the class contains a header and a body, and the header is composed from the public modifier and the keyword class followed by a name of a class etc. etc.

The syntactic rules deal neither with what the program will do, nor with if it would really operate. Those are the rules which you have to fulfill so that the compiler would compile your program.

275. The braces limiting the class body have to be at the separate line?

Not necessarily. Java belongs to languages in which the adjustment of the code to lines is not decisive. With the exception of identifier interior you can include any **whitespaces** or the whole sequence of whitespaces to any place. From the point of compiler's view the code on figure 15.3 is equivalent to a code written at one line

```
public class Empty{}
```

or to the code in which each identifier lies at an individual line separated from others by several empty lines.

276. What are the whitespaces?

Wikipedia says: *"In computer science, white space or whitespace is any character or series of characters that represents horizontal or vertical space in typography. When rendered, a whitespace character does not correspond to a visual mark, but typically does occupy an area on a page."*

Wikipedia defines 26 whitespaces, however in Java is the whitespace defined as the ASCII space character, horizontal tab character, form feed character, and line terminator characters (line feed and carriage return).

However, I return back to the subject. The fact that adjustment of the code is not compulsory does not mean that you can include the code as you wish. One of the very important properties of the good code is its clear code formatting. That's why you should have to keep certain conventions which make the orientation in code easy to others and consequently also to you.

277. Well, well. I will strive to format my code correctly and keep the conventions. But I would be pleased if you stop digressing and would tell me something about how to write the code itself.

Sorry, I was carried away by a problem with which my students are often fighting. Let's return to the code of Empty class. Let it be compiled firstly – e.g. by pressing the button **Compile** at the editor's tool panel. *BlueJ* firstly saves the file, then "thinks over" it and in case of not detecting any fault in it, *BlueJ* writes below in the information panel under the edited text the following message (see figure 15.4):

```
Class compiled - no syntax errors
```

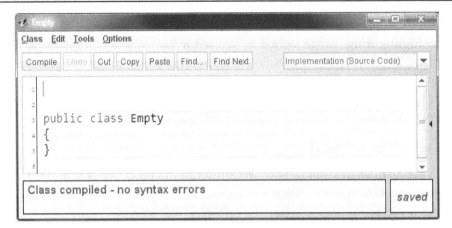

Figure 15.4
The message about the successful compilation

Besides that you should notice that the column with line numbers changed its color and in case you would look into the class diagram, you discover that the empty class is not hatched any more. And now try changing the source code – e.g. cancel the first empty line. The column with line numbers immediately gets grey and *BlueJ* again completes hatching in the class diagram.

In case you would look into the project's folder you would see that after the compilation there are both expected files: Empty.class as well as Empty.ctxt there.

And now, open again the context menu of the Empty class. The new statement appears in it:

```
new Empty();
```

You can enter it immediately and start the standard procedure of creating the instance. *BlueJ* asks you for the name of the reference and after entering it, the reference to an instance of Empty class will appear below in the reference stack.

Constructor

278. **This is somehow strange. In the section *Methods and Constructors* on page 30 you told: *"The method is a part of a program that takes care about an object's reaction to a given message. Each message that the object understands, has assigned to the corresponding method that will take care about the relevant reaction."* But there is nothing programmed in this class. Does it mean that the methods are programmed elsewhere?**

No, as I have told a while ago, it is necessary (contrary to some other languages – e.g. C++) to define everything inside the body of the relevant class. The purpose of this method's existence is somewhere else – the definition of the method reacting to parameterless message requesting to create a new instance is a result of compiler's initiative. The compiler knows that a method responsible for proper creating of its instance has to be defined in each class. As I have told, this method is named the **constructor**.

If the programmer does not define any constructor, the compiler decides to create its simplest possible version and creates an empty parameterless public constructor that is named the **default constructor**. However, its definition is not mentioned in the source code, you can find it only in the class file of the given class.

And that's all for today. Next time we will speak about constructors. And next time we will also go through the animation demonstrating how to create and look into an empty class – it will be a kind of reviewing for you.

Adjustment of Presets

279.   You were speaking about a change of color of a column with line numbers, but I don't have any line numbers there. Why?

You have a different displaying – probably you played with the setting and line numbers were canceled. Enter the command **Tools → Preferences**, which opens the dialog **Preferences** and there check the option **Display line numbers** at the **Editor** card. You can check also other options as you can see at figure 15.5.

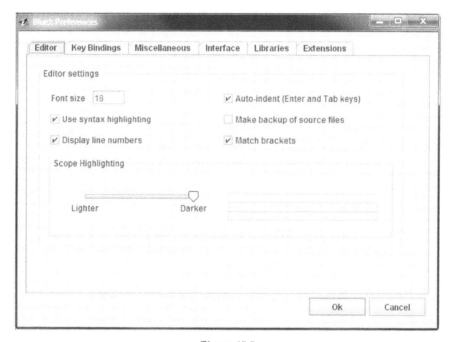

Figure 15.5
Adjusting the editor's options

280.   Why you didn't check the option Make backup copies source files?

Creating the backup copies is off from two reasons:

☞   If I need to return to any previous file version, usually it's the 10th to 20th version back and *BlueJ* is not supporting such long number of backup copies.

☞   Once, when I put on creating back-up copies, *BlueJ* announced that the source code was disturbed every minute. So I switched it off. Since that time the systems of versions administration significantly improved, and they are far better solution of this problem (*BlueJ* 2.5 supports two of them).

281.   Which one?

It would be a long explanation. When you will be advanced I will tell you something more about it and how to use it. But now you have to wait.

Exercise

282.   Which task will you give me today as training?

Today I would recommend you repeating how it is with files in *BlueJ* projects and how you can make a project from a group of files.

And at this occasion you can try also how *BlueJ* will behave when you will delete its source file, but leave the compiled class file and ctxt file. Verify that you can work further with such class and that you cannot see only its source code.

In case you cancel also the ctxt file, the dialog will not contain the documentation comments and the local offers will show you only types of parameters, but not their names.

Review

Let's review what you have learned in this lesson:

☞   You can create the empty class similarly as the test class; you will only turn the switch **Class Type** in the window **Create New Class** to the state **Empty Class**.

☞   When creating the new class, the new text file of identical name with the created class (including the letter size) is created as well as java extension in the project folder. This file contains the source code of the created class.

☞   The syntax is a set of rules describing how you can write the program. These rules deal neither with what such program will do, nor if it would operate. Those are rules which have to be fulfilled so that the compiler could compile the program.

☞   The class definition is composed from the header and the class body.

☞   The public class head contains the keyword public followed by the keyword class and the class name.

☞   The class body is closed by braces.

☞   The source code of a class has to be located in the file with the same name as the class including the capitalization (source file names are case sensitive even in *Windows*).

☞   During compilation of the source code another two files of the same name will appear, but with different extensions, namely class and ctxt.

☞   The compiler will create a file with an extension class and saves the compiled form of the given class in it. This file is marked as **class file** of the given class.

☞   *BlueJ* creates a file with an extension ctxt and saves auxiliary information for increasing the operating comfort in it.

☞   In certain situations several class files can arise during compiling the source file.

☞ You can open the editor with the source code of a class by clicking on the class in the class diagram or by entering the command **Open Editor** in its local offer.

☞ The space, horizontal tabulator as well as line terminator characters (line feed and carriage return) are called **whitespaces** (you can write also *white spaces*) and they are ignored in programs.

☞ You can insert a sequence of whitespaces at any place in a program with the exception of the interior of identifiers.

☞ One of the most important properties of a good program is its clear arrangement.

☞ The programmer has to write the programs so that they might be modified anytime in future.

☞ The method taking care about creating new instances is called the **constructor**.

☞ If there is no constructor defined in a class, the compiler defines **a default constructor**, which is defined as a public, parameterless constructor with an empty body.

Project:
The resulting form of the project to which we came at the end of the lesson after all exercises, is in the 115z_First_code project.

16 The First Constructor

What you will learn in this lesson

In this lesson you will define your first constructor. You will read the explanation how it is with the constructor's name and how the constructor works. You will learn also about the graphic arrangement of the source code and you will create the first more complex objects.

Project:
In this lesson we continue in using the 115z_First_code project.

Definition of the Constructor

283. You told me last time that when the programmer doesn't define any constructor, the compiler creates a default constructor, because the class cannot be without it. When I will create a constructor, the compiler does not add any other, does it?

Exactly, the compiler adds its constructor only in case, when the programmer does not define any one.

284. Well. How can I define my own constructor?

Similarly as the class definition, the constructor's definition consists of the header and the body closed in braces. But its header as well as its body looks out a little bit different.

The header of the public constructor, i.e. of the constructor which would be accessible to all, begins (equally as the header of the public class) with the keyword public. It's followed by the name of the class whose instances are created by the constructor (i.e. the class in which you define the constructor) ensued by the list of parameters closed in parentheses. These parentheses have to be quoted even when the constructor does not have any parameters – in such case the parentheses will be left blank.

You can see the possible definition of the Empty class with explicit definition of the implicit constructor in the listing 16.1.

Listing 16.1:   The class Empty with an explicit definition of the implicit constructor

```
public class Empty
{
    public Empty()
    {
    }
}
```

285. What kind of a phrase is "an explicit definition of the implicit constructor"?

The public parameterless constructor is called a *default constructor* (certain authors use also the term *implicit constructor*) even when it is not defined by the compiler, but you define it, i.e. when it is defined explicitly.

Name of the Constructor

286.   The constructor does not have its name in the header?

No, the constructor's internal name is <init>, but this name opposes to rules for creating identifiers, and so it can have such name really only internally. This internal name is assigned to it automatically by the compiler. But the constructors are declared as methods without a name in the source code.

287.   I've heard or read somewhere that constructors have the same name as the class whose instances they are constructing.

You are true, it's often written in textbooks. If you look at other commands in context menus of classes and their instances (see figure 16.1), you will see that firstly the return value type is quoted, followed by the name of the message (and thus of the relevant method) and by parentheses with a possible list of parameters.

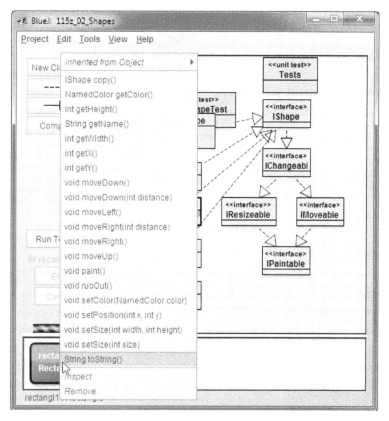

Figure 16.1
The commands initializing a message sending

These commands represent headers of methods, which are called out after calling the relevant message (you saw the method's header in the dialog of methods with parameters). In case you look at the constructor's header, you discover that you can choose if you say that it concerns the method without any name, or on the contrary, it concerns the method in the definition of which the type of return value is not quoted.

It's true that majority of authors prefer the second description. But, as I already told, when you have a look into the compiled code (or when you read *The Java™ Virtual Machine Specification*) you discover that the method representing the constructor has in fact a name <init> (soon you will see it for yourself). Because this name violates the rules for creating the identifiers, it has no applicable name in the program.

Nevertheless, it is not so important how we will speak about the constructor. Simply it's a special method with special properties. Let's have a look how to define it and how to use it.

The Working Constructor

288.   You are true. Let's return to our program, which is not yet operating. I think it's the best time to teach it something.

Yes, of course. Let's add a certain statement to the constructor. We will create e.g. a new ellipse. The statement sending the request for creating a new instance to Ellipse class is very similar to the command which we know from the class context menu. It starts with the keyword new followed by the class name with values of parameters in round brackets. To have the statement as simple as possible, we will send the message without parameters. We complete the whole statement with a semicolon. The class definition is in the listing 16.2.

Listing 16.2:   *The* Empty *class with its own version of a parameterless constructor*

```
public class Empty
{
    public Empty()
    {
        new Ellipse();
    }
}
```

Compile the class once more and enter the command for creating its instance. *BlueJ* locates the reference for created instance into the reference stack, but at the same time it opens the canvas window and draws an ellipse in it. (I remind that we left the canvas manager in the previous project and for few lessons we returned to an ordinary canvas, at which the objects don't have to be registered.)

At the conclusion I would like to remind once more that the programmers mostly do not speak about *sending the message*, but they prefer the expression *calling the method* (or sometimes *invoking the method*). Thus we could say about our default constructor that it calls the default constructor of Ellipse class.

All, what we have spoken about in connection with the source code and the constructors in this as well as the previous lessons, I tried to show you in an accompanying animation.

Animation 16.1: An empty class – OOPNZ_116_A1_PrazdnaTrida
The animation shows creating of a new class, opening its source code and creating a parameterless constructor.

Source Code Formatting

289. **I noticed that any time you start to write braces, you indent the text a little bit to the right. However, at the beginning you told that Java doesn't take care about how the code is formatted. I don't know how I should understand it.**

This is a general convention: **As soon as you write down a code between braces, you should indent the text.** It is one of the generally respected rules which increase the good formatting of the code.

290. **Isn't the permanent indentation of the line beginnings two laborious?**

Don't be afraid, the editors of source codes support this convention and enable you to keep it easily. And you will see how in the animation at the end of the lesson.

291. **How big the indentation should be?**

An indentation by four characters is used most often. However, the book authors sometimes use smaller indentation due to a lack of place.

292. **Isn't it wasting of place, when the whole line is taken by a brace only?**

Truly, the advanced programmers mostly save the place and include the opening brace at the end of the previous line. However, for beginners, it is more suitable to put the opening brace at an independent line, because they can find much easily a mistake caused by a bad coupling of braces which is the very frequent beginner's fault.

Authors of editors know the "popularity" of this fault and therefore they add a function into their editors which stresses the geminate brace to the brace after which the cursor is located. Try to go gradually through the source code with the cursor and notice that any time when you shift the cursor behind any braces, the editor stresses its counterpart by framing.

293. **Why the code should be transparent? The computer has no problem with sloppily formatted code and I think the most important is to be functional and effective.**

We have already discussed about it in the subchapter *Interface as a Data Type* on page 80 and again in the last lesson. As I have said, the only one what you can rely on during programming is the fact that soon everything will be different. A client orders a program and during its development he changes his assignment several times. When you complete and deliver the program he comes with further requirements for amendments and improvements in a while. Only such programs are left without any amendments which are sewage, and the client wants to get rid of them so quickly that he better pays long money for a new program than asking for any amendments.

It doesn't matter, if the client is anybody else or you yourself, i.e. if you prepare the program for you. Each program which is a little bit worthy will undergo amendments in future. That's why you have to write it in the way so that these modifications would be as easy as possible. In case you will be able to adapt your programs quickly and cheaply, you obtain a competitive advantage.

Don't fall prey to an illusion that you are acquainted with your programs. After a year's working on other programs, your own older program will be as strange as someone else's. Implementing certain conventions and their consistent keeping will oil the wheels of your orientation.

This principle was splendidly formulated by Martin Fowler who wrote: *"Any fool can write code that a computer can understand. Good programmers write code that humans can understand."*[5]

More Complex Example

294.   The example with an empty class was tremendously simple. Could we try something more complicated?

Well. But for now all examples will be simple. I will show you, how you could define the class Arrow, whose instance you can see at figure 16.2. The arrow is defined so that it would be located in the left upper corner and could be put into a square area with a side of 50 points. We will have to call constructors with parameters in its definition, but I suppose that after previous experience you will have no problems. You can compare your program with the listing 16.3.

Listing 16.3:   *The Arrow class with the parameterless constructor*

```
public class Arrow
{
    public Arrow()
    {
        new Rectangle(  0, 15, 25, 20, NamedColor.BLACK);
        new Triangle ( 25,  0, 25, 50, NamedColor.BLACK, Direction8.EAST);
    }
}
```

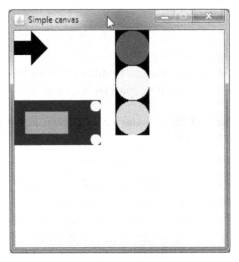

Figure 16.2
Pictures of objects entered for programming

---

5   FOWLER, Martin. *Refactoring. Improving the Design of Existing Code.* Addison-Wesley, © 2000. 430 pp.

Exercise

295.   If I understood it properly, I should define the remaining two pictures myself.

Correct, create the empty classes Car and TrafficLight from figure 16.2 and define their parameterless constructors. Locate the instances created by these constructors to the left upper corner of the canvas and define them so that the car's length would be the double of its width and the height of the traffic light would be the triplication of its width.

And one advice at the conclusion. Do not use a multishape for constructing neither the car nor the traffic light. As you know, the multishape is composed from copies of entered objects, so that you have no chance to influence them, it means you could not enter which lights of the traffic light should shine.

In case you don't dare to define the more complex classes yourself, you can firstly have a look at the sample solution, which can be found in the project 116z_First_Constructor. I recommend you to think out your own graphic shape and define its class. You can send your proposals into a conference about which I was speaking in the preface.

Review

Let's repeat what you have learned in this lesson:

☞   In case the programmer defines any constructor, the compiler would not supplement any other one.

☞   The constructor's definition contains the header and the body of the constructor.

☞   The constructor's header contains the optional keyword public followed by the class name and parentheses for values of possible parameters.

☞   The statement requesting to create a new instance is composed from the keyword **new** followed by the class name whose instance we are requesting and round brackets with values of possible parameters. The statement is completed with the semicolon.

☞   The text inside the braces has to be indented contrary to its environment.

☞   The programs should be written in such way so that they would be as transparent as possible.

Project:
The resulting form of the project to which we came at the end of the lesson after completing all exercises, is in the 116z_First_Constructor project.

17 Parameters

What you will learn in this lesson
In this lesson I will firstly explain you what is the difference between formal and actual parameters and you will define your own constructors with parameters. Then I will show you how it is possible to rename the class and what you have to watch out. And finally the test class of your new class will be defined.

Project:
In this lesson we continue in using the 116z_First_Constructor project.

Parameters and Arguments

296. **I've already coped with the constructor without parameters. In what the constructor with parameters is more complicated?**

When using the parameters you have to realize their dual character. You have to differ:

☞ when you define what the method will do with the parameter, after this parameter will be delivered to it (e.g. that the delivered whole number parameter will be used for adjusting the horizontal coordinate), and

☞ when on the contrary you are calling the already defined method and you need to adjust the initial values of its parameters (e.g. you need to tell the method that the horizontal coordinate is 7).

The beginning programmers have problems with it from time to time. Therefore when explaining the work with parameters you should differ:

☞ the **parameters** (sometimes called *formal parameters*), which are names (identifiers) declared in the method header and used in its definition, and

☞ the **arguments** (sometimes called *actual parameters*), which are values passed to the method during calling it.

You have to install (to declare) the formal parameters in the method header. In the parameter's declaration you quote its type followed by its name (identifier). Individual declarations should be separated by commas. In the method body you will mark the places, where the given parameter (better said its value) will be used, with the parameter's identifier.

Arguments (the actual parameters) are values, which you enter to the called method and which define the initial values of the corresponding parameters. Java requires entering the initial values of all parameters of the called method. These values are quoted in parentheses behind the name of the called method. The required order of presenting these values is unambiguously determined by the order of declarations of corresponding parameters.

297. Well, I admit, it's not much clear to me. Maybe it would be best to show it at an example.

Well, let's adapt our constructor from the previous lesson. We will add a possibility to adjust the coordinates of the depicted ellipse and at the same time we will adjust the calling of its constructor so that not an oval would be drawn at the canvas, but a circle of the entered diameter. The adapted definition might look as the definition in the listing 17.1.

Listing 17.1:   *The double-parametric constructor of* Empty *class entering the position of the depicted ellipse*

```
public Empty(int x, int y)
{
    new Ellipse(x, y, 50, 50);
}
```

The constructor declares two parameters. Both are of int type, i.e. both are the whole numbers. The first of them is named x, the second one y. The user can derive from their names that the first one will represent an x- (horizontal) and the second one a y- (vertical) coordinate of the instance.

The body of the method continues to contain the only one statement – the calling of the ellipse constructor. But this time you do not call the parameterless constructor, but the constructor with four parameters. We assign the values received in the x and y parameters of the defined constructor to the first two parameters of the called constructor, the number 50 will be assigned to the remaining two parameters. Thus we request to create (and depict) the ellipse, which will be located on coordinates [x, y] and will be wide and high 50 points – it means it will be a circle with a diameter of 50 points.

298. Well, and now explain me once more at this program, how it is with those formal and actual parameters.

So once more. The *formal parameters* are names which you write down into the program – in this case "*x*" and "*y*". The *actual parameters* (*arguments*) are values, which the called program "delivers" to these parameters in the moment when this constructor is called.

The parameters in the method header (in this example the x and y parameters) are always the *formal parameters*. You declare here the names and other properties of individual parameters, with the assistance of which you will mark the places in the method body, where the relevant values (the actual parameters, arguments) will be assigned (substituted) after your constructor will be called.

Contrary to it, the parameters in calling the constructor of Ellipse class are *actual parameters (arguments)*, because we say which values we pass to the called constructor.

299. This is somehow strange. The x and y parameters are once formal and next time they are actual. How is it?

The x and y identifiers are the formal parameters. After somebody will call the constructor, it gives two values – the actual parameters (arguments). In the constructor definition of the Ellipse class the identifiers x and y (= formal parameters) mark the places, where the virtual machine has to pass the relevant values of these parameters (the actual parameters, arguments) to the called constructor, when it will be called from this place.

I will try to outline it once more at a life example. Imagine car races. Every car has a crew consisting from a *driver* and a *navigator*. In case you define a constructor of RacingCar class, you define formal parameters carNubmer, carBrand, driver and navigator in it.

You start the program and the racers start to enroll. Each crew announces the number of their car, the car brand, the driver's and the navigator's names. These will be the actual parameters, i.e. values, which you will substitute to formal parameters of your constructor and it creates the relevant car based on these values.

In other words: the calling method passes the actual parameters (values) to the called method, and it will use them in the programs at places where the corresponding formal parameters (names) are quoted in the code. To train it once more, let's add a constructor, which will assign the color of the depicted ellipse besides its position as in the listing 17.2.

Listing 17.2:   *The constructor of the Empty class adjusting a position and a color of the created instance*

```
public Empty(int x, int y, NamedColor color)
{
    new Ellipse(x, y, 50, 50, color);
}
```

300.   And now I have another question. Why did you adapt the parameterless constructor at the beginning and did not define a new one? The classes can have more constructors, haven't they?

I wanted to show you that after a constructor's definition with parameters the statement for calling the parameterless constructor will disappear from the class local offer. In other words I would like to show that the compiler will add an implicit constructor really only in case that the class has no defined constructor.

Add the parameterless constructor to the code once more and try if all three will operate.

Renaming the Class

301.   It looks that we will add further and further code into the class. Should we rename it when we know that it will not be empty anymore?

It is a good idea. Let's agree that its instance will represent the lights, which will switch on and off and which will be later apart of some more complex objects. Let's rename the class to the Light.

302.   How will we do it?

Simply – we rename the class in the source code. In the more complex code we would have to adjust also all references which refer to this class and its instances. Luckily we don't have such references, so it will be easy.

303.   You told that the class source code has to be situated in a file of the same name. So we will have to re-name its source file.

BlueJ will take care about it during saving the file. And because the file is saved before each compilation, we can rely on the fact that all will be O.K. during the compilation. But you can check it yourself:

1.   Open the project folder in your favorite file manager and find there the three files connected with the Empty class, which means the files Empty.java, Empty.class and Empty.ctxt.

2.   In the source code change the class name in the class header to Light.

3.   In the editor window enter the command **Class → Save** or press CTRL+S.

4.   Check that the class in the class diagram was renamed.

5. Now have a look in the project folder and check that all "Empty" files disappeared and opposite to it the file Light.java appeared.

6. Compile the file and the remaining two "Light" files (i.e. the Light.class and Light.ctxt) will appear.

304. **I tried to compile the class, but the program stressed the header of the first constructor and wrote me that it's an invalid declaration of the method in an information panel (see figure 17.1).**

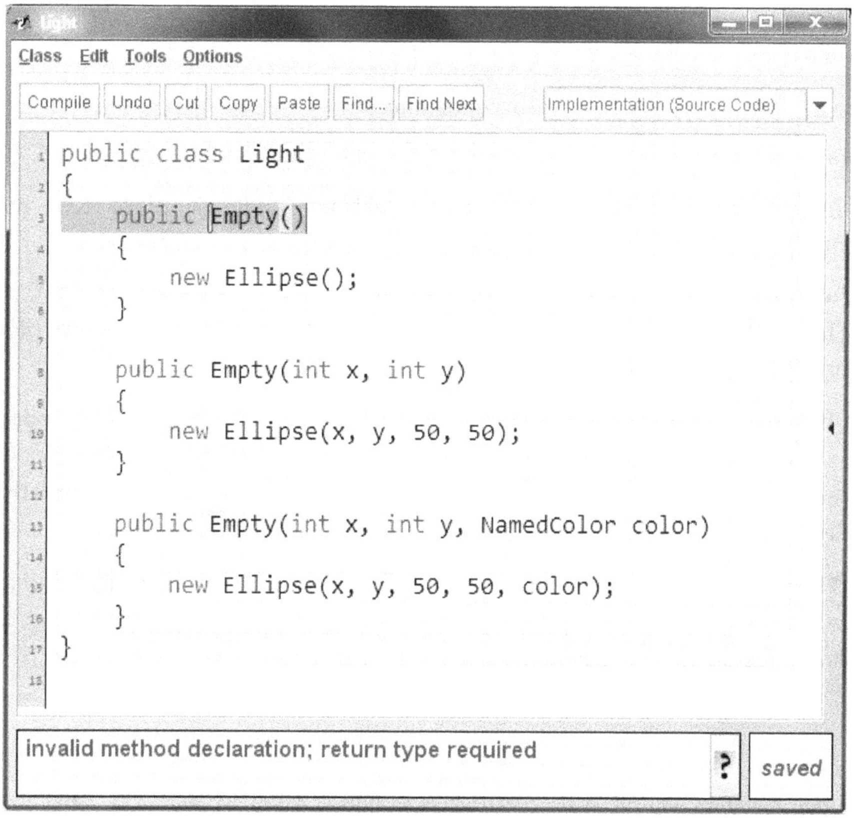

Figure 17.1
The incorrect head of a constructor

That's because you renamed the class, but you did not adapt the type of constructors' return values. The constructors, i.e. nameless methods, may return only instances of the class, in which they are defined. Therefore, the compiler considers our definition as a definition of current methods. But the methods have to quote their name between the return value type and the list of parameters. Correct the return types in constructors' headers (i.e. change Empty for Light) and everything will fit.

The Test Class of the `Light` Class

305.   You are true, now the compilation went without any comments. And at present I can test it.

You will test it many times and therefore I would recommend you to create a test class for the Light class. We will work with it during the course and the tests will make the checking of our program correctness easier. In case you forgot how they are created, you can remind it at the section *Test Class of the Class* on page 91.

306.   I've created a test class. What now?

Define a fixture for it in which you create three instances:

☞   Create the first one with the parameterless constructor and name it light0.

☞   Create the second one with the constructor Light(int x,int y), place it on the position [50, 50].and name it according to the constructor parameters' names lightXY.

☞   Create the third one with the constructor Light(int x, int y, NamedColor color), place it on coordinates [100, 100] and adjust the yellow color to it. Name its variable lightXYC (it's again according the parameters' names).

Create the test fixture interactively as we were doing until now. (Don't be afraid, soon you will learn to program it as well).

I tried to present all what we have debated here again in the accompanying animation. Go through it and train everything once more.

> *Animation 17.1: The formal and the actual parametres – OOPNZ_117_A1_FormalniASkutecneParametry*
> *The animation repeats, what was explained in course of the lesson, i.e. it shows, how the constructors are defined and how it is possible to use parameters in these definitions.*

Exercise

307.   I suppose that today we will fill in the constructors to classes which we started to define previously. Can you show it firstly at the arrow?

You are supposing correctly. In case we fill in a constructor into the Arrow class and it will place it to an entered position, its definition will be as the definition in the listing 17.3.

Listing 17.3:   *The Arrow class with a definition of the parameterless constructor and with the double-parametric one*

```
public class Arrow
{
    public Arrow()
    {
        new Rectangle( 0, 15, 25, 20, NamedColor.BLACK);
        new Triangle (25,  0, 25, 50, NamedColor.BLACK, Direction8.EAST);
    }
```

```
    public Arrow(int x, int y)
    {
        new Rectangle(x,     y+15, 25, 20, NamedColor.BLACK );
        new Triangle (x+25, y,    25, 50, NamedColor.BLACK, Direction8.EAST);
    }


    public Arrow(int x, int y, NamedColor color)
    {
        new Rectangle(x,     y+15, 25, 20, color);
        new Triangle (x+25, y,    25, 50, color, Direction8.EAST);
    }
}
```

Notice that I shifted all coordinates used for the arrow located in the left upper corner. Nothing else has changed in the definition. In the third constructor I substituted the default color by a color assigned in the parameter.

This class also is worthy of having its own test class. When naming the instance, use the convention from light testing and call the individual instances as arrow0, arrowXY and arrowXYC. Don't forget to announce that the arrows are prepared in the window at the end.

And now supplement similarly the definitions of TrafficLight and Car classes by the constructor with two parameters, in which the coordinates of the created object will be entered, and by the constructor with three parameters, in which you will enter also a color besides coordinates. However, this parameter will enter only a chassis color of the car (the cabin and the lights will remain the same), and only the color of the traffic light's box where the lights are placed. Create a test class to each class so that you could check quickly and simply each of its future improvements.

To try that you can use also the class which you defined in your classes, don't use an ellipse for the traffic light's lights, but use an instance of the Light class for them. I don't force on you in case of the car, because the constructor adjusting the lights' diameter was not defined yet. But if you want, you can supplement it and test it. (However, the car still uses ellipses for lights in the sample solution.)

After adding the test classes it starts to be a little bit overcrowded, so that you can re-arrange the class diagram, e.g. according to figure 17.2. Thus the final project with sample solutions is arranged.

Review

Let's review what you have learned in this lesson:

☞ When working with parameters you have to remember their dual character. We differ as follows:

   ☞ the **parameters** (sometimes called *formal parameters*), which are names (identifiers) declared in the head of the method used for its definition, and

   ☞ the **arguments** (sometimes called *actual parameters*), which are values given over to the method during its calling. These values are used for initializing the relevant parameters.

☞ In case we will not need to differ between the formal and the actual substance of the given parameter in further text, we will use only the term the *parameter*.

☞ All parameters have to be declared in the method header within the parentheses.

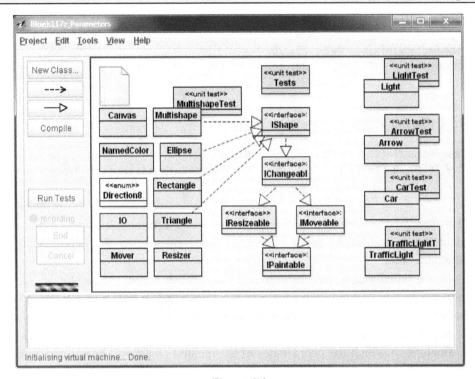

Figure 17.2
The new arrangement of the class diagram

☞ The declaration of a parameter consists of the name of its type followed by an identifier of the given parameter.

☞ Individual declarations are separated by commas.

☞ During calling the method the actual parameters have to be quoted in the same order, in which the corresponding formal parameters were declared.

☞ When renaming the class we have to rename also all its constructors.

☞ When renaming the class we do not have to take care about renaming the relevant source code in *BlueJ* environment, because it will be done by the development environment itself.

Project:
The resulting form of the project to which we came at the end of the lesson and after completing all exercises is in the 117z_Parameters *project.*

18 The Fields and the Methods

What you will learn in this lesson
In this lesson you start teaching your light. And I will show you that you need to install the fields for it. Therefore we will speak about encapsulation and implementation hiding. You will also learn how to assign a value to attributes. Then you will define the first methods. We will speak about qualification of fields and of methods and at the conclusion I will indicate one of the possible ways, how to solve the conflict of names of fields and of local variables.

Project:
In this lesson we continue in using the 117z_Parameters project.

The Light Has to Learn

308.   I have already defined several classes. I would say it's high time to show me how they can be used as well as their instances.

For the beginning I would stay at our simple class Light and what you learn with it you will examine once again with more complex classes. For the time being the lights know nothing. However, each proper object should know something. Therefore, before we start using the lights, we should teach them something first of all.

309.   What you would like to teach the light? The current light doesn't know anything.

How, it doesn't know anything! It knows to shine and to be off! Therefore, we will learn it to switch on at the request and switch off at the request.

310.   Aha – and how we will teach it?

We will define a method for them which would change its color to a color of the switched off light. Which color would you like for the switched off light?

311.   Of course black. So we will define a method which would simulate switching off the light by recoloring it to black?

Yes. But there is a little hitch – we cannot ask the ellipse representing the light to recolor.

312.   Why not? The ellipse knows to change its color, you showed it to me!

The ellipse knows to change its color, but we cannot ask it. To request it we should have to get a reference through which we would send our request. When we were creating an ellipse, we called the new operator. It allocated the memory and passed a reference to the constructor to initialize the freshly created instance. The ellipse constructor made the requested, and passed the reference to the applicant who requested for creating the instance, i.e. the light constructor, as its return value. But we were contented with creating an ellipse in its definition and we ignored the returned reference. We have to retrieve it first of all.

Introducing Fields

313. This means that we have to retrieve the light constructor, so that it would remember a reference which the ellipse constructor would return to it.

Exactly, but first of all we have to declare a field for this reference to which the light constructor will save the reference obtained from the ellipse constructor. Then the method, which is to realize switching off the light, takes out the reference from this field and requests the referred ellipse for the change of the color.

314. Well – how should I declare this field?

The fields are declared similarly as parameters of methods: firstly there is a value type quoted followed by a name of the given field. The whole declaration is completed by a semicolon.

Contrary to parameters also the *access modifier* is quoted at fields, which specifies who can work with the given field. We have already discussed it in the section *Field Accessibility* on page 71.

315. Yes, I remember – we were speaking about two of them: public and private. Is the word public, which we wrote at the beginning of the class head and its constructors, also the access modifier?

Yes. The access modifiers are used for data types (classes, interface types and enumerative types), methods as well as fields. As you surely remember, the public access modifier which we used up until now announces that the designated object can be used by anybody. When we name the class with it, we declare that anybody can send a message to the given class. When we name a constructor with it, we declare that anybody can ask the given class for creating its instance through this constructor.

But the purpose of installing the fields is different. We do not install them to offer something but in order to be able properly react to certain messages. Fields serve mostly for saving information about its object state, but objects mostly don't wish so that anybody else would see their state or even change it. This information should serve for the object's private need, so that it would be able to do what the surrounding program requires. Therefore we mark the fields with the private access modifier. Then we can access to such field only from the code defined within the given class.

Encapsulation and Implementation Hiding

316. What should I do if I'd need to change the attribute's value? For example when I'd like to switch off the light, I should tell to the ellipse in a field to change its color, shouldn't I?

No. I have already told that other program parts don't care about the fact that you depict the light as an ellipse. When somebody intends to handle the light, he has to ask directly the light, not to command the ellipse "through the backdoor". Concerning this, remember two important principles of object oriented programming:

☞ First of all it is encapsulation; this means the fact that we strive to put both data as well as the code that works with these data into one box. This box is a class. In case all fields will be private and anybody will be able to work with them only when he asks the owner for the relevant action (he calls the relevant method of the given object), the class author would be able to provide far better that only correct operations will be done with these dates.

☞ The second important principle is **the implementation hiding,** which says that nobody would take care about how I (the object) organized that I know what I know. When the environment knows nothing about the way of my work, I can change it anytime (e.g. I discover a more effective method of solving problems) without influencing the activities of objects with which I communicate. But, when I would tell them about the way of my work, they could make use of this information and I could not change the disclosed way of work, because I would impact the work of all those who took into account that I am working in an introduced way.

Both principles are very close so that certain authors unify them and as encapsulation they understand both encapsulation itself, as well as implementation hiding.

317. How these principles will appear in our program?

As I have told, we cannot ask the ellipse for anything because we did not remember the reference to it. Therefore we will install a field to which the reference for the created ellipse will be saved. Let's call it bulb and mark it as private so that we can have an access to it only within the Light class body. Its declaration looks as follows:

```
private Ellipse bulb;
```

318. Are there any rules for where the attribute's declaration should be placed?

The only one rule is that the field cannot be declared within the method. You can declare it wherever between methods. But it's a good habit to place the declarations of fields either at the beginning of the class body or on the contrary at its end.

319. And what's better?

There is no accord among the programmers. Each group has its reasons why they prefer their own solution. I prefer to place the declaration of fields at the beginning of the class body, as is stated in the recommendation of *Code Conventions for the Java Programming Language* which you can download at the address http://java.sun.com/docs/codeconv/index.html. This will be also the way of declaring the fields in all programs of this course.

The proponents of fields at the end of the program are in minority, but they also have their reasons why they prefer this arrangement. I am speaking about this possibility primarily so that you would not be surprised during reading programs of somebody else that the fields are defined at the end.

The Assignment of the Value to the Field

320. Well, so how the program will look out now?

Look at the following source code. At the beginning of the class definition there is the bulb field declared and the reference returned by the ellipse constructor is saved in this field in the constructor's definition – see the listing 18.1.

Listing 18.1:   *The Light class with the bulb field and three constructors*

```
public class Light
{
    private Ellipse bulb;

    public Light()
    {
        bulb = new Ellipse();
    }

    public Light(int x, int y)
    {
        bulb = new Ellipse(x, y);
    }

    public Light(int x, int y, NamedColor color)
    {
        bulb = new Ellipse(x, y, 50, 50, color);
    }
}
```

321. I'm not very clear about why you write that a bulb is equal to the new ellipse.

It is an assignment statement. This is what we write down in the program when we want to save certain value. Notice, how we write down that something is assigned to somewhere.

☞ The = sign (equal sign) represents the **operator of assignment**. It announces to the compiler that we will save something at certain place.

☞ To the right of the equal sign we will write an expression by evaluating of which we receive the value that is subsequently saved. In this case the expression is a request for creating an instance of an ellipse (new Ellipse) followed by the constructor's calling which prepares the given instance for using and returns a reference to it. The value that is saved is the received reference to the created instance.

☞ To the left of the equal sign we will write the name of the memory place where we will put the result– in our case the name of the bulb field.

☞ The whole statement is then completed with a semicolon.

Whenever, when the computer meets the assignment statement, it evaluates the value of the expression on the right of the equal sign and saves the result into the memory place assigned on the left of the equal sign.

322.   Can you explain me what does it mean the word operator?

It is derived from the word operation. In case you want to enter carrying out of an operation, you have to enter an **operator**, which is a denomination of what will be done, and **operands**, which are data with which the operator will work.

For the assignment operation the operator is = (the sign of equation) and the left operand is the memory into which it will be assigned (mostly a variable) and the right operand is the expression defining the value which will be assigned.

Method Definitions

323.   We have already remembered the reference to the bulb, so we can switch off.

You are true. We define the switchOff() method which asks the bulb to color in black. Look at the listing 18.2 how such method can be defined.

Listing 18.2:   *The definition of the switchOff() method in the Light class*

```
public void switchOff()
{
    bulb.setColor(NamedColor.BLACK);
}
```

Notice that the method is defined similarly as the constructor. The only one difference is that the method has to have a name.

In this lesson we will define only methods that return nothing. I remind that these methods declare the return type void.

324.   Where should I locate the method's definition? Is there any recommendation for location of methods?

For now we will agree that the instance definitions of methods will be located behind the definitions of constructors. In some of the future lessons we will speak about the locating of individual parts of the code in details.

The Qualification

325.   I would like to ask for the interior of the method in which you call another method. Should I always call the method by writing the field, dot, name of the called method and possible parameters?

Not always. But it's everything more complicated so let me start with the theory again. When we worked in an interactive mode, I did not emphasize that each message has its addressee. When we wanted to send a message to anybody, we opened his local offer, found a command corresponding to this message and entered it. The addressee of the message was then an object in whose local offer we selected the entered command.

But when writing the program in text, it's not so clear, and therefore, we have to quote explicitly the message addressee. Quoting those to whom we are sending the message, i.e. those, whose method we are calling, is named a **qualification** and it is separated by a dot from the name of the called method or used field. In case we address the instance, the result of qualification has to be a reference to an announced object, in case we address the class the qualification is the class name.

Theoretically we could address the class by a reference to its instance, but using such qualification is considered as unmoral – it is one of the programmer's sins. When reading the code it can evoke a false imagine that it is a method or a field of the given instance.

Each method which you want to call and each field whose value you want to discover or adjust you have to qualify. The only exception is methods and attributes of the owner of the given code. You can leave out the qualification and the compiler will supplement it instead of you. There are three ways of qualification used in our method:

☞ The bulb field is "the property of the code's owner", i.e. the field of the same instance whose method I have just defined and therefore I skipped its qualification.

☞ The calling of the setColor method is qualified by a reference received from the bulb field. In other words the method of the object to which the bulb field is referred is called.

☞ The BLACK field is qualified by the name of the NamedColor class.

326. You told that you skipped over the qualification of the bulb field. How it would look out if you would not skip it?

In case the owner of the given code is an instance (e.g. in the instance method) you qualify it with the keyword this. In case the code owner is a class, you qualify it with the name of this class. The statement in the previous method could be also written in the form as follows:

```
this.bulb.setColor(NamedColor.BLACK);
```

327. But now there are two dots.

Yes, because to get the reference qualifying the setColor method I needed the bulb field, which was also needed to be firstly qualified (it doesn't matter if it was done by me or by the compiler). You will meet statements during the course in which the way to qualification will be more complicated and the number of dots will be increased.

Let's leave the rules of language syntax and let's return to improving our light. Don't be afraid we are not leaving them fully. After you will supplement several definitions of classes with methods, we will discuss them again.

The Conflict of Names of a Field and of a Parameter

328. When we switched off the bulb we could switched it on, couldn't we?

We could, but we have to solve firstly the same problem as a while ago. This time we did not remember the color of the bulb on and so we cannot say to which color it should change. We have to install again a field (let's call it perhaps color), in which we remember this color.

**329.   I wanted to adjust the program myself but I did not know which color I should remember at the first two con-
structors and, at the third one, I was surprised that the field is named equally as the parameter. I am afraid
that the statement** color = color; **is not the proper one.**

You are true, it is not. There are several possible solutions. For now I advise you to rename the parameter of the constructor to a mere b. Soon I will teach you more elegant (and more used) solution, but
firstly I have to explain several other items, and that's why we will postpone it for now.

As far as remembering the ellipse color is mentioned, which you did not adjust yourself, the solution is simple: as soon as you create the ellipse, you ask it immediately and you will remember the returned color. You will reach it by inserting the following statement behind the initializing the bulb
field into the constructor:

```
color = bulb.getColor();
```

330.   I'd say it's clear now. Will you define another method?

The third time we could define the blink() method, which switches on the given light, lets it shine for
half a second and then switches it off. It will be a little demonstration of the method, which calls other
methods of the same instance.

You will be able to try that in case the instance method calls another method of the same instance,
it does not need to address anybody and it is sufficient only to quote the method calling. The compiler
provides the needed addressing instead of you.

If you possibly could not remember how to arrange so that the program would wait for half a second I would like to remind you the section *The Animation* on page 56. Due to the fact that this time it
concerns of the message sent to a class, you have to address the IO class. You will achieve it with the
following statement

```
IO.pause(500);
```

I recommend you to wait also after you switch the light off, because then it would be easier to make
several subsequent blinks. And yet another recommendation: the blink method may be more
understandable, when you write the action and the following asking for pause at the same line.

331.   I'll try to write the resulting form of the program myself. Is the program in the listing 18.3 correct?

Listing 18.3:   The Light class with switchOn(), switchOff() and blink() methods

```
public class Light
{
    private Ellipse bulb;
    private NamedColor color;


    public Light()
    {
        bulb  = new Ellipse();
        color = bulb.getColor();
    }


    public Light(int x, int y)
    {
```

```
        bulb  = new Ellipse(x, y);
        color = bulb.getColor();
    }


    public void switchOff()
    {
        bulb.setColor(NamedColor.BLACK);
    }


    public void switchOn()
    {
        bulb.setColor(color);
    }


    public void blink()
    {
        switchOn ();      IO.pause(500);
        switchOff();      IO.pause(500);
    }
}
```

Great, it's good! I see you have even lined up the statements located one below the other for better arrangement. (I know that *BlueJ* helps you, but a significant number of students do not bring such simple operation off.)

And now only the relevant test method should be completed into the test class. You can try it in a single method, which we can call e.g. blink. The fixture you created in the previous lesson leaves all lights on. Therefore, you should request one light after another to switch off and then request one light after another to blink. If you would like to have everything perfect, you can wait a half second before blinking so that you could see that all lights really switch off. Let the program wait again half a second after blinking and switch on all lights at the end.

Exercise

332.   So what you will show me today with the arrow? I suppose we will not switch it on and off.

Let's try something different: we will teach the arrow to become translucent (partially transparent), i.e. so that we could at least partially look through (suspect) the objects which are under it. In case you look to methods offered by the NamedColor class, you find the translucent() method among them, which will return a translucent version of the given color (in case the color already is translucent, it returns itself). The objects colored with a translucent color do not cover its ground but will filter the colors below. The new version of Arrow class then might look out as in the listing 18.4.

It will be a bit more complicated with the test method, because when you only recolor the arrows you cannot recognize if they really get translucent or not. I advise you to draw firstly a rectangle at the canvas (at the best a white one), which will interfere into all arrows. In case you will draw translucent arrows, you will see through them the edges of the rectangle. (It will not be evident if the rectangle

Listing 18.4:   *The Arrow class with three fields and three methods*

```
NamedColor NamedColor NamedColor public class Arrow
{
    private Rectangle  body;
    private Triangle   head;
    private NamedColor color;


    public Arrow()
    {
        color = NamedColor.BLACK;
        body  = new Rectangle( 0, 15, 25, 20, color);
        head  = new Triangle (25,  0, 25, 50, color);
    }


    public Arrow(int x, int y)
    {
        color = NamedColor.BLACK;
        body  = new Rectangle(x,    y+15, 25, 20, color);
        head  = new Triangle (x+25, y,    25, 50, color);
    }


    public Arrow(int x, int y, NamedColor c)
    {
        color = c;
        body  = new Rectangle(x,    y+15, 25, 20, c);
        head  = new Triangle (x+25, y,    25, 50, c);
    }


    public void setColor(NamedColor color)
    {
        body.setColor(color);
        head.setColor(color);
    }


    public void translucent()
    {
        body.setColor(color.translucent());
        head.setColor(color.translucent());
    }


    public void restoreColor()
    {
        setColor(color);
    }
}
```

filters through the arrows, or the arrows through the rectangle, but you will have to believe to your program – in future we will improve the test.) Then open the dialog (i.e. call the IO.inform(Object) method), in which you will ask the user to verify that the arrows really shine through and return the original color to arrows at the end.

333.   Well, probably I understood the arrows. But what should I do with the car and the traffic light?

You will not teach the car any methods today (but you can define its fields and adjust the constructors), but you will teach the traffic light new methods. You will teach using colored combinations you know from traffic lights at crossroads. Define the following methods:

☞   stop() – the red light is on,

☞   getReady() – the red and orange lights are on,

☞   go() – the green light is on,

☞   attention() – the orange light is on,

☞   allLightsOff() – all lights are off,

☞   allLightsOn() – all lights are on (it is not a real state, but it is useful for testing),

☞   cycle(int stop, int getReady, int go, int attention, int lightsOff) – gradually to switch on separate combinations and let them shine as much milliseconds as the value of the relevant parameter is,

☞   cycle() – is a test equivalent to the previous method in which the traffic light remains in each state just half a second, i.e. 500 milliseconds.

The test method will be simple – you will call the test cycle for each created traffic light.

334.   I understand the first methods, simply some lights switch on and the others off. But how did you mean it with the cycle? How can I leave the light shine for a while?

Did you forget that the IO class knows to pause the program for a while? Let's ask it to wait for a certain time and then switch on another combination. The resulting version of both cycles can be as in the listing 18.5.

Listing 18.5:   *Two version of the cycle method for instances of the TrafficLight class*

```
public void cycle(int stop, int getReady, int go, int attention, int lightsOff)
{
    stop();        IO.pause(stop);
    getReady();    IO.pause(getReady);
    go();          IO.pause(go);
    attention();   IO.pause(attention);
    allLightsOff(); IO.pause(lightsOff);
}


public void cycle()
{
    cycle(500, 500, 500, 500, 0);
}
```

In the first version of the method I wrote two statements at each line. Writing more statements at one line is generally not recommended, except the program would become more transparent, as in this case.

335.   Why the last parameter does not have the same name as the corresponding method, i.e. switchOff?

Perhaps I should tell: "Because I did not think it up better." Take it as the previous method names are not names of commands for the traffic light, but more names of commands for cars, controlled by the traffic light. But for the last method I did not think up any corresponding name. The traffic light occurs in this state not only when it's switched off, but also half of the time when the amber light is blinking. So at the end I solved it as you can see here.

Review

Let's review what you have learned in this lesson:

- ☞ Each proper object should have certain abilities. We can teach the object new skills by defining a method which realizes the object's reaction to a relevant message.

- ☞ In case the object should cooperate with some other objects, it has to have a reference to them at its disposal.

- ☞ Objects remember the necessary information in their fields.

- ☞ The fields are declared similarly as parameters of methods. Contrary to parameters we do not declare them as outside methods and mark them as access modifiers.

- ☞ The access modifiers specify who can work with the marked class, method or field.

- ☞ As far as fields are concerned, mostly we don't want to announce that we are using them, and therefore we mark them with the private access modifier.

- ☞ We can approach to entities marked with the access modifier private only from the code inside the class body.

- ☞ Encapsulation means saving the data and the code which works with these dates to a common box – a class or an instance.

- ☞ Hiding the implementation means a highest concealing of how the given function of an object is programmed.

- ☞ Encapsulation of data and of a code belongs together with implementation hiding to the most important principles of object oriented programming.

- ☞ Certain authors unify the terms encapsulation and implementation hiding and they understand this term as both the encapsulation itself, as well as the implementation hiding.

- ☞ The fields are defined according to a convention at the beginning of the class body before definitions of constructors.

- ☞ Marking of to whom I am sending the given message, i.e. whose method I am calling, is named a qualification.

☞ The qualification is separated from the name of the qualified method or the field by a dot.

☞ In case we address an instance, the result of the qualification has to be a reference to an addressed object, in case we address a class, we qualify with the class name.

☞ Theoretically, we could address the class by a reference to its instance, but using such qualification is considered as inappropriate, because the program is non-transparent.

☞ We have to qualify each method which we want to call as well as each field whose value we would like to recognize or adjust. The only one exception are methods and fields of the owner of the given code, whose qualification is completed by the compiler.

☞ In case we want to qualify the owner, we should use the keyword this for an instance, for the class we use its name.

☞ There is an operator and operands in each operation.

  ☞ The operator is an identifier or a character sequence saying what will be done.

  ☞ The operands are data with which the operation is carried out.

☞ The assignment statement is used for remembering the value.

  ☞ The sign of equation = is used as an assignment operator.

  ☞ We write the expression whose value we want to save to the right of the equal sign.

  ☞ We specify a place in the memory where the value would be saved to the left of the equal sign.

  ☞ We complete the whole statement with a semicolon.

Project:
The resulting form of the project to which we came at the end of the lesson and after completing all exercises, is in the 118z_FieldsAndMethods *project.*

19 Implementation of an `interface`

What you will learn in this lesson
In this lesson you will see at an implementation example how the interconnection of class diagram and the source code operates in BlueJ. *Then you will be explained how to define the methods required by the implemented* `interface` *and you will become acquainted with the* `@Override` *annotation. Finally you will see how the interior of the test class look out.*

Project:
In this lesson we come back to the `114z_CanvasManager` *project.*

336.   So which improvement you prepared for me today?

Today I would exploit that you have already learnt defining methods with parameters, and I would return to the project in which the shapes at the canvas do not mutually wipe off, i.e. to the project with a canvas manager. At this occasion we have to change a little bit the classes and for the first time you will see the interior of the test class.

Interconnecting the Source Code with the Class Diagram

337.   Wonderful, go on. I've already downloaded the project and imported the `Light` **and** `LightTest` **classes in it.**

You made it very well. In addition remove the classes `House`, `Face` and `Robot`; we will not use them anymore.

If you remember, in this project only instances of classes implementing the `IPaintable` interface can appear at the canvas. In case we wish the instances of these classes would be drawn, these classes have to implement this `interface`.

When I presented interface types I showed you how the `interface` implementation can be declared in *BlueJ* by only drawing the implementation arrow. These actions immediately appear also in the source code. You can test it right now. Open the source code of `Light` class in the editor so that the editor's window did not hide the project's window and you could see the class header in the editor's window. Then draw the implementation arrow in the class diagram from the `Light` class to `IPaintable` interface.

338.   I see. After drawing the arrow the text `implements IPaintable` **appeared in the header behind the class name. This is what you want to show me?**

Yes, *BlueJ* keeps the link between the class diagram and the source code permanently up-dated. Let's try a reverse procedure. However, copy the `implements IPaintable` declaration into the clipboard before that, so that you should not have later to write it in hand (copy it together with the space behind the class name). Then wipe off the implementation arrow in the class diagram. The declaration immediately disappears from the class head.

339. It really operates! But why I copied the text to a box?

Because I wanted to show you that it operates also in reverse. Move to the editor and put the declaration from the box to the class header. This change will not appear yet in class diagram, because *BlueJ* knows that until you edit the file, you will be concentrated to a text. But save the edited file (i.e. enter the command **Class** → **Save** or press CTRL+S) and then click at the project window (the second possibility is to compile the class and you don't need to click anywhere). Promptly an arrow appears in the class diagram.

Return once more to the editor and wipe off the declaration. Now it is sufficient only to save the file (i.e. you don't need to click anywhere nor compile the file) and the arrow in the class diagram disappears.

340. It operates, as you are saying. And I have one more question: why I saved the declaration to a box if it was sufficient to enter a command Back and the editor would supplement it instead of me?

Because I thought you might be overpowered by an impression that the command **Undo** refers to class diagram and therefore I wanted so that you would really insert the requested letters into the code. Of course, the commands **Undo** and **Redo** in the **Edit** menu can be used as well.

And I will tell you a specialty. Until now we only saved the modified source code. However, before compilation of the class, the class automatically will firstly be saved and immediately also the class diagram is up-dated.

The Abstract Methods and Classes

341. I wanted to compile the class and the compiler announced an abstract mistake. What is it?

I see. It wrote as follows:

```
Light is not abstract and does not override abstract method paint(Painter) in IPaintable
```

I will explain it a little bit broader. As I told you in the chapter *The Interface* on page 77, the interface has no implementation. Methods which it declares are therefore not the concrete methods, but only declarations about how the method should look out if anybody would implement it. Thus we say that the methods which the interface declares are only abstract (what would be if…).

We told that by declaring the implementation of some interface the class pledges to implement all methods declared in it. We could say that all methods declared by the implemented interface become the part of the interface of the implementing class. The class which implements certain interface has either to implement all declared methods, or it has to designate itself as abstract, not fully valuable class which is not able to fulfill all what it promises in its interface.

However, you did not do any of these possibilities, i.e. you neither implemented the method declared by IPaintable interface; nor you designated the class as abstract. Therefore the compiler had objections towards your code.

342. How did you mean it that the abstract class is not fully valuable?

The abstract class has not implemented all methods, which are quoted in its *interface* (this time I mean really the general *interface* of the given class). Therefore you cannot create its instances because they would not be able to react to certain messages which are part of their interface and which could be sent to them by surrounding objects. We could say that the abstract class is a hybrid between a classic class and the "interface". The abstract class can have certain methods implemented as a classic class and at the same time some methods can be only declared (and therefore abstract) as in interface. A number of consequences ensue from it and that's the reason why I postpone the explanation of abstract classes to the next book.

For the time being you should remember that the above quoted statement means that your class does not implement all methods declared by interface which is implemented by a given class. The compiler strives to help you in finding the mistake by saying which method is not implemented by the class and which interface declares the given method.

Implementation of a Method Declared by an Implemented Interface

343. By other words I should implement the paint(Painter) method. But how?

I personally do it by dividing the implementation into two periods: in the first period I copy the head declaration from the source code of an implemented interface into my code and in the second period I supplement the body of a given method. Open the IPaintable interface in an editor and switch the editor to depicting the implementation, i.e. to depicting the source code. You should receive a window as in the figure 19.1.

344. Phew – it's complicated. What's in?

Don't be afraid, majority of texts are comments – we will speak about them next time. When you skip all blue and green you will receive the definition in the listing 19.1.

Listing 19.1:   *The definition of IPaintable interface after removing comments*

```
public interface IPaintable
{
    public void paint(Painter painter);
}
```

And it does not look so complicated, does it?

345. Well, this is far simpler. Please, explain me what is what.

As you see the interface header (the line 22 in the figure 19.1) looks similarly as the class header, only instead of the class keyword there is the interface keyword.

Only single method is declared in the interface body. Notice that its header looks identically as the method header which we defined in the previous lesson. The only one difference is that the method does not have a body and instead of it there is only a semicolon in the code.

Theoretically there might be another two changes in the head:

☞ The public keyword could be missing because all methods declared in an interface are automatically public and will be public even when we would not quote the public access modifier. I quote it in my source codes of the interface so that copying of headers to the source code of implementing classes – where this keyword must be – would be simpler.

```
4    /****************************************************************
5     * Interface {@code IPaintable} must be implemented by all classes,
6     * which want their instances be accepted as manageable
7     * by an instance of the class {@link CanvasManager}.
8     * It is the only way, how to reach the painting the instance
9     * on display.
10    * <p>
11    * This interface requires the instances have a method {@link #paint(Painter)}
12    * that paint the instance by force of the obtained painter.
13    * <p>
14    * In addition the implementing class promises,
15    * that their instances will immediately inform canvas
16    * about any change of their appearance by calling the method
17    * {@link CanvasManager#redraw()}.
18    *
19    * @author Rudolf PECINOVSKÝ
20    * @version 2.00.4006 — 2013-06-13
21    */
22   public interface IPaintable
23   {
24   //== CONSTANTS ===========================================================
25   //== DECLARED METHODS ====================================================
26
27       /****************************************************************
28        * Paints the instance by force the specified painter.
29        *
30        * @param painter Painter drawing the instance
31        */
32   //       @Override
33       public void paint(Painter painter);
34
35
36   //== INHERITED METHODS ===================================================
37   //== EMBEDDED DATA TYPES =================================================
38   }
```

Figure 19.1
The source code of IPaintable *interface*

☞   I told you that methods declared in interface types are only abstract (they don't have any body – there is only a semicolon in the source code instead of it). We could stress this fact by adding the abstract modifier at the beginning of the head. Its quoting is optional because the declared methods must be abstract, so authors of the language forgive quoting this modifier.

     I don't quote this modifier in declarations, because I would have wipe it off after copying the header to the source code of an implementing class. If I don't quote it, I simplify the copying.

346.   Well, you say that I should copy the method header into the source code of the Light **class.**

Yes, copy it together with the documentation comment – those are the five lines with the blue text above the method definition. I usually transport or copy the methods (or their headers) together with the previous line as well as the next one so that I would have two empty lines among them. Thus for me the code is significantly better arranged.

347.   I've copied it and I return to the original question: "How should I implement the method?"

Simply: Wipe off the final semicolon, fill in the braces surrounding the method's body and insert a statement in which you request the bulb to paint itself by the given painter. By painting the bulb logically the whole light is painted. Therefore the definition of the method will be quite simple (I quote it with the documentation comment) – see the listing 19.2.

Listing 19.2:   *The definition of the paint(Painter) method in the* Light *class*

```
/******************************************************************************
 * Paints the instance by force of the specified painter.
 *
 * @param painter Painter drawing the instance
 */
//@Override
public void paint(Painter painter);
```

The @Override **Annotation**

348.   Under the blue text there was a green line with a text @Override. **Why did you wipe off those two leading slashes?**

The @Override is one of the so called **annotations** and it announces to a compiler that the following method is declared also in a supertype – in this case in the IPaintable interface. The compiler can thus check if I made a typing error by defining another method instead of the one which I wanted to define.

Theoretically this annotation is not compulsory, but I welcome each cue provided to the compiler so that it could check already during compilation if I made a mistake. The error which occurs during the run-time is far more difficult to be found and if it becomes evident to a client my reputation is needlessly spoiled. Thus, the moment I spent by adding the @Override annotation is fully returned.

349.   What are those annotations like?

Annotations are special interface types, which mostly do not relate directly with the program's activity but can serve as e.g. auxiliary information for the compiler. You will use them in the source code by writing the @ character in front of their identifier. I will not tell you more because working with them belongs to more advanced programming skills. This is the only one annotation which we will use in our programs. In this introductory course we will use yet several annotations in the test classes, nothing more.

350.   I will ask you once more: "Why did you wipe off those two slashes?"

As long as those two strokes were there, the compiler understood the given line as a comment, i.e. as a text which should be ignored (as I have already told, comments will be explained in the next lesson). It should be in an `interface` because it does not inherit this method, but declares it. The annotation can be only before the header of an inherited method.

The slashes are in the interface, because the annotation is there prepared just for copying to classes which will decide to implement the given `interface` and the presence of this annotation is useful for them. Then it is sufficient to wipe off those two slashes and the comment changes to a program – a reference to an annotation in this case.

The `Interface` **and the Class File**

351.   How the `interface` is compiled? When it has no implementation, it has probably no class file. Do I understand it well, that the `interface` definition is only information for the compiler?

No, it's not true. The interface types are compiled to class files equally as classes. The information saved in them tells to the virtual machine to what the class implementing the given `interface` is pledging.

Test Class

352.   I will return to this project. The compilation succeeded, and I see it was really simple. If I remember it well we have to adjust the fixture so that the created lights could be enrolled at the canvas manager.

You remember it well. However, this time we will not modify the test fixture in the interactive mode, but I will show you its source code and you will adjust it directly. Open the source code of the `LightTest` class in an editor – it should correspond to the listing 19.3. Don't pay attention to introductory lines with stars at the left side; it is a comment which will be explained in the next lesson.

Listing 19.3:   *The definition of the `LightTest` class*

```
/******************************************************************************
 * Testing class {@code LightTest} serves as a complex way to test
 * the class {@link Light}.
 *
 * @author Rudolf PECINOVSKÝ
 * @version 2.00.4006 – 2013-06-13
 */
public class LightTest
{
    private CanvasManager CM;
    private Light light0;
    private Light lightXY;
    private Light lightXYC;


    //== PREPARATION AND CLEANING THE FIXTURE ====================================

    /******************************************************************************
```

```
 * Prepares the tested instances and performs the actions,
 * which should be performed before each test.
 */
@Before
public void setUp()
{
    light0    = new Light();
    lightXY   = new Light(50,  50);
    lightXYC  = new Light(100, 100, NamedColor.RED);

    CM = CanvasManager.getInstance();
    CM.add(light0, lightXY, lightXYC);

    IO.inform("Lights prepared");
}


/****************************************************************************
 * Cleans up after the ran test and performs the actions,
 * which should be performed after each test.
 */
@After
public void tearDown()
{
}


//== THE TESTS =================================================================
//
//      /****************************************************************************
//       *
//       */
//      @Test
//      public void testXXX()
//      {
//      }
//

@Test
public void testBlink()
{
    light0    .switchOff();
    lightXY   .switchOff();
    lightXYC  .switchOff();
    IO.pause(500);
    light0    .blink();
    lightXY   .blink();
    lightXYC  .blink();
    IO.pause(500);
    light0    .switchOn();
    lightXY   .switchOn();
    lightXYC  .switchOn();
}
}
```

353.   What do mean those lines of equal signs?

All lines starting with double slash // are comments too (we talked about them in connection with annotation @Override). Those with equal signs are navigation comments which indicate where you should insert the separate parts of the program. Its location is not obligatory, it is only a recommendation but when you get used to placing individual parts of the program in a certain way, you will be better oriented in your programs. We will debate it in details in the next lesson. This time you should only remember that all lines starting with two slashes should be ignored.

354.   Well, I will pay no attention to them. But tell me, what I should pay attention to.

I am sorry that this class contains so many unknown things. But when I was considering if I should include the explanation today or after all necessary will be completed, I decided as more useful to show you how the test class looks like inside, because then you will have better idea how to utilize it.

The test classes use certain expressions in their work which are considered as a kind of programming witchcraft by a lot of programmers. So reconcile that certain features will be not explained in details, but I will only tell you what you need to know for successful creating of tests. The source code of test classes created by the *BlueJ* environment consists of the following parts:

☞ At the beginning of the class body there are private fields declared – the variables, to which the references to instances creating the fixture are saved. Those are the light0, lightXY and lightXYC fields in this example.

☞ The setUp() method takes care about creating the fixture. Whenever you ask *BlueJ* to create a fixture based on the existing activity, *BlueJ* wipes off the body of this method and substitutes it by a program that realize what you did since the last restart of the virtual machine. As I have said already, this method starts to run before starting the test method.

The method name is not important – it is given by convention. Important is the annotation @Before that tells to the test library, that this is the method creating the fixture.

☞ The method tearDown() takes care about cleaning after the test. We did not use it up to now, so that its body is empty. Soon we will add the body also to this method.

Also this method name is given by convention. Important is the annotation @After that tells to the test library, that this is the method responsible for cleaning up after the test.

☞ The tearDown() method is followed by particular test methods. In case you yourself would decide to define any of them you, you have to keep the following rules:

    ☞ The method should be annotated by the @Test annotation.

    ☞ The method has to be public.

    ☞ The method must return nothing, i.e. the return type void must be defined.

    ☞ The method must have no parameters.

    ☞ The method name is not important, but according to conventions it should start with the word test. When you request *BlueJ* to create a test method it will ask you for the test name. After the user demonstrates the test *BlueJ* creates a test method which fulfills all the above stated requirements.

355.   I understand the structure of the test class. Show me, how I should adjust it.

As you properly recall, we have to enroll the created instances at the canvas manager. We solved it in the interactive mode by sending the message paint() to each created instance and this message enrolled the given instance. The Light class does not have such method. We could define it, but it will be easier when we enroll the instance directly at the canvas manager.

As you surely remember the instances are enrolled at the canvas manager by sending the add(IPaintable...) message. But to be able to send it a message, we need to have a reference to it. For the time being we do not have it. Therefore we add the following declaration at the beginning of the body of the LightTest class:

```
private CanvasManager CM;
```

Then we adjust the setUp() method into the form in the listing 19.4 (I skip over the introductory annotation as well as documentation comments).

Listing 19.4:   *The modified version of the setUp() method in the LightTest class*

```
@Before
    protected void setUp()
    {
        light0    = new Light();
        lightXY   = new Light(50,  50);
        lightXYC  = new Light(100, 100, NamedColor.RED);
        CM = CanvasManager.getInstance();
        CM.add(light0, lightXY, lightXYC);
        IO.inform("Lights prepared");
    }
```

Exercise

356.   I would say that it was enough today and it would be good to repeat it at more complicated classes. I suppose that my task today would be to convert also the Arrow, Car and TrafficLight classes together with their test classes into the new project.

You suppose it well. I would say that I don't have to give you a clue today. I would like to recommend you addressing gradually all parts of the given instance in the paint(painter) message, and those that should be drawn beneath have to be addressed before those that should be drawn atop. This method for an arrow would look as in the listing 19.5.

Listing 19.5:   *The definition of the paint(Painter) method for an arrow*

```
public void paint(Painter painter)
{
    body.paint(painter);
    head.paint(painter);
}
```

Besides that I would recommend you – do not ask for association of the imported test classes with their corresponding tested classes because they take too much place in the diagram and it has to be increased. I prefer to see also other things at the screen besides the class diagram – e.g. I consider as useful to see the source code together with the class diagram and not to cover one by the other.

Despite you will not associate the tested classes with the test classes, the diagram will be full and you have to re-arrange it – e.g. according to the figure 19.2.

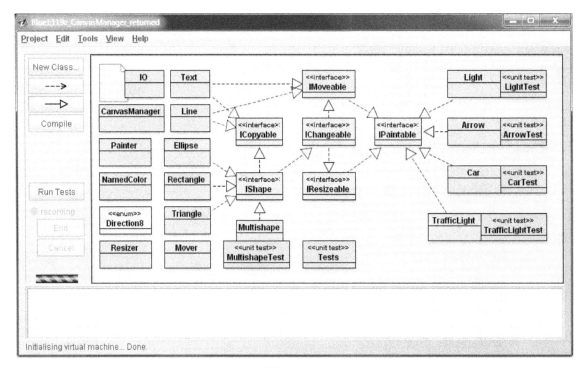

Figure 19.2
The project with newly arranged class diagram

357. I rearranged the diagram and I started to work with the source codes. Hopefully I grasped the definition of paint(Painter) **method. I think that I properly adjusted the** setUp() **method in the test class. But when I start the test, no rectangle appears and the arrows only get matt for a while.**

Because you did not enroll the auxiliary rectangle at the canvas manager. But I have to help you with it, because you cannot enroll it as you did it until now. The canvas manager leaves to redraw the object in the order in which they enrolled, and thus the lastly enrolled objects are on the top. Fortunately, it defines also such methods with the assistance of which you can include the newly added object among objects that enrolled before it. Use the method as follows:

```
boolean addBehind(IPaintable presentShape, IPaintable addedShape)
```

you will pass the object to it which is already enrolled in the first parameter and the newly included object in the second parameter. The method then locates the newly added object closely under the object quoted in the first parameter.

As long as you named the variable that keeps the reference to a canvas manager also as CM and if you enrolled the arrow0 object at the manager as the first one, then the test method should start with the statement:

```
Rectangle ground = new Rectangle(25, 25, 100, 100, NamedColor.WHITE);
CM.addBehind(arrow0, ground);
```

The rest of the test can be left as it is.

Review

Let's review, what you have learned in this lesson:

☞ *BlueJ* synchronizes the source code with the class diagram.

☞ When drawing or wiping off the arrow in the class diagram the change is immediately projected into the source code.

☞ By including the change into the source code this change will appear in the class diagram after saving the given source file and subsequent click into the class diagram, resp. after an attempt to compile the given class.

☞ In case the class does not implement all methods declared by an implemented interface, the compiler considers it as an abstract one.

☞ The abstract class is not fully valuable. All its methods need not to be implemented, and therefore it cannot have any instance. Therefore we will not use the abstract classes in this course.

☞ One of the simple ways how to define a method implementing the "parent version" declared in the implemented interface is to copy the declaration from this interface, and replace the closing semicolon with the method's body.

☞ The annotation is a special kind of an interface which mostly does not relate to the program's operating itself. One of its possible functions is to provide additional information to the compiler or to some library in use.

☞ We refer to annotations in the source code by writing the @ character in front of the name of the given interface.

☞ The test class consists of several parts:

☞ the head,

☞ the declaration of private fields creating a fixture,

☞ the method annotated by the @Before annotation, which creates the test fixture before each test and which name is setUp() according to conventions,

☞ the method annotated by the @After annotation, which cleans up in a necessary way after each test and which name is tearDown() according to conventions,

☞ the test methods which have to be public, parameterless, returning void and annotated by the annotation @Test. According to convention their names should start with the word test,

☞ possible further fields and methods which you need for the test definition.

☞ In case of more complicated shapes composed of several parts we define their re-drawing by graduate re-drawing of separate parts one by another.

☞ In case we need to insert a new part to another place then atop the heap of depicted shapes, we can use the addUnder(IPaintable, IPaintable) method sent to the canvas manager.

☞   The @Override annotation announces to the compiler that you define your own version of certain
      inherited method, so that the compiler could check if you are not defining quite new method
      only due to a typing error.

Project:
The resulting form of the project to which we came at the end of the lesson and after completing all exer-
cises is in the 119z_CanvasManager_returned project.

20 Comments

What you will learn in this lesson
This lesson is devoted to comments, their definition and usage. Firstly you will see how to comment a part of the code, then you will be presented individual kinds of comments and then you will see how the templates of a standard class look like. And finally you will see how the javadoc tags are used including their usage at the example of our class.

Project:
In this lesson we continue in using the 119z_CanvasManager_returned *project.*

Commenting Parts of a Code

358. You mentioned comments in the last lesson and you told that we would speak about them the next time. And the next time is just now.

You are true, let's go on. As I already indicated, the comments are those parts of the source code which serve only for the programmer's information and the compiler ignores them. Originally they were used only for making notes that would enable better orientation in a program or remembering the reason, why the particular code is defined in such way.

Later on, the programmers realized that with the help of the comments they can cover that part of the program which is not needed at the moment, but on the other hand, they don't want to get rid of it definitely, as it might be useful in future. *Commenting* of the program's part is an elegant way how to arrange that the recorded statements would be remained in a program, but the compiler would ignore them and you could "revive" them only at the time when you would need them.

359. For this, as you say, *"commenting the program's part"* the ordinary comments are used or the special ones?

.There are no special comments for commenting the part of the code. You can use for it any kind which Java defines, despite the line comment that is used for commenting the @Override annotation in interface types is the most available for it and therefore the development tools offer such usage

360. How do they offer it?

Majority of development environments have a command for commenting a group of neighboring lines. This is offered also by *BlueJ*.

361. Aha! It looks interesting – show it!

Select a block which would reach to all the lines you would like to comment (the border lines need not to be chosen at the whole, it is sufficient when the selected block reach into them only). Then press the key **F8** or enter the command **Edit → Comment**. *BlueJ* spreads the block to whole lines and comments all lines in this extended block, i.e. it inserts two slashes (and a space, despite it's not necessary) at their beginning.

In case you would activate this code later on, you select the block again, so that it would reach all activated lines and then you press the key **F7** or you enter the command **Edit → Uncomment**. *BlueJ* again spreads the block so that it would contain whole lines, and uncomments the lines in a block, i.e. it deletes the initiating two slashes (and the possible space).

Comments in Java

362.   It operates perfectly. You indicated that Java has more kinds of comments.

Java installs three kinds of comments:

☞   **The line comment** begins with the character twins // and finishes at the end of the line. The line comments are used mostly when we would like to supplement some statement with a note (or we want to make commenting of a part of the code similarly as we did a while ago).

☞   **The Block comment** starts with the character pair /* and finishes by the inverse pair */ – these pairs serve as the comment brackets. Everything what the compiler finds between them is ignored and thus it is not included into the realizing program for the virtual machine. Thus the block comment can be spread through several lines.

☞   The special case of block comments are **documentation comments**, which start with the triplet of characters /**. These comments are used for automatically created documentation. A program **javadoc.exe**, which knows to go through marked files and which creates a proper documentation from documentation comments found in these files, can be found among programs contained in a JDK set. Therefore the documentation comments are also known informally as *"doc comments"* or *"javadoc comments"*.

363.   Where in the program I can write a comment?

Anywhere, where you can write a space, you can write any succession of whitespaces and/or comments. We could have a look at it also in reverse: the only one place where you cannot insert any comment (or whitespace) is in the middle of an identifier.

364.   When you showed me the source code of the IPaintable interface I noticed that some comments are green and the others are blue. Does it have any meaning?

The colored differentiation of comments is a part of syntax highlighting about which we spoke in the section *The Source Code of the Empty Class* on page 137. *BlueJ* differentiates documentation comments from others. In our configuration the documentation comments are blue, other comments are green.

365.   Why so much kinds of comments are installed? One would be sufficient according to my opinion.

In the original C language, which is a "grandfather" of Java, there was really only one comment at the beginning – the block comment. However, the programmers were bothered to write a closing comment bracket even behind short comments which were at only one line. The C++ language author, who came out of C language, added a line comment which does not need any closing bracket, because its closing bracket is the end of the line.

Authors of Java then came with a brilliant idea how to increase the probability that the program is properly documented and introduced into their language the special documentation comments.

Documentation Comments

366.   Why they are so brilliant?

There are two brilliant ideas at documentation comments: the first one that they are in a close neighboring of the documented code so that the programmer or the documentarist can clarify how the described program is made out and what is necessary to know about it.

The second brilliant idea was to supplement the development environment with a tool which would create a professional documentation from program's comments. Moreover, this program can overtake a lot of published data directly from the code and provide correctness of the relevant part of documentation. Then there is no danger that incorrectly written class names, their methods nor types of their parameters could appear in the documentation.

367.   I think the importance of the documentation is not so high. Majority of programmers which I know insist on that the most important thing is to write a good code and that writing of documentation only detains.

A number of programmers really have this idea. However they don't realize that during writing the programming documentation they can e.g. realize what the developed code should precisely do and possibly how it should do it. It is a commonplace that the programmer proposes certain method and then he works on another part of the code; subsequently when he should use this method, he doesn't realize what precisely is the contract (we spoke about the contract in the section *Signature versus Contract* on page 112), for which the method was proposed and he starts to use the method in a little bit different way. Immediately he spends far more time by discovering and rectifying the mistake than writing the relevant documentation comment.

And there is one more reason. As I have indicated several times the programmer's experience shows that any program which is a bit worthy will not be kept forever in the form in which it was developed. Our classes are relatively small but they increase and soon we might lose orientation, especially when we would return to them after a longer time. And how we might grope in case these classes would become really large.

A good programmer believes that his programs are as good as they are worthy for further developing. At the same time he feels that many of those future modifications will be done by somebody else because he will be engaged in more ambitious tasks. And even when he himself would do amendments in the program, after half a year of working on another program, his own program becomes strange for him. Therefore he writes his programs so that his colleagues could modify them because otherwise his programs would be included into programs that are not modifiable. Thus he writes readable and well commented programs (we spoke about that already and I will remind it to you repeatedly).

Everything is developing and the assignment could be changed, new technologies may come or new reasons for program innovation can appear. Then it will be necessary to decide which program should be taken as the base of the new product. In prevailing majority of cases such programs are preferred which are possibly not so perfect in their first version, but are easily understandable and thus they are modifiable to new conditions.

I have already mentioned the motto of Martin Fowler who used to tell: *Any fool can write code that a computer can understand. Good programmers write code that humans can understand.* Documentation comments are one of the ways how to provide so that other people would understand to your program.

Documentation of the Classes and the Whole Project

368.   I am afraid that I can expect producing and using of such documentation after I will work at some larger projects and that I cannot do without them now during my first steps.

The reverse is true. We use the programmer's documentation since the very beginning. I told you that the comments in *BlueJ* dialogs are the documentation comments. Moreover, I showed you in the section *Interface vs. Implementation* on page 78 how you can depict the class documentation in an editor. And further, I showed you in the section *Documentation of the Project* on page 116 how you can request generating of the full project's documentation and how you can look at it in your favorite browser. This created documentation looks identically as the documentation which you can download from JDK. The only one difference insists in the fact that there are far more classes and interface types described in JDK (the JDK version 7 describes 4024 of them).

With the other words: we utilize the advantages of the documentation already now and I will force you to make the detailed documentation of your programs since the very beginning. In case you will not get used to it you will hardly learn it later.

369.   Well, show me how I can prepare a professional documentation with my contemporary knowledge. Because there was a number of various tables, tinged titles and other things that I don't know to create in the documentation you showed me.

Practically all formatting which you have seen was provided by the javadoc program which created the given documentation. I really only delivered just the documentation comments of separate classes, interface types, fields and methods, in which I briefly descried the contract of each documented entity. All my formatting consisted in using few tags of HTML language and of the javadoc program. You will see there is nothing difficult.

370.   You twist my arm. So show me how simply such documentation can be made out.

I will show it to you at an example of the Light class. First of all you have to rename it, e.g. to LightX so that we could define it once more, this time completed by a documentation comment. Don't rename constructors, rename really only the class and ask the editor to save it. We will not bother about mistakes because we will not compile it – it will be only a source of texts for our new class. Therefore leave the editor's window open.

The Standard Class Template

371.   I renamed it, what else?

Press the button **New Class** and enter in subsequently opened dialog that it will have the name Light (we can afford it because we renamed the original light; in case we did not do it, *BlueJ* would now revolt). Leave the switch in the state **Standard Class** and confirm your entering.

BlueJ will create a new class according to the pattern of the standard class and locates it somewhere to the class diagram. Leave it where it is (we will move it after we will remove its predecessor, i.e. the current LightX class), only draw the implementation arrow to IPaintable interface. First of all we have to move the code into the new class from the original one. Open the new class in the editor (its source code should correspond with the listing 20.1) and arrange both editors' windows at the area so that you could easily move the text among them.

Listing 20.1:   *The Light class created with the standard class template*

```
/*****************************************************************************
 * Instances of class {@code Light} represent ...
 *
 * @author   author name
 * @version 0.00.0000 - 20yy-mm-dd
 */
public class Light
{
    //== CONSTANT CLASS ATTRIBUTES ===========================================
    //== VARIABLE CLASS ATTRIBUTES ===========================================
    //== STATIC INITIALIZER (CLASS CONSTRUCTOR) ==============================
    //== CONSTANT INSTANCE ATTRIBUTES ========================================
    //== VARIABLE INSTANCE ATTRIBUTES ========================================
    //== CLASS GETTERS AND SETTERS ===========================================
    //== OTHER NON-PRIVATE CLASS METHODS =====================================


    //########################################################################
    //== CONSTUCTORS AND FACTORY METHODS =====================================


    /*****************************************************************************
     */
    public Light()
    {
    }




    //== ABSTRACT METHODS ====================================================
    //== INSTANCE GETTERS AND SETTERS ========================================
    //== OTHER NON-PRIVATE INSTANCE METHODS ==================================
    //== PRIVATE AND AUXILIARY CLASS METHODS =================================
    //== PRIVATE AND AUXILIARY INSTANCE METHODS ==============================
    //== EMBEDDED TYPES AND INNER CLASSES ====================================
    //== TESTING CLASSES AND METHODS =========================================
    //
    //      /*****************************************************************
    //       */
    //      public static void test()
    //      {
    //          Light instance = new Light();
    //      }
    //      /** @param args Command line arguments - not used. */
    //      public static void main(String[] args) {  test();  }
}
```

372.   Before I start moving anything you should explain me first of all why the standard class looks as it looks.

You are true, I should do it. The source code of the class you create as a standard one begins with the documentation comment of a class. There is a pre-defined empty parameterless constructor in the class body, and a number of line comments which separate individual sections of the source code before and behind it. Through these comments I try to navigate you to arrange all source codes in the same way. When you get accustomed to such arrangement, you will be better oriented in them.

For the time being don't ask me what the comments – which you do not understand – mean. I will explain them step by step. And I also admit in advance that you may feel this template as too complicated. Most of students tell it. However, after some time they admit, that they accustomed to this arrangement and that it helps them. Afterwards they ask for similar templates also for professional development environments, with which we work in subsequent courses.

373.   There is a whole part of commented program at the end.

I use it only when I need to test something simpler to which it is not worthy to define a whole test class. Don't be afraid we will comment these methods during the course as well. And now let's have a look how to make a resulting documented class from this empty standard class.

Formatting of the Documentation Comments

374.   I vote for it. I have the windows with both source codes at the area, one along the other, and we can start.

.Before we begin showing and commenting I would like to tell you something about documentation comments generally, so that we would not lose our time

First of all I will say that each documentation comment has to be located closely before the documented entity in the program. The class documentation comment has to be located before the class header; the method's comment before the method's header and the field's comment has to be located before the declaration of this field. From this implies that each entity has its own documentation comment (more precisely it can have it – depending on if you create it).

The resulting documentation is a group of HTML files mutually connected with references. The javadoc program creates only the total outlook of the documentation and its dividing into sections. It does not take care about formatting individual sections of the documentation. But if you know that you will look through the documentation via the browser, you quickly realize that you can use any HTML tags in your documentation comments. Therefore in case you would like to insert a new line into the explanation, put the tag <br> at the given place in the comment, in case you would like to create a new paragraph, insert <p>. Similarly you can use a pair of tags <b></b> for marking the text that should be printed bold etc. You are limited only by your knowledge of HTML language.

Each documentation comment contains two sections and any of them may be empty:

☞   There is a basic explanation describing the contract of a given entity at the beginning, i.e. what is its purpose in the program or how it is suitable to use it.

☞   At the end there is a section of block tags (see further) containing texts that will be located in individual sections in the resulting documentation.

Javadoc Tags

The documentation comments can contain **javadoc tags**. They can be divided into two groups:

☞ The **block tags** are inserted in documentation comments after the basic explaining text. All are in the form @tag and introduce the text which will be placed in certain independent section entitled identically as the given tag (you will see it soon) in the resulting documentation.

☞ On the contrary the **inline tags** are inserted into the basic explaining test and determine such part of the text which should be formatted or interpreted differently. Their form is as follows {@tag text}.

375. It looks simple until now. It depends on how many doc tags there will be.

Only a few and furthermore, majority of them will be prepared in patterns. Let's come from theory to practice.

We will start with a class documentation comment with which the source code of a standard class begins. The class function should be described in it as well as its instances in the program. We can find three tags in this comment.

You will find the name of the created class inside braces starting with the tag @code immediately in the first line. Thus you can mark the text which you want to write with a monospaced font, i.e. with letters which are used for example for program texts. It is used when you quote the names of classes, methods, variables or other parts of the program inside the ordinary text.

In case you would like to examine the effect of this tag, try to write again the class name before the brace or behind it, switch on to a documentation mode and have a look what is the difference between both styles.

376. I tried and grasp it. I would say that the meaning of those two remaining ones is obvious.

Surely, the @author tag introduces the name of author (or authors) of the code. You can sign the class you are creating. In case your class arose by modifying someone else's class, it is suitable to quote also the author of the class which you used as a base to your class. All what the javadoc finds behind this tag is copied in the documentation's introduction behind the title **Author**. (Write what you want and switch the editor to a documentation mode to see, where javadoc places your text.)

The @version tag works similarly and you can write behind it the number of the version, its name and date and anything else. All what javodoc finds behind this mark is copied in the documentation's introduction behind the title **Version**. (Again you can try it immediately.)   .

377. The class documentation comment is clear. Will you tell me anything more before going on?

Nothing concerning the class comments, but I will describe block tags which are used in documentation comments of methods. We will use again only two of them in this course, as follows:

☞ The @param tag is determined for the description of one particular parameter – the name of the corresponding parameter should follow. Explaining text follows this name. Each parameter should have its own @param tag in the documentation comment.

☞ The @return tag introduces the text explaining what the given method returns. But this tag is not used for constructors, because everybody knows that the constructor returns a reference to the created instance and there is nothing to describe. Therefore if you would use this tag in the constructor's comment, javadoc would ignore it.

Comments Marking Sections of the Source Code

378. Now you outrun a little bit, but I understand that you want to have all tags explained at the same time. Hopefully I will not forget them until I will really need them. And now, please explain me the meaning of those line comments behind the class head.

As I have told, these comments introduce the code sections to which you should insert the relevant parts. As far as I insert nothing, I leave the line comment "glued" to its descendant. If I insert something I should separate it from the introductory line comment with an empty line, and with three empty lines from the following comment.

Nothing that could belong to the first three sections is used in the Light class for the time being and we can leave it empty. We will be interested in the section CONSTANT FIELDS OF INSTANCES. We know that the lights have two fields: bulb and color. We fill in both of them during creating an instance and then we will never change its content. Thus we could consider them as constant. Therefore we insert both declarations behind this comment.

Thus we have declared the first two fields. But we should comment them. Because both fields are private and the documentation comments of private entities are mostly not inserted into the documentation (we would have to request javadoc explicitly for it), we can choose from two possibilities:

☞   We will describe the field with a classic documentation comment.

☞   We will describe the field with only a line comment.

I mostly prefer the classic documentation comment because when I return to an older program which should be adjusted, I ask javadoc to include also comments of private entities into the result and made out a complete documentation. I can orientate in this documentation quicker than in the source code where the code itself diverts me, and at that moment I am really not interested in how I programmed it a year ago, but what the method or the field serves for.

On the other hand I have to admit that I am not consistent and sometimes I describe certain fields with only a line supplement due to my laziness.

379. Well, we finished the fields. And now the constructors are on.

We have prepared a parameterless constructor, but at this moment it will be surely easier to copy all three constructors from the old class into the clipboard and then replace the body of the parameterless constructor in the new class with this triplet.

I would recommend you again to establish a convention for the order of constructors' definition and to keep it. In case you will get back to the class which has more constructors, you will have better orientation in it. I try to start with a parameterless constructor and continue with more general constructors, which enable to enter some parameters. The more general is always put behind the less general.

380. I think I will follow you with this convention. So only the methods remain. Where should I insert them?

The methods of the light defined until now are not the accessory methods (getters and setters) – we will debate them in some of the future lessons. Therefore they belong to a section OTHER NON-PRIVATE METHODS OF INSTANCES.

I try to increase the transparency of the program by ordination of individual methods according to alphabet even at this place. Supposing we have three methods it looks as a useless detail but after our classes will contain hundreds of lines, you will appreciate such delicacy when searching a certain method.

You can see the resulting form of our class in the listing 20.2. Compile all and examine it by starting the test of the test class (it should not notice the change). After all will operate, remove the renamed original class which is not yet needed and move the newly created class to a place suitable for you.

Listing 20.2:   *The resulting form of the Light class*

```
/******************************************************************************
 * Instance of the class {@code Light} represents simulated lights
 * which can be turned on and off.
 */
public class Light implements IPaintable
{
    //== CONSTANT CLASS FIELDS ================================================
    //== VARIABLE CLASS FIELDS ================================================
    //== STATIC INITIALIZER (CLASS CONSTRUCTOR) ==============================
    //== CONSTANT INSTANCE FIELDS ============================================

    /** Color of the light when turned on. */
    private NamedColor  color;

    /** Shape representing the light on the canvas. */
    private Ellipse bulb;



    //== VARIABLE INSTANCE FIELDS ============================================
    //== CLASS GETTERS AND SETTERS ===========================================
    //== OTHER NON-PRIVATE CLASS METHODS =====================================

    ///#############################################################################
    //== CONSTUCTORS AND FACTORY METHODS =====================================

    /******************************************************************************
     * Creates a new light with the default size and color,
     * which will be placed into the upper left corner.
     */
    public Light()
    {
        bulb  = new Ellipse();
        color = bulb.getColor();
    }
```

```
/*************************************************************************
 * Creates a new light with the default size and color,
 * which will be placed at the given coordinates.
 *
 * @param x  Horizontal coordinate
 * @param y  Vertical coordinate
 */
public Light(int x, int y)
{
    bulb  = new Ellipse(x, y, 50, 50);
    color = bulb.getColor();
}



/*************************************************************************
 * Creates a new light with the default size, the entered color,
 * which will be placed at the given coordinates.
 *
 * @param x      Horizontal coordinate
 * @param y      Vertical coordinate
 * @param b      Color of the turned on light
 */
public Light(int x, int y, NamedColor b)
{
    color = b;
    bulb  = new Ellipse(x, y, 50, 50, color);
}




//== ABSTRACT METHODS =================================================
//== INSTANCE GETTERS AND SETTERS =====================================
//== OTHER NON-PRIVATE INSTANCE METHODS ===============================

/*************************************************************************
 * Turns the light on for 500 milliseconds and then turns it off.
 */
public void blink()
{
    switchOn ();     IO.pause(500);
    switchOff();     IO.pause(500);
}



/*************************************************************************
 * Paints the instance by force of the specified painter.
 *
 * @param painter Painter drawing the instance
 */
@Override
public void paint(Painter painter)
{
    bulb.paint(painter);
}
```

```
/****************************************************************************
 * Turns the light on, that means it will set its color
 * to the light-on-color.
 */
public void switchOn()
{
    bulb.setColor(color);
}


/****************************************************************************
 * Turns the light off, that means it will set its color
 * to the light-off-color.
 */
public void switchOff()
{
    bulb.setColor(NamedColor.BLACK);
}



//== PRIVATE AND AUXILIARY CLASS METHODS ====================================
//== PRIVATE AND AUXILIARY INSTANCE METHODS =================================
//== MEMBER DATA TYPES ======================================================
//== TESTING CLASSES AND METHODS ============================================
//
//      /*********************************************************************
//       * Test method.
//       */
//      public static void test()
//      {
//          Light inst = new Light();
//      }
//      /** @param args Parameters of command line - unused. */
//      public static void main(String[] args)  {  test();  }
}
```

381.   I would like to ask you why you start the documentation comments of classes and methods with a line of stars when you told at the beginning, that two are sufficient.

Because I want to have a visible break – again only due to the better orientation in the program. And when I started to write the line of stars for methods, I write them also for the classes. I have chosen a briefer version only for fields.

Empty Method's Pattern

382.   This lesson is as long as two others. I would say we should have finish.

When it's so long, one prolongation should not bother you. I would like to tell you that not only classes and interface types have their patterns, but also the methods have their patterns. In case you will have the task to define a new method in future, get to a place where you want to put the method in the source code, press CTRL+M. *BlueJ* will insert an empty method with prepared documentation comment with the mostly used tags which you can see at the listing 20.3.

Listing 20.3:   *The method's pattern*

```
/*************************************************************************
 * Empty method
 *
 * @param  x    Parameters description
 * @return      Return value description
 */
public void method()
{
}
```

Take into account that the pattern keeps the indentation of the cursor at the moment you inserted it. If you forget it and you will want to change this indentation, remember that the procedure of increasing or decreasing of the indentation is similar as for commenting and uncommenting of a block. It differs only by using the key shortcut: increasing of indentation by pressing **F6**, decreasing by pressing **F5**.

This is really the end for today.

Exercise

383.   **I guess that my today's exercise will be converting all my previous classes to the versions with documentation comments.**

You could earn your money as an illusionist – your estimation is exact.

Review

Let's review, what you have learned in this lesson:

☞   In case we want the compiler would ignore certain lines during compiling, we can *comment* them.

☞   Lines are commented by putting the pair of strokes // at its beginning.

☞   When working in *BlueJ* you can make the work easier by selecting a block which would interfere into all commented lines, then press the key **F8** or enter the command **Edit → Comment**.

☞   When you would uncomment the commented lines later, it is sufficient to remove only the initial pair of slashes.

☞   For uncommenting several subsequent lines you can select a block in *BlueJ* so that it would reach all the selected lines and then you can press the key **F7** or to enter the command **Edit → Uncomment**.

☞   Java recognizes three kinds of comments as follows:

  ☞   The line comments starting with the pair of slashes // and finishing with the line end.

  ☞   The block comments starting with the character pair /* and ending with the pair */.

☞   The documentation comments are block comments beginning with the character triplet
      /**.

☞   The documentation comments are inserted before the definitions of documented entities – of
      classes, fields and methods.

☞   The documentation comments are converted to HTML text. Therefore, you can format their text
      through HTML tags.

☞   Special tags may occur in the documentation comments. These tags are divided into two groups
      as follows:

    ☞   The block tags introduce a text for which an independent section will be created in the re-
          sulting documentation.

    ☞   The inline tags adjust only formatting and possibly the interpretation of the marked text.

☞   The documentation comments contain an explanation section followed by a section of (block)
      tags.

☞   For now we explained the following block tags:

    ☞   @author, which is valid only in the class documentation and introduces the list of authors
          of a given class,

    ☞   @version, which is also valid only in the class documentation and introduces the text spec-
          ifying the product's version,

    ☞   @param, which is valid only in methods' documentation (including constructors) and
          serves to describing the significance of particular parameters,

    ☞   @return, which is valid only in the documentation of current methods and serves for
          describing its output value.

☞   From the inline tags I have explained only the tag {@code text} which causes that the text will be
      typed with the monospaced font.

☞   In case we will create a new class as the standard one, we receive a source text generated ac-
      cording to the pattern that contains a number of auxiliary comments.

☞   The line comments in the pattern of the standard class introduce sections where the code char-
      acterized by the text of a given comment should be incorporated.

Project:
*The resulting form of the project to which we came at the end of the lesson and after completing all exer-
cises is in the 120z_Comments project.*

21 Using of this

What you will learn in this lesson
This lesson is devoted to the hidden parameter this. *I will explain you its presence as well as its usage. Then I will tell you why it is not suitable to copy the code and you will have a detailed look at the work of the constructor and you will see how its work can be defined using the statement* this.

Project:
In this lesson we continue in using the 120z_Comments *project.*

The Hidden Parameter this

384. Today I would like to ask you two questions which you skipped over in previous explanation. We touched the first one in the section *The Conflict of Names of a Field and of a Parameter* on page 162. You advised me to re-name the parameter and you told me you will explain me the more elegant and used solving of this conflict in future.

The solving is relatively simple and I mentioned it indirectly in the section *The Qualification* on page 161. It uses the fact that instead of the shortened name of the field you can use its full name, i.e. including its qualification. Then both names will differ.

385. So I already knew everything! Why you did not tell it directly?

It was not necessary. Renaming of the local variable is also a good solution. Particularly I was afraid of sinking into theory and not having enough of time for programming anything useful. The keyword this needs a lot of explanation around.

386. What's so interesting in it?

The keyword this marks an implicit hidden parameter which all constructors have as well as the instance methods, and which contains the reference to an instance, in whose method or constructor the program is situated just now (which is just running).

387. You say "in whose method", which I understand as "in the method belonging to a given instance". But all methods are defined together in the class body and there is no information concerning to whom the given method belongs.

We told that the method is the part of a code defining how the object will react to certain message. In Java (equally as in majority of contemporary languages) all instances of the given class react to a given message in the same way. Therefore only one code can be defined in the class body for each message which is shared by all instances.

When accomplishing this code the computer has to know which instance reacts to a given message, because within the framework of accomplishing the code there may be a need to use or set the value of this instance fields or to send some other message to this instance. The reference to the instance for which the given method is just working, is received by the method in the mentioned hidden parameter this. Then whenever it needs to turn to an instance, for which it is just working, it turns to it through this reference.

388.   Why is this parameter hidden?

The authors of the language knew that the programmers don't want to write any useless code (they were also programmers), and they didn't want to force anybody to copy something which is always included and everybody knows it.

Moreover, they defined the language syntax so that in case you don't address an object in the instance method to which you are sending a message (you ask this object's field or you call its method), i.e. you don't qualify the asked field or called method, the compiler completes the qualification with the parameter this.

When we would rewrite e.g. the blink() method without skipping over the qualification, it would look out as in the listing 21.1.

Listing 21.1:   *The blink() method in the Light class using the parameter this*

```
public void blink(/*Light this*/)
{
    this.switchOn ();        IO.pause(500);
    this.switchOff();        IO.pause(500);
}
```

For greater clearness I completed the declaration of the hidden parameter to a comment in the previous example. As you see, in the first and the third statement the instance addresses itself just through this parameter; in the second and the fourth statement it addresses the IO class.

389.   This results that the parameterless methods of instances are not parameterless because they have the hidden parameter this.

Exactly, and because they have them every time, it is not quoted in the head and everybody have to deduce it. The programmers welcome it because they don't have to write it in each method.

390.   We somehow digressed from the more elegant solving of conflict between the parameter and the field names.

Never at all. This solution uses just the parameter this. Using it we could rewrite the constructor adjusting the light color to the form (I quoted again the declaration of the hidden parameter in the comment) as in the listing 21.2.

Listing 21.2:   *Solving of name crash using this*

```
public Light(/*Light this,*/int x, int y, NamedColor color)
{
    this.color = color;
    this.bulb  = new Ellipse(x, y, 50, 50, color);
}
```

As you surely remember, I told you that in case of name crash the compiler always prefers the name which is logically closer in the program – in our case to the parameter's name. So the right operand of the equation expression in the first statement refers to the parameter.

But in the left operand I addressed the instance through the (hidden) parameter this and thus I asked it for the reference for the color field. The result of the whole first statement is that the value of color parameter was saved to the color field.

Quoting this in the second statement was not necessary because the compiler could not mix up the bulb field with anything else. I used this only due to the code looked better. In other words: By explicit quoting of the parameter this we can solve the impending crash of names of a parameter and a field. As far as the crash of names does not impend, the decision on an explicit qualification through this depends quite on you.

391. You told me that you will show me a more elegant solution. But I don't see anything elegant on it.

The elegance consists in the fact that you can use the identical name for the two different variables which contain the value of the identical meaning. The program becomes more transparent by this, because you can see at the first sight, which two variables belong together. That's why this solution is so frequently used by programmers.

392. How often the programmers use this facultative this?

It depends on whom. I know companies which require quoting this facultative this from their programmers because it is quite clear what is a field and what is something else. But majority of programmers skip them over (in addition certain IDEs allow distinguishing the parameters from the fields through colors in syntax highlighting). You can often meet what I showed you in the program 21.2: in case this is quoted at certain fields, because with its help a crash of names is solved, it is quoted at all others as well.

393. You told me that the methods of instances have the hidden parameter this. But this was a constructor and _BlueJ_ includes it among the class methods.

The constructors are somewhere between methods of instances and methods of a class. They have the common aspect with class methods, namely that they define answers to messages sent to a class and that you can call them even when no instance exists; the hidden parameter this is a common aspect with methods of instances. This hidden parameter fulfills the virtual machine with a reference to a constructed instance when the constructor is called. Thus the constructor can turn to its fields and methods via this parameter.

Unsuitable Copying of the Code

394. Leaving the parameter this I will remind you another problem which you avoid to explain. When you assigned me topics for an independent work at the end of the 17ᵗʰ chapter on page 154 in the section _Exercise_, you wanted me to define the traffic light's lights as the instances of the Light class. Immediately you also told me that I don't have to do it for the car because the lights don't have the constructor defined for adjusting the size. Why we did not fulfilled it?

Because I wanted to postpone the question of increasing the number of constructors to a time when we will be able to look how it is possible to supplement further constructors more effectively.

395. How more effectively? I simply copy the old constructor and I add or adjust what's necessary. It can be done somehow more effectively?

Copying of the code and subsequent minimal (or even no) adjustments is just what you should avoid. Using the same or nearly the same code at more places of the program is considered as one of the biggest programmer's sins. A number of design patterns deals with how to avoid copying the code. The typical example is e.g. the pattern *Servant* which I presented you in the section *Servant* on page 102.

396. Why using the same or the similar code is so reprobated? When I examine that certain code is well operating, I consider as advantageous to use it somewhere else.

You can use it but not copy it. In case it is necessary to execute the same action on several places we should define it and then call this definition from each relevant place.

I mentioned the main reason of reprobating this practice several times – it is my favorite statement (I mentioned it already on page 80): *"The only one constant of contemporary programming is the certainty that the assignment will soon* **change.***"* And I add another one from the programmers' Murphy's laws: *"The probability of the necessity to change a part of the code is directly proportional to the number of client's assuring that the given function will be never touched."*

When you change certain part of the code, you have to change simultaneously (or at least to check) all what is dependent to this part, together with parts arisen as copies of the changed program's part. In case you discover that the copied part of the code has to be changed, you have to change probably also those copies. The problem is that often you don't remember to which parts you copied the code that is being changed and so you are in a danger that you will forget some of them during corrections or you will change them in a different way than is needed.

Good programmers therefore keep the principle marked with the abbreviation **DRY – Don't Repeat Yourself**. I like to call this the **DRY Rule**, because as soon as you break it, you are potentially soaked in a future pickle.

The Details of the Constructor's Work

397. Well, what should I do not to repeat the code when all constructors provide nearly the same?

You will call one constructor from the other one, similarly as I showed it in the program 18.5 on page 166, where one method was calling the other one and adjusted the values of parameters to it.

398. How one constructor can call another one? I am afraid that using the new statement will maybe not the proper way.

No, it is really not the proper way, because each new statement creates a new instance. The virtual machine creates a new instance before entering into the constructor's body. If you would call another constructor being in certain constructor with the assistance of new, e.g. as follows:

```
public Light()
{
    new Light(0, 0);
}
```

the virtual machine would create a new instance before entering into its body and the calling new would create another instance inside the body. There is really no way this direction.

399.   **You confuse me. In the section *Constructor* on page 140 you told me that the constructor is the method responsible for the proper creating of an instance of the given class. How it can be responsible for creating an instance when someone creates it even before the constructor starts to carry out?**

I have already explained it to you in the section *Methods and Constructors* on page 30. Creating of the new instance could be divided into two phases. In the first phase the memory manager allocates for the instance under creation the needed space at the heap. In the second phase the object is initialized – the allocated space is filled with relevant data and if need be another needed operations are done (e.g. the light depicted itself at the canvas). The constructor is responsible for the second phase of creating. To be able to correctly initialize the creating instance, the constructor should know where the initialized memory is allocated. It becomes the reference to it in its hidden parameter this.

The whole action creating the new instance would be probably more understandable when I would rewrite the program into the following form

```
public Light()
{
    new Light
    (/*Light this,*/ 0, 0);
}
```

At the first line of the body the new keyword instructs the virtual machine to create the instance of the Light class, and at the second line the nameless method (= the constructor) "gets it into operation".

400.   **So what creates the instance, the virtual machine or the constructor?**

I have explained it as well. If you would remember I compared the object's construction to creating a jug: the virtual machine designates and initiates the memory – prepares the clay. Until we don't have the clay (the memory), we cannot create any mug (the object). However, creating the jug is of the potter's (the constructor's) competency. The constructor tailors the designated memory to such form so that it could serve as the required object.

401.   **I understand, but why a special (and a nameless) method have to be installed due to this initialization? Could be an ordinary method used for it?**

Some languages do it, but it brings a lot of problems. The constructor has to provide certain special tasks during initializing an instance. Therefore it has certain special privileges and on the other hand certain limitations. You will be presented some of them during further explanation, and some of them will be expecting you in the next book.

For now we will remain at the fact that the constructor's calling has to follow obligatorily after the new operator; no other method can be used there. On the other hand the constructor cannot be called at a different place, only as the part of the initialization following the application of the new operator.

402.   **You say as the part of the initialization, but I could call it from another constructor, because when the constructor is being carried out, initializing is on. If I would throw away the first line creating another instance from the last program, would it be good? In other words, would the following program be o.k.?**

```
public Light()
{
    (0, 0);
}
```

Nearly, the only one problem is that an isolated bracket presents certain expression in the program, not calling the method. We will substitute it similarly as in name crashing, i.e. we add the addressing this.

If I would write it down as the calling of a current method, the constructor's calling would look out as follows:

```
this.(0, 0);
```

But in this case, the authors of the language deleted using the dot due to syntactic rules, so that the properly written calling of the constructor is as follows:

```
this(0, 0);
```

Adjustment of the Constructors Using this

403. **I understand from the previous explanation that the parameterless constructor slips out of the initializing by entrusting its colleague – the double-parametric constructor, to which it says to create an instance of coordinates [0, 0]. But the light double-parametric constructor produces rounded lights, and the parameterless one creates elliptic lights.**

It's the highest time to change it. You don't meet elliptic lights many times. Let's agree that since this time all lights will be rounded. We can also make an agreement that the implicit color of the light will be yellow, not blue. Our three constructors could be therefore rewritten into the form from the listing 21.3.

Listing 21.3:   *The constructor in the Light class using delegating of the responsibility through this*

```
public Light()
{
    this(0, 0);
}


public Light(int x, int y)
{
    this(x, y, NamedColor.YELLOW);
}


public Light(int x, int y, NamedColor color)
{
    this.color = color;
    this.bulb  = new Ellipse(x, y, 50, 50, color);
}
```

And now ask the LightTest class to create a fixture or to run some of the test methods. Thus you can verify that all your adjustments were correct.

404.   I've adjusted and examined the program. But I admit that I don't understand it much.

Well, let's show how it will react to the calling of a parameterless constructor.

1.   In the previous definition the parameterless constructor delegates the responsibility for instance initializing to the constructor with two integer parameters and pass two zeroes as arguments to it.

2.   The addressed constructor also doesn't want to start the initializing and delegates the responsibility to the third constructor to which it passes its first two arguments (coordinates) as its first two arguments and as the third argument (color) it passes the default, i.e. yellow color.

3.   The statement this only delegates the responsibility for carrying out the task to something else. But the given work has to be done at the end. The last constructor has no colleague to which the responsibility could be delegated and so this last one has to take care about the initializing.

405.   I would like to know if further statements could be in the constructor's body besides the statement this.

Could be, although it is not used much often. Mostly it is really sufficient to prepare parameters for a "colleague" and then to delegate the responsibility for initializing of the created instance to it. The rule is that the constructor with fewer parameters calls the more general constructor and the values of parameters, which are common to both of them, are only passed and implicit values are assigned to the remaining parameters of the called constructor. Sometimes adding of further statements is useful. But as I already told, it is not too often.

In case you will decide to add further statements to the constructor's body, you have to add them **behind** transferring the responsibility for the initializing to a colleague (to another constructor). As ensues from the expression *initializing*, it is something what should be done at the beginning. As far as one constructor repudiates its responsibility and delegates it to its colleague, it can start further activities only after the addressed colleague would finish the initializing and would give back the control to the calling constructor.

However, these problems will be surely debated in further explanation and therefore I will say you only good bye today.

Exercise

406.   I will switch on my prophetic skills and I will estimate that today my task is to adjust the classes Arrow, TrafficLight **and** Car **in the way so that their constructors would give over responsibility for initiating through** this.

Exactly, notice that the definition of constructors will simplify. The light constructor is very simple and it cannot be simplified further. But the traffic light's and car's constructors have changed far more significantly

Next time you will see how adding of new constructors and their possible adjustments will be simplified after the above mentioned adjustments.

Review

Let's review what you learned in this lesson:

☞ The instance methods have the hidden parameter this referring to the instance to which a message was sent and the instance reacts at this message by calling the given method.

☞ Also the constructors have the hidden parameter this; in their case it refers to the just constructed instance.

☞ Any identical or a very similar code should not occur in programs at several places.

☞ In case it is possible to make the same action at several places, you should define it and subsequently call this definition from each place separately.

☞ The principle of not repeating the code is usually marked with an abbreviation DRY, i.e. *Don't Repeat Yourself*.

☞ The object construction is made in two steps: in the first step the new operator allocates the memory for instances of the class, which it obtains as an argument, in the second step the constructor initializes this memory.

☞ Constructor can delegate the responsibility for initializing the instance to its "colleague" through the statement this(???), in which it sets the arguments for the called "colleague".

☞ Besides delegating the responsibility for initializing to another constructor there might be also other statements in the constructor's body. However, they always have to follow after this initialization carried out by another constructor.

☞ Completing further statements is not much used. Mostly the more concrete constructor, i.e. the constructor with fewer parameters calls only the more general constructor, whilst the values of parameters which both constructors have are only passed and the default values are assigned to the remaining parameters of the called constructor.

Project:
The resulting form of the project to which we came at the end of the lesson and after completing all exercises is in the 121z_Using_this project.

22 Overloading

What you will learn in this lesson
In this lesson you will add further constructors to your class and you will learn what it means the over-loading of methods. The significance of identifiers of parameters will be explained as well as how the internal identification of the given method might look out. Finally the basic arithmetic operators will be introduced.

Project:
In this lesson we continue in using the 121z_Using_this *project.*

407.   Why this chapter has the name *The Overloading*?

The overloading is a term for defining several methods with the same name but with various sets of parameters. For now we used them mostly for constructors, but in case you will have a look into the documentation, you will see that majority of classes from our project have also other overloaded methods.

Further Constructors

408.   When we know how to pretty economically create the overloaded constructors (see how quickly I am learning ☺), we could create also the lights with the entered size.

Yes, of course, and when it is so simple, we can add immediately two: the first one will enable to install the light's position and its diameter, the second one its position, diameter and color. To have it more interesting, we will add the constructor enabling to set not only the color of the switched on light, but also the color of the switched off light. If we would install these extensions in definitions which would not use this we would be obliged to adjust all of them. By using this we can adjust only the definitions of the most general constructor.

You can see the new set of constructors (with skipped comments) in the listing 22.1. Notice, how our original, the most general constructor used the possibility to give over the responsibility for initializing with the assistance of this in the new configuration and passed it to a four-parameter one which passed the responsibility to the five parameter constructor. It is just the most general where all ways are ending.

Listing 22.1:   *The innovated set of constructors of the* Light *class*

```
public Light()
{
    this(0, 0);
}
```

```
public Light(int x, int y)
{
    this(x, y, NamedColor.YELLOW);
}


public Light(int x, int y, NamedColor color)
{
    this(x, y, 50, color);
}


public Light(int x, int y, int diameter)
{
    this(x, y, diameter, NamedColor.YELLOW);
}


public Light(int x, int y, int diameter, NamedColor color)
{
        this(x, y, diameter, color, NamedColor.BLACK);
}


public Light(int x, int y, int diameter, NamedColor color, NamedColor switchedOff)
{
    this.color      = color;
    this.switchedOff = switchedOff;
    this.bulb        = new Ellipse(x, y, diameter, diameter, color);
}
```

409. Adding of color of the switched off light requires adding of the switchedOffColor **field and modify the definition of the** switchOff() **method.**

Of course, but I think those are so simple modifications that you will be able to do them without any assistance.

410. I looked at the context menu of the Ellipse **class to discover which parameters can be used. The class offers the constructor with parameters** height **and** width**. However, you recommended the** diameter **parameter for setting the size. How can I detect which parameters can be used for certain constructor?**

You mixed now two faces of parameters. Remind the section *Parameters and Arguments* on page 150, where we spoke about the fact that each parameter has two faces which are marked as formal and actual parameters (parameters and arguments). The formal parameter is a name by which you mark places in the program's definition, where the argument value (the value of the actual parameter) will be used during the program's operating. This actual value is passed to the called program by the calling program.

The names width and height are names of (formal) parameters used in the definition of an ellipse constructor. Opposite to it diameter is the name of the parameter (i.e. a formal parameter) of the light constructor. But when I mention this name in calling of the ellipse's constructor, I say that I pass the value (the actual parameter), which I receive in the parameter diameter during the program's operation, to an ellipse constructor as the value of parameter at the corresponding place in the parameter list. In our case this value is passed twice – as the value of parameters with the names width and height.

Quite different item are the types of parameters, they have to be observed. If the constructor requires e.g. a whole number in the third parameter, you have to enter a whole number or something, about which you are sure that the compiler will automatically turn to a whole number.

411. Is the number of constructors somehow limited?

No – it's not limited if you do not consider the number 65535 as limiting. The only one real limit in creating the constructors is the fact that no two constructors can have the same set of parameters. In other words, the constructors have to differ in the number and/or the types of their parameters. Otherwise the compiler could not recognize which constructor should be called to react to your message.

412. And now we should examine if it's all operating.

Good, we will replenish the new fields into the test class and the relevant statements to the setUp() method. To examine functionality of the new lights, we will extend also the testBlink() method. In case we leave out comments as well as the unused tearDown() method, the test class should correspond to the listing 22.2.

Listing 22.2: *The class LightTest after including the test of added constructors*

```
import org.junit.After;
import org.junit.Before;
import org.junit.Test;

public class LightTest
{
    private CanvasManager CM;
    private Light light0;
    private Light lightXY;
    private Light lightXYC;
    private Light lightXYD;
    private Light lightXYDC;
    private Light lightXYDCF;

    @Before
    public void setUp()
    {
        light0    = new Light();
        lightXY   = new Light(50,  50);
        lightXYC  = new Light(100, 100, NamedColor.RED);
        lightXYD  = new Light( 0, 100, 100);
        lightXYDC = new Light(100,   0, 100, NamedColor.BLUE);
        lightXYDCF= new Light(150, 150, 150, NamedColor.MAGENTA, NamedColor.NO);

        CM = CanvasManager.getInstance();
        CM.add(light0);
        CM.add(lightXY);
        CM.add(lightXYC);
        CM.add(lightXYC);
```

```
        CM.add(lightXYDC);
        CM.add(lightXYDCF);

        IO.inform("Lights prepared");
    }

    @Test
    public void testBlink()
    {
        light0     .switchOff();
        lightXY    .switchOff();
        lightXYC   .switchOff();
        lightXYD   .switchOff();
        lightXYDC  .switchOff();
        lightXYDCF.switchOff();
        IO.pause(500);
        light0     .blink();
        lightXY    .blink();
        lightXYC   .blink();
        lightXYD   .blink();
        lightXYDC  .blink();
        lightXYDCF.blink();
        IO.pause(500);
        light0     .switchOn();
        lightXY    .switchOn();
        lightXYC   .switchOn();
        lightXYD   .switchOn();
        lightXYDC  .switchOn();
        lightXYDCF.switchOn();
    }

}
```

413.   You adjusted the NO color for the switched off light of the lightXYPBZ object — what is this color like?

We could call it the color of invisibility. When you will adjust it to certain object, it stops to be seen. Run the blinking text and you will see – the big violet light will disappear during switching off.

Overloading of the Methods

414.   How the compiler recognizes which constructor should be called?

This is decided according to the number and type of parameters. Precisely: it is decided in the way so that the types of parameters on corresponding positions would concur.

We defined two constructors in the Light class with the same number, but with different types of parameters – the Light(int x, int y, NamedColor color) constructor and the Light(int x, int y, int diameter) constructor. The compiler will decide between them according to if the last actual parameter is the whole number or it is the instance to a color.

415.   What will the compiler call when in the third parameter will be something different?

In case it will be possible to convert the given value according to the known language rules to a whole number or to a color, the compiler will do it and will call the relevant constructor. In the opposite case it announces a compile-time error – the so called *syntax error*. Due to these rules try to envisage all possible situations, they are relatively complicated and therefore I will not explain them. However, you will meet majority of them during further lessons.

The Identifiers of Parameters

416.   There is one thing I don't understand. You say that the compiler decides about which message I have sent and which method should be called only based on the number and types of parameters of the given message. This would mean that names of parameters are not crucial. How the compiler can recognize if I wanted to call the method Light(int x, int y) **or** Light(int y, int x)**?**

This is just what the compiler cannot identify and therefore you cannot define a couple of methods with the identical number of parameters and the identical types of corresponding parameters. In case you will do it, the compiler announces a compile-time error (syntax error). Methods differing only by the order of parameters can be defined entirely in the case their types of separate parameters vary. Thus we could define a couple of constructors Light(int diameter, NamedColor color) and Light(NamedColor color, int diameter).

It is also logical. In case you would define the constructors Light(int x, int y) and Light(int y, int x), then in reaction to the statement

```
new Light(20, 30);
```

it could not be decided which of them should be used. Therefore, in the common text (e.g. in the documentation) the authors often do not quote identifiers of their parameters in references to methods. Our two-parametric constructor could be therefore characterized as the Light(int,int) constructor. But we spoke about it in the section *Briefer Record of Messages* on page 65.

417.   So what are the identifiers for?

I have already told that the identifiers of parameters, i.e. the formal parameters serve entirely to marking places in the source code where the relevant value (actual parameter, argument) will be used in carrying out the given code. We could say that they serve for the better orientation of a programmer. Neither the compiler, nor the virtual machine needs them because they mark individual parameters by the order of quoting them in the declaration.

When we have defined the Light(int x, int y) constructor, we will use the x identifier everywhere in the source text of the method's body, and after calling a method the first of the passed values (the actual parameters) will be used. At those places where the y identifier will be used in the source code, the second of the passed values will be used.

The Identification of the Called Method

418. **I already understand why the order of parameters is so important during passing them. The virtual machine doesn't know anything else about them only their order and type. But I would be interested in how the machine can orientate in those methods.**

You can imagine that the method names used internally by the compiler and the virtual machine insist of the method's name itself completed with names of types of individual parameters. In case you know that the internal name of the constructor is <init> you can simply imagine that the internal names of our constructors are as follows:

```
<init>(),
<init>(int,int),
<init>(int,int,int),
<init>(int,int,NamedColor)
<init>(int,int,int,NamedColor)
```

The Basic Arithmetic Operators

419. **I expect that today my task will be to fulfill constructors into the exercise classes which know to set the object's size as well as the position.**

Your expecting are proper, but it will be more complex. And it's not so simple; that's why I have to explain you something. When you would like to enter also the object's size, the mutual distances of its individual part will change depending on the adjusted size of an object. Therefore you have to count firstly their coordinates as well as the size.

Adding and subtracting is simple – it is marked equally as in mathematics. Therefore I used it several times not to bother you with explaining. But it's little bit more complicated with multiplying and dividing.

In all programming languages which I know the symbol * (a star) is used as an operator of multiplying. At the same time, similarly as in mathematics, multiplying has a preference over adding and subtracting which means the expression (1+2*3) has the value 7 even in the program.

In Java the symbol / (a slash) is used as an operator of division. In case both operands, i.e. the dividend as well as the divisor are whole numbers, also the result is the whole number, which will be a whole part of a quotient. Thus it is valid that (3/2) is 1 and (2/3) is 0.

When entering the arithmetic expressions you have to be careful that the arithmetic expressions in Java are treated always from the left to the right. Therefore the result may depend on how you order the individual operations. The expression (2* 3/4) has the value 1, because (2*3) is 6 and (6/4) is 1. Opposite to it the expression (3/4*2) has the value 0, because (3/4) is 0 and (0*2) is always 0.

In case you have an expression where multiplying and dividing of whole numbers is alongside, usually it is more advantageous firstly to multiply all and only then divide the resulting product. So that you could use this rule, the intermediate result (the product) may not be bigger than the biggest permissible whole number. (I remind that in the section *Primitive and Object Types* on page 35 we told that whole numbers can acquire values ranging roughly between $\pm 2.10^9$, i.e. ± 2 billions.)

420. You say that the result of dividing is the whole part of the quotient. It means that having a quotient and a divisor I cannot detect the dividend.

The whole part of the quotient is the result only in case you divide two whole numbers. If one of those two numbers is the real number, i.e. if it is of double or float type, the result will be also a real number.

And as far as receiving the dividend by return is concerned, even this is possible. But you need an **operator of a remainder after division** for which the % (percentage) sing is used and which is sometimes called **modulo operator**. So always it is valid as follows

```
a == (a / b) * b  +  a % b
```

421. One equal sign fell down there.

It did not fall down. Java uses one equal sign as an operator of assignment and double equal sign as an operator of comparison. I know that the beginners are sometimes confused but we can hardly do anything with it – nothing is perfect.

422. I am afraid not to be drowned. Could you show me using of these terms at an example?

Yes, of course, I will show you how it is possible to define four-parametric constructor of a car (it is maybe the most complicated). Look at its definition in the listing 22.3. Notice that I leaved ellipses and the car's lights are instances of the Light class. I enter only the length of the car to the constructor, its width will be one half of the length.

Listing 22.3:   The definition of the most general constructor in the Car class

```
/****************************************************************************
 * Creates a car with the given size,
 * and with the given color of the chassis,
 * which will be placed at the given coordinates.
 *
 * @param x                Horizontal coordinate
 * @param y                Vertical coordinate
 * @param length           Length of the car
 * @param chassisColor     Color of chassis
 */
public Car(int x, int y, int length, NamedColor chassisColor)
{
    chassis = new Rectangle(x, y, length, length/2, chassisColor);
    cab     = new Rectangle(x+length/8, y+length/8, length/2, length/4,
                                              NamedColor.GRAY);
    lightL  = new Light(x+7*length/8, y,            length/8);
    lightR  = new Light(x+7*length/8, y+3*length/8, length/8);
}
```

423. Well, this was a little bit complicated for me. Could you explain me the formulas in details?

It's not so complicated. Look at the figure 22.1, where I let draw the car in a net so that the relative sizes of car's individual measures could be simply deduced. Then you can simply derive from the figure as follows:

☞   The car's width is one half of its length.

☞ Horizontal as well as vertical distance of the cab's roof towards the chassis is equal to one eighth of the car's length.

☞ The cab's length is equal to one half of the car's length and its width is equal to a quarter of the car's length.

☞ The horizontal distance of both lights is 7/8 of the car's length.

☞ The left light has identical coordinate y as the chassis, the right light has coordinate y pushed towards the chassis by 3/8 of its length.

And it's all. This I recorded to parameters and the program in listing 22.3 came out from it.

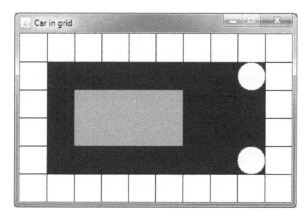

Figure 22.1
The car depicted in a net for deriving the measures

424.   It's easy to be understood, but I wouldn't think it out myself.

Maybe not now, but don't be afraid, soon you will consider it easy.

Exercise

425.   So what have you prepared for me?

You have already estimated that you will fulfill the constructors. I will add a couple of supplementing information:

☞ Enter only one size parameter for an arrow – you can call it maybe a module. It will signify the length of the square's side, in which the arrow is located. By other words the total length as well as the width of the arrow will be the same.

☞ Enter only one size parameter for the traffic light (you can call it module as well): the traffic light's width which is also an average of its lights. Use the light definition to which you will set the NO switched off color. By this you will unify the outlook of the switched off lights independently to the color of the box – the switched off lights simply will be not seen.

☞ When we decided to switch from ellipses to lights in the Car class, don't forget that you have to change also the types of relevant fields. Fulfill the methods as follows:

☞   `switchOff()` – switches off both lights

☞   `switchOn()` – switches on both lights

☞   `blinkLeft()` – blinks with the left light

☞   `blinkRight()` – blinks with the right light

Review

Let's review what you have learned in this lesson:

☞   The definition of several methods with the same name but of various sets of parameters is called the *overloading*.

☞   During calling the methods the actual parameters have to be quoted in the same order in which the corresponding formal parameters were declared.

☞   When defining several versions of methods with the same name (i.e. overloaded methods) the individual versions have to differ by the number of parameters and/or by the parameter's type at certain position.

☞   When calling an overloaded constructor or a method the compiler picks up the proper version so that the types of parameters at corresponding positions would match.

☞   In case the types of parameters do not correspond with any existing versions, the compiler tries to convert the parameters to another type according to language rules. If no version of the called method complies then a compile-time error (syntax error) is announced.

☞   Names of parameters have the meaning only for a programmer. The virtual machine does not use them and internally signifies the parameters by their order.

☞   The number of defined constructors is practically not limited.

☞   For multiplying the operator * (a star) is used in programs.

☞   For dividing operations Java uses the operator / (a slash).

☞   Similarly as in mathematics multiplication and division is preferred to addition and subtraction.

☞   The result of dividing two whole numbers is the whole part of their quotient (e.g. (5/3) is 1); the result of a quotient of a real number with any other number is a classic quotient, i.e. again the real number.

☞   By applying the operator % (percent) we receive a remainder after division – e.g. (5%3) is 2.

☞   It is possible to receive back the dividend from the whole number quotient and the remainder after division, i.e. it is always valid as follows:

    a == (a / b) * b   +   a % b

☞   An operator == is used in Java as an operator of comparison.

☞   Java interprets the arithmetic expressions entirely from the left to the right.

☞   During a series of multiplying and division it is advantageous to arrange the whole expression in such way that firstly the multiplying comes, followed by dividing. However, this procedure can be used only if the midst result is not too big number.

Project:
The resulting form of the project to which we came at the end of the lesson and after completing all exercises is in the 122z_Overloading project.

23 The Local Variables

What you will learn in this lesson
In this lesson you will see how tests that were assigned as exercises in the last lesson can be written down more effectively. Then you will learn how to use local variables and you will read what the difference among fields, parameters and local variables is. And finally you will be informed about inappropriate using of magic values and appropriate substituting them by constants.

Project:
In this lesson we will continue in using the `122z_Overloading` *project.*

The Auxiliary Methods

426. I've already made all methods of the car which you assigned me as an exercise in the previous lesson. But I didn't want to write a test method which would examine the lights functioning for each of the five instances in the fixture. Would you mind to test only one car?

Theoretically it would be sufficient but let's admit that a test of only one car is nearly as complicated as the test of all five.

427. No, it's not. When I need to test five cars, I have to write the car test five times.

No, you don't have to do it. I hope you remember that in the section *Unsuitable Copying of the Code* on page 196 I said that repeating of the same or nearly the same code belongs to great programmer's sins. And you say now that you have to write something five times.

428. You are true but how should I do it, when I would explain to five objects that they are obliged to do the same?

Use the fact that the test class is a class as any other and that you can define also other methods in it, not only those test methods. Define the auxiliary method which would verify blinking of one car – you will enter it as a parameter. Then call this method for each car. You can see the possible definition of this auxiliary method as well as of the following test in the listing 23.1.

Listing 23.1:   *The definition of the blinking test in the* Car *class*

```
private void auxBlink(Car car)
{
    car.lightOff();       IO.pause(500);
    car.blinkLeft();      IO.pause(500);
    car.blinkRight();     IO.pause(500);
    car.lightOn();        IO.pause(500);
}
```

```
public void testBlink()
{
    auxBlink(car0);
    auxBlink(carXY);
    auxBlink(carXYC);
    auxBlink(carXYM);
    auxBlink(carXYMC;
}
```

429.   When I see it's completed I admit that it looks simple. And I will only ask why did you define this auxiliary method as private**? Until now we used the** private **modifier only for fields.**

Because this method is only an auxiliary one. When we were speaking about this topic in the section *Interface vs. Implementation* on page 78, I told you that we should do programming in such way so that the colleagues of our objects would know what these objects know, but they would not know how it is programmed.

The code of the listing 23.1 makes the test public so that everybody can ask the class to start the test. At the same time it hides (with the aid of private modifier) that an auxiliary method was defined for processing the test.

Try to keep the general principle: if something should not be private, there must be a rational reason for it.

The Local Variables

430.   Well, we have simplified the test definition. Would it be possible to simplify somehow also the constructor's definition? The repeated entering of formulas to parameters really bothered me. And moreover, the same code is repeated at several positions.

You are true and it could be simplified, it means to simplify it in the sense of cancelling the code duplicities. For this purpose you can use the **local variables**, which means the named positions in the memory that can be used within the method and after closing the method they are at anybody else's disposal.

431.   Can you explain why they are called just *local variables*?

They are called *local* because nobody knows about them except the interior of a given method and therefore you can use them really only locally within the given method. They are called *variables* because their content can change. Thus you can gradually put various values into them as the program course will require.

432.   How such local variable is declared?

Contrary to fields which are declared outside methods, as well as to parameters which are declared within parentheses in the method's head, the local variables are declared inside a method, i.e. inside the braces bounding this body. The following rules are valid for declaration of local variables:

☞   Each variable has to be declared before it is used.

☞   The declaration should contain the name of a given variable (i.e. the name of the value's type which you can put into it) followed by its name (identifier).

☞   In case you decide to initialize the local variable immediately (and this is warmly recommended), you add the equal sign followed by the expression whose value is put into the variable. However, the initialization is not compulsory.

☞   The whole declaration should be completed by a semicolon.

In case we would use a local variable in the car constructor that I showed you previously, it could look as in the listing 23.2. I introduced four local variables in the program: d1, d2, d4 and d8, which represented frequently occurring fractions of the basic length. (It's true that the variable d1 was not necessary to be introduced and I could use the length parameter, but I did not resist the temptation to install identifiers of all fractions in the same form.)

Listing 23.2:   The four-parametric constructor of the Car class using the local variables

```
public Car(int x, int y, int length, NamedColor chassisColor)
{
    int  d1 = length;
    int  d2 = length/2;
    int  d4 = length/4;
    int  d8 = length/8;

    chassis = new Rectangle(x,     y,    d1, d2, chassisColor);
    cab     = new Rectangle(x+d8, y+d8, d2, d4, NamedColor.GRAY );

    lightL  = new Light(x+7*d8, y,      d8);
    lightP  = new Light(x+7*d8, y+3*d8, d8);
}
```

The new code has more lines (the declaration of local variables was added) but the callings of constructors are a little bit more readable.

Fields × Parameters × Local Variables

433.   I see that local variables have a lot common with fields and parameters. Could you somehow summarize, what are the differences among the fields, the parameters and the local variables?

Let's divide my answer into several topics.

The Applicability (The Range of Validity)

A **field** (attribute) belongs to its object (a class or a class instance) and can be used in all its methods. If it is not private, also other object can join it. But usually we don't want it because the objects should be responsible for their data and cannot be dependent on what anybody can do with them behind their back. Therefore we should declare the fields always as private.

Opposite to it the **parameters** and the **local variables** are the property of their method and nobody else can use them. Therefore the access modifiers (public, private) are not quoted at parameters and local variables, because we cannot choose – they are always the private property of their method.

434. Wait a minute, you told that nobody should adjust the class fields and its instances. But we did it. For example the setStep(int) **method adjusted the value of the** step **field at all shapes.**

This is something different. I said that nobody can adjust these values behind the back of the class or the instance, so that they would not know about it, i.e. to change directly e.g. the value of the relevant field. In case someone would ask the class or the instances for the new adjustment by calling their methods, the addressed object knows about it and can check if the required change of the field can be permitted – e.g. that you do not try to adjust a reverse step.

435. You also told that the parameters and the local variables are the private property of their method and nobody can use them. But when I call a method, then I use them, don't I?

No, when you call a method, you write down expressions into parentheses, which the virtual machine counts and assigns the results to parameters as their initial values. But the calling method never comes to a direct contact with the parameter.

The Initialization (Assigning the Initial Value)

436. Well, what are further differences?

The **parameters** are initialized during calling the method – its initial value will be provided by the calling method. As soon as you enter the method, you can immediately use it.

You have to assign the initial value to the **local variables** in the method's body. You can choose if you assign it immediately in a declaration, as I have showed you in the last example, or if you only declare it and you assign the initial value sometimes later in an independent statement. The compiler will take care not to use it in a program before you assign them the initial value. Using a variable to which the initial value was not yet assigned is considered as a syntax error (compile-time error).

The possibilities of initializing the **fields** are the most manifold. You can choose if you will initialize them already in a declaration (their syntax is the same one as of the local variables) or in an independent assigning statement in the constructor, or you will not initialize them at all.

☞ The initialization in a declaration will be chosen if the initial value of the field doesn't depend on values of constructor's parameters. (The values of our fields were dependent on parameters and therefore we did not use the initialization in the declaration for now. However, soon we will meet such situation.)

☞ In case the initial value of the field depends on constructor's parameters, you can initialize only the field with an assigning statement in the constructor's body.

☞ The virtual machine resets the memory of the instance during its allocation and therefore the fields, which are initialized neither in the declaration, nor in the constructor, will have a zero value.

The fields, the zero initial value of which suits to us, theoretically do not need to be initialized at all, but it's not recommended. Generally, it is considered as far advantageous to initialize these fields explicitly directly in the declaration so that it would be evident that the fields are zero because their zero initial value is the required value, not because the programmer forgot to set the appropriate value.

437. You say that the virtual machine resets the memory of a created instance. So if we would not initialize the `bulb` field in the `Light` class, it would have a zero value. How then such zero bulb would look out?

I would like to run through all possible eventualities:

☞ The zero value of numerical values of primitive types is really zero.

☞ The zero of `boolean` fields is interpreted as the value `false`.

☞ At characters, it is the character with the code 0.

☞ The zero content of object type fields is interpreted as an empty reference, i.e. as a reference to nowhere. Java installs for it the identifier `null`. You can assign this value into the variable also in the program and you say by it that you don't need the reference which was hold there. If nobody else needs the referred object (i.e. no other variable points to it), the object becomes a candidate for removing and for recycling its memory by the garbage collector.

The Lifetime

The **fields** are born (i.e. a position in the memory is assigned to them) together with their object and live for the whole period of the object's life.

Opposite to it the **parameters** and the **local variables** receive a memory only at a moment of their initialization – parameters during calling a method, the local variables during the first assignment of the value. They finish their life in a moment when the program leaves a block in which the local variable has been declared.

438. Which block?

Oh, I am little bit ahead. In the section *Block* on page 385 I will show you that inside the method's body you can use another pair of braces to which you put certain statements – we call such part of code a **block**. A declaration of local variables may be a part of any block. These variables "die" in the moment when the program leaves the block where they were declared.

Generally it is recommended to minimize the life period of the variables, i.e. to declare them as late as possible and finish their life as soon as possible. The code is then more transparent.

439. From what you have told me I understand that parameters differ from local variables only by the fact that they are initialized by a calling method, whilst the local variables have to be initialized inside its body.

You understand it quite properly. Remember: **Parameters are local variables initialized by the calling method.**

Position and Module Setting

440. Before you show me certain exercise, I would like to see some usage.

You are true. Let's stay at the car because it is our most complicated object. You will learn to adjust its position as well as size. If you remember the convention about which we were speaking in the section *The `getXxx` and `setXxx` Messages/Methods* on page 40, then these methods should be named according to it `setPosition` and `setModule`. And because those are methods for setting the values of instance properties, you will locate it in the source code into the area introduced by a relevant comment. You can find their possible form for the car in the listing 23.3.

Listing 23.3:   *The definition of the methods setPosition(int,int) and setModule(int) in the Car class*

```java
//== INSTANCE GETTERS AND SETTERS =============================================

/****************************************************************************
 * Sets the given coordinates.
 *
 * @param x  Horizontal coordinate
 * @param y  Vertical coordinate
 */
public void setPosition(int x, int y)
{
    int d8 = chassis.getWidth() / 8;    // One eight of car's length

    chassis.setPosition(x,      y);
    cab    .setPosition(x+d8,   y+d8);
    lightL .setPosition(x+7*d8, y);
    lightR .setPosition(x+7*d8, y+3*d8);
}


/****************************************************************************
 * Sets the basic size from which we will derive all the gauges
 * of the object &ndash; in the case of the car it is
 * the car's length.
 *
 * @param module   The set module (the car's length)
 */
public void setModule(int module)
{
    int x  = chassis.getX();
    int y  = chassis.getY();
    int m1 = module;
    int m2 = m1/2;
    int m4 = m1/4;
    int m8 = m1/8;

    chassis.setSize(m1, m2);

    //Other parts of the car change their sizes as well as position.
    cab.setPosition(x+m8, y+m8);
    cab.setSize(m2, m4);

    lightL.setPosition(x+7*m8, y);
    lightR.setPosition(x+7*m8, y+3*m8);
    lightL.setModule(m8);
    lightR.setModule(m8);
}
```

441.   I am taken by surprise due to the program's complexity. And moreover, there is an error in it, because the compiler refused to compile it.

It's true; the definition is a little bit more complicated, but understandable. Adjustment of the position is simple, because all objects will really only shift. The chassis will move to a target position and other objects will keep their relative position towards the chassis. Therefore it is possible to take over the co-ordinates setting from the constructor, or derive it from the figure 22.1 on page 209.

Adjustment of the new size is worse because during the size change also the position of all parts is changing except the chassis. Therefore the chassis really changes only its size, but other parts, i.e. the cabin and the lights, have to shift so that they would move to a proper position on the new size chassis.

If it is still strange to you, try to draw a small car at a squared paper and a big one according to the figure 22.1 on page 209 and then go through the program and check that it counts the size properly.

442.   You try to gloss over the error somehow.

But there is no error in the program. The program only supposes that the Light class has already defined the methods setPosition(int,int) and setModule(int). I intended to leave their definition for the exercise. To make sure that the newly defined methods work properly, I fulfill the missing methods myself. But they are so simple that I will not quote them. First of all, try to derive them yourself, how they should look out and then look into the source code and check your estimations.

Instead of quoting the mentioned methods I will show you how you could define an auxiliary method for the test of changes in positions and car size. The method in the listing 23.4 receives the tested car in a parameter, moves it to the position which I selected so that it would not clash with other cars. It waits a moment after moving, then increases the car, then waits a moment again, subsequently it decreases the car, waits and finally it asks the canvas manager to cancel the car from the canvas. At the end it waits again so that you have time to realize that the car really disappeared before another one will move to this position.

Listing 23.4:   *The auxPositionSize(Car) method in the Car class*

```
private void auxPositionSize(Car car)
{
    final int ms = 500;
    car.setPosition(50, 200);    IO.pause(ms);
    car.setModule(200);          IO.pause(ms);
    car.setModule(25);           IO.pause(ms);
    CM.remove(car);              IO.pause(ms);
}
```

The Constants and the Magic Values

443.   Why the declaration of the ms variable begins with the word final?

By this I announce to the compiler that I will not change the value of this variable, i.e. that I will take it as a constant. The compiler then takes care about keeping this promise.

444.   And why did you define the constant local variable? You will neither save anything nor make it significantly better arranged.

Because I am keeping the *DRY rule*. (Do you remember it? If not, read once more the section *Unsuitable Copying of the Code* on page 196.)

445.   Perhaps it doesn't matter if you copy 500 or ms.

But it does matter. Imagine that I would like to change the period of waiting. In this way I only change the adjustment of the variable value and all values are immediately changed. But if I would not use the variable, I would have to go through the whole method and find all five hundreds which mark the period of waiting and change them properly. These simple methods are not so big problem but if this value would be spread along the whole (and possibly large) class, it would be far worse.

One of the very important programmer's rules says: **The magic values inside the code are forbidden!**

446.   But the five hundred is no magic value.

How no magic value. Perhaps you know what is the optimal time of waiting, not too long and not too short? And could you guarantee that tomorrow or after a year you will still consider the same value as optimal? The five hundred is just anticipated optimal value. Moreover, in a bigger program you only hardly estimate which five hundred represents the period of waiting and which one means e.g. a minimal amount you would like to have in your wallet.

By other words: all numbers except zero and one (and in some situations even these numbers) are considered as "magic" as well as nearly all values of object types except the empty reference null. Whenever you will need to use certain fixed value in a program, you should firstly define a constant and then use this constant instead of the value.

I know that this rule is often not observed – mainly when this value is used in a program only once or when the author is convinced that it will never change (very often it's not true, only he is persuaded). You can meet not keeping this rule often particularly in tests.

I recommend you to keep it in your mind and to observe it. Define the constants for immutable values which are used several times. Often it is advantageous to define the constants even for values which you will use only once because this will enable you to concentrate all declarations at one place. I will come back to this question during the explanation of the final class fields.

447.   You told me that "nearly all values of object types" are considered as "magic" – what does it mean nearly?

Until now we did not meet any "non-magic" object value. But I can tell you that e.g. empty string, i.e. a string which does not contain any mark – "" belongs among these values. Generally, we could say that objects which in their class have the same or analogous meaning as zero among numbers are "non-magic". (For example if we would define the Fraction class, then we could consider the zero fraction is a non-magic object value.) However, I am afraid that further in the course we will not meet such values.

Exercise

448.   I am afraid that today's exercise will be very demanding. I am expecting that I will add the setPosition(int,int) and setModule(int) methods even into the classes Arrow and TrafficLight.

Your expectations are proper, but it will not be so complicated. Both classes are simpler and there are only few recounts. If you understand how the car is defined, extending the arrow and the traffic light will be just playing for you.

Then think out a test method for all classes, similar to those one which I showed you for cars.

Review

Let's review what you have learned in this lesson:

☞ In case you should execute the very similar code many times, it is advantageous to define an independent method for such code and divergences of separate "accomplishments" should be provided through parameters.

☞ Auxiliary methods defined only for better definition of the code of the given class should be declared as private, i.e. with the private modifier.

☞ In case you need to save temporarily certain value in a method, you can declare a local variable for it.

☞ In local variable's declaration firstly its type, followed by a name and if need be an initialization should be stated. The whole declaration is completed by a semi-colon.

☞ You can use local variables only inside methods or blocks.

☞ You cannot use a local variable until you assign an initial value to it. Using of local variable without any initialization is a syntax (compile-time) error.

☞ The parameters are local variables whose initial value is provided by a calling method.

☞ After the method closes its work, its local variables finish to exist.

☞ In case you would forget to initialize a field, the zero value is left in it.

☞ The zero value is interpreted differently according to each data type.

    ☞ Numerical data types interpret the zero value as the number zero.

    ☞ The logic type boolean interprets it as the value false.

    ☞ The type char interprets this value as so called empty character, i.e. the character with the 0 code.

    ☞ Object data types interpret it as a not existing reference (a reference to nowhere) marked with the keyword null.

☞ It is recommended not to use "magic values" in programs. All numerical values except zero and one are considered to be the "magic values". Similarly all object values with the exception of the empty reference null and the empty string ("") are considered to be "magic values".

☞ By quoting the final modifier I announce to the compiler that the variable is in fact a constant and that I will not change its value any more.

☞ You should use a constant whenever when you would like to use one value in the program at many places.

Project:
The resulting form of the project to which we come at the end of the lesson and after completing of all exercises is in the 123z_LocalVariables project.

24 Methods Returning a Value

What you will learn in this lesson
At first you will learn what is the difference between fields and object properties. You will come to know about the accessory methods and about the properties whose values are saved in fields, respectively obtained by a calculation. Finally you will see problems caused by wrongly defined equality of objects.

Project:
In this lesson we continue in using the 123z_LocalVariables project.

Fields versus Properties

449. **At the end of the last lesson you asked me to put the created methods among the accessory methods of instance properties. How do you recognize that something is a property? I read that the object's properties are defined as fields and its abilities as methods, but somehow it does not fit to me.**

A lot of programmers really confuse fields with properties, but mostly it is not convenient. The relation between a field and a property could be compared with a relation between an implementation and an interface:

☞ The **property** is something for what we can ask the object or what we can adjust at the object. Some properties can be detected as well as adjusted (e.g. a position of our graphic shapes), the others can be only detected (e.g. the name of a direction) and exceptionally there are also properties which can be only adjusted (there is no such property in our project). Object's properties are included into its interface.

☞ Opposite to it the **fields** are a matter of implementation (therefore they are declared as private). They serve for an internal need of the class and its instances for saving values which we need to be remembered. They are defined so that programming would be possible or so that the programming would be easier.

At the same time I told you that no one should be informed about how the task will be solved and therefore the fields are defined as private. Firstly this conceals how the task is solved and secondly it ensures that anybody could manipulate with the saved values behind your back.

450. **Should I understand it that besides fields and methods there is yet another kind of entity – properties?**

Some languages define properties as a special entity. However, Java authors came to the conclusion that asking for current value of properties identically as requirements for its setting are ordinary messages and therefore they are defined as ordinary methods in the program; they only defined certain conventions for making out their names – this was explained in the section *The getXxx and setXxx Messages/Methods* on page 40.

The Accessory methods

451.   When they are only ordinary methods, why we are speaking about them so long?

Well, they are not so ordinary. They are ordinary only from the compiler's view, because they look out equally as other methods. But from the programmer's view they have rather exceptional position because they know to reveal and set information about the internal state of objects.

Due to the fact they enable us to access to (in other respect secret) interiors of objects, we call them the **accessory methods** – we talked about them in the section *The getXxx and setXxx Messages/Methods* on page 40. Those methods which reveal the current state of objects are called **accessors**, and those which adjust the new state of objects are called **mutators**. You may remember that programmers prefer to call them **getters** and **setters**.

The relation between a field and a property can be of three types:

☞   There may be fields "covered" by a property – e.g. it is a color field of our graphic objects, whose value we detect by the getColor() method and adjust by the setColor(NamedColor) method.

☞   Then there may be fields with which no property corresponds and therefore their value can be neither read nor set from outside. These fields are the matter of implementation only. E.g. it is the bulb field of our light or fields that are parts of arrows, cars and traffic lights.

☞   On the other hand we can have properties, that are not "covered" by any fields, because it is not worthy to remember them and it is better to detect their value only by a query (by evaluation of an expression). Such property is e.g. an information concerning if the given light is just on or off.

The accessory methods (getters and setters) are often considered as a special group of methods. They have their own conventions for creating their names and usually they are placed together in the source code. Therefore there are the line comments in the standard class pattern, quoting the sections of the accessory methods of class properties and of the accessory methods of instance properties.

452.   You told that values of properties can be detected or adjusted. Last time we have only adjusted them. Why we did not join both activities?

When detecting values of properties we have to solve the problems in some cases, which we will not meet during adjusting the values. Therefore I postpone detecting the values into a separate lesson to have time and debate them in a little bit more detailed way.

The Properties Saved in the Fields

453.   Would it be possible to include something problem-less at the beginning of the lesson?

Yes, of course. Let's start with the simple properties which essentially do not bring any problems – e.g. by determining the color of our light. We remember the color in the color field, so that it is sufficient to write the method which will take the content of this field and pass it to the calling method.

454.   When it passes the value, I cannot use it anymore. How I will switch on the light next time?

Don't be afraid, by passing the value you are not losing it. You only announce to the calling method what the value is. It is similar as when somebody would ask you how much money you have in your pocket. By saying this amount you are not losing the money.

455.   Well, so how I tell to the calling method what is the value for which it is asking?

As the last statement of the method you will write the return keyword followed by an expression whose value is given over to the calling method, and you will complete the whole statement with a semi-colon. (This statement is called the *return statement* according to the introductory keyword.)

Thus, if you would like to define the method returning the color of the switched on light, you should write return followed by the name of the field in which the reference to the relevant color is saved. When carrying out the return statement, the program looks into this field and returns the found value (in this case the reference to a color), i.e. it returns this reference to the calling method.

I remind that when defining the method which returns certain value you have to quote the type of the returned value in its header instead of the existing void, so that the compiler could disclose some of your possible faults. Then the definition of the method returning the color of the given light might look out as in the listing 24.1.

Listing 24.1:   *The definition of the getColor() method in the Light class*

```
/****************************************************************************
 * Returns the color of the light when turned on.
 *
 * @return  Color of the light when turned on
 */
public NamedColor getColor()
{
    return color;
}
```

I would like to remind that in case the program would be more understandable, you can write the above mentioned return statement in the following form:

```
return this.color;
```

456.   Why there is the second line in the documentation comment? It says the same as the first one.

The documentation comment begins with the description of what the method makes. Then the information follows quoted by a relevant javadoc tags about which we were speaking in the section *Javadoc Tags* on page 187. It's true that in a number of cases these descriptions are very near. However the javadoc program processes each of them by a little bit different way. *NetBeans* which I use for programs development always warns me if I miss using some of these tags and thus I have learned to use them. But I will not press on you to do it as well, especially if you would only repeat what you wrote a while ago.

Returning of the Values Obtained by Calculation

457. I would be interested in another point. You told that there may be an expression behind the `return` **keyword. Please, show it at an example.**

The name of the field which we used in the last method is also an expression; despite it is a very simple one. But I understand that you would like to see something more complex. Let's look how we would define the getDiameter() and isOff() methods.

Let's start with the getDiameter() method. The diameter is a whole number, which means the method's return value is of the int type. The light's diameter is not saved which means that first of all you have to ask the bulb ellipse for it. It will not tell us its diameter, but due to the fact we know that it is a circle, we can ask its height or its width instead of it. Then the definition of the method might look out as in the listing 24.2.

Listing 24.2:   The definition of the getDiameter and isOff methods in the Light class

```
/****************************************************************************
 * Returns the diameter of the light.
 *
 * @return Diameter of the light
 */
public int getDiameter()
{
    return bulb.getHeight();
}


/****************************************************************************
 * Returns information if the light is currently on or off.
 *
 * @return If the light is turned off, it returns {@code true},
 *         otherwise it returns {@code false}
 */
public boolean isOff()
{
    return bulb.getColor().equals(switchedOffColor);
}
```

Object Equality Testing

When detecting if the light is on or off the situation is even more complicated. First of all you will ask the bulb for its current color and then we will ask this color if it is a color which the given light has saved in the switchedOff field. Please, notice at this example that even the ordinary test of objects equality leads to sending the equals (Object) message (to calling the method).

In this example we met for the first time using of the equals(Object) method which was mentioned in the section *The Class Object* on page 60 as one of methods inheriting all objects from the Object class. The reference to the object is given over in the method's parameter where it is necessary to discover if the object is equal to the addressed object, i.e. to the object to which the given message was sent (whose method was called).

A number of beginners would solve the mentioned example by dividing it into two to three statements similar to the following sequence:

```
NamedColor color = bulb.getColor();

boolean    swOff = color.equals(switchedOff);
return     swOff;
```

But I wanted to show you that in case you receive certain reference from the constructor or the method, it is not necessary to firstly save it and only consequently use it, but that you can use it directly. You can, but you do not have to. Choose yourself which way is more acceptable (or better said more understandable) for you.

458. You told in the section *The Basic Arithmetic Operators* on page 207 that the value equality is tested by the `==` operator. Why do not use it now and why you use the `equals(Object)` method?

The operator `==` tests if it is the same instance. Contrary to it the `equals(Object)` method tests if both objects represent the same value. It is the same at instances of certain objects. Our `NamedColor` class watches over so that two different instances representing the same color would not be created, but such classes are rather exceptional. Therefore, when comparing the values of objects we prefer using of the `equals(Object)` method and the operator `==` is used only in cases if you really ask whether it is the same object.

You know that I am always repeating that the only one thing what you can rely on in the program, is the fact that the assignment will soon change. During including of such change it can happen that the class, where the equality of values may be tested as the equality of instances, will lose this property (the instance is equivalent only to itself). However, the code using the `equals(Object)` method will probably be operating even after this change properly. We will get back to this topic in details in the section *Problems with Objects Comparing* on page 251.

Test of Returning the Proper Value

459. We have defined two methods and we could try how they operate.

You are true. Let's define another test. I will show you how you can verify if the test method returns the proper value.

460. Wonderful – I am going to open the test class.

Not yet, we are returning to the interactive mode and we will leave the test definition to *BlueJ* to which we will only show what should be programmed. Then you will have the look at the result and you can write the next test yourself.

461. Well, so what should I show?

Let's go step by step to review the interactive test creating:

1. Compile the class with the newly defined methods. Thus you simultaneously restart the virtual machine which means no garbage can creep in the test definition.

2. Enter the command **Create the Test Method** in the context menu of the `LightTest` class. *BlueJ* opens a dialog, where you should enter `testGetColor` as the test method name.

3. The test class creates a test fixture and opens a dialog reporting, that the test fixture is ready. Confirm the window and ask the lightXYDC instance (this is the big blue one in the middle up) about its color, i.e. send the getColor() message to it.

4. *BlueJ* opens the dialog, in which the reference to the returned color can be obtained, and through the checkbox **Assert that** it asks if the returned value should be checked. Leave it checked and into the input field enter that the returned color should match with the NamedColor.BLUE color (see figure 24.1). Then press the **Close** button.

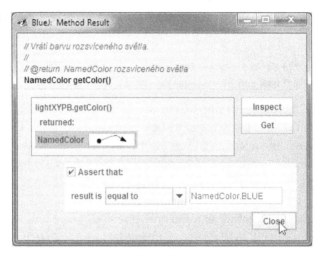

Figure 24.1
Entering of the return value test

5. Make the same procedure with the light created by the default constructor, i.e. with the light light0. Tell it that the light should be blue; despite we know it is wrong.

6. Complete defining the test method.

Figure 24.2
The report on the cause of the test failure

When you run the right now defined test method, *BlueJ* opens the window **Test Results**, in which the red color of the central zone means that the test did not pass. In case you click on the test up, you will see the following message below:

```
expected <blue> but was <yellow>
```

The message says that the test method expected the blue color (according to your entering), but that the called method returned the yellow color (see figure 24.2).

In case you press the button **Show Source** beneath, the editor's window will open with the source code of the LightTest class with the emphasized line where the test stopped. The test looks as follows:

Figure 24.3
The source code of the test with highlighted fault

Please notice that *BlueJ* tests the return value so that it calls the method assertEqulas(?,?), to which it passes the expected value in the first parameter and in the second parameter the value which it receives by calling the relevant method.

462. What the two question marks mean in the method assertEqulas(?,?)?

I just indicated that it is a method with two parameters whose type we do not know yet. I can tell you that the method has a lot of overloaded versions and surely the one which you need for your test is among them.

463. This means that when I revise the test definition, the test will prove to be correct.

Yes, it is sufficient to replace the wrongly expected blue color in the second statement with the yellow one and the test will pass through. If you revise the second statement to the following form:

```
assertEquals(NamedColor.YELLOW, light0.getColor());
```

everything will be o. k.

464. Shouldn't we test also what the method returns with the switched off light?

Good, we should do it. Try to fulfill statements for switching off both instances into the method and then test once more what the method returns to you.

465.   It's not operating. When switched off, the big light was black, but it insisted that it is blue.

But it is good. The method getColor() always returns the color of the switched on light, even in the case when the light is switched off. Look at its definition. The testing statements before and after switching off have to look out quite identically.

Exercise

466.   Oh, I see, I am slow on the uptake today. Better give me examples for exercising and let's finish for today.

Last time you defined methods to all our classes for setting a position and a module. Now add to all four classes (i.e. including the Light class) the methods returning the current position and module of their instances, i.e. define the following methods:

☞   getX(), which will return the horizontal coordinate of the given instance,

☞   getY(), which will return the vertical coordinate of the given instance and

☞   getModule(), which will return that the module which was adjusted to the method setModule(int), i.e. the width or the height of the arrow (it is the same in this case), the length of the car and the diameter of the traffic light lights.

Implement the IMovable interface by all classes. Then define the test method testSmoothMovement testing the correctness of your implementation through a smooth movement mediated by a mover in each test class. I recommend you to make them translucent at first, because then you will be able to see how one is floating under the other one.

Don't forget to add the annotation @Override in front of the relevant methods during the interface implementation – we were speaking about it in the section *The @Override Annotation* on page 173. At the same time I would recommend you to cancel (now useless) implementation of the IPaintable interface, because it is a logic consequence of implementing its subtype – the IMovable interface. Even without it the project will look out a little bit stuffed and that's why I recommend you to re-arrange the class diagram according to the figure 24.4 and thus prepare it for the classes which we will add in the next lessons.

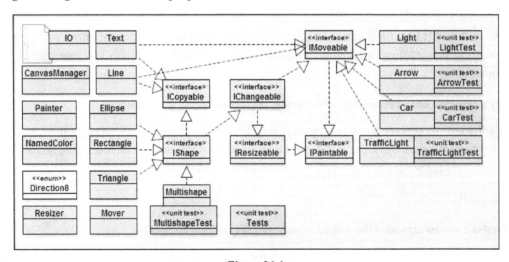

Figure 24.4
The project window with the newly arranged class diagram

467. But the class `Light` already has the method for detecting its dimension – we have defined the method `getDiameter()`.

So we shall have two of them. Sometimes it is advantageous, if the object has two various methods that make the same (we could mark them as synonyms). I don't say that in this case it is especially advantageous, but I wanted to show you that you can meet also such things.

468. But you told me that the code should not be repeated.

So don't repeat it – call one method from the other one.

Review

Let's review what you have learned in this lesson:

- ☞ We do not realize a lot of properties and abilities of objects we are meeting in current life, because they are absolutely self-evident. However, we have to equip our objects in the program with all properties that we will need in the program and teach them all necessary abilities.

- ☞ The field serves for the internal need of the class and its instances, and in most cases we conceal them from surrounding objects.

- ☞ This, what the objects are willing to tell about themselves to their vicinity, is described as a property. Something what another object can ask for or even what another object can adjust.

- ☞ Objects ask for properties and set them by calling the **accessory methods**.

- ☞ The methods which return the current state of their objects are called **accessors**, and those which adjust the new state of their objects are called **mutators**.

- ☞ Java established a convention according to which the identifiers of accessors start with the word **get** followed by the name of the detected property. In case the detected property is a logic value, the word **get** can be replaced by the word **is**. The identifiers of mutators should start with the word **set**.

- ☞ Programmers prefer to call the accessory methods *getters* and *setters*.

- ☞ Properties usually correspond to fields, but it is not a strict rule. Some properties may not have the corresponding field, and opposite, some fields may not have the corresponding properties.

- ☞ The mutators (setters) are mostly defined as methods with parameters, in which the calling object enters the required value of the given property.

- ☞ It is necessary to decide if reading and/or adjusting of each property can be allowed.

- ☞ The tests should be programmed in such way so that their evaluation would not bring overabundance of various kinds of information.

- ☞ If a method should return certain value, it has to finish with a statement consisting from the keyword `return` followed by an expression whose result will be returned, and closed with a semi-colon.

- ☞ We have to quote the type of the returned value (the return type) in the method's header.

☞   The test method can verify if the called method returns the proper value.

   ☞   When defining the test method in the interactive mode we ask for checking the obtained
       value by setting the option **Assert that** and writing down the expected value into the
       joined text field. When we don't want to check it, we should clear the option.

   ☞   In the direct definition of the test method we verify the returned value by calling the
       method assertEquals(?,?), to which we pass the expected value in the first parameter, and
       the value returned by the tested method in the second parameter.

☞   When the test does not pass, *BlueJ* opens the window **Test Results** with a red central zone. You
    can click in it at the crashed test at the upper panel and *BlueJ* will show you in the lower panel
    what the mistake in the test was and where it is located.

☞   By pressing the button **Show Source** in the **Test Results** window the editor's window with the
    source code of the test class opens with an emphasized line where the test stopped.

Project:
The resulting form of the project to which we came at the end of the lesson and after completing all exer-
cises is in the 124z_ReturningValues project.

25 The Crate

What you will learn in this lesson
In this lesson you will learn about passing the parameters by value and by reference. Then you will be presented with the design pattern Crate and you will learn its basic requirements. At the conclusion the methods will be defined which return the crate as their return value.

Project:
In this lesson we continue in using the 124z_ReturningValues *project.*

The Fields Representing a Set of Values

469. When I ask an object about its position I have to ask twice. Would it be possible to arrange that I could ask about its position only once?

Yes, it would be possible. Similarly as the position we could detect also the size. Both characteristics are represented by the couple of values. The methods which are to give us this information should return these two values at the same time. The problem is that Java does not know it (as well as most other languages) and we have to use a trick advised by the design pattern *Crate*. I will show you how it is possible to define the method getPosition(), which will return current position of an object, i.e. its horizontal as well as vertical coordinate, and the method getSize(), which will return its current size, i.e. its height and width.

Passing Parameters by Value and by Reference

470.   I've heard that it's possible to return the values also in parameters.

There are various ways of transmitting parameters to the called methods. The most used are the following two:

☞   The term *call by value* (or *pass by value*) means that the method gets just the value that the caller provides. More precisely the copy of the passed value is created and it is set as the initial value of the parameter of the called method. Because during this way of value passing the called method works with only the copy of the passed value, no changes of the passed values can influence the original value in the calling method.

☞   Contrary to it, the term *call by reference* (or *pass by reference*) means that the method gets the location of the variable that the caller provides. Thus, the method can modify the value stored in the variable that is passed by reference. We could say that the calling method loans the place to the called method. The called method then uses this (lent) memory place as its local variable. Because this memory place is the property of the calling method, the called method will not cancel it during its return, as is usually done with current local variables. Therefore, after finishing the called method the calling method can look into this variable and learn which value the called method left there.

471.　I think I understand but I would appreciate an example.

Imagine that you will find Sudoku in newspapers, which you cannot solve. Therefore you will ask an experienced friend to tell you if the given riddle is solvable. So that he could answer your question you have to give him Sudoku as a parameter.

☞　In case you will give the riddle over through a value, you will write it down on a paper and you will pass him this paper. Your friend will solve the riddle and will tell you that it is solvable. After that you can start solving it as well. His solution did not influence your Sudoku in any way.

☞　In case you will give the riddle over through a reference, you will tell to your friend: "In this newspaper there is Sudoku which may be not solvable. What do you think about it?" You did not give him a copy but you directly showed him (i.e. you gave him a reference) the object of your interest. Your friend will take the newspapers, will solve Sudoku and will tell you that it is solvable. But now you have nothing to solve, because your Sudoku is already solved. You can only look at the changes made by your friend.

472.　But this means that if we would pass several parameters through a reference we could obtain several values in these parameters – one value in each of them.

No, we couldn't, because Java passes all parameters by value. Certain languages enable calling by reference but a number of programmers refuse them because the program is less transparent. Therefore the Java authors rejected this possibility and chose a different solution.

473.　You told me that at instances of object types the program knows only a reference to this instance. The instances of object types are therefore given over through a reference.

Yes and no, if the parameter is of object type, the caller really passes the reference to the relevant object. But this reference represents the given object for us – this is the passed value. Whenever we are working with an object in the program, in fact we are working with a reference to this object and thus the object is passed to the called method by value, i.e. only a copy of reference to it is passed. In case we would like to pass it through a reference, we would have to pass a reference to the memory place, where the reference to the object is saved (a reference to this reference).

　　In other words: when passing an object (better say a reference to an object) by value it can happen that the called method changes certain properties of the given object (e.g. it changes the shape size), but it cannot happen that – after returning from the called method – the field or the local variable will refer to a different object than particularly to that we have passed as a parameter.

　　But if I would pass an object through a reference, the called method might change the content of the allocated memory place and the passed field or local variable may then refer to a different object. As I've said, Java does not support calling by reference and thus nothing like that can happen to us.

474. Well, I did not absorb it fully, but I will try to continue and concentrate on what is valid for Java. So how Java solves the need to send several values at once?

Java solves these situations with the assistance of crates; they are instances of the special class that defines an individual field for each of transferred values. Whenever you need to pass or return a group of relevant values, you create the instance of the given class (the crate) and you fill in its attributes with transferred values and you pass this object to the calling method or return it to the caller. From the compiler's view you pass or return the only one value – the reference to the crate but in fact you pass or return all values which you wanted to pass.

475. What is the advantage of this way compared to passing the values in parameters?

As I have already told you: it is far transparent. Parameters serve to one thing: so that we could pass the data for work to the called method. The return value serves for returning the result of the called method work. As soon as the methods start returning some results in the return value and the others in parameters, we are on the best way to install a lot of faults into our program.

Besides that the crate can serve not only for returning the requested values but also to keeping data for their further passing to the called methods or transporting these values. Therefore this design pattern is often called *Transport Object*.

Crate / Transport Object

476. Well, show me how such crate is used.

Before we start using the crate, we have to make it:

1. First of all you have to clarify which values you would like to collect into the crate.

2. You define a class in which you declare a corresponding field for each of the passed values. It's a habit to define these fields as public constants.

3. Then you define a constructor which initializes all crate's fields.

477. You told that "it's a habit to define fields as public constants". But in the section *Introducing Fields* on page 158 you said that nobody should know which fields the class uses and therefore the fields should be declared as private.

Each rule has its exceptions and the crate is such exception. The only purpose of the crate is to enable saving and/or transporting of certain set of values. It is generally known which attributes the crate has – and there's no reason to hide it.

If I should compare it to a life example, I would tell that if you need to bring few trifles from a room to a garage you will use a suitable crate. But if you decide to send these things to your friend by mail, you will carefully pack them so that nobody could see what is inside the package and would not be lured to "borrow" them.

On the other side it is good if you can rely on values put into the crate, i.e. that the values cannot change. Therefore the fields of the crate are defined as constants.

478.   How the attributes in the crate could change?

Easily, as I said many times, methods in Java never return an object, but always only a reference to an object. Therefore you cannot guarantee that your reference is at the disposal of anybody else (and it does not matter if he obtained them on purpose or by a mistake). Then there is a danger that this person can change the value of certain field, and your crate stops to correspond with the reality without you would know it.

479.   Don't spook me. You always make a detective story and a spy novel from the programming.

But it's the life. As I have told you several times the greatest enemy of your programs is you yourself and your human substance making faults. And moreover, when you learn creating programs ensured against faults of those who do not want to harm them, it will be easier for you to secure your programs against those who want to break them.

The Constants

480.   Well, you told me that the fields should be defined as public **constants. How to do it?**

The constants in Java are defined by adding the keyword final among their modifiers – you met this already in the listing 23.4 on page 218. You can define a field, or a parameter or a local variable as a constant. Their value can be assigned to them only once. Mostly it is assigned to them in the declaration, but often you do not know the value of fields in the time of declaring, thus you can do it in the constructor and initialize the value there. As soon as the constant receives the assigned initial value, the compiler considers any further attempts to assign other value as the compile-time (syntax) error.

In case you would define a class whose instances – the crates – would serve for saving coordinates of current position, you would define their fields in the part CONSTANT FIELDS OF INSTANCES. Then the whole definition might correspond with the listing 25.1 (the line comments quoting unused sections are left out):

Listing 25.1:   *The* Position *class*

```
/******************************************************************************
 * Instances of class {@code Position} are transport objects (crates)
 * containing coordinates.
 * Their attributes are therefore defined as public constants.
 */
public class Position
{
    //== CONSTANT INSTANCE FIELDS ===============================================

    /** Horizontal coordinate. */
    public final int x;

    /** Vertical coordinate. */
    public final int y;


    //== CONSTUCTORS AND FACTORY METHODS=========================================
```

```
/****************************************************************************
 * Creates a crate containing given coordinates.
 *
 * @param x Horizontal coordinate
 * @param y Vertical coordinate
 */
public Position(int x, int y)
{
    this.x = x;
    this.y = y;
}
}
```

In case you want to check the properties of constants, you can initialize certain field in the declaration (e.g. to zero it) or to add the statement

```
this.x = 0;
```

at the constructor's end. You will see that the compiler marks it as a syntactic fault and announces that the given variable was not initialized:

```
Variable x might already have been assigned
```

When you delete the statement, it will be o.k. again.

481. You said that I can define also a local variable as a constant. Isn't it a little bit contradiction in terms?

Don't deal with it. Take it as a variable to which you can write its value only once – it is similar to CD-ROM. After this initialization you can only read it.

482. So the crate's fields are not treated through the accessory methods?

Mostly not, but the frequently used crates are equipped with getters, so that you can choose. And we shall equip with them also the instances of the Position class as well. Sometimes I will show you to which they may suit to us.

Methods Working with the Crate

483. Well I've created a crate. What to do with it?

Let's supplement two methods to the lights which will work with the crate. The first one will return the crate with a current position and the second one will adjust the position passed in the crate. Look at the definition in the listing 25.2.

Listing 25.2: The methods getPosition() and setPosition(int,int) in the Light class

```
public Position getPosition()
{
    return new Position(getX(), getY());
}
public void setPosition(Position p)
{
    this.setPosition(p.x, p.y);
}
```

484.   Oh, you took me by surprise a bit. Why the new position is made out in the first definition? After all the light already has its position.

The light has its position, but it is not saved. Therefore, when somebody asks this position, it is necessary to make out a crate into which the necessary information would be put. In other words, a new instance of the Postion class has to be created where its horizontal as well as vertical coordinates are saved. Then this crate can be returned to the calling method as the asked position.

485.   I don't understand the second definition as well. There is this as if the method would call itself?

The method does not call itself, but it calls the overloaded version of the newly defined method, i.e. it calls the method setPosition(int,int), which we have already defined (you can find it in the source code). I put the optional this into the definition to make it obvious that the instance calls its own method.

You can often meet whole sets of overloaded methods in programs which make the same and differ only in the composition of their parameters. These sets of methods are mostly defined in such way that one of them is defined in a classic style and the rest only prepares a set of parameters and call any of their colleagues. It is a usual construction, similar to those we used in the definition of overloaded versions of constructors. The only difference is that the dot behind this is missing in case of constructors whilst it is used in case of methods.

486.   And the next step is testing, isn't it?

Good, let's prepare a little test in which the couple of lights will change their positions. Again we will compose it from an auxiliary method in which we explain to two lights –to their parameters – how they should change their positions. The test method will call this auxiliary method and pass the selected candidates exchanging their positions to it. Simply a little *puss-in-the-corner*. You can find the definition of both methods in the listing 25.3.

Listing 25.3:   *The methods auxSwapPositions(Light,Light) and testSwapPositions() in the LightTest class*

```
public void auxSwapPositions(Light s1, Light s2)
{
    int ms = 1000;

    s1.switchOff();
    s2.switchOff();
    IO.pause(ms);

    Position p1 = s1.getPosition();
    s1.setPosition(s2.getPosition());
    s2.setPosition(p1);

    IO.pause(ms);
    s1.switchOn();
    s2.switchOn();

    IO.pause(ms);
}
```

```
public void testSwapPositions()
{
    auxSwapPositions(light0,    lightXYPB);
    auxSwapPositions(lightXYB, lightXYP);
    auxSwapPositions(lightXYP, light0);
}
```

487.   I wanna ask about the auxiliary method. Why did you define a variable for the position of the first parameter and none for the position of the second one?

Because in the following statement I am moving the first light to the position of the second one. During this moving I can obtain the required position by asking the second light for its position. However, when the first light will be already moved, I would have no chance to ask for its original position. Therefore I had to remember this position in a local variable before moving, so that I would be able to pass it to the second light as its required target position.

Exercise

488.   Oh, which exercise will you give me today? I guess I will be asked to fulfill the methods getPosition() **and** setPosition(Position) **into the remained classes and exchange their instances.**

You estimated treating with the accessory methods right, but only partly. Your today's task has three phases:

1. Put the project 125b_Crate_Start into operation

Open the new project called 125b_Crate_Start and put it into operation. At the first view this project looks out as the previous one but it cannot be compiled, because there are new versions of graphic classes in it which take into account the crates Position, Size and Area. But the classes Size and Area are not yet the part of the project which means you have to define them firstly. There is a place prepared for them close to the class Position. Your task will be as follows:

☞   To define the class Size with the fields width and height, which will be an equivalent of our class Position, only the size of instances will be saved in it instead of the position.

☞   To define the class Area with the fields x, y, width and height, whose instances will represent the crates saving simultaneously both the position as well as the size. This class will have two constructors:

  ☞   Area(int x, int y, int width, int height)
  ☞   Area(Position pozition, Size size)

As I have indicated, until you would define these two classes, it will be not possible to compile the project because a number of classes rely on their existence.

2. Import the classes `Light`, `Arrow`, `TrafficLight` and `Car` and put them into operation

You start the second phase with importing our four classes from the previous project. You will discover that they cannot be compiled. The reason is the different definition of the `IMovable` interface. Look at its documentation – I can help you saying that there are two differences:

☞ It doesn't require implementation of methods `getX()` and `getY()` from implementing classes.

☞ Besides the previously required method `setPosition(int,int)` it requires implementation of the methods `getPosition()` and `setPosition(Position)`.

Several tasks ensue from these requirements. Try to solve them yourself and in case you would not succeed, have a look at further items as a help. You have to do the following:

☞ Cancel the annotation `@Override` of all classes of the methods `getX()` and `getY()`, because they do not override any supertype's method.

☞ Define the method `setPosition(Position)` in them and I recommend you to add immediately the annotation `@Override`.

☞ Supplement the definition of the method `getPosition()` at those classes which still do not have this method defined, and again I recommend you to supplement it with the annotation `@Override`.

3. Supplement and Test these Classes

Moreover, in all four classes I will ask you to implement the method `getSize()`, which returns the current size of the given instance, i.e. the instance of the `Size` class with the fields containing the current width and height of the given instance (i.e. the car's width will be twice bigger than its height and on the contrary, the traffic light's height will be three times bigger than its width).

The new form of the `IMovable` interface leads to the new `Mover` class. Thus, in the second phase, you can verify the correctness of the implementation through exchanging the positions of both objects by moving them smoothly from one position to the other with the new mover.

> **Note:**
> The `IResizable` interface passed a similar change as the `IMovable` interface – it started to use the method `getSize()` instead of methods `getWidth()` and `getHeight()` and added the method `setSize(Size)`. The new `Resizer` adapted to this change. We are not using it in our examples, but nothing prevents you to make out your own examples in which you will use it.

489. Oh, I think I will have work for the whole week-end.

It's not as difficult as it looks at the first sight. If you will start you will finish with it in a while.

Review

Let's review what you have learned in this lesson:

☞ The programming languages mostly use passing parameters by value and/or by reference.

    ☞ When passing parameters through a value, the copy of the value of the actual parameter (argument) is passed to the called method. The calling method does not learn anything about possible changes of the value.

    ☞ When passing parameters by reference, the reference to the place in a memory is passed, which the called method uses as a parameter. After finishing the called method, the calling method will find the resulting value at this place.

☞ Returning output values in parameters makes the program less transparent. Therefore Java did not install this possibility and uses only passing parameters by value. In case of object parameters the reference to an object is passed by value.

☞ Certain properties of objects are represented by a group of values. Therefore the method, which should return a value of such property, should return several values at the same time.

☞ Detecting of the value of such property can be programmed in two ways:

    ☞ Ask for each coordinate separately.

    ☞ Think out a way how to pass all parts of information at the same time.

☞ In Java, such situations are solved with the help of crates which are instances of a special class that defines its own field for each of the stored value.

☞ The fields of a crate are usually defined as public constants.

☞ The crate enables not only to obtain a set of values in one step, but also to transport this set in one step and pass it to the called method as a parameter.

☞ The constant fields and the local variables are defined by adding the keyword final among their modifiers.

☞ For keeping the position we have defined the class Position with int fields named x and y holding the horizontal and vertical coordinates respectively.

☞ For keeping information about the size we have a similar class Size with fields width and height.

☞ For keeping information about the position and the size together we have the Area class with fields x, y, width and height.

Project:
The resulting form of the project to which we came at the end of the lesson and after completing all exercises is in the 125z_Crate project.

26 Strings and How to Work with Them

What you will learn in this lesson
In this lesson we will go back to problems with comparing the objects. You will see how the strings are as-sembled and how the object can define its text signature. Then I will explain you expressing of non-standard characters and you will become acquainted with a standard output and a standard error output.

Project:
In this lesson we continue in using the 125z_Crate project.

Problems with Comparing the Objects

490. **I have to tell you that you took me by surprise with the change of the project in which I should participate. I hope we will hold this new project for a long time.**

Yes and no. It should last until the end of the book to certain extent, but we will do some tiny changes in it and I suppose that you will help me with them again.

Now I would like to go back to the class Position and to the way how our objects adjust it. Previously we defined the test for lights in which the instances mutually moved to their positions so that you could see that they really reach the proper position. Today I will show you that if we consider two positions as equal it does not mean that also the computer consider them as equal.

I prepared an innovated version of our last test in which I let the computer check after each moving if the reached position is the same as the required one (I showed you how it is done in the section *Test of Returning the Proper Value* on page 225). You can see its source code in the listing 26.1.

Listing 26.1: *The test of moving the lights with checking the position correctness in the LightTest class*

```
public void auxSwapPositionsWithCheck (Light l1, Light l2)
{
    Position p1 = l1.getPosition();
    Position p2 = l2.getPosition();

    auxSwapPositions(l1, l2);

    assertEquals(p1, l2.getPosition());
    assertEquals(p2, l1.getPosition());
}
```

As you can see I didn't write the auxiliary method once again, but I used the previous one. I remembered the positions of both lights and called the method which exchanged the lights and after returning from it I let the program check if the new light's position is really equal to the original (remembered) one of its counterpart. The test itself is practically the same one as the previous, it only calls a different auxiliary method and I didn't copy it.

491. **And it finished as you predicted. The lights relocated as previously, but the test was not o.k. Similarly as before, the window Tests Results opened with a red central bar and after a click at the test line *BlueJ* announced:**
expected <Position@c59ad5> but was <Position@13829d5>
What a strange number is it?

This number indicates that we did not teach the positions to "sign" so that a text signature inherited from the Object class is used in which the class of the given instance is quoted followed by the mark @ and a number which can vary in each running of the program. Let's forget for a while that the program considers the same positions as different, and first of all I will show you how you can teach the objects to "sign". But before it we will speak about the text strings (i.e. about instances of the String class) and how to work with them.

Concatenation of the Text Strings

492. **From what you have explained until now I understand that the text *string* is certain sequence of characters. What can I do with them?**

The most frequent operation with the text strings is their concatenation. The operation is based on two rules:

☞ The text strings can be "summed" with the aid of an operator +. By adding two strings a new string ensues, e.g. from adding "abc"+"123" the new string "abc123" arises.

☞ In case you add anything else to a text string (more precisely any expression, the result of which is not a string), a text representation (I call it a *text signature*) of what you add is added. In case there will be a value 50 in the integer variable average, the result of the addition

    "Diameter = " + diameter

will be the string

    Diameter = 50

Notice that when I wanted to have a space after the equals sign, I really had to write it down in the given string. Neither the compiler nor the virtual machine will add supplementary spaces and on the opposite it will not delete any surplus spaces. Everything will be recorded exactly as you ordered.

493. **May I sum more than two summands?**

Of course, in the total you can have as many summands as you need.

Text Representation (Text Signature)

494. **You told me that when I add to the string something what is not a string, a signature of what I added is concatenated with the string. What is added to it when I add a color? In other words: what is the text signature of the color?**

If I will answer you now your color question, you will ask for something else in a while. Therefore I will explain you fully what is the text representation of primitive values as well as object types (if you would forget you can remind them in the section *Primitive and Object Types* on page 35) in Java:

☞ The **whole numbers**, i.e. the values of int, long, byte and short types are the simplest – their text representation is the written form of the number which you know from mathematics. The value *one hundred and twenty three* is therefore "signed" as 123, the value *minus three hundred and twenty one* is signed -321.

☞ The **real numbers**, i.e. the values of double and float types are a little bit more complicated. The numbers around one are written in the similar way, which you know from the school – e.g. 12.3 or 0.45. For the very large or very small numbers the so called *scientific notation* is used, which you know from calculators. In this notation the number $1.23.10^4$ is displayed as 1.23E4.

☞ The **logic values**, i.e. the values of boolean type are again simple because the values true and false are signed as true and false. How simple.

☞ The **characters**, i.e. the values of char type are mostly also simple, because their text representation is the character itself. Only in some special cases (e.g. when the character has no representation in the font in use) it can be a little bit different – I'll explain it soon.

☞ Well and only the objects remain. It is again relatively simple: the signature (i.e. text representation) of all objects is the text returned by their method toString(). What it will be depends on the object's own decision. The instance of NamedColor class, you were asking for, is signed with the name of the given color.

495.   But our instances do not have any toString() method.

They do have – they inherited it from the Object class (we were speaking about it in the section *The Class Object* on page 60). It expresses each instance as a name of its class followed @ and by the hash-code of this instance in the hexadecimal numeral system by the character. (The hash-code is an integer number that – to a certain extent – represents the instance.) That is just the number on which you were asking at the lesson's beginning.

As you see the inherited version of the signature does not bring too extensive information. Therefore the programmers mostly equip their classes with their own version of the method toString(), which generates a signature reasonably characterizing the relevant instance.

496.   So in case I'd define the method toString() in the Position class, it will write me something more reasonable?

It will write you exactly what the method toString() returns. Let's define it e.g. as shown at the listing 26.2.

Listing 26.2: The definition of the toString() method in the Position class

```
/***************************************************************************
 * Returns a string representation of the instance.
 * It is used mostly for debugging purposes.
 *
 * @return String representation of the instance
 */
@Override
public String toString()
{
    return "Position[x=" + x + ", y=" + y + "]";
}
```

497.   Well, I cannot say that the expression describing the return value would be one of the most transparent, but with a bit of endeavor it may be readable.

I admit that the last statement is not so well arranged because you cannot recognize which part of the text is inside quotation marks and therefore it will be copied, and which part is an expression written outside of quotation marks and therefore it will be replaced by the text representation of its value.

I know that if the statement would be written at more lines it would be more transparent but the programmers mostly write it as quoted above. That's why I will not spoil you; on the contrary I will ask you to learn reading it.

Examine the statement in detail and notice where the commas are written. If we know that there is no space before comma and that it should be placed immediately behind the number, we have to write it behind the quotation marks in the next string. The comma will be followed by a space and the name of another parameter in the value of which we are interested.

And now run again the test `testSwapPositionsWithCheck` and you will see that the error will stay but you will receive more extensive information about the position with which the test method has problems.

498.   You are true. When I opened the test now, the following record appeared in the window Tests Result
`expected:<Position[x=0, y=0]> but was:<Position[x=0, y=0]>`
This is far more readable but I can see that *BlueJ* makes things up because the positions are the same.

Unfortunately they are not the same – you can see it from the previous message (different hash-codes indicates different instances). But I will explain it in the next lesson in which you will also hear how to repair it. Now I would like to continue in speaking about the text strings. You will need it for further work.

499.   I would like to continue in solving the fault but I try to skip it. So what you would like to tell me?

Create the instance of the `Position` class representing e.g. the coordinates [10, 20] and send the message `inform(Object)` to the I0 class to which you will pass this position as a parameter. You should obtain a window as in the figure 26.1.

Figure 26.1
The signature of the position on coordinates [10, 20]

Line Ending

500.   Well, what should I do if I would like to write several of these positions at once?

No problem, but you have to use a character for ending the line. It cannot be put into the text as an ordinary character you met until now. You have to insert this character into a text as \n. In case you create the variables p1, p2 and p3 in the interactive mode which will gradually refer to positions [1, 2],

[10, 20] and [100, 200] and if you enter the parameter to the inform(Object) message in the following form

     p1 + "\n" + p2 + "\n" + p3

the IO class depicts a dialog as in the figure 26.2.

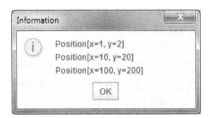

Figure 26.2
Signatures of three positions, each of them at the separate line

501.   When I would like to leave a line should I write the line end character twice, one after another "\n\n"?

Yes, and I remind you can write it to an arbitrary place in the string. Whenever the program meets it, it lines in the output text.

The Escape Sequence

502.   Why the new line character is written as the pair of different characters?

All is coming from the fact that according to syntax rules each text string has to finish at the same line on which it started. Because there are further special characters, the unified notation – so called *escape sequence* – has been defined for them.

Each such sequence begins with a backslash followed by an identification character. Java defines the following escape sequences:

\b   *Backspace* (deletes the previous character – it operates on few devices only).

\t   Horizontal tabulator (moves the text cursor to the next tabulation position at the line).

\n   Line feed (enters an end of line and continues writing on the new line)

\f   Form feed (enters an end of page and continues writing on the next page).

\r   Carriage return (returns the text cursor to the beginning of the line). However, certain systems (e.g. old Mac) use this character as a new line; certain others (e.g. *Windows*) use it as a part of two character sequence \r\n representing end-of-line.

\"   Quotation marks (so that it would be possible to write quotation marks inside quotation marks).

\'   Apostrophe (so that it would be possible to enter apostrophe inside apostrophes – '\'').

\\   Backslash (when alone it marks a beginning of an escape sequence).

\uHHHH Whichever character including those that are not possible to write from the keyboard (HHHH marks four numbers of the character's code in the hexadecimal radix [hexadecimal – that's why H is used] – e.g. the ± character can be written as \u00B1).

503.   I did not understand why the apostrophe is among escape sequences.

As I've already said the char type, whose values are characters, is included into primitive data types. And now I will tell you that its values are entered closed in apostrophes – e.g. 'a'. But this brings a problem how to write down an apostrophe. In case you would not like to record it directly in the code (i.e. '\u0027'), you have to use an escape sequence and write it down as: '\''. And this is the reason why the apostrophe received its own escape sequence.

504.   Should I enter the apostrophe in such way also in text strings? It is closed there in quotation marks, which means there is no problem.

Inside the text strings you really can write it without using the escape sequence – it means e.g. as follows

```
"'apostrophes' in a text string"
```

505.   Why the character code in the last escape sequence is written in the hexadecimal system?

The hexadecimal numeral system has a number of advantageous properties, which significantly facilitate expressing of various values. I will not ruminate on it because we will not need it now. I just want to supplement the list of possibilities. I know a number of programmers who never used the hexadecimal numeral system, but on the other hand, I know also a number of situations, in which it is good to know it. Sometimes we may get back to it.

506.   Tell me please, why I should write u after the backslash.

Because Java uses the *Unicode* character set. It strives to comprise all characters which people were using and are using now. You can find there all alphabets including Chinese, Japanese and Korean characters, Braille script, Egyptian hieroglyphs, musical notation, cartographic signs etc. etc. Totally there are comprised more than 100 000 characters. Probably you cannot find a currently used character which would not be there.

507.   Please, leave the theory and show me, how I could use the escape sequence in the program.

Firstly examine it in the interactive mode: send the message inform(String) to the IO class with the following parameter:

```
"We are using for quotation marks \\\",\nfor new line \\n,\nfor aspostrophe \\\'"
```

After sending this message the dialog will open as in the figure 26.3.

Figure 26.3
Information text divided into more lines

508.   **The result really corresponds with the picture, but I don't know why the backslashes are multiplying there?**

From time to time it happens in the text strings. In case you want to enter a backslash to a string you have to write it as a couple of backslashes, because if you would put down only one, it would be an introductory character of some escape sequence. But if you have a look at the previous list of escape sequences you will see that the character pair \" have to be written into the string as a quartet \\\" – the first two characters represent the backslash and the other two represent the quotation mark. I suppose you will derive further characters yourself.

The Standard Output

509.   **When I know to write down nearly everything, I would be interested in whether my programs could write their messages so that they would not disappear after I will read them. The dialogs are spectacular, but sometimes I would welcome if I could get back to my texts after finishing the program and read them once again.**

You are true, often it may suit. The simplest solution of such requirement is to print texts to the standard output. This is an object which is a public field of the System class and which is named out.

510.   **This is interesting but we do not have the class** System **in our project.**

The System class is a part of the standard library identically as the classes Object and String. Therefore you can use it as if it would be a part of your project.

   But I will go back to the standard output. It has two sets of useful overloaded methods (I quote the question marks in the list of parameters because you can add whatever as its parameter – mostly the text strings are passed to them):

☞   the methods print(???), which print a text signature of their parameter and

☞   the methods println(???), which make the same but moreover, they terminate the line at the end.

And we can try it immediately. After long ignoring we can remind again our Tests class and enhance it by the method testStandardOutput which we could define e.g. as shown at the listing 26.3.

Listing 26.3: The test of printing to the standard output in the Tests class

```
@Test
public void testStandardOutput()
{
    System.out.print  ("Without line termination - ");
    System.out.println("with line termination");

    System.out.print  ("Rectangl0: ");
    System.out.println(rectangl0);

    System.out.print  ("Ellipse0:    " + ellipse0);
    System.out.println();
    System.out.println("Triangle0: " + triangle0);

    System.out.println("\nRectangl1: " + rectangl1 +
                       "\nEllipse1:  " + ellipse1  +
                       "\nTriangle1: " + triangle1);
}
```

☞ The first two statements show how the behavior of the methods print and println differ.

☞ The third and the fourth statements show the same but I wanted to present you that string doesn't have to be necessarily the parameter in the fourth statement. The fourth statement prints the signature of the smaller rectangle.

☞ Another triplet of statements inform about the remaining two objects of the smaller picture. Notice the middle statement – it shows that the println method calling without parameters can be used for entering empty lines.

☞ The last statement shows very frequent usage of a method in which the longer text is gradually put together from smaller parts and the string that arises as a "sum" is passed to print.

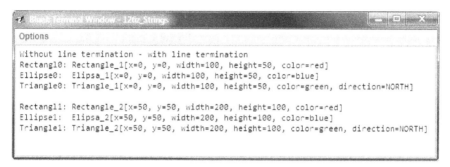

Figure 26.4
The terminal's window with the test result

Terminal Window

After starting the test and confirming the dialog announcing the creation of a test fixture the terminal's window is opened (see figure 26.4), into which the text is printed. This window does not lose its content after finishing the method or the test; it only closes after closing the project. Moreover, you can pick up its content (or part of it) and insert to any place through the box.

When you open another test or method, the new text will be written behind the first one. If you mind it and you would like to write to an empty window, you can enter the command **Clear** in the menu **Options** of the terminal window (see figure 26.5) (if need be you can use also the shortcut CTRL+K).

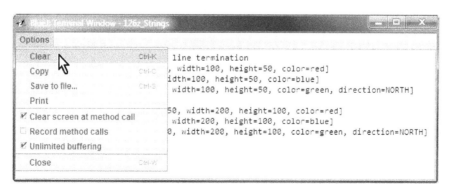

Figure 26.5
Local offer of the terminal's window

As you surely noticed you can enter that the window will be automatically cancelled before the method's calling in the local offer. Unfortunately this choice is not related to tests.

At the same time you noticed that I ticked the choice **Unlimited buffering**. In the opposite case the terminal's window remembers only last 47 lines (I really don't know why just 47). Mostly you do not need more and you do not need to overfill the memory with your historical listings. In case the listing of your program is longer and you need to see them whole, you surely appreciate this choice.

I will not present further possibilities, only I will tell you that in case you would close the window by mistake, you can open it again by ticking the relevant choice in the offer **View** (see figure 10.3 on page 82).

The Standard Error Output

511.   When there is a standard output, probably there is also a standard input, isn't it?

Yes, the standard input also exists, but we will not use it because working with it is difficult. When we would need any input, I will teach you something better.

When we already started speaking about the standard output, I should point out that there is also a *standard error output*. For example all error messages are sent into it. We did not meet it until now, because our methods were tested through the test methods in the test classes and they have their own mechanism of catching the error reports. However, in case an error would occur in the program, which you would start directly from the local offer of certain object, the message about this error would be written just into this standard error output.

In case we will send anything to the standard error output in *BlueJ* the second panel will open in the terminal's window, into which *BlueJ* will write everything in red for emphasizing. In the moment when you ask for cancelling the terminal's window, *BlueJ* cleans up the standard error output and closes it.

But not only system can write into the standard error output, you can write there as well. It is sufficient when you use the field err instead of the field out in the System class. Try to add the following statements at the end of the previous test

```
System.err.println("This is written into the error output");
System.out.println("\nHowever this goes to the standard one");
```

Listing 26.4:   *The definition of the test for making lines in the standard output and in the standard error output in the Tests class*

```
public void testNewLine()
{
    System.out.print("Before new line");
    System.err.print("After new line");
    IO.inform("Before new line");

    System.out.println(" - second part");
    System.err.println(" - second part");
    IO.inform("After new line");
}
```

In case you would really intend to use the standard error output, you have to count that *BlueJ* writes into it only after ending the line. This can be proved with `testNewLine` which you will find in the listing 26.4.

Exercise

512.   Well don't beat me with various kinds of information and let me know what I will train today?

I thought you discovered it already with your visionary abilities. I will ask you to define the method `toString()` in the remaining crates and in all our classes. Use the way which is shown in the listing 26.2 – the method returned the class name followed by enumerated values in brackets, which the constructor received in parameters. Choose the most general way for classes with more constructors, i.e. the constructor adjusting the position, the module and the color of our classes. If the instance does not remember the value of the given property in the field, it can call its own accessory method.

It will be a little bit more complicated for the light because there are two colors adjusted. The light has also the property `isOff`, which informs if it shines or not. It should be shown in its signature.

513.   We have set also the translucency of the arrow.

Yes, but it was not installed as a property. In case we would add the method `isTranslucent ()` to the arrow, we would speculate about including translucency into the signature.

But I would go back to our task. Go into the definition of the test fixture before the last statement announcing that the test fixture is prepared. Add a statement at this place writing signatures of all instances in the fixture to the standard output; each signature at a separate line introduced with the name of the given instance.

Try to think out e.g. how the statement for printing in the `CarTest` class should look out, so that the following text would be written into the standard output during opening of the lastly defined test:

```
====== Instances in the test fixture
| CM: CanvasManager(step=50, width=6, height=6, background=creamy)
| car0:    Car[x=0, y=0, module=128, color=blue]
| carXY:   Car[x=50, y=100, module=128, color=blue]
| carXYB:  Car[x=150, y=25, module=128, color=black]
| carXYM : Car[x=200, y=100, module=64, color=blue]
| carXYMB: Car[x=0, y=172, module=256, color=black]
======
```

Review

Let's review what you have learned in this lesson:

☞   The text strings can be "summed" with the + operator. A sum of two strings is a string originated by concatenating them together, e.g. by adding `"abc"+"123"` the string `"abc123"` arises.

☞   The sum can have any number of members.

☞   In case we add an identifier to a text string, not this identifier is added, but the text signature of the object represented by this identifier. Then if the value of `diameter` parameter is 50, the sum's result (`"Diameter = " + diameter`) is the string `"Diameter = 50"`.

☞ Each class has its own idea about how its instances should be converted to a string which would inform the user about the given instance as best as possible.

☞ The text, which is the value of the string, is entered in quotation marks.

☞ Transfer to a new line is inserted into the string as a pair of \n characters.

☞ Characters that cannot be simply inserted into the string are entered with their *escape sequence*.

☞ Each escape sequence begins with a backslash followed by an identification character.

☞ The mostly used escape sequences are: '\n', '\t', '\"', '\'', '\\'.

☞ All characters can be entered by the escape sequence in which we write down a backslash, a letter u and four hexadecimal digits representing its code.

☞ The field out of the System class represents a standard output.

☞ Everything what is printed to the standard output is depicted by *BlueJ* in terminal's window.

☞ We can write into the standard output through the following statements
System.out.print(xxx);
and
System.out.println(xxx);
where xxx is the value of any primitive or object type. The second of the mentioned method terminates the line after printing the passed text.

☞ Making the new line can be reached by the following statement
System.out.println();

☞ The field err of the System class represents a standard error output.

☞ The standard error output is depicted by *BlueJ* also in terminal's window only in the second bottom panel to which it is written in red.

☞ The panel of the standard error output is opened by *BlueJ* only when somebody is writing in it.

☞ *BlueJ* writes into the standard error output only after making a new line.

Project:
The resulting form of the project to which we came at the end of the lesson and after completing all exercises is in the 126z_Strings project.

27 A Bit of Logic

What you will learn in this lesson
In this lesson you will solve the problems with comparing the objects. Then you will meet a number of mostly logic operators and you will learn what the operator's arity is. Then a contract of the method equals(Object) *will be presented and you will program the method according to this contract. Finally you will learn what the difference between the value object types and the reference object types is, as well as why you should not use the variable value types.*

Project:
In this lesson we continue in using the 126z_Strings project.

Problems with Objects Comparing

514. Well, will you already tell me how I should explain to the computer that two equal positions are really equal?

Let's go on. The problem consists in the way of comparing the instances. We consider two positions as equivalent (equal) in case if they have identical coordinates. However in Java, the instance is *implicitly* (i.e. in case you would not tell that it is different) equivalent only to itself.

515. How is it possible that the colors were operating and the positions are not operating?

Due to the fact, that the NamedColor class takes care about not to create two instances representing the same color. Whenever somebody asks for a special color, the called factory method firstly checks, if such color exists. If it exists, the existing color is returned. The new instance is created only in the case that there is no object representing the required color. Therefore the standard equals operation is sufficient.

The String class uses a different way. It knows, or better said its instances know, how to compare themselves mutually – they have defined its own version of the equals(Object) method.

But we did not explain it yet to the Position class (i.e. we did not define this method in it) and thus it uses the method equals(Object) inherited from the class Object (this was explained in the section *The Class* Object on page 60). As I told you a while ago, this method considers an instance equivalent only with the instance itself.

516. How can I change this implicit setting?

As I have already told – you have to define the method equals(Object) for instances of the given class. This method will compare its instance with the instance obtained as a parameter. As far as the method considers them as mutually equivalent, it returns the logic value true; in an opposite case it returns the value false. Before I will show you a possible definition of this method, I will explain you several operations which I need to use in it and which were not yet debated. And when I start explaining this, I will mention also their relatives which we will not use this time, but which will suit to you soon.

The Cast Operator (Type)

517.   Well, go on.

First of all I will tell you something about an operator of casting. You will use it when you have an instance of one type which does not suit to you because its instances are not able to do something, but you know, that the given object is at the same time an instance of another type which is able to do what you need.

This is directly our situation. We know about the parameter of the equals(Object) method that it's of Object type. But this knowledge does not help us with the comparison. But if this parameter of instances would be of the Position class we could ask it for its coordinates and decide according to them if it is equivalent with our position or not.

Therefore we will ask the virtual machine to **cast** the reference of the Object type instance into the reference of the Position type instance and we will save this cast reference to the auxiliary variable. We ask for casting by writing the name of the target type, closed (separately!) in rounded brackets, before the reference to the cast object, which is in our case as follows:

```
Position p = (Position) object;
```

Then we can ask the object in the variable p for its coordinates.

518.   What? Such simply I can change the type of the object? It means I could make possibly the whole car with lights from only my light.

In no case, you cannot change the type of object. You can change only a type of the reference to it. By casting you announce to the compiler that you know that the given reference refers to the object of the destination type. The compiler inserts a requirement to virtual machine at the place of casting to check if you are true and subsequently treats this reference as if it would really refer to the given object. The compiler knows that in case you would not be true then the virtual machine would announce an error in the previous checking.

Try to program the semi-finished method from the listing 27.1.

Listing 27.1:   *The initial (not yet operating) version of the equals(Object) method for the Position class*

```
public boolean equals(Object o)
{
    Position p = (Position)o;
    return true;
}
```

And now call it in interactive mode and pass parameters of various types to it. If the Position class would not be its parameter, the method finishes with announcing an error – e.g. as follows:

```
java.lang.ClassCastException: Ellipse cannot be cast to Position
```

Numerical Comparison Operators < <= == >= > !=

519.   Well, maybe I understand casting. What you have further?

Then we need to discover if the coordinates of our instance agree with the coordinates of the instance obtained as the parameter. For the identity test of two values Java uses an operator == so that if I would like to detect whether the content of the variable a agrees with the content of the variable b, I will write a==b.

When I started to speak about the operator of comparison, I will present also the others.

☞   a < b – the value a is smaller than the value b

☞   a <= b – the value a is smaller or equal to the value b

☞   a == b – the value a is equal to the value b

☞   a >= b – the value a is bigger or equal to the value b

☞   a > b – the value a is bigger than the value b

☞   a != b – the value a is not equal to the value b

You can use values of all primitive types as operands, but you cannot compare logic values with "illogical" ones. The characters are converted to integers with the value equal to the code of the given character. When comparing logic values, it is valid (false < true).

Operators and their Arity

520.   What is the operand?

I see that you are more forgetful than me. We were speaking about it in the section *The Assignment of the Value to the Field* on page 160, when we were speaking about the assignment operation. I remind that each operation consists of the following:

☞   an **operator**, which is a character or a group of characters, saying which kind of operation it is,

☞   **operands**, which are data with whom the given operation is carried out.

If we take an example of counting up operation, the operator is the + sign and operands are both summands.

I would like supplement my information about the term **operator's arity**, which says with how many operands the operator works. According to arity we distinguish four kinds of operators in Java:

☞   Nullary operators do not need any operand. The example of nullary operators could be constants.

☞   Unary operators have only one operand. E.g. the cast operator which we were debating a while ago is usually included among unary operators. Also the + and – characters placed before numbers (e.g. +2, –4 etc.) are unary operators.

☞   Binary operators have two operands. The arithmetic operators + - * / belong to this group, the operators of comparison about which we were speaking as well as the assignment operator.

☞   Java has also one ternary operator, which uses three operands, but this will be discussed in the next volume.

521.   And what about when I want to sum up more summands?

Then the sum will be evaluated gradually from left to the right and the result of the left sum will become a left operand (summand) of the right sum. So if you write in the program as follows

```
a + b + c + d
```

the compiler compiles it into a sequence of binary operations, i.e. the result ends the same as if you would write

```
(((a+b) + c) + d)
```

Comparison of Objects

522.   I see you drew me into theory. Let's return to our project, I want to ask you: may I compare also objects?

Objects can be directly compared only with the help of the operators == and !=. They compare references to objects so that the result is information if the compared references show the same object. When working with an object the comparing operators cannot be used to anything else.

From what I told you until now you could estimate that the inherited version of the equals(Object) method behaves as if its body would contain the statement as follows (supposing that the parameter will have the name o):

```
return (this == o);
```

In other words: it returns information if the parameter shows an instance whose method equals is just called and to which the hidden parameter this refers.

Logical Complement Operator !

523.   Why a symbol "!=" is used for the operator "not equal"? I think I saw a symbol "<>", and it seemed to me far more logical.

The symbol <> is used for non-equality in e.g. Basic and Pascal. But Java took over a significant part of its syntax from the language C++, which took it from its predecessor C language. Thus the languages C and C++ were used by a majority of programmers and it was reasonable to adapt to their syntax.

524.   And why the authors of C language have chosen such strange operator?

I did not tell you that the! sign (the exclamation mark) serves as an operator of negation that negates its operand, i.e. it says true opposite – (!true == false) and (!false == true). It means the following equality is valid:

```
(a != b)   ==   !(a == b)
```

To express it by words: *a is not equal to b* means the same as *it is not true that a is equal to b*.

525. And may I write down also for example (x !< y)?

No, you cannot. The exclamation mark as "negation" is a part of the operator only at !=. You can use the expression !(x < y), but then it is better to use (x >= y).

Conjunction (Conditional-And) Operators && and &

526. Sure, the exclamation mark was only moved. What you have further?

We still do not know how to explain to the computer that if two positions should be considered as equivalent, both their coordinates, i.e. the horizontal as well as the vertical have to agree. The **operation of conjunction** is used for it (sometimes it's called *logical multiplication* or *logical and*) whose result is true if and only if both its operands are true. For entering this operation I use the operator && (usually it is marked the *operator AND*).

In case I want to save the test result whether the coordinates of my instance (this) are identical with the coordinates of the instance p, into the logic (boolean) variable result, then I insert the following statement into the program:

```
boolean result = (this.x == p.x)  &&  (this.y == p.y);
```

Knowing this we can now improve the definition of our method and set it to the form as in the listing 27.2 (of course you can leave out the qualification this).

Listing 27.2:   *Version of the equals(Object) method which is able to compare two positions (for the Position class)*

```
public boolean equals(Object o)
{
    Position p = (Position)o;
    boolean result = (this.x == p.x)  &&  (this.y == p.y);
    return result;
}
```

527. You indicated in the title that I can choose between one and two & characters. Is there any difference between them?

Yes and a big one! I recommend not to use the operator & and I quote it here only for you would know about it in case you would use it by mistake and you would be surprised that the program operates in a different way that it has.

The result between them insists in the fact that the operator & evaluates both operands whilst the operator && often suffices to evaluate only the left of them. It knows that to reach the true result both operands have to be true as well. In case it discovers that the left operand is not true, it doesn't bother to evaluate the right one and directly announces the result as false.

However the advantage of && operator is not only that it is quicker (the speedup is often nearly immeasurable) but in the fact that in the right operand you can use the fact that the left operand is true. Imagine that e.g. you have to discover if the quotient of two entered non-negative numbers smaller than 10. You can find out the result e.g. as follows:

```
boolean smallerThan10 = (denominator != 0)  &&
                        (numerator / denominator  <  10);
```

I already know that denominator is not zero in the right operand and that I can divide. If the denominator is zero, it's no sense to find out the value of fraction and I can announce with clear conscious that it's not smaller than 10.

528.   When the operator & is used?

It is used in situations when you need to evaluate also the right operand because certain side effect arises in its evaluating with which the following code counts. But using side effects of operations is considered as a great programmer's sin and is tolerated only in extraordinary reasoned cases. I explained you this operator mainly so that you would not be surprised by remodeled running of the program in case you will not write or cancel the second & by mistake.

Disjunction (Conditional-Or) Operators || and |

529.   In school we discussed over and over three logic operations: negation, conjunction and disjunction. I suppose that Java has certain operator also for the third one.

Of course, even here you have two versions at your disposal, namely "intelligent" || and "hardworking" |. I only remind that the result of a **logic disjunction operation** (sometimes we speak about *logical addition* or about the *logical or*) is true (i.e. the result is the value true) in case if at least one operand is true. Its operator is usually called by the programmers as the *operator OR*.

The "intelligent" version knows that it's sufficient if at least one operand is true, and so if it finds out that the left operand is true, it doesn't evaluate the right one and directly returns true. Using "intelligence" of the operator is similar as at its above mentioned colleague.

530.   I suppose that the difference between its one-character and the two-character variant is the same as of the previous operator.

You suppose well. The operator of shortened evaluation evaluates the left operand and if it is true, it does not check the right one and returns the result true.

Type Comparison Operator instanceof

531.   It means we have the equals(Object) method completed, haven't we?

Not so completely. The method's contract requires so that the method would always return some result independently which parameter it obtains. And this is not valid for our method yet.

532.   How not valid yet?

Because the definition in the listing 27.2 crashes at the moment when its parameter could not be cast to the Position type. Therefore we have to adapt our code in such way so that it would be able to solve the situation. In other words only those objects would be cast which are positions.

For this it is necessary to find out at first if the obtained object is a position. The operator instanceof can be used for it. It expects a tested object in the left operand and a type to which the competency should be discovered in the right operand. The result is a logic value announcing if the left operand can be considered as the instance of the right operand. If the object o is an instance of the Position class can be detected e.g. in the following way:

```
boolean isPosition = o instanceof Position;
```

533.   And what about when I will ask for not existing object, i.e. when the left operand will contain an empty reference?

An empty reference is nobody's instance which means that (null instanceof Anything) is always false.

534.   So we know everything and we can start programming.

Yes, we know everything but we have to arrange that in case the parameter will not be the instance of the Position class the method would return false. When you will learn algorithmic constructions I will show you another possibility how to reach it. But for now let's use "intelligence" of the && operator and define the method equals(Object) according to the listing 27.3.

Listing 27.3:   *The operating version of the method* equals(Object) *for the* Position *class*

```
public boolean equals(Object o)
{
    return (o instanceof Position)      &&
           (((Position)o).x == this.x)  &&
           (((Position)o).y == this.y);
}
```

535.   Oh, you have to explain me this code.

Well, if you think about it, you surely would be able to explain it as well, but I will do it.

The method contains the only one statement – return. When this statement starts to evaluate the expression whose value it has to return, it starts with detecting if the parameter is the instance of the Position class. In negative case nothing is necessary to evaluate because the whole expression is false. Thus the && operator returns the value false which the return statement passes to the calling method as the result.

If the parameter is the instance of the Position class the result is not yet obvious and the expression will be further evaluated. It will continue with the second line expression. First of all, the parameter will cast to the Position type (this time we already know that casting is correct), the value of its field x will be detected and will be compared with the value of the corresponding field of the given instance (the optional this only stresses whose field it is).

In case the compared values will not be equal, the result of comparing is false and nothing should be further checked – the return statement can give back false.

In case the previous comparison will be true, also the y field should be evaluated in the same procedure as the x field.

536.   Don't you have rather too many brackets in the casting?

There are really many brackets in the expression, but those who are probably mostly bothering cannot be cancelled. I have to respect operator's priorities, i.e. which operator is preferred to the other one. The basic school knowledge is that multiplying is preferred to adding, and rising to a higher power is preferred to multiplying. There is no operator of rising to a higher power in Java but there is a wide range of others and totally there are 14 levels of priority. Therefore I recommend to students not to think over operator's priority and rely on brackets because then each expression is clear even for these people who do not remember the proper ordering of those 14 priorities.

Contract of the `equals(Object)` Method

537.   Well, we are ready and we can examine it.

Oh, there are few things left. Above all, it would be suitable to supplement the annotation `@Override` before the method's definition because it is a method overriding the method inherited from a parent. As I have already said this annotation is optional but it enables to the compiler to check that what you have defined is really the covering of the inherited method.

538.   Well, and what else?

Further we should check if the method fulfills the contract.

539.   We have already fulfilled it. You told me that it has to react correctly to any parameter and we arranged it with the help of `instanceof`.

You know, the contract is a little bit more complicated. Besides the fact that the method may never end with an error the following five conditions have to be fulfilled:

☞   It has to be **reflexive**, i.e. the object has to be equivalent with itself. In other words: the expression `object.equals(object)` has to return `true` for each `object`.

☞   It has to be **symmetric**, i.e. the object has to be equivalent with another one at the moment when the second one is equivalent with the first one. In other words: the following expression has to be always true (supposing of course that both objects do exist):

    `object1.equals(object2)  ==  object2.equals(object1)`

☞   It has to be **transitive**, i.e. if one object is equivalent to the second one and the second one with the third one, then the first one has to be equivalent also with the third one. In other words the following expression has to be true for all existing objects o1, o2, o3:

    `(o1.equals(o2) && o2.equals(o3))  <=  o1.equals(o3)`

☞   It has to be **consistent**, i.e. when you ask twice if one object is equivalent with the second one, you have to receive the same answer every time. When e.g. two positions are equal today, they should be equal also tomorrow.

☞   For each `object` the following expression `(objekt.equals(null) == false)` has to be valid, i.e. no object can be equivalent with an empty reference.

Having a look at our definition in the listing 27.3, you may estimate that it fulfills all of the above mentioned rules. I specified them so that you would have them in your memory when you will define the `equals(Object)` method for some of your own classes.

540.   I didn't catch the expression for transitivity. Should the arrow be on reverse? The mathematics teaches us that when something emerges from the other thing, then the arrow faces to the emerging one.

When you have a look at the table of implication values (you can find it e.g. at http://en.wikipedia.org/wiki/Material_conditional#Truth_table), you discover that if the implication is true, the assumption (hypothesis) does not have bigger logic value than the statement. So if the mathematician says "T comes from P" (the statement comes from the assumption) and writes it as (P => T) you will write to the program (P <= T), i.e. P is smaller or equal to T.

In our case there was a premise that the first object is equivalent to the second one and at the same time the second one is equivalent to the third one. A statement originated from this premise that the first object has to be equivalent to the third one. That's why the record looked out as it did. Don't bother about it – it is sufficient to know what it is about, you do not have to remember how to write it down.

Value Types and Reference Types

541.   Fulfilling of the first three items is obvious, because it comes from the characteristic of equality, which we learnt in school. The last item is also clear because you told that the operator instanceof **always returns** false **for** null**. But how I recognize if our definition is consistent?**

You will recognize it from the fact that both fields, whose values are compared, are defined as constants and thus they cannot change. When they would be equal or not today, the same will be valid for them any time.

Observing the consistency of the equals(Object) method is related to immutability of value objects. Don't ask about it, I will explain it immediately.

Until now we were dividing the data types to *primitive* and *object* ones. But the object data types can be further divided, to *value types* and *reference types*.

Reference Types

The instances of reference data types are interesting for us only from the view which instance it is. To determine the given instance we need to have only a reference to this instance. We could say that the instance itself is their value and therefore it is sufficient to have the inherited version of equals(Object) method. From classes with which we have been working up until now we could include into this group all graphic objects. E.g. the fact that two rectangles have the same color, the same size and lies in the same coordinates does not seem as a reason for considering them as equal. The rectangles are always two different rectangles which only overlap in the given moment.

Value Types

As the title says the value types serve for representing some value. If we have two instances of value type we can determine if they represent the same value similarly as we can detect at the two variables of primitive data types. We recognize the value types according to the fact that they define their own version of the equals(Object) method which knows how to recognize an equality of represented values.

From classes which we met until now, only `String`, `NamedColor`, `Direction8`, `Position`, `Size` and `Area` are value types. We can look for equality of values of their instances, i.e. if two instances of the `String` class contain the same string or if two instances of the `Position` class denote the same place.

The value classes can be divided into two groups:

☞ **Immutable** types don't offer any possibility how to change values of key fields, i.e. fields which e.g. act in the method `equals(Object)`. As soon as we create their instances, we can rely on the fact that they will always have their initial value. From all classes used until now the classes `String`, `NamedColor`, `Direction8` as well as all crates belong to them.

☞ **Mutable** types will not guarantee invariability of values of its key fields. On the contrary the value, kept in their instance, can change any time. They have defined the `equals(Object)` method but they are not able to guarantee its consistency. Therefore we should avoid using of such classes.

Exercise

542. I suppose that today's exercise will deal with the method `equals(Object)`.

Surely, fulfill the definition of this method to the rest of classes of the crates.

As you surely estimate our classes of graphic objects are of reference type so that they do not need to cover this method. Fill in the method `testSwapPositionsWithCheck` to their test class, so that we could check any time in future that detecting and adjusting of positions continues properly in instances of test classes.

Due to the fact that acting of this method cannot be differentiated from the test without any checking, you can fulfill the auxiliary method by a print of initiating and target positions of shifted objects to standard output.

Review

Let's review what you have learned in this lesson:

☞ When comparing objects you have to differ when you detect if it is the same instance and when it is only an instance representing the same value.

☞ You can use a cast operation in the situation when you have an instance of certain type, but you know that the referred object is simultaneously an instance of another type which is more suitable for your purpose.

☞ You ask for casting by writing the name of the target type closed (separately!) in parentheses before the reference for cast object.

☞ By casting you do not change the object's characteristics, but only our point of view at the given object.

☞ During casting the virtual machine checks if it is possible to cast the given reference, i.e. if the referred object is really the instance of the target data type. If not, a program error is announced.

☞ For comparing in Java the following operators are used: `< <= == >= > !=`

☞ Operators are differentiated according to their arity which says with how many operands they work. Nullary operators have no operand, unary operators have one operand, binary have two and ternary have three operands.

☞ In case you need to express that two affirmations are valid at the same time, you can use a logic conjunction operation. You will write it down using the operator && or &.

☞ The operator && evaluates its left operand and if it is not true it stops evaluating (because the result is obvious) and returns `false`.

☞ The operator & evaluates always both operands. It is used in the situation when the right operand has to be evaluated due to a possible side effect.

☞ Using of side effects is considered as a great programmer's transgression.

☞ For expressing that at least one of the two affirmations is valid, you use a logic disjunction operation which is written by means of operators || or |.

☞ Even in case of disjunction the double-character version uses the shortened evaluation; the one-character version always evaluates both operands.

☞ The operator `instanceof` expects a tested object in the left operand and a type to which you detect the competency in the right operand. The result is a logic value announcing whether the left operand can be considered as the instance of the right operand.

☞ Operations in Java recognize 14 priority levels. In case you want the evaluation procedure would be evident on the first sight, use parentheses.

☞ The `equals(Object)` method is used in situations when equality of two objects is detected.

☞ If two instances of the given class are equivalent only in case that they are of the same instance, it is possible to use the version of the `equals(Object)` method inherited from the `Object` class.

☞ In case you define your own version of the `equals(Object)` method, you have to provide that it will be reflexive, symmetric, transitive, and consistent and will differentiate the object from the empty reference.

☞ Object data types are divided to value types and reference types.

    ☞ The instances of reference types represent only themselves. Therefore the inherited version of the `equals(Object)` method is sufficient for their comparison.

    ☞ The instances of value types represent certain value. Therefore it can happen that two different instances represent the same value. Thus for their comparison you have to define their own version of the `equals(Object)` method.

☞ Value data types can be divided also in two groups:

    ☞ The immutable types do not offer any possibility how to change values of fields acting in the `equals(Object)` method.

    ☞ The mutable data types enable changing of the value of key fields (i.e. fields affecting the returned value of the `equals(Object)` method) and therefore their `equals(Object)` method is not consistent. That's why you should avoid using them.

Project:

The resulting form of the project to which we came at the end of the lesson and after completing all exercises is in the 127z_Booleans project.

28 Class Methods and Fields

What you will learn in this lesson
In this lesson you will firstly see how the class can count created instances and allocate identification numbers to them. You will also see improving the toString() method, so that its ID number would become the part of its signature. At the end you will see how to define a class according to the design pattern Singleton at the Town example.

Project:
In this lesson we can continue in using the project 127z_Booleans.

Counted Objects

543. **The toString() method, which I defined in the last lesson, returns a string beginning with the name of the given class for each instance. Would it be better if the name of the given instance would be quoted instead of the class name?**

Instances have generally no names. Only fields and variables have names, into which, in case of necessity, you save a reference to an instance. But the same reference can be at several places simultaneously and the addressed object is not able to discover through which reference you are addressing it.

In case you unambiguously want to identify an object according to the string returned by the toString() method, it is more advantageous to equip the object at its origination by some unambiguous identifying sign according to which you can recognize it and which the toString() method puts into the resulting string.

One of the most popular procedures is to assign an identifying number (an "ID number") to each instance, according to which you can recognize it. Similarly also the geometric shapes in our project are marked in this way.

Static Fields

544. **It looks interesting. How could I arrange it?**

Do you remember the fields of a class about which we were speaking in the section *Static Fields – Class Fields* on page 73? Then I told you that the class remembers information in these fields that is common to all its instances. The number of instances created until now can be such field.

Each time when the new instance of the given class is created this number increases by one and the result is then assigned to some field of just created instance. This value serves as the identifying number of the given instance. Due to the fact that this number should never change the relevant field should be declared as a constant, i.e. with the final modifier.

545.   This seems simple. But how should I define a field of the whole class?

By adding the keyword static among their modifiers. The class fields are often called *static* due to this keyword.

Order of Modifiers

546.   You have already told me four modifiers: public, private, final **and** static. **Should I quote them in certain order or the order is not important?**

The order you quote them is not important. Nevertheless, it's a habit to quote them as follows: public/private static final. And moreover, I would like to remind that the public and private modifiers cannot be quoted at the same time.

Program Modifications

547.   I would say I already know everything needed and — as you say — we can start creating.

I agree. Let's start with the simplest, namely with the Light class. Add the count field to its class variable fields. We will count the created instances in this field and therefore we initialize it to zero. Then add a field called ID to instance's constants. The instance will save its identification number into this field.

At this occasion I recommend you to define also the fields color, switchedOffColor and bulb as constants (i.e. to add the modifier final to them). The resulting proposal of the declaration (without line comments of not used sections) you can see in the listing 28.1.

Listing 28.1:   *The declaration of fields of the* Light *class*

```
//== VARIABLE CLASS FIELDS =====================================================

/** Number of so far created instances. */
private static int countCreated = 0;


//== CONSTANT INSTANCE FIELDS ==================================================

/** Identification number of given instance. */
private final int ID;

/** Color of the light when turned on. */
private final NamedColor color;

/** Color of the light when turned off. */
private final NamedColor switchedOffColor;

/** Shape representing the light on the canvas. */
private final Ellipse bulb;
```

548.   Why should I declare a bulb as a constant? After all, the ellipse representing a bulb can move and change its measure.

Yes, it can, but it is always the same ellipse. In other words: the reference saved in the field is not changing and we can consider it as constant. As I already told, by adding the modifier final we ask the compiler to check if we don't try to change its value by mistake.

549.   I see, so what should I do further?

Put a statement adding one to the countCreated field into the most general constructor. The constructor knows that it is initializing the newly created instance and so it has to put information into this field that there is one more instance. You write down the following statement:

```
count = count + 1;
```

Thus you express that the computer has to take the value saved in the countCreated field, add one to it and save the resulting value as the new value of this field.

550.   It looks a little bit strange because the left side is not equal with the right one but in case I would think that instead of equals sign there is for example an assigning arrow, it's understandable. I have to accustom to it. What else?

You add another statement immediately behind this one which saves the new value of the countCreated field into the ID constant.

551.   How can I assign a value into a constant? You told that no value can be saved into constants.

But I also told that if you cannot initialize a constant in declaration, you can do it in a constructor. But you can initialize it, i.e. to assign a value to it, only once – and this is what I want you to make. The modified version of the construction might look as in the listing 28.2.

Listing 28.2:   The new version of the most general light constructor

```
public Light(int x, int y, int diameter, NamedColor color,
                                   NamedColor switchedOffColor)
{
    countCreated = countCreated + 1;
    this.ID      = countCreated;
    this.bulb    = new Ellipse(x, y, diameter, diameter, color);
    this.color   = color;
    this.switchedOffColor = switchedOffColor;
}
```

552.   It's strange how you can number instances. You put zero into the count field, then you extend it to one and you assign it into the ID field. This means that there will be always one in this field.

The point is in the fact that the count field is the field of a class (static field), which means it initializes in the moment when program reads its class. Then it is never more zeroed and only one is added by each instance.

The first created instance finds zero in the field count, adds one and saves the resulting one into its ID field. The second instance finds one in the count field. It adds again one and the resulting two saves into its ID field. And it goes further like that.

Innovation of the `toString()` Method

553.   Oh yes, I'm sorry, I forgot. So what expects us now?

Now we can start adjusting the toString method so that also ID of the given instance would be added to a class name. To offer you further matter for speculations let's make a small change in the definition: I will not write the x and y coordinates separately, but I will write directly the whole position. You can see the result in the listing 28.3.

Listing 28.3:   *The innovated version of the `toString()` method in the `Light` class*

```
@Override
public String toString()
{
    return "Light_"     + ID             + "("            + getPosition() +
           ", module=" + getModule() + ", color="     + color          +
           ", switchedOffColor="       + switchedOffColor +
           ", isOff="  + isOff()        + ")";
}
```

When you require creating a fixture, the `setUp()` method writes the following text to the standard output (I made the font smaller to allow the lines not to be wrapped):

```
====== Instances in the test fixture for LightTest@45431f89
| CM: CanvasManager(step=50, width=6, height=6, background=creamy)
| light0:    Light_1(Position[x=0, y=0], module=50, color=yellow, switchedOffColor=black, isOff=false)
| lightXY:   Light_2(Position[x=50, y=50], module=50, color=yellow, switchedOffColor=black, isOff=false)
| lightXYC:  Light_3(Position[x=100, y=100], module=50, color=red, switchedOffColor=black, isOff=false)
| lightXYM : Light_4(Position[x=0, y=100], module=100, color=yellow, switchedOffColor=black, isOff=false)
| lightXYMB: Light_5(Position[x=100, y=0], module=100, color=blue, switchedOffColor=black, isOff=false)
| lightXYMB: Light_6(Position[x=150, y=150], module=150, color=magenta, switchedOffColor=no, isOff=false)
======
```

Town

554.   For now it was more a lesson on how to work with strings. Would you have a practical usage for static fields and methods?

You say practical usage. I would like to use our car as well as a traffic light in the further project in which we could simulate traffic in a town. For this we need a town which might be even greater than the canvas we are now using. We could practically show the implementation of design patterns *Singleton* and *Simple Factory Method* which we discussed in the section *Examples of Design Patterns* on page 101. What do you say?

555.   I'm afraid it will be too complicated for me.

Don't be afraid, start with reminding of what was said about both design patterns and then we will go on with the entering.

Entering

556.   Well, I reminded it. You can start.

As I told, we will define the foundations of the future class Town. The versions you will create today have to fulfill the following requirements:

☞ The town should be able to be painted at the canvas, i.e. it will implement the IPaintable interface.

☞ The town will be defined as a translucent smoky rectangle. Translucent (NamedColor.SMOKY) because the lines of the canvas grid should penetrate through it.

☞ The coordinates in town will not be defined as point coordinates, but as field coordinates. Similarly the town's size will not be quoted in points, but in fields corresponding to canvas' fields. This means the town will have the given number of lines and columns.

☞ In the first approximation the size of the town, i.e. the number of its lines and columns, will be constant during the whole town's life.

☞ The size of the town's field will be derived from the current size of the canvas field. With change of the canvas field size by calling one of the methods setStep(int) and setStepSize(int,int,int) automatically the size of the field in the town will change and thus also the point size of the rectangle representing the town.

☞ One field of the town will be always highlighted as an active one and the town will be always depicted in such way so that the active field would be in the middle of the canvas.

☞ The active field position within the canvas will always be possible to adjust by calling the method activeOn(int,int) to which the column and line of the active field will be passed in parameters.

☞ The active field will be painted as milky (translucent color allowing to see what is under it – NamedColor.MILKY) square which will overlap the marked field at each side by half of its width.

☞ Only one town can meet the requirement to centralize the active field at canvas, except the towns would overlap and this is outside our requirements. Therefore, the instance of Town class has to be a singleton, i.e. it will be possible to create the only one town.

☞ You will ask the town class for the town's instance by calling its static method getInstance().

So what you say? Is it enough difficult and practical?

557.   Don't laugh at me. I can never program something like this. I could do it only having more experience.

Don't underrate yourself. I will persuade you that for programming such class you do not need anything what you would not already know.

An Analysis

558.   I'm just curious. Start persuading me.

Any time when you receive a programming task you should start with an analysis how you would solve individual requirements of the assignment. Each minute spent with analyzing will save you a lot of time uselessly wasted after rash start of programming.

Let's begin with an analysis. I will guide you to see that you could do this analysis yourself with only a little endeavor. That's why we will turn our discussion a bit. I will ask you questions and you will give me answers.

559.   You are asking too much. It's your turn to start.

Well, you should begin with the town's *interface*, i.e. what – according to the assignment – the surrounding objects have to know about the town. In other words: what you have to define as public? Enumerate only what really must be public, because otherwise the task would not be fulfilled. Don't quote anything you speculate it should be public, but the assignment does not say it particularly.

560.   Public? At the beginning you told that the town has to implement the IPaintable **interface, so that it has to have defined the public method** paint(Painter)**. Then it has to have the method** activeOn(int,int) **as well as the static method** getInstance()**. And finally it has to have a constructor which will create it.**

A public constructor?

561.   I see. In your explanation of a singleton you told that the singleton's constructor has to be private and that I should ask for the singleton's instance by using a simple factory method – this is the method getInstance()**. This means only those three above mentioned methods and besides them the private constructor.**

Well, so the full declarations of methods you enumerated could be as follows (you did not tell the constructor's parameters, so I will put question marks instead of them):

```
public static Town getInstance();
private Town(???);
public void activeOn(int column, int row);
public void paint(Painter painter);
```

For now it looks simply, what do you think? And now go through the whole assignment once more and try to think out which fields the town should remember so that the previous methods would work as required.

562.   I am going through from above to down, so I have to know:
        – the rectangle representing the town,
        – the field size of the town, i.e. the number of its columns and lines,
        – the coordinates of the active field and
        – the square representing the active field.
        That's all I think.

I would see one item more as useful in this list. Imagine how the method getInstance() will work and how the repainted town will detect where it should be placed at the canvas.

563. **Aha, I see. I have to remember the created singleton which the method** `getInstance()` **will return each time. I hesitate with the second part but I estimate that I should remember a reference to canvas manager to avoid permanent requiring for it.**

Correct, and you should add that these two fields will be defined as static constants, because they will not change within the class life. When I repeat and precise it, you say that we should declare the following fields:

```
//== CONSTANT CLASS FIELDS ========================================================

    /** Canvas manager painting the town. */
    private static final CanvasManager CM;

    /** The only instance of the town. */
    private static final Town singleton;


//== VARIABLE INSTANCE FIELDS =====================================================

    /** Rectangle representing the town area. */
    private Rectangle ground;

    /** Rectangle highlighting the current field. */
    private Rectangle current;

    /** Current number of the columns in the town. */
    private int columnSize;

    /** Current number of the rows in the town. */
    private int rowSize;

    /** Column of the current field. */
    private int currentColumn;

    /** Row of the current field. */
    private int currentRow;
```

This means the basic framework is finished and we can begin with supplement the construction. The first item you should think is initialization of those static constants. So how would you go on?

564. **The canvas manager is clear; we used it in test classes several times. It means I will put an initialization only to a declaration. But how should I handle with the singleton?**

My advice is: initialize it by inserting a reference returned by new `Town()` into the `SINGLETON` field.

Well, let's go on. How you will program the constructor?

565. **I will determine the town's size and save it to fields. Suppose I will locate an active field to the canvas center so that a half of the town's size can be saved as its coordinate. Then I will detect the size of those rectangles and I will count their positions. Well, I don't know how to do it.**

I advise you a bit. You do not have to enter any sizes nor any positions for the rectangles in the constructor (precisely you can enter any of them), because in case the town should immediately react to changes of the size of canvas field, it would be best if the paint(Painter) method could detect this size itself and adjust the size of both rectangles in the last moment. As far as the constructor is mentioned I would think over if the object should be registered at the canvas immediately after it will be created, i.e. if the registering statement should be saved at the end of the constructor.

And how do you consider the `activeOn(int,int)` method?

566.   It's clear – I will adjust new coordinates of an active field.

It's not sufficient. You have to say to the canvas manager that something has changed and therefore it should repaint itself. And at this occasion you adjust also the position of the town at the canvas.

567.   Oh, yes, you're true. I didn't realize it. So there is only the `paint(Painter)` method, and I hesitate what to do with it.

Because you pay bigger respect to it than it's worthy. Let's take it in proper ordering. Which values, that you need to enter to depicted rectangles, are ensuing from the assignment? (Don't say that it's color.) Look once more into the assignment.

568.   It says that the current field should be in the center of the canvas and that it should overlap the size of canvas field at each side by one half. When it should overlap its size by one half at each side it should be twice bigger. And I will get its field's coordinates by dividing the number of the canvas' columns and rows by two. Then I get its point coordinates by multiplying its field's coordinates by the step length.

Clever student! Now you should only count the position and the size of the rectangle representing the town. I suppose you know how to count its size, and the position will be not so difficult:

1.   When you know the field's coordinates of the current field in the town, you surely know how far the current field is from the left upper edge of the town.

2.   You already know the position of the current field at the canvas – it is in the center, thus (as you told) you obtain its field position by dividing the number of columns and rows by two.

3.   When you subtract the relative coordinate of the field in the town from the absolute coordinate of the field at the canvas you have the town's position at canvas.

4.   Now you only multiply the field coordinates by the field's size and you receive the point coordinates.

569.   But it can happen that the position of the town rectangle will be minus.

Yes, it can happen, but it does not matter. The rectangle opposes to minus position only in the constructor, not in setting the position.

This means we can close the analysis as completed and you can start programming. The sample solution you will find in the listing 28.4. There are some extra constants, but more or less it's as you have just produced it. I would only remind you not to forget to define the `toString()` method which returns the text marked as instance signature.

Listing 28.4   *The class* Town

```
/***************************************************************************
 * Instance of {@code Town}class is a singleton and represents a town
 * in which we will subsequently add objects.
 * The town can be bigger than the canvas and will place itself so that
 * the current field will be in the center of the canvas
 * where the relative position of the current field in the town can be set.
 */
```

```java
public class Town implements IPaintable
{
    //== CONSTANT CLASS FIELDS ====================================================

    /** Initial number of columns. */
    private static final int COLUMN_COUNT_0 = 10;

    /** Initial number of rows. */
    private static final int ROW_COUNT_0 = 10;

    /** Canvas manager painting the town. */
    private static final CanvasManager CM = CanvasManager.getInstance();

    /** The only instance of the town. */
    private static final Town SINGLETON = new Town(COLUMN_COUNT_0, ROW_COUNT_0);


    //== VARIABLE INSTANCE FIELDS ====================================================

    /** Current size of the canvas manager step. */
    private int module = CM.getStep();

    /** Rectangle representing the town area. */
    private Rectangle ground;

    /** Rectangle highlighting the current field. */
    private Rectangle current;

    /** Current number of the columns in the town. */
    private int columnSize;

    /** Current number of the rows in the town. */
    private int rowSize;

    /** Column of the current field. */
    private int currentColumn;

    /** Row of the current field. */
    private int currentRow;


    //################################################################################
    //== CONSTUCTORS AND FACTORY METHODS ====================================

    /********************************************************************************
     * Returns the (only) instance of the town.
     *
     * @return Instance of the town
     */
    public static Town getInstance()
    {
        return SINGLETON;
    }
```

```
/***************************************************************************
 * Creates a new town with the given number of columns and rows.
 * It is not possible to change the size of the town.
 *
 * @param columnSize Number of columns
 * @param rowSize    Number of rows
 */
private Town(int columnSize, int rowSize)
{
    this.columnSize = columnSize;
    this.rowSize    = rowSize;

    currentColumn = this.columnSize / 2;
    currentRow    = this.rowSize / 2;

    ground  = new Rectangle(0, 0, 1, 1, NamedColor.SMOKY);
    current = new Rectangle(0, 0, 1, 1, NamedColor.MILKY);

    CM.add(this);
}


//== OTHER NON-PRIVATE INSTANCE METHODS =======================================

/***************************************************************************
 * Moves the active field into another position in the town
 * and automatically moves also the town on the canvas.
 * The current field should be always in the center of the canvas.
 * As of this moment program does not control,
 * if the field will be in the city.
 *
 * @param column The set current field column
 * @param row    The set current field row
 */
public void setCurrentAt(int column, int row)
{
    currentColumn = column;
    currentRow    = row;
    CM.repaint();
}


/***************************************************************************
 * Paints the instance by force of the specified painter.
 *
 * @param painter Painter drawing the instance
 */
@Override
public void paint(Painter painter)
{
    module = CM.getStep();
    int canvasColumns = CM.getColumns();
    int canvasRows    = CM.getRows();
```

```
        //The current town field should be in the canvas centre
        int curColumn = canvasColumns / 2;
        int curRow    = canvasRows   / 2;

        //The town base position has to be set up in that way, so that
        //the current field would be on the canvas in the calculated position
        int townX = (curColumn - currentColumn) * module;
        int townY = (curRow    - currentRow) * module;
        ground.setPosition(townX, townY);
        ground.setSize(columnSize*module, rowSize*module);

        ground.paint(painter);

        current.setPosition((2*curColumn - 1) * module / 2,
                            (2*curRow    - 1) * module / 2);
        current.setSize (2*module);
        current.paint(painter);
    }
}
```

Exercise

570. Marvelous. I really succeeded to make it out! (To be true, with your little help.)

So until you are in full flow, define the test class for the town (but define it as an independent class, so that *BlueJ* would not associate them because then they would take too much place in the class diagram). Think out tests in which you will change positions of current field as well as the canvas size, and you will check if everything operates according to the assignment.

And I will also ask you to modify all our classes to be able to count their instances. Then adjust their methods toString() in such way so that they would show also instances' IDs behind the class name.

And I will add another little task. Until now all our constructors used the statement this(???) by which they delegated the responsibility for initializing the instances to their colleague in the way that the values of parameters which their colleague had extra, were entered directly – e.g. the double-parametric light constructor entered directly the yellow color to the tri-parametric constructor in the third parameter.

And now the task: adjust the class definitions in the way so that you define the corresponding constants for all these "magic" implicit values. Define these constants in the section CONSTANT CLASS FIELDS and use it instead of direct entering of values. I only remind that according to the convention only block letters are used in identifiers of static constants and individual words are separated with underscores – e.g. CHASSIS_DEFAULT_COLOR.

571. How to change the canvas size?

Learn to look into the documentation. You will find it there. This time I will help you: you will use the method setStepAndSize(int,int,int) which knows to change the step size (and by this also the field's size), as well as the number of lines and columns.

572. **You know, when solving the examples from exercises I noticed that on one hand you explain me not to copy the code, but on the other hand you give me examples which are mainly about copying the code. Would it be possible to make it somehow more skillfully and to decrease the code copying?**

I cannot agree with you so fully. We have defined a number of similar methods with the same signature in our four classes (what does it mean a signature was explained in the section *Signature versus Contract* on page 112), particularly methods for painting their instance to canvas by the painter and methods for getting and setting the position and the size, but each of those method had to react to special terms of the instance of the given class. Even definitions of the toString() method are very similar but only hardly could be unified (at least with your contemporary knowledge).

It is a little bit different in test classes – we defined several auxiliary methods which were nearly or fully identical. We will change it in the next lesson. We will try to unify all these methods into one. But we have already discussed such problem, do you remember? Take it as the second part of the exercise. But look far back – you have to return to time when we were working in the interactive mode. And my next hint: revise the design patterns discussed until now.

Review

Let's review what you have learned in this lesson:

- ☞ An instance cannot discover the name of the variable which refers to it.

- ☞ Some classes equip their instances by a field which helps to their identification.

- ☞ Due to the fact that the value of this field would not change in course of the instance's life, it is defined as a constant.

- ☞ For initializing the identification field the class remembers the number of created instances and the value of this field is derived from the order of creating its instance.

- ☞ The class remembers the number of created instances in the class field.

- ☞ The class fields are declared with the modifier static. Therefore they are called *static*.

- ☞ The order of enumerating individual modifiers is not important, but mostly they are quoted in the order as follows: public/private static final.

- ☞ The class fields are initialized only during installing the class.

- ☞ In case of declaring the variable of an object type as constant it means that the reference saved in it will not change. But the properties of the referred object can change.

- ☞ The value of the variable is increased with the statement of the following type:

      variable = variable + increase;

- ☞ Prior to programming you should always make an analysis of the problem in which you should decide how the task might be solved.

- ☞ In case the class should have the only instance, it is good to use the recommendation from the design pattern *Singleton*.

  - ☞ The constructor is private, so that nobody from outside could create his own instance.

☞   The class defines `private static final` field containing the reference to the only instance of the given class – its singleton. This field is optimal to be initialized immediately in its declaration.

☞   The class offers a `public static` factory method which returns a reference to its only instance, i.e. it returns a reference saved in the above mentioned field each time.

☞   This method is usually called `getInstance` or `getXyz`, where `Xyz` is the name of the class whose instance it returns.

Project:
The resulting form of the project to which we came at the end of this lesson and after completing all exercises is in the 128z_Class_Members project.

29 Refactoring of the Code

What you will learn in this lesson
In this lesson you will learn at first what is refactoring and then you will start adapting test methods entered in the last lesson as an exercise. You will adapt them so that not the same code would be repeated in them.

Project:
In this lesson we continue in using the 128z_Class_Members project.

What is Refactoring

573.   You have a strange word in the lesson's title – what does it mean refactoring?

I will not invent anything and I will only cite Martin Fowler, who wrote in his famous book *Refactoring* the following: *Refactoring is the process of changing a software system in such a way that it does not alter the external behavior of the code yet improves its internal structure. It is a disciplined way to clean up code that minimizes the chances of introducing bugs. In essence when you refactor you are improving the design of the code after it has been written.*[6]

Maybe it is said a little bit sophisticated but you surely understand. Last time you were complaining that our test classes are badly proposed because nearly the same code is repeated in them. I promised you to arrange the code so that it would be better designed. The function of classes and their public methods (i.e. tests) will not be touched. In other words: you will do refactoring.

574.   It's interesting that I never heard this word neither from friends who are programming a long time. And I've heard a lot about programming from them.

Maybe it is caused by the fact that refactoring is nearly not presented. Maybe the teachers assume that they can teach their students programming so well that the students cannot need any refactoring. But as I have already told: *The only one thing what you can rely on in programming is certitude that the assignment will be soon changed.* The old conception does not have to suit to the new assignment and then you can only refactor the program even when it was designed for the original assignment well.

575.   Well, well. So let's start refactoring our test classes.

Yes, if you remember, I asked you to seek in your memory at the end of the last lesson (answer to the question 572) and try to suggest how to unify the auxiliary methods in our test classes.

---

6   FOWLER, Martin. *Refactoring. Improving the Design of Existing Code.* Addison-Wesley, © 2000. 430 pp.

How to Solve Our Problem

576. You are true, I found it. And for change I'll cite you (I found it on page 102): *The design pattern Servant solves the problem how to add a supplementary functionality to a group of classes without inserting nearly the same method into each of them and violating by this the principle not to repeat the same or the very similar code.*

Bingo! You surely read how to proceed.

577. The pattern *Servant* advises to define a class whose instances will operate as servants, and an `interface`**, in which these servants specify their requirements for objects they are willing to control. With which will you start, with a class or an** `interface`**?**

Let's have a look into test classes for their auxiliary methods to clarify which of them are repeated and therefore it would be good to delegate their function to a servant. Then we will view these methods in detail to derive how to define the necessary `interface`.

The `IModular` Interface

578. There are three repeating auxiliary methods: `auxSmoothlySwapPositions`**,** `auxPositionSize` **and** `auxSwapPositionsWithCheck`**. I cannot do anything else with tested instances only to adjust their size, and detect and adjust their position. The arrows become translucent and back not translucent.**

Well, we will not notice the translucency of arrows at present, only in the second round. Methods for detecting and adjusting the position are declared by the `IMovable` interface which means you could define our `interface` as its child.

Then you told that you adjust the size of instances. A small correction: due to the fact that all our instances are determined for location into the canvas square fields, you adjust only a module. However, to put only adjustment of module into the `interface` is not the best variant, because then you would define them in too one-purpose way. To keep the possibility to use this new `interface` to other purposes as well, you should declare also its getting besides setting.

Now you could think out which name you will give them. Due to the fact that you will declare only the methods for working with the module in it, it should be named IModular. And that's all. You can see the resulting definition in the listing 29.1.

Listing 29.1: The IModular interface

```
/****************************************************************************
 * Instances of interface {@code IChangeable} represents geometrical shapes
 * that can reveal and set their positions and module.
 * The object's module is the basic size from which we derive
 * all the gauges of the object. The module of a shape is mostly defined
 * as the size of its circumscribed square.
 */
public interface IModular extends IMovable
{
    //== CONSTANTS ===============================================
    //== DECLARED METHODS ========================================

    /************************************************************
     * Returns the module &ndash; the basic size from which we derive
```

```
             * all the gauges of the object.
             *
             * @return The object's module
             */
//      @Override
        public int getModule();


        /*****************************************************************************
         * Returns the module &ndash; the basic size from which we derive
         * all the gauges of the object.
         *
         * @param module   The set module
         */
//      @Override
        public void setModule(int module);




        //== INHERITED METHODS =====================================================
        //== EMBEDDED DATA TYPES ===================================================
}
```

579.   Well, we have completed the `interface`, **so we can get back to the class of servants.**

Not fully, to complete this step you have to implement this interface by all classes whose instances
will be controlled. It means you have to draw the implementation arrows from all four classes. At the

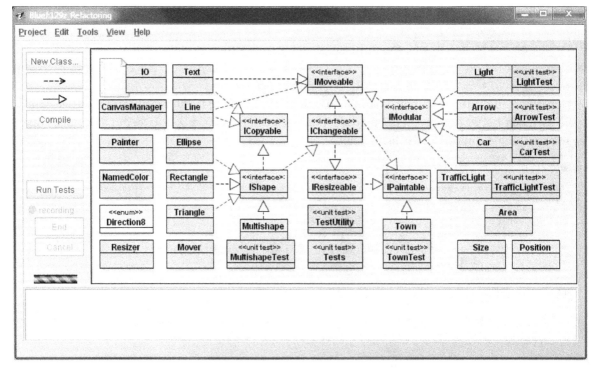

Figure 29.1
The project window after including the IModular interface

same time you can remove the implementation arrows to the IMovable interface because it is a parent of IModular and therefore the classes implement them from the grounds of interface inheritance (the project may look as in the figure 29.1). And when you will draw and remove the implementation arrows it would be suitable to open each class and add the annotation @Override before the heads of methods getModule() and setModule(int).

A Servant Class

580.   I have already made the arrangements. Tell me now what's your advice for the servant class.

I advise you to make a little step aside. Don't define the class whose instances would act as servants but define it in such way so that the class itself would be directly the servant. That's opportunity to practice definitions of static methods and how to work with them as well as the definition of the utility class (if you remember it – you can remind it on page 101).

581.   What should be the name of the class?

It is a test class according to the *Utility class*, so I recommend the name TestUtility. Create it, open it and make the arrangements I told you a while ago (the private constructor, deleting of methods for working with a fixture). Then open one of our test classes, e.g. the ArrowTest class, copy the auxiliary methods which are repeated in all classes i.e. methods auxSmoothlySwapPositions(Arrow, Arrow), auxPositionSize(Arrow) and auxSwapPositionsWithCheck(Arrow, Arrow) into the section OTHER NON-PRIVATE CLASS METHODS.

582.   You have indicated that the class will have no instances and that I'll train the static method definitions. Does it mean that it will be the library class (utility) and that (according to the section *Library/Utility Class* on page 101) I should define its constructor as private?

Excellent, I gape. I explained that the library class may not have a public constructor and when you don't define any, the compiler creates the default one (and it is public). Thus the only way, how to make the creation of an object impossible from outside, is to define the constructor as private.

When you are so excellent, I jump ahead in my explanation for a while and I suggest inserting of the following statement at the beginning (more precisely between the starting comment and the class javadoc comment):

```
import static org.junit.Assert.*;
```

This statement allows you to use the assertEquals(???) methods that were mentioned in the section *Test of Returning the Proper Value* on page 225. (In the chapter *Static Import* starting on page 360, I will explain why this statement helps.)

The Method auxSwapPositionsWithCheck

583.   It's inserted, and what now?

Have a look at the three enumerated methods carefully. You discover that the method auxSwapPositionsWithCheck is only an improved version of the method auxSmoothlySwapPositions, which means that you could keep the more perfect method and not install the simpler one.

584. Should I cancel it?

NO! Don't be rash. I told you to watch it carefully. You can see that the auxSwapPositionsWithCheck method calls the first one. In case you would delete the first one, nothing would operate. You have to take the content of the first method and put it into the second one on the place from which it is called, more precisely instead of this calling. The new form of the method should correspond with the listing 29.2. I commented the old calling and surrounded the inserted body by comments to make it clearer.

Listing 29.2:   *The method auxSwapPositionsWithCheck after inserting the body of the called method (the TestUtility class)*

```
private void auxSwapPositionsWithCheck(Arrow a1, Arrow a2)
{
    Position p1 = a1.getPosition();
    Position p2 = a2.getPosition();

    System.out.println("Start: " + p1 + " <--> " + p2);

    //auxSmoothlySwapPositions(a1, a2);  <- We replaced this call
    //The method body, which substitutes the calling, starts here
    Mover mover = new Mover(10);
    Position p1 = a1.getPosition();
    a1.translucent();
    a2.translucent();
    Mover.moveTo(a2.getPosition(), a1);
    Mover.moveTo(p1,              a2);
    a1.restoreColor();
    a2.restoreColor();
    //End of the inserted body

    System.out.println("Target:  " + a1.getPosition() +
                       " <--> " + a2.getPosition() + "\n");

    assertEquals(p1, a2.getPosition());
    assertEquals(p2, a1.getPosition());
}
```

585. It became a little bit more complicated.

It is only temporary. Look at the code now, how it should be modified. You will surely notice that the variable p1 is declared and initialized twice. Moreover, in the second declaration it is initialized by the value, which it already has. The best solution is then to delete the second declaration. When you try to compile the class now, you should succeed. Only then you can delete the first method.

586. Oh, now you swallowed the hook. It couldn't be compiled because in the method auxPositionSize(Arrow), which I copied, the canvas manager is used, and it was not yet declared. When I added its declaration, the compilation really passed.

As you can see, nobody is perfect. Try now to estimate what should be adjusted.

Generalization of a Method

587. Well, it would be a method not only for arrows, but it should enable to enter instances of all our classes.

Correct, and it concerns not only of our module classes. These tests are concentrated only to moving which means you could use this method for verification of position functions of any movable object. Replace the type `Arrow` by the type `IMovable` in both parameters.

There are two modifications left: you have to replace the modifier `private` by `public` one and you have to add the modifier `static` so that it became a class method. Otherwise the others will not be able to use it (you know that the utility class has no instances).

588. I arranged everything but the compilation did not pass. It says:
```
cannot find symbol - method translucent()
```

I see, you are not concentrated. You could discover it yourself. The method `translucent()` is called only in the arrow test. Other classes do not know this method. I recommend you to comment these statements (reminder: key F8); and comment also the statements calling the method `restoreColor()` because this method can be used also only with arrows. Later on I will show you how to modify the `ArrowTest` class to utilize the transparency of arrows in its test.

Besides that I would recommend to shift the mover's declaration up to position declarations and you can even delete comments with which I marked the borders of inserted code to you. I would say that then the code might be a bit better arranged.

And now you can replace the calling of auxiliary methods in definitions of our classes by the calling of an auxiliary method of the `TestUtility` class. Due to the fact that you did not qualify the method's calling with the help of `this`, it is sufficient to only add the `TestUtility` qualification before the method's calling. Compile the arranged classes and examine them.

589. Wow, it's already running! So now can I delete the auxiliary methods in all classes and call methods of the same name in the class `TestUtility`?

I would re-name the method. I would delete the prefix aux from the beginning, because it was put at this place to differentiate the test methods from the auxiliary ones. Now you can differentiate it easily: you can call the method from utility class `TestUtility`. To keep Java conventions, you should change also the first letter of the remaining identifier to a small one. Then the method could have the name `swapPositionWithCheck`.

At the same time you can guide the calling of the original method `auxSmoothlySwapPositions` to it – any extra checking might do well.

Adjustment for Arrows

590. Let's go to delete the auxiliary methods of test classes and adjust their tests in such way, so that they would call the methods of the `TestUtility` class instead of those deleted auxiliary methods.

Where do you hurry up? Don't rush. It's not so simple. At first you surely remember that you did not succeed to compile the original version of the method testing the fluent exchange of arrows. Let's go and have a look at it (fortunately the critical statements are only commented, which means you know where they have been).

591.   Sorry, I forgot. I promise to be concentrated. How should I solve it?

You have to try to do such arrangement that the changes of getting translucent and getting back not translucent would be executed by the calling method itself. If you would succeed to adjust the code so that the commented statements would be moved to its beginning and to its end, it's our triumph because it means that we can get them out of the method. Those, that need to carry out the commented statements (arrows in our case) can execute them before and after calling the method and the others are convenient without their presence in the method.

   We have luck by chance. Nothing will happen when you firstly make the arrows translucent, then you will carry out the whole method body and finally you return the original color to arrows. This means that making the arrows translucent and not translucent can be extracted from the method and transferred to the method that will call it.

592.   This means we should adjust the test method.

Neither this is an optimal solution because in the test method we call the auxiliary method several times one after another and we would have to make the pair of exchanged arrows firstly translucent, then call the method in the utility class and at the end return again to the original color of both arrows. It means repeating of the code would be back which we don't like much. We have already solved such repeating of a code – do you remember how?

593.   By chance yes: we defined an auxiliary method which executed the repeating code and we told it in parameters with whom it should do it.

Correct, marvelous! The test method testSwapPositionsWithCheck in the ArrowTest class calls the auxiliary method auxSwapPositionsWithCheck for each couple of moved arrows. Let's use it, we leave the test method as it is and define all necessary operations in the body of an auxiliary method. We delete its original body and replace it by a code according to the listing 29.3, i.e. making the arrow translucent, calling the method in the utility class, which exchanges the positions of arrows and tests, if it returns the original color to arrows after returning from this method.

   We did not avoid the auxiliary method but its part which is identical with other classes, is now common. In case you would like to change it sometimes in future, you will change it at the only one place and not in each class separately.

Listing 29.3:   *The adapted method auxSwapPositionsWithCheck in the ArrowTest class*

```
private void auxSwapPositionsWithCheck (Arrow a1, Arrow a2)
{
    a1.translucent();
    a2.translucent();
    TestUtility.swapPositionsWithCheck (a1, a2);
    a1.restoreColor();
    a2.restoreColor();
}
```

Adaptation of Test Classes

594. **So the test method of arrows will not change because it will continue in calling its auxiliary method. And as far as the others are mentioned, will the calling of their auxiliary method be replaced by calling a method from the** TestUtility **class?**

Exactly, you should go through the substituted auxiliary method in all adjusted classes once again, but you will discover that the remained auxiliary methods are already equal and its functionality corresponds with the method defined in the TestUtility class. Then, in other class it will be sufficient to change the method testSmoothlySwapPositions (). E.g. in the CarTest class the adjusted test method will look out as in the following listing 29.4.

Listing 29.4:   *The method* testSwapPositionsWithCheck() *in the CarTest class*

```
public void testSwapPositionsWithCheck()
{
    TestUtility.swapPositionsWithCheck(car0,   carXYB);
    TestUtility.swapPositionsWithCheck(carXYB, carXYM);
    TestUtility.swapPositionsWithCheck(carXYM, carXYMB);
}
```

After you will run these tests and verify they operate you can delete the auxiliary methods (of course with the exception of the one we have adjusted in the Arrow test class). And you can delete also the test methods testSmoothlySwapPositions and connected auxiliary methods because we came to an agreement that they do the same except checking the positions after the shift.

595. **At the beginning of adjustments you told me that I should enter the** IMovable **type to method's parameters because the method doesn't work with a module. We could use it for any movable object. I should remind our historical test classes.**

Correctly! The Tests class is not much suitable for this purpose because the smaller shapes would be hidden under the big ones after the shift, but the fixture in the MultishapeTest class enables an elegant exchange of positions of both multi-shapes. Therefore you should supplement the test even for multishapes and you can examine operating of our class even with them.

The testPositionSize **Test Method**

596. **It means we have two thirds behind us. It was a bit more complicated than I expected. But on the other side I converted one of the tests by its deleting which means the total result is quite good. I hope the conversion of the third test method will be simpler.**

Well, I wouldn't be so sure. My experience is that the computer and its programs are always ready to present a surprise. Look through the individual steps of your last adjustments once again and try to proceed according to them.

Generalization of a Copied Method

597.   **I looked at it. First of all we adjusted the copied method to be public and static and we changed its parameters so that it would accept any element that would implement the `IMovable` interface. Finally we renamed the method. Now I made the same with the `testPositionSize` method; only instead of `IMovable` I entered `IModular`. And what now?**

The beginning is good. And now go through the auxiliary methods in all classes and check if they are identical or if there is a similar surprise hidden as the arrow transparency was in the previous method.

598.   **The methods are quite identical.**

Identical? Look at them once again and more sharply.

599.   **They are really identical. They differ only in values of parameters.**

Just only in values of parameters. We had to choose a little bit different position in each class according to its fixture; the objects of its fixture will move to this position and will there increase and decrease. The position is chosen in such way so that the objects would not hinder one to another and would not shade mutually. Also the modules, to which the objects increase, are different. Only the module of the decreased object is common.

There are no values that would suit to all. Therefore, each test class should have the possibility to send its objects to the position that suits to it and to let the objects increase to the size suitable for it.

Adapting the Method to Different Requirements

600.   **I admit I did not think of it. How to solve it?**

Basically there are two possibilities. The first one is to add parameters to the method in which you pass over the required position as well as the module. I dislike this way because the test class would have to pass over the same values to the called method during each calling (as you might notice I have certain aversion against repeating). We could define these values as constants so that it would be possible to change them in bulk at one place if need be, but I would like to show you also another possible procedure.

In case we know we will call the method several times for the identical values of the target position of the big module as well as the small one it can be better to define another method in the utility class, to which we pass over the required values before the series of calling, and this method will save them into fields established for this purpose. Then the called method will hand over the needed values from them. This solution seems to me more suitable and therefore I recommend you to go this way.

601.   **Should we define another method in the `TestUtility` class?**

Yes, and I would call it maybe `testPositionModules` and it would have three parameters: the required target position, the module for increasing and the module for decreasing. I know that the decreasing module is the same for all tests but I take into account that it might change in time. I suppose that I do not have to quote the source code of this method.

602.   I know you will not like it but the method with several parameters seems to me good.

Why not – we can define both of them. The parameterless method can call the parametric one and it can find the values of parameters in fields. You use the parametric method in case you would like to call the test method only once and you use the parameterless method in case you would like to call it more times one after the other with the same parameters. Then you have to remember calling the method `testPositionModules(Position,int,int)` before the given series and adjust the necessary parameters in it.

After you will adjust the test methods within the exercising, try both variants.

603.   I tried to program both versions of the methods but I didn't succeed to compile them. The compiler says that `non-static variable Position cannot be referenced from a static context`

Because you forgot to declare the position field as static. Go through the whole source code once more and check that all fields and methods are declared as static (nothing else has a meaning in the utility class). Then the compilation should be completed. Have a look at the listing 29.5, in which the pattern solution is quoted.

Listing 29.5:   The *TestUtility* class

```
import static org.junit.Assert.*;


/***************************************************************************
 * Library class {@code TestUtility} contains a set of auxiliary methods
 * used by test classes of objects implementing the {@link IModular} interface.
 */
public class TestUtility
{
    //== CONSTANT CLASS FIELDS ===========================================

    private static final CanvasManager CM = CanvasManager.getInstance();


    //== VARIABLE CLASS FIELDS ===========================================

    /** Position, where the tested object will move
     *  in the {@link #positionSize(IModular)} method. */
    private static Position position;

    /** Size of the smaller of the two modules,
     *  which are going to be set up to object
     *  that is tested in method {@link #positionSize(IModular)}. */
    private static int smallModule;

    /** Size of the bigger of the two modules,
     *  which are going to be set up to object
     *  that is tested in method {@link #positionSize(IModular)}. */
    private static int bigModule;


    //== CLASS GETTERS AND SETTERS =======================================
```

```
/***************************************************************************
 * Tests the changes of position and sizes of entered object;
 * parameters of test has to be set by method in advance
 *
 * @param position  Position where the tested object will move
 * @param small     Small sized module
 * @param big       Big sized module
 */
public static void setPositionsModules(Position position,
                                       int small, int big)
{
    TestUtility.position    = position;
    TestUtility.smallModule = small;
    TestUtility.bigModule   = big;
}



//== OTHER NON-PRIVATE CLASS METHODS =========================================

/***************************************************************************
 * Tests the changes of position and sizes of entered object;
 * parameters of the test has to be set by the method in advance.
 *
 * @param object Tested object
 */
public static void positionSize(IModular object)
{
    positionSize(object, position, smallModule, bigModule);
}



/***************************************************************************
 * Tries the changes of position and size of entered object with entered
 * parameters.
 *
 * @param object    Tested object
 * @param position  Position where the tested object will move
 * @param small     Small sized module
 * @param big       Big sized module
 */
public static void positionSize(IModular object,
                                Position position, int small, int big)
{
    final int ms = 500;
    object.setPosition(position.x, position.y);     IO.pause(ms);
    object.setModule(big);                          IO.pause(ms);
    object.setModule(small);                        IO.pause(ms);
    CM.remove(object);                              IO.pause(ms);
}



/***************************************************************************
 * Will exchange positions of the entered objects and will check
 * if the objects really exchanged their positions.
```

```
    *
    * @param o1 1st object
    * @param o2 2nd object
    */
   public static void swapPositionsWithCheck(IMovable o1, IMovable o2)
   {
       Mover mover = new Mover(10);
       Position p1 = o1.getPosition();
       Position p2 = o2.getPosition();

       System.out.println("Initial: " + p1 + " <--> " + p2);

       mover.moveTo(p2, o1);
       mover.moveTo(p1, o2);

       System.out.println("Target:   " + o1.getPosition() +
                           " <--> " + o2.getPosition() + "\n");

       assertEquals(p1, o2.getPosition());
       assertEquals(p2, o1.getPosition());
   }



   //#####################################################################
   //== CONSTUCTORS AND FACTORY METHODS ========================================

   /** Private constructor blocks the creation of instances. */
   private TestUtility(String name) {}
}
```

Exercise

604. **This means that we are going to cancel the auxiliary methods from test classes and adjust their tests. And thus we could finish today.**

I agree and I would say that all tasks for exercise were quoted during the explanation. I only remind that your assignment is to adjust the tests in all four test classes in such way so that they would use the TestUtility class methods. Don't forget to call the method testPositionModules(Position,int,int) at the beginning.

Add the new test into the MultishapeTest class in the first part and try to think out an analogous test for objects in fixture of the Tests class.

Review

Let's review what you have learned in this lesson:

☞ Refactoring is accomplishing of such changes which improve the program design but do not influence its operating.

☞ When unifying several similar methods, it is good to find out if it is possible to "push" those parts of the code, in which the individual versions differentiate, at the edge of the code. Then there is no problem to entrust the calling method to carry them out.

☞ In case several very similar methods differ in only values used in the code they can be unified by adding these values as parameters.

☞ The second way of solving the previous problem insists in the definition of fields into which the calling method firstly saves the required values by calling a special adjusting method. Subsequently the called method can hand over the necessary values of these fields.

☞ When defining the class fields and methods the keyword static cannot be forgotten.

Project:
The resulting form of the project to which we came at the end of the lesson and after completing all exercises is in the 129z_Refactoring project.

30 Static Constructor – Class Constructor

What you will learn in this lesson
This lesson will be probably the most difficult from the whole book for somebody. You will learn in details how the class can get into the memory and how it is initialized there. After that you will see in details the activities of constructors. During it you will become acquainted with static as well as instance initializa-tion blocks and you will see where and how you can use them.

Project:
In this lesson we continue in using the 129z_Refactoring project.

Note:
This lesson as well as the next one may seem to some people too detailed. The truth is that even a number of more advanced textbooks do not explain the topic of constructing the objects and classes to such depth. However, my students persuaded me about their endless invention in us-ing not yet explained constructions which logically lead to arising apparently not comprehensi-ble mistakes. The deeper knowledge of processing the construction of objects and classes ena-bles to explain many of them naturally.

The second reason for such detailed explanation is that one of the best ways of learning is a study of foreign programs. A number of these programs (even the simpler ones) use the knowledge of principles explained in this lesson and students who work with them have some-times problems with understanding their function or with the author's aim.

In case any reader will find out the lesson too detailed he/she can skip it over and get back to it after he/she will think he/she may find an explanation of strange acting of certain program. Anyway, I would recommend to everybody not to skip over the whole lesson but read the sec-tions started with *What Should Be Remembered* at page 302. These sections summarize how to act. The preceding explanation shows what could happen if you would not act like that.

Class Constructor – Static Constructor

605. In last two lessons we were playing with static fields and methods. I tried to add a modifier static **to a con-structor, but it was not accepted. I think the class should also have its constructor, because you told that the class is also an object.**

Let's admit that the class is a little bit (well, better say a lot) non-standard and in a number of ways. There are different rules valid for it than for the rest of the world. Primarily (at least in Java and simi-lar languages) the classes do not act as instances of some common parent class that would define which fields and methods they have. Each class plays for itself and has its own set of fields and methods.

However, in a number of other aspects it does not differ from current objects. Even the class has its constructor. I've told that the constructor of instances has (in Java) the internal name <init>. The constructor of the class has (in Java) the internal name <clinit> (surely you will deduce that it's a shortcut from *class init*) and that it is created by a compiler by putting together all initializations of static fields and static initializers.

606.   Static initializers? What is it?

The **static initializer** (often called only *static block* or *static initializer*) arises when you write the key-word static followed by braces – a block – at the place where you can declare a field or a method. You can write a code into this block which should be executed after the class will be loaded into the memory and its class-object will be constructed.

607.   You are good! You explain one term using two others, not yet explained. What is the class-object and what does it mean that the class is loaded into the memory? I thought it's there all the time.

No, it's not. Java counts with creating the **class-object**, i.e. an object representing the given class in the program (as any object), only in a moment when somebody will need it. In other words, until anybody does not need the given class, the class does not hinder in the memory.

In the moment when somebody needs a class, a special object – the **class loader** (an instance of the ClassLoader class) – is called which returns the class-object of the given class. In case the class loader discovers that the class-object of the given class does not yet exist, it **loads the class into the memory**, i.e. it finds its class file, loads it and creates the needed class-object on the basis of information saved in it. At this occasion the class loader calls the static constructor of the given class and it initializes the class.

During this initialization the individual declarations of static fields as well as static initializers are executed in the order in which they are placed in the source code. Then the created class-object is given over to the applicant.

608.   You forgot to tell that the not initialized are zeroed.

They are not zeroed in the static constructor (if you don't write such initialization). They are already zeroed a long time ago by the virtual machine. You know that the virtual machine allocates the memory for an object and it zeroes it before giving it over. Therefore, when starting the initializing of a class the entire needed memory is already zeroed.

609.   Is it possible to verify that the class loading operates exactly as you told?

Of course, and we will do it in two parts: in this lesson we will consider the class loading and con-struction of its instances from outside, in the next lesson we will have a look from inside. I prepared an experimental class CCI for this research work (its name is a shortage of Construction of Classes and Instances) – you can see its source code in the listing 30.1 and you can find it in the subfolder Extension_30. The class contains a code for experiments on loading and constructing of a class as well as for experiments on constructing its instances. For now we will deal with only a construction of a class, i.e. we will take into account only fields, methods and initializers marked with the modifier static.

Listing 30.1:   *The CCI class*

```
/***********************************************************************************
 * Class {@code CCI} and its instances serve for demonstrations and experiments
 * when explaining the
 * implementing and initialization of classes and construction of its instances.
 */
public class CCI
{
    static  // Opening static initializer
    {/*##_1_##*/
        String me = "\nSTART of the class constructor (= static initializer)" +
                    " of the CCI class";
        IO.inform(me);
        printStaticFields(me);
    }

    //Opening instance initializer
    {/*##_2_##*/
        String me = "\nSTART of the initialization of the creating " +
                    "CCI instance\n" +  this;
        IO.inform(me + " of a new CCI instance\n\nSTART");
        System.out.println("\n-------------------------------------" +
                        "\n" + me + " - START for " + this);
    }


    //== CONSTANT CLASS FIELDS ===================================================

    static  //Before declaration of constants
    {/*##_3_##*/
        //Use of undeclared constant is a syntax error,
        //even if the constant value was assigned in the compile-time
        //System.out.println("COMPILED:    " + COMPILED);

        //Nevertheless, the hidden use works as can be seen in the block ##_1_##
    }

    /** Constant initialized in the compile-time -
     * if the value of a constant is known in the compile-time.
     * compiler initializes it during compilation. */
    private static final String COMPILED = "COMPILED";

    /** Constant initialized during the class loading. */
    public static final Class<?> CLASS_OBJECT = CCI.class;

    /** Constant initialized in a static initializer. */
    public static final String INITIALIZED;

    static  //After declaration of constants
    {/*##_4_##*/
        //The not initialized constant can't still be used as well
        //System.out.println("INITIALIZED: " + INITIALIZED);
```

```
            INITIALIZED = CLASS_OBJECT.getName();

        //After the initialization constants can be used
        System.out.println("\nxxx Print after the initialization" +
                            " of class constants:" +
                    "\n    - COMPILED:      " + COMPILED +
                    "\n    - CLASS_OBJECT: " + CLASS_OBJECT +
                    "\n    - INITIALIZED:  " + INITIALIZED);
    }

    //Static (= class) field can also refer to an instance of the class
    //But it's needed to initialize such field after all static fields,
    //which are used during its initialization.
    //The following declaration has problems with constant field LOADED
    //as well as with variable field countCreated.
    //Problems are solved by shift of this field initialization
    //behind all fields used in its initialization.
    //public static final CCI ME = new CCI();


    //== VARIABLE CLASS FIELDS =============================================

    static //Before declaration of instance variables
    {/*##_5_##*/
        //Undeclared variable may not be used
        //System.out.println("variable: " + variable);
    }

    private static String variable;
    private static int    countCreated = 0;

    static  //After declaration of variables
    {/*##_6_##*/
        //Variable can be also used if uninitialized,
        //because the compiler is not able to recognize it
        System.out.println("\nxxx Print after declaration of class variables:" +
                        "\n    - variable:    " + variable);
        variable = "VARIABLE";  //As of this moment variable is reinitialized
    }


    //== STATIC INITIALIZER (CLASS CONSTRUCTOR) ===========================
    //== CONSTANT INSTANCE FIELDS =========================================

    private final int ID;
    //Instance ID has to be counted at first
    {/*##_7_##*/
        countCreated = countCreated + 1;  //Increase of static field
        ID = countCreated;                 //and save its current value
        //The hidden parameter this can be used in the initializers ...
        System.out.println("ID field initialized: " + this);
    }

    private final CCI THIS = this;  //... as well as in field initialization
```

```
//In the following initialization I ask the instance for its class-object
String name = "[" + this.getClass() + "]";     //Temporary name




//== VARIABLE INSTANCE FIELDS =================================================

//In the initialization of the instance fields we can use only
//already declared instance fields and already initialized constants.
//On the other side all class fields can be used,
//because they were already defined during the class loading.
private String time = LOADED;

String source;


//== CLASS GETTERS AND SETTERS ================================================
//== OTHER NON-PRIVATE CLASS METHODS ==========================================

/****************************************************************************
 * Prints all static attributes of class to standard output.
 * The compiler does not recognize, if this method is used
 * before the used fields are declared and/or initialized.
 *
 * @param title Header of the particular prints
 */
public static void printStaticFields(String title)
{
    System.out.println("\n" + title +
                    "\n   - COMPILED     = " + COMPILED +
                    "\n   - CLASS_OBJECT = " + CLASS_OBJECT +
                    "\n   - variable     = " + variable +
                    "\n   - countCreated = " + countCreated +
                    "\n   - LOADED       = " + LOADED
                );
}



//###########################################################################
//== CONSTUCTORS AND FACTORY METHODS ==========================================

/****************************************************************************
 * Parameterless constructor for test of initialization.
 */
public CCI()
{
    String text = " of the body of the parameterless constructor of ";
    System.out.println("Beginning" + text + this);
    source = "Parametereless";
    System.out.println("End" + text + this);
}
```

```
    /****************************************************************************
     * One-parametric constructor for test of responsibility delegation.
     *
     * @param name Name of the generated instance
     */
    public CCI(String name)
    {
//        //Before the delegation of the responsibility there can be nothing
//        System.out.println("One parametric for " + this);
        this(name, prepare("One-parametric"));
        System.out.println("END parameter one");
    }



    /****************************************************************************
     * Constructor with 2 parameters for test of responsibility delegation.
     *
     * @param name   Name of the generated instance
     * @param source Characteristics of applicant
     */
    public CCI(String name, String source)
    {
        this(name, prepare("2-parametric"), source);
        String local = "2-parameters";
        System.out.println("END " + local);
    }



    /****************************************************************************
     * Constructor with 3 parameters for testing of responsibility delegation.
     *
     * @param name       Name of the generated instance
     * @param source     Characteristics of applicant
     * @param presource Second part of attribute value {@code source}
     */
    public CCI(String name, String source, String presource)
    {
        String text = " of the body of the 3-parametric constructor";
        System.out.println("Beginning" + text + this +
        "\n    Title=" + name + ", Source=" + source +
                            ", Presource=" + presource);
        String unused;
        String underlinning;
        this.name    = name;
        String sum   = "«" + presource + " -> " + source + "»";
        this.source  = sum;
        String local = "END" + text + "\n    this=";
        underlinning = "\n~~~~~~~~~~~~~~~~~~~~~~~~~~~~~~~~~~~~~~~~~";
        System.out.println(local + this + underlinning);
    }


    //== ABSTRACT METHODS =======================================================
    //== INSTANCE GETTERS AND SETTERS ===========================================
```

```
    //== OTHER NON-PRIVATE INSTANCE METHODS =======================================

    /*****************************************************************************
     * Return the object's text signature.
     *
     * @return The object's text signature
     */
    @Override
    public String toString()
    {
        return "CCI_" + ID + "(name=" + name + ", source=" + source +
               ", ##time=" + time + ")";
    }



    //== PRIVATE AND AUXILIARY CLASS METHODS =======================================

    /*****************************************************************************
     * Auxiliary static method serving for registration of the moment,
     * in which the parameters are evaluated.
     *
     * @param text Header before particular prints
     */
    private static String prepare(String text)
    {
        System.out.println("  === Preparing: " + text);
        return text;
    }




    //== PRIVATE AND AUXILIARY INSTANCE METHODS =================================
    //== MEMBER DATA TYPES =====================================================
    //== TESTING CLASSES AND METHODS ===========================================

    {/*##_8_##*/
        String text = "END of the initialization part of\n    " + this;
        System.out.println(text + "\n----------------------------");
        IO.inform(text);
    }

    //Static attribute declared as far as at the end of the body
    private static final String LOADED = "" + new java.util.Date();
    static
    {/*##_9_##*/
        String me = "\nEND of the class constructor (= static initializer)" +
                    " of the CCI class";
        printStaticFields(me);
        System.out.println("=============================\n");
        IO.inform(me);
    }
}
```

610. Wow, it's a nice podge!

It only seems to you here in the book. In fact you have programmed a far longer one – e.g. the class TrafficLight. Moreover, the CCI class does not have so complicated code as you would guess at the first sight, because a significant part of it consists of comments which are part of the explanation.

611. Well, so tell me what I will find out of it.

We will go through step by step. But now I would like to draw your attention to static initialization blocks at the beginning and at the end of the CCI class. The introductory block opens the dialog announcing that the constructor of the given class is opening, and after confirmation of this window it writes a message on starting the work of class constructor to the standard output. On the contrary, the closing static block writes there firstly a message on closing the work of class constructor and then opens the dialog, in which it announces the end of the class constructor work.

Inside the class body there are further static initializers serving for demonstration of some other properties and possibilities. They don't open any dialogs, but they write down a message to the standard output, but only in certain cases. As I have told you, we will go through all of them and explain them.

Besides static initializers you can find also instance initializers in the class – those are blocks without the modifier static before the braces. We will speak about them in the second part of the lesson.

To be precise which part of the program we are just now debating, I inserted a comment into all initializers behind their opening braces. This comment is in the form /*## ? ##*/, where the middle question mark represents the ordinal of the block. The comment form utilizes the advantage that the authors of *BlueJ* program use comments starting with /*# for stressing certain information and use a different color for it. For better orientation I shaded these comments in the listing 30.1. Therefore you can find them much better in the source code.

612. What is the strange declaration after the third initializer? Why is the text <?> in the following statement?
```
public static final Class<?> CLASS_OBJECT = CCI.class;
```

The Class class is declared as a *generic type* (we will discuss them in the section *Generic Types and Type Parameters* on page 412). The text <?> is not necessary, however if it would not be there, the compiler will send the following warning:

```
found raw type java.lang.Class
  missing type arguments for generic class java.lang.Class<T>
```

Program with the <?> is more pure and does not force any warnings.

613. For what are the static initializers used in practice?

Mostly they are used in situations when some class fields cannot be initialized directly in a declaration because it is necessary to carry out some more complex code within their initialization. The existence of static initializers is important above all for class constants which due to certain reason cannot be initialized immediately in the declaration. For class constants as well as for constants of instances there is the same valid rule: you can initialize them only in the declaration or in the appropriate constructor – the class constants in the class constructor, i.e. in its static initializer.

The second reason for using the static initializers is the need to analyze in detailed way the running of the class during its loading into memory. Further static initializers were inserted into the CCI class just from this reason. Therefore they are more frequent, because they enable us to follow the course of initialization. Using more than one static initialization blocks in other than test cases is considered as inappropriate. That's the reason why these blocks should be deleted or at least commented after revealing and removing the error (which is the reason why they were defined).

The Call class

614.	**You say that thanks to static initializers I can follow how the class is loaded into memory. It's interesting. Start showing.**

Besides the CCI class you can find also the Call class (see listing 30.2) in the subfolder of the project folder. There are also four static methods in it (they are static so that we should not produce instances due to calling these methods):

☞	The method nothingNeeded() only opens the dialog in which it announces its invocation. I included it only so that you could see that as far as we will work with those parts of the program which do not use the CCI class; it will not be installed and initialized.

☞	The method classNeeded() also opens the dialog announcing its invocation, but then it requires the CCI class for its field CLASS_OBJECT whose signature is depicted in the opened dialog. It is a method which arranges that if the class is not yet installed into memory, it will be installed after calling this method.

☞	The introductory dialog can be open also by the instanceNeeded() method. It requires the CCI class for a new instance whose signature is shown in an opened dialog. The instance is here to examine the class behavior during creating the instance. If the class is not yet loaded into the memory, it is loaded during requiring an instance, and only then it starts to create instances. In case it is already loaded, only instances are created.

☞	The last method testInvocation() will be used in the next lesson. It calls the one-parametric constructor of the CCI class and we know that it delegates the responsibility for initializing to its colleague. We will see how the succession of mutual calling of methods in the program can be observed in it.

Besides that the class contains also the private method which accompanies each opening of a dialog with the framed text printed to the standard output so that once more we could remind particular steps after running the whole action.

Listing 30.2:	*The Call class with deleted line comments quoting not used sections*

```
/*****************************************************************************
 * Library class {@code Call} serves for demonstration of behavior
 * of class KTI when used for the first time and afterwards and for
 * demonstration of behavior of its constructors.
 */
public class Call
{
```

```java
//== OTHER NON-PRIVATE CLASS METHODS =========================================

/****************************************************************************
 * Method does not use class CCI
 */
public static void nothingNeeded()
{
    window("nothingNeeded", "I was executed\nand I need nothing.");
}



/****************************************************************************
 * Method uses only class CCI, not its instances.
 */
public static void classNeeded()
{
    window("classNeeded", "I require a class-object.");
    Object clso = CCI.CLASS_OBJECT;
    window("classNeeded", "I recieved an object\n\n" + clso);
}



/****************************************************************************
 * Method needs instance of class CCI.
 */
public static void instanceNeeded()
{
    window("instanceNeeded", "I require an instance.");
    Object inst = new CCI();
    window("instanceNeeded", "I recieved an instance\n\n" + inst);
}



/****************************************************************************
 * Method calls one-parametric constructor of CCI and knows,
 * that it will call the 2-parametric one,
 * that will call the 3-parametric one.
 * Method serves for explanation and demonstration of work with a debugger.
 */
public static void testInvocation()
{
    CCI inst = new CCI("Experiment");
    System.out.println("\n=================================" +
                       "\nCreated instance: " + inst +
                       "\n=================================");
}



//###########################################################################
//== CONSTUCTORS AND FACTORY METHODS =========================================

/** Library class without accessible constructor. */
private Call() {}
```

```
//== PRIVATE AND AUXILIARY CLASS METHODS =====================================

/***************************************************************************
 * Prints the given text to standard output and afterwards also in a dialog.
 *
 * @param method Calling method name
 * @param text   The additional text
 */
private static void window(String method, String text)
{
    System.out.println("\nvvvvvvvvvvvvvvvvvvvvvvv" +
                       "\nMethod: " + method + " - " + text +
                       "\n^^^^^^^^^^^^^^^^^^^^^^^");
    IO.inform(text);
}
}
```

Loading and Initializing of a Class

615.   I'm afraid a bit if I will not be lost in those printed texts but I'm going to try it. What should I do?

Let both classes compile. You can verify that it's sufficient to ask for compilation of the Call class, because it uses the CCI class and therefore it is dependent on it and thus the compilation of the Call class force the compilation of the CCI class before it. With regards that it is dependent on the CCI class (it calls its method), *BlueJ* can arrange firstly to compile CCI which means that both of them will be compiled.

Now you can start experimenting. Today's experiments will all run in an interactive mode. We will send messages to the Call class and watch the program's answers in dialogs and in the terminal window. Therefore I recommend you to open the terminal window (you should remember the command **View → Terminal** or CTRL+T hotkey) and set the **Clear screen at method call** and **Unlimited buffering** in its **Option** menu.

616.   I am ready, let's start.

Reset the virtual machine before the beginning of the experiment. Then send the nothingNeeded() message to the Call class. A message on standard output is written and the dialog created by the invoked method is opened. And it's all. The situation will be the same not depending on how many time you will send this message, i.e. how many times you invoke the corresponding method.

617.   You are true, it's boring. Give me something more interesting.

Send the classNeeded() message to the Call class. Even now the called method announces its invocation at the standard output and in the dialog, but after your confirmation the dialog appears announcing the entry into the constructor of the CCI class, and the second one appears announcing its completing. Only then the classNeeded() method receives what it asked for, and opens the dialog with the description of the received class-object.

The course of further callings of this method is then briefer and will open only dialogs opened by the given method and the relevant listing on standard output. The CCI class is already installed and initialized so that its constructor is not started.

As you have surely noticed, until the CCI class was not needed, its initializing was not started. Maybe you will believe me that it was not in the memory at that time. It was loaded and initialized (i.e. its static constructor was activated) only after it was needed – in our case when the classNeeded() method hungered for its public field or when the instanceNeeded() method needed to call its constructor. It would be similar when you would like to call its public static method. The class is loaded and initialized during the first addressing and then it only provides for what it was asked.

Try to reset the virtual machine. By this you clear the memory again and you can try once more that classes will be installed after the first addressing.

Details of Class Initializing

618.   It's as you say. After each resetting the class is initialized only in its first using.

And now I would like to draw your attention to the code of class constructor itself. Let's go through its source code and explain what you should remember during defining your own classes. For now we have seen the first and the last static initializer which pointed us at its activation by opening a dialog. Come to have a further look– at a block /*##_3_##*/. I want to draw your attention on the fact that using the not yet declared field is a syntactic error. It's valid for constants as well as for variable fields.

The warning comment is followed by a commented statement which strives to print a value of COMPILED constant. Despite the fact that the compiler assigned this value already during compilation, which means it exists and has its value but you cannot use it before its declaration. When you delete the comment and you will try to compile the class, the compiler gives the following announcement

```
illegal forward reference
```

The compiler says by this message that you use not allowed forward reference.

619.   Which forward reference?

As I have already told, during class initialization its code is passed through from the beginning up to the end, and in initializers as well as in field initializations you can use only the fields which were already declared and in case of constants also initialized. As soon as you would like to use a field which only **will be** declared, you refer ahead to something what will be declared and that's why this reference is named as forward.

620.   How is it possible that in case of methods it does not matter when I use a method which only will be defined, whilst for fields it does matter?

Because during field initialization each action has to be carried out immediately (you need to prepare the data that should be stored in the initialized field) whilst the methods can be prepared prior and aside. In the moment when the method is called the compiler has already everything prepared and knows where the method can be found independently if it was defined prior or after the method which calls this method.

621.   I return to our program. How do you know that the given constant already exists and has an assigned value, when the compiler says that it's not true?

Because I played a trick on it. When you look into the block /*##_1_##*/, you discover that besides calling the method IO.inform(Object) it calls also the method printStaticFields(String). It prints values of all fields regardless if they were declared and initialized. Look at the standard output at the first print after entering into the static constructor – and you will find the following:

```
START of the class constructor (= static initializer) of the CCI class
    - COMPILED     = COMPILED
    - CLASS_OBJECT = null
    - variable     = null
    - countCreated = 0
    - LOADED       = null
```

As you can see, the constant COMPILED already has its value whilst other fields are kept in the initial zero state.

622. How is it possible that the field COMPILED already has initial value assigned and the others not?

Because it is a **constant evaluated in the compile-time**. In its declaration after the block /*##_3_##*/ the expression specifying the initial value is so clear that the compiler was able to evaluate it and compile this field a little bit different – not as a standard field, but as a different name for the value "COMPILED".

We say that the assigned value is specified as a *constant compile-time expression*, i.e. an expression, which can be evaluated in compile-time. As the compiler discovers such expression, it doesn't compile it, but evaluate it and puts the result into the compiled program instead of the compiled original expression.

Constants initialized by a constant compile-time expression (we will name them *compile-time constats*) have a special position. Due to the fact that those are only different names for fixed values (we could say *only declaration, no implementation*), they may be declared also in an interface. We shall speak about them in course of further explanation. Now I would like to skip it. Take this constant similarly as all others and you surely will not make any mistake.

623. Well. How is it possible that the method did not print the values of fields, which – as the compiler said – do not yet exist?

Due to the fact that the place for these fields already exists – it was prepared by the virtual machine when reserving the place for future object. The compiler took into account these fields during compiling the method, which means the method works with the place in memory, where the given fields will be located after they will officially exist.

If I would like to be ironic I would say that the forward reference is used so clumsily in a commented statement that the compiler did notice it and therefore it announced an error during uncommenting. The fact I used the same fields in the method which I called from the static initializer was outside its view. The compiler doesn't reveal the inappropriate using of fields there, because otherwise it should analyze each method called during initialization including methods called from these methods. This would uselessly complicate the compiler.

624. So should I move using the fields to methods?

No, NO, **NO!** The fact, that I showed you that such premature usage of fields is not revealed by a compiler, does not mean that it is correct. Our method only printed signatures of fields, and the fact, that some of them were not initialized, only led to a null in the printed listing. But, if the method should have certain critical action as task, the whole program might finish with a crash. Take it like I wanted to draw your attention to some of the popular mistakes which the beginners make from time to time and then they explain that there is an error in the compiler.

Look at the standard output to where the method `printStaticFields(String)` prints the texts during its operation. You will see how the values of some fields declared as constants are currently changing. This can have really fatal consequences for the program.

When you will read the source text further you can find another notice to various principles which you should keep during declaring and initializing of static fields. As I showed you at the example a while ago, you can avoid majority of them with a bit of effort but you are asking for troubles which are not worthy when you try to achieve "victory over the compiler".

What Should Be Remembered

625. Well, I shall try to keep them. But could you summarize them not to have them spread in a source code?

Well, let's do a small summarization. However, I will not differ between what you have to do because the compiler forces on you, and what you should do because different way goes to hell.

☞ Begin the field declarations with declaring the static constants. Declare the variable fields only after it. I recommend using sections in the standard class pattern.

☞ Initialize individual constants in declarations only with direct assigning of the value of reasonably simple expressions (it's up to you what you understand as "reasonably").

☞ You can use only previously declared and initialized fields in initializing expressions. And be careful to use the variable fields after their initialization. The compiler does not analyze when you initialize the variable field and when you only assign another value to it. Therefore, it allows you to use the variable field also before its factual initialization (see block /*##_6_##*/).

☞ In case you need to gain the assigned value by some more complicated way, transfer its calculation to a static initializer.

☞ If you declare and initialize a static field which is an instance of a given class (e.g. see the source code of the Town class and the definition of singletons generally), please, realize that you activate a constructor in such moment when the class is not yet fully initialized. Therefore you have to keep an eye open so that everything what you need for constructing the instance would be already prepared.

In case you would like to examine how such creating fields is operating, uncomment the declaration of ME field behind the block /*##_4_##*/. Then, when the class will be initialized, you will see how the constructor of their instances is called, and the initialization of the class is completed only after it.

☞ Insert the static initializer after all declarations of static fields and before declaration of instance fields. A section introduced by a line comment is reserved for the static initializer in the standard class pattern. I recommend you to put the possible static initializer just here in case your class will need it.

☞ You should use at most one static initializer for initializing the class (the best variant is when you do not need any block, but sometimes you cannot avoid to it).

☞ Take care about the fact that the methods you are calling from the static initializer should use only those static fields that are already initialized.

The rule of the only one permissible static initializer has one exception, which is the situation when you insert the static initializer into the program only so that it would help you in analyzing when exactly the class is initialized and how it behaves. (In the CCI class the introductory as well as the closing block might serve for this purpose). Faults caused by unexpected (i.e. premature) or bad initialization are usually very treacherous and can be hardly detected. The static initializer is an invaluable tool in searching for them.

In case you use such auxiliary initializers in your program, don't forget to delete them after the completed analyze or (if you expect you might use them soon again) at least comment them. Don't adjust anything in these auxiliary blocks, only inform – e.g. by using prints to standard output.

Procedure of Instance Creating

626. **Hopefully I mastered using the static initializers. And now show me please what you have prepared for instances.**

Before I start showing you how the construction of instances can be analyzed, I would like to review what you know about constructing the instances.

Details on Constructing an Object Once Again

627. **You said that constructing of an object proceeds in two phases: in the first phase the operator new allocates the memory, i.e. reserves it, cancels it out and assigns it to the given object; in the second phase the constructor of the given object initializes this memory.**

Good. I would only remind that this initialization, i.e. the constructor's work runs also in several phases (I admit I have only outlined them for now):

1. The constructor parameters are evaluated (by the calling the program).

2. If the constructor's body starts with the calling this(???) delegating the responsibility for initialization to a colleague, the constructor prepares all parameters for the colleague and gives over the control to this colleague. It starts again with the item **2**, i.e. by determining if it starts or not by calling this(???). After the colleague completes its activity, controlling returns into this constructor and item **3** follows.

    When the constructor's body does not starts with calling this(???), the constructor goes through all fields and instance initializers (i.e. those without the modifier static) in the order in which they are declared in the source code. The constructor calculates the initializing expression of fields which are initialized already in the declaration and assigns the resulting value to them.

3. It carries out the remaining statements of the body.

4. After completing the body, the constructor passes the parameter this to an applicant for creating the instance as its return value.

628.   I thought that the constructor makes only what is in its body. From what you have said it looks now like it takes care also about all declarations in the rest of the file.

The constructor, as each method, makes really only the statements in its body. But its real body is in fact very often bigger than that quoted in the code. When you have a look into the class file what the compiler has created from your program, you discover that at the constructors which do not begin with this(???) it inserted all initializations and bodies of instance initializers, found in the rest of the class body, in front of what you wrote in the constructor body.

And that is another reason why to use the statement this(???). The compiler copies the initializing part into all constructors which do not delegate their responsibility to anybody. As many of such constructors are in the class, as many times the initializing code is copied.

629.   Aha, it didn't cross my mind. Probably that's why the constructor's parameters are evaluated firstly and only then the fields are initialized which are already initialized in declaration. When you say that initializations in declarations are in fact parts of the constructor's body, then I could use their parameters in them, couldn't I?

It's not possible. The compiler had to check if the used parameters have the same name in all constructors, into which the initializing code will be copied. And this might be too much.

The quoted condition (i.e. having the same name in all constructors) is fulfilled by only one parameter, and it is the hidden parameter this. You can use it in initialization of fields and instance blocks.

This is important e.g. for using the value of certain field in another one. For example if you say the following in your program:

```
int a = 5;
int b = a;
```

then you know, that the compiler converts your program into the following form

```
int a = 5;
int b = this.a;
```

Nothing will happen when you minimize its work and when you use the parameter this explicitly.

During initialization of instance fields the same is valid also for the static ones: you can use only fields which are already declared and initialized. And again you have to be careful for calling of methods which could work with not yet initialized fields. As an example of bad using of methods I can quote various callings of the toString() method in the constructor and initializers in the CCI class. You can see again how the value of constants is changing in course of initialization.

630.   But there are no callings of the toString() method.

On the contrary, but they are hidden – the method toString() is called during the preparation of a parameter for the method println(String). This is often printed together with certain text in initializers as well as in the constructor. As you surely remember in counting up of the object with a string there is a signature inserted instead of an object which is received by calling the method toString().

631.   In the section VARIABLE FIELDS OF INSTANCES you assigned the value of LOADED field which was declared as the second one to the time field.

But it was a static field and they are processed during class installing. Therefore the static fields are contemplated separately and the instance ones also separately. Nevertheless, each decent programmer declares firstly all static fields and only after them the instance ones. Then the chronological succession corresponds to the succession of placing in the source code.

The only one exception is when there is such static field which contains a reference to an instance of its own class (we were speaking about it a while ago). Such fields should be declared really as the last ones in the section of static fields.

632. At the beginning as well as at the end of the CCI class definition you placed instance initializers. Are they also used to analyzing the code's behavior?

Yes, and it is their exclusive meaningful usage. Other instance initializers in the listing 30.1 only showed what you can and what you are forbidden to do.

Instance Instruction

633. Which principles are valid for initialization of instances and instance initializers?

Due to the fact that these principles have a lot of common with principles valid for static initialization, I will shorten it to two items as follows:

☞ There is the same rule for initialization of instance fields in declarations as for the static fields: they should be initialized by only simple expression using only initialized fields. All more complex initializations should be moved to the constructor's body.

☞ **Instance initializers should not be used.** They may be used only in case when you need to analyze the course of class initialization; then they should be canceled or at least commented. The whole initializing code which is too much complex for placing directly in declarations should be moved to the constructor's body. It will be placed there anyway – and in this case you will have everything ready together and you will be able to use all parameters.

Exercise

634. I wonder which exercise you prepared for me today.

The today's exercise is throughout practical one. Pass through the source codes of both classes and experiment with them to realize how the initializations are running from the outer point of view. Next time I will show you how you could see the initializations as well as other program's operating from inside.

Review

Let's review what you have learned in this lesson:

☞ The classes behave as non-standard objects. They do not have e.g. a common parent that would determine their fields and methods.

☞ The class constructor is internally named ‹clinit› and it is created by a compiler composing all initializations of static fields and static initializers.

☞ An object representing a class in the program is marked as a class-object.

☞   The class-loader is an instance of the ClassLoader class which is responsible for installation here-tofore not used classes into a program, their initialization and creating of their class-objects.

☞   During initialization the separate static fields as well as static initializers are passed through in the order in which they are registered in the source code. At that time the fields with an assigned initialization are initialized and the static initializers are carried out.

☞   Java does not install the class into memory until it is not needed.

☞   As soon as the class is in memory, it is not installed again when required once more, but the previous loading is used.

☞   The static initializer consists of the keyword static followed by braces with the body of the given block.

☞   In initializations as well as in initializers the fields cannot be used sooner than they are declared and the constant fields are initialized.

☞   If the not yet declared field is used in the called method, the compiler does not consider it as an error (but we do!). The fields not yet initialized have zero initial value.

☞   The initialization of a static field realized by calling a method should be placed into the static initializer.

☞   Static initializers are used for initialization of static fields that cannot be simply initialized in declaration. There should be at most one static initializer in the class and it should be inserted after declarations of all static fields.

☞   The second reason for (temporary) use of initializers is the need to analyze the course of class initialization. You can define more of those blocks, especially when you need to monitor the course of initialization. But these blocks should be canceled after detecting and removing the error, or at least commented.

☞   The instance is created in two phases: the virtual machine allocates and cancels out the memory in the first phase, in the second one it calls a constructor to which it passes over a reference to the allocated memory.

☞   The constructor initializes an instance in several phases:

   ☞   The constructor's parameters are evaluated.

   ☞   In case the body begins with the calling this(???), it gives over the management to its colleague and after the called colleague finishes, it continues in the work by another item.
       In case the body does not start with this statement, it carries out all initializations and instance initializers in the order in which they are quoted in the source code.

   ☞   It accomplishes the rest of its body.

   ☞   It returns this as its return value.

☞   The body of the constructor consists of all initializing statements and instance initializers in the class body followed by statements of the constructor's body in the source code.

☞   You can use the hidden parameter this in initializations of fields and in instance initializers.

☞ The instance initializers should be used **only** for testing and harmonizing purposes.

☞ All initializations except the simplest ones should be place into the constructor's body.

Project:
The resulting form of the project to which we came at the end of the lesson and after completing all exercises is in the 130z_Class_Constructor project.

31 Debugger

What you will learn in this lesson
In this lesson you will continue in analyses of class loading and creating its instances. Then a debugging tool will be introduced which enables to observe the whole process from "inside". At this occasion you will learn what the return stack is and why the local variables finish their existence after finishing the method.

Project:
In this lesson we continue in using the 130z_Class_Constructor project.

The Importance of Debugger

635.   At the end of the last lesson you told that next time you will show me how the initialization and other behavior of the program can be seen from inside. How did you mean it?

Let's start from scratch. Each of us can make a mistake in our programs. Searching these mistakes and their subsequent removing – the so called debugging is probably the most unpleasant activity for programmers. Therefore they create various tools that can help them with in this searching. These tools are often named debuggers. One of their most important properties is the ability to step through the running code according to your instructions and to show what the program really makes. And that is what I wanted to show you today.

A simple debugger is a part of the development environment *BlueJ*. Today I will show you how it is used. At this occasion you can verify that our programs really operate as we said and, above all, that your future programs will act as you plan.

Activating of the Debugger

636.   Marvelous, so show me the miracle. How to start it?

You are not asking for starting it directly. You are using the **breakpoints** which you place into the program. When *BlueJ* meets the breakpoint while running the program, it stops the program and opens the debugger's window. You can get information you are interested in with its help (due to which you inserted the breakpoint into the program).

637.   How to put the breakpoint into the program?

Simply – you click to the left into the column with line numbers in the editor at the line with a statement before which you want to stop the program. Then the editor draws a picture of the traffic sign STOP at the given place – see figure 31.1.

But it really has to be a line with the statement which will be executed. It means it cannot be an empty line, neither the line where only a comment lies nor the declaration without initialization.

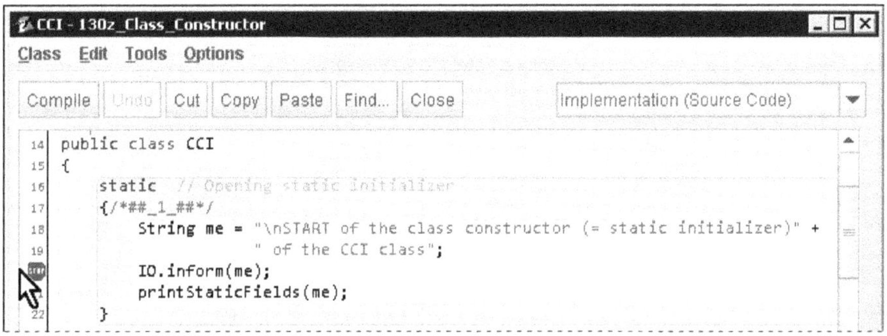

Figure 31.1
Inserting the breakpoints into a program

638.   Shall we stop the program in CCI class?

I would say it can show us at the best how the mechanisms, explained in the previous lesson, work.

639.   I clicked into the column with line numbers according to your advice. I am clicking and clicking but no stop appears.

Because your class is not compiled. Look down at the information panel – *BlueJ* warns you:

    Class should be compiled to set breakpoints

You recognize if the class is compiled according to the color of the stripe with line numbers. When the class is compiled, it has the same background color as the code. As soon as you start adjusting the code, the color of this column is changing.

640.   I've compiled the class but it doesn't operate.

Because you are clicking one line up – there is only the opening brace introducing the block. It would be the same when you would click at the line with not yet initialized declaration, with procedure head or the comment itself. When you would have a look down again into the information window, you would see that

    Cannot set breakpoint: no code in this line

You have to remember that the breakpoint can be set only at the line in which certain executable statement is contained.

641.   You are true – the stop already appeared. What now?

Now activate the program – for example send the classNeeded() message to the Call class. When the statement at the line where the breakpoint is located (see figure 31.1) should be executed, i.e. when the CCI class is loaded and starts its initialization, *BlueJ* stops executing the program and activates debugger, better said it opens its window (see figure 31.2).

Debugger's Window

642.   A window with many panels really appeared here.

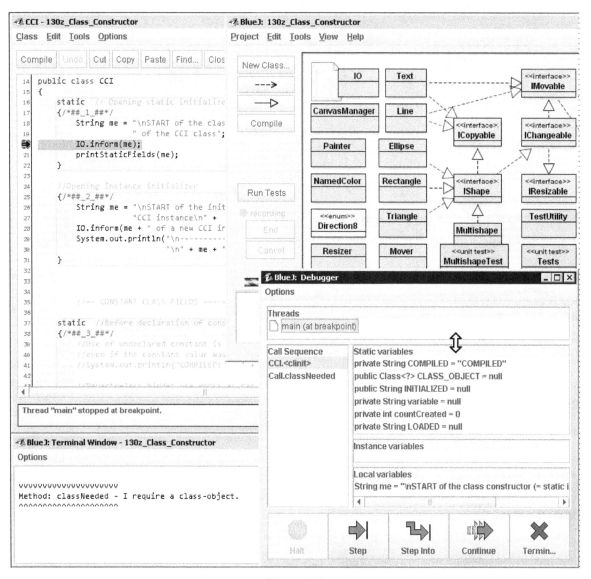

Figure 31.2
The debugger's window

This is just the window of the debugger. It has a number of panels in which various kinds of information appear. However, I will postpone describing them for a moment and I will explain firstly the buttons at the bottom.

Stop Halt	The button **Halt** is not active in this moment because the program is just standing. The button revives when the program is running. (In our case it "revives" e.g. when the program will expect your confirmation that you have read the dialog). The running program can be temporarily stopped with its help so that it could run again by pressing the button **Continue**.
Step	The button **Step** allows the program to execute the following statement and to stop again. As you can notice at the figure 31.2, the line with a statement in the editor's window waiting for being executed is highlighted.
Step Into	The button **Step into** enables you to move into the just called method (I will show it in a moment). If the "waiting" statement is not the calling of the method in a class, that is a part of the project and whose source code is available for *BlueJ*, the operation will be the same as after pressing the button **Step**.
Continue	Pressing the button **Continue** runs the program and let it continue in its operating until the next breakpoint. In case of zero breakpoint it operates until the end.
Terminate	Pressing the button **Terminate** finishes the activity of the tested program and closes up the whole tested application

Stepping through / Tracing the Program

643.   I already know functions of the buttons which means I could examine them, couldn't I?

Let's go on. As you see at the figure 31.2, we are going to open the dialog, more precisely to call the inform(Object) method of the IO class. Press the button **Step** to see what will happen.

644.   A window opened with a report that the constructor of CCI class is starting. When I pressed O.K., the program stopped again and the highlighting in editor moved to the next line.

Shift the content of the editor's window and place the breakpoint to the line with the declaration of the CLASS_OBJECT field. Then press the **Continue** button.

645.   The program runs a bit and the highlighting moved to the line with a breakpoint.

And now look into the panel entitled **Static Variables** in the right part of the debugger's window. You will see types and names of the first three fields. Go with your mouse to the upper edge of this panel so that the mouse indicator would get a form of double vertical arrow (see the figure 31.2) and then take this edge and pull it up. Then take its lower edge similarly and pull it so that you can see all class fields in the panel.

Notice that null is quoted as the value of the CLASS_OBJECT field. Now press the **Step** button. Highlighting will move to another statement and the field will be initialized – the <object reference> will appear. In other words: the reference to an object has been saved to the field.

Try to double click at the field. A dialog will open looking into the interior of the relevant class-object. I will not explain you what is there because the class-object analysis belongs to really advanced course. I only wanted to show you how you can look into the object's interior in the debugger.

646.   You told that the highlighting will move to the next statement, but it skipped it over and stopped inside the initializer.

Good, the declaration itself is not a statement. The declaration does not do anything, the pure declaration only announces. The previous declaration was connected with the initialization and the debugger stopped at this initialization. And now it again stopped in the place where the program is expecting for further work.

Press again the **Step** button. The highlighting will move again and the class name as a value is assigned to the field INITIALIZED (an answer of the class-object after sending the message getName()).

You can continue step by step like that, if need be you can place a breakpoint again and run over the whole segment up to it. Or you can decide that you learned everything what you wanted to learn, then press the **Continue** button and let the program run to the end.

647.   It all operates excellently. I have already examined also the operating of the Terminate button. However, the function of the Halt and Step into buttons is not clear to me.

I am already going to explain it. I want to show you their functioning in the delegated calling of constructors. Open the source code of the Call class and insert the breakpoint at the beginning of the testInvocation() method's body, i.e. at the line with the statement

```
CCI inst = new CCI("Experiment");
```

And now call this method. The program's running should stop just at the breakpoint you inserted in.

We intend to create an instance of the CCI class with the help of the one-parametric constructor. Now it is the moment for the **Step into** button. Press it.

648.   The program stopped at the beginning of the class definition at the place as previously.

Because you reset the virtual machine and the class had to be firstly loaded. I supposed that you will call the method after **correct** ending of the previous program, i.e. after a regular loading of the class which then will wait for another command.

649.   I did not reset anything.

You pressed the **Terminate** button which causes a non-standard finishing followed by resetting of the virtual machine. In case you wish that the class would be kept loaded in memory, you have to let the program run until its end. The class is not loaded again when another method is called and directly this method is run.

650.   I let the class to be loaded and I asked for its instance after it. This time the program stopped inside one-parametric constructor at the statement this.

A lot of things happen:

☞   All instance fields have been written in the right middle panel entitled **Instance variables** – not yet initialized, i.e. zeroed.

☞ In the right bottom panel entitled **Local variables** (it shows the parameters and local variables of the method in which we are just now occurring) a new item representing the method's parameter appeared.

☞ Another item – CCI.<init> appeared in the left panel entitled **Call sequence** which announces in which method we occur just now. When we stepped through the class constructor of the CCI class, its name CCI.<clinit> was shown (see the figure 31.2 on page 310). Now we are in the constructor of instances of the CCI class, therefore the name CCI.<init> is depicted. The item Call.testInvocation is under it (being there also sooner) and reporting from where this constructor was called, i.e. from the method testInvocation in the Call class.

651. I understand to the content of the panel Instance variables – I see there the prepared instance fields and I am waiting that they will be initialized, similarly as previously. But why the lower panel has the name Local variables and not Parameters?

We have already spoken about it in the part *Fields × Parameters × Local Variables* on page 214, where you yourself discovered at the end that the parameters are local variables initialized by the calling method.

The Call Sequence Panel

652. You told that in the panel Call Sequence I can find out where I am and what called this method. But I already know it, don't I?

Where you are – you surely know, but who called this method, is not always so sure. Now you know it, because you came to it "step by step" but it's not the usual way. This panel has also another function. To show it, let's dive a little bit deeper. Press the **Step into** button once again.

653. It did not dive me into the double-parametric constructor, but into the method prepare(String)**.**

Good. Now you may be interested how you've got there. Simple to answer you. As you see, another item marking our current position in the program appeared at the panel **Call Sequence**; the item marking the position you have been a while ago moved under it. Click at the item CCI.<init>.

654. Oh! We moved back to the previous position.

Yes, you can see here in which state the program occurred before calling the method to which you jumped in debugger. When you look at the statement, you will find the calling of the prepare(String) method in the second parameter. This calling serves for verifying that firstly the parameters are prepared and only then the calling of the method comes. And because within the preparation of parameters the method is called, the debugger firstly dove you into it.

655. Does it mean that when I press now Step, the statement will be carried out without inserting?

No, we did not return in time, this debugger is not so clever. We only looked from where we came to our current position. When you click at the item Call.testInvocation you move to a place where we started with our tracing. On the contrary, when you click at the item CCI.prepare you move to the place where we are just now.

After pressing the stepping buttons you always continue from the current position, i.e. from the position to which the upper item in **Call Sequence** panel is showing. As I have already told other items enable you only to discover how you have got into place. The method in which you are just now occurred atop, the method which called is below it, and the method which called the first method is again below it and so on.

Return Stack

656. Does it mean that whenever I call certain method, a new item appears and when I leave the method, the item is again deleted?

Exactly. This list is one of the key internal data structures of the virtual machine. The programmers call it **return stack** or shortly **stack**, because the addresses of program's places to which the program will return after completing the executed method are located here.

657. You have just explained why "return", but why a stack?

The stack is a name of a data structure which operates similarly as a stock or pile of papers to which you put your further notes. The newly added items are then "put on the top" and the oldest are "at the bottom" of the stack. In the moment when you take away the last item, i.e. the item from the bottom of the stack, the program is ending.

You can simulate it. Imagine that you are a virtual machine and you execute the program. Suddenly you discover you have to invoke certain method (let's call it A), which means to get into another part of the program – to the place where the code of this method is. You make a note at a piece of paper, where you are just now and where you will return after you will execute the method. And you place the paper with the note at the top of the pile-stack.

However, you discover during executing the A method, that this method calls another method – let's call it B method. Then you make another note again at a piece of paper concerning your position and where to return to continue in your work. You put the piece of paper again at the top of the stack.

You start to carry out the B method and you meet another method's calling – let's say C. You again make a note about the return address and put it in the stack. Supposing the C method does not call any further method. When you complete it, you take the piece of paper of stack's top to see where you should return. The paper says you that you have to return to B method behind calling the just completed C method.

You move to B method and continue your work at the place from which you went out a while ago. If calling of further methods is a part of B method, you will act similarly as in calling C: you put the return address to a stack, to know from where you should continue after executing it, and you are going to execute the relevant method.

After you complete your work on B method, you again have a look at the stack's top where a paper is laying with the return address aiming to the A method. You take the paper and continue in carrying out the A method. After completing it you again look into the stack and you find the last paper with a reference to the place where the whole anabasis started.

Take a piece of the code, prepare the papers and you can examine it. You will discover that it is simple and nicely operating.

658.   Perhaps I understand how the virtual machine works with the stack. But what's good on the stack for us?

I have already shown it to you. The places where you are supposed to return are at the same time places from where the method was called (well, just closely to). Looking into the code parts, to which the items from the stack are referring, enable us to see the history of program's coming to a place where we are just now located. And this is what is interesting for us very often.

When I already touched this topic, I can tell you also confidentiality from the kitchen of the virtual machine. Not only return addresses, but also parameters as well as local variables are saved on the return stack. Debugger does not depict them at the stack (there is a panel allocated for it), but they are saved there. As we have explained, after completing the method its item is deleted from the stack to have enough of place for another one.

It implies that after completing the method not only its return address ends its existence, but also its local variables. Their place is immediately taken by something else. When the method is called next time, a new place at the stack is allocated for the method and all variables have to be initialized once again. If the method wants to remember something between its callings, it has to be saved in a field.

Examine, that whenever you click at any of the items on the stack, at the same time the content of the panel of **Local variables** start to show values of local variables of that method into which you moved by clicking. If the owner of the method changed, i.e. you moved into the method of another instance of another class, surely the content of panels with the relevant fields will change. Thus you can learn, in which situation the calling method was as well as its data in the moment of calling.

659.   I wanted to step into the `println` method, but I did not succeed. *BlueJ* made it as if I would enter only Step.

The debugger can pace out only those methods the source code of which you provided. And method from the standard library does not belong to them, which means you cannot look into them.

660.   What a pity that the parameter types are not shown in the Call Sequence panel. I have three `CCI.<init>` items shown and I cannot easily discover which version calls which version.

You are true. You have to detect such information in the source code. It is important especially in the case of recursive calling (we spoke about it in the section *Recursion* on page 130 and we will return to this subject in the section *Recursion* on page 366).

661.   I dived into the four-parametric constructor and I was surprised that, contrary to previous stops, the program stopped at the opening brace, not at the first statement. The opening brace does not represent any code.

Braces sometimes stand in for invisible code which has to be carried out in the given place. You surely remember from the last chapter that the constructor's body consists of two parts: from initializations and the body itself. By stopping at the opening brace the debugger announces you that you are going to execute the given constructor which means you move to the first statement of initialization in the next stop.

662.   You are true. I pressed Step and the mark moved to the block `/*##_2_##*/`, which is the first instance initialization block. And now I will continue in stepping through initialization.

Well, and at this occasion you can examine how the buttons operates. The initializer prepares the `me` variable and calls the `IO.inform(Object)` method, which opens a dialog. In the moment when the computer waits for your pressing the button, only the **Halt** button is explicitly deactivated. Other buttons are seemingly living, but when you press any of the "green buttons" (i.e. **Step**, **Step Into** and **Continue**), nothing happens. Only the **Terminate** button works and really terminates the application.

In addition the highlighting of the current statement disappears and all panels are cleared to emphasize that the program is now blocked by the operation from a standard library and that you should firstly satisfy the library's request and the control will be returned to your traced program.

Local Variables

663.   I am back in the constructor's body and I am going to print.

I wanted to show you how the program behaves towards the local variables. There are four local variables used in the constructor: unused, underlining, sum and local. Step through its body and notice how each local variable appears after its initialization in the **Local variables** panel.

The variables sum and local are initialized directly in the declaration, maybe nothing surprises you there. But the variable underlining is declared behind the print statement and initialized already in the last but one statement. As you can see, the debugger ignores the declaration itself – it is information for the programmer. The compiler takes it in its mind, but until you initialize the variable, the compiler acts as it is unknown. There is no information about it in the compiled program and that's why the virtual machine doesn't know about it as well. Therefore, you cannot be surprised that also the debugger registers the local variable underlining only in the moment when it is initialized, i.e. closely before the final print. Until this time the variable is unknown and it cannot be seen in the panel. Therefore, the debugger cannot learn about the variable unused, due to the fact it is not initialized.

664.   That's it. Local variables really appear in the panel only after their initialization.

Which means only the final rising up expects you. Step further and observe how you will rise up to methods from where the current method has been called. And notice at this occasion how the content of panels with fields and local variables change. At the same time you can also notice that the debugger always stops at the closing brace before return from the method, so that you could see, in which state the program is closely before the return from the given method.

Stepping through Test Methods

665.   I have to say that it was informative and I learned a lot about how it's acting inside. Do you think that I should know more about stepping through the program which was not yet debated?

I would like to draw your attention to one item. Until now we were stepping through the current calling of methods. If you would like to step tests, be prepared that at the bottom of the stack, i.e. at the lower end of the list of the **Call Sequence** panel there will be a number of items showing into the *JUnit* library which is responsible for carrying out tests. Take care about only your items atop of the stack and don't mind those below. In case you would accidentally touch and click on any of them, *BlueJ* opens a dialog warning you that there is no source code of these programs and therefore you cannot see anything concerning them. Don't mind of it, there are only references to classes which you would not understand for now.

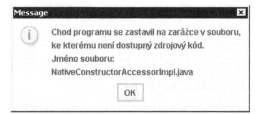

Figure 31.3
There is no source code to the given class

Exercise

666.   What you have prepared for my today's exercise?

We spent today's lesson in an interactive mode and I prepared an accompanying animation in which I tried to repeat and show today's pile. Start it and examine everything once more. Then I recommend you to use the debugger at your own examples.

> *Animation 31.1: Debugger and how to work with it – OOPNZ_131_A1_Debugger*
> *The animation will repeat what was explained during the lesson, i.e. it will show how to work with debugger which is a part of BlueJ.*

Review

Let's review what you have learned in this lesson:

☞ Searching mistakes is one of the most unpleasant activities in program development. We call it debugging the program.

☞ Special *tools* called *debuggers* help us during the code analysis and its debugging.

☞ A simple debugger is a part of the development environment of *BlueJ*.

☞ For marking places in the code where we want to analyze the course of the program in details we use *breakpoints*.

☞ The breakpoint is placed in an editor by clicking to the left into the column with line numbers at the line number with the statement before which we want to stop the program. Then the editor depicts the traffic sign STOP.

☞ *BlueJ* does not allow us to put the breakpoint into a code of not yet compiled class nor to the line which has no beginning of feasible statement.

☞ When *BlueJ* meets a breakpoint during executing the program, it stops the program and opens the debugger's window.

☞ At the lower edge of the debugger's window there are five buttons, with the help of which we can control starting and stopping the program.

☞ Above the line of buttons there is a set of panels providing information on the program's state and depicting data with which the program works.

☞   The panel **Local variables** show values of local variables and of parameters.

☞   The panel **Call sequence** contains a list of references to places from where the currently executed method was called, from where the method which called the method was called etc.

☞   This list is usually named the **return stack**, because it contains (among other things) also the addresses to which the course of the program will return after completing the currently executed method.

☞   Together with the return addresses also the local variables as well as parameters are saved on the stack.

☞   After clicking at the stack's item you can see the part of the code to which the given item refers including its local variables as well as current fields of an instance and of a class.

☞   Local variables will be depicted in their panel only after they are initialized. The fields are in their panels for the whole time.

☞   During stepping through tests you will see items referring to methods from the standard as well as from the test library. These items cannot be open.

Project:
We did not change the project and therefore we end with the project 130z_Class_Constructor in the state, in which we began to work with it.

32 Creating of an Standalone Application

What you will learn in this lesson
This lesson is a closing lesson of the second part. You will create your first standalone application – a game which will be running at all computers in which the Java environment is installed. At this occasion you will get to know how the files JAR are created and what they are for, and you will learn to create these file from the BlueJ environment.

Project:
In this lesson you open a new project entitled 132a_UFO_Start.

667. Until now you were showing me only which properties has this or that, how to program it or where certain treacherousness is awaiting us. Only learning, now playing. Would you be able to show me, how to program something useful?

You are true. I closed the part in which I showed you how to code simple object constructions. Before I will pass to the more complicated, you could program a simple game.

668. Well! Gladly accepted. At last something interesting. And what it will be?

With regards to what you know until now it cannot be anything too much complicated. You can see the game window at figure 32.1. The game runs in the universe. Each player has a task to put several UFOs to aprons ("UFO-ports") at the lower edge of the game's window. All UFOs will be available at the starting apron in the left upper window's corner. The game (including the UFO's engine) will be controlled from the keyboard. However, you have to take into account that until UFO's engine is running; it is always accelerating (speeding up) or decelerating (slowing down). Therefore it is not so simple to get UFOs quickly to aprons. You need certain training because in case you are not lending sufficiently slowly, you hang over the apron and you disappear from the observable part of the cosmos. And it is very hard to get back.

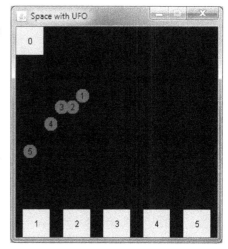

Figure 32.1
The application's window of the game

But you will not program the game fully, only two classes. It is the same as in practice: usually the programmer's task is to create only a part of a larger project – so you can try it just now. Beforehand I assure you that the classes will be sufficiently simple so that you could do it.

Assignment

669.   I am very curious. Describe what is expecting me.

The project contains classes as follows:

☞   NamedColor – a class which you know from our application working with graphic objects.

☞   Space – its instance is a singleton and it is responsible for creating and depicting of application window representing the universe, where the whole game is running. This class is as service class and your class will not communicate with it.

☞   Dispatcher – a key class of the whole application. Its instance is responsible for opening of the relevant universe and controlling of the traffic in it. You start the game by creating an instance of the Dispatcher class – a dispatcher. Then you ask this instance to prepare a new UFO at the starting apron from where you will try to get it into some of the target aprons.

☞   Apron – its instances represent starting and landing (target) aprons which are able to catch and park the landing UFOs at the dispatcher's command. Neither with it will your instances communicate at the time being.

☞   Number – an instance of this class is able to paint a number which you enter to its constructor. This number serves for identification of UFO (each UFO should bear its number) as well as landing aprons. Probably from all methods, which are offered by instances of the Number class, you will use only a method for adjusting the position and painting of the given number.

☞   ISaucer – the saucer represents one from the UFO's parts (UFO is composed of the saucer on which the number is depicted). It offers only methods for detecting and adjusting its position, and a method paint() which knows how to paint the saucer in the space.

☞   IUFO – an interface specifying what such a UFO has to know. If you have a look into its documentation, you discover it quite a lot. On the other hand, all its abilities can be rather easily programmed. **Your task is to define a class, which implements this interface.**

☞   IUFOFactory – an interface specifying what an object which you will use as a factory for UFO has to know. The requirements on such object are rather simple: it has to define a method, which is able to create operating UFOs. **Creating such a factory is your second task.**

☞   UFOTest – a test class which will verify your solution. This class is not yet operating, because its fixture is not yet defined. This fixture will contain the only object: a factory for UFOs. As soon as you will create it you can start testing.

670.   It is not as simple as you indicated. Surely I cannot produce immediately those two classes. I am afraid that you did not teach me so much. Try to navigate me for a while.

Don't be afraid. Before I will let you go to the world, I will help you to analyze the whole project, so that you could know what you can expect from your neighborhood and what the other will expect from you.

The Dispatcher Class

671.   Well, I know the color, the space is supposedly outside me, so what about to start with the dispatcher.

As I have already told you, the Dispatcher class is a key class of the whole application. Let's have a look at methods, which it offers to you.

☞   public static Dispatcher getDispatcher(IUFOFactory factory)
Due to the fact that the Dispatcher class wants so that it's instance would be a singleton, it will not offer you a constructor, but only this simple factory method, to which you will over an instance of the UFO factory. This simple factory method will arrange creating of the whole space with the dispatcher and will return a reference to the created dispatcher. You can call this method only once because there may be only one universe with only one type of UFO (and so only one UFO factory). Not a lot of them – at least at this game's version.

☞   public IUFO prepareUFO()
prepares UFO made out by the previously assigned factory for UFO at the starting apron. Calling of this method is the only one way how to create a UFO which will join the game. In case you would try to create it directly with the assistance of a constructor, the dispatcher will not know about it and so you will not be able to control it from the keyboard, nor to ask the apron for parking.

☞   public void stop()
It stops all animations. This method exists only for the case that in case someone would interrupt you in playing or the control of flying UFOs would get out of your hands.

☞   public void start()
It starts again all animations.

The IUFOFactory Interface

672.   Why is there the factory for UFO?

Because producing of UFO has to be assigned by a dispatcher so that it could include an instance into all auxiliary structures which provide the proper animation in time. If you would create UFO, you would have to enroll them at the dispatcher similarly as you do it at the canvas manager. Moreover you would have to look after when the user – handling by keyboard – pressed a key requiring creation of a new UFO. Thus it is simpler. The keyboard is observed by a dispatcher and when the user asks for a UFO, the dispatcher requires creating a new UFO from the factory and prepares it at the starting apron.

673.   But why a special factory? It is sufficient to call the constructor for creating a new UFO.

So that the dispatcher could call a constructor your class should have already exist. And it would be limited to only one particular class. But I would like if this example might be solved by a number of students.

   In case the assignment uses an interface, then the dispatcher via this interface only announces its requirements. And anybody who defines a class corresponding to these requirements (i.e. class implementing this interface) can include them into his project and examine them. It means you can define several different pairs of factory-UFO and examine which of these pairs is better operating. It is sufficient when you pass the factory from a pair which you want to examine to the getDispatcher method.

Design Pattern *Factory Method*

**674.	The way, you tell it, impresses that the factory is only a cover around a constructor so that the dispatcher could order which parameters should be passed to a constructor.**

Exactly, in our case the factory method really only calls the constructor and passes the parameters. I can tell you that this using of factories is one of the possible implementations of the design pattern *Factory method*. Until now you met its simpler variant – *Simple factory method*. It recommends defining a static method which returns the reference to an instance of its own class.

The not simplified *Factory method*, applied just now, is more general. It solves a problem how to get an instance of a class from which you know only an interface. The pattern recommends defining an *interface* (we will call it *factory interface*) for creating an object, but let the implementing classes decide which class should be instantiate. We will call the class implementing the factory interface as *factory class*. Instances of such factory class will offer a method that would create the required instance. It means that when you declare using of factory (i.e. an instance of a factory interface) as a moment ago, you do not know what the given factory will return you. You only know that the received instance will implement the given interface. But what type the returned instance will be of, it will be decided by an addressed factory.

And our project is operating exactly thus. You can produce a set of pair's factory-UFO and according to which factory you deliver to the dispatcher, those UFOs the dispatcher will prepare.

The IUFO Interface

**675.	I start to understand it. Please, describe me in details, what the class implementing the IUFO interface should know.**

Most of those things you have in the documentation, but I can tell it by different words. Before I start to list particular methods and their purpose, I want to draw your attention to one thing: please, notice that all parameters as well as the return values are of the double type. Logically it ensues from it that in case you would like to save anything into fields, you probably will have to declare also these fields as double numbers.

**676.	Why everything has to be double? Until now we also animated and whole numbers were sufficient.**

No, it was not sufficient, it was only hidden. The instances assigned its initial and target position with the whole numbers. However, the Mover worked already with numbers double. That's to say when it should change the coordinate by 0.75 point; it could change it neither by 0 point, nor by 1 point. It has to count up the three quarters and three times move an object by one point and the fourth time by zero. In the longer movement the result look out equally as if the object would be shifted constantly by ¾ point.

677.   Well, I am defining double **fields. Which one would you recommend me?**

You can look at the required methods. Methods getX(), getY(), getXSpeed(), getYSpeed(), getXThrust(), getYThrust() are nearly asking for defining of homonymous attributes and save into them the horizontal as well as vertical coordinate, a speed and tensile load.

When you discover that you have to define also a method setSpeed(double, double), I suppose you know that this method will adjust the horizontal as well as vertical speed.

And the definitions of methods right(), left(), up(), down(), which have to increase or decrease the thrust (and thus also the acceleration) in the given direction, will be identically clear. To proper adjustment of a new thrust you have to know only that the required increasing or decreasing is adjusted in an interface as the DIF_THRUST (difference of the thrust) constant.

678.   Wait a minute! A constant in an interface? **But you told that there might be only declaration in an** interface **and constants are data. How it is possible that a constant can be in an** interface?

Remember a section *Details of Class Initializing* on page 300. I told you that there is a special kind of constants – the compile-time constants – the value of which can be evaluated in the compile-time, and which can occur even in interface types because they are not data saved in the memory, but only different names of their values.

679.   Oh yes, I recall. This means that at each calling of some of the quoted methods the value of the relevant thrust fields will change by DIF_THRUST.

Directly, these four methods are completed by the stopEngine() method, which zeroes both thrust fields.

The move(int) **Method**

680.   I understand the adjustment ad returning of attribute values. But your explanation what the attributes are for and how it operates would be welcome. I put them in only because the interface **declared methods which adjust and return their values.**

The whole UFO's function is hidden in the method move(int). To understand its function you have to repeat a bit of physics. I experienced that majority of students, beginners in programming, would like to program computer games full of animated subjects. In case you belong to them, the following small theoretical explanation might be useful.

You were explained in the school that the speed is defined as a track traveled within a time unit. The speed of animated objects is composed of two parts: the horizontal and vertical one. The horizontal part says how quickly the object is moved in the horizontal direction, and the vertical part describes the speed in vertical direction.

In case any animated object has a defined speed as a number of points by which it has to move in a second, its position changes by the required number of points in each second. However, in case you want to move the object relatively fluently, you cannot change its position within one second, you have to change it more often.

That's why you can often find the frequency of re-drawing the animated pictures. It says how many times the picture is re-drawn in a second. (Because it significantly influences the calculation of next position, the method move(int) is given the same frequency of re-drawing as a parameter). It means if he object has to move fluently in the horizontal direction with an xSpeed points in a second, its position has to be changed within two re-drawings of xSPeed/frequency points.

Your UFOs (equally as current rockets and satellites) are controlled by rocket motors which control not their speed, but manage their acceleration. If the motors are off, the rocket moves in the space with the same speed (contrary to rockets we know from movies in which their authors do not know physics and think that to move with the same speed through the space, the rocket has to have motors always operating). As soon as you switch on the motors, the rocket will permanently speed up or slow down. In case the braking motor will be on even after you will stop the rocket, it becomes a speed up motor and the rocket starts to speed up the opposite direction.

The acceleration of the rocket depends only on its weigh and on the motor's thrust. Let's agree that your UFO will have just such a weight so that its acceleration would be the same number as the motors' thrust.

The acceleration is similar as the speed from the animation point of view. The acceleration is defined as a change of a speed in a time unit. The speed will increase in a second by as much as the acceleration is big. If your UFOs movement should look out as a real one, their speed cannot change by a jump. If the object has to uniformly accelerate in a horizontal direction with acceleration xThrust and if you know the frequency of redrawing, the horizontal speed of the moving object has to change between the two re-drawings of the screen by xThrust/frequency.

And now the whole calculation starts to emerge. When somebody asks you for re-drawing, you will look at the parameter to know with which frequency he is asking you. Then you calculate a new speed and when you will know it, you can calculate the new position. You will move the UFO to this position.

681.   **Well, it was demanding to go after you, but I will try to orient in it. From what you told I understand that the program for adjustment of a new position should look out roughly as follows:**

```
speed    = speed    + (thrust / frequency);
position = position + (speed  / frequency);
```

The speed and the position have to be counted for each direction separately. And after I count a new position, I can move UFO to it.

Exactly.

A Constructor

682.   **Now I'm thinking about: what I will move? When I don't know how the UFO will look out. How I will make out the UFO?**

Come out of the documentation an interface of a factory class. You know that your constructor will receive a saucer and an order of a given instance from its factory method, and it is required so that the UFO had this order written on itself. The procedure is analogous as when you created the arrow or the car: simply you compose the object from several others – in this case from a plate and an order. You only have to remember that in case you would like to draw the order at the plate, you have to make out an instance of the Number class, which is the only one that knows to paint the assigned number. You have to remember references to objects, from which your object is composed, so that you could refer to them when you will move the object or draw at it.

This gives you also how the method paint() will look out – you will draw a saucer and paint a number on it. Shortly, all well-known things. So can you start?

Controlling by Direct Message Sending

683.   I am going to try it. Please, explain me the game.

You can run the game in two modes. In the simpler one you control all with addressing instances in the reference stack of *BlueJ*. Thus you can make acquaintance (e.g. with the help of debugger), how the UFO and the dispatcher communicate one with the other. And, you can send the UFO, which goes adrift, return to the visible part of the universe by sending a suitable message.

First of all you ask the dispatcher for preparing the further UFO to the starting apron by sending the prepareUFO() message. Then you adjust the speed in the horizontal as well as vertical direction with suitable sending the setSpeed(double,double) messages, and you try to lend with your UFO on some apron. If you fly sufficiently slowly to an apron, the lending mechanisms should provide automatic parking.

To be successful with parking, the UFO cannot have bigger sum of speed in the horizontal and vertical direction in driving on the apron, than is the size of its saucer which is adjusted to 20 points. (If you will change it in the Dispatcher class, you change also the measures of the whole universe.)

Controlling from a Keyboard

684.   I suppose that the other mode controls everything from the keyboard.

Exactly. In this variant you ask for preparing of another UFO by pressing the key ENTER. In the prepared UFO you operate the motor's thrust with cursor's keys. If you press e.g. key with the arrow to the right, the UFO starts to speed up to the right. With each pressing the arrow key you increase the thrust in the given direction and thus also the acceleration.

685.   And how I will stop it?

It cannot be stopped. You can only switch off the motors. Then it will not speed up, but it will move with the same speed. Then you can switch on the motors to the other direction and the UFO starts to decelerate and so slow down. But you have to stop pressing the arrow in time, so that the slowing down would not change into speeding up in the opposite direction.

The lastly prepared UFO reacts to the cursor's keys. But nothing prevents you to ask for preparation of another UFO before you succeed to part the previous one. The prepared UFO immediately seizes the keyboard and starts reacting to pressed keys. In case you will manage several UFOs simultaneously, you switch on managing of the relevant UFO by pressing the key with its number (the program reacts to numbers adjusted from the main as well as the numeric field). Theoretically you can control simultaneously up to 9 UFOs. But it is really only theoretically.

Creating a Standalone Application

686.   **Somehow I succeeded to run it, but my parking is not the best so far. I would welcome if the program could be opened as an ordinary application and I could avoid *BlueJ* for its operating. Is it possible to make an exe-file in Java?**

Exe-files can be run only under *Windows* operating system and/or under their emulations. But Java has something better: it can save its programs into a compressed archives file with an extension jar (an abbreviation from **J**ava **AR**chive). You can open it as other executable files – e.g. by clicking on its icon. The only one condition for its running is to have an installed JRE (Java Runtime Environment – we were speaking about it in the section JDK and JRE on page 6). Its main advantage is that it is significantly smaller than JDK, which is used for creating programs.

687.   **And how such a jar-file can be made out?**

It's quite simple, but for the time being it will be useless for you, because you do not have an executable application produced. First of all you have to arrange it so that the application could be opened and only then you can look after how to deploy it into jar.

The Main Class of an Application

688.   **Well, so how can I make out an executable application from my project?**

An application that can be run from the system has to contain a class with the method of the following signature (you know that the parameter's name can be changed):

```
public static void main(String[] args)
```

This method serves as an entry point into the application. The virtual machine starts this method and it has to arrange all others. (Don't bother with the strange parameter type; you will not use this parameter for this time, and thus you don't mind that its origin is not clear. Don't be afraid, after you will know more, I will explain you how to use it.)

And now let's have a look at how as easy as is possible to make out the **Main class of application**, as the class with a method main(String[]) is sometimes called. The procedure is simple and well-known to you: you ask for creating a new class. *BlueJ* opens the **Create New Class** window. The only difference towards the current habit is that you put the switcher **Class type** into the state **Application main class**. Enter certain name (e.g. Main) and confirm the adjustment.

689.   **I see it is quite ordinary class. Only it has prepared an empty definition of a method** main(String[]). **If I would give the method into another class, would it also operate?**

Of course, you can put the method main into any class. And you can have it in each class as well. When you look at the end of the class created according to a standard pattern, you will find it in a section for lightning tests preparations. The standard pattern puts the main method into each class commented.

I recommend defining the separated main class of an application because each proper class should be responsible only for one aspect. In case you add it to any other place, you add besides its standard responsibility also a responsibility for starting the application. And when you would return to your program after some time and would like to modify it, you would ruminate which class you marked as the main one.

690.   So why the method main is at the end of each class?

It serves for writing a quick and simple test and testing the given class. When you are not working in *BlueJ*, you cannot call methods as you wish, and you have to add the method main into the class and call the requested method from this one.

691.   Well, I created a new class and named it Main. How should I define the main(String[]) method's body?

Simply: you create an instance of your factory and then you call a method Dispatcher.getDispatcher(IUFOFactory), to which you pass the freshly created instance as a parameter. That's all.

Creating Executable Archives

692.   It's really simple. So when I have the main class, the executable archives can be created.

Yes, it can be created. Enter the command **Create Jar File** in the **Project** menu. A dialog from figure 32.2 will open. You pull down the list **Main class** in it and enter the application main class – in our case the class Main.

Then you have to think over if you would like to add source files and project files into the archives. In case you want to create only an executable program, you will add nothing. In case you would like to save the whole project into a form in which you can transfer it to another computer, add the source files.

When everything is adjusted, press the key **Continue**. A standard window will open for saving the files. You enter a name and location of the created JAR-file; confirm your entering and it's ready. The created JAR-file can be started wherever where Java is installed.

693.   Even including the telephone?

In case the class Space would be adjusted a little bit, you could compile the application also for telephones. But I will not show it to you, because I would have to explain you certain specialties of the program's development for telephones.

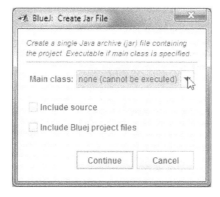

Figure 32.2
The dialog for creating a JAR archives

694.   Could it be seen what have I saved into the archives?

Yes, it can. The JAR archives are files compressed in a ZIP format, which means you can watch them through any program which is able to look through the content of ZIP-files. The only one problem remains in titles of files using some "exotic" (i.e. non ASCII) letters. Java saves them in a form so that it could open up the archives properly and independently to a platform to which you saved the file and from which you open the file. You could experience it in the self-opening archives in which the accompanying programs are prepared. However, not all browsers of ZIP-files are prepared to cope with it.

Exercise

695.   Do you have an exercise for me today?

I have such a little exercise for you. Copy your class e.g. under a name UFO_P and extend the method setSpeed(double,double), so that it would write the current values of attributes to standard output. Define its factory and examine how the dispatcher works with the new factory.

Review

Let's review what you learned in this lesson:

☞   The design pattern *Factory method* is a more general version of the simple factory method. It solves the problem how to get an instance of a class from which only an interface is known.

☞   In case a change is realized in an animation, then the change among separate animation snaps can be received by dividing of the change planned for one second by the animation frequency in the time unit.

☞   The applications programmed in Java are saved into archives which are files with the extension jar compressed in ZIP format.

☞   When saving the executable application you have to mark the main class of an application, i.e. a class which contains the static public method main(String[]), which serves as the introductory point into the application.

☞   The virtual machine starts the application by starting the method main(String[]) in the defined class. This class is called the application main class.

☞   The prepared application in *BlueJ* environment is saved into the executable JAR-file by assigning a command **Create a JAR file** in the **Project** menu.

Project:
The resulting form of a project to which we came at the end and after completing all exercises in is the 132z_UFO_App project.

Part 3:

Advanced Creating of OO Programs

The program which you created up until now is so big that it starts to be difficult to keep its classes together all the time. Let's divide them therefore into several cooperating class groups called packages. The group, in which only classes and interface types developed through the existing teaching will be contained, will be further improved and thus you can learn further principles of object oriented programming together with techniques that enable creating programs with possible future perfecting.

33 Packages

What you will learn in this lesson
This lesson opens the last part of the textbook. You can recognize the problems to which big applications are facing and how it is possible to solve these problems. You will meet the conception of packages and you will learn how to create and use the packages.

Project:
In this lesson you will return back to the 130z_Class_Constructor *project, which will serve only as a source of source files for the newly created project.*

696.   I'm very curious what you prepared for me today. The project is now quite big. With the number of classes, contained in it, even the implementation arrows can be hardly displayed. Therefore I am afraid that to make place for another class will not be able without extending the project's window.

It will be able and this is just what I prepared for you today.

697.   It means I should diminish the classes or to put them in a line.

Nothing like that. I will show you how it is possible to divide a big project into several smaller, mutually cooperating parts. I will explain you what the packages are like and show you how you could arrange your previous project into packages.

Packages and Folders

698.   You say divide into packages? This reminds me the X-mas shopping – I usually have my presents divided into so many packages, that I cannot look over them.

But it is a different dividing here. In many aspects it reminds dividing of PC files into folders. Files which are somehow connected are placed into the same folder. Files which concern with different topics are placed into different folders. In case you would have all files of your PC in one pile, you never can orient in them.

699.   But the files at the disc are well divided due to the folders can have subfolders. Can the packages have also sub-packages?

The packages create a hierarchic tree structure similarly as folders at a disc. Even the connection of packages with folders at a disc is very tight. The language definition says that in case you have compiled files saved at a disc, the division of classes into packages has to correspond with the division of their class files into folders. The folder name has to correspond **precisely including the capitalization** to the package name (as you know, all names in *Java* are case sensitive) into which the data types belong, whose class files are located in the given folder (it's valid also in *Windows*!). And because the package is a program's object, it has a logical implication that names of these folders have to correspond with rules for creating of identifiers.

700. You told: "if you have compiled files saved at a disc". Where I might have the files saved somewhere?

Maybe in a database or at a net. The programs in Java can run also in the way that they are located at several computers and objects in individual computers communicate among themselves. But this is not our case – let's stay therefore at files located at a disc.

Big Programs and Their Problems

701. When the language definition takes it into account, then it's surely important. And what is its advantage, besides the fact that all data types could be put into one window?

Problems with complexity of professional programs are far bigger than yours. You have to realize that such programs have hundreds and thousands of data types[7]. The experience proved that the time needed for creating the program increases exponentially with its size. If, in a stroke of genius, you will be able to create a program of one thousand lines within one day, it does not mean that you would be able to create the 5-thousand lines program in a week and 20-thousand lines in a month. Rather can be expected that you will need a month to create the 5-thousand lines program and you will succeed to create the 20-thousand lines program within half of a year or even in one year.

Therefore one of the targets of a good proposal is to divide the program into several smaller parts which will be connected only minimally. Then each part can be developed relatively independently and you can test the proper cooperation of individual parts in suitable intervals.

One of such parts is the class. However, it is too tiny part (despite it can have several thousands of lines) and when creating really extensive programs such division is not sufficient (as you will soon see, it is not sufficient even in smaller programs). Therefore it is needed to create parts of the higher order. And the package is such part.

With proper division of the program into packages the advantage can be used that the classes within one package can share a part of their implementation's secret, so that they could use this knowledge for increasing their effectiveness. This supposes that the author of all classes within the given part is one or few programmers who know their code and therefore the risk of incorrect modification of the code is significantly smaller.

Conventions for Project Names

702. Well, well, you've already persuaded me. Show me how I should divide the project into these packages.

You will divide the project twice in this lesson. First of all you will divide it as simple as possible, just to realize which key problems you can expect during this dividing. Then you will divide it into the form in which the project will be handled for several future lessons.

---

[7] We mentioned that the Java standard library has just more than 20,000 classes. A lot of them are auxiliary, but even when we would count only those that are public, documented and you can use them any time, Java 7, which I used in the time of writing this book, had 4024.

Let's start with opening quite new project in *BlueJ* environment. Enter the command **Project → New Project**, find the folder in the opened window where you saved your projects and let it create a project entitled 133b_Packages_Start.

703.   Why just this title?

You can name it as you wish but with the name defined like that it will fit inside the others. Names of projects for this textbook respect the following convention:

☞   The first digit means the volume of the textbook – this is the first volume – the first part.

☞   The next two digits represent the chapter – now it is chapter 33.

☞   The next figure has the following meaning:

    ☞   The letter a marks the introductory project of the lesson, i.e. the new project determined for the lesson.

    ☞   The letters b, c, d… mark projects which arose during the lesson's course. We started with the b letter and each subsequent project created in the given lesson is marked with the next letter.

    ☞   The letter z marks the final project with sample solutions of tasks which were adjusted as exercises.

☞   These four characters comprise the project identifier (ID). They are followed by the underscore separating the ID from the descriptive part indicating the subject demonstrated by this project.

☞   The possible last word "Start" indicates that this is the first project of the sequence containing projects touched with the indicated subject. The sequence ends with a project that has no suffix after the indicated subject.

Creating Packages in *BlueJ*

704.   I see it's sophisticated. I will accommodate to your convention and I will create the project 133b_Packages_Start. What else?

Click with the right button at the class diagram area. The local menu opens (see figure 33.1) in which you can choose if you would like to create a new class or a new package. Select the command **New Package** and name the created package manager. Enter it with only small letters because this is the convention for packages names. Then an icon in class diagram occurs which remembers an increased icon of folders known from the file manager. This icon represents the package in the class diagram.

Then create another package and call it town. When you diminish the project window so that it would not take too much place and you adjust positions and size of icons (I remind that you diminish the icons so that *BlueJ* could not hide the possible imported type or package under them), you can have the class diagram as in the figure 33.1.

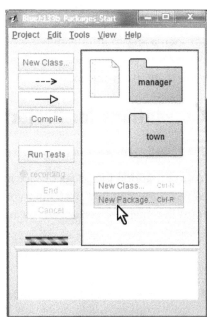

Figure 33.1
The window of the
133b_Packages_Start project

705.   I have a project with two packages. What now?

And now I will show you two ways how to fulfill the package with source files. Let's start with the way in which you use only *BlueJ*. Double click on the package manager icon or enter the statement **Open** in its local menu. A new window opens (*BlueJ* takes each package as a separate project).

Now enter the statement **Edit → Add Class from File**. Then find the 130z_Class_Constructor project and import all classes from it. (The simplest way how to select all is to click at any of them and then press CTRL+A.) *BlueJ* imports the entered files into the current package in a casual order. As is demonstrated at the figure 33.2, this arrangement is not applicable. As you see, this is not the proper way.

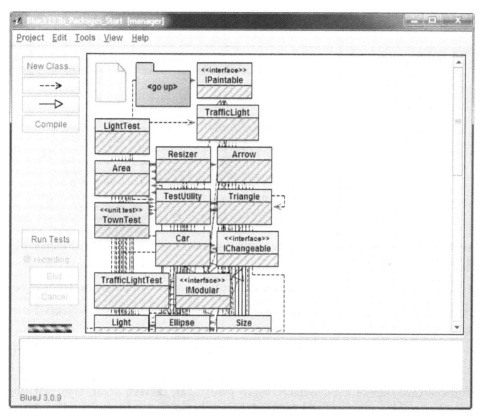

Figure 33.2
The arrangement of the class diagram of the 133b_Packages_Start project after the import of files from the 130z_Class_Constructor project

706.   Where the package `<go up>` **left up occurred? I did not install it into the project.**

It represents the parent package. Its icon cannot be shifted nor deleted. But as you see at the figure 33.2, *BlueJ* avoids it when placing the types. But you can move your types to it.

707.   Well. You told that this is not the proper way. So what should I do?

If you remember the animation OOPNZ_115_A1_SouboryVProjektechBlueJ, in which I showed you the file structure of the project, you might have the idea that you can create packages without *BlueJ*, only with the help of some file manager or use it to fine-tuning. And this is today's way. Proceed as follows:

1. Enter the command **Project → Save as** and save the copy of the current project as a new project named 133c_Packages_Arranged. Leave the original project for the future comparison.

2. Close the newly created project and start your favorite file manager. Open the manager subfolder of the project folder of the just created project.

3. Copy the package.bluej file from the project folder of the project 130z_Class_ Constructor into this folder (the manager subfolder).

4. Open again the project 133c_Packages_Arranged and open its manager package. Its class diagram will be now almost the same as the class diagram of the 130z_Class_Constructor project (see figure 29.1 on page 278). The only difference will be that the parent package icon will appear behind the classes in the upper left corner (see the figure 33.3).

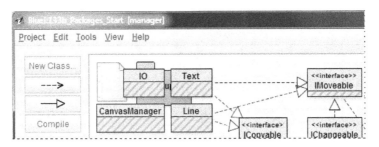

Figure 33.3
Parent package shown behind the classes in the upper left corner

708. You are true; however the project complexity is still the same. I don't see any simplification, but rather additional complexity coming with the packages.

We are just going to make it simpler. Let's continue with our modifications. Few steps remain only.

5. Leave the current project as a backup and create its copy named 133d_Packages_Separated by entering the command **Project → Save as**.

6. Close the newly created project and open its folders manager and town in your favorite file manager.

7. Select the source files of the classes Arrow, ArrowTest, Car, CarTest, Light, LightTest, Town, TownTest, TrafficLight, TrafficLightTest, and TestUtility in the manager folder and move the selected files into the town folder.

8. Copy the package.bluej file from the manager folder into the town folder and replace the original version of this file by it.

9. Close the file manager and open again *BlueJ* with the last project.

Is it O. K.?

709. I succeeded to move everything as you advised. Both packages now look out like my original project in which certain classes are missing.

Good, and now let's go to make the new project operating. Open the manager package and ask *BlueJ* for its compilation.

710.   The PC did not compile the class MultishapeTest. **It says:** cannot find symbol - variable TestUtility.

This is because the TestUtility class is in a different package. For the time being, don't pay attention to it; I will soon show how to correct it. Comment provisionally the problematic statement (and thus hide it for the compiler) and compile the project again. Now the compilation should succeed.

711.   You are right. It really succeeded.

Let's move into the package town. Here your requirement for compilation will finish much worse because here you are not able to compile any class, because each class contains an error.

Before starting to remove the errors we will make (for the last time) a copy of the current project. Name it 133e_Packages_Compiled. We leave the previous project as the backup for the case that we would make an error, the removing of which would be more laborious than the new start of the modifications.

The package statement

712.   Well, let's have a look what is the problem.

To proceed in the same way activate the window with a source file of the TestUtility class, because other test class use it and therefore we should start with its repairing. Notice the change in the first line. There is the following statement

    package town;

As you see, this statement consists of the keyword package, followed by a package name (to be precise I should say full package name, but I will explain it later on) and a closing semicolon. This statement has to be the first statement of the source code. Before it you can put only whitespaces or a comment.

You would find the same statement in all other source files. All files that are in a different package, than in the root one, have to begin with the package statement. *BlueJ* knows it and accommodates you, and supplements the relevant package statement at the beginning of the imported file. Thus you have fewer sorrows.

Tree of Packages

713.   You somehow forgot to tell me what the root package is.

As I already told, packages have the same tree structure as folders. Components in the tree structure always have one **parent** and can have several **children**. The parent of the hard disc folder (if need be of another medium with the similar address structure – e.g. the flash memory) is the folder in which the given folder is located; folders and files which it contains, are its children. When you will look for the parent of the tree element, and for the parent of this parent etc., you will arrive to an element that has no parent – and this is the tree root. It is a root folder at the disc.

Similarly it is with packages. The package that has no parents, i.e. it is not a sub-package of another package, is called the root package. All other packages have to be located in certain package which we call their **parent package**. All packages besides the root one must have a name. The only one root package does not have any name (or better said it has an empty name). But it doesn't need it, because the root package can be the only one package.

Look at the figure 33.4, on which I showed you the arrangement of source files of the Java standard library which, as you know, corresponds to the arrangement of its packages. The root package is located in the SRC folder. It has six children – the packages com, java, javax, launcher, org and sunw. I opened the java package which has 13 children. The most important of them being lang package, where all key data types are located. They are not seen at the figure but you can see that besides these invisible children (data types) this package has another five sub-packages. And you could continue like this throughout the whole tree.

Figure 33.4
The structure of packages
of the standard library

714. But how I can recognize in which folder the root package is placed? The SRC **folder is not the root folder at your disc.**

Java establishes certain rules for determining of folders in which the root package occurs. However, each development environment defines certain way, how to make easy the determination of the root package for the user as much as possible. As you could see a while ago, when you create a new project in *BlueJ*, firstly its root package is opened in which you can define its separate sub-packages and in each of them sub-package of this sub-package etc.

When you build up a package tree through the file manager, please remember, that each folder, representing a package, contains its own package.bluej file that has the key information about this package. In case you will find the package.bluej file in its parent folder, it means that also the parent folder represents some package, and then its child folder represents its sub-packages. The folder, whose parent folder doesn't contain the package.bluej file, represents the root package.

715. If I understood properly, you told that Java establishes rules for determination of FOLDERS in which the source package is located. Does it mean that it can be spread in several folders?

Yes, the standard library is located at a certain place and it has also its root folder there. But our project has its root at a different place. Beside that we can use some other auxiliary programs, each of them can be divided into a set of packages and each of them will have its root somewhere. The virtual machine unifies all these trees and makes out one big tree of them with which it works.

Simple and Full Names

716. And what happens when the same package will be in the second tree as in the first one? Will the packages also be unified after unifying the trees?

It depends on whether their full names will be equal. If yes, they will be unified and the virtual machine will perceive them as one big package.

717. Second time you are speaking about some full name, but you did not tell me, what it is. What is the difference between a simple name and a full one?

The **simple name** of a package, a class, an interface or an enumeration type (in further text I will call them overall as entities) is the name which we always used when we asked *BlueJ* for creating a class, an interface or a package. The simple name is an identifier. It means it has to correspond with rules for creating the identifiers.

The **full name of an entity** consists of the full name of a parent package (the package in which the given entity is located) followed by a dot and a simple name of the given entity. It means that when there will be the Cls class located in the bbb package, which is a sub-package of aaa, that is in the root package, then the full name of this class will be aaa.bbb.Cls, the full name of the package bbb will be aaa.bbb and the full name of the aaa package will be also aaa, because packages in the root package have the same full names as the simple ones. Other entities from the root package do not have any full name.

718. Other entities of the root package do not have any full name? Why?

Take it as that the root package is degenerated and can be used only in two situations. First of all it is in introductory courses of programming when students do not know packages, and second, in the moment when you need to instantly examine some idea and you know that you will again immediately delete the created classes as well as the interface. Not to divert you to use it for something more serious, the authors declared it as a degenerated package in the 1.3 version (Thanks God!). Thus, you can use the data types defined in the root package again only in the root package.

Package java.lang

719. A while ago you told that the compiler did not like when I worked with a class from a different package. Now you tell me that the root package is nearly not used. How is it possible that the compiler did not protest when I used the classes String and System? Are these classes in the root package?

No, they are not there. Another exception applies to their package. When I showed you the tree of the standard library packages a while ago, I told you that the most important package is java.lang because there are all key data types in it. Without this package you cannot program anything. That's why it has an exception and data types of the java.lang package can be "addressed" only with their simple names.

You can, but you do not have to. Try that when you use the full name, i.e. java.lang.String, resp. java.lang.System, everything will operate. Also the class java.lang.Object, which you met several times, comes out of this package, and you even met its full name in the part *Return Stack* on page 314.

The import Statement

720. Allow me to get back to the incorrect programs. Please, explain me how can I correct the errors.

As I have already told you, the errors announced by the compiler are caused by using data types which are in another package. Until you are operating within one package, you suffice with simple names of data types. However, as soon as you get to another package (of course, with the exception of java.lang package), you have to use for its "children" quite different names.

Ask for compilation of the opened class (TestUtility class). The compiler stops at the declaration of the CM field announcing:

```
cannot find symbol - class CanvasManager
```

It's clear – the CanvasManager class is not in this package. Modify the declaration of the CM field into the following form:

```
private static final manager.CanvasManager CM = manager.CanvasManager.getInstance();
```

Then ask once more for compilation of this class.

721.   Oh yes, this error disappeared. But several lines later the same error appeared in declaration of the position **field. Looking into the rest of this file as well as into other files I discovered that there are dozens of such corrections needed. If I will rename each appearance of each class, I have to stay here up to morning.**

Don't be afraid, Java offers you another possibility, which is the import of the entered types. If you know that you will use a data type from another package in the source code, you can insert the import statement behind the package statement (if it's not there, then at the beginning of the file), which consists of the keyword import followed by the full name of the imported type and completed by a semicolon. Then you will be allowed to use a simple name in the source code and the compiler itself will convert it to a full name based on information from the import statement. For example open the Light class and insert the following line behind the introductory package statement

```
import manager.CanvasManager;
```

Be sure, the compiler will be satisfied.

722.   It's satisfied with the canvas manager, but it doesn't like Position. **Should I write it behind the** CanvasManager?

No, you can import only one data type in each import statement. But you can add the Position import behind the color import and imports of further classes as well as interface types behind it about which the compiler will tell that their names are unknown.

723.   It helped. The class light is already compiled. Its beginning now looks out as follows:

```
package town;

import manager.CanvasManager;
import manager.IModular;
import manager.IMovable;
import manager.IO;
import manager.Mover;
import manager.Position;
```

724.   Should I modify also further classes like that?

I advise you something quicker. As I told you that now the project is divided into packages only in rough outlines, so that you would learn how to do it, I allow you using a speeded up version of the import statement. If you write a star instead of the data type name in the import statement behind the full package name and the following dot, you will import all names of data types from the given package. For that reason place the following statement into other classes

```
import Manager.*;
```

Then let compile all of them and examine if the tests are operating.

725. Wonderful! Everything is compiled and everything is operating. Perfect! So now I should get into the manager **package and correct similarly the class** MultishapeTest**.**

You can do it as an exercise, but as I told you, this correction was only in rough outlines. So after you will do the corrections, we will try the real one. So that you could control that you understood and executed everything properly you can compare your converted files with files of the project 133c_Packages_Arranged.

Package Name Convention

726. It's revised – the following statement helped

```
import town.TestUtility;
```

727. Well, and now let me know, in what our compilation is imperfect and why you call it a compilation in rough outlines?

It is one-purpose and does not correspond to conventions. If our project would increase (and it will increase), it would complicate further development.

728. Don't be vague and tell me what's wrong with it.

I will start with those conventions. When Java starts, it was abundantly used at an internet. You could create a program and include it into a web page as an applet. Anybody who looked at this web page with a reasonably intelligent browser (i.e. with such that was able to open applets) could open your code in that page.

However, to do it, it's good to provide so that two programs downloaded from various sources would not quarrel in the computer only due to the fact that their authors decided to give the same name to their classes. Therefore the Java authors decided to establish conventions for such package names, to prevent the situation that there will be two data types with the same names.

729. I've heard that applets are not much used now.

Applets are really used more at intranet, but the convention remained. It is just the same when the programs are quarreling for a name at internet or at the client who had the bad luck that he bought two programs with identical identifiers. Therefore, if you name packages according to internet domains and sub-domains in your web address (in case you do not have a web address, you can use your e-mail address), then the full name of the resulting package will not collide with the package name of anybody in the world. And you yourself are responsible for uniqueness of names in your domain.

Packages, in which the programs are located, have the names according to web address of the product or its author. In case the product is developed in a company or at a school, then the given company or the school are considered to be the author. So when my web address is pecinovsky.cz, I know that the cz.pecinovsky package will be unique and no one who respects the quoted conventions can have it.

730.   And does everybody respect these conventions?

You know – everywhere there are wrongdoers. Companies, at least those, whose products I met, observe this convention. The authors of open-source projects are not so careful. E.g. the source code of *BlueJ* should be in the org.bluej package, but authors skipped the initial org and put it into the bluej package. And you can find more of such examples. However, this is not the reason to do it. I would recommend abiding these rules.

731.   Does it mean that all programs for this course are at your PC in the package cz.pecinovsky**?**

It is a little bit more complicated. As you know I deal above all with teaching and I often develop the same program in several languages for various language versions of the given course or textbook. Therefore it can happen that names of data types in several languages will be equal (the IO class is a hot aspirant). Therefore I add sub-packages according to the used language.

In addition each of my books on programming has its own sub-package inside each language package. When starting to write this textbook I called it *Learn Object Oriented Thinking and Programming*, which means the "root" package of accompanying program for the English version has the name

    cz.pecinovsky.english.lootp

In this package and its sub-packages you will find all files, which you receive from me including sample solutions of all exercises. It's up to you if you will define for your programs your own "package way" or if you will locate them somewhere along those mine ones.

Let's show how you could prepare a project, using *BlueJ* and the file manager, according to conventions which I indicated a while ago.

732.

Change in Package Dividing

733.   When I asked you what is so imperfect in my transfer into packages, you told me that it is single-purpose and does not correspond with conventions. You explained the conventions. But did you mean by this single-purpose something else?

Yes, I did. In this project there were data types gathered from several groups, as follows:

☞   The class CanvasManager, graphic classes, which directly cooperated with it (Ellipse, Rectangle...), certain servant classes (Mover, Resizer) and interface types which supported their mutual cooperation.

☞   Classes which you proposed within the lessons – those were transferred into the town package.

☞   Classes which were universal and could be useful also to classes that don't cooperate with the class CanvasManager. All three crates (i.e. Position, Size and Area), NamedColor and Direction8 belong here. All of them cooperate for example with objects in projects that don't use CanvasManager, but Canvas.

☞   The auxiliary and single-purpose classes Tests, MultishapeTest, CCI and Call.

Each of those groups is worthy to have an independent package.

734. I don't understand fully why, but let's believe you. So what shall I do?

Create a new project and call it 133z_Packages. Make a sub-package cz, another sub-package pecinovsky in it, in this package another sub-package english with a sub-package lootp. Create four sub-packages: town, manager, tests and util in the package cz.pecinovsky.english.lootp. And import the source files of separate classes into them from the project 130z_Class_Constructor according to the listing 33.1. Then try to run everything.

Listing 33.1: *Location of the source files as well as the auxiliary files in separate folders of the 133z_Packages project*

```
133z_Packages
133z_Packages\package.bluej

133z_Packages\cz
133z_Packages\cz\package.bluej

133z_Packages\cz\pecinovsky
133z_Packages\cz\pecinovsky\package.bluej

133z_Packages\cz\pecinovsky\english
133z_Packages\cz\pecinovsky\english\package.bluej

133z_Packages\cz\pecinovsky\english\lootp
133z_Packages\cz\pecinovsky\english\lootp\package.bluej

133z_Packages\cz\pecinovsky\english\lootp\town
133z_Packages\cz\pecinovsky\english\lootp\town\Car.java
133z_Packages\cz\pecinovsky\english\lootp\town\CarTest.java
133z_Packages\cz\pecinovsky\english\lootp\town\package.bluej
133z_Packages\cz\pecinovsky\english\lootp\town\IModular.java
133z_Packages\cz\pecinovsky\english\lootp\town\Town.java
133z_Packages\cz\pecinovsky\english\lootp\town\TownTest.java
133z_Packages\cz\pecinovsky\english\lootp\town\TrafficLight.java
133z_Packages\cz\pecinovsky\english\lootp\town\TrafficLightTest.java
133z_Packages\cz\pecinovsky\english\lootp\town\Light.java
133z_Packages\cz\pecinovsky\english\lootp\town\LightTest.java
133z_Packages\cz\pecinovsky\english\lootp\town\Arrow.java
133z_Packages\cz\pecinovsky\english\lootp\town\ArrowTest.java
133z_Packages\cz\pecinovsky\english\lootp\town\TestUtility.java

133z_Packages\cz\pecinovsky\english\lootp\canvasmanager
133z_Packages\cz\pecinovsky\english\lootp\canvasmanager\package.bluej
133z_Packages\cz\pecinovsky\english\lootp\canvasmanager\Line.java
133z_Packages\cz\pecinovsky\english\lootp\canvasmanager\Ellipse.java
133z_Packages\cz\pecinovsky\english\lootp\canvasmanager\IChangeable.java
133z_Packages\cz\pecinovsky\english\lootp\canvasmanager\ICopyable.java
133z_Packages\cz\pecinovsky\english\lootp\canvasmanager\IPaintable.java
133z_Packages\cz\pecinovsky\english\lootp\canvasmanager\IResizable.java
133z_Packages\cz\pecinovsky\english\lootp\canvasmanager\IMovable.java
133z_Packages\cz\pecinovsky\english\lootp\canvasmanager\IShape.java
133z_Packages\cz\pecinovsky\english\lootp\canvasmanager\Resizer.java
133z_Packages\cz\pecinovsky\english\lootp\canvasmanager\Painter.java
133z_Packages\cz\pecinovsky\english\lootp\canvasmanager\Multishape.java
```

```
133z_Packages\cz\pecinovsky\english\lootp\canvasmanager\Rectangle.java
133z_Packages\cz\pecinovsky\english\lootp\canvasmanager\Mover.java
133z_Packages\cz\pecinovsky\english\lootp\canvasmanager\README.TXT
133z_Packages\cz\pecinovsky\english\lootp\canvasmanager\CanvasManager.java
133z_Packages\cz\pecinovsky\english\lootp\canvasmanager\Text.java
133z_Packages\cz\pecinovsky\english\lootp\canvasmanager\Triangle.java

133z_Packages\cz\pecinovsky\english\lootp\tests
133z_Packages\cz\pecinovsky\english\lootp\tests\package.bluej
133z_Packages\cz\pecinovsky\english\lootp\tests\CCI.java
133z_Packages\cz\pecinovsky\english\lootp\tests\MultishapeTest.java
133z_Packages\cz\pecinovsky\english\lootp\tests\Tests.java
133z_Packages\cz\pecinovsky\english\lootp\tests\Call.java

133z_Packages\cz\pecinovsky\english\lootp\util
133z_Packages\cz\pecinovsky\english\lootp\util\yellow.java
133z_Packages\cz\pecinovsky\english\lootp\util\package.bluej
133z_Packages\cz\pecinovsky\english\lootp\util\IO.java
133z_Packages\cz\pecinovsky\english\lootp\util\Area.java
133z_Packages\cz\pecinovsky\english\lootp\util\Position.java
133z_Packages\cz\pecinovsky\english\lootp\util\README.TXT
133z_Packages\cz\pecinovsky\english\lootp\util\Size.java
133z_Packages\cz\pecinovsky\english\lootp\util\Direction8.java
```

When you will build up those packages and sub-packages, please notice that in the title bar of the project window the package is quoted in square brackets after the project's name, whose class diagram is displayed in the window. And as you can see at the figure 33.5, you will find statements for moving to any parent and grandparent packages in local menu of the parent package.

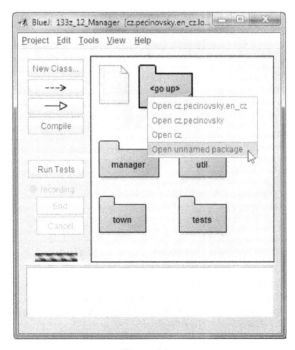

Figure 33.5
Local menu of the parent package

Why the Star Notation is Unsuitable

735. Did I understand it properly, that now I should run the whole new project, i.e. go through all data types and complete properly the imports to all, so that they may be compiled?

Yes, but don't use the star notation in the import statements – it is not considered as appropriate and it is tolerated only in experimental codes. In case you use a star in an import, you don't know what exactly you are importing. It can happen that there is a type added to the imported package, which has the same name as certain type in your package, and, because the imported ones are preferred, this type will be used instead of your one. And you will be surprised, why your program suddenly does not operate.

736. Well, I am surprised. So you say the imported type is preferred to the type of its own package?

Exactly, and that's one of reasons why using the star notation in import statements is not recommended. I understand that it is far more writing, but using the advanced development environments (e.g. *NetBeans*, which will be used in the next volume) you will avoid this writing because these environments are able to produce the needed imports independently.

   And not to press much on you, if you will not like it, you can close the project and copy the not-yet-ready-part from the 133z_Packages project in which the sample solution is completed. But it would be good to run at least the data types in the town package.

737. Isn't the division into sub-packages uselessly complicated? Like this, I will have to go through three layers of packages in each opening of the project where there is nothing.

No, you will not have to go through it. *BlueJ* takes it into account and when it finds during opening of the project, that the given package contains only one sub-package and nothing else, it automatically moves to this sub-package and repeats the possible test (and if need be also the corresponding move) up to that package, where are no sub-packages, or where more sub-packages are contained, or where also classes are contained besides the sub-packages. Try it.

738. You are true. When I closed the project and opened it again, it opened only in the package with four sub-packages. But what should I do when I would like to open the project in certain particular sub-package?

It is possible in several at once. When you open several packages and you enter the statement **Project → Quit**, *BlueJ* will remember this configuration and next time it will open in the same configuration (i.e. the same packages in identically located windows), in which you closed the project.

Exercise

739. I would say that the last task, i.e. running the new project, was acting as an exercise.

Yes, but I would have one suggestion for you. Try to create your own hierarchy of packages acceding to conventions (if you do not have your own web page, you can use your e-mail address as a basis) and insert into it your solutions from previous lessons.

Review

Let's review what you have learned in this lesson:

☞ The time need for creating a program grows exponentially with its size. Therefore, one of the targets of the good proposal is to divide the program into several smaller parts, which will be minimally dependent one on another (they should be minimally coupled).

☞ Packages create hierarchical tree structure, similarly as the folders at a disc.

☞ All but one elements of the tree structure have only one parent. The element that has no parent is called a root.

☞ If the files are saved at a disc, the placing of classes into packages has to correspond precisely with the placing of their class files to folders.

☞ Folders, in which the root package is located, have to be specified in Java. Majority of development environments make this instead of the user.

☞ There may be more folders keeping the root package. The virtual machine unifies contents of all such incurred trees into one common tree.

☞ *BlueJ* considers as the root folder such folder, which contains the `package.bluej` file, but its parent folder doesn't contain it.

☞ The package, in which certain entity (a class, an `interface`, an enumeration type or another package) is located, is called a parent package of the given entity.

☞ A simple name of an entity is an identifier by which we name the given entity.

☞ The full name of entities is composed of the full name of their parent package, followed by a dot and a simple name of the given entity.

☞ The root package is degenerated. The full names of packages in the root packages are identical with the names of the simple packages. Data types in the root package do not have full names.

☞ According to the convention the parent package of all parts of certain product is the package the name of which is derived from the web address of the product or of the author. A company (a school) is considered as an author of the company's (school's) program.

☞ Packages can be created directly in *BlueJ*, as well as externally with the assistance of certain file manager.

☞ Source files of all data types which are in the different than in the root package, have to start with the `package` statement, in which the full name of the parent package of the given data type is quoted after the `package` keyword and the statement is finalized by a semicolon.

☞ In the source file you can refer with a reduced name only to those data types which are in the same package or are quoted in the `import` statement. To other data types you have to refer with their full name.

☞ The only exception from the previous rule is the data types from the `java.lang` package, which are all implicitly imported.

☞ The import statement consists of the keyword import followed by the full name of the imported data type and the finalizing semicolon.

☞ One import statement can import only one data type. Therefore it is necessary to insert one import statement for each imported type.

☞ In the import statement you can use the star notation, in which instead of the finalizing simple name of the data type you quote a star. Then all data types of the given package are imported.

☞ Using of star notation decreases the lucidity of the program. Therefore you should use it only in training projects. In real projects you should avoid using it.

Project:
The resulting form of the project to which we came at the end of the lesson and after completing all exercises is in the 133z_Packages project.

34 Linking of Instances

What you will learn in this lesson
In this lesson you will see how it is possible to define a road along which cars will drive. You will see how you can use the advantage of linking of instances, when each instance in the closed chain knows its descendant and how it is possible to create a closed chain. At the same time you will be presented a design pattern Builder and you will learn how it is possible to define creating rings for our cars. At the conclusion you will learn how to use a static import.

Project:
In this lesson you continue in using the 133z_Packages project.

Note:
Since this lesson you will deal only with constructions to which the *BlueJ* environment does not offer any "added value". Those who would like to use some more professional development environment; it is now the proper time to transfer to it. However, I don't like to lose a number of pages with explanations of the new development environment and therefore I will continue in using the *BlueJ* environment until the end of this textbook. I introduce the *NetBeans* IDE in the next volume.

Conditions, the Future Objects Have to Meet

740.   **In the previous lesson you really succeeded to simplify our project (or better said to simplify the part containing objects created during the course) and thus I expect that today something will be added to them.**

You are expecting properly. We will further improve the town package. There are cars and traffic lights in it and it's the proper time that some routs should appear in it as well. That's why today the class Road will be proposed which will enable us to define the road at the canvas along which your cars as well as other objects will drive. During next lessons we will improve our project, so that it would be possible to make races at these roads.

741.   **It looks nice. However, for races it would better, if it would not be a route, but a ring. Formula F1 is also running along a ring.**

Surely, it will be a ring. Let's think how to make out such ring. To slow down a little bit your flowering ideas to areas which might be over your programming abilities, let's set basic, initial limits (which will be elaborated in near future) as follows:

☞   Entire visible processes will take place at the canvas managed by the canvas manager.

☞   Let's use the square grid displayed at the canvas by the manager and let's insert all objects into this squared grid.

☞   So that we could make the grid finer in case of necessity (to place more fields at the canvas) without crashing the general outlook of the canvas, all objects have to be able to accommodate to this change. Therefore all depicted objects will be created with implementing the IModular interface.

742.   I am afraid that two meaning of the term *field* would confuse me. You use it once time for the object's data and the other time for the area at the canvas.

You are true it can confuse a bit, especially when we soon add the third field – the road-field. Maybe you remember that I explained that classic OOP uses the term *attribute* for the object's data. Certain textbooks prefer it (me too), but I wanted to accommodate the Java habits and therefore I use the term *field*. Not to confuse you, when a misunderstanding may occur, I specify if I talk about an attribute or about a field on the canvas or about a field of the road.

Nevertheless, let's return to our program – what do you think about the above mentioned limits?

743.   It looks reasonably, despite the fact that in case of a road it is limiting. On the other side, I precisely know how to program it – I will set it up from grey rectangles (or maybe squares).

When you are producing an object you shouldn't be limited only to how it will look out. You have to think over how it will operate and how it will communicate with other objects. It's not much wise to make out clever objects at every price, but sometimes a bit of intelligence is suitable for each object.

Think over the fact that it might be profitable if your road would communicate with cars (if need be also with other objects) which will go along it. For example it may tell them when and where the objects should turn to. Then the cars may go alone and the next version could be arranged so that the player could compete with the computer.

The RoadField **Class**

744.   I admit that I have no idea. I should know precisely in each moment where the car is on the road and where this part of the road is going to. I think I should program also some maps as well as GPS.

GPS? No, you need nothing like that. It's sufficient to define the road as a chain of small parts – segments, where each of them knows to which direction it goes and what is its descendant. The object that follows the road receives the reference to the first segment and it can start going. The object asks the received segment to which direction it should go and what its descendant is. Arriving to the descendant, the object asks once again and this is repeated until the object arrives to the aim.

745.   Oh yes! It might be operating! And when you told that everything should be in the squared grid of the canvas, one part (the road-field) could be a square occupying one canvas field bounded by the grid. And now I have to think out only how to compose the route from those road-fields.

Thinking over how to compose the road from road-fields has certain sense only when you have a basic idea what one road-field is. Let's define the RoadField class and let's think over what it should know.

746. It will have to know to draw itself which means it will have to implement the IModular interface according to your limits. Then you told that it should know its direction and its descendant. But the descendant will be again the RoadField instance. Does it matter if one instance will have another instance of the same class as a field (an attribute)?

No, it doesn't matter and it's used relatively often. Sometimes these objects are called **linked lists**. Our road-fields will make just such list.

Well, do you think that's all?

747. I think that for the beginning it's quite a lot.

You properly say *for the beginning.* You never know what can appear in course of further parts and what will push you to change or extend the originally proposed definition. To summarize what you thought out for the RoadField class and its instances, I say the following:

☞ The road-field has to know how to draw itself. Remembering the light, we surely will have the idea to define a field (an attribute) – a rectangle this time. (In fact it will be a square, but as there is no class of squares, the rectangle class is quite suitable.) And you know that this square will not change (i.e. it will be not replaced by another square), which means it can be defined as a constant.

☞ The class has to implement the IModular interface which means the road-field has to know its coordinates and its module. However, other attributes (fields) don't have to be defined, because (similarly as at the light) you can ask the just defined rectangle.

☞ The road-field should know the direction of riding. And that's why it is necessary to define the attribute containing this direction.

☞ The road-field also should know its successor, i.e. which road-field is the next one. So it is necessary to define an attribute for this as well.

☞ It should be possible to ask for the direction as well as for the successor. Therefore we should define also the accessory methods that will provide this information as well.

You already know which methods and attributes the RoadField class will need and you can start thinking over the definition of a constructor. First of all which parameters it should have. Do you have some idea?

748. I would say that parameters are clear: we need the position, the size, the color, the direction and the successor.

Unfortunately the parameters are not clear. The first what comes on my mind are problems with the successor. To get a reference to a successor, it is necessary so that it would exist. So first of all you have to create the successor, but it needs again to know its successor. And it would stretch to infinity. You have to bypass it somehow.

I advise you to define three constructors as follows:

☞ The first constructor (let's call it an *opening* one) will be used in the definition of the first road-field of the future ring. That's why you will set its position, module, direction and its color. But you will not adjust its successor because no one still exists.

☞ The second constructor (let's call it a *continuing* one) will be used for defining the following arrays of the ring. You will set a predecessor of the created array as well as the direction in which the given array should be crossed over. The constructor will ask the color as well as the module of the predecessor, because it should be the same.

The constructor will use the help of its predecessor also as far as the position of the created array is mentioned, because knowing where the predecessor is located and in which direction you can drive through it, the constructor can derive where the created road-field should be placed so that the joint object would arrive to it. (In a moment I will tell you how to derive it.)

The parameter referring to the predecessor will serve also for another important thing. The constructor knows that the created road-field is a successor of the set predecessor so that it can initialize the predecessor's attribute (field) referring to its successor which is the just created object.

The constructor does not know the successor of the just created object, and that's why it leaves the relevant field (attribute) not initialized and expects that the future successor will initialize it retrospectively in the moment of its birth – similarly as it initialized the "successional" attribute (field) of its predecessor.

☞ The third constructor (let's call it a *closing* one) will be used for the definition of an array which closes the whole ring. Besides the direction and the predecessor you have to give also its successor to this constructor. After this road-field you will not create other road-fields and thus you need an alternative way how to set a successor for this array.

Fortunately we know the successor of the last road-field – it is the first road-field of the ring. Therefore you pass this road-field to the closing constructor and it will set the successor of the created array alone.

749.   It is clever! And maybe I would be able to program it myself. Can anything surprise me?

No surprise, but two advices for you:

☞ For calculation of the created road-field's position based on the position as well as the direction of its predecessor you should call the method nextPosition(Position,int) of the direction of the given road-field. When you pass the predecessor in the first parameter and the module (the road-field size) in the second one, the method will return you the position of the neighboring road-field in the given direction.

☞ Don't try to define everything in one constructor, to which the remaining two will refer through this. It was possible in all classes which you defined until now. In this case it would be possible as well, but it would be quite clumsy. The closing constructor can refer to the continuing one because then it will need to supplement only the successor of the created road-field. But the opening and continuing constructors will differ and you should program them both once again.

☞ To unify the names, call the method, which will return the successor of the given road-field, getNextPosition.

And you can start creating. You can compare your result with the sample solution in the listing 34.1. I stated in this listing only the declarations of fields (attributes) and the definitions of constructors. You will not find definitions of instance methods in it, because I thought they are quite clear. But, in case you would see them, you can look at the final project of today's lesson.

Listing 34.1:   *The fields (attributes) and constructors of the RoadField class*

```
/*******************************************************************************
 * Instances of class {@code RoadField} represent parts,
 * from which the roads are built.
 * Each instance knows the direction in which it is driven through,
 * and its descendant that is a sibling, where the driven through cars arrive.
 */
public class RoadField implements IModular
{
    //== CONSTANT CLASS FIELDS ===================================================

    /** Canvas on which the instance will be painted. */
    private static final CanvasManager CM = CanvasManager.getInstance();


    //== CONSTANT INSTANCE FIELDS ================================================

    /** Rectangle representing the field's area at the canvas. */
    private final Rectangle area;

    /** Direction in which the field can be driven through. */
    private final Direction8 direction;


    //== VARIABLE INSTANCE FIELDS ================================================

    /** Descendant is a {@code RoadField,
     *   where the driven through cars arrive. */
    private RoadField next;


    //##########################################################################
    //== CONSTUCTORS AND FACTORY METHODS =========================================

    /*******************************************************************************
     * Creates a starting field with the given position, direction and color.
     * <p>
     * Because a ring building starts with this constructor,
     * we call it the "<i>starting constructor</i>".
     *
     * @param position    Field position
     * @param direction   Direction in which the field will be driven through
     * @param color       Field color
     */
    public RoadField(Position position, Direction8 direction, NamedColor color)
    {
        int  module = CM.getStep();
        this.area   = new Rectangle(position.x, position.y,
                                    module,      module,      color);
        this.direction = direction;
    }
```

```
/*****************************************************************************
 * Creates a field following the field given as an argument
 * ({@code predecessor}), and being driven through in the given direction.
 * The created field borrows its size and color from the {@code predecessor}
 * and it also derives its position from the predecessor's
 * position, size and direction.
 * <p>
 * Because a ring building continues with these constructors,
 * we call it the "<i>continuing constructor</i>".
 *
 * @param predecessor Field, which will be followed by this field
 * @param direction    Direction in which the field will be driven through
 */
public RoadField(RoadField predecessor, Direction8 direction)
{
    int        module   = predecessor.getModule();
    Position   position = predecessor.direction.
                          nextPosition(predecessor.getPosition(), module);
    NamedColor color    = predecessor.area.getColor();

    this.area = new Rectangle(position.x, position.y,
                              module,      module,      color);
    this.direction   = direction;
    /** Set itself as a successor of its predecessor */
    predecessor.next = this;
}


/*****************************************************************************
 * Creates a field following the field given as an argument,
 * being driven through in the given direction,
 * and being followed by the given successor.
 * The created field borrows its size and color from this predecessor
 * and it also derives its position from the predecessor's
 * position, size and direction.
 * <p>
 * Because a ring building ends with these constructors
 * (it closes the created ring),
 * we call it the "<i>closing constructor</i>".
 *
 * @param predecessor Field, which will be followed by this field
 * @param direction    Direction in which the field will be driven through
 * @param successor    Field, which will follow this field
 */
public RoadField(RoadField predecessor, Direction8 direction,
                 RoadField successor)
{
    this(predecessor, direction);
    this.next = successor;
}


//Instance method are omitted
}
```

The `Ring` **Class**

750.   Well, I had to look at it a bit, but I think I succeeded to do it. Can I test it somehow that it's operating?

I would say that the best testing will be if you would compose a ring of those arrays. Let's think over which properties and abilities the rings should have. When building the ring you will also test if you programmed properly the `RoadField` class.

751.   Well. Let's define the `Ring` class. What such ring has to know? I think it should know which road-fields belong to it.

Good, but it doesn't have to remember them all. It's sufficient to know only the initial one, because the "traveler" can ask for the next array and so on.

   You told what it should to know, however you forgot to tell also, what it should be able to do. Let me to tell it instead of you. It will be not much demanding. To start up along the ring, it's sufficient so that the ring would return its starting road-field at a request and that it will be able to paint itself.

   From the previous we can derive that also the ring's constructor might be simple: it may have only one parameter, in which it receives a reference to the initial road-field and remembers it so that it could be passed at a request.

   Due to I would like to add something into this class definition, I will not show it to you at once. But if you are burning from eagerness you can find it in the listing 34.3 on page 357.

The Design Pattern *Builder*

752.   You told that the constructor gets only a reference to the initial road-field in the parameter and remembers it. I thought that the constructor will have the task to build up this ring.

Oh, it's a bit more complicated with this building. If the ring should know to build up itself, we should have to equip it with several methods, and with calling them step by step we might build it up. But these methods would be useless during operating and on the contrary, by casual calling the whole ring might be disrupted.

   Such situations can appear in practice. Therefore the design pattern *Builder* recommends separating building of complex constructed objects from their running. When building the ring you should define a special class, the instances of which would take care about this building. The result of the whole process then will be a new ring which cannot be further changed nor disturbed.

The `RingBuilder` **Class**

753.   Oh, it really wouldn't cross my mind. So your advice is to define an independent class for building the rings — e.g. `RingBuilder`? I'm afraid I have no idea how to propose this class. You should give me some clue.

Considering this class you can proceed e.g. as follows:

☞   When you create a new builder, you should equip it immediately with basic information about the ring which the builder should create. For example a position as well as a color of the created ring belongs to this information. It could be passed to the constructor in parameters, so that the constructor could save them in fields (attributes).

☞ Then you have to define methods with which you will create the ring. Because you remember that the RoadField class, which will provide its instances for composing the ring, has a special constructor for opening, continuing and closing road-fields, you can estimate that three methods will be needed. These methods could be satisfied with an only parameter – a direction in which you can go through the inserted array. Then you could define the methods startTo(Direction8), continueTo(Direction8) and closeTo(Direction8).

☞ When all arrays will be composed the builder will have to deliver also the created ring. Therefore define the getRing() method returning the freshly created ring.

754. It crossed my mind that I don't know, ho to paint such ring. I should probably paint it field by field, but I don't know how to program it.

In my university courses the advanced students would now shout, that it can be solved by a loop. Yes, it can, but we try to do without it, because (as you will see) such solution is simpler in the final result. When you start to think about the possibilities, how to ensure depicting of the created road-fields at the canvas, you probably come upon to three possible solutions:

☞ Include the registration at the canvas manager into the RoadField constructor.

☞ Register the road-field at the canvas manager in the above mentioned creating methods of the builder.

☞ Don't take care about any registration and set up a multishape from the created road-fields. This multishape can be passed to the created ring as the second argument. The ring will implement the IPaintable interface and define its painting by delegating it to the obtained multishape.

I prefer to leave the registration in the calling hierarchy as high as possible and therefore I recommend the third mentioned possibility with the multishape.

755. You advise well, however I remember, that we can add into the multishape only the instances implementing IShape. Should we therefore add this implementation to the RoadField definition?

It would be uselessly too much work. Let's use another way. The builder creates an empty multishape and will pass it to the RoadField constructors (we should add there a parameter – add it at the end of the parameter list in all three constructors). These constructors add the square representing the road-field's area to this multishape. Thus, this multishape will be a visual representation of the ring and its road-fields. We only should ensure that the positions and sizes of the multishape and particular road-fields will be modified synchronously in the future.

I would say that after all these clues you could define the builder alone. Test it. You can compare your definition with the sample solution in the listing 34.2 (you can check the correctness of the RoadField constructors' modification in the accompanying project).

756. One more question: "What did you mean by saying that you would leave it in the calling hierarchy as high as possible?"

In the calling hierarchy the calling method is always higher and the called method is lower. When you define certain method, you operate in a higher level of abstraction than when you think how to define methods which you will call from this method. Let's show it in an example.

☞ You were operating in the highest level of abstraction when you started to speculate over the possibility to program organizing a race.

☞ Then you came lower ruminating what is necessary for such race. It is necessary to have racers (they already exist more or less) and the racing ring.

☞ Then you came lower again and you begin speculating how to define the racing ring. You came to the idea that it would be good to define the route's array of and the builder, who will build a ring from these arrays.

☞ Then you came again lower starting to mediate over what the route's array should know. And now, you are going to solve the question, how the builder should be defined.

Generally, there are things that are suitable to be inserted in the calling hierarchy higher, and besides them, there are things which should be inserted lower. However, I wouldn't like to ruminate about this question because you could sink in theories as to understand it you don't have enough of experience.

Listing 34.2:   *The RingBuilder class*

```
/*******************************************************************************
 * Instances of class {@code RingBuilder} represent builders
 * that are able to build ring compound from the {@link RoadField} instances.
 */
public class RingBuilder
{
    //== CONSTANT CLASS FIELDS ==================================================

    /** Canvas on which the instance will be painted. */
    CanvasManager CM = CanvasManager.getInstance();

    /** The default road color. */
    private static final NamedColor DEFAULT_COLOR = NamedColor.GRAY;


    //== CONSTANT INSTANCE FIELDS ===============================================

    /** Position, where the first road-field will be placed. */
    private final Position startPosition;

    /** Color of the created ring. */
    private final NamedColor color;


    //== VARIABLE INSTANCE FIELDS ===============================================

    /** Multishape containing all the ring fields. */
    private Multishape multishape;

    /** The ring starting field.
     * When the ring is closed, it is also the last field. */
    private RoadField startField;
```

```
/** The ring end field.
 *  When the ring is closed, it is also the starting field. */
private RoadField lastField;



//###########################################################################
//== CONSTUCTORS AND FACTORY METHODS ========================================

/****************************************************************************
 * Creates a builder that will build the ring
 * with the default color starting at the given position.
 *
 * @param startPosition Starting field position
 */
public RingBuilder(Position startPosition)
{
    this(startPosition, DEFAULT_COLOR);
}



/****************************************************************************
 * Creates a builder that will build the ring
 * with the given color starting at the given position.
 *
 * @param startPosition Starting field position
 * @param color         Road color
 */
public RingBuilder(Position startPosition, NamedColor color)
{
    this.startPosition = startPosition;
    this.color         = color;
}



//== INSTANCE GETTERS AND SETTERS ===========================================

/****************************************************************************
 * Returns the just created ring.
 *
 * @return Created ring
 */
public Ring getRing()
{
    return new Ring(startField, multishape);
}



//== OTHER NON-PRIVATE INSTANCE METHODS =====================================

/****************************************************************************
 * Adds the first road-field of the created ring.
 *
 * @param direction Direction in which the field will be driven through
 * @return This instance for chaining the calls
```

```java
     */
    public RingBuilder startTo(Direction8 direction)
    {
        multishape = new Multishape();
        lastField  = new RoadField(startPosition, direction, color, multishape);
        startField = lastField;

        return this;
    }


    /****************************************************************************
     * Adds a next road-field to the created ring.
     *
     * @param direction Direction in which the field will be driven through
     * @return This instance for chaining the calls
     */
    public RingBuilder continueTo(Direction8 direction)
    {
        lastField = new RoadField(lastField, direction, multishape);

        return this;
    }


    /****************************************************************************
     * Adds the last, closing road-field to the created ring.
     *
     * @param direction Direction in which the field will be driven through
     * @return This instance for chaining the calls
     */
    public RingBuilder closeTo(Direction8 direction)
    {
        lastField = new RoadField(lastField, direction, startField, multishape);
        multishape.creationDone();

        return this;
    }


    /****************************************************************************
     * Returns a string representation of the object &ndash; its text signature.
     *
     * @return A string representation of the object
     */
    @Override
    public String toString()
    {
        return "StringBuilder_(start=" + startPosition + ", color=" + color +
               ", first=" + startField + ", last=" + lastField + ")";
    }
}
```

Creating of Rings

757. **I really don't like to open any theory, because I think now I am able to make out some ring. Besides that, until the ring class will not be defined, we cannot compile the** `RingBuilder` **class.**

You are true. And when the class Ring is so simple (see the part *The Ring Class* on page 352), you can entrust it with creating the rings. For each produced ring you will define a special static method that will be able to create the ring at adjusted coordinates. When you will call this method several times with various coordinates, you will receive several rings looking similarly. You can even add a parameter that enables defining the ring's color, so that individual instances of the given ring could be easily identified.

Then you can organize races in which each racer will have his/her individual ring. All rings will be equal and the racers will compete who will go through his/her ring quicker. How to program the application that would enable such races will be the topic of some future lessons.

758. **But, a moment ago you told me that it's not good if the class alone would build complicated instances.**

A moment ago I told that if the Ring class would know to build its instances it would have to offer such methods enabling to create the required ring's instance to all who would like to create certain ring. These methods were moved to the RingBuilder class. Now I want to insert two sample methods into the Ring class that will show how it is possible to create a ring with the help of a builder. You can see them in the listing 34.3.

I admit that it would be more pure from the programming aspect if I would install quite new library class, but I didn't want to overload the class diagram. If you would like to define more of those rings, it would be better to establish such class. But as I've told, I only wanted to offer you two sample methods demonstrating how the rings should be created.

In the newSquareRing method I show that in special simple cases it is possible to create the builder, let it create the ring and return the created ring in one statement. The newLShapeRing method creates a more complex ring and therefore its creation is divided into three statements: the first statement creates the builder, the second one explains to the builder, how to create the ring, and the third one returns the created ring.

In both methods you can learn, how it is possible to chain the methods returning a reference to its instance.

Listing 34.3:   *The Ring class*

```
/************************************************************************
 * Instances of class {@code Ring} represent road rings,
 * where the players can travel or race.
 */
public class Ring implements IPaintable
{
    //== CONSTANT INSTANCE FIELDS ================================

    /** The road starting road-field. In case of closed road (ring)
     *  the starting field is the same as the final one. */
    private final RoadField startField;
```

```
/** The shape representing the ring at a canvas. */
private final Multishape shape;


//== OTHER NON-PRIVATE CLASS METHODS ==========================================

/***************************************************************************
 * Creates the smallest possible ring at the given position.
 * The ring has the square shape, it will have the default, gray color
 * and it will start from its left upper corner to the east (right).
 *
 * @param  startPosition Position of the ring start field
 * @return The created ring
 */
public static Ring newSquareRing(Position startPosition)
{
    return new RingBuilder(startPosition)
            .startTo   (EAST)
            .continueTo(SOUTH)
            .continueTo(WEST)
            .closeTo   (NORTH)
            .getRing();
}


/***************************************************************************
 * Creates an L-shape ring at the given position.
 * The ring will have the given color
 * and it will start from its left upper corner to the south (down).
 *
 * @param  startPosition Position of the ring start field
 * @param  color         Color of the created ring
 * @return The created ring
 */
public static Ring newLShapeRing(Position startPosition, NamedColor color)
{
    RingBuilder builder = new RingBuilder(startPosition, color);
    builder.startTo    (SOUTH).continueTo(SOUTH).continueTo(SOUTH)
            .continueTo(EAST ).continueTo(EAST ).continueTo(EAST)
            .continueTo(NORTH).continueTo(NORTH)
            .continueTo(WEST )
            .continueTo(NORTH)
            .continueTo(WEST ).closeTo    (WEST);
    return builder.getRing();
}


//##########################################################################
//== CONSTUCTORS AND FACTORY METHODS ==========================================

/***************************************************************************
 * Creates a new ring-road beginning at the given road-field.
 *
 * @param startField  The start field of the future road
```

```java
 * @param shape         The shape representing the ring at a canvas
 */
public Ring(RoadField startField, Multishape shape)
{
    this.startField = startField;
    this.shape      = shape;
}


//== INSTANCE GETTERS AND SETTERS ============================================

/****************************************************************************
 * Returns the starting road-field of the ring.
 *
 * @return Ring starting field
 */
public RoadField getStartField()
{
    return startField;
}


/****************************************************************************
 * Paints the instance by force of the specified painter.
 *
 * @param painter Painter drawing the instance
 */
@Override
public void paint(Painter painter)
{
    shape.paint(painter);
}


//== OTHER NON-PRIVATE INSTANCE METHODS =====================================

/****************************************************************************
 * Returns a string representation of the object &ndash; its text signature.
 *
 * @return A string representation of the object
 */
@Override
public String toString()
{
    return "Ring_(start=" + startField + ")";
}
}
```

Static Import

759. I tried to define the class, but the compiler told me that it doesn't know these directions and importing the `Direction8` class didn't help me as well.

The import will help you only when you intend to use data types. I did not use data type in this program, but the open static fields (attributes) of certain type – in this case of `Direction8` type. There are two possibilities in this case: either you will refer to these fields through the given type (e.g. `Direction8.EAST`), or you will use the static import.

760. The static import? What does it mean?

We met it in the section *A Servant Class* on page 279 when we included the statement

```
import static org.junit.Assert.*;
```

to make the assert???(???) methods family available. Generally the static import enables you to import names of static elements (fields, methods) of a given class. In case you would use the static import, you can use simple versions of these names, i.e. to act as if these names would be defined within your class.

761. How such static import is defined?

You could see it in the mentioned statement – it is defined similarly as the current import, you only have to add the keyword `static`. Also at the static import you can use either a directly imported name – for example:

```
import static cz.pecinovsky.english.oopnz.utility.Direction8.EAST;
```

or you can use the star convention and import all static members of the given class:

```
import static cz.pecinovsky.english.oopnz.utility.Direction8.*;
```

762. I looked into the closing project of the lesson and I saw that you used the star convention which you traduced in the last lesson. Is it different for the static import?

Let's precise that generally using of static import should be limited at a maximum, because it can invoke a false impression of the reader, that certain element of the given class has been used. Using of the static import is tolerated in cases when the imported identifiers are used within the class body quite often; and when it is suitable so that these identifiers themselves would indicate that they symbolize something which does not belong into members of the given class. In such case even using the star convention is considered as acceptable.

But I would remind once again: the static import should be used as little as possible and only when you are sure that the reader of the code will easily identify the imported identifiers as names of objects which are elements of other classes.

The RingTest Class

763.   And now it remains only to show how the cars will drive along the rings.

I would not send the cars at rings for now, because they do not know to turn. You can examine it at for example lights. They are round so it doesn't matter that they cannot turn. Create the class RingTest and let's define a little test in it.

764.   I've got a test class. Shall I do a fixture?

Yes, but it will be not created in an interactive mode, but it will be programmed directly. It's due to the fact that only hardly the position would be assigned in an interactive mode – you would have to assign its full name, and as you know, it's quite long. You could supplement the overloaded versions of static methods in the Ring class, which would expect two integer coordinates instead of one Position, but I am not much keen into it (but of course, you can try it).

As I already told, enter the preliminary fixture by hand, at least you will verify that it's really possible. Open the RingTest class and define the fields (attributes) in it:

```
private CanvasManager CM;
private Ring ringSquare;
private Ring ringLShape;
```

Then move into the body of the setUp() method and insert the statements:

```
CM         = CanvasManager.getInstance();
ringSquare = Ring.square    (new Position(0,0));
ringLShape = Ring. ringLShape(new Position(100, 100), NamedColor.BROWN);
CM.add(ringSquare, ringLShape);
```

Now you can compile the class and examine the fixture.

Exercise

765.   Oh, yes! Really two rings were created, one grey and the second one brown.

Driving the lights along the ring is your today's exercise. I advise you the following procedure:

1.   Create an instance of the mover with a reasonable speed.

2. Request the ring for its initial array.

3. Ask the received array for its position.

4. Create an instance of the light at the received position.

5. Ask the initial array for its successor.

6. Ask the successor for its position.

7. Request the mover to move the light at this position.

8. Make an initial array from the successor, i.e. save it to the variable in which you saved the initial array.

9. Repeat the actions from point 5.

766. I suppose that the repeating part should be defined as an independent auxiliary method.

Your suppositions are good – call it for example auxMove. I would recommend you to define it with the following signature (in case you forgot what it is a signature, look at the part *Signature versus Contract* on page 112):

```
private RoadField auxMove(RoadField field, Mover mover, IMovable ip)
```

767. Why should I return the road-field?

Because you will add the returned array as the first parameter during the next calling, which means it will move to another one. By repeating calling you can drive along the whole ring.

Define also the whole procedure as an auxiliary method which I described you a while ago – possibly as a method with the following signature

```
private void auxDriveRound(Ring ring)
```

As you surely estimate, the parameter is a ring in which you will drive your light. Then you can define two test methods. You will call this method with the parameter ringSquare in one of them, and with the parameter ringLShape in the second one.

768. But even with this there will be a lot of repeating. Before I succeed to run around L, I will have to call the method twelve times.

I have another trick for it, but I will explain it only in the next lesson. Try to program the test with what you know and you can compare it with the sample solution in the listing 34.4.

Listing 34.4:   *The RingTest class*

```
/****************************************************************************
 * The class {@code RingTest} serves
 * for a complex test of the class {@link Ring}.
 */
public class RingTest
{
    private CanvasManager CM;
    private Ring ringSquare;
    private Ring ringLShape;



    //== PREPARATION AND CLEANING THE FIXTURE ====================================

    /****************************************************************************
     * Creates a test fixture, i.e. a set of objects that will be prepared
     * before each run test.
     */
    @Before
    public void setUp()
    {
        CM        = CanvasManager.getInstance();
        ringSquare = Ring.newSquareRing(new Position(0,0));
        ringLShape = Ring.newLShapeRing(new Position(100, 100),
                                        NamedColor.BROWN);
        CM.add(ringSquare, ringLShape);
```

```
        IO.inform("Rings prepared");
}


/****************************************************************************
 * Clean-up after - this method is called after each test.
 */
@After
public void tearDown()
{
}



//== PRIVATE AND AUXILIARY INSTANCE METHODS ===================================

/****************************************************************************
 * Runs around the given ring with a light;
 * version with repeated call.
 *
 * @param ring Ring where the light should run
 */
private void auxRunRound(Ring ring)
{
    RoadField startField = ring.getStartField();
    Position   position   = startField.getPosition();
    Light      light      = new Light(position.x, position.y);
    Mover      mover      = new Mover(10);

    CM.add(light);
    startField = auxMove(startField, mover, light);

    //...  The previous statement can be repeated as needed

    startField = auxMove(startField, mover, light);
    startField = auxMove(startField, mover, light);
    startField = auxMove(startField, mover, light);
    startField = auxMove(startField, mover, light);
    startField = auxMove(startField, mover, light);
    startField = auxMove(startField, mover, light);
    startField = auxMove(startField, mover, light);
    startField = auxMove(startField, mover, light);
    startField = auxMove(startField, mover, light);
    startField = auxMove(startField, mover, light);
    startField = auxMove(startField, mover, light);
}


/****************************************************************************
 * Moves the given movable object with the given mover
 * from the given field to its successor
 * and returns a reference to this successor.
 *
 * @param field    Starting field
 * @param mover    Mover drawing the moved object
```

```
 * @param movable Moved object
 * @return Successor of the current field = object's destination
 */
private RoadField auxMove(RoadField field, Mover mover, IMovable movable)
{
    RoadField nextField = field.getNext();
    Position  position  = nextField.getPosition();
    mover.moveTo(position, movable);
    return nextField;
}


//== THE TESTS ===============================================================

/***************************************************************************
 * Tests how the light runs around the L-shape ring.
 */
@Test
public void testLShapeRing()
{
    auxRunRound(ringLShape);
}


/***************************************************************************
 * Tests how the light runs around the square-shape ring.
 */
@Test
public void testSquareRing()
{
    auxRunRound(ringSquare);
}
}
```

Review

Let's review what you have learned in this lesson:

☞ Meditating on the planned graphical object you cannot limit only to the fact how the object will look out, but you have to ponder, how it will act and communicate with other objects.

☞ Objects which, at the first sight, seem too much complicated often can be divided into a number of very simple objects that can be easily put together.

☞ An object can contain another object of the same instance as a field (an attribute). Groups of objects connected in this way are usually named linked lists.

☞ Sometimes it is advantageous not to pass the responsibility in a constructor by the statement this, but to define the whole constructor.

☞ The design pattern *Builder* recommends not mixing the construction of complex objects with their current usage because for construction you use methods that cannot be used later on.

☞ The *Builder* recommends a definition of a special class, the objects of which will be responsible for constructing. The constructed objects can thus concentrate only to their acting.

☞ Using of objects from different packages brings problems in the *BlueJ*'s interactive mode, because full names of their classes have to be used.

☞ In case you often use static elements of some other class, you can avoid repeating of their qualification by using the static import.

☞ In the static import you have to add the keyword static behind the keyword import.

☞ You can use either the particular imported name in the static import, or the star convention.

☞ The static imported identifiers should significantly mark that they are not proper members of the class in which you use them.

☞ The static import should be used as little as possible. Before using it you always should ruminate if you will not invoke a false idea that imported identifiers are not identifiers of the members of the given class.

Project:
The resulting form of the project to which we came at the end and after completing all exercises is in the 134z_Instance_chaining project.

35 Decorator

What you will learn in this lesson
In this lesson you will learn analyzing of error messages of the virtual machine. Then you will see how you could effectively define cars which will drive along the rings created in the previous lesson. You will become acquainted with the design pattern Decorator *and you will read how in some cases this pattern can substitute advantageously the inheritance.*

Project:
In this lesson you will open a new project named 135a_Decorator_Start. *It differs from the previous project only by the enriched packages* manager *and* util.

Recursion

769. Last time you were speaking about a trick due to which I will not have to repeat the same calling of a method. I was told that a loop is used for it.

A loop is immensely useful construction and it might become useful in the test mentioned at the last lesson. But I would like to make do without it for some time. Don't be afraid we will get to it within few lessons. Today I prepared for you several improvements, for which the loop would not simply suffice: moving of several objects simultaneously. I will adapt the tests so that several moving objects could run about mutually at the ring.

770. Oh, it seems interesting. And what will be today's topic?

We will improve the class RingTest. Before I start the explanation of the improvement, I would like to present you another construction: the recursion, because you will use its certain form. I remind that the recursive calling of method means that the method calls directly or indirectly (vicariously) itself. You met this method in the section *Recursion* on page 130 when you learn how the multi-shapes operate.

771. I remember. You mentioned the recursion when you explained that a multi-shape can be a part of another multi-shape. So you say that by a recursion I can substitute the loop.

It's possible, but mostly it's not the best solution. Each of the constructions has its own area where it can be used as the best solution. Nevertheless, at the beginning I would like to show you how you can replace the loop by the recursion, i.e. how you can use the recursion so that a code's part would be executed repeatedly. It will be not an optimal solution, but it should show you, how such recursion is operating.

**772.		Well, show it.**

First of all I will show you how you can adapt the auxMove method from the previous lesson so that you should not repeat its calling because the method will call it itself. To compare both solutions, copy the method and re-name the copy to auxMoveRecursive. You can do the same with the auxDriveRound method, re-name its copy to auxDriveRoundRecursive, and possibly also with the tests. Don't forget to change the name of the called method to the recursive one in these copies (i.e. to the re-named one).

**773.		I've copied and re-named all, go on.**

The auxMove method returns a reference to the target road-field so that the calling method could call it once again and declare this being target road-field as the current initial one. But when the method already knows the target road-field (and thus also the new initial one) , you could save its transferring by one floor up and back, and leave it inside the method. Replace the closing return statement in the auxMoveRecursive method body with a statement in which the method calls itself and passes the new initial array as a parameter. You can see the source code of the new method in the listing 35.1.

Listing 35.1:		*The endless version of auxMoveRecursive method in the RingTest class*

```
private void auxMoveRecursive(RoadField field, Mover mover,
                              IMovable movedObject)
{
    RoadField nextField = field.getNext();
    Position  position  = nextField.getPosition();
    mover.moveTo(position, movedObject);
    auxMoveRecursive(nextField, mover, movedObject);
}
```

**774.		When the method calls itself at the end, does it start once again with new values of parameters?**

Yes, try it in the debugger. Step the method and whenever the method would like to call itself, you have to step inside. Another possibility is to insert a breakpoint into the method and the program stops at this in each method's calling.

**775.		Another item appears left in the sequence of callings with each method's calling (i.e. in the stack – I still remember that). Does it matter?**

Of course, it does matter. It is immensely important to observe when the recursion should finish because otherwise the memory will be overloaded and the program will collapse. Finish the application, comment the third statement requiring the mover for a fluent moving of the light into a new position (that's why the program accomplishes slowly) and run the test once again.

Analysis of Error Message

**776.		The program stopped immediately and a window of test results appeared announcing an interesting error** no exception message. **And there is written** java.lang.StackOverflowError **under it. When I wanted to display the source code it took me somewhere to the** Position **class.**

Let's explain what *BlueJ* announces you. The message no exception message announces that the program itself did not declare any error. But this is nothing strange because you make only undemanding operations.

The message java.lang.StackOverflowError says that the virtual machine announced an overflow of the stack. As you have heard already in the part *Return Stack* on page 314, the virtual machine saves the address in each calling of method, to which it will return after its accomplishing, and at the same time it reserves also a place for its local variables. Then, if one method is calling the other one and never returns, no wonder that the memory reserved for the stack is filled up in a while.

Don't bother if the program shows an error in the Position class. In case of the stack overflow, the virtual machine shows the error position at the just executed place in the code.

777. And can it be recognized, where the error is?

You have to read the error message further. Each message line speaks about one method's calling. The Java error messages have standard forms. The error messages announced during accomplishing the tests are displayed by *BlueJ* in the window **Test results**, the error messages received during current sending of messages are displayed in the standard error output. This time there is a message starting with:

```
java.lang.StackOverflowError
      at cz.pecinovsky.english.oopnz.utility.Position.<init>(Position.java:41)
      at cz.pecinovsky.english.oopnz.manager.Rectangle.getPosition(Rectangle.java:195)
      at cz.pecinovsky.english.oopnz.town.RoadField.getPosition(RoadField.java:144)
      at cz.pecinovsky.english.oopnz.town.RingTest.auxMoveRecursive(RingTest.java:144)
      at cz.pecinovsky.english.oopnz.town.RingTest.auxMoveRecursive(RingTest.java:144)
      at cz.pecinovsky.english.oopnz.town.RingTest.auxMoveRecursive(RingTest.java:144)
   ...
```

You can start decoding. The first line indicates what kind of error it is. You have already detected it – a stack overflow. All other lines have the following structure:

at ClassName . MetodName (FileName : LineNumber)

The second line announces that the error appeared in the class fully entitled cz.pecinovsky.english.oopnz.utility.Position, in its constructor (the method <init>) at the place which can be found in the source code of the file Position.java, line 41.

The third line announces that the above mentioned constructor was called from the method getPosition of the Rectangle class (you will supplement the package) and you can find the source code of this calling in the file Rectangle.java, line 195.

778. It shows me a different number.

Probably you are using a little different source code. The number you find in the error message is valid. The line marked by the message witnesses about something what evoked the exception. Of course, it does not mean that the error is just here. The real originator of this state might be an action that happened a long time ago. Therefore, sometimes you have to read also other lines to find the real originator.

Each further line announces from where the method mentioned at the previous line has been called. Thus you can arrive up to the place where the real cause of the error announced in the first line has been born. You can see in the listing that messages are repeating since the fifth line which means that at that place the method called itself. The error of your last program consisted in fact that you did not finish this recursive calling in time.

779.   So how we will solve it?

Let's utilize the fact that the IO class offers a method with a signature (I remind that the signature explanation is presented in the section *Signature versus Contract* on page 112):

```
public static void endIf(boolean end, String message)
```

This method tests the first parameter and if it's true, it opens an information dialog with a message passed in the second parameter. After pressing the **OK** button the application is finished. Therefore in front of the recursive calling you insert the calling of this method, to which you announce that the program should be finished when you return to the initial array.

780.   Well, but where should I take the initial road-field?

You will add it as another parameter of the method. The modified method then shall have the form displayed in the listing 35.2.

Listing 35.2:   *The final version of auxMoveRecursive method in the RingTest class*

```
private void auxMoveRecursive(RoadField field, Mover mover,
                              IMovable movedObject, RoadField endField)
{
    RoadField nextField  = field.getNext();
    Position  position   = nextField.getPosition();
    mover.moveTo(position, movedObject);
    IO.endIf(nextField.equals(endField), "Ring ran around");
    auxMoveRecursive(nextField, mover, movedObject, endField);
}
```

You can see that the method received a road-field in the fourth parameter, where its journey along the ring started. Then it detected the next road-field and moved the light to it. Then it passes the expression

```
        nextField.equals(startField)
```

to the closing method in the fourth line of the body. It is true only when the road-field nextField is equal with the road-field startField; it means only when we run around the whole ring and arrived again to the start. Until these arrays are different, the method makes nothing and only goes over to the fifth line with the recursion calling. The method passes over to itself the array where the light is now located as well as the mover and the moved light. Then, in the fourth parameter, it passes the initial array of the ring, so that the called method would close the whole anabases after reaching it.

781.   I tried it and it really operates. I have to admit that the program looks simple, but I don't understand it fully.

Try to examine it in debugger and have a look through the inspector into the interior of those road-fields with which the method cooperates. Maybe you will more understand to its functions.

782.   I will leave it for the next time. At the beginning you enticed me to a parallel movement of several objects and then you digressed and dealt with a simple recursion which is, however, solving the problem of moving of an only one light. And you also told me that it's not an optimal solution. So why you presented it to me?

I wanted just to show it to you at this simple example and above all to point out its danger. My students – usually by mistake – use the recursive calling (most often they incorrectly copy certain methods and do not register it) and then they are surprised why the stack is overloaded. However, in the solution I prepared for you today you will use the recursion, but the indirect one, which means that the method will not call itself but it will call somebody who will call the method.

Multimover **Class and** IMultimovable **Interface**

783.   Oh, it again reeks of a programming black magic! I suppose that you will again pick up some new servant from your hat.

I see, you know me well. As I have mentioned at the lesson's beginning, a new project will be opened today. At the first sight it looks as a continuation of the previous one, but it differs with one detail: classes in the packages canvasmanager and utility are cleverer and there are several new data types added in them.

In today's lesson we shall deal above all with two new data types: the Multimover class and the IMultimovable interface. The Multimover class offers (among others) two pairs of methods. These methods

```
public void  moveInTime(double seconds, IMovable object, Position position)
public void  moveInTime(double seconds, IMovable object, int xn, int yn)
```

will move the object to the given position in the given number of seconds. Opposite to it, the methods

```
public void  moveWithSpeed(int speed, IMovable object, Position position)
public void  moveWithSpeed(int speed, IMovable object, int xn, int yn)
```

will move the ip object to an entered position with an entered speed which is quoted in a number or traveled points in a second. At the same time the real distance is considered, which means that the movement along the diagonal of the square of 100 represents a distance of 141 points.

Both methods do not wait until they succeed to shift the object, but they return immediately, whilst the addressed multi-mover moves your object somewhere at the background and your program can do something quite different. In case you will call some of the quoted methods once again and you will pass another object to it, both objects will move simultaneously. You can repeat it several times one after another, and at the end the wide range of objects can move at the canvas.

784.   Well, thus I can arrange so that several objects will move simultaneously, but I will be able to send them only to the neighboring array. How you want to arrange so that they would go around the whole ring?

The IMultimovable interface which is a successor of a IMovable interface comes together with the Multimover class and adds its own method moved()to the inherited methods, which serves just to multi-mover. The multi-mover offers one additional function: if the shifted object is not only an instance of IMovable interface, but if it is an instance IMultimovable, then the multi-mover calls its method moved() after completing the movement. The object then can decide in the method what it will make further – e.g. it can be moved once again.

785. **I see. It means that the method calls the mover, and the mover – after shifting the object – calls back the method. Is this the recursion you were speaking about?**

Yes, but there is a tiny difference: the multi-mover knows to plant the recursive calling so that the return address stack would not be filled up. And this is just the bit of magic you were speaking about a moment ago.

But it is important that the method of each of the moved objects will be called in a moment when this object arrives to the aim independently to the state of movement of other objects. Therefore each object moves independently to others.

Ambitions of Objects

786. **It means that we will improve the light so that it would implement the** IMultimovable **method and we could launch several of them at the ring.**

Oh, no, one of the important programming principles is to define the objects purposefully, i.e. so that they would focus to one key task and would not unnecessarily be distracted. The light's purpose is to be fixed in certain object and to be either on or off. The fact that you use its properties to testing the rings does not mean that its range of methods will be extended by methods that would enable to travel along the rings. This traveling in rings does not belong to its main tasks.

787. **My programming friends told me that when I have an object and would like to equip it with certain functionality, the best way how to do it is to define a successor which would be able to function equally as the parent, but will have this added functionality as a bonus.**

Although it is very popular procedure, in this case it is not the suitable one. In case you would now make out a successor of a light, next time you should have to make out also a successor of the arrow and of the car which will also drive along the rings. With each object that would be sometimes added, it would be necessary to make out also a successor that is able to drive along the ring. The classes would be dangerously multiplied. And moreover, very similar methods would be defined in all successors, and it would evoke a dispute with the DRY rule, i.e. with the principle not to repeat items.

788. **Oh yes, I was told something like that. Supposedly if I would not be programming in Java, but in some decent language, I could inherit the needed functionality from another parent.**

Oh, your friends are evidently programming in C++ or Python. Anyway, not the multiplied inheritance will prevent the classes of multiplication. It will prevent you repeating the same code, and even only partially. But as I told you already in the part devoted to inheritance of interface types, the inheritance of classes is very delicate matter and the inheritance of classes with several parents is even more delicate.

Believe me, I was programming in C++ for about 15 years. It is an excellent language with the only disadvantage: the programmer has to be permanently very careful. And due to the fact that majority of programmers cannot be so attentive their productivity compared to Java is only half effective. This was also the reason why I converted to Java 10 years ago. I prefer the language which looks after me and thus I can concentrate to developing the code. But this is a digression, let's return to our topic.

Design Pattern *Decorator*

789.   You stopped that by using the inheritance, the classes would multiply.

You are true. It is far worse with this multiplying the classes, then you can see at the first sight. Each class would have its double. But what would happen when functionality is added – maybe the ability to automatically accommodate to the canvas step (and this is expecting us as well). To have free hands, you would need three successors for each class:

☞   The class whose instances are able only to ride along the ring.

☞   The class, whose instances are able only to accommodate to the size of the canvas step.

☞   The class, the instances of which are adaptable and know to ride along the ring.

With each added functionality the number of needed successors would multiply. Can you imagine how it would increase?

790.   So what's your advice?

Let's choose another procedure, similar to the one which you used with the light. The light is an object envelope of an ellipse, which takes over certain methods (e.g. setting of the position and the size) and adds some others (e.g. switching on and off). You will now do it similarly, but the constructor of this new object will be not creating the light, the constructor will receive it in a parameter, as e.g. the UFO saucer.

This procedure is proposed by the design pattern *Decorator*, which derived its name from the fact that the wrapping object decorates the wrapped object with a new functionality. (Sometimes this design pattern is called *Wrapper*, because it wraps the decorated object.) In our case the decorator decorates its wrapped object with an ability to be shifted by a multi-mover along the rings.

The advantage of this solution is that the decorator is not limited only to decorating the lights, but it can decorate any object that implements the set interface with a new functionality. In our case the interface would be IMovable.

But I don't like to solve it alone. Try to propose, how such a decorating class (let's call it for example Circular, because it will be responsible for driving along the ring) should be defined.

791.   Well, but what would happen when you add another functionality?

Then only a new decorator will be added. You will use either the original object or an object decorated by the first or the second decorator, according to which combination of functionality you will use. In case you will need an object with both added functionalities, you will create an object decorated with the first and the resultant object with the second decorator. The solution is to wrap up one object into the other one and this one to the third one – something like the Russian folklore doll Matrioshka.

You can see the general class diagram at figure 35.1. The arrows leading from decorators to interface types mean that the decorators are willing to accept any instance of the given interface as the wrapped object (the constructor's parameter).

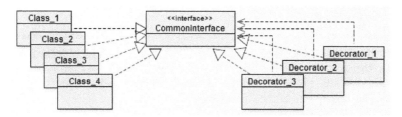

Figure 35.1
The principle of the design pattern Decorator

792. The picture is too general. Could you precise it to our terms?

There are three basic classes implementing the IMovable interface and their functionality should be extended so that they would implement the IMultimovable interface. Let's use the decorator, called Circular for it.

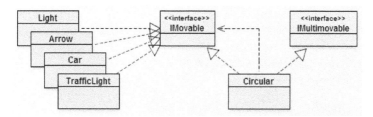

Figure 35.2
The application of the design pattern Decorator in the project

793. From what you told I understand that the resulting decorator object has to implement the IMultimovable interface so that the multi-mover would inform it after arriving to the planned target. Its constructor will have the parameter of IMovable type, in which it receives the decorated object which it wraps and decorates with its additional functionality. It defines the methods of IMovable interface type in such way that it calls the corresponding method of the decorated object in their body, identically as we did with the lights. And the moved() method will be then defined similarly as the auxiliary methods were defined in the test class.

I'm amazed! You estimated it quite precisely. So you can see that it really is not so complicated. Well, the grounds of the circular object are proposed. You know how to create it and how to implement it. And now you could ruminate if some further properties and abilities should be added.

The Circular **Class**

794. How should be added? It already knows everything what's needed, doesn't it?

For example we were not thinking about how to put the circular object at the ring where it should go around. Therefore you should add the methods which will execute it.

Besides that the multi-mover always requires to be informed by which speed the shifted object will move or which time it would take before the object will arrive to its aim. This means that the circular object should be able to set up the speed.

I will not examine you further. Look at the sample solution at the listing 35.3, go through all its methods and check if their definitions are really clear.

Listing 35.3:   *The Circular class*

```
/*******************************************************************************
 * Instances of the {@code Circular} class represent movable object decorators
 * that decorate the wrapped objects with the ability to circulate at rounds.
 * By this circulation the circulated objects don't change their shape
 * together with the direction of their movement.
 */
public class Circular implements IMultimovable
{
    //== CONSTANT CLASS FIELDS ================================================

    /** Default speed of objects moving. */
    private static final int DEFAULT_SPEED = 100;

    /** Manager of the canvas on which the instance will be painted. */
    private static final CanvasManager CM = CanvasManager.getInstance();


    //== CONSTANT INSTANCE FIELDS =============================================

    /** Decorated object that will circulate at a round. */
    private final IMovable decorated;


    //== VARIABLE INSTANCE FIELDS =============================================

    /** The object's current moving speed. */
    private int speed = DEFAULT_SPEED;

    /** The field the object leaved last time. */
    private RoadField field;


    //###########################################################################
    //== CONSTUCTORS AND FACTORY METHODS ======================================

    /*******************************************************************************
     * Creates a new instance decorating the given object.
     *
     * @param decorated Wrapped and decorated object
     */
    public Circular(IMovable decorated)
    {
        this.decorated = decorated;
    }


    //== INSTANCE GETTERS AND SETTERS =========================================

    /*******************************************************************************
     * Returns instance of the class {@code Position} with current position.
     *
     * @return Current position
```

```
 */
@Override
public Position getPosition()
{
    return decorated.getPosition();
}



/*****************************************************************************
 * Sets a new position of the instance.
 *
 * @param position    The set position
 */
@Override
public void setPosition(Position position)
{
    decorated.setPosition(position);
}



/*****************************************************************************
 * Sets a new coordinates of the instance.
 *
 * @param x   The newly set horizontal coordinate,
 *            left canvas border has x=0, coordinate increases to the right
 * @param y   The newly set vertical coordinate,
 *            upper canvas border has y=0, coordinate increases to the down
 */
@Override
public void setPosition(int x, int y)
{
    decorated.setPosition(x, y);
}



/*****************************************************************************
 * Sets the speed for the next moving.
 *
 * @param speed   The set speed
 */
public void setSpeed(int speed)
{
    this.speed = speed;
}



//== OTHER NON-PRIVATE INSTANCE METHODS ===================================

/*****************************************************************************
 * Paints the instance by force of the specified painter.
 *
 * @param painter Painter drawing the instance
 */
@Override
```

```
public void paint(Painter painter)
{
    decorated.paint(painter);
}


/***************************************************************************
 * Sets the decorated object at the given ring
 * and starts to circulate with it.
 *
 * @param ring The ring for circulating
 */
public void goRound(Ring ring)
{
    RoadField start = ring.getStartField();
    continueFrom(start);
}


/***************************************************************************
 * Puts the decorated object at the given field
 * and moves to its successor.
 *
 * @param field The starting field
 */
public void continueFrom(RoadField field)
{
    this.field = field;
    Position position = field.getPosition();
    decorated.setPosition(position);
    CM.add(this);
    moved();
}


/***************************************************************************
 * Method called by multimover in the moment,
 * when it brings the object to the requested target.
 * It starts the moving of the decorated object to the next field.
 */
@Override
public void moved()
{
    field = field.getNext();
    Position position = field.getPosition();
    Multimover m = Multimover.getInstance();
    m.moveWithSpeed(speed, this, position);
}


/***************************************************************************
 * Returns a string representation of the object &ndash; its text signature.
 *
 * @return A string representation of the object
```

```
    */
    @Override
    public String toString()
    {
        return "Circular_(" + decorated.toString() + ")";
    }
}
```

Test Completing

795. Now it would be good to make a handy little test which would verify all.

Good, to make it simpler for you, I suggested the test myself – both methods which are creating the test can be seen in the listing 35.4. The screenshot of the window with the running test you can see at the picture 35.3.

Listing 35.4:   The methods for testing the ring objects in the RingTest class

```
/*****************************************************************************
 * Wraps the given movable object into a circular one,
 * places the resulting circular object at the given field,
 * runs its move and returns a reference to the field after the next.
 *
 * @param field    Road-field, where the wrapped object should be placed
 * @param movable Wrapped movable object
 * @return The descendant of the descendant of the field
 */
private RoadField auxPutOnRing(RoadField field, IMovable movable)
{
    Circular circular = new Circular(movable);
    circular.continueFrom(field);
    return field.getNext().getNext();
}


/*****************************************************************************
 * Puts instances of several movable types on both rings.
 * The put instances will be wrapped into circular objects and will be put
 * in the way that among the running objects will be one empty field.
 * Besides the equidistant instances running with the same speed
 * also one instance with the half speed and one with the double speed
 * will be put.
 */
@Test
public void testMovingGroup()
{
    RoadField field = ringSquare.getStartField();
    int module = field.getModule();

    field = auxIntroduce(field, new Light());
    field = auxIntroduce(field, new Triangle(0,0,50,50));

    field  = ringLShape.getStartField();
    module = field.getModule();
```

```
field = auxIntroduce(field, new Car(0, 0, 50));
field = auxIntroduce(field, new Ellipse(0, 0, 50, 50));
field = auxIntroduce(field, new TrafficLight(0, 0, 50/3));
field = auxIntroduce(field, new Rectangle(0, 0, 50, 50, NamedColor.GOLD));
field = auxIntroduce(field, new Arrow(0, 0, 50));
field = auxIntroduce(field, new Line(0, 0, module, module, NamedColor.WHITE));

//One slow multishape
Multishape m = new Multishape("Triple-shape", new Rectangle(),
                              new Ellipse(), new Triangle());
m.setSize(50);
Circular o = new Circular(m);
o.setSpeed(50);
o.goRound(ringLShape);

///One quick text
o = new Circular(new Text(0, 0, NamedColor.YELLOW, " FLYER"));
o.setSpeed(200);
o.goRound(ringLShape);

IO.inform("When you check it, press OK");
Multimover.getInstance().stopAll();
}
```

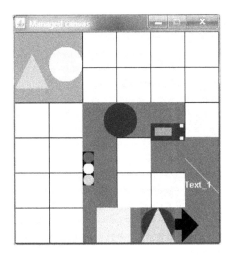

Figure 35.3
The course of the group test

796.   Why didn't you define its own test class for the circular class, but you put its tests into the class RingTest**?**

I do not place the tests according to whom I'm testing but according to in which class the most advantageous test fixture is located. The fixture defined in the RingTest class is optimally suitable for this test and that's why I put the test there.

Exercise

797. What shall I train today?

Your task today will be to examine once more the source codes and try to program your own equivalent data types – for example that you will add the prefix My to their names.

Review

Let's review what you have learned in this lesson:

☞ When the method calls either directly or vicariously itself, then we speak about the recursive calling of methods.

☞ Each method's calling consumes part of the stack's memory.

☞ It is necessary to provide so that the recursive calling would finish at certain time.

☞ The error messages in Java have a standard form as follows:
     at *ClassName* . *MethodName* (*FileName* : *LineNumber*)

☞ The error messages announced during accomplishing the test are displayed by *BlueJ* in the window of test results, the error messages received during current message sending are displayed in the standard error output.

☞ The first line beginning with at announces where the error occurred. Each further line announces from where the method mentioned at the previous line has been called.

☞ One of the most important programming rules is to define the purposive objects, i.e. so that they would focus to only one key task and would not be diverted uselessly.

☞ The design patter *Decorator* advises to add a new functionality to a group of classes so that a new class (decorator) is defined, the instances of which will be responsible for adding this functionality to class instances of the original group. (Decorating of the instance of the original class with a new functionality.)

☞ Constructors of these decorators then receive an object as a parameter, which they wrap and decorate it with a new functionality.

☞ Adding of new functionality brings only a necessity to define a new decorator.

☞ The decorated objects can be folded up one into the other, similarly as the Russian Matrioshka.

☞ Bodies of methods not influenced by the decorator can be defined by only calling the corresponding method of the folded object.

Project:
The resulting form of the project to which you came at the end of the lesson and after completing all exercises is in the 135z_Decorator project.

36 Teaching Cars to Turn

What you will learn in this lesson
Your objects are able to drive along the rings but yet they cannot turn. In this lesson you will read how to
teach the cars properly move in all directions using a method in Direction8 *class. At the same time you*
will become acquainted with blocks and you will learn how to deal with re-drawing a canvas effectively.

Project:
In this lesson you continue in using the 135z_Decorator project.

798. The previous test in which a number of various objects rides along the ring was perfect. Only the cars as well as the arrows should know to turn.

Last time I really strived to show you that thanks to the decorator all can be programmed so, that any movable object can circulate along the rings.

Besides that I wanted to show you why I'm dealing only with the interface inheritance and I'm not going to deal with the class inheritance. If you will learn it too early, you would apply it in cases where it should not occur. That's why I want to present you several solutions, that are possible without any class inheritance, and after we shall speak about it in the next course, you will be far better able to estimate where its usage is really useful.

Reference Area and Relative Coordinates

799. Well, well. Will you show me today how should I arrange so that my cars and arrows would turn along the ring?

I will try it. Again I will dig deep into the hat and I will pull out a surprise from there. If you will look into the documentation of Direction8 class, you will find there an interesting method with a signature, as follows:

    public Area turnInArea(Area inner, Area ref)

By calling this method you are asking the direction to return you the area in which an object should be drawn after some bigger object, whose part the given object is, would turn into the direction which you asked (to which you sent the given method). The turned object is supposed to be originally turned to the east.

800. Oh, if you think that I understood anything from your explanation, then be sure that I didn't understand a word.

I understand that when I told it so generally, it looks rather not understandable. I try to show it at an object – at an arrow at the best, because it is quite simple.

The entire arrow is located in the square area with identical coordinates and identical module as the arrow has. This area is called a **reference** area. And towards it, precisely said towards its upper left corner you will enter the so called **relative coordinates** of individual parts of the arrow (of a body and a head), which could be understand as their offset towards the beginning of the reference area. The real coordinate is then calculated as a sum of the corresponding coordinate of the reference area and the relative coordinate (the offset) of the given part.

Look at the listing 36.1. You will find there the current form of the most general constructor in the design definition of the Arrow class. Please, notice the parameters of the rectangle constructors creating the body as well as the triangle creating the arrow head. You can derive from them relative coordinates of each part towards the entire arrow.

The rectangle relative coordinate representing the arrow body is [0;m3], because it has the same horizontal coordinate as the whole arrow; its vertical coordinate is by m3 larger that the coordinate of the whole arrow. Its horizontal size (width) is a half of the module and its vertical size (height) is one third of the module. The relative area, in which it is located towards the entire arrow, could be received by the following statement:

```
Area relRecBody = new Area(0, m3, m2, m3);
```

In case you would apply similar speculation on the triangle representing the arrow's head, you could realize that the relative area in which the triangle is located could be received by the following statement:

```
Area relRecHead = new Area(m2, 0, m2, module);
```

Is it clear up to here?

Listing 36.1:   *The current form of the most general constructor of the Arrow class*

```
public Arrow(int x, int y, int module, NamedColor color)
    {
        countCreated = countCreated + 1;
        this.ID      = countCreated;

        int m2 = module / 2;
        int m3 = module / 3;

        this.body  = new Rectangle(x,     y+m3, m2, m3,     color);
        this.head  = new Triangle (x+m2, y,     m2, module,color, Direction8.EAST);
        this.color = color;
    }
```

801. I understood that I can get the relative coordinates of the head or of the body, when I subtract the coordinate of the whole arrow from the coordinate of the given part. The sizes of the relative area are the same as the sizes of the corresponding object.

Exactly, the arrow shows to the east and that suits to us because the method I was speaking about, does not need such an initial direction. And now imagine that the whole arrow will be turned for example to the left, i.e. to the north. At that time the area, where the whole arrow is located (the reference area) cannot be changed, but its parts have to be drawn somewhere else and in a different direction – their relative area will change. Its width changes to the height and on the contrary, its height changes to its width. Previously the head had the same vertical coordinate as the entire arrow, now it will have the same horizontal coordinate. Simply a lot of speculations how to modify separate coordinates as well as measures, so that the turned arrow would be drawn properly. And the method I was speaking about can get rid of speculating.

Creating of Objects Turned to Entered Direction

802.   I believe you that you can get me rid of this speculating but still I have no idea how to do it.

I will show you a new form of the arrow's constructor and I will explain you how to arrange so that the constructor would be able to create an arrow turned to the entered direction. Look at the listing 36.2 and let's analyze how it differs compared to the previous listing.

Listing 36.2:   *The new form of the most general constructor in the* Arrow *class*

```
public Arrow(int x, int y, int module, NamedColor color,
                                        Direction8 direction)
{
    Arrow.countCreated = Arrow.countCreated + 1;
    this.ID = countCreated;

    this.xPos      = x;
    this.yPos      = y;
    this.module    = module;
    this.color     = color;
    this.direction = direction;

    int m2 = module / 2;
    int m3 = module / 3;

    Area ref = new Area(x, y, module, module);
    Area part;

    //Body = Rectangle
    part = new Area(0, m3, m2, m3);
    part = direction.turnInArea(ref, part);
    this.body = new Rectangle(part, color);

    //Head = Triangle
    part = new Area(m2, 0, m2, module);
    part = direction.turnInArea(ref, part);
    this.head = new Triangle(part, color, direction);
}
```

803.   Why did you suddenly start to name the field (the attribute) countCreated **as** Arrow.countCreated**?**

Because I wanted to stress that it is a class field. But when you leave the statement in the original form, nothing would happen. There is no substantial change. However, the change comes immediately in the following statements. There are several fields (attributes) added which should be initialized. Before that, the values of coordinates as well as of the module could be detected by an inquiry concerning the arrow's head or body, but now, when the arrow can be turned to any direction, you should laboriously think whom to ask. Which means it's far simpler to remember the coordinates as well as the arrow's module.

You could continue in detecting the direction from the triangle which creates the arrow's head, but according to me, if the fields for other data could be created, then it is possible to create a field also for the direction.

And now I'm coming to the code's core. I created a reference area, i.e. an area, towards which you can quote relative coordinates of particular arrow's part. This area has the coordinates as well as the size of the whole arrow. The reference of the created area has been saved into the variable named ref.

Then I declared the variable part, into which I intend to save the relative areas of particular arrow's parts. I declared it without initialization so that the program of individual parts would be as similar as is possible.

I started with the arrow's body. I created its relative area, about which we were speaking a moment ago. Then I called a method of the direction to which the arrow should be turned and I passed to it the relative area of the body together with the reference area towards which the relative area has been detected. Then the method returned me the absolute area in which the body rectangle should be displayed in the arrow turned to the entered direction. Then I saved this area to the rectangle constructor and I declared the created rectangle to be the arrow's body.

I made the same with the head in the next step. The only difference was in the fact that during creating the triangle I had to enter also the direction to its constructor, to which the created triangle will be turned.

804. **The resulting program looks simply but it's not so simple for understanding. Well, there's an arrow turned to the required direction. But when the arrow will drive along the ring, it needs to turn during driving. How to do it?**

Let's define the method setDirection(Direction8), in the body of which the areas will be re-calculated where the particular parts will be drawn after turning into the required direction. The definition of this method will be immensely simple – you can find it in the listing 36.3. As you see, the method only entered the new direction of turning and all responsibility was "thrown" to the method setModul(int). It utilized the fact that identical re-calculations have to be done in each module's change.

Listing 36.3:   *The method setDirection(Direction8) in the Arrow class*

```
public void setDirection(Direction8 direction)
{
    this.direction = direction;
    this.head.setDirection(direction);
    this.setModule(module);
}
```

I suppose that you are able to make out the definition of the setModul(int) method, which places the particular arrow's parts to their new positions. Don't forget to enter also a new value into the modul field. You can inspire by the constructor's definition. First of all try yourself to suggest it and then compare it with the sample solution in the listing 36.4. I prepared a surprise for you.

Listing 36.4:   *The method* setModul(int) *in the Arrow class*

```
public void setModule(int module)
{
    int x  = getX();
    int y  = getY();
    int m  = module;
    int m2 = m / 2;
    int m3 = m / 3;

    Area ref = new Area(x, y, m, m);
    Area part;

    CM.stopPainting(); {
        //Body - Rectangle
        part = new Area(0, m3, m2, m3);
        part = direction.turnInArea(ref, part);
        this.body.setArea(part);

        //Head - Triangle
        part = new Area(m2, 0, m2, module);
        part = direction.turnInArea(ref, part);
        this.head.setArea(part);
    } CM.returnPainting();
    this.module = module;
}
```

Effective Re-drawing of Modified Objects

805.   Well, I understood that the definition of module's setting differs from the constructor's definition only in the fact that instead of creating new instances only new positions and sizes of their parts are set. I only set the position and the size separately, because I didn't notice that it could be done together. But what you did with this painting?

When the object composed of several parts changes its outlook, for example when the arrow turns, it gradually moves particular parts. If we would let the canvas manager repaint the canvas after moving of each individual part, the changes might look jerky, especially at slower computers.

Therefore the class CanvasManager installs the possibility to stop repainting for a while. You can reach it by calling the method stopPainting(). However, the problem is how to arrange the repeated beginning of the painting in the proper time. You cannot simply ask the canvas to continue painting because you don't know if your complex object is not a part of some more complex object which also asked for stopping the repainting of the canvas. If you, as a part of this more complex object, would say to the canvas, that it can start painting again, because you are completed with your modifications, the canvas might start repainting prior the modifications of other parts of that more complex object, and we could start once more from the beginning.

Therefore the method returning the original state does not have the name paint, but returnPainting(). By calling this method you require the canvas to get back to the state in which it was when you asked for its temporarily stopping. In case you stopped the painting, it starts to repaint. In case you were a part of some more complex form, it starts to repaint only after the repainting is permitted by who stopped it originally.

Block

806.   Well, but I didn't catch why there are the braces and why the statements are indented.

I told you that you are sufficiently advanced so that another programming construction could be introduced. A pair of braces in the code does not bound only the bodies of classes, interface types, methods and of initializing blocks, but you can insert it anywhere into the code. A group of statements closed in braces is then marked as a **block**.

The whole block, i.e. braces including their content is understood by the compiler as an exclusive statement. In certain time we shall speak about programming constructions which require only one statement despite you would prefer having more statements. The braces enable you to put inside a whole number of statements and to pass off such group as an exclusive statement.

807.   It's nice, but I'm afraid that such situation did not happen. You can insert as much statements between two method's callings, as you wish.

I try to solve another problem with the help of a block. Each statement stopPainting() needs to have its playfellow which returns drawing to its original state. The canvas manager can only look after the fact that you stopped drawing fewer times than you asked returning to its original state. But it cannot look after that somebody stopped drawing and forgot returning to switch on.

Therefore I took the compiler for help and I insert braces behind each requirement for stopping the redrawing – I open the block. When I withdraw again the restriction, I close the block before the withdrawing statement. And I write the brace bounding the block at the same line as the restriction or its withdrawal.

As I told you I took the compiler for a help. It takes care so that the number of opening braces will be the same as the closing ones and moreover, they will be formally properly coupled. Then if I would forget to withdraw the restriction of drawing, the compiler would miss one brace and my default would occur as a syntactic fault.

If you want so that your moving pictures would be displayed at the canvas as good as possible and if you would use the possibility to stop redrawing of canvas for the time of modifying the outlook of objects, I would recommend you to use this little tool. And when you keep the convention, that the code will be indented behind each opening brace, your programs will be more reliable and transparent.

To train it, try to define a new form of the setPosition() method for the arrow. Its individual parts have to move gradually there. But fortunately the moving is not as complicated as setting of a new size. It is sufficient to discover at the beginning, by how much the entire object has to move in the horizontal as well as vertical direction and then to move each part of the shape by the given bit. At the conclusion you cannot forget saving of new coordinates into relevant fields. Try it alone and then compare your solution with the designed one, which you can find in the listing 36.5.

Listing 36.5:   *The method* setPosition(int,int) *in the* Arrow *class*

```
public void setPosition(int x, int y)
    {
        int dx = x - getX();
        int dy = y - getY();
        CM.stopPainting(); {
            body .moveRight(dx);
```

```
                body .moveDown  (dy);
                head.moveRight(dx);
                head.moveDown  (dy);
            } CM.returnPainting();
            xPos = x;
            yPos = y;
        }
```

Generally I would recommend you to take always into consideration this construction whenever you will need to insert some statements which compulsorily occur in the couple – to open–to close, to switch on–to switch off etc. Then the compiler can help you not to forget completing its closing playfellow to the initial "opening" statement.

808. Could I shift also the declaration of variables into the block?

Yes, you could. But you have to take into account that these variables will cease existing in the moment when you leave the given block – but I indicated this in the part *The Lifetime* on page 216. I don't use local variables outside the block, which means they might be shifted also inside. But I really get used to leave there really only the subsequence of drawing statements. But if you give them there, it will be quite good.

The IDirectable **Interface**

809. Now the arrow knows to turn and move and I believe that when I'll concentrate a little bit, I should be able to teach it also the car. And now we should teach them to drive along the ring. I suppose that certain decorator will be defined.

Yes, but leave the decorator Circular for its great success in the state in which it is, and let's define a new decorator for objects that know how to turn. However, the precise specification of what are the objects that know to turn is missing. Let's define an interface which announces it and let's name it IDirectable. How would you propose it?

810. I'd say that each object that's shifting and that can set its direction at the same time.

It would be sufficient for smart driving along the ring with those objects. So that it would be really smart, such object should for example fit at the road. It means it should be able to set its size. And when you are able to set certain characteristic you should think over the possibility to determine it as well. In case of the direction, surely yes. Therefore let's define the IDirectable interface as shown in the listing 36.6.

Listing 36.6:   *The IDirectable interface*

```
/*******************************************************************************
 * The {@code IDirectable} instances represent modular instances
 * which are able to turn in the defined direction.
 * These instances are mostly intended for going through the winding roads,
 * however, they may be also stationary instances,
 * which should be turned to a specified direction.
 */
public interface IDirectable extends IModular
{
```

```
    //== DECLARED METHODS =========================================================

    /***************************************************************************
     * Returns the direction to which the instance is turned.
     *
     * @return Direction to which the instance is turned
     */
//    @Override
    public Direction8 getDirection();


    /***************************************************************************
     * Turns the instance to the given direction.
     *
     * @param direction The direction, instance should be turned to
     */
//    @Override
    public void setDirection(Direction8 direction);
}
```

811. Why did you write that it may be also stationary instances? For what it would be when an instance, that doesn't move, can turn?

It is not important if it is able to turn during its life, but so that it could be placed to a canvas (and to a town in future) directed to certain direction. Look at the traffic lights for example. They are defined directed to the north. If they should be located along the ways so that they could simulate controlling the traffic, they should be also defined as directable ones.

Decorator DirectableCircular

812. Oh yes, you are thinking about the next version of the program. I'm glad that I'm handling the current one. Well, we have the interface, **at least the arrow is able to implement. Now only the decorator should be prepared which makes all directable instances moving along the ring.**

Let's call the class of this decorator maybe DirectableCircular. It will be immensely similar to the decorator Circular of the previous lesson. So similar that you may take over the bigger part and copy it. It will be a transgression against the DRY principle, but I would like to postpone the constructions which would enable us to get rid of this copying to the next volume.

813. Well, I created a new class DirectableCircular **and I copied the body of the class** Circular **into it. What should be changed?**

I will start with pettiness.

☞   Add an IDirectable interface into implemented interface types.

☞   Change the type of the field decorated to IDirectable.

☞   Change also the type of the constructor's parameter to IDirectable.

☞   Add the definitions of methods getModule() and setModule(int).

☞   Add the definitions of methods getDirection() and setDirection(Direction8).

Those were more formal modifications. The only one modification that would require at least a bit of thinking is the definition of a new form of the method moved(), which has to turn the shifted object into the direction in which you can get out of just reached canvas field. But I think it is so simple that you could try defining it alone. The sample solution you can find again in the listing 36.7.

Listing 36.7:   *The modified moved() method in the DirectableCircular class*

```
@Override
public void moved()
{
    Direction8 direction = field.getDirection();
    decorated.setDirection(direction);
    field = field.getNext();
    Position position = field.getPosition();
    Multimover m = Multimover.getInstance();
    m.moveWithSpeed(speed, this, position);
}
```

Then I would add one tiny modification: so that you would not take care how big object you will release at the ring, insert the following statement prior adding the instance into the administration of canvas manager in the method continueFrom(RoadField field)

```
decorated.setModule(field.getModule());
```

Thus the decorator will arrange that the objects running along the ring will be automatically as big as they would fit to its canvas fields.

814.   I pondered the direction of the object and I saved the correction. So only a test remains which will show if everything is well programmed.

I prepared an auxiliary method to the TestUtility class (you can find it in the listing 36.8). I named it runRing and it should make it easy to test each of the modified classes. Firstly the method removes all objects of the fixture from the canvas and then, it puts a little quarter ring at a clear canvas and sends a turnable object along it which you will pass to it as a parameter. Then, it is possible to define a simple test method into each of the test classes of our new turnable objects, and this method creates an instance of its test class with the help of the implicit constructor and passes this instance to this auxiliary method.

Listing 36.8:   *The auxiliary test method runRing(IDirectable) in the TestUtility class*

```
public static void runRing(IDirectable object)
{
    CM.removeAll();
    int k = CM.getStep();
    Ring  ring  = Ring.newSquareRing(new Position(k,k));
    //Ring  ring  = Ring.newLShapeRing(new Position(k,k));
    DirectableCircular rotable = new DirectableCircular(object);
    rotable.goRound(ring);

    IO.inform("When you check it, press OK");
    Multimover.getInstance().stopAll();
}
```

Exercise

815.   I estimate that today's exercise will be to make also the cars as well as traffic lights turnable.

Of course – you could not expect anything else.

Review

Let's review what you have learned in this lesson:

☞   Speaking about relative coordinates of an object, it means the size of offset towards some reference point.

☞   Block closes a group of statements to braces and then it acts as one statement towards the surrounding program.

☞   To any place in the code, where the statement could be inserted, also a block could be inserted.

☞   The statements within the block are indented towards surrounding statements.

☞   If you need to provide inserting both statements of a certain pair into the code, you can use connecting the initial statement with the opening block's brace and the closing one with the closing brace. The compiler will look after coupling of braces and thus it guards also coupling of our statements.

☞   Similar constructions are used in our projects to temporary suppression of redrawing of the canvas and its repeated switching on.

Project:
The resulting form of the project to which you came at the end of the lesson and after completing all exercises is in the 136z_Turning_Cars project.

37 Controlling from Keyboard

What you will learn in this lesson
As the name of the lesson indicates, cars will be created which will obey the commands from the keyboard.
And moreover, you will learn how to use a conditional statement and at the same time how to premature-
ly leave the method with the aid of the return statement. You will also learn how to measure the time and,
at the end, you will read the explanation concerning the explicit as well as implicit conversions of primi-
tive type values.

Project:
In this lesson you will continue in using the 136z_Turning_Cars project.

The Controller

816. Last time we taught the cars turning and this time we should taught them listening to commands from a keyboard. Do you have some servants prepared for it?

This is a frequent task and thus there is a servant prepared for it. You will find it in the package manager and its name is Controller. And as a proper servant it declares also an interface which has to be implemented by all who want to be served – the IControllable interface. This interface requires so that the object would implement seven methods which will define reaction to seven keys. (We should not learn general rules for controlling a program from the keyboard and therefore I've prepared a servant allowing to control the served object with a subset of all possible keys.)

817. Seven? Why just this number?

Implicitly there should be the following adjustment:

☞ The first four are cursor keys and they will control the movement.

☞ The fifth and the sixth is a space and ENTER and they control some functions defined by the user, e.g. shooting.

☞ The seventh key is implicitly the ESCAPE key and by pressing it the whole game stops.

However, the Controller class offers also the possibility to define your own set of keys. Various controllers can control committed objects by way of various keys, and you can use it for programming games controlled by several players. A student has programmed a game for four players with one keyboard. There was a little bit lack of place, but it was possible to play the game.

818. **Shall we program controlling our cars? I estimate after previous experience that you will again recommend me to use the decorator.**

And I recommend you to make several of them, each of them with a little bit different control. One can e.g. move your turnable objects directly, with a jump from one canvas field to another one (I would start with this as it is the simplest), another can move them more smoothly or even can enable to change the speed. Not to be pushed to think out a sophisticated name for each of them, you can choose a unified base and differentiate individual versions with the suffix – e.g. Vehicle_A, Vehicle_B etc.

819. **This is a good idea. I also have problems with producing names. So I will try to suggest the simple one which jumps with our car to the neighboring canvas field.**

Not to have it so simple, I advise you to add an adjustable class property speed, which will specify by how much the car will move after pressing the key *forward*. Besides that I would recommend riding a bit forward with it after pressing the key with an arrow up, and turn it by 90° after pressing keys with arrows left and right. You can leave the bodies of remaining methods empty.

As usually, I will ask you firstly to try definitions by yourself. But before you start creating your solutions, look into the documentation of the Direction8 class and above all at its method nextPosition(Position position, int distance). It will suit you for detecting the position to which you should move your car (we used it already when defining the RoadField class).

Similarly the class Direction8 will help you in adjusting a new direction of the turned car. When you send the message leftTurn() to the direction to which the car is turned, you will receive the direction, to which it will be turned after this turn.

You can compare your solution with the sample solution in the listing 37.1. I was of the opinion that testing of this class is so easy that I did not define any special test class, and I did not add any other test to any of the existing classes, but I used the commented method which is prepared at the end of the standard class pattern.

When you would like to test your class, don't forget that the application window has to be active to react to commands from the keyboard. In case your car will not react to the keyboard, check if the window of the canvas manager is really active. (Clicking on it makes it active).

Listing 37.1:   *The Vehicle_A class*

```
/******************************************************************************
 * Instances of the {@code Vehicle_A} class represent movable objects
 * that can be controlled from a keyboard.
 */
public class Vehicle_A implements IControllable
{
    //== CONSTANT CLASS FIELDS =================================================

    /** Manager of the canvas on which the instance will be painted. */
    private static final CanvasManager CM = CanvasManager.getInstance();


    //== VARIABLE CLASS FIELDS =================================================

    /** The movement speed, i.e. how much the object moves after one command. */
    private static int speed = CM.getStep();
```

```
//== CONSTANT INSTANCE FIELDS ================================================

/** The decorated object that will be controlled from a keyboard. */
private final IDirectable decorated;


//###########################################################################
//== CONSTUCTORS AND FACTORY METHODS ========================================

/***************************************************************************
 * Wraps the given directable object and adds an ability
 * to be controlled from a keyboard to it.
 *
 * @param wrapped Decorated object
 */
public Vehicle_A(IDirectable wrapped)
{
    this.decorated = wrapped;
}


//== OTHER NON-PRIVATE INSTANCE METHODS =====================================

/***************************************************************************
 * Reacts to the right arrow key or its equivalent.
 */
@Override
public void right()
{
    Direction8 direction = decorated.getDirection();
    decorated.setDirection(direction.rightTurn());
}


/***************************************************************************
 * Reacts to the left arrow key or its equivalent.
 */
@Override
public void left()
{
    Direction8 direction = decorated.getDirection();
    decorated.setDirection(direction.leftTurn());
}


/***************************************************************************
 * Reacts to the up arrow key or its equivalent.
 */
@Override
public void up()
{
    Position position = decorated.getPosition();
    Direction8  direction  = decorated.getDirection();
```

```
        position = direction.nextPosition(position, speed);
        decorated.setPosition(position);
    }


    @Override public void down()   {}
    @Override public void enter()  {}
    @Override public void space()  {}
    @Override public void escape() {}


    /***************************************************************************
     * Paints the instance by force of the specified painter.
     *
     * @param painter Painter drawing the instance
     */
    @Override
    public void paint(Painter painter)
    {
        decorated.paint(painter);
    }


    /***************************************************************************
     * Returns a string representation of the object &ndash; its text signature.
     *
     * @return A string representation of the object
     */
    @Override
    public String toString()
    {
        return "Vehicle_A_(" + decorated.toString() + ")";
    }


    //== TESTING CLASSES AND METHODS =============================================

    /***************************************************************************
     * Tests, that the instance can react to commands entered from a keyboard.
     */
    public static void test()
    {
        Arrow      arrow      = new Arrow();
        Vehicle_A  va         = new Vehicle_A(arrow);
        Controller controller = new Controller(va);
        IO.inform("After you take a ride, press OK");
        System.exit(0);
    }
}
```

820. **After your delicate clues I really succeeded to make it. But you told that the controller enables playing of the game to several players. How is this arranged?**

You will not create the controller with the help of a constructor, but you will ask the simple factory method – createFor(IControllable) for it. First of all it will ask the user how the keys for individual functions will be used and then it passes the object of its racer to the controller. The controller then will call its methods after pressing keys, entered by the user before.

Preparation of the Race

821. **In case I will drive the arrow or the car only along the canvas, it will be operating. But how I should arrange to drive them along the ring without being able to short the way? Otherwise I cannot run the race.**

In case you would like to prevent the racing cars to shorten the way, you have to add a referee to the race who will (equally as in the life) check if all runs according the regulations. This referee should be able to detect the needed circumstances from the racers.

Therefore you will create a new class named for example Race. The instance of this class will act as an organizer as well as a referee in one object. You will pass the ring to this instance, where the race will take place as well as the racer who will try to drive as quickly as possible along the given ring.

To be able to check if the racer really went through the given ring, the referee will prepare several transit controls. Not to think too much about their arrangement, you can take each road-field as a control and you can require so that the racer would announce reaching each road-field to you. Thus the duty to prove going through each road-field will fell to the racer and the referee can only check if the racer stands in the proper road-field.

822. **Does it mean that the racer will have to announce to the referee that he reached the following road-field?**

Exactly. Let's equip the referee with a method, called for example checkpoint and the racer will call it each time when he would like to announce reaching another road-field.

823. **I understand how you mean it but I'm not sure how the racer will announce that he reached the required position when we didn't tell him which position he should reach. This is known only to the person who manages the racer, because only this person can see the racing circuit drawn at the canvas.**

Not to force the user or the racing object to think whether he reached the road-field or not, you can simply program a moving method so that it would call the checkpoint method each time when the racer moves a bit with its car – for object of Vehicle_A type it would be after each pressing the key with arrows up. The transit control would verify if the racer's position corresponds with the road-field's one which should be reached. In case it would correspond, the race would remember that next time the racer has to reach the following road-field and that the race would check reaching the next road-field.

824. **And if the racer's position would not comply?**

You mean when the racer would rush over and drove out of the circuit, or on the contrary, would like to shorten the circuit. Then the race would wait until the racer would arrive to the proper road-field. Only after that it would be willing to present internally the following consecutive aim and expect it at the next road-field.

Conditional Statement – the `if` Statement

825.   Everything is understandable, but I don't know how to program this "if".

Majority of languages have defined a special programming construction called a **conditional state-ment**. Often it is named according to the characteristic keyword the `if` **statement**. This statement serves for programming the decision making.

The conditional statement in Java has two forms. The **simple conditional statement**[8] solves a situation when certain action should be carried out only when a certain condition is fulfilled. In case you would like to use it, you will write the keyword `if` in the program followed by a condition in round brackets, which should be fulfilled, so that the statement quoted after the brackets with the condition is written. This statement is called the **body of the conditional statement**. The syntax of a simple conditional expression can be written as follows:

> **if** (*<condition>*) *<statement>*

As you see, there is the keyword `if`, followed by a condition in parentheses and the statement itself after the brackets that should be executed if the condition is fulfilled.

826.   And what about when I need to do something only when the condition is not fulfilled?

Then you will use a negation of the given condition. We were speaking about it, as well as about further operations which you can use for defining of more complex conditions, in the section *A Bit of Logic* on page 251. The condition can be arbitrarily complex as you wish.

827.   And what about when I need to do more things than only one statement?

Then you will use what we were speaking about last time. You will put all these statements to braces and then this block acts in the program as one statement. However, the contemporary trends in programming prefer using a block any time, i.e. also in cases when a simple statement appears in a block.

828.   Could you give me an example?

Of course, I told you that the racer has to announce to the race going through particular control points. This means you could define the method `checkpoint(IRacer)` in the `Race` class and by calling it, the racer (the object, not the user) would ask the race for checking if the racer is at a proper place. The race will receive a racer in a parameter and asks it for its current position. The racer will return it and the race will compare it with the required position. If both positions match, the race will prepare the next position for the racer. The simple version of this method is shown in the listing 37.2.

As you can estimate from its source code, the race remembers the road-field which the racer should achieve in the field `finish`. When it discovers the racer reached this road-field, it replaces the road-field with the following road-field and next time it will check if the racer will reach this successor.

---

[8]   Java Language Specification calls it *if-then statement*.

Listing 37.2:   *The first version of the checkpoint(IRacer) method in the Race class*

```
public void checkpoint(IRacer racer)
{
    Position racerPosition  = racer .getPosition();
    Position targetPosition = target.getPosition();
    if (racerPosition.equals(targetPosition)) {
        target = target.getNext();
    }
}
```

Using a Block

829.   I understand and I noticed that you followed your own advice to use a block despite there is only one statement in it. Why?

Because quite often you need to change the program and add another statement to this present sole statement. Mostly you don't realize that the body contains a sole statement and therefore it is not closed in a block braces and you simply write the added statement after it. Mostly you indent it to keep the graphic layout but after that you forget to close both statements to braces. Then the computer accomplishes the first statement only if the entered condition will be fulfilled, and the second statement will be carried out in each case.

It is evident, that the program operates in a different way than is supposed. Usually the programmer starts to check the source code. He finds the indented statement and assumes that it is in a common block of statements with the previous one. The programmer does not realize that the compiler cannot react to indentation, because it needs to have both statements closed in a joint block – and in this case they are not closed together.

The situation I have described is so typical that modern development environment enables you to enter checking if all bodies will always be composed of a block, even when only one statement will be present in this block.

830.   Can you have a block with no statement in it?

Yes, you can, but it is used only in case when due to certain reason you decide to comment the statements contained in it for a while. Using it is not recommended.

The IRacer Interface

831.   In the listing 37.2 you defined a method with the parameter of IRacer type and you did not mention what will this interface (at least I assume according to the initial I that it is the interface) require from implementing classes.

It is simple – I still don't know what it will require. Surely you will think out why the future racers should be equipped with certain method. And furthermore, there should be the possibility that the object could proclaim itself a racer. Therefore I would define them as the interface that is a successor of the interface types IDirectable and IControllable, because in advance it is obvious that each racer has to have such qualities.

For the time being it occurred to me only that each racer should be able to register at the race. Do you have any other idea?

832.   Maybe that in case there will be several racers, each of them should have its own name, so that we could be able to differentiate them.

It's a good idea. Let's add the methods getName() and setName(String) to requirements. If you would remember another method in course of time which you would require from all racers, you should supplement its declaration into the interface. The current definition of this interface you can find in the listing 37.3.

Listing 37.3:   *The IRacer interface*

```
/*****************************************************************************
 * Instances of the {@code IRacer} interface represents racers,
 * which register themselves at races and compete in them.
 */
public interface IRacer extends IDirectable, IControllable
{
    //== DECLARED METHODS ======================================================

    /*************************************************************************
     * Returns the instance name.
     *
     * @return   Instance name
     */
//    @Override
    public String getName();


    /*************************************************************************
     * Sets new instance name.
     *
     * @param name   New instance name
     */
//    @Override
    public void setName(String name);


    /*************************************************************************
     * Registers the racer at the given race.
     * The racer then should report the reached positions to this race.
     *
     * @param race Race, where the racer registers
     */
//    @Override
    public void registerFor(Race race);
}
```

Premature return

**833.	How the method can recognize that a registered racer is reporting his positions and not a cheater passing off as a racer?**

The race remembers who is registered. The method compares the reference to the racer received in the parameter with the reference remembered from the registration. If the instances are different, the race will not take into account this calling.

It can be programmed by two ways. The first possibility is to make out one big conditional statement into the body of which the whole original body of the method would belong. This body will be executed only in case when the racer will be equal to the registered one.

The second possibility is to turn the condition from the beginning and ask on the contrary, i.e. to ask if the racer received in the parameter is different than those who have been registered. If this turned condition is fulfilled, I will not try to verify anything and I will directly leave the method's body.

To leave prematurely the method's body you should use the return statement, which you met only at methods returning the value. You used it only at the end of methods. However, you can use it whenever in the body of the method, but then you have to provide that no statement will follow – it would not be carried out.

**834.	If there will be nothing after it, so it will be at the end.**

Not exactly – the return statement can be also the last statement in the block which creates the body of the conditional command. And when this body is executed, the command return is carried out at the conclusion and completes accomplishing of the method. Unless the program would step into the body of the if statement and skips it over, then the statements that follow after this block can be carried out.

**835.	You told that I met the return statement only with methods that return the value. Does it mean that I can use it also with methods that return nothing?**

Yes, it is just used for the premature leaving of their body. And with these methods you write only the keyword return into the program, followed by a semicolon completing the statement. In the new version of the transit control I chose this second version, because I consider it as more transparent – you can see it in the listing 37.4, just at the beginning.

**836.	What is the strange arrow there?**

The calling of return statement in the middle of the body is a nonstandard continuation. Therefore I add a comment in my programs with ten equation marks followed by a "greater than" mark to see at the first sight where it is possible to leave the method prematurely.

Embedded Conditional Statement

837. **The way, as it was programmed until now, means the racers can drive round and round and would never recognize that they reached the finish. How it should be arranged that reaching the finish, the racer (the user) would for example stop and could see how much time the way took to him/her?**

Let's start with the first half, i.e. how to arrange that reaching the finish the racer would stop and could not continue further. You need to detect if – after the racer reaches the advancing checkpoint – this checkpoint is at the same time the finish of the whole race. Therefore you insert another test into your current test. If the reached field is at the same time the finish of the whole race, you can make the necessary arrangements. The modified source code is in the listing 37.4.

Listing 37.4:   *The second version of* checkpoint(IRacer) *method in the Race class*

```
public void checkpoint(IRacer racer)
{
    //Check, if it is the same racer - therefore the operator !=
    if (this.racer != racer) {
        return;                          //==========>
    }
    Position racerPosition  = racer .getPosition();
    Position targetPosition = target.getPosition();
    if (racerPosition.equals(targetPosition)) {
        if (target.equals(start)) {
            finishRace(racer);
            return;                      //==========>
        }
        target = target.getNext();
    }
}
```

838. **You told that I should compare the objects through the method** equals(Object) **and suddenly you compare it with an operator** !=**. Why?**

I don't compare the values of objects, but the fact if it is an instance which was registered. Therefore I ask if it is the same instance regardless to which value it might have. In this case you would receive the same result, but in other cases you could receive a different one. Therefore you have to differentiate when an identity of instances is detected and when it is an equality of their values.

839. **Is it a problem when another conditional statement is in the body of the conditional statement?**

The conditional statement is a statement as any other one. Therefore you can insert it into the body of another conditional statement. And I can tell you that you can meet it quite often.

840. **When reaching the starting road-field you call the method** finishRace**, which was not yet defined.**

I try to keep the principle, about which I was already speaking, that each entity has to be focused on a single matter. (I like the expression that each entity has to be goal-directed, as I already mentioned.) To provide the termination of the race does not belong to the responsibility of the transit control – it has only to recognize, when the end comes. How to handle with the end is left for a specialized method.

A lesson for you: don't be afraid to define a new method, although you know that you will use it only once in the surrounding code. Take it as that the most important criterion of well-designed program is its transparency. In case you feel that installation of certain construction might make the program more transparent, do it.

Time Measurement

841. Oh, again you are giving general instructions and you forgot to answer the second part of the question. You didn't tell me how to arrange so that the racer would recognize the time spent for driving along the ring.

Well, I forgot. The time can be measured in a lot of ways. I will show you the simplest one. By calling the method

```
System.currentTimeMillis()
```

you get a number of a long type, which contains the system time and which means a number of milliseconds passed from the midnight starting on January 1st, 1970. When you remember the time of the race start and you measure it again at the finish of the race and you subtract both values, you receive the number of milliseconds spent by the racer during driving the ring.

When you would like to use more precise measurements, I would like to warn you that the millisecond accuracy of time is only fictitious. Contemporary processors are able to carry out a million of operations during one millisecond, however, a number of operating systems does not keep such precision and provides data concerning the time with roughly 10 ms plus/minus.

842. It will be sufficient to measure the time of our race in tenths of a second. Which means will I get the time of the race by inquiring the system time before the race and after the race and subtracting both numbers?

Well, but once more I remind that for the system time you have to prepare a variable of long type. As soon as you subtract both times you can return to the variable of int type – more than two billion milliseconds can get in it, which is slightly more than three weeks. And you surely will not hold the race so long. But you have to keep on your mind that the compiler automatically converts only smaller types to bigger ones. Transfer from long to int is from the bigger to the smaller and therefore you have to do it explicitly using the casting operator. The part of the code dealing with the time then might look as follows:

```
long now = System.currentTimeMillis();

this.controller.stop();
this.racer = null;
int time    = (int)(now - time0 + 50) / 100;
System.out.println("\n\nThe racer " + racer.getName() +
        " ran the race in time " + time/10 + "," + time%10 + " second");
```

843. Could you explain me the last line?

In the last but one statement I divided the number of milliseconds by one hundred to get the number of second's tenth. Due to the fact that the integer's division does not round, but only cuts the decimal fraction, I add fifty to the measured time. Thus I received the rounded number of second's tenths. Remember this way of rounding (i.e. to add a divisor's half to a dividend), it's useful.

In the last statement I firstly divide the received time by ten and thus I get the number of seconds. Then I put the decimal point followed by the remainder of dividing by ten, i.e. the number of second's tenths.

Automatic and Explicit Casting

844. I would like to get back to the conversion from long numbers to the ordinary ones. When you were speaking about casting in the section *The Cast Operator* (Type) on page 252, you did not mention any automatic casting from smaller to bigger.

You are true. The best time to do it now. Java distinguishes two types of casting:

☞ An **implicit casting**, which can be realized by the compiler without your requirement, but which can be used only in several particular situations:

  ☞ At object types the compiler is willing to cast a child to its parent. And the implemented interface is considered as a parent of those classes which implement this interface (as presented in the section *Three Types of Inheriting* on page 110). Therefore it is used e.g. for the following statement:

    IMovable im = new Ellipse();

  ☞ At primitive types the compiler implicitly casts in the direction of arrows at the figure 37.1. In case of primitive types we are not speaking about casting, but about a conversion, because the change of type is connected with the change of an internal representation of the given value.

☞ An **explicit casting** (or conversion), which you enter through the cast operator. You have to choose it in situations, when the automatic casting cannot be used.

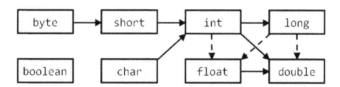

Figure 37.1
An implicit conversion of primitive type values

845. Why some arrows are dashed at the figure?

Because these conversions can be connected with losing of precision. When you have a look at the overview of primitive types in the section *Primitive and Object Types* on page 35, you can see, that the numbers of int type can acquire the value about ± 2 billion (±2.10⁹), and the biggest of them can have up to 10 valid figures. But despite the float type keeps far bigger numbers, it keeps them with the precision only to 6 figures. Therefore during the conversion from int type to float type you can lose several significant figures. It is analogous with the other "dashed conversions".

Finishing the Race Class

846. Let's return to the race. I can control the racer during the race and I can finish the race. Can I start racing?

The constructor is not yet defined, nor the racer's registration. The constructor is quite simple – there will be an only parameter: the ring where the race is running. You only have to remember to initialize the fields used in the above defined methods. The resulting form of the Race class you will find in the listing 37.5.

Again I completed the class with a simple test which verifies if the race is able to cooperate with the racer that is an instance of the Vehicle_B class, and your task is to define this class.

Listing 37.5:   *The class Race*

```
/*******************************************************************************
 * Instances of the {@code Race} class represent races that can be attended.
 * The race is characterized by the ring where the vehicles run.
 * The racers can subsequently register at the race.
 * The next racer can register only after the previous one finished the race.
 */
public class Race
    {
    //== CONSTANT CLASS FIELDS =================================================

    /** Manager of the canvas on which the instance will be painted. */
    private static final CanvasManager CM = CanvasManager.getInstance();


    //== CONSTANT INSTANCE FIELDS ==============================================

    /** Ring, where the race takes place. */
    private final Ring ring;

    /** Road-field, which the racer starts from. */
    private final RoadField start;


    //== VARIABLE INSTANCE FIELDS ==============================================

    /** The checked racer that tries to run through the ring
     *  as quickly as possible. */
    private IRacer racer;

    /** Controller, mediating control from a keyboard. */
    private Controller controller;

    /** Next field, which the racer should reach
     *  and reaching of which will be checked. */
    private RoadField target;

    /** System time of the start. */
    private long time0;
```

```
//############################################################################
//== CONSTUCTORS AND FACTORY METHODS =========================================

/****************************************************************************
 * Creates an instance that will be able to organize race at the given ring.
 *
 * @param ring Ring, where the race should be organized
 */
public Race(Ring ring)
{
    this.ring    = ring;
    this.start   = ring.getStartField();
}



//== OTHER NON-PRIVATE INSTANCE METHODS ======================================

/****************************************************************************
 * Registers the given racer, places it at the race start
 * and registers it as a keyboard listener.
 *
 * @param racer Registering racer
 */
public void register(IRacer racer)
{
    if (this.racer != null) {
        IO.inform("At this race the racer\n" + this.racer +
                  "is already registered.\n" +
                  "You have to wait with your registration" +
                  "until this racer run to the finish.");
        return;                              //==========>
    }
    Position   position  = start.getPosition();
    int        module    = start.getModule();
    Direction8 direction = start.getDirection();

    racer.setPosition(position);
    racer.setModule(module);
    racer.setDirection(direction);

    this.controller = new Controller(racer);
    this.target     = start.getNext();
    this.racer      = racer;
    this.time0      = System.currentTimeMillis();

    //Ensure, that both, racer as well as its ring, will be visible
    CM.add(ring);
    CM.addAbove(ring, racer);
}


/****************************************************************************
 * Checks that the racer reaches the correct running position (checkpoint).
 * If yes, prepare the next running position, if no, do nothing.
```

```
     *
     * @param racer Racer announcing reaching the next position
     */
    public void checkpoint(IRacer racer)
    {
        //Check, if it is the same racer - therefore the operator !=
        if (this.racer != racer) {
            return;                              //==========>
        }
        Position racerPosition  = racer .getPosition();
        Position targetPosition = target.getPosition();
        if (racerPosition.equals(targetPosition)) {
            if (target.equals(start)) {
                finishRace(racer);
                return;                          //==========>
            }
            target = target.getNext();
        }
    }


    /*****************************************************************************
     * Returns a string representation of the object &ndash; its text signature.
     *
     * @return A string representation of the object
     */
    @Override
    public String toString()
    {
        return "Race_(ring=" + ring + ", racer=" + racer + ")";
    }


    //== PRIVATE AND AUXILIARY INSTANCE METHODS ==================================

    /*****************************************************************************
     * Finishes the race for the given racer.
     *
     * @param racer Racer finishing the race
     */
    private void finishRace(IRacer racer)
    {
        //Check, if it is the same racer - therefore the operator !=
        if (this.racer != racer) {
            return;                              //==========>
        }
        long now = System.currentTimeMillis();
        this.controller.stop();
        this.racer = null;
        int time = (int)(now - time0 + 50) / 100;
        System.out.println("\n\nThe racer " + racer.getName() +
                " ran the race in time " + time/10 + "," + time%10 + " second");
    }
```

```
//== TESTING CLASSES AND METHODS ============================================

/***************************************************************************
 * The test method.
 */
public static void test()
{
    Arrow  arrow = new Arrow(0, 0, NamedColor.WHITE);
    Vehicle_B vb = new Vehicle_B(arrow);

    //The racing ring can be selected by uncommenting appropriate line(s)
    Race  race = new Race(
//                    Ring.newLShapeRing(new Position(0,0),
//                                       NamedColor.BROWN));
                    Ring.newSquareRing(new Position(50,50)));
    vb.setName("Racer");
    vb.registerFor(race);
    }
}
```

847.   I did not understand why you tested the field for null **in the** register(IRacer) **method.**

I wanted to ensure that no other racer (the object) can be registered until the previous one would finish its race. Until now we define our race so that only one racer can compete in the given moment. As soon as the racer is registered, it can immediately go at the ring and its time is measured. When it finishes, the field is adjusted back again to null, and another racer can register.

I used the fact that the newly created object has an empty reference – the value null in all not initialized fields of object type. Until this value is in the field racer, no one is registered. As soon as someone is registered, the reference just to the registered racer is entered into the field. When the racer finishes the race, again null is entered into the field and thus the previous state is returned when anybody else can register (or just the same).

Exercise

848.   It means my task is to create a car which would be able to run the race, i.e. to implement the IRacer **interface.**

You are true, but a bit of complications: The instance of Vehicle_A class defined last time could run out of the canvas borders. This will be not allowed to instances of Vehicle_B classes, which you will define. Because you already know the conditional statement, you should be able to set its acting so that in case of statements from the keyboard it should leave the canvas area; it will stop and will not move. And supplement the ability of moving backwards as a reaction to pressing the arrow down, so that the hot-headed racers could get back to the track.

Review

Let's review what you have learned in this lesson:

☞ For programming an action which has to be carried out only under certain condition you should use a *conditional statement*, which is often called the *if statement*.

☞ The syntax of a simple conditional statement is as follows

```
if ( <condition> ) <statement>
```

☞ The condition can be created by any complex logic expression.

☞ In case it is necessary to make more statements under the condition, all of them are closed into a *block* which then acts as a sole statement and which will be executed only after fulfilling the entered condition.

☞ The block does not have to contain any statement, but this possibility is mostly not used.

☞ The best practice suggests closing even a single statement into the block. Thus we lower the probability of errors by future modifications.

☞ The conditional statement is a statement as any other one. Therefore you can put it into the body of another conditional statement.

☞ For premature finishing of the method's running you can use the return statement.

☞ In methods that return nothing you will write no expressions after the keyword return; only the closing semicolon.

☞ Immediately after the return statement no other statement can follow because it would never be executed.

☞ The premature leaving of the method is a nonstandard continuation which should be highlighted in the code – for example by a characteristic comment.

☞ Each method should concentrate at one point. If further duties are part of its activity, it is suitable to define separate methods for them, which the given method would only call.

☞ The current system time can be determined by calling the method System.currentTimeMillis(), which will return the value of long type. This value represents the number of milliseconds passed from the midnight of January 1st, 1970.

☞ The time is quoted in milliseconds, but mostly its precision is of lower-order.

☞ The empty reference null, which is an initial value of non-initialized fields, can be used for a test if the field was already initialized.

Project:
The resulting form of the project to which you came at the end of the lesson and after completing all exercises is in the 137z_KBD_Control project.

38 Containers and Maps

What you will learn in this lesson
In this lesson you will become acquainted with containers – objects for saving other objects. First of all you will see maps and you will read how they can be used for arranging the race in which several racers simultaneously compete.

Project:
In this lesson you continue in using the 137z_KBD_Control project.

Containers and a Library of Collections

849. When you explained me how to arrange so that the objects would be controlled from the keyboard, you told me that several racers could participate. Last time the program has been created in which individual racers were competing step by step. How should I modify the program so that several racers could compete simultaneously?

There are several possibilities. One of them is that you would use special objects, named **containers**. The containers are objects that are determined for saving other objects. You have already met one of them, do you remember?

850. An object for saving other objects? I have no idea.

I will give you a clue: until now you saved mostly only values of primitive types in it. What? No idea? It's a crate! This was an object which did not serve for nothing else than to put values which you wanted to save or transport into it.

Generally there are containers of two types: static and dynamic ones. They are differentiated according to how they are able to change their size during their life course, i.e. the space to which they save the objects.

☞ The **static containers** are born with a definitive size and will not change it through their life. This limitation is balanced with high effectiveness. The crate belongs to the static containers, because already in the definition of its class it was clear for how many elements the space will be prepared. Further you will meet also an array.

☞ Opposite to it the **dynamic containers** can change their size within their life (can does not mean they have to). Mostly they are born empty and only within their life they increase their "volume". Objects can be inserted into them and removed again during their life. Nevertheless, sometimes it is useful to "freeze" the dynamic container and thus forbid to add or extract anything from it. You will see it further.

In times of my programming beginning mostly the static containers were used and the dynamic ones appeared in programs rather exceptionally. At present the situation is vice versa and the dynamic containers prevail. The standard Java library offers a wide range of dynamic containers which vary with their properties and suitability of using in particular situations. Due to the fact that all of them implement the `java.util.Collection` interface or cooperate with it intensively, the library is usually named a **collection library** or **collection class library** (despite it includes also interfaces).

Classes and interfaces of this library are located in the package `java.util`. All collections of this library have one common: they are willing to save only values of object type. Fortunately it does not matter, because each primitive type has its own **wrapping type**, which wraps its value into an object. In a number of cases it will be done by the compiler, but it's good to know it. I would skip over the details, as they are not necessary at present.

Dictionaries and Maps

851.   I see that you are again digressing to the theory. Which of the collections I could use for my program?

For your purpose the map would be suitable. It does not belong to pure collections, but it is a part of the collection library. The map is not limited to only saving objects, but it offers also an effective way, how to find quickly the saved object.

The elements are saved to a map in pairs. The first item is called a **key** and according to it you can find the saved **value**, which is the second element of the pair. The map then could be proclaimed as a collection of key/value pairs, in which the *key* serves for quick identification of the given pair and the *value* contains the saved data.

852.   Why is it called a map?

Because it maps the key for the value, i.e. it connects the key with the value. Any of the saved values can be received simply by saying the key to the map under which the required value is saved and the map returns the saved value.

853.   I admit I hear the word "mapping" for the first time. What should I imagine by it?

The term *mapping* is taken over from mathematics and it is understood by the programmers as assigning. You can meet also the term "mapping of discs" which means assigning of individual items of network discs to items in your computer. And a value is assigned to the key in the container named a map.

In some other libraries this data structure is also marked as *a dictionary* – there are also data in the key/value pairs saved in it. The key represents a known word in the initial language, and its translation is a value. You enter the key here (the original) and the dictionary will find you its value – the translation.

854.   And now please explain me why just the map would suit to me.

You surely remember from the previous lesson that there were several data concerning the racer and the course of this race. (I remind that in our current discussion the racer is an object.) Go through them once again and remind what you should have on your mind to be able to program a reasonable simulation of a race.

855. We had to know the ring along which the racer was going; to check if it was really our object and nothing else; to which road-field it should have arrived. We also remembered its controller unit to be able to disconnect it from the keyboard at the end.

You have to keep such information about each racer. When the racer is coming to the checkpoint, you have to pull out its data and verify if it is going properly and when you can expect it at next time.

And there is just the map for it. The racer is the key and the whole saved information is the saved value. Whenever the racer reports at the control we pull out all necessary values from the map and we check it.

Member Classes

856. I am somehow confused by your jumping between the singular and the plural. Just now you've told that the map is in fact a collection of pairs (a key; a value). Then you started to speak about values which I have to remember concerning the racer. Does it mean that several values can be saved to one key?

Not in the ordinary map and there is no other than just the ordinary map in the standard library. But it does not matter, because you can use the same procedure as you used when you needed so that the method would return several values – let's define a crate for these values.

But there is a little problem: in case you would like to keep the principle of concealing the implementation, you should define the crate so that nobody else would know about it. The crate is really needed only for the race to save the necessary information into the map.

Let's use one special possibility. In Java the data types can have three sorts of members:

☞ Data members – the fields (attributes).

☞ Functional members – the methods.

☞ Type members – the member data types.

For type elements the same characteristic is valid as for the remaining two. Among other things they can be declared as private, which means nobody outside will know about them.

Member data types are a special case of the **nested types** that include also the types, which are not members, because they are defined inside blocks.

And when I am speaking about the terminology, I add also that the data type, in the body of which the given nested type is defined, is called the **outer type** of the given nested data type.

857. So you want to define the crate for needed values as a member class?

Exactly, to be precise, I would like to define it as a static class. Also the internal data types can be defined as static or instance. The static ones will be called **embedded**, the instance are called **inner**.

Whenever you don't need so that the instances of member data type would know to which instance of its outer type they belong, you should define the member data type as a static one (embedded). The non-static nested (inner) data types may be only classes (the instances of the non-static member classes need to remember a reference to their outer class instance and certain implementation is needed for it). The work with inner classes is a little bit more complicated, and that's why I will not speak about it in this volume.

858.   When you say embedded, so I accept it. But tell me, how such an embedded member class is defined.

In the same way as the normal one. The only difference is that you define it inside another class, similarly as if you would define fields or methods in it.

But it's good to define all member types regularly at certain place, known beforehand. Equally, as we used to define fields at the beginning of the code (and the static before the instance ones and constants before the variables), the member data types will be defined at the end. When you have a look at the definition created according to the standard class pattern, you can find as the last but one the section, introduced by the comment MEMBER DATA TYPES. Put your private crate just at this place.

Let's agree that for the race enabling parallel running of several racers a new class will be defined to compare the today's solution with the previous one. Let's call the class RaceLShape. The name expresses that the class will provide the race only at the *L-shape* ring in this lesson. You can try to program wider range of rings in some next lesson.

But let's get back to the embedded class. If a private embedded (i.e. static member) crate called Info would be defined in the newly created standard class, the class definition would be as in the following listing 38.1.

Listing 38.1:   *The semi-finished class* RaceLShape *with the defined internal crate* Info

```
/********************************************************************
 * Instances of the {@code RaceLShape} class represents races that can be run.
 * All such races are taken at an L-shape ring, which means a ring created
 * by the {@link Ring#newLShapeRing(Position, NamedColor)} method.
 * Several racers can be registered at one race and all will be run
 * simultaneously, each at its own instance of the ring.
 */
public class RaceLShape implements IRace
{
    //== CONSTANT CLASS FIELDS ===========================================

    // ...Not used sections omited


    //== MEMBER DATA TYPES ===============================================

    /********************************************************************
     * Internal crate containing the basic needed information
     * about racer and its current state.
     */
    private static class Info
    {
        /** Ring, where the race takes place. */
        private final Ring ring;

        /** The starting field and thus also the finish field. */
        private final RoadField startField;

        /** The next running target.  */
        private RoadField targetField;

        /** Controller, mediating control from a keyboard. */
        private final Controller controller;
```

```
/**************************************************************************
 * Define a new crate and initialize its fields.
 *
 * @param ring          Ring, where the race takes place
 * @param startField    The starting field and thus also the finish field
 * @param targetField   The first checkpoint
 * @param controller    Controller, mediating control from a keyboard
 * @param roundsNumber  Number of rounds
 */
Info(Ring ring, RoadField startField, RoadField targetField,
     Controller controller)
{
    this.ring        = ring;
    this.startField  = startField;
    this.targetField = targetField;
    this.controller  = controller;
}

}


//== TESTING CLASSES AND METHODS ===================================================

// ... Remaining, not shown, code
}
```

859. You forgot to state that the field targetField **is a constant.**

No, I didn't. The target is moving by one road-field after each arrival. I broke the principles of creating the crate by this, but due to the fact that this crate will be a private one, it is not a big fault. Generally, rather milder demands are placed on private internal classes. They can be watched more easily and their internal classes as well as their instances are handled more correctly.

860. Then you told that the crate's fields are defined as public so that they could be used without accessory methods. In this case, they are private; but the class doesn't have any accessory methods. How to approach to them?

The field private only excludes the access to certain elements for all who are out of the outer class body. However, inside it there is no difference between the "private and more private". There is only one level of privacy within the whole class. It means that if you define another class within the class and you install private elements in it, these elements are visible also from the outer class.

861. I see that the internal class can be decorated with modifiers which I met until now at only fields and methods. Does it have other special properties?

I present you two of them but they result from what you already know. I've already spoken about the first one, so only reminder. You can make the internal class invisible with a field private and only other elements of its outer class will know about it and its elements. Thus, you can hide that the class needs certain auxiliary class for fulfilling its tasks.

The second specialty is also connected with visibility. Due to the fact that the internal class is inside the body of its outer class, it has an access to private fields and methods of its outer class similarly as all that are defined within its body. This is usually a frequent reason why the internal classes are defined. But I would like to finish it and get back to the race.

The Map<K,V> Interface and the HashMap<K,V> Class

862.   Well, so the crate is ready and now the map could be declared and you could show me how to put everything into it and how to pull it out again.

There are several little surprises waiting for you. First of all I will present the declaration and then I will explain individual divergences from what you already know. If the map will be called racer2info, its declaration connected with the immediate initialization would look out as follows:

```
Map<IRacer, Info> racer2info = new HashMap<>();
```

863.   I see that you use a SMS-shortcut in identifier.

Yes, I accustomed to name all maps according its keys and values. Because this map maps racers to appropriate info, I named it racer2info.

Generic Types and Type Parameters

864.   What are the increasing and decreasing characters doing there?

This is the first divergence. As I said already, containers serve for saving the objects. But the objects can be of various types. It would be suitable, if you could somehow specify which objects belong to the container and which not.

Until Java 5.0 it was not possible to specify what belongs into the container so that the compiler could check it. Java 5.0 brings an innovation – the **generic types** which means the data types certain properties of which can be specified at the last moment, when the variable of the given type is declared.

The **type parameters** are quoted after the generic type name in angle brackets. In case of containers they specify, what is the type of objects saved in the container.

865.   Why these types are called generic?

The word *generic* means general, generally used. It means that generic types are the types that are not specialized for work with certain particular data types. They are defined generally, and the data type with which you will work should be entered in type parameters in the declaration of an object of the given generic type.

Having a look into the documentation, you will see that the Map interface is quoted as Map<K,V>, K means the type parameter for the key and V means a parameter for the value. In the declaration which I stated a moment ago, I mentioned particular values: the data of IRacer type will be the key and the data of Info type will be the values. If I would use data of another type, the compiler announces a syntactic error.

866.   In the section *Class Constructor – Static Constructor* on page 289 you have used a question mark instead of type argument and you promised to explain it in this section.

You are true. The compiler checks, if the generic types are always used with the type arguments. However, sometimes you don't know which type to insert there. In such case you can use the ? (question mark) sign as a wildcard representing all object types.

More detailed explanation overlaps borders of this volume; I will explain it in the next volume.

Interface vs. Implementation

867.   But why do you declare the variable as an instance of the Map<IRacer,Info> **class and save a reference to an object of** HashMap<> **type into it?**

If you declare any variable in the program or the type of the return value, you would use for it the most general type that suits in the situation. Then you have far more space in case of possible consequent changes of a program.

To keep this generality, the variable should be declared as an instance of certain interface. And the object which should be saved in it should be an instance of particular class. Therefore afterwards, when some other class implementing the given interface is more suitable for your program, you only change the initialization. You do not have to change the rest of the program, because it handled the given object as an instance of the declared interface the whole time, and it did not change with the new initialization.

That's what I did in this declaration. I declared the field as an instance of the Map interface and I saved into it the reference to an object that was an instance of the HashMap class. If I would discover later on that some other implementation of the Map interface is more suitable for this purpose, e.g. LinkedHashMap, is it sufficient to change only the initialization in the declaration. The rest of the class will work with the given object as with the instance of the Map interface. Until the change will touch this part of the declaration, you don't have to take care about the rest of the program.

868.   Why you didn't quote the type parameters at type names in this explanation?

Because what I told is not dependent on particular values of type parameters. Before you learn more, please, remember that the type parameters quoted in the type of the declared variable as well as the type parameters quoted in the class constructor used in initialization should be the same.

869.   You still didn't explain why the interface has the type parameters and the class doesn't have it. I mean the declaration:
    Map<IRacer, Info> racer2info = new HashMap<>();

When you declare the type arguments at the left side of the assignment operator, it is clear that at the right side there will be the same arguments. Therefore, Java 7 allows delegating their specification to the compiler. Therefore the best practice suggests leaving the angle brackets empty in such case and let the specification on the compiler that doesn't make typos.

Initialization

870.   Does the map constructor create an empty map?

Yes, you can rely on it; when the non-parametric constructor of some collection or of a map is used, an empty collection or map will be created. The constructors that fill in the container immediately at the beginning, always have some parameters which say what should be filled in the container during the initialization.

871.   Tell me please, what the map knows.

The instance of Map<K,V> interface declares (among other things) the methods with the following signatures (I remind that K is the key type and V is the saved values type):

☞ void clear()
   removes all of the mappings from this map.

☞ boolean containsKey(Object key)
    returns true if this map contains a mapping for the specified key.

☞ boolean containsValue(Object value)
    returns true if this map maps one or more keys to the specified value.

☞ V get(Object key)
   returns the value to which the specified key is mapped, or null if this map contains no mapping for the key.

☞ boolean isEmpty()
   returns true if this map contains no key-value mappings.

☞ V put(K key, V value)
   associates the specified value with the specified key in this map. If the map previously contained a mapping for the key, the old value is replaced by the specified value.

☞ V remove(Object key)
   removes the mapping for a key from this map if it is present. Returns the value to which this map previously associated the key, or null if the map contained no mapping for the key.

☞ int size()
   returns the size of the map, i.e. the number of key-value mappings in this map.

The Registration

872.   The empty map is prepared and thus the racers could start registering.

Yes, they can. Have a look at the listing 38.2 with the source code, with the register(IRacer) methods and let's speak about it.

Listing 38.2:   *The register(IRacer) method in the Race class*

```
public void register(IRacer racer)
{
    if (registered >= maxRacers) {
        IO.inform("It is possible to register only : " + maxRacers +
                " racers");
        return;
    }
    if (racer2info.containsKey(racer)) {
        IO.inform("The racer cannot be registered twice: " + racer);
        return;
    }
    Ring        ring      = prepareNextRing();
    RoadField   start     = ring.getStartField();
```

```
    Position   position  = start.getPosition();
    Controller controller = Controller.createFor(racer);
    RoadField  target     = start.getNext();

    Info info = new Info(ring, start, target, controller);
    racer2info.put(racer, info);

    racer.setPosition(position);
    racer.setModule(module);
    racer.setDirection(start.getDirection());

    //Ensure, that both, racer as well as its ring, will be visible
    CM.add(ring);
    CM.addAbove(ring, racer);

    controller.start();
}
```

As you see, the test of the second racer registration was replaced by a test, if the registered racer still fits to the maximum permissible number of racers registered simultaneously. There is also a test if the racer doesn't try to register the second time. Its condition is as follows:

```
racer2info.containsKey(racer)
```

Thus I am asking the map if there is an item the access to which is through the entered key. If the map answers that there is such an item, I know, that the racer tries to be registered the second time. Equally as the previous test I announce him his violation in a dialog and finish the registration.

Then I prepare values which I will save to the map, I will create a new instance of the crate and I will put it into the map. At the conclusion I place the racer at the starting position at its ring and start its controller, i.e. I begin controlling it from the keyboard.

873. There are two methods, which I don't know. I will start from the last one – how do you create the controller?

The class Controller offers the createFor(IControllable) factory method which asks the user, which keys he/she would like to use, and then it creates a controller which will manage the object in reaction to the entered keys. Thus several players will be able to play at one keyboard, if need be at several keyboards connected to the same computer.

874. I see. The second method unknown to me is prepareNextRing(). I suppose that similarly as previously you don't want to "distract" the methods and therefore you defined part of their duties into an auxiliary method. What does it do?

Your supposition is correct. The auxiliary method prepares its own ring for each racer. Then it puts individual rings one along the other one, and knows that the constructor arranged sufficient place for all of them. (That's why the number of racers is limited.) You can find its source code in the listing 38.3.

As you see, the method is simple. It multiplies the order of the registered racer by the width of the ring and deduces the ring's position at the screen. For better orientation of the racers each ring will have another color. The color will be given by the NamedColor class as a method with an index smaller by one than is the order of the registered racer. Then it increases by 1 the number of heretofore registered racers before returning the created ring so that the ring for the next racer will be drawn the needed bit aside.

Listing 38.3:   *The prepareNextRing() method in the RaceLShape class*

```
private Ring prepareNextRing()
{
    int x = registered * RING_WIDTH * module;
    Position position = new Position(x, 0);
    Ring ring = Ring.newLShapeRing(position,
                            NamedColor.getNamedColor(registered));
    registered = registered + 1;
    return ring;
}
```

The Check of Transits

875.   The racers are registered and they can start and report at checks. How did you solve it?

Have a look at the listing 38.4. I would like to draw your attention to the beginning where I ask the map for an object saved under the racer key by the following statement

```
racer2info.get(racer)
```

Afterward I test if the map did not return me an empty reference. This would mean that I am asking an information from a racer who did not register and therefore he is not saved in the map.

Listing 38.4:   *The checkpoint(IRacer) method in the RaceLShape class*

```
public void checkpoint(IRacer racer)
{
    Info info = racer2info.get(racer);
    if (info == null) {
        return;                        //===========>
    }
    Position racerPosition  = racer.getPosition();
    Position targetPosition = info.targetField.getPosition();
    if (racerPosition.equals(targetPosition)) {
        if (info.targetField == info.startField) {
            finishRace(racer, info);
            return;                    //===========>
        }
        info.targetField = info.targetField.getNext();
    }
}
```

876.   Why don't you announce the error in the dialog as during the registration?

Because this error occurred in the middle of the race and I don't want to spoil the race to other racers. It means I will simply ignore the not registered racer.

The End of the Race

877.   I see that you also give information about the racer to the `finishRace(IRacer)` **method. Why?**

This method uses only the reference to the controller to which the method announces that the action finished and monitoring of keyboard can be closed.

However, this method has more interesting aspect: Notice, that there is the following statement after announcing the time of the given racer printed at the standard output

```
racer2info.remove(racer);
```

By this statement I ask the map to remove the couple (a racer; information on him). After this statement I am asking the map, if it is empty. In case it returns `true`, it means that it removed the last racer, i.e. that all racers finished. Therefore an announcement about finishing the race is written in the standard output.

878.   This closing announcement could be written into the dialog, couldn't be?

Yes, it could be, but I take into account that another group of racers might come and consequently compare their times and pick up according to time, which of them will proceed to the finals. This announcement clearly differs among separate groups.

879.   Compared to the previous lesson the method `getName()` **occurred. Last time it was not there.**

Last time there was only one racer and thus it was not necessary to differentiate him. Now there are further methods for detecting and adjusting the racer's name in the `IRacer` interface, so that it would be possible to distinguish separate racers in such mass racers.

The `IRace` Interface

880.   Do you have further methods on stock?

I think I don't have to analyze each detail. I would say you will understand the rest from the source code in the final project of this lesson. The only one what I would like to mention, is the fact that I added an implementation of the `IRace` interface, which implemented also the race of the last lesson. It was due to the reason that the racer could register at any of them.

For this reason also the `IRacer` interface changed, and now the method `registerFor` expects the parameter of `IRace` type.

Exercise

881.   What you have prepared for my today's exercise?

Read once again the source code of the RaceLShape class and above all using of maps and of embedded classes. Try to think out some simple dictionary with methods as follows:

☞   void addWord(String source, String translation)

☞   String findTRanslation(String source)

☞   void remove(String source)

Examine the class functioning in an interactive mode. And if you will be diligent, you can define also a test class. Check, if, after adding a new value with a key which already is in the map, the map would change the old value assigned to this key by the new one.

Review

Let's review what you have learned in this lesson:

☞   Containers are objects determined for saving other objects.

☞   Containers are divided into static and dynamic ones.

   ☞   The static containers have the same size for their whole life, which means the same number of objects fits into them.

   ☞   The dynamic containers are mostly born as empty and they fill up and clear out dynamically during their life.

☞   The crates belong among static containers.

☞   The library of collection is defined in the package java.util in a standard library.

☞   Containers of the library are willing to work only with values of object types.

☞   Each primitive type has its wrapping type, which "wraps" its value into the object.

☞   A map is the container that serves to saving objects and their quick searching.

☞   A map stores key/value pairs. The key serves for identifying the given couple; the value contains the saved data. You can find a value if you provide the key.

☞   This data structure is called in certain libraries as a dictionary.

☞   In case it is necessary to save more values to one key of the map, they should be put into a crate.

☞   Data types can have three kinds of members:

   ☞   Data members – fields.

   ☞   Function members – methods.

   ☞   Type members – member types.

☞   Member types are a special group of more general nested types. Nested types include also the types declared inside blocks.

☞ Member types are divided to embedded (static) and inner (instance) ones.

☞ The data type in the body of which a nested type is defined, is called an outer type of this nested type.

☞ Member data types can have the same modifiers as fields and methods.

☞ According to our conventions the member data types are located at the end of the source code in the relevant section.

☞ The member class, the instances of which do not need to know to which instance of their outer class they belong, should be defined as static (embedded) ones.

☞ The classes of containers use to be defined as generic data types which have angle brackets after their name with a list of names of type parameters.

☞ The type parameters of containers enable to enter such types of values which are allowed to save into the given container.

☞ When declaring the variable, the type parameters of its type have to be the same as the type parameters of the constructor which create the value saved in the variable. To avoid typos we can let this list empty and let its specifying to the compiler.

☞ The type of the declared variable should be chosen as general as possible to have a minimum of problems with consequent modifications.

☞ The object saved in this variable can have more precious type.

☞ In case it is necessary to receive instances of various types in the parameter of certain method, an interface can be declared, which would be implemented by all these types and then this interface will be proclaimed as the type of the relevant parameter.

☞ When working with maps it is possible to use (among other things) the methods with the following signature (K and V represent the type parameters for the key and the value):

 ☞ void clear()
 ☞ boolean containsKey(Object key)
 ☞ boolean containsValue(Object value)
 ☞ V get(Object key)
 ☞ boolean isEmpty()
 ☞ V put(K key, V value)
 ☞ V remove(Object key)
 ☞ int size()

Project:
The resulting form of the project to which we came at the end of the lesson and after completing all exercises is in the 138z_Containers project.

39 Further Programming Constructions

What you will learn in this lesson

The organization of the race programmed in the previous lesson was not perfect. In this lesson you will see how it can be improved. You will become acquainted with collections with the colon for loop, *then increment as well as decrement operators will be presented, and finally you will learn how to throw exceptions.*

Project:

In this lesson you continue in using the 138z_Containers *project.*

---

882. **When I tried the race programmed in the last lesson with my buddies, sometimes only the last prepared racer was competing. We figured out that it happens when I assigned the same key to the unused methods. I thought it cannot be a problem.**

You made one fault, because you used the same key for finishing the reaction to pressing the keys for the next racer. Therefore, when you entered the hot key for the subsequent racer, you pressed at the same time the key to which the preceding racer (properly) reacted in the way that he switched off.

This behavior is a result of one imperfection of the previous program. If you look at the listing 38.2 on page 414, you will see that the last statement is switching on the controller. Since this moment the given racer reacts to the keyboard. If you would like to program it better, you should activate all controllers after all racers would be registered. But you didn't have sufficient skills for that.

Collections that Can Be Received from a Map

883. **And what was missing?**

I didn't explain you how to repeat certain action or how to use a cycle. I think that it's the proper time to make it now. But before that I will tell you about certain methods of maps. As I said, the map is a collection of key/value pairs. (We call these pairs **entries**, because they are instances of the Map.Entry interface.)

But the map does not operate as this collection. It is specialized above all to saving and subsequent withdrawing of values according to the entered key. Nevertheless, it offers methods which will return a collection of keys, of values or of whole entries. The methods are as follows:

☞ Set<Map.Entry<K,V>> entrySet()
   returns a set of entries – instances of the Map.Entry<K,V> interface.

☞ Set<K> keySet()
   returns a set of the keys contained in the given map.

☞ Collection<V> values()

returns a collection of the values saved in the given map. If some value is saved more times (it is in several pairs with various keys), it will be contained more times in this collection.

The above mentioned returned collections (as you know, sets belong to collections) are backed by the map, so changes to the map are reflected in the set, and vice-versa.

884. What is the type Map.Entry<K,V> **about?**

In the previous lesson I presented member data types. The internal crate which we have created was declared as a private one and therefore nobody outside the class knew about it. However, sometimes it is useful so that the member types would be declared as public, and this is just the case of Map.Entry. This is an interface which is defined within the Map interface. As you see, I refer to it similarly as to other members of classes and of interface types – they are qualified by their owner, i.e. we write the name of the outer type, dot and the name of the member. The Entry interface is defined within the Map interface and that's why its name is Map.Entry for all around.

Collection Library

885. Why the first two methods return sets and the last method a collection? And what does it mean a set?

A set is a collection which guarantees that no element will be contained twice in it. It means it is a special type of a collection and therefore the Set interface is a descendant of the Collection interface. And because you will soon meet further collections, you should have a basic idea about the structure of the standard collection library. You can see the class diagram of the most important interface types at the figure 39.1.

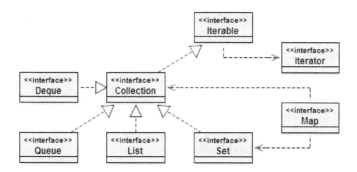

Figure 39.1
The class diagram with the most important interface types of the collection library

886. Ah, I see that you should at least introduce individual interface types to me.

You're true. Let's go on.

☞ Collection – The most general collection. The container to which you can save objects and withdraw them again. You know nothing about it. In a while I will show you the list of the most important methods.

☞ Set –As I have already told you, it is a collection which guarantees to you that each element is contained only once in it. When you would try to save the element second time, it will not accept it. It will not add any other method to those which are inherited from the general collection. The difference is only in the above mentioned contract.

☞ List – A collection, in which the elements are lined up which means you can ask for example for its first or its last element. The list is the mostly used dynamic container.

☞ Queue –A collection used for simulating of the classic queue. The element which you save as the first in it, you will also receive as the first one, when you ask for any saved element.

☞ Deque – A queue, where you can add new elements to (and remove them from) both ends (deque is short for "double ended queue").

☞ Map – You already became acquainted with it.

As you see, the map is standing a bit aside. It has a common aspect with collections that it knows to return collections of elements which you saved into it. Therefore, for certain operations with elements saved into the map, we have to get firstly the collection of them and only after that we can work with it.

887.   Once more: why the first two methods return sets and the last one returns a collection?

Each key may be only once in the map. Therefore you know in advance that the collection of keys is in fact a set. It's the same with the collection of entries, because two entries with the same key cannot be contained in any map.

It's not strictly valid for values, because you can have a map in which the same value will be assigned to several keys, so that you would have several entries with various keys, but with the same value. But as I have described in functioning: if any value is contained in the map more times, i.e. if it is contained in more entries, it will be more times also in the resulting collection of values. It has a logical implication that returning of the set cannot be promised and therefore the method promises only returning of a general, unspecialized collection.

888.   What can I do with such a collection?

Above all you can save objects into it and withdraw them again. All collections offer (among other things) a kit of important methods with following signatures (E means a type parameter of the collection and represents the type of saved elements):

☞ boolean add(E e)
ensures that this collection contains the specified element; returns true if this collection changed as a result of the call.

☞ void clear()
removes all of the elements from this collection.

☞ boolean contains(Object o)
returns true if this collection contains the specified element.

☞ boolean isEmpty()
returns true if this collection contains no elements.

☞   `boolean remove(Object o)`
    removes a single instance of the specified element from this collection, if it is present; returns true if this collection changed as a result of the call.

☞   `int size()`
    returns the number of elements in this collection.

The `for(:)` Loop

889.   I already know what the collection is and how I can get it from the map. And now please show me how to use it for solving my problem.

I will show it to you directly at the method `start()`. I have told you at the beginning that the problems you complained on were caused by a premature activation of the controller. Remove the closing statement from the end of the `register(IRacer)` method, which deals with its activation, find the method `start()` and compare it with the definition in the listing 39.1.

Listing 39.1:   *The new form of the method* `start()` *in the RaceLShape class*

```
public void start()
{
    IO.inform("Press OK to start measure the time");
    Collection<Info> infos = racer2info.values();
    for (Info info : infos) {
        info.controller.start();
    }
    time0 = System.currentTimeMillis();
}
```

890.   Several statements were added between displaying the message and measuring the time.

Two of them were added. The first statement asks the map for a set of all saved values and saves it into the variable `infos`, which is the collection containing crates with information on each racer.

The second statement is the **loop statement**. It enables you to execute operations repeatedly, in a loop. It is introduced by a keyword `for`, and therefore sometimes it's named *colon for* or the *for each* statement, because the analogous loop statements are named in this way in other languages. This statement enables to execute the required action with each element of the entered collection. Its syntax is as follows:

```
for ( <ElementType> <element> : <container> ) <statement>
```

As you see it is composed of the keyword `for` followed by parentheses and a statement. The collection from which you will take one saved element after another (you will not remove but only borrow them) is quoted on the right of the colon (still in parentheses), and on the left hand from the colon there is a declaration of the variable into which the reference to the withdrawn element is saved.

The keyword `for` together with the following parentheses is sometimes named the **loop header**, the executed statement as the **loop body**. The head specifies how many times you will carry out the loop body and with what, i.e. with which object. The variable on the left hand from the colon is named a **loop control variable**. (Therefore it is sometimes called the **loop with a parameter**.) Before each entry into the loop body a reference to another element from the container to the right of the colon is put into the parameter. Working with the loop control variable proceeds inside the body.

The content of the opened collection cannot be changed inside the loop body, i.e. the elements could be neither taken away nor added. After finishing the loop the elements should be the same as in the moment when you entered in it; only their properties may change.

891. Why the content of the opened collection could not be changed?

Because transferring of individual instances from the container is provided by a special object called an *iterator* that keeps a view of elements – which of them were already distributed and which only will be distributed. When you add or remove anything from the collection, the iterator might be confused and could install an exception (exceptions will be discussed further on). Therefore the content of the opened collection can be changed only in a permitted way; however, this will be presented in the next volume.

Let's return to the example in the listing 39.1 and let's look at its loop. From the head you can see that objects saved in the collection infos will be gradually withdrawn. These objects are crates with information on separate racers. The name of the loop control variable is info. A reference to the next element of the collection (to the next crate) is saved into it before each entry into the loop body. Then the controller, to which a reference is saved in the received crate, is started in the loop body. Thus the controllers of all racers are started and the race can begin.

Race for Several Rings

892. I tried this repair and it's marvelous. I assigned the same keyboard shortcuts to all racers and then, when I tapped at the keys, they all went altogether. So now I could try to extend the race so that the racers could go several rounds. It will also be a cycle, won't it be?

You will be surprised, but no. Not each repeated operation means a loop. The bigger number of rounds which you require does not lead to any loop in the program. At least, not to a loop that would be programmed with the help of the loop statement.

893. So how should I program it?

You should amend the transit control so that it would decrease by one the remaining rounds to the racer when it goes through the start. When it would have no remaining round, the racer would reach the finish and you would "flag it down", i.e. you would call the method finishRace(IRacer) for it.

894. But when we would decrease by one the remaining round to the racer, we should put down somewhere how many rounds remain. When we keep complete information about the racer in that crate, we should put this info there as well, shouldn't we?

Yes, you should add another field into the crate as well as add a corresponding parameter to its constructor. Besides it you should also enter information how many rounds the race would have. This should be best included into the constructor. It receives a parameter determining the number of rounds and we also add the field into which you save the entered number of rounds.

If you would have written more programs working with the class RaceLShape, such change would be very unpleasant, because you should have to modify all of them. That's why the requirement for increasing the number of parameters of certain method is solved in practice by adding a new method with an increased number of parameters and the definition of the original method is amended so that it would call the new method and would enter some implicit value as the added parameter.

You will modify the program by adding a new constructor which will enable to set the number of race rounds. The body of the old constructor will be modified so that it would call the new constructor and will enter one as a number of rounds.

895. **I'd say I can handle the constructor alone, maybe with some tiny corrections. But show me please, how I should modify the method** checkpoint.

When you will amend the constructor, don't forget to modify also the crate which should have to remember the remaining rounds (add the field roundsLeft into it and add the relevant parameter into its constructor), as well as the method register(IRacer), which fulfills this crate.

Neither the method checkpoint will be too much complicated. There will be only another embedded conditional statement added. You can see its new form at the listing 39.2.

Listing 39.2:   The innovated version of the checkpoint(IRacer) method in the RaceLShape class

```
public void checkpoint(IRacer racer)
{
    Info info = racer2info.get(racer);
    if (info == null) {
        return;                          //==========>
    }
    Position racerPosition  = racer.getPosition();
    Position targetPosition = info.targetField.getPosition();
    if (racerPosition.equals(targetPosition)) {
        if (info.targetField == info.startField) {
            info.remainingRounds--;
            if (info.remainingRounds > 0) {
                endOfRace(racer, info);
                return;                  //==========>
            }
        }
        info.targetField = info.targetField.getNext();
    }
}
```

Increment and Decrement Operators

896.   **What does it mean the statement** info.roundsLeft--?**?**

This is the statement for decreasing the variable's value by one. This statement would correspond in this case with the following statement

```
info.roundsLeft = info.roundsLeft - 1;
```

897.   I see, it is briefer. Why you didn't use it a long time before?

It' not so simple. It's one of the four operators which have several special characteristics. All four are rated among unary operators because they have only one operand equally as for instance the negation operator. Contrary to other unary operators you can choose if you would like to locate it before or after the operand.

I told that there are four operators, but I should better tell that there are two pairs of operators. The ++ operator is called an **increment operator**, because it adds one to its operand, and the -- operator is called a **decrement operator,** because it subtracts one from its operand.

If you put the operator before an operand, they are named **preincrement** / **predecrement** operators. In case you put them after an operand, they are named **postincrement** / **postdecrement** operators.

If the operation is the only one in the statement, the difference of operator's location will not become evident. But if this operation is a part of more complex expression, then preincrement operator firstly adds one to the variable and this increased variable is used in the expression, whilst the postincrement operator firstly uses the increased variable in the expression and only after that it is increased by one. The same is valid for decrementation.

To make it more illustrative, I prepared a simple little program demonstrating the above mentioned and you can see it in the listing 39.3 (the source code can be found in the package tests). After starting it the dialog will open as at the figure 39.2. Having a look at it you will surely understand the operators best. Since this time I will use it.

Listing 39.3:   *The Xkrements class*

```
/*****************************************************************************
 * The class {@code Xkrements} should demonstrate the behavior
 * of the increment and decrement operators.
 */
public class Xkrements
{
    //== VARIABLE CLASS FIELDS ==============================================

    /** i, j, k are defined as static fields,
     *   to allow their sharing with the method show(String). */
    private static int     i, j, k;

    /** Serves as an accumulator of the created string. */
    private static String  all = "";


    //== OTHER NON-PRIVATE CLASS METHODS ====================================

    /*****************************************************************************
     * Demonstrates that the operators behave as was explained.
     */
    public static void test()
    {
        //Static fields are zeroed at start => it suffices to set the "i"
        i = 1;              show("Initial values:");
        j = i++;            show("After (j = i++)");
        k = ++i;            show("After (k = ++i)");
        k = i-- + j--;      show("After (k = i-- + j--)");
        k = --i + --j;      show("After (k = --i + --j)");
        IO.inform(all);
        System.out.println(all);
    }
```

```
//##########################################################################
//== CONSTUCTORS AND FACTORY METHODS ========================================
/* Blocks a constructor usage. */ private Xkrements() {}


//== PRIVATE AND AUXILIARY CLASS METHODS ====================================

/**************************************************************************
 * Auxiliary method showing the last action and printing
 * through the method {@link IO.inform()} values of all numeric fields.
 * In addition the printed text is added to accumulator
 * that will be printed at the end.
 */
private static void show(String text)
{
    text = text + ":  i=" + i + ",  j=" + j + ",  k=" + k;
//      IO.inform(text);
    all = all + "\n" + text;
}
}
```

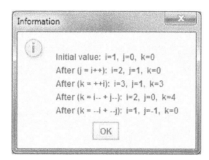

Figure 39.2
The dialog depicted with the test() *method in the* Xkrements *class*

898. Ah, again we get off our race a bit. Show me please, how I should modify the program to make the race at different rings and not only at the L-track.

It's rather longer explanation which I would better postpone to the next lesson. Today I want to repeat what you learned until now. I would say that it was quite a lot of things in last three lessons, starting with the simple conditional statement through working with collections and maps up to the colon for loop. Let's go through individual classes in the package town and let's look in which of them you could apply what you learned until now with advantage. Try to open one class after another in the class diagram (you can skip interface types) and look where you could apply the simple conditional statement.

Exceptions and Their Throwing

899. **It's quite a good idea. For example immediately up in the class** Town **I could check if the current road-field which I want to display is actually in the town.**

Good, and if you would announce that there is an error, you should learn how it is usual in Java, i.e. through throwing an expression.

900. **Throwing an expression? What does it mean?**

The expression is an object which bears the necessary information concerning the situation when an error or another exceptional situation occurred. When you discover an error, you should create an exception (even the exception is an object) and throw it.

Throwing the exception is a special operation when a method passes an exception's object to the virtual machine and asks to find somebody who knows what to do with it. If the virtual machine would not find anybody like that, a message is issued at a standard error output which is analyzed in the part *Analysis of Error Message* on page 367.

901. **How this exception is thrown?**

There is a special throw statement for it. You write the exception you will throw behind this keyword. You will throw out an instance of one of the following classes in our program (all are of the package java.lang, that's why I quote only their simple names):

☞ IllegalArgumentException

Throwing of this exception signalizes the forbidden value of a parameter (e.g. a negative width).

☞ IllegalStateException

This exception is thrown by the method only if the instance is in such state when it is not able to react to the sent message.

☞ IndexOutOfBoundException

An index with senseless value has been entered – maybe minus the first column of the town.

☞ NullPointerException

The attempt for addressing an instance through en empty reference – for example:

```
Direction8 direction = null;
direction.leftTurn();
```

☞ UnsupportedOperationException

An attempt for accomplishing the operation which the addressed object declares, but not supports. Throwing this exception is inserted into bodies of new methods, the bodies of which will be defined sometimes in future.

Second typical usage is bodies of methods whose object has to be defined because the implemented interface requires it, but their calling is not supposed. Bodies of these methods create only throwing the exception UnsupportedOperationException, so that the offender would be warned that he is calling an unsupported method.

I mentioned e.g. collections to which nothing can be added nor taken out. But the `Collection` interface required an implementation of adding and taking away methods from all collections. Therefore these invariable collections throw out an exception `UnsupportedOperationException` in the attempt for a change of their content.

☞ `RuntimeException`
Common parent of all exceptions reacting to current errors in the program. I recommend throwing this exception when an error occurs in the program to which any of the previous exceptions should not be applied (its name doesn't reflect the nature of the occurred state). Nevertheless, in the error situation you should always decide if any of the above mentioned exceptions can be applied.

All quoted exceptions have a parameterless constructor and one-parametric constructor, to which you pass the string that becomes a part of the output report. You should suitably describe the error in this string, which occurred, to give a clue to the user for its correction.

902.   Oh, now you took me by surprise. How the user can correct an error in my program?

Saying a user I don't mean the end user who is using the program, but the user of your part of the program, i.e. the programmer who uses your classes and calls their methods.

In case the error got up to the screen of the end user, it is dishonor, but it can happen to anybody. When the end user announces such an error, you can only politely ask him to copy the error message and send it to you, so that you could make the corrections.

903.   I still don't know how such exception is thrown.

I will show it at an example of the method `activeOn(int,int)` in the class `Town`, which you can see in the listing 39.4. I test at the beginning of the method, if the entered coordinates belong outside the town's borders, and if yes, then I throw an exception.

Listing 39.4:   *The modified version of the `activeOn(int,int)` method in the `Town` class*

```
public void activeOn(int column, int row)
{
    if ((column < 0)  ||  (this.columnSize <= column)  ||
        (row    < 0)  ||  (this.rowSize    <= row  )  )
    {
        throw new IllegalArgumentException("\n" +
            "Position outside the town border.\n" +
            "Coordinates have to be >=0, column < " + columnSize +
            ", row < " +  rowSize + '\n' +
            "However the column=" + column + "and row=" + row +
            "were entered.");
    }
    currentColumn = column;
    currentRow    = row;
    CM.repaint();
}
```

As you see, creating an exception, i.e. calling of the `new` operator followed by the constructor's calling is executed as a part of the `throw` statement. Of course, you can firstly create the exception, then save the reference into the variable and then you can throw the created exception. However, creating the exception as a part of the throw statement requires less writing and therefore the programmers prefer it.

I tried to show you at the same time how such report about the error could look out. I'm used to begin the reports at the new line, because the announcement to a system, that precedes it, is usually quite long and the report is then written somewhere far to the right.

Further Corrections in Older Classes

904. **I perceived the exceptions and I would return to those corrections. When I went through further classes, I realized, that closing the ring, their builder could verify if the two fields are really connected one with the other. But I've no idea how to arrange it.**

This control cannot be provided by the builder or at least not in such simple way. It would be far more suitable if the constructor of RoadField class would be appointed to do this checking, which creates the closing field. Look at it – you surely would discover the solution. Then you can compare it with the sample solution in the listing 39.5.

Listing 39.5:   *The modified RoadField(RoadField, Direction8, RoadField, Multishape) constructor*

```
public RoadField(RoadField predecessor, Direction8 direction,
             RoadField successor,   Multishape multishape)
{
    this(predecessor, direction, multishape);
    Position next = direction.nextPosition(getPosition(), getModule());
    if (next.equals(successor.getPosition())) {
        this.next = successor;
    } else {
        IO.inform(
            "The first and the last ring fields are not correct neighbors");
    }
}
```

905. **Nothing important crosses my mind. Do you see any further corrections there?**

I see two of them. But the first is in the package util. The previous versions of the methods equal(Object) uselessly retyped the received parameter. When you already know a simple statement, you can change the whole definition so that the retyping would be only once. You can find the new definition for the Area class in the listing 39.6. Similarly also methods of other crates are modified.

You are meeting these new versions since the time you started to use the library's version under the code 13. I only did not tell you.

Listing 39.6:   *The new version of the method equals(Object) in the Area class*

```
public boolean equals(Object object)
{
    if (! (object instanceof Area)) {
        return false;                  //==========>
    }
    Area compared = (Area)object;
    return (compared.x      == x)      && (compared.y      == y)      &&
           (compared.width == width) && (compared.height == height);
}
```

Exercise

906. You were speaking about two corrections.

The second correction is your today's exercise. Add controls into the methods setSize(int,int) for inflatable objects if the values of parameters are meaningful, for example if somebody tries to enter a zero or even negative size. The negative position is chosen, when the object should travel outside the canvas borders.

At the same time add a control into the method setDirection(Direction8) for turnable objects, if somebody enters a direction into which the given instance does not know to turn, i.e. if it turns the instance into one of the four cardinal points. The method isMain() of the Direction8 class can help you with the control. Find in documentation what it precisely can do.

907. Would it be better to solve the measure control in classes Size and Area?

The instances of classes Size and Area are pure crates which don't have any idea for what the given application needs the saved data. I can imagine for example an application which will understand setting of negative measure as a statement for a mirror overturn of the given application's picture. Therefore let's leave the decision what is good and what's wrong on the class because it knows what the controlled data are for.

Similarly I would not insert the controls into classes of decorators. You can suppose that the decorated instance will take care about everything. Then the turnable decorator will be able to decorate in future also those turnable instances which are able to turn into all eight points.

And so that you would really train, add a control into the method activeOn(int,int) in the Town class that the active field is within the town. But it would be suitable to supplement the method getFieldSize(), which returns the field measurement of towns (i.e. the number of its columns and lines), so that the program that intends to set this active position could firstly determine the limits in which the setting can be done.

As the last exercise go through all source codes in the town package and find, where you can use increment and decrement operators (e.g. by counting the created instances).

Review

Let's review what you have learned in this lesson:

☞ The map offers three methods which return collections of saved objects as follows:

  ☞ Set<Map.Entry<K,V>> entrySet()

  ☞ Set<K> keySet()

  ☞ Collection<V> values()

☞ The Map.Entry<K,V> interface is a nested interface of the Map interface. Its instances are key/values pairs saved in maps.

☞ The standard library defines an interface specifying collections of several types as follows:

  ☞ Collection – The most general collection. The container to which objects can be saved and withdraw again. It does not guarantee anything else.

☞   Set – The collection that guarantees that each element is contained only once in it.

☞   List – The most used dynamic container. Elements in it are arranged in an order.

☞   Queue – The container which is used for simulating of a classic queue.

☞   Deque – The container representing double ended queue.

☞   The most important methods offered by the general collection are the following:

    ☞   boolean add(E e)

    ☞   void clear()

    ☞   boolean contains(Object o)

    ☞   boolean isEmpty()

    ☞   boolean remove(Object o)

    ☞   int size()

☞   For looking through elements saved in collection you use the loop named *colon for* or *foreach*
    loop. Its syntax is as follows:
    for (<ElementType> <element> : <container>) <statement>

☞   The keyword for with following parentheses is named *a loop header*; the following statement is *a
    loop body*.

    ☞   Inside the parentheses of the header, on the right side of the colon you can find a container
    from which you select the elements. On the left from the colon there is the so called *loop control
    variable*. It's a variable to which you save the reference to the next element selected from the
    container on the right. You are working with the cycle's parameter inside the body.

☞   Within the loop body you cannot change the content of the opened collection, i.e. you cannot
    withdraw any elements, nor to add.

☞   The operators ++ are named *increment*, because they add one to their operand, the operators --
    are named *decrement*, because they subtract one from their operand.

☞   In case the operator is located before the operand, it is called *preincrement* or *predecrement*
    operator, if it is located after the operand, it is called *postincrement* or *postdecrement* operator.

☞   The preincrement and predecrement operators change the value of its operand and then the
    changed value is used in the expression.

☞   The postincrement and postdecrement operators also change the value of their operand, but the
    original value before the change is used in the expression.

☞   The exception is an object which bears information about the situation in which the error or
    some other exceptional situation occurred.

☞   Throwing the exception is a special operation during which the method passes the object of the
    exception to the virtual machine and asks to find somebody who is able to handle the exception.

☞   If the virtual machine will find nobody, it issues a standard error report at the standard error
    output.

☞   When creating an exception you should use its one-parametric constructor, in the string parameter of which you suitably describe the error, to give a clue to the user for its correction.

☞   The most important exceptions are as follows:

   ☞   `IllegalArgumentException`

   ☞   `IndexOutOfBoundException`

   ☞   `IllegalStateException`

   ☞   `NullPointerException`

   ☞   `UnsupportedOperationException`

   ☞   `RuntimeException`

Project:

The resulting form of the project to which we came at the end of the lesson and after completing all exercises is in the 139z_Algorithmic project.

40 The Factory Method Second Time

What you will learn in this lesson
In this lesson you will improve the organization of your race. You will see how you can define the class organizing the race by using the factory method, so that the class would not be fixed to one ring, but you would be able to enter any ring along which the race will be run. At this occasion you will learn how to use a complete conditional statement, methods with variable number of parameters and the classic for loop.

Project:
In this lesson you will continue in using the 139z_Algorithmic project.

Problems with Variant Rings

908.   You promised in the previous lesson, that today you will explain how the race should be arranged, so that I could input not only the participants, but also the ring along which the race will drive.

The problem in inputting the ring is that your temporary knowledge (and above all the time possibilities) does not allow you to define the race so that all participants would drive along the same ring and could mutually pass. To provide a relative impartiality of such race is quite complicated problem.

We have chosen a strategy in which each racer has its own instance of the racing ring which he/she tries to drive through as quickly as possible. No one blocks his/her way which means no crashes have to be solved and we can only watch if the racer is out of the track.

By this access we save a lot of work with solving the passing and possible collisions, but you have to know how to create a set of equal rings. The class RaceLShape solved it simply: driving will be possible only along an L-shape ring which can be created by a static factory method of the Ring class. If we would like to enable entering the type of the ring to a constructor as a parameter, we can meet a problem that nothing else than an object can be entered as a parameter.

Similar problem we solved in the lesson *Creating of an Standalone Application* on page 319, when it was needed to explain to the dispatcher, which UFOs should be created in this game – mine or yours. The solution was that a special factory class was created the instance of which was able to create the required object and this instance has been given over to the constructor as a parameter. Now you could use a similar procedure.

Recall now how we proceeded in defining the game UFO and tell me how you should proceed in defining the race on various rings.

The IRingFactory **Interface**

909. **I was looking at it. At that time we made out UFO by means of UFO factories. The dispatcher's parameter required an instance which implements an** interface **for these factories. The factories implemented this** interface **and each of them created UFO of its author.**

Good, and now you will do it the same way. Define the IRingFactory interface, in which you will define your requirements for an instance that would be able to produce rings. The factory interface with the only required method has been already examined with UFO, and thus you can increase your requirements and ask more methods. Let's propose the interface as is shown in the listing 40.1.

Listing 40.1: *The IRingFactory interface*

```
/*****************************************************************************
 * Instances of the {@code IRingFactory} interface represent factories
 * intended for creating rings, where various vehicles can run.
 */
public interface IRingFactory
{
    //== DECLARED METHODS ======================================================

    /*****************************************************************************
     * Creates a ring with the default color and with the starting field
     * at the given starting position.
     *
     * @param startPosition Starting field position
     * @return The created ring
     */
//    @Override
    public Ring createRing(Position startPosition);


    /*****************************************************************************
     * Creates a ring with the given color and with the starting field
     * at the given starting position.
     *
     * @param startPosition Starting field position
     * @param color         Color of the created ring
     * @return The created ring
     */
//    @Override
    public Ring createRing(Position startPosition, NamedColor color);


    /*****************************************************************************
     * Set the default color for the future rings-
     *
     * @param color The set default color
     * @return The default color before the new was set
     */
//    @Override
    public NamedColor setDefaultColor(NamedColor color);
}
```

910. I see that the method setDefaultColor(NamedColor) **returns the previously adjusted implicit color. This is the first time when some adjusting methods return something.**

It's not the first time, you met it when I was speaking about maps and their methods put(K,V) and remove(K). I wanted to show you one of the possibilities how the only one accessory method to certain property can be sufficient. Sometimes you can meet such setting method designed like that (see the mentioned methods of maps). It is worthwhile in a situation when you exceptionally ask for the value of the given property and you only adjust the property without detecting what is its current value.

The adjusting method which will return you the previous value is one of the possible ways how you can do without the detecting method. In case you need only to find out a color, you can set any color and then set again the previously set color.

More Complex Factory

911. It's an interesting idea, but I would like to get back to the race. If I understand it properly, first of all various ring factories should be created, and then the class of races can be created the instances of which will organize the race with rings produced by the factory delivered to them as a parameter.

You understand it properly. I would say that you could create factories for producing L-shape rings alone, because as I've already told you, its methods only call the prepared static methods in the Ring class. Therefore it will be your exercise. Do it just now to obtain some experience in this way before we will continue. I think that it is so simple task that I don't need to show the possible solution – you can compare your solution with the LShapeFactory class in the final project of this lesson.

912. I defined the MyLShapeFactory **class and I have to admit that the task was really simple.**

Well, let's have a look, how you could create certain more complex factory.

913. More complex factory? I would understand more complex ring, but why more complex factory? According to me, the individual factories will vary only in the length and the extent of twisting the ring.

On the contrary, I would choose the simplest possible ring – something as in Indianapolis – a simple, rectangle track with four curves. We name the class OShapeRingFactory.

At the first sight such task looks very simple, but just this simplicity enables to set parameters for it. The constructor will find out of how many lines and columns the track will consist and if the driving along it will be clockwise or counterclockwise. The created instance will produce and locate at the entered positions the track specified like that.

914. I admit that you surprised me. I see that you are able not only make the complex things simple, but also the simple things complex. Nevertheless, I think that I would be able to define the constructor, because it will remember only those three items you were speaking about.

I have chosen this extension, because it is relatively simple, but you have to learn a new construction for the solution. So, let's go and agree that three fields will be defined:

☞ The fields of columns and rows will define the width and the height of the ring quoted in a number of occupied road-fields.

☞ The field direction will remember the direction from the starting road-field, which will be always located in the left upper corner of the ring. It will have only two permissible values: EAST and SOUTH. The first one will represent driving clockwise, i.e. with curves turned to the right, the second one driving counterclockwise, i.e. with curves turned to the left.

When you will be defining the constructor, don't forget to check, if the required number of lines and columns is not less than 2. Check also, that the parameter for setting the direction has the value EAST or SOUTH. In case of anything else, throw the IllegalArgumentException.

Complete Conditional Statement

915. **I created the class and I prepared the fields as well as the constructor including the requested verifications. I also defined the** setDefaultColor(NamedColor) **method, because I think it was not complicated. And please, show me the rest now.**

I prepared the definition of the creatingRing(Position, NamedColor) method, which you can see in the listing 40.2. (I suppose that you can define the one-parametric version of this method alone.) I used one new construction which was not yet presented and that's why I explain it in this example.

916. **Do you mean the** else **statement?**

This else, you are speaking about, does not create an independent statement, but only introduces the second part of the complete conditional statement. Until now we were using only a simple conditional statement, in which we could impact if it makes something or not. The **complete conditional statement**[9] has two branches and therefore it enables to specify even what should be done, if the condition is not valid. The syntax of the complete conditional statement could be written as follows:

    if (<condition>) <statement_1> else <statement_2>

When the computer will meet this statement, it evaluates the condition. If it is valid, the computer executes <statement_1>; if it is not valid, the computer executes <statement_2>.

I created a builder in the method and I started building the road with this builder. However, the procedure of building depends on the direction where the ring will turn (clockwise or counterclockwise). This depends on the starting direction which you will choose. If you start to the south, you call the method for creating the ring with different parameters compared to starting to the east. As you see, I gradually enter the number of road-fields which are necessary to be built at separate sites.

Listing 40.2:   *The createRing(Position, NamedColor) method in the OShapeRingFactory class*

```
public Ring createRing(Position startPosition, NamedColor color)
{
    RingBuilder builder = new RingBuilder(startPosition, color);
    builder.startTo(direction);
    if (direction == Direction8.SOUTH) {
        completeRing(builder, rowSize-1, columnSize, rowSize, columnSize-1);
    }
    else {
        completeRing(builder, columnSize-1, rowSize, columnSize, rowSize-1);
```

---

[9]   Some authors call it *general conditional statement*; Java Language Specification calls it *if-then-else statement*.

```
    }
    return builder.getRing();
}
```

917.   Ah, I don't see anything. Why do you subtract one from the number of lines and columns?

It is decreased to simplify the method for creating the side of the ring. Look at it, how the builder makes the ring. Firstly it creates the first field, and then a series of continuing fields and at last the closing connecting field. That's why I suppose that the method createRing creates initially the first road-field, which means, for the first line (or column) one field less remains.

Well, we turned. In the second and the third side all fields are the continuing ones and so the full number of fields should be created. As the last side is mentioned, I know that I have to leave the last field empty, because it is added in the different way – it is the closing field of the circle. Thus I again ask for a side shorter by one field.

918.   When you explain it in this way, I can understand it. So it means that the createRing method creates the required ring with the builder, and at the end it asks the builder for the created ring and returns it as its own product.

Exactly.

Methods with a Variable Number of Parameters

919.   When I skip over the speculations about the proper number of road-fields which have to be created at individual sides, it seemed to me quite simple. I create a builder, I ask somebody to help him building instead of me, and then I brag about the result. I start to be interested in the last method.

The last method is really interesting, because there are two not yet explained constructions in it. The first one is the definition of the method with the variable number of parameters. Look at the method's head in the listing 40.3.

920.   I see there three dots. You spoke about them in the section *Variable Number of Parameters* on page 93, when you showed me how to create a multishape. I only do not know why you installed the variable number of parameters when you knew that the parameters are always four.

I used the fact that the parameter sizes is only a container to which all passed parameters are saved whose number is not known in advance. If I would take over the parameters individually, I would have to turn each of them separately and thus I would have to program the same several times. As you see, I avoid this situation if it is possible a little bit.

Due to the fact that all values of parameters are in one container, I can use the colon for loop, withdraw one parameter after another from the container and let the builder create as much road-fields, as the given parameter requires.

Listing 40.3:   *The method* completeRing(RingBuilder, int...) *in the* OShapeRingFactory *class*

```
private void completeRing(RingBuilder builder, int... sizes)
{
    if (sizes.length != 4) {
        throw new IllegalArgumentException(
                "\nFour sizes should be entered");
    }
```

```
        Direction8 currentDirection = direction;
        for (int size : sizes) {
            for (int i=1;   i < size;   i++) {
                builder.continueTo(currentDirection);
            }
            if (direction == Direction8.SOUTH) {
                currentDirection = currentDirection.leftTurn();
            } else {
                currentDirection = currentDirection.rightTurn();
            }
        }
        //The last direction should be turned back because I am
        //at the last but one field and so I should not turn yet
        if (direction == Direction8.SOUTH) {
            currentDirection = currentDirection.rightTurn();
        } else {
            currentDirection = currentDirection.leftTurn();
        }
        builder.closeTo(currentDirection);
    }
```

921. Well, so if I define a method with a variable number of parameters, the parameter after the triple-dot is always a container in which all those values are saved?

Yes, this container is established as an array. I can speak about it more detailed in some of the following lessons. For now it's sufficient to know, that it is a container through which you can pass with a help of the colon for loop, and that you receive individual parameters exactly in the order in which they were quoted during the method's calling.

In case you would sometimes decide to define your own method with a variable number of parameters, then remember, that the container for the variable number of parameters always has to be quoted as the last one. Logically it results that you cannot have two of them.

922. But if there maybe any count of those parameters, the method can receive less than four or on the contrary more. Could it be a problem?

Be sure, that if I would not take care about it, it really would be a problem. Therefore, before entering the loop I ask the array, how many elements it has. This information is saved in the array's public constant length. If there are not four elements, I throw an exception.

It's true that the method is private and that I could look after such things within the class source code, but it does no harm if the programmer inserts also guarding of his own possible errors into the program.

The Classic for Loop

923. Well, I comprehend the container and the colon for loop. But what about the next for – you didn't tell anything about it.

This is also a loop – I call it a *classic for loop*, because Java took it over from its grandfather, the C language. You can see that the C language was developed by programmers for programmers (better said for themselves). The beginners sometimes complain that they have troubles with remembering the meaning of its separate parts. Its syntax is the following one:

```
for ( <initialization> ; <condition> ; <modification> ) <statement>
```

The keyword for with the following braces constitutes the loop **header**; the `<statement>` constitutes the loop **body**. A declaration of a loop control variable or some expression can occur in the part named `<inicialization>`. This part will be executed only once before the first entry into the loop body. Mostly the loop control variable is declared and initialized there; which is the variable used within the loop body and its value is modified before each next execution of the loop body (better said before testing the condition).

It's good to remember that **the variable declared in the header is visible only in the header and in the loop body**, not further. In case you intend to use the variable in a loop which would be accessible even after finishing the loop, you have to define it before the loop header. This is a popular error of the beginners.

In the middle part you write a condition which is evaluated before each execution of the loop body. You enter into the loop body only in case if the condition is true. If it's not true, executing of the loop ends and you continue with the first statement after the loop body. If the condition is not true for the first time, the loop body is not executed at all.

If the condition is not quoted, it is evaluated as always-true and the loop is executed until the time when some statement would jump out. (How it is possible to jump out from the middle of the loop you will see in the next lesson.)

The part named `<modification>` is the place where the express specifying what should be executed after going through the loop body. Mostly you can find here a statement defining how the value of the loop control variable should change. If there is nothing, nothing is done after completing the loop body and the execution continues with the next evaluation of the condition.

924. **You told that there may be nothing in each part. Does it mean that despite I will write nothing into the head, it will be good?**

You mean when you will write neither the initialization, nor the condition, nor the modification, because you have to write the semicolons into it. Yes, it will be proper. This will be a head of an endless loop – for(;;). It is so characteristic, that I recommend its using to everybody, and wherever the endless loop is needed. It is more conspicuous in the code than other variants of the endless loop. You will train how to use it in the next lesson.

925. **May I skip also the statement?**

You cannot skip the statement because then the next statement would be used as a body. But you can quote an empty statement after the head, which is created by the only semicolon or the empty block. Sometimes it's suitable, because there are loops, which execute all necessary already in the head, and then their body is created by only empty statement.

As you see, the empty header has a sense and an empty body as well. Both are sometimes used. But it's no sense to use an empty head together with an empty body, i.e. a statement for(;;);. Such program has an only function: to block. It does nothing, but it does this nothing all the time.

926.   Well, and now apply this general talking to this program.

It is simple. You will find a declaration int i = 1 in the initializing part, which defines the variable i as a loop control variable and initializes it to 1.

The condition tests, if i < size. Because the parameter i is increased by one in the following modification part, this condition tests, when the constantly increasing i will reach the value size.

To summarize: this header says that the loop body will be executed just (size-1) times. The builder adds another road-field to the ring in the entered direction, so that as many road-fields is added to the built side of the ring as is stated in the variable size.

927.   I think if the control variable acquires subsequently the values from 1 up to size, the body will be executed size times.

However, the control variable acquires the accepted values from one up to size-1. When it gets the value size, the condition i < size will be evaluated as false and the loop ends. It should be done in this way, because the last road-field of the side is shared with the next side and because this field is turned to the next side's direction, we create it as the first road-field of the next side. Therefore this loop is defined to create only the (size-1) road-fields.

928.   Well, I will have to digest it. But I understand that the for loop is a statement as any other and therefore I can insert it into another loop; I believe that also into another conditional statement.

You can insert it anywhere, where you can insert a statement.

929.   At the end of the colon for loop you are changing the current direction and when you leave the loop, you change it back. Why?

At the end of the colon loop I arrived just in front of the ring's corner and I need building of another side the direction of which is turned by 90° to the right or to the left according to the circulation. In the next passing I take the next side size and I start building the next side of the ring.

After I go around the whole future circuit, I have to place only the last road-field which has to be connected with the initial one, so that I could go around the whole circuit. This last road-field has the same direction as its predecessors. The initial road-field, which is the corner field, will have a new direction. However, the if statement mentioned a while ago at the end of the colon loop has already turned the direction. Therefore firstly I have to return this turned direction back, so that the builder would know, that also this road-field would continue in the given direction.

930.   Well, when I go through your method, I take gradually one entered size of the side after another and I make one less road-fields in the row as is the value of the given size. Then I look in which direction I started and according to it I turn to the right or to the left. And thus I make nearly the whole circuit. Before creating the last closing road-field I give back the turn which was eagerly made by the last loop's statement, and I close the whole circuit.

You say it better than me. It means we have finished another factory of optional circuits. But it's not the end. The race now has conditions for creating any number of circuits, but information for placing these circuits one along the other is missing. However, explanation will continue the next time, as there is a lot of things remained.

Exercise

931. Aha, it's time for exercising. So with what I will be entrusted today, when the race with optional rings is not finished yet?

Complete the classes that are in the work and define the RaceRing class, the instances of which will be able to organize the race in ring created by instances of the RingFactory class. Proceed from the definition of the RaceLShape class and take into account that instances of the wheel factory know the measures of circuits they create, which means it is sufficient to equip them only with methods that announce this measurement when asked.

Review

Let's review, what you have learned in this lesson:

☞ If the method should create instances of a class unknown to the author in time of its constructing, it is suitable to pass the factory instance, which is able to create these instances, to the method as a parameter.

☞ Sometimes it is suitable to unite the getter and setter in the way that the setter returns the previous value of the adjusted property.

☞ The complete conditional statement is used in the moment when based on the condition you have to decide which of the two actions will be executed.

☞ The syntax of the complete conditional statement is the following one
`if ( <condition> ) <statement_1> else <statement_2>`
where the `<statement_1>` is executed when the condition is fulfilled and the `<statement_2>` when it is not fulfilled.

☞ In case you don't need to detect the distance between two points, but the length of their connecting line, one has to be added to the difference of their coordinates.

☞ In the method with variable number of parameters, the values of parameters whose number is not known in advance are saved into a container, the name of which is stated in the head of a method behind triple-dot.

☞ Values saved in a container can be withdrawn and processed one after another.

☞ The container for a variable number of parameters has to be quoted always as the last.

☞ A classic for loop inherited its syntax from the C language. This syntax is as follows:
`for ( <initialization> ; <condition> ; <modification> ) <statement>`

☞ The keyword for with the following braces constitutes the loop *header*; the `<statement>` constitutes the loop *body*.

☞ The part called `<initialization>` will be executed only once before the first entry into the loop body. There may be a declaration of a control variable or certain expression located there.

☞ The `<condition>` has to be evaluated prior each entry into the loop body. If it is not true, the loop is finished and you continue with the first statement after the loop.

☞ The ⟨*modification*⟩ will be executed after each passing through the loop body. Here you will write an expression modifying the value of loop control variable for the next execution of the loop body.

☞ All parts of the loop header can be skipped so that only two semicolons will be left. The for(;;) header will be used as a header of an endless loop.

☞ In case all necessary actions are defined already in the head, probably you will need no body with statements. Then you can use an empty statement as a body, i.e. the only semicolon.

☞ Using the statement for with an empty head and an empty body has no sense – it evokes only freezing of the program.

☞ The for loop is a statement as any other one, and you can use it in all cases where you can use a statement.

Project:
The resulting form of the project to which we came at the end of the lesson and after completing all exercises is in the 140z_Factory2 project.

41 The Loops

What you will learn in this lesson
In this lesson an improvement of the race, which will be not bound to a particular circuit, will be completed. You will read what it means a lazy initialization, you will learn how to use the break *statement for premature leaving the loop and how to define a decision sequence* if ... else if. *I will also explain you the side effects of methods and I will present how to use the loop with the final condition.*

Project:
In this lesson you continue in using the 140z_Factory2 *project.*

Size of a Road-field

932. Last time you started an improvement of the race, so that it would not be limited to one ring. You told that the necessary modifications are too large to get into one lesson. What is missing?

We prepared conditions so that the race can create any number of rings (however, they will be equal for the given race), but you miss information to place these rings reasonably one along the other.

933. But we know the number of lines as well as columns of each of them.

Maybe we know it, but the race is not able to discover it. When you have a look at the class RaceLShape, you see, that it has to know how many lines and columns takes the given ring so that its instances could display individual rings one along the other and to prepare a sufficiently spacious canvas for them. In this class we could save these sizes into constants, but the instances which should be able to arrange races at various rings need to have a chance to get such information directly from the ring or to discover it in some other way.

Therefore it is necessary to supplement the ring with the method getFieldSize(), which returns the size of the area taken by the ring measured in fields (i.e. the number of lines and columns of the smaller rectangle into which the ring fits – we will call it a circumscribed rectangle).

Then the method getStartRelFieldPosition() is added which returns a relative field position of the ring's starting road-field measured as an offset to the position of the circumscribed rectangle, i.e. by how many lines and columns you have to move to get from the upper left corner field of this rectangle to the ring's starting road-field.

To show it at the existing rings, the square ring has the field size [2×2], and ringShapeL [4×4]. Both of them have the ring's start at the left upper corner of the circumscribed rectangle, which means that the relative position of the beginning is [0, 0] for both of them.

934.   I start to understand. It means now the class Ring will be improved, won't it be?

Exactly, you have to teach the ring to run through all its road-fields when required and derive the occupied area (circumscribed rectangle) from the location of these road-fields.

935.   Would it be sufficient to remember the number of columns and lines that were entered during its construction?

You entered these numbers only to O-shape ring factories. When you intend to create other factories, you have to equip them with an ability to find the size of the created ring. It will be simple because all discovering will be concentrated at one place – the ring is able to discover its size itself.

936.   I know – it asks the remembered multishape. So where is the problem?

Unfortunately, asking the multishape is not the right way. I suggested using the multishape to allow you obtaining important information that otherwise you were not able to discover at that time. However, we plan to place several rings on the display and therefore we can expect that we will need to change the size of the grid-field, i.e. the canvas step size.

As a consequence of this change the sizes and positions of particular rings would be changed. To change the position and size of the multishape representing the ring at the canvas is not a problem. However, you should change also the positions and sizes of all the road-fields in the ring and you have to program it. I advise you that you would certainly discover that you should better avoid the multishape services. Otherwise you need to modify the multishape as well as the represented road-rings and in addition you should keep these modifications synchronized. That's why we now remove the multishapes and replace their using with our own code.

So, to return to our program, we try to explain to the ring, how to detect (and later also how to set) its size.

The Lazy Initialization

937.   I am afraid that it (I mean the ring) will have to ask all of its road-fields and count the result according to the obtained information. It will take some time.

You are true. Let's teach the ring to make this going around only at the first requirement and then, to return simply the value discovered in the first round. This is used in practice quite often – for example instances of some classes are saving their text signature in this way. For instances, the signatures of which are laboriously created and are not changed in course of their life, is worthwhile to reserve a special field (attribute) for their signature.

After the first requirement the instances create their signatures and save them into this field. In case of any other requirements they only withdraw the signatures and return them. Similarly you can program also determining of the area and offset of rings.

938.   How the instance recognizes that someone asks for the first time?

The instance looks into the designated area and if there is only null, it is clear that nothing has been prepared. Then it prepares necessary information. Next time there will be already a reference to a prepared object instead of null, which the relevant method will only return. This procedure is called a **lazy initialization**, because the relevant field is not initialized by a constructor, but it is postponed to the time when it is really needed.

939.   Show me, please, how I could program determining of the needed area.

You can see the method's definition in the listing 41.1. It shows also the definitions of the ringPosition, ringFieldSize and startFieldOffset fields (attributes), where the instance remembers the counted results not to be urged to count them again in the next calling. As I said above, it's reasonable to explicitly "zero" these fields at the beginning. I know that they obtain the null value during the memory allocation, however, I wanted to emphasize this initial value and so I used the formally needless assignments in its declaration.

As you can see, the method is created by two statements. Firstly the big conditional statement discovers if the field ringFieldSize (the area dimension) contains only an empty reference and if yes, it counts it and saves the created Size object into the field. Then the field's content returns the second statement as a functional value independently to the fact if it was just saved or prepared in the moment of the method's calling.

Listing 41.1:   *The getFieldSize()method in the Ring class*

```
//== VARIABLE INSTANCE FIELDS =================================================

    /** Ring position, which is the position of the circumscribed rectangle. */
    private Position ringPosition = null;

/** Relative field position (field offset) of the starting road-field.
 *  This means the position measured relatively to the left top corner
 *  of the circumscribed rectangle. */
private Position startFieldOffset = null;

/** Ring field size (size measured in fields),
 *  which is the field size of the circumscribed rectangle.. */
private Size ringFieldSize = null;


//== INSTANCE GETTERS AND SETTERS =============================================

/*****************************************************************************
 * Count the field size of the ring if it is not yet counted,
 * otherwise it returns the previously counted value.
 *
 * @return Field size of the ring
 */
public Size getFieldSize()
{
    if (fieldSize == null) {
        RoadField field    = startField;
        Position position = startField.getPosition();
        int minx = position.x;
        int miny = position.y;
        int maxx = minx;
        int maxy = miny;
        for (;;) {
            field    = field.getNext();
            position = field.getPosition();
            if (field == startField) {  //All fields were used
                break;                         //---------->
```

```
        }
        //Tests horizontal coordinate
        if (position.x < minx) {
            minx = position.x;
        } else if (position.x > maxx) {
            maxx = position.x;
        }
        //Tests vertical coordinate
        if (position.y < miny) {
            miny = position.y;
        } else if (position.y > maxy) {
            maxy = position.y;
        }
    }
    //Pixel coordinates are counted, we may count the field coordinates
    int module      = field.getModule();
    ringPosition    = new Position(minx, minx);
    ringFieldSize   = new Size((maxx - minx) / module + 1,
                               (maxy - miny) / module + 1);
    startFieldOffset = new Position((position.x - minx) / module,
                                    (position.y - miny) / module);
}
    return fieldSize;
}
```

Determining of Lower and Upper Limits

940.   You say two statements, but the first one is quite big.

Yes, it's a little bit extensive, because it makes several things simultaneously. It needs to detect the smallest and the biggest horizontal as well as vertical coordinate for deducing the occupied area. But let's go on step by step.

First of all it discovers the position of the starting road-field, and inserts the corresponding coordinates of this beginning into the variables, in which it will remember the found minima and maxima. Then it enters into the loop in which particular road-fields are analyzed and according to them the discovered limits of coordinates' values are adjusted.

The variable field, initialized before the entry into the loop, is in fact a loop control variable and therefore it theoretically could be declared and initialized in the initializing part of the header. However, we need to initialize some other auxiliary variables and therefore we have to define it before the loop. Nevertheless, I recommend in all cases in which you would skip the condition in the loop head and define an endless loop, to skip over even this initialization (you should "factor it out" before the loop) as well as the modification (you should move it into the loop body). Then it will be far obvious that it is an endless loop.

Leaving the Loop from Inside of Its Body

941.   But this loop should not be endless. After passing through all road-fields, it should finish.

Of course, the loop, which would be really endless, is used rather exceptionally in programs. Mostly the endless loop is used in the way that, when somewhere in the middle of the loop you discover that everything what was needed is arranged, you recall its premature finish.

And it is also in this case. Your loop starts with a modification in which you move to another road-field and determine its position. If this further road-field will be at the same time the starting road-field, i.e. the road-field where you started measuring, you know that you passed through all road-fields and therefore you can finish. You insert the break statement into the program, which helps you jumping out of the loop and then you continue with the first statement after the loop.

942.   If I understand it properly, you have chosen the endless loop instead of the classic one due to the fact that modification is done at the beginning, whilst in the classic loop it is done at the end. If you would add the modi-fication statement
        `field = field.getNext();`
also before the loop, you could use the classic one about which you spoke last time.

Yes, I could, but then the modification would be twice in the program – before the loop there would be a code which would be executed before starting the loop, and then the modification which would be executed after each finishing the loop body would be in the header. Furthermore, we would add also the statement

`position = field.getPosition();`

(This statement should be added behind the loop.) Some programmers propose the loops like that but I prefer not to have the same code at two places despite the fact that I have to jump out from inside of the loop body.

943.   Is the statement break **responsible for jumping out of the endless loop?**

No, the statement break is responsible for jumping out of any loop. In each loop you can discover that it is going to finish and you need to jump out, despite it is premature from the head point of view. Then you use the statement break. Remember, that for break the same is valid as for return: it has to be the last statement of the given block.

944.   And why the same statement is not used in both cases?

Because each of them is doing something else. The return statement finishes the method, whilst the break statement finishes only the loop and remains in the method. When you use the break statement, further statements can follow after the loop. On the contrary, when you leave the loop by the return, you jump out not only from the loop, but directly from the whole method.

The Sequence of `if … else if`

945.   Well, I came to another road-field and I know that I didn't finish yet. What now?

Now you verify if coordinates of the given field are not smaller than the minima, or bigger than the maxima found until now. Notice that the test is created with two complete conditional statements and both of them have again a conditional statement in their `else` part, but this conditional statement is not as embedded as usually. You can meet this construction quite often and I would like to digress for a while from your program to an explanation of the used construction.

Listing 41.2:   *The sequence of comparison with standard alignment*

```
if (small) {
    //What to do if it is small
}
else {
    if (big) {
        //What to do if it is not small, but it is big
    }
    else {
        if (fat) {
            //What to do if it is not small, nor big, but it is fat
        }
        else {
            if (thin) {
                //What to do if it is not small, nor big, nor fat, but it is thin
            }
            else {
                //What to do if it is not small, nor big, nor fat, nor thin
            }
        }
    }
}
```

Listing 41.3:   *The sequence of comparison with better formatting*

```
if (small) {
    //What to do if it is small
}
else if (big) {
    //What to do if it is not small, but it is big
}
else if (fat) {
    //What to do if it is not small, nor big, but it is fat
}
else if (thin) {
    //What to do if it is not small, nor big, nor fat, but it is thin
}
else {
    //What to do if it is not small, nor big, nor fat, nor thin
}
```

You surely know the classic one-liner that somebody is not small, nor big, nor fat, nor thin. When you would like to write a program which would select a proper action for anybody, it would look out in standard alignment as the program in the listing 41.2. But a program with such alignment is not well formatted and moreover, bodies of the embedded statements are gradually shifted to the right. Therefore, the alignment showed in the listing 41.3 is preferred in such comparing string. Both programs are entirely equal from the compiler's point of view. They only differentiate which one of them is better formatted.

The described more effective formatting is used also in the code in the listing 41.1. First of all I always ask, if the given coordinate is smaller than the smallest found until now, and if not, I ask on the contrary, if it is bigger that the biggest found. Due to the fact that it cannot be smaller and bigger at the same time, it's obvious, that only one correction will be done. Then the same is done with the other coordinate.

946. What about when I would write the "ifs" one below the other, without any else? Would then it be simpler, wouldn't it?

The record will be simpler, but the program will mostly do something quite different. I tried to show you both versions procedures of evaluation at the figure 41.1. The left figure shows an evaluation procedure of the listing 41.2, respectively 41.3; the right figure shows the procedure in case when else before if is missing. As you see at the left figure, the program moves to the end after completing the relevant action, whilst at the right figure another condition can be evaluated. Even when any other condition would not be true, the program at least is delayed with their evaluating.

I met several programs in which the programmers made this particular mistake. And consequently, when removing the error, they laboriously modified conditions, so that all other conditions would not be true, instead of simple inserting else.

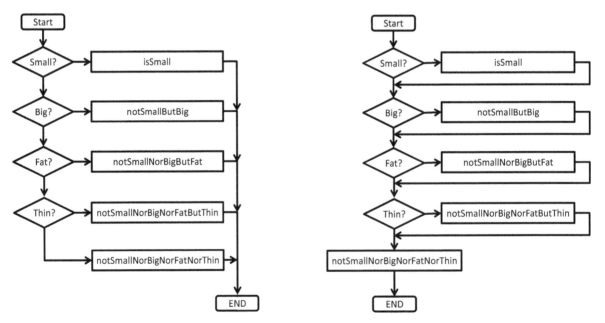

Figure 41.1
Different meaning of the construction if ... if compared to the construction if ... else if

Side Effects of Methods

947.   Please explain me the statements behind the loop.

I calculate the distance between positions that I subtract the smaller one from the bigger one. Due to the fact that I want the field distance, i.e. the number of fields, I divide the determined point distance by the size of a road-field and I get the number of fields between these two coordinates. But I'm not interested in the number of fields between them, but the total number of road-fields, and it is always bigger by one. Train it at some simple example.

948.   And why do you count the relative position when nobody asks you for it?

Because I have all necessary intermediate results at my disposal, otherwise I would have to count them again. If we don't use the multishape, the method for discovering the relative field position of the starting field would test if this position (the `startFieldOffset` attribute) is calculated and if not, it should call the method for determining the field size of the ring, because it knows that the calculation for required relative position will be the side effect of this method – see the listing 41.4. (The `getPosition()` method should be modified in the similar way.)

Let's admit that creating of methods with side effect is considered as a programming transgression because they make the program less transparent. Nevertheless, they are profitable in certain special situations. And I thought this time it was just such special situation, because the calculations are almost the same and when I have prepared the needed intermediate results for the first one, I can easily count also the second one without any possible danger for the rest of the program.

Listing 41.4:   *The getStartRelFieldPosition() method in the Ring class*

```
public Position getStartRelFieldPosition ()
{
    if (startFieldOffset == null) {
        getFieldSize();   //Method counting both the field size and the offset
    }
    return startFieldOffset;
}
```

949.   The side effect is something what the method should not do?

The method with a side effect is such a method which is responsible for one aspect and it makes also something else. And such program proposal is considered as immodest, in which – due to receiving this side effect – you have to call a method, whose official determination is quite different. It reminds a little bit the old jokes, in which an old lady asks the houseman to bring her a piano, because she forgot the car key laid at it.

Calculation of relative field position of the starting field is a side effect of the method for calculating the ring field size in this case, but from outside, i.e. outside the class, nobody knows it. Information that for discovering the relative position of the beginning you have to calculate firstly the size is internal information of the Ring class and the surrounding programs cannot use it, nor misuse it. When somebody asks the ring for the relative position of its beginning, he will not be informed that the called method entrusted somebody else to discover this information as a side effect of his activities.

Loops Taxonomy

950.   Does it mean that now the race could be arranged so that the racers may drive along any ring?

We are close to it, but I would like to add some further improvements. We add the method getLength(), which counts and returns the total length of the ring, i.e. the total number of its road-fields.

951.   What will be this method for?

The main purpose of introducing this method is to have an example for demonstrating the remaining kinds of loops. Now you know certain loops, and I want to complete this explanation.

Java offers several kinds of loop. The for loop we used in the last lesson is the most complex one. Besides it there are another two simpler loops:

☞   The while loop – the loop with a condition at the beginning, i.e. with the condition tested before each entering into the loop body.

☞   The do-while loop – the loop with a condition at the end, i.e. with the condition tested after each executing of the loop body.

952.   Why there are so many types of loops? Why one type doesn't suffice?

Theoretically one would suffice, however then we should make some compromises. Each loop type has its situations, in which it is the best one.

I will gradually present several versions of the same method; each of them defined with different type of loop to demonstrate the difference between them. At first I will show the version with the for loop I've already explained. You can see it at the listing 41.5.

Listing 41.5:   *The countFieldsUsingFor() method in the Ring class*

```
public int countFieldsUsingFor ()
{
    int length = 1;
    for (RoadField field = startField;
         field.getNext() != startField;
         field = field.getNext())
    {
        length++;
    }
    return length;
}
```

This method firstly declares and initializes the counter i, where we will count the number of fields. Then the loop starts.

☞   In its initialization part the field control variable is declared and initialized.

☞   In its condition we test, if the field variable refers to the last not counted road-field. If its next field is the starting field with which we begun the counting, we know, that the last counted field was the last one and we can end the counting and thus also the loop.

☞   In its modification part we move the control variable to refer to the next road-field in the ring.

At this example we can show, how the method will behave in some boundary situations.

If the ring would have no road-field (I know, that it is impossible, however, please accept this possibility for a while), it means if the value of the startField would be null, the method will end with the NullPointerException whilst trying to execute the expression field.getNext().

If the ring would have only the starting road-field, this road-field should refer to itself as its next field. Thus the condition will be false even before the first attempt to execute the loop body and therefore the loop body will not be executed at all and the method returns the initial value of the length variable, which is 1.

As an exercise try to derive similarly, what happens, when the loop will have two or three road-fields.

The while Loop – the Loop with a Condition at the Beginning

953.   I tried it and think that I understand despite the mentioned border conditions could never happen.

I know, but as I said, I wanted to explain, that when the condition is false immediately from the beginning, the loop body would execute zero times.

Let's go on to the second example, where I show the method using the while loop. Its syntax is simple as follows:

```
while (  <condition>  )  <statement>
```

The keyword while with the following condition is called loop header and the statement is the loop body.

The semantics of the while loop is simple: first of all the condition is evaluated, and if it is true, the statement creating the loop body is executed. Then again the condition is evaluated and it continues round and round, until the condition is false. It finishes the execution of the loop body and the next first statement after the loop continues. If either the first evaluation of the condition is false, the loop body is not executed at all.

The while loop has a lot of common with the for loop. You can write one with the help of the other and on the contrary. The while loop works equally as the for loop with the head

```
for (  ;  <condition>  ;  )  <statement>
```

As I've already told, it is true also vice versa – you could write down operating of the classic for loop with the help of the while loop as follows:

```
<initialization>;
while(  <condition>  )  {
    <statement>
    <modification>;
}
```

I think that with this information you are able to write the countFieldsUsingWhile() without any help. You can compare your solution with the solution at the listing 41.6. I think that the behavior of this method needs no further explanation.

Listing 41.6:   *The* `countFieldsUsingWhile()` *method in the* `Ring` *class*

```
public int countFieldsUsingWhile ()
{
    int length = 1;
    RoadField field = startField;
    while(field.getNext() != startField) {
        length++;
        field = field.getNext();
    }
    return length;
}
```

The do … while **Loop – the Loop with a Condition at the End**

954.   I understand that while **loop and** for **loop are interchangeable and that it is on my decision, what I prefer in particular situations.**

It is true for languages from the C-family, because the C-language authors defined this statement in a more general way compared to other languages.

Let's go on to the third example. As the last one I explain the do … while loop. Its syntax is as follows:

```
do <statement> while (  <condition>  ) ;
```

In this case the loop body is the statement between the keywords do and while. The keyword while with the following condition is called a *loop footer*.

This loop firstly executes its body and then evaluates the condition. If it is true, it starts once again from the beginning (i.e. once more it evaluates its body), if it is not true, it finishes the loop's running, and executing of the code continues with the following statement. Thus you can derive, that this loop body will be always executed at least one times. You can see the solution in the listing 41.7.

Listing 41.7:   *The* `countFieldsUsingDoWhile()` *method in the* `Ring` *class*

```
public int countFieldsUsingDoWhile ()
{
    int length = 0;
    RoadField field = startField;
    do {
        length++;
        field = field.getNext();
    } while(field != startField);
    return length;
}
```

Before entering into the loop body the method will initialize a loop control variable, it means the field local variable, with a reference to the ring's starting road-field. In the loop body the number of the found round-fields is increased for the current field and the control variable is then "redirected" to the successor of this field. So the loop body ends and we test, if this successor differs from the starting field. If it differs, we again enter the loop body, add the length for this successor by one and redirect the field variable to the successor of this successor. So we continue until we reach the starting point.

You can see, that this third loop is a little simpler than the previous two, because we evaluate the condition in the right time (or, if you want, at the right place) and thus we need not to compare the starting field with the successor of the current field, but just with the current field.

955. I believe I understand everything. So, on what will we embark now?

I think that you can train your new skills by defining the paint(Painter) method. Define the first three version of this method named paintUsingWhile, paintUsingFor and paintUsingDoWhile. Define all these methods as private and modify the paint(Painter) method to call one of these three methods. Be watchful, the solution is not so simple, as you can think. You can compare your solution with the definitions in the listing 41.8.

Listing 41.8: *Three versions of the painting methods in the Ring class*

```
private void paintUsingDoWhile(Painter painter)
{
    RoadField field = startField;
    do {
        field.paint(painter);
        field = field.getNext();
    } while(field != startField);
}

private void paintUsingFor(Painter painter)
{
    RoadField field = startField;
    for (;
        field.getNext() != startField;
        field = field.getNext())
    {
        field.paint(painter);
    }
    field.paint(painter);
}

private void paintUsingWhile(Painter painter)
{
    RoadField field = startField;
    field.paint(painter);
    field = field.getNext();
    while(field != startField) {
        field.paint(painter);
        field = field.getNext();
    }
}
```

956. You were true. When I've defined the second and the third methods mechanically, one of the road-field was not painted.

In this case there is a problem in loops with conditions tested before entering the loop body. I wanted to show you that there are situations, when one kind of loop is significantly better than the others.

The switch **Statement**

957.   When two of these methods use not an optimal kind of loop, should I remove them?

No, I want to present the last algorithmic construction that we didn't use yet. This is the switch statement. You would use it whenever you need to decide which one of several possible continuations to
choose. Its syntax is far most complicated from all constructions you met until now. I was hesitating if
I should postpone its explanation into the next volume, but then I realized, that you would reproach
me if you would meet it somewhere in a program and you would not know what it is about. The
syntax of the switch statement is as follows:

```
switch( <integer_expression> )
{
    case <value_1>:
        //Code executed when the value of the <integer_expression> is the <value_1>
        break;

    case <value_2>:
        //Code executed when the value of the <integer_expression> is the <value_2>
        break;

    //...    Next possible branches

    default:    //This part is optional
        //This code is executed when the value of the <integer_expression>
        //is not equal to any of the declared <value_i>.
}
```

In the previous definition you should distinguish **a header** created by the keyword switch and by an
integer expression in parentheses, and **labels,** which are parts quoted by the keyword case and ending
with a colon. The default: is also considered as a label. There are several rules for the switch statement:

☞   The term *<integer_expression>* quoted in parentheses after the keyword switch indicates that really an integer (value of the int type) has to be the result of this expression. If the result type can
be automatically converted to an integer (for example if the result is of char type), the compiler
converts it instead of you. In opposite case (if for example it is the long or double type), you have
to explicitly convert it yourself (probably by the cast operator). Otherwise the compiler announces a compile-time error.

☞   The values quoted after the keyword case have to be integer constants, the value of which is
known in the compile time. Therefore they cannot be current constants to which the initial value
is assigned by a constructor. This quite strict requirement is placed on the program so that the
compiler could decide if the given statement will be converted to a classic sequence of conditional statements, or if certain optimized strategy how to quickly jump to the beginning of the
code which should be executed would be used.

☞   Labels can be quoted in any order and it's not necessary to keep the increasing order or their
values. Similarly it is not necessary to quote the optional label default: as the last one, despite it
is usual practice.

☞ The same value of two various labels cannot be quoted in one switch statement. (The compiler could not choose what to do sooner.)

☞ The statement break, with which each branch is finishing in the previous illustration, is facultative. But if you would not quote it, the program would not jump out of the switch statement and would continue in executing the code in the next branch. Sometimes it is suitable, but in prevailing number of cases the break statement will be contained there.

958. You were true, it is really complicated. Could you find a really simple little example for me to understand it better?

I show you how you can use this statement for choosing the right code performing the task of the method paint(Painter). We have three methods. At first we need to assign some indexes to them. Let's define the following constants that can be evaluated in the compile time:

```
private static final int DO_WHILE=0, FOR=1, WHILE=2;
```

In the listing 41.9 you can see the version using the if … else if sequence and in the listing 41.10 you can see the version using the switch statement.

Both versions are equivalent in their functions. They both define the method which invokes the desired method (the method, the index of which is in the index variable). But the first of them gradually tests all possibilities until the selected one is found, whilst the switch version jumps directly into the relevant branch. As you see separate branches don't have to finish with the statement break. If I skip over the possibility not to quote the break statement, because I want so that executing of the code would continue with the next branch, I have also other possibilities of finishing. In this case I concluded each branch with the return statement, because after jumping out of the switch statement nothing had to be done.

959. Isn't the defined solution too complicated?

Yes, it is. However, I defined it in this way to show you all kinds of loops and differences among them as well as the switch statement. You find it in the final project in this lesson; however, you don't need to keep it for the future. On the other hand the only drawback of this solution is its length. The speed of execution is almost the same as the speed of the paint(Painter) method defined directly with the do…while loop.

Change of the Module for Ring

960. I'm afraid that the ring's modifications do not finish by defining the method paint(Painter).

You are true. To use this ring fully, it should implement the IModular interface. And for this you are still missing several methods. I will show you the definition of the method setModule(int). Defining the remaining methods will be your exercise. You can train the loops in these definitions, so be careful.

I will present you the definition of the method setModule(int) to show you that adjusting the module is not as simple as you could imagine for the first sight. To give you in illustrative idea, I advise you to draw a square grid and draw e.g. the known L-shape ring into it. And now draw another square grid over it, the fields of which will have their sides twice or four times bigger and realize what you will have to modify to re-draw the ring from one square net into the other one. You will have to change not only the size of individual road-fields, but also their positions. Due to I was afraid you may have problems in defining this method I prepared it in the listing 41.11. Let's explain the definition.

Listing 41.9:   *The paint(Painter) method using a sequence of the* if ... else if *sequence*

```
public void paint(Painter painter)
{
    int index = DO_WHILE;
    if (index == DO_WHILE) {
        paintUsingDoWhile(painter);
    }
    else if (index == FOR) {
        paintUsingFor(painter);
    }
    else if (index == WHILE) {
        paintUsingWhile(painter);
    }
    else {
        throw new RuntimeException("\nUnknown method type: " + index);
    }
    return
}
```

Listing 41.10:   *The paint(Painter) method using the switch statement*

```
public void paint(Painter painter)
{
    int index = DO_WHILE;
    switch (DO_WHILE)
    {
        case DO_WHILE:  paintUsingDoWhile(painter);     return;
        case FOR:       paintUsingFor(painter);         return;
        case WHILE:     paintUsingWhile(painter);       return;
        default:
            throw new RuntimeException("\nUnknown method type: " + index);
    }
    return
}
```

Listing 41.11:   *The setModul(int) method in the Ring class*

```
public void setModule(int newModule)
{
    double oldModule = getModule();
    double ratio     = newModule / oldModule;

    CM.stopPainting(); {
        RoadField field = startField;
        //Sets the new module and positions to all road fields
        do {
            Position pixelPosition = field.getPosition();

            //Derive its relative position
            double relX = (pixelPosition.x - ringPosition.x);
```

```
                double relY = (pixelPosition.y - ringPosition.y);

                //Derive the pixel position from the field position
                field.setPosition(ringPosition.x + (int)(relX * ratio  +  .5),
                                  ringPosition.y + (int)(relY * ratio  +  .5));
                field.setModule(newModule);
                field = field.getNext();
            } while (field != startField);
        } CM.returnPainting();
}
```

1. First of all it asks the ring for its current module and saves the obtained value as the oldMOdule. As you surely remember, this method counts also the position as its side effect.

2. For a while it forbids the canvas manager re-painting to avoid the situation that the user would see how the ring's size and position changes field by field, because its intention is to move the entire ring altogether. At this place I would like to draw your attention to useful unification of pair commands (e.g. stopPainting – returnPainting) with brackets surrounding the block. If these commands would stay lonely as any other, most likely you would forget the second command in such long methods.

3. It defines the loop it has used in defining the drawing method. At first the loop control variable field is defined and initialized. At the end of the loop body this variable is modified and behind the body it is tested to reveal, if the loop body should be executed once more.

4. In the loop body it counts the relative position of the current field to the whole ring. Only this relative position (offset) should be changed according to the module. The counted new relative position is then again added to the ring position to obtain the field absolute position.

961.   Why did you declare the relX and relY variables as double when you converted the result back to int later on?

I wanted to eliminate the possible rounding errors. As you certainly remember, the result of division of two integers is also an integer – 1/2=0. So if you want to resize the module to one half and declare all variables as int, the ratio would be zero.

962.   Why do you work with relative positions? Isn't it uselessly complicated?

No, it is not. When you change the module (i.e. the size) of an object, you change not only the sizes of its parts, but also their distances and so their positions. However the position of the whole object (i.e. the position of the circumscribed rectangle) should not change. Thus, when the object size changes, only the offsets if its parts to the object origin changes. (Have a look at the section *Position and Module Setting* on page 216.)

963.   Well, you've got me again. Go on.

The modifications of the Ring class are almost done. Don't forget to remove the last parameter in the constructor (the Multishape) – we stopped to use it. Remove also the shape field. Then compile the class and if you forget to remove using of the shape field somewhere, the compiler shows it as a syntax error.

964.　But when I modified the Ring class, I have to modify also other classes.

Yes, but it should be much simpler. For example in the RingBuilder class you remove the notion about Multishape and you should do the same in the RoadField class. Everything should be compiled and the old test should run.

965.　I would like to see, how the module setting is operating.

There's nothing easier. I modified the class RingTest. And I added a test method in which firstly both rings are reduced and then again enlarged. To notice the change better there is a translucent rectangle drawn over them, the module's change has no influence at it and thus it has a constant size and constant location. You can find the definition of the method in the listing 41.12.

Listing 41.12:　The testModuleChange test method verifying the ring's ability to change the module size in the RingTest class

```
@Test
public void testModuleChange()
{
    class Wrapper implements IPaintable
    {
        IPaintable paintable = new Rectangle(50, 50, 100, 100,
                                    NamedColor.BLUE.translucent());
        @Override
        public void paint(Painter painter)
        {
            paintable.paint(painter);
        }
    }
    CM.setSize(8, 7);
    CM.add(new Wrapper());
    IO.inform("Reference rectangle shown");
    for (int krok = 25;   krok < 150;   krok += 75) {
        CM.setStep(krok);
        ringSquare.setModule(krok);
        ringLShape.setModule(krok);
        IO.inform("Step modified to " + krok);
    }
}
```

966.　Why did you define the Wrapper class inside the test method? Why did not you use directly the Rectangle?

I needed an object that is not influenced by changes of canvas step. When the canvas step is changed, the canvas manager asks all objects implementing IChangeable and IModular to adapt to the new step size (our rings are also asked). So I needed an object that is only paintable, nothing more. Thus I defined a class that implements only the IPaintable interface and therefore the canvas manager does not ask its object to adapt.

Thus you can check that only the positions and sizes of our rings change. The position and size of the reference rectangle is all the time the same.

The `ParallelRace` **Class**

967. **The rings really change the size of their road-fields and move them into the relevant canvas fields. Does it mean the race can be started?**

I think yes. But I suggest few tiny improvements. Let's use the fact that you can set the required ring position and you will not enter in advance how many racers can apply. You will simply take on new racers and prepare rings for them, despite the fact that you would know they do not fit at the implicit canvas. When somebody stops registration of further racers and starts the race, the starting method discovers how large canvas can be created and asks the canvas manager to adjust the needed number of columns and change suitably the step size (I remind that the module overtakes this size), so that individual rings would fit at the canvas after these changes.

968. **How the program recognizes how big canvas should be created?**

You declare the class fields that will remember the maximal permissible size of the canvas. This size can be set any time. The starting method will use the size which will be valid in time of its running.

969. **Shall we create a new class?**

Yes, we will create a class called `ParallelRace`, because it will be able to organize races, where several racers compete on parallel rings. You can see its definition in the listing 41.13. I tried to comment it sufficiently, so that you would understand all. Go through it and tell me what is clear and unclear to you.

Listing 41.13: *The ParallelRace class*

```
/*******************************************************************************
 * Instances of the {@code Race} class represent races
 * that can be attended.
 * The race is characterized by the ring where the vehicles run.
 * This ring is created by a factory object passed to constructor in parameter.
 * The racers can subsequently register at the race.
 * All registered racers compete together in parallel,
 * each on its own ring instance.
 */
public class ParallelRace implements IRace
{
    //== CONSTANT CLASS FIELDS ===========================================

    /** Manager of the canvas on which the instance will be painted. */
    private static final CanvasManager CM = CanvasManager.getInstance();

    /** Default maximal available canvas width, where all the rings should fit.
     *  Each racer has a ring of its own and particular rings
     *  are separated with an empty column. */
    private static final int DEFAULT_MAX_CANVAS_WIDTH = 1000;

    /** Default maximal available canvas height, where should each ring fits. */
    private static final int DEFAULT_MAX_CANVAS_HEIGHT = 700;
```

```
//== VARIABLE CLASS FIELDS ========================================================

/** Maximal available canvas width, where all the rings should fit.
 *  Each racer has a ring of its own
 *  and particular rings are separated with an empty column. */
private static int maxCanvasWidth = DEFAULT_MAX_CANVAS_WIDTH;

/** Maximal available canvas height, where the ring should fit. */
private static int maxCanvasHeight = DEFAULT_MAX_CANVAS_HEIGHT;


//== CONSTANT INSTANCE FIELDS =====================================================

/** Map mapping the racer to the crate with information about this racer. */
private final Map<IRacer, Info> racer2info = new HashMap<>();

/** Number of rounds of the race. */
private final int roundNumber;

/** Factory generated the rings. */
private final IRingFactory ringFactory;


//== VARIABLE INSTANCE FIELDS =====================================================

/** Currently set canvas module. */
private int module;

/** System time of the start. */
private long time0;

/** Number of registered racers. */
private int racersNumber = 0;

/** Number of columns and rows of the ring in use. */
private int ringColumns, ringRows;


//== OTHER NON-PRIVATE CLASS METHODS ==============================================

/*****************************************************************************
 * Remember the maximal allowed canvas size.
 *
 * @param width  Max allowed pixel width
 * @param height Max allowed pixel height
 */
public static void setMaxCanvasSize(int width, int height)
{
    ParallelRace.maxCanvasWidth  = width;
    ParallelRace.maxCanvasHeight = height;
}



//###########################################################################
```

```
    //== CONSTUCTORS AND FACTORY METHODS ==========================================

    /********************************************************************************
     * Creates an instance that will be able to organize
     * one ring race on rings generated by the given factory.
     *
     * @param ringFactory  Factory creating rings for the race
     */
    public ParallelRace(IRingFactory ringFactory)
    {
        this(ringFactory, 1);
    }


    /********************************************************************************
     * Creates an instance that will be able to organize race
     * with the given number of rounds on rings generated by the given factory.
     *
     * @param ringFactory  Factory creating rings for the race
     * @param roundNumber  Number of rounds of the race
     */
    public ParallelRace(IRingFactory ringFactory, int roundNumber)
    {
        this.ringFactory = ringFactory;
        this.roundNumber = roundNumber;
        this.module      = CM.getStep();     //Temporary value until the start
    }



    //== OTHER NON-PRIVATE INSTANCE METHODS ==================================

    /********************************************************************************
     * Opens a dialog announcing start
     * and after closing it, starts measuring the time.
     */
    public void start()
    {
        Collection<Info> infos = racer2info.values();
        prepareCanvas();     //Sets it size so that the rings would just fit
        for (Info info : infos) {
            info.controller.start();
        }
        IO.inform("After confirming this window\n" +
                "the time starts to be measured");
        time0 = System.currentTimeMillis();
    }


    /********************************************************************************
     * Finishes the race, terminates all registrations
     * and prepares for the new ones.
     */
    public void stop()
    {
        racer2info.clear();
    }
```

```
/***************************************************************************
 * Registers the given racer, places it at the race start,
 * learns its needed keys
 * and registers its controller as a keyboard listener.
 *
 * @param racer Racer registering for the race
 */
@Override
public void register(IRacer racer)
{
    if (racer2info.containsKey(racer)) {
        IO.inform("The racer cannot be registered twice: " + racer);
        return;
    }
    Ring       ring       = prepareNextRing(); //Modify number of racers
    RoadField  start      = ring.getStartField();
    RoadField  target     = start.getNext();
    Controller controller = Controller.createFor(racer);

    Info info = new Info(ring, start, target,
                         controller, roundNumber, racer);
    racer2info.put(racer, info);

    //Ensure, that both, racer as well as its ring, will be visible
    CM.add(ring);
    CM.addAbove(ring, racer);
}

/***************************************************************************
 * Checks that the racer reaches the right running target (checkpoint).
 * If yes, prepares the next target position, if no, does nothing.
 *
 * @param racer Racer announcing reaching the next position
 */
@Override
public void checkpoint(IRacer racer)
{
    Info info = racer2info.get(racer);
    if (info == null) {
        return;                          //==========>
    }
    Position pz = racer.getPosition();
    Position pc = info.targetField.getPosition();
    if (pz.equals(pc)) {
        if (info.targetField == info.startField) {
            info.roundsLeft--;
            if (info.roundsLeft == 0) {
                finishRace(racer, info);
                return;                  //==========>
            }
        }
        info.targetField = info.targetField.getNext();
    }
}
```

```java
/*****************************************************************************
 * Returns a string representation of the object &ndash; its text signature.
 *
 * @return A string representation of the object
 */
@Override
public String toString()
{
    return "ParallelRace(factory="      + ringFactory  +
                    ", racersNumber=" + racersNumber +
                    ", module="       + module        + ")";
}


//== PRIVATE AND AUXILIARY INSTANCE METHODS ==================================

/*****************************************************************************
 * Prepares the next ring and returns it.
 *
 * @return The requested ring
 */
private Ring prepareNextRing()
{
    int x = racersNumber * (ringColumns + 1) * module;
    Position position = new Position(x, 0);
    Ring      ring    = ringFactory.createRing(position,
                            NamedColor.getNamedColor(racersNumber));
    racersNumber++;
    if (racersNumber == 1) {
        Size ringFieldSize = ring.getFieldSize();
        ringColumns = ringFieldSize.width;
        ringRows    = ringFieldSize.height;
    }
    return ring;
}


/*****************************************************************************
 * Finishes the race for the given racer.
 *
 * @param racer Racer finishing the race
 * @param info  Crate with information about racer
 */
private void finishRace(IRacer racer, Info info)
{
    long now = System.currentTimeMillis();
    info.controller.stop();
    int time = (int)(now - time0 + 50) / 100;
    System.out.println("The racer " + racer.getName() +
            " finished the race in the time " +
            time/10 + "," + time%10 + " second");
    racer2info.remove(racer);
    if (racer2info.isEmpty()) {
        System.out.println("Race finished");
    }
}
```

```
/*****************************************************************************
 * Prepares the canvas so that all rings just fit in it.
 */
private void prepareCanvas()
{
    int  canvasColumns = (ringColumns + 1) * racersNumber  -  1;
    int  xStep = maxCanvasWidth  / canvasColumns;
    int  yStep = maxCanvasHeight / ringRows;
    this.module = Math.min(xStep, yStep);
    CM.setStepAndSize(module, canvasColumns, ringRows);

    CM.stopPainting(); {
        Collection<Info> infos = racer2info.values();
        for (Info info : infos) {
            Ring ring = info.ring;
            ring.setModule(module);
            CM.add(ring);
            info.racer.setDirection(ring.getStartField().getDirection());
            info.racer.setPosition (ring.getStartField().getPosition());
            info.racer.setModule(module);
        }
    } CM.returnPainting();
}



//== MEMBER DATA TYPES =======================================================

/*****************************************************************************
 * Internal crate containing the basic needed information
 * about racer and its current state.
 */
private static class Info
{
    /** Ring, where the race takes place. */
    private final Ring ring;

    /** The corresponding racer. */
    private final IRacer racer;

    /** Controller mediating the control from a keyboard. */
    private final Controller controller;

    /** The starting (and also finishing) field. */
    private final RoadField startField;

    /** The next running target field with a checkpoint
      *  checking, if the racer really runs through it. */
    private RoadField targetField;

    /** Number of remaining rounds. */
    private int roundsLeft;
```

```
    /***************************************************************************
     * Defines a new crate and initializes its fields.
     *
     * @param ring        Ring, where the race takes place
     * @param startField  The starting (and also finishing) field
     * @param targetField The first checkpoint
     * @param controller  Controller, mediating the control from a keyboard
     * @param roundsNumber Number of rounds
     * @param racer       Racer, information of which the crate holds
     */
    Info(Ring ring, RoadField startField, RoadField targetField,
         Controller controller, int roundsNumber,
         IRacer racer)
    {
        this.ring       = ring;
        this.startField = startField;
        this.targetField= targetField;
        this.controller = controller;
        this.roundsLeft = roundsNumber;
        this.racer      = racer;
    }
}


//== TESTING CLASSES AND METHODS =============================================

/***************************************************************************
 * The test method.
 */
public static void test()
{
    int racers = 4;
    int size   = racers * 100;
    int rounds = 2;
    ParallelRace.setMaxCanvasSize(size, size);
    IRingFactory iFact = new OShapeRingFactory(2, 2, Direction8.SOUTH);
    ParallelRace race  = new ParallelRace(iFact, rounds);

    for (int i=1;   i <= racers;   i++) {
        Arrow  arrow = new Arrow(0, 0, NamedColor.WHITE);
        Vehicle_B vb = new Vehicle_B(arrow);
        vb.setName(NamedColor.getNamedColor(i-1).getName());
        vb.registerFor(race);
    }
    race.start();
}
//    /** @param args Command line arguments - not used. */
//    public static void main(String[] args)  {  test();  }
}
```

Exercise

970.   I overtook your class from the closing project of the lesson and it does not work.

Because you did not finish the implementation of the interface IModular with the Ring class which I gave you as an exercise. After you will supplement it, it will be operating.

Review

Let's review what you have learned in this lesson:

☞   The postponed initialization means that the field is not initialized by a constructor, but its value is adjusted in the moment when somebody needs it.

☞   In case you need to use a loop whose closing is decided somewhere inside its body, you will use an endless loop. Leaving the loop is the realized by the statement break.

☞   You should align the set of decisions if … else if … else if … when all expressions else are aligned under the initial if.

☞   The method which – besides its main task- makes also something else is called a method with side effects.

☞   You should avoid using of methods with side effects if possible. In case you would use them, then their side effects should be used only inside the definition of their class.

☞   The loop with an end condition i.e. the do-while loop has the following syntax:
do ⟨statement⟩ while (⟨condition⟩) ;

☞   The loop with the end condition tests fulfilling the condition after executing the body and therefore executes its body always at least once.

☞   The syntactic definition of the loop while is as follows
while (⟨podmínka⟩) ⟨příkaz⟩

☞   The loop while can be simply converted to the for loop and on the contrary.

☞   The switch statement is used in case you need to decide among one of several follow-up possibilities.

☞   The definition of the switch statement is created by a head and by a set of notices with constants that have to be evaluated in time of compilation.

☞   The switch statement can decide according to the value of the integer expression or according to the value of the reference to an object of enum type.

☞   When adjusting the object's module you have to realize that by changing the module not only the object's size, but also its position is changed.

> *Project:*
> *The resulting form of the project to which we came at the end of the lesson and after completing all exercises is in the 141z_Loops project.*

42 Lists and Their Ordering

What you will learn in this lesson
In this lesson you will develop factories for producing rings, so that they would be able to catch the possible incorrect user inputs. You will become acquainted with the enumerated (enum) types and you will learn to define their simpler version. After that you will see the state diagram of UML *language and how it is possible to program solving of certain problems. Then you will learn the work with lists and how to sort them. Next I will explain what is the native sorting and you will become acquainted with the design pattern Command. Finally you will see how it is possible to use this pattern for ordering a list in case when the native sorting does not suit.*

Project:
In this lesson you continue in using the 141z_Loops *project.*

Enum Types

971. When I tried to define factories for some more complex rings, it happened several times that I forgot to close the ring and to my surprise the builder passed over such ring. Shouldn't I teach the builder to produce only properly constructed rings?

That's a good idea. And you immediately will learn how to create your own **enumerated types** (also called **enumeration** or **enum** types). Until now you worked with only enum type Direction8. I would say it's the proper time to learn creating your own ones.

972. Remind me once more, why they are called enum.

I already explained it in the section *Enumeration Type – Multiton* on page 102 – they have this name because they have their instances defined by an enumeration. All their instances are listed in the class definition and you cannot change this set, i.e. you cannot add nor remove any further instance.

973. How can I create my own enum type?

It is simple as follows:

1.   you press the button requiring creating a new class,

2.   in the subsequently opened dialog **Create New Class** you will set the switch **Class Type** to the value Enum,

3.   and then you confirm your complete assignment.

BlueJ opens the file created according to the enum type design. I would say that it is too complicated for your today's training, because besides the definition of values it takes into account that you will equip the instances of a given type with methods and various further abilities.

Today I wouldn't like to analyze all possibilities of the enum type, but I would show you how it is possible to define the simplest variant which will offer nothing more than the most essential things. Ask *BlueJ* to define an empty class and modify it according to the listing 42.1, where you will find the definition of an enum type and with which you will further work.

Listing 42.1:   *The enum type* `BuilderState`

```
/****************************************************************************
 * Instances of the {@code BuilderState} represent particular states,
 * in which an object can be.
 */
public enum BuilderState
{
    /** Ready for start ring building. */  READY,
    /** Building started, we can add.  */  BUILDING,
    /** The ring was finished (closed). */  FINISHED;
}
```

As you can see, the keyword `class` in the enum type definition is replaced with the keyword `enum` and the body starts with the list of values of this type separated by commas and finished with a semicolon. After this list the same members (fields, methods, types) can follow as in other classes (it is sufficient to see the type `Direction8`), but for now we will continue in enum types containing only a list of values.

Enum Type Using

974.   I see three names with documentation comments in the definition – I suppose that they are those listed values of the enum type.

Yes – they are names of stages in which the ring builder can be found. Each of its building method is applicable only if the builder is in the proper state. Let's define a field in which the current state of the builder will be saved. Then the method will ask if the builder is in the proper state and according to the answer it will execute the required items or throws an exception.

975.   It's not necessary to define a new type for it. I can mark individual states as 1-2-3 and define the state field as an integer.

Of course, you can do it and formerly it was done like that. But there are several disadvantages. The most significant is that you cannot provide that some number would not get into the given field by mistake – you cannot provide the type control of used values. Generally, modern programming recommends using the enum type anytime, when the number, which you would use, should not serve really for calculating.

The State Diagram

976.   Well, I will use values of enum type for representing the state. Could you explain me, how do you mean it with those states?

The ring builder can be in three clearly defined states as follows:

☞   At the beginning, after the creating, it is in the state READY, prepared to build a new ring. The only "building" message you can send to it in this state, is startTo(Direction8), which asks locating
of the first road-field of the future ring, passing through in the entered direction.

☞   When opening the building of a new ring by locating the first road-field, the builder transits to
the state BUILDING. In this state it can accept two messages:

   ☞   the continueTo(Direction8) message, after which it adds another road-field and continues
   to stay in the state BUILDING, or

   ☞   the closeTo(Direction8) message, after which it closes the ring and ends its building. After
   processing of this message it transits into the state FINISHED.

☞   The builder in the state FINISHED waits until it receives the message getRing(), in which it is asked
for freshly built ring. Reacting at this message the builder transits again to the state READY and is
prepared to start building another ring.

Whole this transferring among states can be illustratively displayed in the state diagram, which is one
of the UML diagrams. You can see the builder's state diagram at the figure 42.1. The rounded rectangles represent states and the arrows show transitions among them.

   I think that having this information you might be able to modify individual methods of the builder
alone, but to be sure, I will show you how to modify the definition of getRing() method in the listing 42.2.

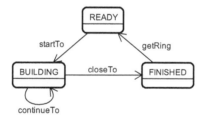

Figure 42.1
The state diagram showing transitions among individual states of the ring builder

Listing 42.2:   *The method getRing() in the RingBuilder class*

```
public Ring getRing()
{
    if (state != FINISHED) {
        throw new RuntimeException(
            "\nRing building is not finished yet; it is in the state: " +
            state);
    }
    state = READY;
    return new Ring(startField);
}
```

The Lists

977.   **The race is already nearly perfect. Only announcing of results is missing. Could we add it?**

The class is not yet prepared for reporting the results, but you can help with it. The first what you have to do is to prepare a container which would be ordered according to the achieved results. There are two of currently used containers, suitable for this purpose, namely:

☞ the list about which I was already speaking as one of the collections, and

☞ the array, which is a static container with properties very similar to the list ones.

I would choose the list, because it is more general and you will not have to learn any new syntactic constructions.

978.   **When you are speaking about sorting, we could create three result documents. The first one would be sorted according to who arrived as the first, the second one according to racers' names and the third one according to rings, which they followed.**

Oh, a good idea, but fortunately it will be not so complicated. However, you will have to create another field, because you have to remember the finish times of individual racers even after you will leave the method finishRace, to wait the finish of another racer.

You define a field – a list named finishes, to which you will save everything. But you should think over what you will save in it. Principally you have two possibilities:

☞ To save only references to the racers and any time you will need to get some information you will draw it up from the map racer2info.

☞ To save crates with information concerning the racers into it – there are also references to relevant racers in them since the last lesson.

Have a look at the current definition of the finishRace method and tell which possibility you would choose.

979.   **When you give me hints like that, I've finally found it. I have to save infos (instances of the Info class) there because the finishRace method removes the racer's record from the map after his arrival.**

You say it well, although we could choose also the other possibility, which is not to remove the racer from the map and count the racers who have already arrived to the finish. But I will incline to what you suggest. Therefore the field finishes will be declared as follows:

```
/** List with the racers ordered by their finishing time. */
private final List<Info> finishes = new ArrayList<Info>();
```

Notice, that I again declared the field through the interface (in this case java.util.List) and I initialized it by the newly created instance of java.util.ArrayList class.

I would like to recommend the ArrayList class to your attention. It is the most used class of the collection library. It is used not only as a list, but also as a general collection. In case that certain method returns a general collection on which no special requirements are laid, it uses very often an instance of the ArrayList class for it. I recommend it to you as well.

980. **You always digress to general principles. I'd like to get back to the race. This list is initialized immediately in a declaration and also the map is initialized in the same way. Therefore I suppose that it's a habit of collection fields.**

The fields which are collections are really often initialized already in the declaration, where an empty collection of the relevant type is assigned to them. In the course of the program's operating this collection is filled in and, if need be, it is also cleared again.

Modifications of the `ParallelRace` **Class**

981. **Well, the field is installed. Where will something be inserted in it?**

I would not start with where something will be inserted in it, but on the contrary, where it will be cleared, not to have references of the previous race in it. Try to think over where you would clear it out?

982. **After I will write all result documents and I will not need the saved info.**

That's one possibility. The second one is to clear it out before starting each new race. The advantage of this variant is that the whole time since the finish of one race until the start of the next race you will have the relevant info to your disposal, if you would like to create some other result document by chance.

Let's choose this version (because it's my idea ☺). Add the following statement at the beginning of the start() method

```
finishes.clear();
```

which will clear out the possible previous result document (precisely it will clear out the content of the list that was a background for the result document), which means the list will be pretty empty in time of the next race finish.

983. **When I changed the starting method, should I change also the registration, which is immediately behind it?**

You will have to modify it slightly, because of what you have thought out you would need to remember the info concerning the given racer together with his starting number (and thus also the number of his ring), as well as the resulting time and the order in which he arrived to the finish. Therefore you have to extend your private crate Info by these three fields and you have to add a parameter to its constructor, in which the racer's starting number (it is the number of its ring as well) will be saved. And that's all in the registration.

984. **The checkpoint probably will not change.**

You are true. Skip it over and go immediately to the finishRace method. You will save the arrival time and the order in which the racer arrived to the finish into this info. After the arrival of the last racer – instead of previous simple printing of the announcement – you call the evaluateRace method, which will take care about the required evaluation.

985.   Why should I save to info in which order the given racer arrived? It can be recognized according to his place in the list, can't be?

No, you can recognize it only at the beginning where the list is ordered according to rings' numbers. Then we should remember it, because you intend to print several result documents ordered according to different rules. If you will quote the racer's placing also in documents ordered according to names or rings, you have to save them in info.

You can see in the listing 42.3, where I put the new version of this method, that the new item was added into the list with the help of calling the method add(E) which is common for all collections (I remind that E is the type parameter of the collection and it indicates the type of saved elements).

The list has in its contract that the added element will be always placed at the end of the list. It means that if you will insert racers into the list according to their arrival, the list will remember this order and after you will open it, the list will keep this ordering.

Listing 42.3:   *The modified version of the method* finishRace *in the* ParallelRace *class*

```
private void finishRace(IRacer racer, Info info)
{
    long now = System.currentTimeMillis();
    info.controller.stop();
    int time = (int)(now - time0 + 50) / 100;
    System.out.println("The racer " + racer.getName() +
            " finished the race in the time " +
            time/10 + "," + time%10 + " second");

    //Remeber the racer's info with its finish time
    info.time = time;
    finishes.add(info);
    info.placings = finishes.size();
    racer2info.remove(racer);
    if (racer2info.isEmpty()) {
        evaluateRace();
    }
}
```

986.   Should I understand it that if I select components from a set or from a general collection in the loop, I receive them randomly?

Neither the general collection, nor the set guarantee the order in which they would pass you the saved elements. Just now I don't want to expand it; I will explain it in details in the next volume including the reasons.

987.   Hmm. Your code is strange. I see that you save the arrival time into info and then you add info into the list. I understand it. But I don't understand why after saving you insert the size of the list into its field finishes.

Because there are as many elements in the list at the given time, as how many racers arrived to the finish. I save the racer and then I ask how many of them are in the list. When I've inserted the racer in the list, the whole number of racers in this list is the same as the order of the just added racer.

988.   But it's strange why you save information into the saved info.

Realize that info does not know that it is saved. It is sitting somewhere at heap and does not move. There is no saved instance of Info class in the list; there is only a reference to this instance (similarly as in your variables). Therefore it's the same if you work with it before saving or after. It means the following statement

```
info.rank = finishes.size();
```

will be executed as if no info would be saved. The only difference is in the fact that after adding the instance the size of the list will increase so that the list contains as many elements as how many racers arrived to the finish. If you would like to enter the racer's order into the list before saving this info, you should remember it and increment after each racer's arrival, or you would have to add one to the list size before saving the racer.

989.   Oh, pretty nice tricks. I don't know if I will learn using of such tiny tricks in my programs.

Don't be afraid, it will come. When you are learning a foreign language, you often have the feeling that there are many things which you cannot remember, and when you start speaking, you use them without realizing it.

But let's leave general contemplation and let's return to the topic. The method evaluateRace is responsible for writing the complex result document (see the listing 42.4). It allows to the list to be sorted according to the required criterion and then it asks the writeResults method, to write down the sorting list, and at the same time it passes a message in the parameter describing the subsequently printed table of records.

Listing 42.4:   *The method evaluateRace in the ParallelRace class*

```
/*****************************************************************************
 * Evaluates the whole race, i.e. writes the records of particular racers.
 * The first list will be ordered according to their placing,
 * the second according to the alphabet
 * and the third according to numbers of their rings.
 */
private void evaluateRace()
{
    writeResults("Resulting placement:");

    Collections.sort(finishes);
    writeResults("Results according to alphabet:");

    Collections.sort(finishes, new CompByRings());
    writeResults("Results according to the ring numbers:");
}
```

990.   I see that it will be more complicated with the sorting, so I will ask you firstly to demonstrate me the writeResults method.

I agree. But I would say that the method is so simple that you surely would be able to write it alone – see the listing 42.5. Firstly it prints the new line followed by the message and then, in the loop, it takes one list item after another, discovers whole necessary information and prints it.

Listing 42.5:   The method writeResults(String) in the ParallelRace class

```
/****************************************************************************
 * Write a report followed by information about particular racers
 * ordered by the list {@link #finishes} to the standard output.
 * Each racer will be written on a separate line
 * with its final placing, ring's number, time and name.
 *
 * @param title Title starting the whole report
 */
private void writeResults(String title)
{
    System.out.println("\n" + title);
    for (Info info : finishes) {
        int    placing = info.placing;
        String name    = info.racer.getName();
        int    time    = info.time;
        int    number  = info.number;
        System.out.println(placing + ".  o"  + number   + " - " +
                         time/10 + ","     + time%10 + " - " +  name);
    }
}
```

Sorting the List Content

991.   It is really simple. So explain me the sorting.

'In the listing 42.4 you can see calling the writeResults method at the beginning without sorting the elements before that. I told you that it is possible, because when the racers were entered into the list (to be precise info about them) in the order in which they arrived to the finish, and the list remembers this sorting, and provides it in the loop in the writeResults method.

But for other two scorecards you have to order the list yourself. There are two overloaded versions of the method sort for list sorting, located in the librarian class java.util.Collections. (Please, notice the final s in the class name – it is the only difference from the name of the java.util.Collection interface specifying general collection properties.)

Native (Natural) Sorting

992.   But how the method recognizes according to which criterion the components should be listed? When I remind for example a telephone list of companies – it has two volumes. The first one contains companies according to the names, the second one according to areas of their activities.

The programmers solve the similar problem. To arrange a list of numbers is simple. Each schoolchild knows which number is higher and which is lower. But even here they have to solve the question whether arrange the numbers in ascending or descending order.

In case of objects it's a little bit more complicated, because various aspects can be taken as a basis. In majority situations the most advantageous is to let the decision to one of the compared object.

Java defines interface types java.lang.Comparable<T> that is implemented by classes, the instances of which know to decide which of them is "bigger". The Comparable interface requires an implementation of the method:

```
public int compareTo(T object)
```

This method defines the so called **native sorting** (sometimes it is called also **natural sorting**) of instances of its class. It returns:

☞ the negative integer in case if this is considered as lower than the parameter,

☞ zero, if both instances are equivalent, and

☞ the positive integer in case if this is considered as higher that the entered parameter.

Similarly as the contract of the method equals(Object) also the contract of this method requires fulfilling of several conditions, with which the mathematicians characterize the inequality. (The term contract was not used for a long time – you can remind its meaning in the section *Signature versus Contract* on page 112.) I will not analyze these conditions, because the currently defined methods always fulfill them. If sometimes you would define certain inequality, you can see these conditions in documentation any time.

993. **I would say that it's quite clear how the objects define which of them is bigger. It means now you could use this program as an example of such definition.**

You are true; the one-parametric version of the sort method supposes the native sorting. Therefore the list of instances of Info type is given to it in the listing 42.4. If the compiler should not announce a syntactic error, the Info class has to implement the interface Comparable<Info>. Then the relevant declaration should be completed into the class header as well as the definition of the compareTo(Info) method should be added into the class body according to the listing 42.6.

Listing 42.6:   *The definition of the method compareTo(Info) in the ParallelRace.Info class*

```
/***********************************************************************
 * Compare the racer's name
 * with the name of the racer obtained in argument.
 *
 * @param o Object for comparing
 * @return If this name is less, returns negative number,
 *         if it is equal, returns zero
 *         and if it is grater, returns a positive number.
 */
@Override
public int compareTo(Info o)
{
    //return this.racer.getName().compareTo(o.racer.getName());
    String myName  = this.racer.getName();
    String itsName = o    .racer.getName();
    return myName.compareTo(itsName);
}
```

At the beginning of the method's body there is a commented statement which solves all. Due to I was afraid that you might not understand it; I itemized it into several statements. You can verify that by uncommenting it and by commenting next three statements you get the same result.

I repeat again, that I don't press on you to write the programs in such condensed way, but it's good to know that the more experienced programmers do it and you should be able to "decode" such statement.

994.   Passing over those ciphers you sometimes provide me, I ask you, for what the just defined method is serving besides the compiler needs it for compiling the method.

When the method sort orders the items in a list, it needs to recognize which item do you consider as the higher one and which is lower. Therefore it used the known principle of the servant and declared the interface that has to implement items to be ordered. Thus, by implementing this method you tell your idea, how to recognize which of the compared objects is the bigger, to the sorting algorithm and, by that you influence the sorting.

995.   And why this way is called the native sorting?

The word native is taken from Latin *nativus* – natural. The classes and their instances are born with this way of sorting, because the method compareTo is one of their methods.

In the method of the listing 42.6 the sorting according to the racer's name has been announced as the basic (inborn) way of sorting the instances of the Info class. In case you would like to sort these instances in any other way, you have to choose alternative solution.

Alternative Sorting and the Design Pattern *Command*

996.   The alternative solution is the two-parametric version of the sort method, isn't it?

Yes, it is. The two-parametric version of the method implements the design pattern *Command*. You use it in situations, when you know that at the given place you will have to do something, but you don't know what. You know only the contract of the required operation.

The design pattern *Command* suggests asking for the given code as a method's parameter. In languages, which don't know passing the code as an argument, it is necessary to wrap the code into a method and the method into an object. To make clear, what the given object should know, you have to define the interface, in which you declare requirements for this object, i.e. what the signature of the method, which will be responsible for executing this command, will be, and, of course, also the relevant contract.

When some object would like to call a method with a command parameter, it will precisely know, what exactly should be carried out. It wraps the appropriate code into a method and this method into an object. Then it passes this object to the called method in the command parameter. The called method then asks the obtained object at relevant places to execute the required operation.

997.   To hear it so generally, it looks interesting, but I would like to get again an example – best of all just the ours.

When some object doesn't want to order instances according to their "inborn" sorting (and it doesn't matter if it is not suitable or if the given class instances have no native sorting defined), it has to specify, how to recognize, which instance should be ahead and which at the back of the sorted list. This decision, what is higher and what is lower, is just the action, about which the author of the sort method knew it would be executed many times, but he/she did not know how. Therefore he/she used the above described design pattern *Command*. He defined the interface Comparator<T>, in which the type parameter T represents the object type that has to be compared. This interface always requires an implementation of the method with the signature as follows

```
public int compare(T o1, T o2)
```

This method receives two objects and returns the result of their comparison - similarly as the compareTo method defining the native sorting used for returning. In case you would sort certain list in your special way, you should call the method sort, to which you pass the given list in the first parameter and the comparator in the second parameter, and the method will always ask the comparator which of those two entered elements is higher.

998. **Aha. It means in addition the comparator will have to be defined.**

Yes, and due to the fact that any from the surrounding classes should not be bothered with the fact that the ParallelRace class needs a comparator for making out perfect scorecards, you should again define it as its private static class. You can see its definition in the listing 42.7.

Listing 42.7: The class ParallelRace.CompByRings

```
/****************************************************************************
 * Class implementing the {@literal Comparator<Info>} interface.
 * Its instance compares two infos according to our criterion -
 * in this case according to the ring used by the racer.
 */
private static class CompByRings implements Comparator<Info>
{
    /************************************************************************
     * Compares the given infos and takes as the greater that one,
     * the ring of which has grater number (it is placed more to the right).
     *
     * @param i1 First compared info
     * @param i2 Second compared info
     * @return If {@code i1.number} is less than {@code i2.number},
     *         it returns negative number, if they are equal,
     *         it returns zero, otherwise it returns a positive number.
     */
    @Override
    public int compare(Info i1, Info i2)
    {
        return i1.number - i2.number;
    }
}
```

999. **If I understood it properly, so as soon as certain class implements the** Comparable **interface, I can sort its instances. And when I get a foreign class, which does not implement this** interface, **I can define a comparator for it and again I can sort its instances.**

You understood it properly. You only have to find the instances which you wish to order in certain container, whose content can be sorted. Until now I was speaking about lists only. In the next lesson I will present an array, the content of which can be sorted as well. But for now I am finished.

1000. **I have few unclear items. You told that when working with objects, it does not matter if they are saved in a container, because in the given container there is only a reference to an object that continues to stay at its original place at the heap. It means, that I can have more references to an object and I can sort these references in various ways in various containers, e.g. according to different fields. But when the field is changed, sorting in the container loses its sense.**

Well, but the fields according to which you compare should be defined as constants. We were speaking about that in the section *Value Types and Reference* Types on page 259. In case you need to sort the objects according to the variable field, you should firstly think over if you have any error in the program proposal, because such requirement is always suspicious. But in case you are solving one of the extraordinary problems, when you really need something like that, you have to take into account that such sorting will be valid only until the first change of such field of any of the sorted objects. But as you can see, those are more advanced questions dealing with the project proposals and I would really prefer to postpone it to the next volume.

1001. **We were speaking a long time about sorting the elements in a container, but before that you told, that I cannot rely on sorting of elements in containers (at least some of the containers). So there is a bit of chaos in it.**

It's no reason for it. Each container type has a definition in its contract to what you can rely on. Generally, a set does not guarantee an order, in which the saved elements will be given to you (despite some special sets which do guarantee it), but the list guarantees it. In case you need to discover, if the element is already in the container, choose a set. In case you need to have the possibility to sort elements and to have the guarantee that you can go through the container in the entered order, choose the list. In case you would have any other requirement, find such container, which can meet your requirement, or define your own one. But this is again a topic for the next volume.

Exercise

1002. **Will I have another task besides the one to make the new version of the** ParallelRace **class run?**

For some time, you have been playing with arrows and rings, driving with cars along them and you disregard the traffic light. Let's return to it. Define the enum type TrafficLightState and add the methods getState() and setState(TrafficLightState) to the traffic light. To test, how all lights are shining, add the allLightsOn() method to the traffic light which switches all lights. Then the traffic light should be in one of the following states LIGHTS_OFF, ATTENTION, STOP, GET_READY, GO and LIGHTS_ON.

Then I would recommend you to examine sorting of elements in the list. Define the method in the TestUtility class with the following signature

```
public void  sortList(List<IModular> list);
```

The method will sort objects in the parameter list according to the module size (the bigger is prior to the smaller). Then objects of the same size will be ordered firstly according to the horizontal coordinate (and for change the smaller will be prior to the bigger), and in case of equality, according to the vertical coordinate (again the smaller is prior to the bigger). (I suppose it's obvious you have to define a comparator for such sorting.) After that, press the resulting list at the standard output.

Then call this method from individual test classes of module objects and add the list of objects from the fixture to it. At this occasion you can examine that in case you will include one element twice into the list, it will remain there twice. After sorting both elements one will be along the other.

Unfortunately you cannot examine functioning of the last decision (the same module and the same horizontal coordinate), because there are no equally big instances with either the equal horizontal (nor vertical) coordinate in it. But you can supplement them.

Review

Let's review what you have learned in this lesson:

☞ The instances of enum types are defined by an enumeration. When the program is running, you cannot neither create any new instance, nor delete any existing one.

☞ The class keyword is replaced by the enum keyword in the definition of the enum type, and the body starts with the list of values of this type, separated by commas and finished with the semi-colon.

☞ The enum type can contain the same members as other classes.

☞ The state machine diagram is one of the UML diagrams. The rounded rectangles in it represent the states and the arrows mark transfers among them.

☞ The list is a collection which keeps information about the order of saved objects.

☞ Properties of the general list are defined by the java.util.List interface.

☞ The List interface is implemented for example by the ArrayList class, which is the most used implementation of the list and often also of the general collection.

☞ Mostly they are initialized immediately in the declaration as empty during using collections, and during the program course they are fulfilled, and if need be, again cleared out.

☞ The add(E) method, where E is the type parameter of the list, adds the new element at the end of the list.

☞ When working with objects, it does not matter whether they are already saved in certain container, because in the given container there is only a reference to an object that stays at its original place at the heap.

☞ For sorting of lists there are two versions of the sort method in the java.util.Collections class.

☞ The one-parametric version requires so that the elements in the list would be instances of classes implementing the java.util.Comparable interface.

☞ The Comparable interface requires from its instances the definition of the compareTo method, whose parameter is an object with which you compare the given object. The method returns a negative integer, zero, or a positive integer when this object is less than, equal to, or greater than the specified object.

☞ Ordering specified by the compareTo method is named as native or natural.

☞ In case you need to sort elements in a list according to the different criterion, you should use double-parametric version of the sort method, to which you pass a comparator in the second parameter.

☞ The comparator is an instance of the class implementing the java.util.Comparator interface. It requires from its instances implementing of the int compare(T o1, T o2) method, which compares its two parameters and returns a negative integer, zero, or a positive integer when the first argument is less than, equal to, or greater than the second one.

☞ Using of comparator is an application of the design pattern *Command*.

Project:
The resulting form of the project to which we came at the end of the lesson and after completing all exercises is in the 142z_Lists project.

43 The Array

What you will learn in this lesson

In this lesson you will become acquainted with the arrays and how to work with them. You will see how they are used for defining the method with the variable number of parameters. You will read the explanation that they can be sorted similarly as the lists and you will see the class which uses arrays for converting numbers to words. At the conclusion you will see also the loop while and the statement switch.

Project:

In this lesson you continue in using the 142z_Lists project.

Declaration of an Array Variable

1003. In the previous lesson in the section *The Lists* on page 472 you told that besides the list also an array would be suitable for preparation of the scorecard. You mentioned the array also when you started to explain what containers mean. But until now you did not explain what the array means.

Well, I will rectify it immediately. As I have already told, the arrays are static containers. When you create them, you have to announce how many elements fit into them, and this count cannot be changed. On the other side, you can insert into them not only references to objects but also values of primitive types.

1004. My friend told me that arrays can change their size in Basic.

But then they are not classis arrays, but more lists. The fact they are called arrays in Basic, is only a marketing matter which has to persuade amateurs that this language is better. In fact their array is only an equivalent of the class ArralyList, which I presented to you in the last lesson.

But I stop slander other languages and I return to the array. The main advantage of arrays compared to dynamic containers, with which you were working up to now, is that they have the direct support in the machine code of the used processor. Therefore they enable very quick carrying out of certain operations. If you would have a look at the source code of dynamic containers, you will see that their efficiency is very often programmed just with the help of arrays.

1005. Finish your general speeches and show me how such array is used in a program.

The array is declared in such way that, behind the type of elements which will be inserted in it, you write empty square brackets followed by the name of the variable in which the reference to the given array will be saved – for example as follows:

```
int[]      aInt;    //Array of integger
String[]   aStr;    //Array of strings
IMovable[] aImo;    //Array of objects implementing IMovable
String[][] aaStr;   //Array of array of strings (array of string array)
```

As I tried to show in the last example, the array's element can be anything including another array. This is suitable for example in case you need to save values of certain table. You can use the lastly declared array aaStr for example in case you would have a table with first names in its first column, surnames in the second one and e-mail addresses of given persons in the third one. Then you define the array of the table's line and this line will be the array of texts.

Then often a number of dimensions of the given array are mentioned. The number of dimensions means the count of squared brackets. Therefore in the previous example the first three arrays are one-dimensional, the fourth array is two-dimensional.

1006. How many dimensions can have the array?

Theoretically 256, but in practice it usually has one or two dimensions, exceptionally three. Practically you cannot meet more dimensions.

Creating and Initializing an Array

1007. I have declared an array. How I will create it?

The array is an object. Therefore it is created with the help of the operator new, and you can choose, if you will create it uninitialized (precisely explicitly uninitialized, i.e. with zeroed elements) or initialized. In the first case you say the required size of the created array to the operator new by writing an expression into square brackets after the type name. Value of this expression specifies the size (number of elements) of the created array, e.g. as follows:

```
aInt = new int[5];        //Creates an array with the first five prime numbers
aStr = new String[5][3]; //Creates a table with 5 rows and 3 columns

//We can count the size of the created array in the nick of time:
aaStr = new RoadField[2 * (columns + rows)];
```

As I have already said, the array created in this way is not initialized, which means it contains only zeros that may represent also null, false or empty character. You have to realize this, especially in case of arrays of objects. These arrays do not contain any objects, i.e. they contain really only null-s. Very often the programmers who are coming to Java from other languages – e.g. C++, Pascal or Delphi – are surprised by this.

1008. And when I would like to create initialized arrays?

Then you have two possibilities. Either you want to write down the creating as well as initializing the array as a part of its declaration, or you create and initialize the array somewhere within the code. If creation and initialization of the relevant array is a part of a variable declaration, you can skip over calling of the operator new and you can write squared brackets with the list of values separated by commas after the equation mark.

```
int[] a5p = { 1, 2, 3, 5, 7 };   //Array of the first five primes
String[] season = {"spring", "summer", "autumn", "winter"};
String[][]address = { {"Tom",     "Jones",   "tom.jones@gemail.com"  },
                      {"Elvis",   "Presley", "ep@yahoo.com" },
                      {"Michael", "Jackson", " michael@email.org} };
```

The compiler will understand that it has to create an array, and it will derive the array's size from the number of values. If you will initialize a more-dimensional array, i.e. an array the elements of which are again arrays; you again quote such element as a list of values closed in squared brackets.

1009. And what about the other possibility, when I would like to create and initialize the array in the code?

In this way you have two possibilities even now. Let's start with the more complicated one, which you can use anywhere. In case you are outside of a declaration and you would come to the opinion that just now it is suitable to create an initialized array, you start equally as with the uninitialized, i.e. you call the operator new and write down the type of the created object after it including the empty squared brackets, similarly as in the declaration. Then you put braces with initializing values. If I would not use the quoted initializations in the declaration but somewhere in the middle of the code, it would look out as follows:

```
a5p     = new int[] { 1, 2, 3, 5, 7 };    // Array of the first five primes
season  = new String[]   {"spring", "summer", "autumn", "winter"};
address = new String[][] { {"Tom",     "Jones",   "tom.jones@gemail.com"  },
                           {"Elvis",   "Presley", "ep@yahoo.com" },
                           {"Michael", "Jackson", " michael@email.org} };
```

Thus you can assign the created arrays not only to variables but also when passing parameters. Imagine, that for example you need to know, if certain array includes the beforehand known values. Let's say that my task for students is to write down the primes(int,int) method, which returns the sorted array of prime numbers among the entered parameters. When I use the equals(int[],int[])method in the java.util.Arrays class, which compares two entered arrays, the result in my control program can look out as follows (the reference to the object of the tested student is saved in the student variable):

```
int[]   result = student.primes(10, 20);
boolean right  = Arrays.equals(new int[] {11, 13, 17, 19}, result);
```

Methods with a Variable Number of Parameters

1010. You spoke about certain simpler possibility.

You have already met it– you can use this simpler possibility when you are using a method with a variable number of parameters. The "triple-dot" parameter is in fact an array, with which you can work in the middle of the method as just with the ordinary array.

1011. And this reminds me that you explained in details, how to create the array, but I don't know anything how to use it.

You already know something – I showed you that you can use the colon loop for working with values in the array. And after all you can try it. At the end of the last lesson I put an exercise for creating test methods added into the test classes of the relevant shapes. These methods should verify if you defined properly the sortList(List<IModular>) method in the TestUtility class. I suppose that similarly as in the sample solution you created an empty list, and gradually you added individual instances of the template and then you pass this list to the test method for sorting.

Now I will show you the alternative possibility. Let's supplement the TestUtility class with the newListIModular method, to which you can add any sum of instances of this interface. You can see the definition in the listing 43.1.

Listing 43.1:   The newListIModular method in the TestUtility class

```
/*****************************************************************************
 * Creates a new list (precisely {@link ArrayList}) of {@link IModular}
 * objects and fills it with values obtained in parameters.
 *
 * @param values  Values initializing the created list
 * @return New list filled with the given values
 */
public static List<IModular> newListIModular(IModular... values)
{
    List<IModular> list = new ArrayList<>();
    for (IModular value : values) {
        list.add(value);
    }
    return list;
}
```

When you would declare in the method's header that the parameter is an array, you have to assign into it the required array similarly as you did it for example in the listing 40.3 on page 438. Then you can define the body of the test method in the class ArrowTest for example as follows:

```
List<IModular> list = TestUtility.newListIModular(
                    arrow0, arrowXY, arrowXYB, arrowXYM, arrowXYMB, arrow0);
TestUtility.sortList(list);
```

If need be you can unify both statements into one and modify the method's body into the form

```
TestUtility.sortList(TestUtility.newListIModular(
                    arrow0, arrowXY, arrowXYB, arrowXYM, arrowXYMB, arrow0));
```

How to Use the Array

1012. I remember that you already showed me using of the colon statement for **in the method with the variable number of parameters. Could the array be used in a different way than in the loop?**

Working with the array elements in the loop is far more frequent, but you can access to elements saved in the array separately. But you have to know, where the element is saved in the array, you have to know its index. All positions in the array are indexed (numbered). The initial array position has the index 0 (zero) and each next one has the index higher by one.

1013. Why the positions are not numbered one, two, three etc.?

Since then a lot of problems you are meeting disappear – for instance why the year 1234 belongs to the 13th century. And moreover, many calculations are more effective. Keep in mind that all good programming languages are indexing from zero. And thus, it follows that the index of the last element in the array is (numberOfElements - 1). Despite the fact laics consider it as strange for the first sight, after some time they become accustomed to it and would not like to return to indexation from one.

1014. Well, so show me certain usage, where I would work with individual array elements.

I will show you the definition of the method, which selects and returns maximum from entered values. Or even better: the definition of this method is your exercise today, and I will show you the definition of a little bit more complicated method, that returns index of the highest element. You can find its code in the listing 43.2. Notice, how I ask for the value of the array element: I quote the array name followed by the index of the element, the value of which I am interested in, and this index is written in squared brackets.

Listing 43.2:   *The* indexOfMax(int...) *method in the* ArrayTest *class*

```
/*****************************************************************************
 * Returns the index of the greatest number among the given numbers.
 *
 * @param ii Analyzed numbers
 * @return Index of the greatest number
 */
public static int indexOfMax(int... ii)
{
    int index = 0;
    int max   = ii[0];
    for (int i=1;   i < ii.length;   i++) {
        if (ii[i] > max) {
            index = i;
            max   = ii[i];
        }
    }
    return index;
}
```

1015. Why didn't you use the colon for**?**

This method cannot use the colon loop for, because at the beginning it remembers the value (as well as the index) of the initial element and then it goes through the array only from the element with the index 1. The colon loop for does not know going through only a part of the array. It works according to the principle all or nothing. As soon as you need to go through only an array's part, you have to use the classic form of the loop for.

Notice also, how the loop is programmed. The program goes through the particular array element by element until it comes to the element which is bigger than the current maximum and proclaims it as a maximum, i.e. remembers its value and its index.

1016. What the length **field which you use in the loop header contains?**

In this (constant) field the array length is placed, i.e. the number of its elements. The quoted header is the typical header of the for loop, through the body of which you pass. If you would go through the whole array, you would only save zero into the loop control variable as an initial value, because (as I already said) the array's elements are indexed from zero.

1017. Do you have an example in which I have to use the classic for loop?

You have to use the classic form of the loop whenever you need to save something into the array. The colon for offers you only what it found in cells, but it does not enable you to change their content. Thus, if you would define a method which receives an array as a parameter and returns another array, whose elements contain the second power of values of the first array's elements, it could look out as in the listing 43.3.

Listing 43.3:   *The square(double[]) method in the ArrayTest class*

```
public static double[] square(double[] dd)
{
    double[] result = new double[dd.length];
    for (int i=0;   i < dd.length;   i++) {
        result[i] = dd[i] * dd[i];
    }
    return result;
}
```

As I already told, the length of the array does not change during its life. Therefore if you save something into the array, you cannot ask to put it at the end, as it was possible with the list. Anytime you read something from the array or you save something into it, you always have to say with which array's cell you want to work, you have to quote its index. Then the virtual machine checks if such cell exists and if yes, it reads the required value or save it. But if the array does not contain such index, it throws the ArrayIndexOutOfBoundsException, and you can read the used false index value in its message.

Sorting of the Array Content

1018. I suppose that you can sort the values in the array similarly as previously in the list.

Yes, the only difference compared to lists is, that methods working with arrays are defined in the class java.util.Arrays. For sorting the arrays you can find here a whole variety of methods differing with the type of elements of the sorted array – for each primitive type there are two methods: one is sorting the whole array and the other only the assigned part of it. Besides that there is another slew of methods for further operations – for example a set of methods equals mentioned at the beginning of the lesson, which compare two specified arrays.

However, among methods for sorting values of primitive types you will not find a version to which you could enter the used comparator. You can find such version only among methods for sorting arrays with values of object types.

How to Express Numbers with Words

1019. Can we try an example for using the array?

I have a little example here, which I used in one of my previous textbooks. It shows how you can define a class the static method of which converts the number to its expression in words. The whole definition (you can find it in the listing 43.4) is based on using the arrays, so go through it. This definition converts numbers only until one thousand. And in the package utility you can find its sister, which is able to convert all positive numbers of the long type.

Listing 43.4:   *The class ByWords*

```java
/*******************************************************************************
 * The {@code ByWords} class allows to translate the integer numbers
 * into text showing how they can be said by words.
 */
public final class ByWords
{
    //== CONSTANT CLASS FIELDS ==================================================

    /** The maximum translatable value */
    public static final long MAX = 999L;

    private static final String UNITS[] = new String[] {
        "",        "one",     "two",       "three",    "four",
        "five",    "six",     "seven",     "eight",    "nine",
        "ten",     "eleven",  "twelve",    "thirteen", "fourteen",
        "fifteen", "sixteen", "seventeen", "eighteen", "nineteen",
    };

    private static final String TENS[] = new String[] {
        "",        "ten",     "twenty",    "thirty",   "forty",
        "fifty",   "sixty",   "seventy",   "eighty",   "ninety"
    };

    private static final String HUNDRED = " hundred";

    private static final String AND = " and ";

    private static final String[] TRIADS = { "",
        "thousand", "million", "billion", "trillion",
        "quadrillion", "quintillion"
    };


    //== OTHER NON-PRIVATE CLASS METHODS =========================================

    /*******************************************************************************
     * Returns a string representing the given number expressed by words.
     *
     * @param number   Converted number
     * @return Word representation of the given number
     */
    public static String number(long number)
    {
        if (number == 0) {
            return "zero";       //=========>
        }
        if (number > 0) {
            return convert(number);
        }
        else {
            return "minus " + convert(-number);
        }
    }
```

```
//##########################################################################
//== CONSTUCTORS AND FACTORY METHODS =======================================

/** Private constructor preventing creation of an instance. */
private ByWords() {}


//== PRIVATE AND AUXILIARY CLASS METHODS ===================================

/***************************************************************************
 * Returns a string representing the given number expressed by words.
 *
 * @param number   Converted number
 * @return Word representation of the given number
 */
private static String convert(long number)
{
    String[] texts = new String[TRIADS.length];
    texts[0] = hundred((int)(number % 1000));
    int triad = 0;
    do {
        int trinum = (int)(number % 1000);
        if (trinum == 0)
        {
            triad++;
            continue;
        }
        String trinumString = hundred(trinum);
        String triadString  = TRIADS[triad];
        texts[triad] = trinumString + " " + triadString;
        triad++;
    } while ((number /= 1000) > 0);
    StringBuilder sb = new StringBuilder();
    for (int i = triad-1;   i >= 0;   i--)
    {
        if (texts[i] == null) {
            continue;
        }
        if (sb.length() > 0) {
            sb.append(" ");
        }
        sb.append(texts[i]);
    }
//      String ret = sb.toString();
    return sb.toString();
}

/***************************************************************************
 * Returns a string representing the given number from 1 to 999
 * expressed by words.
 *
 * @param number   Converted number
 * @return Word representation of the given number
 */
```

```java
    private static String hundred(int number)
    {
        int units    = number % 10;
        int ten_units= number % 100;
        int tens2    = number / 10;
        int tens1    = tens2  % 10;
        int hundreds = tens2  / 10;

        StringBuilder sb = new StringBuilder();
        if (hundreds > 0) {
            sb.append(UNITS[hundreds]).append(HUNDRED);
        }
        if ((tens1 > 0)  ||  (units > 0)) {
            if (hundreds > 0) {
                sb.append(AND);
            }
            if (ten_units < 20) {
                sb.append(UNITS[ten_units]);
            }
            else {
                sb.append(TENS[tens1]);
                if ((tens1 > 0)  &&  (units > 0)) {
                    sb.append(' ');
                }
                sb.append(UNITS[units]);
            }
        }
        return  sb.toString();
    }


    //== TESTING CLASSES AND METHODS ===========================================

    /***************************************************************************
     * The test method.
     */
    public static void test()
    {
        java.util.Random rnd = new java.util.Random();
        for (int i = 0;   i < 100;   i++)
        {
            long n = rnd.nextLong();
        }
    }
    /** @param args Command line arguments - not used. */
    public static void main(String[] args)  {  test();  }
}
```

Exercise

1020. Well, it was enough for me. So what will be today's exercise?

I said your today's exercise during this lesson. Define a method with variable number of parameters which will return the value of the highest of its parameters. And if you dare, you can try a version which will receive a comparator in the first version with the help of which it decides about the remaining parameters and which of them is the biggest.

Then study the Slovy class and think over how to extend it, so that it would be able to convert also numbers bigger than 999. You will find such version in the package utility. However, it uses certain constructions which will be explained only in the next volume.

Review

Let's review what you have learned in this lesson:

☞ Arrays are static containers that enable to save also primitive type values directly, i.e. without using their wrapper objects.

☞ The main advantage of arrays is the direct support of working with them in the machine code of the processor.

☞ The array is declared by writing empty squared brackets after the type of elements that should be saved into it, followed by the name of the variable to which the reference to the given array is saved – e.g.

```
int[] intArray;
```

☞ The number of array sizes (dimensions) is defined by the number of square brackets – e.g.

```
double[][][] threeDimensional;
```

☞ An empty uninitialized array is created with the help of the operator new followed by the name of the array's element types and by squared brackets with quoted number of elements – e.g.

```
intArray = new int[100];
```

☞ You can create an initialized array in a declaration by writing the equals sign behind the name of the declared variable and then you name the initial values of array elements in braces. The array's size will be derived from the number of elements – e.g.

```
String[] initializedArray = { "zeroth", "first", "second" };
```

☞ Arrays created in the code are initialized simply by quoting braces with the list of initial values instead of square brackets behind the operator new and behind the name of array elements type. The array's size will be derived from the number of elements.

```
String sorted = Arrays.sort(new String[] {"John", "Tom", "Mary"});
```

☞ Each array's element has its index. The array elements are indexed from zero.

☞ The index of the last element is always smaller by one than the number of array elements.

☞   The arrays have a constant integer field length, which contains the array's size (number of elements).

Project:
The resulting form of the project to which we came at the end of the lesson and after completing all exercises is in the 143z_Arrays project.

44 The Finale

What you will learn in this lesson
In this final lesson I will only say good bye and I will outline which program I prepared for you in accompanying programs for the concluding self-study.

Project:
In this lesson you continue in using the 143z_Arrays project.

1021. Well, and what you have prepared for me?

I prepared a lot of further things for you, but I think that we should finish at the best. We went together through the very basics of object oriented programming and I showed you how to make object programming in the Java language.

As I told you at the beginning, I tried to look into various areas which enable you to understand how the object oriented programs are developed. But it was just a look into majority of areas, because there was neither space nor time for more systematic explanation.

As I told you during previous lessons, I intend to continue with this topic in another volume of this book in which I would like to explain systematically all areas that were just started. Besides that I promised you to complete the explanation on inheritance as well as inheritance of implementation which is the base of class inheritance. And moreover, I would like to touch several other topics which are rarely mentioned in books for beginners.

1022. What you would advise me to read when I would not like to wait before you finish editing of the second volume?

Probably I will advise you to read something about class inheritance because when studying programs of other people you might meet it. But be prepared that majority of textbooks do not expand on various trickiness you can meet in using the class inheritance. I say "self-critically" that you can become acquainted with this trickiness best in my book *Java 8 – Textbook of the Object Oriented Architecture for the Slightly Intermediate Programmers*. However, there is a disadvantage: roughly two thirds of its content was just explained here.

The both above mentioned books deal more with how to think in object programming. In case you would like to discover something about syntactic rules and supplement your knowledge in Java by topics that were only slightly mentioned (e.g. what the standard library offers), you will find a number of books as well as freely available texts. You can start with *The Java™ Tutorial*

1023. Well, this is the end?

Yes, this is the end. I will be looking forward that you will take fancy to programming and that you will show off your creations at the conference pages that might inspire others.

Index

@After, 176
@Before, 176
@Override, 173
@Test, 176
access
  private, 71
  public, 71
accessor method, 40
animace
  OOPNZ_115_A1_SouboryVProjektechBlueJ, 137
  OOPNZ_116_A1_PrazdnaTrida, 146
  OOPNZ_117_A1_FormalniASkutecneParametry, 154
  OOPNZ_131_A1_Debugger, 317
animation, 4
  LOOTP_101a_Handling, 5
  LOOTP_101b_IDE_BlueJ, 8
  LOOTP_102a_Compilation, 17
  LOOTP_103a_First_messages, 23
  LOOTP_104a_Tests_class, 29
  LOOTP_105a_Return_primitive_value, 35
  LOOTP_106a_Return_object, 48
  LOOTP_107_e1_House, 57
  LOOTP_107_e2_Face, 57
  LOOTP_107_e3_Robot, 57, 75
  LOOTP_107a_Messages_with_parameters, 56
  LOOTP_108_e1_House, 66
  LOOTP_108_e2_Face, 66
  LOOTP_108_e3_Robot, 66
  LOOTP_108a_Object_parameters, 63
  LOOTP_109_e1_House, 75
  LOOTP_109_e2_Face, 75
  OOPNZ_109_A1_DoplneniPripravku, 72
  OOPNZ_109_A2_UtrobyObjektu, 74
  OOPNZ_110_A1_Interface, 86
  OOPNZ_111_A1_Mnohotvar, 98
  OOPNZ_112_A1_ViceRozhrani, 107
  OOPNZ_113_A1_DedicnostRozhrani, 119
  OOPNZ_114_A1_SpravcePlatna, 131

annotation
  @After, 176
  @Before, 176
  @Override, 173
  @Test, 176
apostrophe, 245
application
  creation, 326
  main class, 326
area
  reference, 380
argument, 150
architecture, 115
Architecture First, 2
arity, 253
array
  creation, 484
  index, 486
  initialization, 484
  sorting, 488
  use, 486
arrow
  dependency, 15, 27
  implementation, 86
arrows
  uses
    deny, 83
attribute, 68, 214, 221
  private, 69
  public, 69
  static, 69, 73
backup copy, 141
block, 216, 385
  initializing
    static, 290
BlueJ, 6
BlueJ command
  Compile, 17
  Create Test Method, 28
  Executed actions ▶ Test Fixture, 27

Run Tests, 28
Test Fixture ▶ Object bench, 27
boolean, 36, 242
breakpoint, 308
button
  Compile, 17
  Continue, 311
  Get, 39, 69
  Halt, 311
  Inspect, 69
  New Class, 26
  Replace, 53
  Run Tests, 28, 130
  Show Source, 227
  Show static fields, 73
  Step, 311
  Step Into, 311
  Terminate, 311
byte, 37, 242
call sequence, 313
CanvasManager, 126
casting
  default, 401
  explicit, 401
circumscribed rectangle, 444
class, 11, 15, 16, 20
  associated test class, 92
  defined
    Apron, 320
    Arrow, 192, 200, 209
    Auto, 149
    BuilderState, 470
    Call, 297
    Canvas, 15
    CanvasManager, 126
    Car, 192, 200, 209, 216
    CCI, 291
    Circular, 373
    DirectableCircular, 387
    Direction8, 15
    Dispatcher, 320, 321
    Ellipse, 15
    Empty, 134

House, 65
Info, 410
IO, 15
Light, 163
Mover, 77, 81, 102, 104
MultishapeTest, 128
NamedColor, 15, 320
Number, 320
ParallelRace, 461, 473
Position, 234
Race, 402
RaceLShape, 410
RaceLShape.Info, 410
Rectangle, 15
Resizer, 106
Ring, 352, 357
RingBuilder, 352, 354
RingTest, 362
RoadField, 347
Space, 320
Tests, 26, 27, 127
TestUtility, 285
Town, 266
TrafficLight, 149, 192, 200
TrafficLights, 209
Triangle, 15
Vehicle_A, 391
Xkrements, 426
field, 68
child class, 60
import into project, 84
kind of class, 134
name
  full, 336
  simple, 336
New Class, 26
standard
  Object, 242
standard class template, 184
standard library
  ArrayList<E>, 472
  Arrays, 488
  Collections, 476

Object, 60
System, 246
String, 46
test class, 25
method setUp, 176
of class, 91
type of class, 26
class diagram, 14
class file, 135
class test class, 91
code
source code
comment, 181
formatting, 147
indenting, 147
collection
important methods, 422
command
Comment, 181
conditional
embedded, 399
Uncomment, 182
comment
block comment, 182
documentation, 182, 183
formatting, 186
line comment, 182
comments
javadoc
tags, 187
compilation, 16
Compile, 17
compile-time
constants, 301
expression, 301
conditional statement
complete, 437
simple, 395
constant, 218
compile-time constants, 301
compile-time expression, 301
constructor, 30
definition, 144

header, 144
how it works, 197
name, 145
this statement, 199
container, 407
dynamic, 407
static, 407
context menu, 18
conversion
default, 401
explicit, 401
copy
backup, 141
Crate, 231
cycle
for(
), 423
data type, 80
debugger, 308
call sequence, 313
window, 310
declaration, 50
default
casting, 401
conversion, 401
dependency arrow, 15, 27
design pattern, 100
Command, 478
Crate, 231
Decorator, 366
Enum type, 102
Enumeration type, 102
Library class, 101, 279
Multiton, 102
Prototype, 96
Servant, 102, 277
Simple factory method, 101
Single Factory method, 266
Singleton, 101, 266
Static factory method, 101
Utility class, 101, 279
diagram
class diagram, 14

state machine, 470
documentation
    class, 79
documentation comment, 183
double, 37, 242
Eclipse, 7
encapsulation, 159
enum type, 15, 469
Enum type, 102
Enumeration type, 102
exception, 428
explicit
    casting, 401
    conversion, 401
field, 214
    class field, 263
    initialization, 215
    lifetime, 216
    static, 73, 263
file
    *.class, 135
    *.ctxt, 135
    *.java, 135
    auxiliary, 135
    class file, 135
    compiled, 135
    package.bluej, 135
    README.TXT, 16
    source file, 135
final, 218
fixture
    test fixture, 25
float, 37, 242
Fowler
    rule, 148
French quotation marks, 15
garbage collector, 37, 38, 47
getter, 40, 222
getXxx, 40
guillemets, 15
hatching, 16
heap, 37
Hollywood principle, 122

char, 37, 242
child class, 60
IDE, 6
IDEA, 7
identifier, 20, 36, 39, 43
implementation, 78
implementation hiding, 159
import
    static, 360
import class into project, 84
index, 486
inheritance, 61
inheritance of interfaces, 108
instance, 11, 19, 22
    field, 68
int, 37, 242
Integrated Development Environment, 6
IntelliJ IDEA, 7
interactive mode, 16
interface
    defined
        IRingFactory, 435
        IUFOFactory, 321
    from standard library
        Collection<E>, 421
        Deque<E>, 422
        List<E>, 422
        Map<K,V>, 422
        Queue<E>, 422
        Set<E>, 422
interface, 78, 80, 171
    defined
        IMovable, 104
        IResizable, 106
        ISaucer, 320
        IShape, 77, 81, 102
        IUFO, 320
        IUFOFactory, 320
        UFOTest, 320
    inheritance, 108
interface
    defined
        IDirectable, 386

interface
  standard library
    List<E>, 472
iterator, 424
Java Development Kit, 6
JDK, 6
key, 408
keyword, 44
kind of class, 134
library
  standard library, 36
Library class, 101
Liskov Substitution Principle, 116
list
  linked, 348
  sorting
    native, 476
    natural, 476
local
  variable, 213
local variable, 214, 316
  initialization, 215
  lifetime, 216
long, 37, 242
loop
  endless, 440
  for
    body, 440
    classic, 439
    header, 440
LSP, 116
main class, 326
memory manager, 37, 38
message, 12, 22
  list of messages, 18
  sending, 31
  to IDE, 18
  with parameters, 12
method, 30
  accessor, 40
  accessory method, 222
  auxiliary, 212
  calling, 31

  defined
    auxSwapPositionsWithCheck, 279
  getter, 222
  mutator, 40
  return value, 47
  setter, 222
  setUp, 176
  tearDown, 176
  with variable number of parameters, 438, 485
mode
  interactive, 16
modifier
  final, 218
  usage, 264
Multiton, 102
mutator method, 40
name
  conventions for packages, 339
  full, 336
  simple, 336
names
  conventions, 331
NetBeans, 7
new, 18
New Class, 26
object, 10, 19, 37, 38, 45
  comparison, 240
  state, 68
object bench, 21, 22
object oriented program, 13
object oriented programming, 10
object type, 36
OOP, 10
operand, 161
operator, 161
  !, 254
  !=, 253
  %, 208
  &, 255
  &&, 255
  *, 207
  /, 207
  |, 256

| |, 256

<, 253

<=, 253

=, 160

==, 253

>, 253

>=, 253

assignment, 160

binary, 253

comparison, 253

conjunction, 255

disjunction, 256

division, 207

instanceof, 256

modulo, 208

multiplication, 207

negation, 254

nullary, 253

postdecrement, 426

postincrement, 426

predecrement, 426

preincrement, 426

reminder after division, 208

unary, 253

output

  standard

    error, 248

package, 330, 335

  name convention, 339

panel

  local variables, 316

parameter, 12, 50, 214

  actual, 150

  formal, 150

  initialization, 215

  lifetime, 216

  this, 194

  type, 412

pattern

  design

    Command, 478

    Enum type, 102

    Enumeration type, 102

Multiton, 102

  Singleton, 101

design pattern, 100

  Decorator, 366

  Library class, 101, 279

  prototype, 96

  Servant, 102, 277

  Simple factory method, 101

  Static factory method, 101

  Utility class, 101, 279

primitive type, 22, 36

principle

  dependency injection, 124

  dependency inversion, 124

  Hollywood, 122

  Liskov Substitution Principle, 116

  LSP, 116

program

  tracing, 311

program

  object oriented, 13

  structured, 13

program

  stepping, 311

project, 13

  101a_Shapes, 13

property, 221

Prototype, 96

qualification, 161

  this, 162

quotation marks, 59, 245

README.TXT, 16

rectangle

  circumscribed, 444

recursion, 366

refactoring, 276

reference, 19, 22, 37, 38, 45

  how to get it, 38

return stack, 313

Servant, 102

setter, 40, 222

setXxx, 40

short, 37, 242

Simple factory method, 101
Singleton, 101
source code
  comment, 181
  formatting, 147
  indenting, 147
stack
  return stack, 314
standalone application, 326
standard class template, 184
standard library, 36
state machine diagram, 470
statement
  conditional
    complete, 437
    simple, 395
  import
    star notation, 343
  import static, 360
  loop
    for(
      ), 423
  package, 335
Static factory method, 101
stepping, 311
stereotype, 15, 27
  enum, 15
  interface, 83
  unit test, 27
string
  concatenation, 241
String, 46, 54
structured program, 13
switch
  kind of class, 134
tag
  @author, 187
  @param, 187
  @return, 187
  @version, 187
tags
  javadoc, 187
template

standard class, 184
test
  creation, 28
  return the proper values, 225
test class, 25
test fixture, 25
text representation, 241
text signature, 241
this, 162
this statement, 199
time
  measurement, 400
tracing, 311
type
  boolean, 36, 242
  byte, 37, 242
  double, 37, 242
  enum, 15
  enum type, 469
  float, 37, 242
  char, 37, 242
  immutable, 260
  int, 37, 242
  long, 37, 242
  mutable, 260
  object, 36
  primitive, 22, 36
  short, 37, 242
  void, 36
  wrapper, 408
UFO, 319
UML, 14
  class diagram, 14
  state machine diagram, 470
Unified Modeling Language. UML
Utility class, 101
value
  in map, 408
  magic, 219
  permissible, 36
  return value
    test, 225
variable, 20

local, 213, 214, 316
    initialization, 215
    lifetime, 216
virtual machine, 23

restart, 23, 28
void, 22, 36
whitespace, 139, 182

www.ingramcontent.com/pod-product-compliance
Lightning Source LLC
Chambersburg PA
CBHW080546060326
40689CB00021B/4767